Project Maths

2015 ONWARDS

Text & T 3

Leaving Certificate Ordinary Level Maths

Strands 1–5

O. D. Morris · Paul Cooke · Paul Behan

The Celtic Press

Acknowledgements
I would like to express my deep gratitude to Aidan Raleigh for his invaluable advice at
all stages of the production of this book.

First published in 2012 by
The Celtic Press
Ground Floor – Block B
Liffey Valley Office Campus
Dublin 22

This reprint February 2017

ISBN: 978-0-7144-2011-0

Design: Identikit Design
Layout and artwork: Tech-Set Limited
Cover: Identikit Design

Contents

Preface

Text & Tests 3 covers the complete Leaving Certificiate, Ordinary Level Mathematics course for students taking their examination in 2015 and onwards. The book reflects the overall approach to the teaching of maths as stated in the learning outcomes for *Project Maths*. It encourages the development of not only the students' mathematical knowledge and skills but also the understanding necessary to apply these skills.

There is an excellent range of imaginatively written and probing questions on each topic which will help students to understand what they are doing and to develop their problem-solving skills. A sufficient number of questions in varying degrees of difficulty have been provided to satisfy the needs of the vast majority of students at this level.

The motivating and stimulating full-colour design together with the large number of well constructed diagrams should help the student's understanding of the topic being studied. At the beginning of each chapter there is a list of **Key Words** that students are expected to know and understand when the chapter is completed. Each chapter includes a blue-coloured **Test Yourself** section which provides comprehensive consolidation and revision. The **Summary of Key Points** page in each chapter will remind the student of key facts and important formulae.

The book provides a logical and structured continuation from the new Junior Certificate Ordinary Level course. Every effort has been made to make it accessible to students by addressing the problems encountered by them as they progress from this course to the Leaving Certificate programme. The earlier chapters of the book provide basic but necessary revision and practice in those important fundamental skills which were covered at Junior Certificate level, but which may not be solidly grounded.

O.D. Morris
Paul Cooke
Paul Behan
April 2012

Algebra 1

Key words

integers   expression   term   variable   constant   coefficient

evaluating   linear equation   linear inequality   simultaneous equations

intersection   subject of a formula

Section 1.1 Working with negative numbers

The set of positive and negative whole numbers is called the set of **integers**.
It is denoted by the capital letter, **Z**.

The examples below will help you recall the basic rules when working with integers.

Examples

1. When adding integers with the same sign,
   add the numbers and retain the sign

   (i) $8 + 4 = 12$
   (ii) $-3 - 7 = -10$

2. When adding integers with different signs,
   retain the sign of the numerically bigger
   number and then take the smaller number
   from the bigger number

   (i) $-3 + 8 = 5$
   (ii) $4 - 10 = -6$

3. When multiplying or dividing integers,
   (a) like signs give a positive answer
   (b) unlike signs give a negative answer

   (i) $-5 \times (-4) = 20$
   (ii) $-3 \times 6 = -18$
   (iii) $7 \times (-4) = -28$

Removing brackets

(i) $3(4 + 5) = 3 \times 4 + 3 \times 5$
$= 12 + 15 = 27$

(ii) $5(7 - 3) = 5 \times 7 + 5(-3)$
$= 35 - 15 = 20$

(iii) $-3(7 - 2) = -3 \times 7 + (-3)(-2)$
$= -21 + 6$
$= -15$

> In these examples, we multiply each number inside the brackets by the number outside the brackets.

Order of operations

The graphic below should remind you of the correct order in which to perform mixed operations in arithmetic and algebra.

B	**I**	**M**	**D**	**A**	**S**
Brackets	Indices or powers	Multiplication	Division	Addition	Subtraction

Examples (i) $3 + (5 \times 4) = 3 + 20 = 23$

(ii) $5 + 4 + 3(10 - 4) = 9 + 3(6) = 9 + 18 = 27$

(iii) $(10 \times 3 - 20) \times 6 = (30 - 20) \times 6$
$$= 10 \times 6 = 60$$

(iv) $6^2 + (6 - 2)^2 \times 5 = 36 + (4)^2 \times 5$
$$= 36 + 16 \times 5 = 36 + 80 = 116$$

(v) $4^2 \times 2 - (-7 + 2) = 16 \times 2 - (-5)$
$$= 32 + 5 = 37$$

$-(-5) = 5$

Exercise 1.1

Express each of the following as a single integer:

1. $8 - 3$

2. $-7 + 3$

3. $-7 - 3 + 4$

4. $12 + 4 - 8$

5. $15 - 3 - 9$

6. $14 - 3 - 7$

7. $-8 + 4 + 7$

8. $5 - 9 + 8$

9. $-3 + 7 + 6$

10. $6 - 12 + 8$

11. $-3 - 2 - 7$

12. $-9 + 16 - 10$

13. $-3 - 7 + 12$

14. $-9 - 4 + 6$

15. $-5 - 8 + 9$

16. 12×6

17. -5×6

18. $6 \times (-7)$

19. $-8 \times (-6)$

20. $-7 \times (-9)$

21. -9×7

22. $6 \times 2 \times (-3)$

23. $4 \times (-3) \times (-2)$

24. $(-3) \times (-4) \times (-2)$

25. $\dfrac{18}{6}$

26. $\dfrac{-12}{4}$

27. $\dfrac{-36}{-9}$

28. $\dfrac{63}{-7}$

29. $\dfrac{-6 \times 3}{9}$

30. $\dfrac{9 \times (-6)}{2}$

31. $\dfrac{(-8) \times (-6) \times 3}{-12}$

32. $\dfrac{-2 \times 9 \times (-4)}{8}$

33. $\dfrac{-5 \times 4 \times 9}{-6}$

Using the correct order of operations, simplify each of the following:

34. $3 \times 6 + 3$

35. $5 \times 7 - 8$

36. $35 \div 5 - 6$

37. $5 \times 6 - 4 \times 3$

38. $32 - 8 \times (-5)$

39. $(16 - 4) \div 2 + 5$

40. $4 \times (-2) - (7 - 15)$

41. $\dfrac{4 \times (7 - 2)}{5}$

42. $\dfrac{8 \times (7 - 4)}{1 - (5 - 10)}$

43. $\dfrac{-8 \times (-3) \times 6}{-12}$

44. $15 + 6 \div 2 - 24$

45. $(16 - 4) \div 2 - 8$

46. Find the missing number in each of these calculations:

(i) $-5 \times 3 \times \square = 30$

(ii) $6 + 2 \times \square = -2$

(iii) $(\square - 5) \times 3 = -9$

(iv) $4 + 2 \times \square = 14$

(v) $\square - (-3) \times (-2) = -4$

(vi) $12 + \square \times (-2) = 0$

Section 1.2 Simplifying algebraic expressions

In algebra $2x^2 - 3x + 4$ is called an **expression**.

It consists of three **terms** which are separated by plus or minus signs.

The letter x is called a **variable** because it can have different values in other expressions.

The number 4 is called a **constant** because its value does not change.

The number -3 before the x is called the **coefficient** of x.

The coefficient of x^2 is 2.

Like terms

Here are some **like terms**:

(i) $2x$ and $3x$ (ii) $2x^2$ and $3x^2$ (iii) $3ab$ and $-6ab$.

These are like terms because they contain the same letter or combinations of the same letters or powers of the same letters.

The terms $3ab$ and $3ac$ are not like terms.
Neither are $3x^2$ and $3x$, because the powers are not the same.

> Like terms only may be added or subtracted.

Example 1

Simplify each of the following
(i) $2x - 3y + 4 - 3x + 5y - 2$
(ii) $3x^2 - 2xy + y^2 - 5xy + x^2 - 3y^2$

(i) $2x - 3y + 4 - 3x + 5y - 2 = 2x - 3x - 3y + 5y + 4 - 2$
$$= -x + 2y + 2$$

(ii) $3x^2 - 2xy + y^2 - 5xy + x^2 - 3y^2 = 3x^2 + x^2 - 2xy - 5xy + y^2 - 3y^2$
$$= 4x^2 - 7xy - 2y^2$$

Example 2

(i) Remove the brackets and simplify $(2x - 3)(x + 5)$.

(ii) Hence simplify $2(3x^2 - 2x + 4) - (2x - 3)(x + 5)$.

(i) $(2x - 3)(x + 5) = 2x(x + 5) - 3(x + 5)$
$= 2x^2 + 10x - 3x - 15$
$= 2x^2 + 7x - 15$

(ii) $2(3x^2 - 2x + 4) - (2x - 3)(x + 5)$
$= 6x^2 - 4x + 8 - (2x^2 + 7x - 15)$ ... from (i) above
$= 6x^2 - 4x + 8 - 2x^2 - 7x + 15$
$= 6x^2 - 2x^2 - 4x - 7x + 8 + 15$
$= 4x^2 - 11x + 23$

Exercise 1.2

Simplify each of the following expressions:

1. $4x + 3x + 6x$

2. $7x - 4x$

3. $3a + 8a - 4a$

4. $5a - 3a + 4a$

5. $a - 2a + 3a - a$

6. $6y - 7y + 5y - 2y$

7. $6x^2 + 4x^2 - 5x^2$

8. $x^2 + 3x + 2x^2 - 5x$

9. $3a^2 + b + 4a^2 - 3b$

10. $3x - 7 - 5x + 9$

11. $5a - 4 - a + 8$

12. $9x^2 + 6 - 3x^2 - 8$

13. Remove the brackets and simplify each of these:
(i) $(x + 4)(x + 3)$
(ii) $(2x + 3)(x + 1)$
(iii) $(x + 4)(2x - 3)$
(iv) $(2x - 2)(x + 5)$
(v) $(3x - 1)(2x + 5)$
(vi) $(2x - 3)(x - 6)$

14. Remove the brackets and simplify each of these:
(i) $3x - 5 + 4(4x - 3)$
(ii) $3x(x - 4) - x(x + 5)$
(iii) $3(2x - 4) - (5x - 2)$
(iv) $2(x^2 + 4x - 1) - 2x + 5$

15. Expand and simplify each of these:
(i) $(x + 2)^2$
(ii) $(x - 3)^2$
(iii) $(2x + 3)^2$
(iv) $(3x - 2)^2$

16. Copy and complete each of these:
(i) $3(\square + 5) = 6x + 15$
(ii) $4(\square - a) = 8 - 4a$
(iii) $5(\square - 3) = 20x - \square$
(iv) $2(\square + \square) = 8x + 16$

17. Which of these expressions gives the area of the rectangle?

$\boxed{12x - 4}$ $\boxed{2x - 24}$ $\boxed{12x - 24}$

2x − 4

6

18. For each shape, write an expression for the missing length:

(i)

? | Area = $9x - 6$

$3x - 2$

(ii)

Area = $3a^2 + 18a$ | $3a$

?

19. Write and simplify an expression for
  (i) the area
  (ii) the perimeter
of the given rectangle.

$6a + 2b$

$3b$

20. Simplify: $(3x - 2)(x + 5) - 2(x^2 - 3x + 7)$.

Section 1.3 Evaluating expressions

From your knowledge of algebra, you should know that

  (i) $3x = 3 \times x$

  (ii) $2ab = 2 \times a \times b$

  (iii) $x^2 = x \times x$

  (iv) $2a^2 = 2 \times a \times a$

Having regard to (i), (ii), (iii) and (iv) above, we will now find the values of expressions by substituting real numbers for the letters or variables in the expression.

Example 1

(i) Find the value of $2x^2 - 3y^2$ when $x = 3$ and $y = 2$.

(ii) Evaluate $3x^2 - 5x + 6$, when $x = -2$.

(i) $2x^2 - 3y^2 = 2(3)^2 - 3(2)^2$ ... when $x = 3$ and $y = 2$
$\qquad\qquad = 2(9) - 3(4)$
$\qquad\qquad = 18 - 12 = 6$

> Always square before you multiply.

(ii) $3x^2 - 5x + 6 = 3(-2)^2 - 5(-2) + 6$
$\qquad\qquad = 3(4) + 10 + 6$
$\qquad\qquad = 12 + 10 + 6 = 28$

Exercise 1.3

Evaluate each of the following:

1. $3x - 7$ when $x = 5$

2. $3x + 4$ when $x = -2$

3. $3x + 2y$ when $x = 2$ and $y = 3$

4. $2a + b$ when $a = 3$ and $b = -2$

5. $x^2 + 4x$ when $x = 3$

6. $2x^2 - 8$ when $x = 4$

7. $2x^2 - 6x + 4$ when $x = 1$ **8.** $3x^2 - 5x$ when $x = -2$

9. $3x^2 - x + 5$ when $x = -2$ **10.** $3x^2 + y^2$ when $x = 2$ and $y = -3$

11. $3(x^2 - 2)$ when $x = 5$ **12.** $3(x - 2y)$ when $x = -1$ and $y = 2$

13. What is the value of each expression when $x = -4$?

     (i) $2x^2 + 1$ (ii) $3(2x + 1)$ (iii) $\dfrac{x^2}{2} - 1$ (iv) $\dfrac{x^2 - 8}{4}$

14.

A	**B**	**C**	**D**	**E**	**F**
$2(t - 5)$	$2(t^2 - 7)$	$\dfrac{4t + 3}{-5}$	$5 - t^2$	$3t^2 - 11$	$\dfrac{3t - 17}{2}$

     (i) When $t = 3$, three of the above expressions have a value of -4.
         Find these expressions.

     (ii) When $t = -2$, three of the above expressions have the same value.
         Find these expressions.

15. Find the value of each of the following:

     (i) $\dfrac{5x - 3}{2}$ when $x = 5$ (ii) $\dfrac{10 - 6h}{5}$ when $h = 5$

     (iii) $\dfrac{10 - 2x}{1 - x}$ when $x = -3$ (iv) $\dfrac{3x - 4}{x - 5}$ when $x = -6$

Section 1.4 Solving linear equations ————————————

$3x - 5 = 7$ is an example of an **equation** as it contains an $=$ sign.

Solving an equation involves finding the value of the variable that makes the equation true.

The following two examples will illustrate the steps involved in solving a linear equation.

Example 1

Solve the equation $5x - 3 = 2x + 9$.

$$5x - 3 = 2x + 9$$
$$\Rightarrow \quad 5x - 3 + 3 = 2x + 9 + 3 \;\ldots\; \text{add 3 to both sides}$$
$$\Rightarrow \qquad\qquad 5x = 2x + 12$$
$$\Rightarrow \quad 5x - 2x = 2x - 2x + 12 \;\ldots\; \text{take } 2x \text{ from each side}$$
$$\Rightarrow \qquad\qquad 3x = 12$$
$$\Rightarrow \qquad\qquad\; x = 4 \;\ldots\; \text{divide each side by 3}$$

Example 2

Solve the equation $5(2x - 4) = 3(2x - 1) - 1$.

$$5(2x - 4) = 3(2x - 1) - 1$$
$\Rightarrow$ $\quad 10x - 20 = 6x - 3 - 1 \ldots$ remove brackets
$\Rightarrow$ $\quad 10x - 20 = 6x - 4 \ldots$ simplify each side
$\Rightarrow$ $\quad 10x - 20 + 20 = 6x - 4 + 20 \ldots$ add 20 to each side
$\Rightarrow$ $\quad 10x = 6x + 16$
$\Rightarrow$ $\quad 10x - 6x = 6x - 6x + 16 \ldots$ take 6x from each side
$\Rightarrow$ $\quad 4x = 16$
$\Rightarrow$ $\quad x = 4 \ldots$ divide each side by 4

Exercise 1.4

Solve each of the following equations:

1. $2x = 8$ **2.** $3x = 15$ **3.** $8x = 40$

4. $x - 3 = 5$ **5.** $2x - 3 = 10$ **6.** $3x - 1 = 8$

7. $5x + 2 = 12$ **8.** $3x - 10 = 8$ **9.** $5x - 6 = 19$

10. $7x + 4 = 25$ **11.** $6x - 2 = 4x + 10$ **12.** $7x - 9 = 3x + 11$

13. $3x + 1 = 5x - 13$ **14.** $5x - 2 = 40 - x$ **15.** $3x + 7 = 32 - 2x$

16. $3(2x + 1) = 2x + 11$ **17.** $2(2x + 5) = 5x + 5$ **18.** $4(2x - 3) = 2(3x - 5)$

19. $3(2x - 6) = 2(2x + 1)$ **20.** $3(5x - 2) = 4(3x + 6)$ **21.** $6(1 + 2x) = 5(3x - 1) - 4$

22. $2(x + 2) - 3(x - 3) = x + 7$ **23.** $3(4 - 3x) = 5(3 - 2x)$

24. $4(x + 3) - 3(2x - 5) = x$ **25.** $3(x - 1) = 18 - 5(x + 1)$

26. The figures below show a triangle and a rectangle.

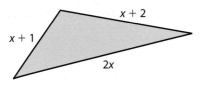 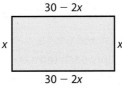

    (i) What value of x gives a triangle with a perimeter of 63 units?
    (ii) Find and simplify an expression for the perimeter of the rectangle.
    (iii) For what value of x are the perimeters of the triangle and rectangle equal?
    (iv) What value of x makes the rectangle into a square?

27. Form an equation and solve it to find the value of x in the given triangle.
Hence write down the measure of each angle.

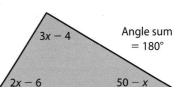

Section 1.5 Solving linear equations with fractions

Consider the equation $\dfrac{2x-1}{5} = 3$.

To get rid of the fraction, we multiply both sides by 5.

$$\therefore\ \frac{{}^{1}\cancel{5}(2x-1)}{\cancel{5}_1} = 3 \times 5$$

$$2x - 1 = 15$$

$$2x - 1 + 1 = 15 + 1 \ \ldots \text{ add 1 to each side}$$

$$2x = 16$$

$$\therefore\qquad x = 8$$

> If an equation contains more than one fraction, we multiply each part by the lowest common multiple (LCM) of the denominators.

Example 1

Solve the equation $\dfrac{4x}{5} - \dfrac{x}{2} = \dfrac{3}{4}$.

The LCM of 5, 2 and 4 is 20.
We now multiply each term by 20.

$$\frac{20(4x)}{5} - \frac{20(x)}{2} = \frac{20(3)}{4}$$

$$\Rightarrow \quad 4(4x) - 10(x) = 5(3)$$

$$\Rightarrow \qquad 16x - 10x = 15$$

$$\Rightarrow \qquad\qquad 6x = 15$$

$$\Rightarrow \qquad\qquad x = \tfrac{15}{6} = \tfrac{5}{2} = 2\tfrac{1}{2}$$

Example 2

Solve the equation $\dfrac{x+4}{3} - \dfrac{x+2}{4} = \dfrac{7}{6}$.

The LCM of 3, 4 and 6 is 12.
We now multiply each term by 12.

$$\frac{12(x+4)}{3} - \frac{12(x+2)}{4} = \frac{12(7)}{6}$$

$$\Rightarrow \quad 4(x+4) - 3(x+2) = 2(7)$$

$$\Rightarrow \quad 4x + 16 - 3x - 6 = 14$$

$$\Rightarrow \qquad\qquad x + 10 = 14$$

$$\Rightarrow \qquad x + 10 - 10 = 14 - 10$$

$$\Rightarrow \qquad\qquad\qquad x = 4$$

Exercise 1.5

Solve each of these equations:

1. $\dfrac{x}{4} = 3$

2. $\dfrac{3x + 7}{5} = 2$

3. $\dfrac{2x + 4}{3} = 6$

4. $\dfrac{x - 1}{5} = 4$

5. $\dfrac{3x - 1}{4} = 8$

6. $\dfrac{3x}{4} = \dfrac{9}{2}$

7. $\dfrac{x + 12}{4} = x$

8. $\dfrac{8x - 3}{7} = x$

9. $\dfrac{x + 18}{2} = 5x$

10. $\dfrac{x + 1}{2} = x - 2$

11. $\dfrac{x + 2}{3} = x + 4$

12. $\dfrac{2x + 3}{4} = x - 3$

13. $\dfrac{2x - 5}{3} = \dfrac{x - 2}{2}$

14. $\dfrac{2x + 1}{5} = \dfrac{x - 1}{2}$

15. $\dfrac{x}{2} + \dfrac{x - 5}{4} = 4$

16. $\dfrac{x + 5}{4} = \dfrac{2x}{3}$

17. $\dfrac{2x}{3} - \dfrac{x}{4} = \dfrac{5}{2}$

18. $\dfrac{x + 4}{3} - \dfrac{x}{4} = 2$

19. $\dfrac{2x - 1}{5} = \dfrac{x}{3} + \dfrac{1}{3}$

20. $\dfrac{2x - 1}{3} + \dfrac{x}{4} = \dfrac{3}{2}$

21. $\dfrac{x}{6} + 1 = \dfrac{x - 4}{4}$

22. $\dfrac{x}{5} - \dfrac{x - 3}{6} = \dfrac{3}{2}$

23. $\dfrac{3x - 2}{5} - \dfrac{x - 1}{2} = \dfrac{3}{10}$

24. $\dfrac{2x - 3}{4} + \dfrac{1}{2} = \dfrac{3x - 2}{5}$

25. $\dfrac{1}{3}(x + 2) = \dfrac{1}{5}(3x + 2)$

26. $\dfrac{x + 1}{2} - \dfrac{5}{12} = \dfrac{4x - 1}{3}$

27. $\dfrac{1}{2}(x - 3) + \dfrac{1}{3}(x + 1) = 8$

28. The length of a rectangle is $(2x + 3)$ cm.
    The width of the rectangle is $\frac{1}{2}(x + 3)$ cm.
    If the perimeter of the rectangle is 49 cm, find the value of x.

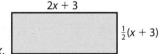

29. The diagram shows an isosceles triangle ABC.
    The lengths of the sides are given in centimetres and $|AB| = |AC|$.

    (i) Write down an equation in terms of x.
    (ii) Work out the length of [AB].

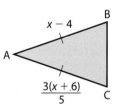

Section 1.6 Adding algebraic fractions

To express $\dfrac{3}{4} + \dfrac{2}{3}$ as a single fraction, we express both fractions with 12 as denominator.

$$\dfrac{3}{4} + \dfrac{2}{3} = \dfrac{9}{12} + \dfrac{8}{12} = \dfrac{17}{12}$$

This can be done more concisely as follows:

$$\dfrac{3}{4} + \dfrac{2}{3} = \dfrac{3(3) + 2(4)}{12} = \dfrac{9 + 8}{12} = \dfrac{17}{12} = 1\dfrac{5}{12}.$$

Similarly $\dfrac{6}{7} - \dfrac{2}{3} = \dfrac{6(3) - 2(7)}{21} = \dfrac{18 - 14}{21} = \dfrac{4}{21}$

> Algebraic fractions can be added or subtracted in the same way as numerical fractions.

Express as a single fraction $\dfrac{4x-3}{4} - \dfrac{x}{3}$.

The LCM of 3 and 4 is 12.

$$\frac{4x-3}{4} - \frac{x}{3} = \frac{3(4x-3) - 4(x)}{12} = \frac{12x - 9 - 4x}{12}$$

$$= \frac{8x - 9}{12}$$

Express $\dfrac{5}{x+3} - \dfrac{2}{x-4}$ as a single fraction.

The LCM of $(x + 3)$ and $(x - 4)$ is $(x + 3)(x - 4)$.

$$\frac{5}{x+3} - \frac{2}{x-4} = \frac{5(x-4) - 2(x+3)}{(x+3)(x-4)}$$

$$= \frac{5x - 20 - 2x - 6}{(x+3)(x-4)} = \frac{3x - 26}{(x+3)(x-4)}$$

Exercise 1.6

Express each of the following as a single fraction:

1. $\dfrac{3}{4} + \dfrac{1}{3}$

2. $\dfrac{3}{5} + \dfrac{7}{10}$

3. $\dfrac{5}{8} - \dfrac{1}{6}$

4. $\dfrac{x}{2} + \dfrac{x}{3}$

5. $\dfrac{3x}{4} + \dfrac{3x}{2}$

6. $\dfrac{5x}{3} - \dfrac{x}{2}$

7. $\dfrac{2x+3}{4} + \dfrac{x}{3}$

8. $\dfrac{3x-1}{3} + \dfrac{x-5}{2}$

9. $\dfrac{4x-3}{5} + \dfrac{x-3}{3}$

10. $\dfrac{3x-4}{6} - \dfrac{2x+1}{3}$

11. $\dfrac{3x-2}{6} - \dfrac{x-3}{4}$

12. $\dfrac{3x-1}{4} - \dfrac{x}{10} + \dfrac{3}{5}$

13. $\dfrac{1}{x+3} + \dfrac{1}{x}$

14. $\dfrac{2}{x+5} + \dfrac{3}{x}$

15. $\dfrac{2}{x+2} + \dfrac{3}{x+4}$

16. $\dfrac{4}{2x-1} + \dfrac{3}{2x-3}$

17. $\dfrac{3}{4x-1} + \dfrac{4}{3x-1}$

18. $\dfrac{5}{3x-1} - \dfrac{2}{x+3}$

19. $\dfrac{6}{3x-1} - \dfrac{4}{2x+3}$

20. $\dfrac{2}{3x-5} - \dfrac{1}{4}$

21. $\dfrac{3}{2x-7} - \dfrac{5}{3x-5}$

22. Express $\dfrac{5}{2x-1} - \dfrac{3}{x-2}$ as a single fraction and verify your answer by letting $x = 3$ in the given expression and in your answer.

23. If $\dfrac{6}{3x-4} - \dfrac{4}{2x+3} = \dfrac{k}{(3x-4)(2x+3)}$, find k where $k \in N$.

24. Write down an expression for the perimeter of these shapes.
Write each expression as a single fraction.

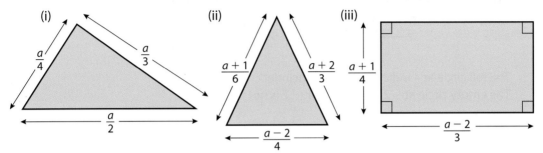

Section 1.7 Linear inequalities

$2x + 4 = 6$ is an example of an equation because both sides are equal.
However $2x + 4 > 6$ is an **inequality** as both sides are **not** equal.

The four inequality symbols are as follows

> **1.** $>$ … is greater than   **2.** $\geqslant$ is greater than or equal to
> **3.** $<$ … is less than   **4.** $\leqslant$ is less than or equal to

The rules for solving inequalities are very similar to those for solving equations. There is, however, one important difference.

> The inequality sign is reversed when both sides are multiplied or divided by the same **negative** number.
> $$3 < 5 \text{ but } 3 \times (-1) > 5 \times (-1)$$
> i.e. $\qquad -3 > -5$

Before solving inequalities, we will revisit the different types of number and how they are represented on the number line.

1. The set of natural numbers, **N** = {1, 2, 3, 4, …}

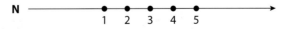

2. The set of integers, **Z** = {… −3, −2, −1, 0, 1, 2, 3, …}

3. The set of real numbers **R** contains all the numbers on the number line. R is represented on the number line by a **bold** line which indicates that all the numbers are included.

R ⟵⟶

Here are two sets of real numbers represented on the number line.

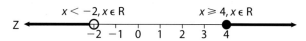

$x < -2, x \in R$ $x \geqslant 4, x \in R$

Z ⟵⟶ −2 −1 0 1 2 3 4

The full circle at 4 indicates that 4 is included.
The empty circle at −2 indicates that −2 is not included.

Example 1

Solve the inequality $5 - 2x < 9, x \in Z$ and illustrate the solution on the number line.

$$5 - 2x < 9$$
$$\Rightarrow \quad 5 - 2x - 5 < 9 - 5 \ldots \text{ subtract 5 from both sides}$$
$$\Rightarrow \quad -2x < 4$$
$$\Rightarrow \quad 2x > -4 \ldots \text{ multiplying both sides by } -1 \text{ results in reversing the inequality sign}$$
$$\Rightarrow \quad x > -2.$$

Illustration on the number line:

−2 −1 0 1 2 3

Example 2

Find the solution set A of $3x + 1 \leqslant 2x + 5, \ x \in R$.
Find the solution set B of $\frac{1}{3} - 2x \leqslant \frac{25}{3}, \ x \in R$.
Find $A \cap B$ and illustrate your answer on the number line.

$$3x + 1 \leqslant 2x + 5$$
$$\Rightarrow \quad 3x - 2x + 1 \leqslant 2x - 2x + 5 \qquad\qquad \frac{1}{3} - 2x \leqslant \frac{25}{3}$$
$$\Rightarrow \quad x + 1 \leqslant 5 \qquad\qquad\qquad \Rightarrow \quad 1 - 6x \leqslant 25$$
$$\Rightarrow \quad x + 1 - 1 \leqslant 5 - 1 \qquad\qquad \Rightarrow \quad 1 - 1 - 6x \leqslant 25 - 1$$
$$\Rightarrow \quad x \leqslant 4 \qquad\qquad\qquad \Rightarrow \quad -6x \leqslant 24$$
$$\Rightarrow \quad 6x \geqslant -24$$
$$\Rightarrow \quad x \geqslant -4.$$

Combining these results we get, $x \leqslant 4, x \geqslant -4$,
i.e. $-4 \leqslant x \leqslant 4$.

Number line:

⟵ −4 −3 −2 −1 0 1 2 3 4 ⟶

Exercise 1.7

1. Match up these inequalities.

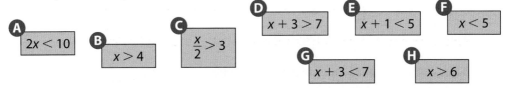

(A) $2x < 10$ **(B)** $x > 4$ **(C)** $\dfrac{x}{2} > 3$ **(D)** $x + 3 > 7$ **(E)** $x + 1 < 5$ **(F)** $x < 5$ **(G)** $x + 3 < 7$ **(H)** $x > 6$

2. Which two of the following are equivalent to $m > 6$?

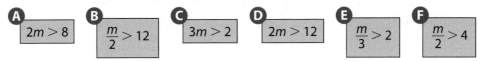

(A) $2m > 8$ **(B)** $\dfrac{m}{2} > 12$ **(C)** $3m > 2$ **(D)** $2m > 12$ **(E)** $\dfrac{m}{3} > 2$ **(F)** $\dfrac{m}{2} > 4$

3. Find the four equivalent pairs in these eight inequalities.

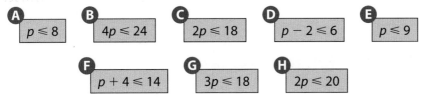

(A) $p \leqslant 8$ **(B)** $4p \leqslant 24$ **(C)** $2p \leqslant 18$ **(D)** $p - 2 \leqslant 6$ **(E)** $p \leqslant 9$ **(F)** $p + 4 \leqslant 14$ **(G)** $3p \leqslant 18$ **(H)** $2p \leqslant 20$

Solve the following inequalities and graph the solution set on the number line:

4. $3x - 2 \leqslant 7, \quad x \in N$

5. $8x - 1 < 5x - 10, \quad x \in Z$

6. $3x + 1 \leqslant 2x + 5, \quad x \in Z$

7. $7 - x > 4, \quad x \in Z$

8. $2x - 5 \geqslant 3x - 2, \quad x \in R$

9. $4(x + 2) < 3x - 4, \quad x \in R$

10. $1 \leqslant 3x - 11, \quad x \in Z$

11. $7 - 4x \geqslant 2x + 1, \quad x \in R$

12. $3 - 2(4 - x) \geqslant 3x, \quad x \in R$

13. $3x \leqslant -2(4 - x), \quad x \in R$

14. $x - 4 \leqslant 4x - 1, \quad x \in R$

15. $4 - 2x > 5(2 - x), \quad x \in R$

16. Solve the inequality $5(2x - 5) \geqslant 1 - 2(11 - 3x), \quad x \in R$.
Now illustrate your solution on the number line.

17. Find the solution set K of $11 \geqslant 3x + 2, \quad x \in R$.
Find the solution set L of $3x + 2 > -7, \quad x \in R$.
Find $K \cap L$ and graph the solution on the number line.

18. Find the solution set P of $2 - 3x \leqslant 4 + x, \quad x \in R$.
Find the solution set Q of $4 + x \leqslant 7, \quad x \in R$.
Find $P \cap Q$ and graph the solution on the number line.

19. Find the solution set A of $x < 3x - 1, \quad x \in R$.
Find the solution set B of $3x - 1 \leqslant 2x + 7, \quad x \in R$.
Now illustrate $A \cap B$ on the number line.

20. Find the solution set C of $2 \leqslant \dfrac{5x - 6}{2}$, $x \in N$.

Find the solution set D of $\dfrac{5x - 6}{2} \leqslant 7$, $x \in N$.

Illustrate $C \cap D$ on the number line.

21. A bus can carry a maximum of 44 passengers.
A school wants to take 5 adults and as many groups of 4 children as possible on the bus.

(i) Given that n represents the number of children, which of these inequalities is true for the bus

(a) $4n + 5 \geqslant 44$ (b) $4n + 5 \leqslant 44$

(c) $4n - 5 < 44$ (d) $4n + 5 > 44$?

(ii) Solve the inequality to find the maximum number of groups of 4 children the bus can carry.

Section 1.8 Simultaneous equations

The linear equations $3x + y = 9$

and $2x - y = 1$

are both satisfied by the values $x = 2$ and $y = 3$.

When two equations are both satisfied by the same values of x and y, they are said to be **simultaneous equations**.

We will solve simultaneous equations by eliminating one of the unknowns as shown in the following example.

Example 1

Solve the simultaneous equations

$$2x - 5y = 9$$
$$3x + 2y = 4$$

We number the equations $2x - 5y = 9$ ①

① and ② for convenience. $3x + 2y = 4$ ②

We now multiply equation ① by 2 and equation ② by 5 to equate the number of y's. (i.e. the y-coefficients)

① × 2: $4x - 10y = 18$

② × 5: $15x + 10y = 20$

Add: $19x \quad\quad = 38 \Rightarrow x = 2$

We now substitute 2 for x in equation ①

$$2x - 5y = 9$$

$x = 2 \Rightarrow \quad 4 - 5y = 9$

$\Rightarrow \quad \quad -5y = 5$

$\Rightarrow \quad \quad \quad 5y = -5 \Rightarrow y = -1$

$\therefore \quad \quad \quad x = 2 \text{ and } y = -1$

(Always substitute these values for x and y in the given equations to verify that they are correct.)

Example 2

Solve the simultaneous equations $\quad 3x - 2y = 19 \ldots$ ①

$$\frac{x}{3} + \frac{y}{2} = 5 \ldots ②$$

We number the equations ① and ② for convenience.

First multiply each term in equation ② by 6 (the LCM of 3 and 2) to eliminate the fractions.

Thus equation ② becomes: $\quad 2x + 3y = 30$

The equations now are $\quad \quad 3x - 2y = 19 \ldots$ ①

$$2x + 3y = 30 \ldots ②$$

Multiply equation ① by 2 and equation ② by -3 to equate the numerical coefficients of x.

① $\times 2 \quad : \quad 3x - 2y = 19 \quad \quad \quad 6x - 4y = 38$

② $\times -3: \quad 2x + 3y = 30 \quad \quad \quad -6x - 9y = -90$

$\quad \quad \quad \quad \text{Add:} \quad \quad \quad \quad \quad \quad \quad -13y = -52$

$$\Rightarrow 13y = 52$$

$$\Rightarrow y = 4$$

Substitute 4 for y in equation ① to find the value of x.

$$3x - 8 = 19$$

$$3x = 27$$

$$\Rightarrow x = 9$$

$\Rightarrow$ The solution is $x = 9$ and $y = 4$.

Exercise 1.8

Solve the following pairs of simultaneous equations:

1. $x + 2y = 6$
   $3x - 2y = 10$

2. $x + y = 7$
   $2x + y = 12$

3. $3x - y = 11$
   $3x - 2y = 13$

4. $2x + 3y = 9$
   $4x + y = 13$

5. $3x - 2y = 1$
   $x - 5y = 9$

6. $2x + y = 7$
   $3x - 2y = 0$

7. $x + 2y = 8$
   $2x + 3y = 14$

8. $x - 2y = 9$
   $3x + 7y = 1$

9. $4x - 3y = 23$
   $2x - 5y = 8$

10. $3x - 2y = 7$
    $4x + y = 13$

11. $2x + 3y = 5$
    $5x - 2y = -16$

12. $x + 2y = 12$
    $3x - 5y = 3$

13. $3x - 2y = -12$
    $2x + 3y = 5$

14. $4x + 5y = 1$
    $3x - 4y = 24$

15. $x = 3 + 4y$
    $y = 2 + 3x$

16. $3x + 4y = 23$
    $y = 2x + 3$

17. $4x = 16 - 5y$
    $6x = 13 - 2y$

18. $x + y = 3 = 2x - y$

19. $3x + y = 9$
    $\dfrac{x}{2} - y = -2$

20. $3x + y = 27$
    $\dfrac{x}{2} - y = 1$

21. $2x - 3y = 24$
    $\dfrac{5x}{3} - \dfrac{y}{2} = 12$

22. ABC is an equilateral triangle. All lengths are in cm.

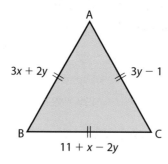

(i) Form two simultaneous equations and solve them to find the value of x and the value of y.

(ii) Now find the length of the side of the triangle.

Section 1.9 Problems and graphs

Simultaneous equations are particularly useful for solving certain types of algebraic problems, as shown in the following examples.

Example 1

James has some ten-cent coins and some twenty-cent coins in his piggy bank.
In his piggy bank he has a total of 18 coins which amount to €2.30.
Work out the number of ten-cent coins and the number of twenty-cent coins James has in his piggy bank.

Let x be the number of 10c coins and y the number of 20c coins.

① $x + y = 18$ ... there are 18 coins altogether

② $10x + 20y = 230$ ... the sum of the 10c and 20c coins is €2.30 (230c)

$$
\begin{aligned}
① \times 10: \quad & 10x + 10y = 180 \\
② \quad & 10x + 20y = 230 \\
\text{Subtract:} \quad & -10y = -50 \\
& 10y = 50 \\
& y = 5
\end{aligned}
$$

① $x + 5 = 18$ ... substitute 5 for y

$x = 13$

James has 13 ten-cent coins and 5 twenty-cent coins.

Using graphs

Simultaneous equations can be solved graphically by drawing the graph of the two equations (or two lines) and finding the coordinates of their point of **intersection**.

The given diagram shows the lines
$x + y = 1$ and $2x - y = -4$.

The lines intersect at $(-1, 2)$.

If we solve the two simultaneous equations we get $x = -1$ and $y = 2$.

This shows that simultaneous equations can be solved by drawing the two lines and writing down the point of intersection of the two lines.

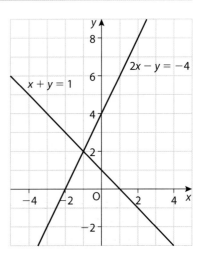

17

Exercise 1.9

1. The sum of two numbers is 9. If twice the first is added to three times the second, the answer is 20. Find the two numbers.

2. The difference of two numbers is 7. When three times the second is taken from twice the first, the result is 11. Find the two numbers.

3. Cinema tickets for 1 adult and 3 children cost €27.
   The cost for 2 adults and 5 children is €48.
   Find the cost of one adult ticket and the cost of one child ticket.

4. A slot machine takes only 20c and 50c coins and contains a total of 43 coins altogether. If the total value of the coins is €13.10, find the number of 20c and 50c coins in the machine.

5. A potter sells large and small mugs.
   Two small mugs and one large mug weigh 758 grams.
   Four small mugs and three large mugs weigh 1882 grams.
   How heavy is each mug?

6. The diagram shows a rectangle. All sides are measured in centimetres.
   (i) Write down a pair of simultaneous equations in a and b.
   (ii) Solve your pair of simultaneous equations to find a and b.

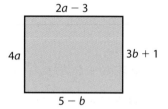

7. Some hens and a herd of cows are in a field.
   Between them they have 50 heads and 180 legs.
   How many cows and how many hens are in the field?

8. Jupiter chocolate bars are made in two sizes: regular and king size.
   2 regular bars and 5 king size bars weigh 760 g altogether.
   1 regular bar and 7 king size bars weigh 920 g altogether.
   (i) How much does a regular bar weigh?
   (ii) How much does a king size bar weigh?

9. Rory has some 2-litre bottles of lemonade.
   Sarah has some 3-litre bottles of lemonade.
   Altogether they have 27 litres.
   Rory has 6 bottles more than Sarah.
   How many bottles does each person have?

10. The diagram shows three lines **A**, **B** and **C**.
    The equations of the lines are:
    A: $x + y = 3$ **B:** $y = 2x$ **C:** $x - 2y = 3$.
    Use the diagram to solve these simultaneous equations:
    (i) $x + y = 3$ (ii) $x - 2y = 3$ (iii) $y = 2x$
        $y = 2x$ $x + y = 3$ $x - 2y = 3$

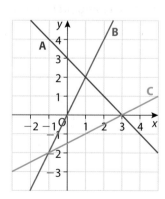

11. (i) Use the graphs to solve each pair of simultaneous
equations.

(a) $y - 2x = 1$ (b) $y - 2x = 4$
$\quad x + y = 4$ $\quad\quad x + y = 4$

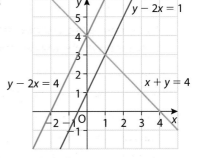

Check each solution by substituting into the
equations.

(ii) How do you know there is no solution to the
following pair of simultaneous equations?
$$y - 2x = 4$$
$$y - 2x = 1$$

12. A fraction is equivalent to $\frac{2}{7}$.
If the numerator and denominator are both increased by 1, the fraction is equivalent to $\frac{3}{10}$.
Find both fractions.

13. The shape ABCD is a parallelogram.
All lengths marked are in cm.
Find the lengths of [AB] and [BC].

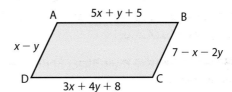

Section 1.10 Changing the subject of a formula

In the equation $x = 2y - z$, we say that x is expressed in terms of y and z, or that x is the
subject of the formula.

If the formula is changed to the form $z = 2y - x$, then z is the subject of the formula.

If we rearrange a formula (or equation) so that there is a different variable on the left-hand
side, we are said to have **changed the subject of the formula**.

The process of changing the subject of a formula
is very similar to the steps we use when solving
an equation.

> An equation remains unchanged
> if the same operation is performed
> on both sides.

The following examples will illustrate the basic
rules for changing the subject of a formula.

Example 1

If $bc - d = a$, make c the subject of the formula.

$bc - d = a$

$\therefore \quad bc = a + d$ ... add d to both sides

$\therefore \quad c = \dfrac{a + d}{b}$ ... divide both sides by b.

Example 2

If $x = \dfrac{3y}{2} - 1$, make y the subject of the formula.

$$x = \dfrac{3y}{2} - 1$$

$2x = 3y - 2$ ... multiply all terms by 2

$2x + 2 = 3y$ ... add 2 to each side

$\dfrac{2x}{3} + \dfrac{2}{3} = y$ ... divide each term by 3

$y = \dfrac{2x}{3} + \dfrac{2}{3} \left(\text{or } y = \dfrac{2x + 2}{3} \right)$

Example 3

If $a = \dfrac{bc}{b + c}$, make c the subject of the formula.

$$a = \dfrac{bc}{b + c}$$

$a(b + c) = bc$ ... multiply each term by $(b + c)$

$ab + ac = bc$ ... remove the brackets

$ac - bc = -ab$

$c(a - b) = -ab$

$c = \dfrac{-ab}{a - b}$

Exercise 1.10

1. Make the underlined letter the subject of the formula in each of the following:

   (i) $2\underline{x} - 4 = y$ (ii) $a = 8\underline{b} - 6$ (iii) $c = 4\underline{d} - 1$ (iv) $h = 2\underline{k} - 2$

2. Rearrange each of these formulas to make the underlined letter the subject:

   (i) $a = 3\underline{b} - 5$ (ii) $b = 4\underline{w} + 2$ (iii) $d = 6\underline{e} - 12$ (iv) $g = 18 - 5\underline{h}$

3. Copy and complete each of the following:

   (i) $v = u + at$

       $v - \square = at$

       $t = \ldots$

   (ii) $ap + bq = k$

       $ap = k - \square$

       $p = \dfrac{k - \square}{\square}$

   (iii) $p = \dfrac{g}{5} + 3h$

       $p - \square = \dfrac{g}{5}$

       $\square(p - \square) = g$

       $g = \ldots$

4. Make x the subject of the formula in each of these:

(i) $x - y = 2z$ (ii) $3x - b = 4c$ (iii) $6y + 3x = 7$ (iv) $\frac{x}{3} - 2y = 8$

5. Make a the subject of the formula in each of these:

(i) $2a - b = \frac{1}{2}$ (ii) $ab - 3a = 5$ (iii) $7(a - 3) = 4b$

6. (i) Make a the subject of the formula $k = \frac{a}{b} - 2$.

(ii) Make v the subject of the formula $s = \frac{u}{v} + 10$.

7. Make the letter in brackets the subject of the formula in each of the following:

(i) $c = \frac{a}{2} - 4b \dots (a)$ (ii) $2(a - 2b) = 3c \dots (a)$ (iii) $2x - \frac{1}{3} = \frac{y}{3} \dots (x)$

(iv) $5(b - 3) = \frac{a}{2} \dots (b)$ (v) $x = \frac{y - 2z}{3} \dots (z)$ (vi) $a = \frac{b}{2} - \frac{3c}{4} \dots (b)$

8. (i) Make a the subject of the formula $ma = n(m + a)$.
(ii) Make n the subject of the formula $b = a + (n - 1)d$.

9. Make the letter in brackets the subject of the formula in each of the following:

(i) $\frac{3x}{4} = 5(y + z) \dots (y)$ (ii) $\frac{ab}{3} = \frac{b}{2} + c \dots (b)$

(iii) $t = \frac{x - 2y}{z} \dots (y)$ (iv) $\frac{p}{q} = \frac{q}{t} + 1 \dots (t)$

10. Make the letter in brackets the subject of the formula in each of these:

(i) $x = \frac{a + b}{a - b} \dots (a)$ (ii) $y = \frac{3x + 4}{x - 1} \dots (x)$ (iii) $p = \frac{qr}{q - r} \dots (r)$

11. Make k the subject of the formula $ab = \frac{dk}{k - e}$.

12. Which of the following are correct arrangements of $s = w - \frac{g}{r}$?

A $w = s - \frac{g}{r}$

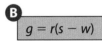

B $g = r(s - w)$

C $r = \frac{g}{s - w}$ **D** $r = \frac{g}{w - s}$

E $w = \frac{g}{r} + s$ **F** $g = r(w - s)$

13. By squaring each side, make the letter in brackets the subject of the formula in each of these:

(i) $x = \sqrt{a + b} \dots (b)$ (ii) $a = \sqrt{\frac{x}{y}} \dots (y)$ (iii) $k = 2\sqrt{\frac{a}{b}} \dots (b)$

14. If $C = \frac{5}{9}(F - 32)$, make F the subject of the formula.

15. (i) Make q the subject of the formula $t = \frac{8(p + q)}{pq}$.

(ii) If $m = \frac{cab}{a - b}$, express b in terms of a, c and m.

Test yourself 1

1. (i) Solve the equation $2(3x - 1) = 7 - 3(3x - 2)$.
   (ii) Solve the simultaneous equations
   $$3x + y = 13$$
   $$x - 2y = -5.$$
   (iii) Make b the subject of the formula $ax + by = c$.

2. (i) Solve the equation $7(x - 1) = 21 - 3(x + 1)$.
   (ii) Which of the following inequalities are equivalent to $a \geqslant 10$?

   A $a - 5 \geqslant 5$ **B** $2a \geqslant 20$ **C** $a + 5 \geqslant 5$ **D** $\frac{1}{2}a \geqslant 5$ **E** $a + \frac{1}{2} \geqslant 10\frac{1}{2}$

   (iii) Evaluate $\dfrac{2}{x + 2} + \dfrac{3}{2x + 1}$ when $x = \frac{1}{2}$.

   (iv) Solve the simultaneous equations
   $$2v = 31 - 3w$$
   $$3v + w = 64$$

3. (i) Simplify $(2x - 3)^2 - 2x(2x - 5)$.

   (ii) Solve the equation $\dfrac{2x + 1}{3} = \dfrac{1}{2}$.

   (iii) Solve the inequality $5 - (3x + 4) \geqslant 4, x \in Z$ and illustrate your answer on the number line.

   (iv) The diagram shows the dimensions of a rectangle. The perimeter of the rectangle is 18 cm. Find the value of x.

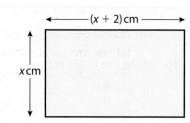

4. (i) Evaluate $2x^2 - 3xy$ when $x = -2$ and $y = \frac{1}{3}$.

   (ii) Solve the equation $\dfrac{3x}{4} = \dfrac{4x - 1}{5}$.

   (iii) Find the solution set A of $2x - 4 \leqslant 6, x \in N$.
   Find the solution set B of $4 - 2x < 0, x \in N$.
   Illustrate $A \cap B$ on the number line.

   (iv) The diagram shows three lines **A**, **B** and **C**.
   (a) Match the three lines to these equations.
   $$y = 2x$$
   $$x + y = 3$$
   $$x - 2y = 3$$

   (b) Use the diagram to solve these simultaneous equations.

   (i) $y = 2x$ (ii) $x + y = 3$
       $x + y = 3$ $x - 2y = 3$
   (iii) $y = 2x$
       $x - 2y = 3$

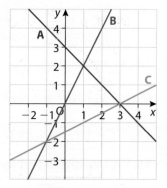

5. (i) Solve the inequality $8x - 1 \leqslant 5x - 10$, $x \in R$ and graph the solution on the number line.

(ii) The formula $h = \dfrac{a}{k} + j$ gives h in terms of a, k and j.

Which of the following are correct rearrangements of the formula?

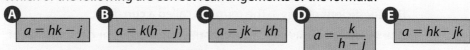

A $a = hk - j$ **B** $a = k(h - j)$ **C** $a = jk - kh$ **D** $a = \dfrac{k}{h - j}$ **E** $a = hk - jk$

(iii) Solve these simultaneous equations:
$$a = 2b + 1$$
$$5a + 2b = 29.$$

(iv) Express $\dfrac{1 + 3x}{3} + \dfrac{x - 5}{2}$ as a single fraction and simplify your answer.

Hence solve the equation $\dfrac{1 + 3x}{3} + \dfrac{x - 5}{2} = \dfrac{25}{3}$.

6. (i) Solve the equation $\dfrac{3x - 4}{6} - \dfrac{1}{3} = \dfrac{x - 1}{3}$.

(ii) Where do the lines with equations $2x + 3y = 1$ and $5x - 2y = 12$ intersect?

(iii) Find the largest possible integer value of x if $2(4x - 1) < 11$.

(iv) The volume of a cone, in cm³, is given by $V = \dfrac{\pi r^2 h}{3}$.

r is the base radius and h is the height, both in cm.

(a) Rearrange the formula to make r the subject.

(b) Use your rearrangement to work out the base radius of a cone of volume 100 cm³ and height 8 cm.
Give your answer to one decimal place.

7. (i) Find the value of $\dfrac{1}{p} - \dfrac{1}{q}$ when $p = \frac{1}{2}$ and $q = \frac{1}{3}$.

(ii) Megan thinks of a number. She adds 15 and then doubles her result.
Olivia's starting number is 5 more than Megan's starting number.
Olivia trebles her number and then takes off 6.
Both Megan and Olivia end up with the same number.
What numbers did each of them think of?

(iii) If $p = \dfrac{3qr}{q + r}$, express r in terms of p and q.

(iv)

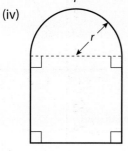

This doorway is formed by a semicircle on top of a square.

(a) Show that a formula for the perimeter, P, of the doorway can be written $P = \pi r + 6r$.

(b) Make r the subject of this formula.

(c) What is the height of a doorway with a perimeter of 10 metres?
Give your answer in terms of π.

Summary of key points...

1. **Algebraic expressions**

   $3x^2 - 4x + 2$ is an **algebraic expression** consisting of 3 **terms**.

   The **coefficient** of x^2 is 3. The term 2 is called a **constant**.

   Like terms are terms which contain the same letters or combination of letters.

   Like terms only may be added or subtracted; $3x + 4x + 7x = 14x$.

   $2ab + 3ac$ cannot be added as they are not like terms.

2. **Order of operations**

   BIMDAS is a mnemonic to help you remember the order of operations:

   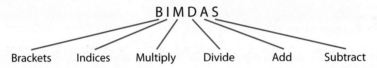

   | Brackets | Indices | Multiply | Divide | Add | Subtract |

3. **Inequalities**

   $>$ means **greater than** $<$ means **less than**

   $\geqslant$ means **greater than or equal to** $\leqslant$ means **less than or equal to**

   The inequality $-1 \leqslant x < 2, x \in R$ is shown on the given number line.

   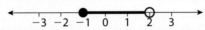

4. **Simultaneous equations**

   When you solve a pair of linear simultaneous equations you are finding the point where the lines cross.

   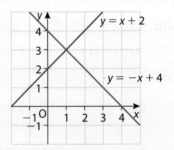

5. **Changing the subject of a formula**

   The **subject** of a formula appears on its own on one side of the formula and does not appear on the other side.

   For example $x = 4y + 4$ can be rearranged to give $y = \dfrac{x - 4}{4}$.

   $\downarrow$ $\downarrow$

   x is the subject y is the subject

Key words

quadratic expression	**perfect squares**	**difference of two squares**
roots	**parabola**	**the quadratic formula**	**simultaneous equations**
power	**index**	**surd**	**rational**	**irrational**

Section 2.1 Factorising quadratic expressions

An expression of the form $ax^2 + bx + c$, where a, b and c are numbers and $a \neq 0$, is called a **quadratic expression**.

Since $(x + 5)(x + 2) = x^2 + 7x + 10$, we say that $(x + 5)$ and $(x + 2)$ are the factors of $x^2 + 7x + 10$.

We factorise a quadratic expression by 'trial and error' to find numbers such that the product of the outside terms added to the product of the inside terms gives the middle term of the quadratic expression.

outside terms

$(x + 5)(x + 2)$

inside terms

Example 1

Factorise $3x^2 + 13x + 4$

The factors of $3x^2 + 13x + 4$ will take the form $(3x + ?)(x + ?)$

$$3x^2 + 13x + 4 = (3x + 1)(x + 4)$$

These are the correct factors as   (i) $3x(x) = 3x^2$

           (ii) $12x + x = 13x$

           (iii) $4 \times 1 = 4$

Factors of 3:

3×1

Factors of 4:

4×1

or 2×2

Example 2

Factorise   (i) $3x^2 + 10x + 8$ (ii) $8x^2 + 10x - 3$

(i) $3x^2 + 10x + 8$

     The factors of $3x^2 + 10x + 8$ will take the form $(3x + ?)(x + ?)$

$$3x^2 + 10x + 8 = (3x + 4)(x + 2)$$

     These are the correct factors since $6x + 4x = 10x$.

     $\therefore \; 3x^2 + 10x + 8 = (3x + 4)(x + 2)$

(ii) $8x^2 + 10x - 3 = (4x - 1)(2x + 3)$

$\qquad 12x - 2x = 10x$ (correct)

$\qquad \therefore \ 8x^2 + 10x - 3 = (4x - 1)(2x + 3)$

Expressions of the form $ax^2 + bx$

To factorise $x^2 - 5x$, we divide each term by the highest common factor, i.e. x.

$\qquad x^2 - 5x = x(x - 5)$

Similarly (i) $3x^2 - 6x = 3x(x - 2)$ (ii) $9x^2 - 15x = 3x(3x - 5)$.

Difference of two squares

Numbers such as 1, 4, 9, 16, … are called **perfect squares**.

$\qquad 1 = 1^2, 4 = 2^2, 9 = 3^2, 16 = 4^2, \ldots$

Similarly $9x^2$ and $16y^2$ are **squares** since $9x^2 = (3x)^2$ and $16y^2 = (4y)^2$.

An expression such as $9x^2 - 16y^2$ is called **the difference of two squares**.

If we multiply $(x + y)(x - y)$ we get $x^2 - y^2$.
Thus the factors of $x^2 - y^2 = (x + y)(x - y)$.

$$x^2 - y^2 = (x + y)(x - y)$$

Example 3

Factorise   (i) $2x^2 - 3x$ (ii) $x^2 - 25$ (iii) $9x^2 - 16y^2$

(i) $2x^2 - 3x = x(2x - 3)$
(ii) $x^2 - 25 = (x)^2 - (5)^2 = (x - 5)(x + 5)$
(iii) $9x^2 - 16y^2 = (3x)^2 - (4y)^2 = (3x - 4y)(3x + 4y)$

Exercise 2.1

Factorise each of the following:

1. $x^2 + 7x + 6$
2. $x^2 + 7x + 12$
3. $2x^2 + 5x + 2$

4. $2x^2 + 9x + 4$
5. $2x^2 + 15x + 7$
6. $3x^2 + 8x + 4$

7. $3x^2 + 7x + 4$
8. $5x^2 + 17x + 6$
9. $4k^2 + 8k + 3$

10. $4x^2 + 13x + 3$
11. $10x^2 + 17x + 7$
12. $6x^2 + 23x + 10$

13. $x^2 - 7x + 12$
14. $x^2 - 13x + 36$
15. $2x^2 - 7x + 3$

16. $2x^2 - 19x + 9$
17. $2x^2 - 7x - 15$
18. $8x^2 + 10x - 3$

19. $6x^2 - 11x + 3$
20. $8x^2 - 10x - 3$
21. $8x^2 - 14x + 3$

22. $3x^2 + 13x - 10$ **23.** $2x^2 - 21x + 54$ **24.** $6x^2 + x - 22$

25. $24x^2 - 2x - 15$ **26.** $6x^2 - 19x + 3$ **27.** $15x^2 - 14x - 8$

28. $x^2 - 4x$ **29.** $x^2 + 8x$ **30.** $2x^2 - 3x$

31. $x^2 - y^2$ **32.** $x^2 - 25y^2$ **33.** $16x^2 - 1$

34. $16x^2 - 25y^2$ **35.** $49x^2 - 100$ **36.** $36x^2 - 49y^2$

Section 2.2 Using factors to solve quadratic equations ——

Take the equation $x^2 - 5x + 6 = 0$.

When $x = 2$, then $x^2 - 5x + 6$ becomes
$$(2)^2 - 5(2) + 6, \text{ i.e., } 4 - 10 + 6 = 0$$

When $x = 3$, then $x^2 - 5x + 6$ becomes
$$(3)^2 - 5(3) + 6, \text{ i.e., } 9 - 15 + 6 = 0$$

When $x = 2$ or $x = 3$, both sides of the equation are zero.

When this happens, we say that $x = 2$ and $x = 3$ are **solutions** or **roots** of the equation.

Solving a quadratic equation involves finding the values of x which satisfy the equation.

When a quadratic equation is in the form $ax^2 + bx + c = 0$, we express the left-hand side as the product of two linear factors and then solve the equation, as shown in the following examples.

Example 1

Solve the equation $x^2 - 5x - 14 = 0$.

$x^2 - 5x - 14 = 0$

$\Rightarrow (x - 7)(x + 2) = 0$ ... factorise the left-hand side

$\Rightarrow x - 7 = 0$ or $x + 2 = 0$ ... let each factor $= 0$

$\Rightarrow x = 7$ or $x = -2$

$\therefore x = 7$ or $x = -2$

Example 2

Solve these equations:

(i) $2x^2 - 9x = 0$ (ii) $4x^2 - 25 = 0$

(i) $2x^2 - 9x = 0$

     [This equation contains no number term (i.e. no constant) and is factorised by taking outside the bracket the highest factor common to both terms.]

     $2x^2 - 9x = 0 \Rightarrow x(2x - 9) = 0$

     $x = 0$ or $2x - 9 = 0$

     $\Rightarrow x = 0$ or $x = 4\frac{1}{2}$

     $\therefore x = 0$ or $x = 4\frac{1}{2}$

(ii) $4x^2 - 25 = 0$

$\Rightarrow (2x - 5)(2x + 5) = 0$ ... the difference of two squares

$\Rightarrow 2x - 5 = 0$ or $2x + 5 = 0$ ... both factors $= 0$

$\Rightarrow 2x = 5$ or $2x = -5$

$\Rightarrow x = 2\frac{1}{2}$ or $x = -2\frac{1}{2}$

Discovery

The curve on the right is called a **parabola**.

It is the graph of $y = x^2 - 5x + 6$.

> Can you use the graph to solve the equation $x^2 - 5x + 6 = 0$?
> Factorise $x^2 - 5x + 6$ and then solve the equation $x^2 - 5x + 6 = 0$.
> What are the links between your answers and the graph?

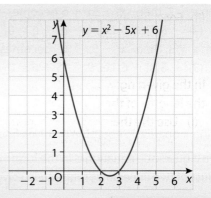

Exercise 2.2

Solve each of the following equations:

1. $(x - 4)(x + 1) = 0$
2. $(2x - 1)(3x + 6) = 0$
3. $x(2x - 5) = 0$
4. $x^2 - 2x - 3 = 0$
5. $x^2 - 8x + 12 = 0$
6. $x^2 - 4x - 5 = 0$
7. $x^2 - 2x - 8 = 0$
8. $x^2 + 2x - 15 = 0$
9. $2x^2 - 5x + 2 = 0$
10. $6x^2 - x - 2 = 0$
11. $4x^2 - 29x + 7 = 0$
12. $9x^2 - 9x - 28 = 0$
13. $4x^2 - 12x + 5 = 0$
14. $3x^2 - 13x - 10 = 0$
15. $6x^2 + 17x - 3 = 0$
16. $x^2 - 7x = 0$
17. $2x^2 - 5x = 0$
18. $3x^2 + 4x = 0$
19. $2x^2 - 9x = 0$
20. $3x^2 + 10x = 0$
21. $5x^2 - 12x = 0$
22. $x^2 - 9 = 0$
23. $x^2 - 49 = 0$
24. $4x^2 - 9 = 0$
25. $4x^2 - 25 = 0$
26. $9x^2 - 16 = 0$
27. $4x^2 - 1 = 0$
28. $(x - 3)(x - 2) = 20$
29. $(2x - 5)(x - 2) = 15$
30. $2x(x - 2) = 3(x + 10)$

31. (i) Show that the area of this rectangle in cm^2 is equivalent to $2x^2 + 5x + 2$.
    (ii) If the area of the rectangle is $14 \, cm^2$,
        (a) form an equation in x and solve it.
        (b) write down the length and width of the rectangle.

$(2x + 1)$ cm

$(x + 2)$ cm

32. The rectangle and triangle below each have the same area.

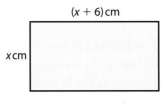 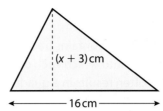

    (i) Write an expression in x for
        (a) the area of the rectangle   (b) the area of the triangle.

   (ii) Form an equation and solve it to find the value of x.
        Hence find the dimensions of the rectangle.
        Why did you take only one value for x?

33. In the given right-angled triangle,
the lengths of the scales are given.

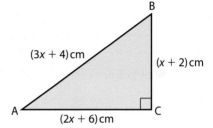

    (i) Use the theorem of Pythagoras to write
       down an equation in x.
   (ii) Solve this equation.
  (iii) Write down the length of [AB].

34. Three parabolas are shown here.

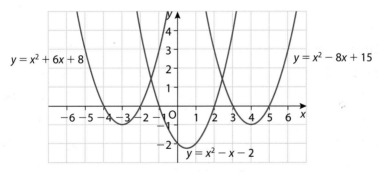

   Use the graphs above to solve the following equations (each has two solutions).
   (i) $x^2 - 8x + 15 = 0$ (ii) $x^2 + 6x + 8 = 0$ (iii) $x^2 - x - 2 = 0$

35. The diagram shows a shape in which
all the corners are right angles.
The area of the shape is 48 cm².

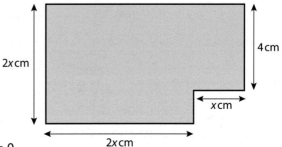

    (i) Form an equation, in terms of x,
       for the area of the shape.
       Show that the equation can be
       simplified to $x^2 + x - 12 = 0$.
   (ii) Solve the equation $x^2 + x - 12 = 0$
       and hence calculate the perimeter of the shape.

Section 2.3 Solving quadratic equations involving fractions

To solve an equation which contains fractions, we multiply each term of the equation by the smallest number into which each of the denominators divide (i.e. the LCM of the denominators). This often results in a quadratic equation as the following examples illustrate.

Example 1

Solve the equation $\dfrac{x-3}{3} + \dfrac{12}{x} = 4$.

The LCM of 3 and x is $3x$.
We now multiply each term by $3x$.

$$\frac{{}^{1}\!3x(x-3)}{{}_{1}3} + \frac{3x^{1}(12)}{x_{1}} = 4(3x)$$

$\therefore \qquad x(x-3) + 3(12) = 4(3x)$

$\therefore \qquad\quad x^2 - 3x + 36 = 12x$

Take $12x$ from each side: $x^2 - 3x + 36 - 12x = 12x - 12x$

$$x^2 - 15x + 36 = 0$$

Factorise: $\qquad\qquad\qquad (x-3)(x-12) = 0$

$\therefore\ x - 3 = 0\ $ or $\ x - 12 = 0$

$\therefore\ x = 3\ $ or $\ x = 12$

Example 2

Solve the equation $\dfrac{2}{x-1} - \dfrac{1}{x+2} = \dfrac{1}{2}$.

The LCM of the denominators is $2(x-1)(x+2)$.
We now multiply each term by $2(x-1)(x+2)$.

$$\frac{2(2)(x-1)^{1}(x+2)}{(x-1)_{1}} - \frac{2(x-1)(x+2)^{1}}{(x+2)_{1}} = \frac{2^{1}(x-1)(x+2)}{2_{1}}$$

$$4(x+2) - 2(x-1) = (x-1)(x+2)$$

$$4x + 8 - 2x + 2 = x^2 + 2x - x - 2$$

$$2x + 10 = x^2 + x - 2$$

$$-x^2 + x + 12 = 0$$

$\therefore \qquad\quad x^2 - x - 12 = 0 \ldots$ multiply each term by -1

$\therefore \qquad\quad (x-4)(x+3) = 0 \ldots$ factorising

$\therefore\ x - 4 = 0\ $ or $\ x + 3 = 0$

$\therefore\ x = 4\ $ or $\ x = -3$

Exercise 2.3

Solve each of the following equations:

1. $x - 5 + \dfrac{4}{x} = 0$

2. $x - 7 + \dfrac{12}{x} = 0$

3. $\dfrac{x + 7}{3} + \dfrac{2}{x} = 4$

4. $\dfrac{15}{x} + 2 = x$

5. $\dfrac{2x}{2x - 1} + x = 3$

6. $\dfrac{x + 1}{3} - \dfrac{1}{x} = 1$

7. $\dfrac{1}{x + 1} + \dfrac{x}{5} = 1$

8. $\dfrac{4}{x} + \dfrac{1}{x - 1} = 3$

9. $\dfrac{6}{x} - \dfrac{5}{x + 1} = 2$

10. $\dfrac{5}{x - 2} - \dfrac{3}{x + 2} = 2$

11. $\dfrac{2}{x - 2} + 3 = \dfrac{1}{x}$

12. $\dfrac{5}{2x - 1} + 1 = \dfrac{6}{x}$

13. $\dfrac{9}{x + 8} + \dfrac{1}{x} = 1$

14. $\dfrac{2}{x - 1} + \dfrac{3}{x - 3} = 2$

15. $\dfrac{5}{x - 4} - \dfrac{2}{x - 2} = 2$

16. $\dfrac{5}{x + 2} + \dfrac{4}{x - 1} + 6 = 0$

17. $\dfrac{5}{2x + 1} + \dfrac{6}{x + 1} = 3$

18. $\dfrac{3x + 3}{x - 1} = \dfrac{1}{x} + 1$

19. Each of these equations has only one root. Find it in each case.

(i) $\dfrac{2x}{x + 3} + \dfrac{1}{x} = 2$ (ii) $\dfrac{2x}{2x + 1} + \dfrac{1}{x - 1} = 1$ (iii) $\dfrac{1}{x + 1} + \dfrac{x}{x - 1} = 1$

Section 2.4 Using the quadratic formula

In the previous sections of this chapter we used factors to solve quadratic equations of the form $ax^2 + bx + c = 0$.

If the expression $ax^2 + bx + c$ cannot be factorised, the equation can be solved by using the quadratic formula which is given below.

The quadratic formula

> The roots of the quadratic equation $ax^2 + bx + c = 0$ are
> $$x = \frac{-b \pm \sqrt{b^2 - 4ac}}{2a}$$

Example 1

Use the quadratic formula to find the roots of the equation $5x^2 + 7x - 3 = 0$, correct to two decimal places.

In the equation $5x^2 + 7x - 3 = 0, a = 5, b = 7$ and $c = -3$.

$$x = \frac{-b \pm \sqrt{b^2 - 4ac}}{2a}$$

$$= \frac{-7 \pm \sqrt{49 - 4(5)(-3)}}{2(5)}$$

$$= \frac{-7 \pm \sqrt{49 + 60}}{10}$$

$$= \frac{-7 \pm \sqrt{109}}{10} = \frac{-7 \pm 10.44}{10} = \frac{-17.44}{10} \text{ or } \frac{3.44}{10}$$

$\therefore\ x = -1.744$ or $x = 0.344$

$\therefore\ x = -1.74$ or $x = 0.34$

Exercise 2.4

Solve the following equations using the formula $x = \dfrac{-b \pm \sqrt{b^2 - 4ac}}{2a}$.

Give your answers correct to two decimal places.

1. $x^2 + 4x + 2 = 0$
2. $x^2 + 6x + 4 = 0$
3. $x^2 + 2x - 5 = 0$

4. $x^2 - 2x - 7 = 0$
5. $4x^2 + 2x - 1 = 0$
6. $3x^2 - x - 1 = 0$

7. $3x^2 - 6x + 2 = 0$
8. $3x^2 + 7x - 5 = 0$
9. $5x^2 - 4x - 2 = 0$

10. $3x^2 + 8x + 2 = 0$
11. $6x^2 - 9x - 4 = 0$
12. $3x^2 + 7x = 2$

13. $4x^2 + 3x = 5$
14. $2x^2 = 7x - 4$
15. $3x^2 + 5x = 3$

Express the following equations in the form $ax^2 + bx + c = 0$, and hence solve the equations, giving your answers correct to one place of decimals.

16. $x + \dfrac{2}{x} = 7$
17. $\dfrac{12}{x + 2} - \dfrac{1}{x} = 2$
18. $\dfrac{7}{x} = 3 + 2x$

19. $\dfrac{3}{x - 1} - \dfrac{2}{x + 3} = 1$
20. $\dfrac{3}{2x - 3} = \dfrac{5x + 7}{x + 1}$
21. $\dfrac{1}{x + 1} + \dfrac{2}{x - 3} = 4$

22. The diagram shows a rectangle with length $= x + 4$ and width $= x - 1$.

    All measurements are in centimetres.
    (i) Express the area of the rectangle in terms of x.
    (ii) If the area is 10 cm², write an equation in x and solve it.
    (iii) Find the length of the rectangle, in cm, correct to two decimal places.

$x + 4$

$x - 1$

Section 2.5 Simultaneous equations – one linear, one quadratic

To solve a pair of equations, one of which is linear and the other quadratic, we use the method of **substitution** as follows:

1. In the linear equation, express one variable in terms of the other, e.g. $x = 2y - 1$.

2. Substitute this value for x (or y) in the quadratic equation and then solve the equation.

Example 1

Solve the equations
$$x + y = 3 \dots ①$$
$$x^2 + y^2 = 17 \dots ②$$

From equation ①: $x = 3 - y$

Substituting $(3 - y)$ for x in equation ② we get:

$$(3 - y)^2 + y^2 = 17$$
$$\Rightarrow 9 - 6y + y^2 + y^2 = 17$$
$$2y^2 - 6y - 8 = 0$$
$$y^2 - 3y - 4 = 0$$
$$(y - 4)(y + 1) = 0$$
$$\Rightarrow y - 4 = 0 \quad \text{or} \quad y + 1 = 0$$
$$\Rightarrow y = 4 \quad \text{or} \quad y = -1$$

Substituting these values for y in equation ① we get

$$y = 4 \Rightarrow x + 4 = 3 \quad \text{or} \quad y = -1 \Rightarrow x - 1 = 3$$
$$\Rightarrow x = -1 \qquad\qquad \Rightarrow \quad x = 4$$

The solutions are: $x = -1, y = 4$ or $x = 4, y = -1$

In Example 1 above, $x + y = 3$ represents a straight line and $x^2 + y^2 = 17$ represents a circle.

The solutions to the two equations, i.e.,

$$x = -1, \quad y = 4 \qquad \text{and}$$
$$x = 4, \qquad y = -1$$

Represent the points $(-1, 4)$ and $(4, -1)$.

These are the points where the line intersects the circle.

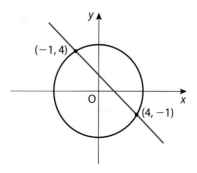

Example 2

Find the coordinates of the points of intersection, A and B, of the line $y = 2x + 3$ and the curve $y = x^2$.

To find the points A and B we solve the equations

$$y = x^2 \ldots \text{①}$$
$$\text{and} \quad y = 2x + 3 \ldots \text{②}$$

Substituting $(2x + 3)$ for y in equation ① we get,

$$2x + 3 = x^2$$
$$x^2 - 2x - 3 = 0 \ldots \text{rearrange}$$
$$(x + 1)(x - 3) = 0$$
$$x + 1 = 0 \quad \text{or} \quad x - 3 = 0$$
$$x = -1 \quad \text{or} \quad x = 3$$

Substituting these values for x in equation ② we get:
When $x = -1, y = 2(-1) + 3$, i.e., $y = 1$
When $x = 3, y = 2(3) + 3$, i.e., $y = 9$

So the line intersects the curve at the points

$$A(-1, 1) \text{ and } B(3, 9).$$

Exercise 2.5

Solve the following equations:

1. $x^2 + y^2 = 5$
$x + y = 3$

2. $x^2 + y^2 = 10$
$x - y = 4$

3. $x^2 + y^2 = 18$
$x - y = 0$

4. $y = x^2$
$y = 3 - 2x$

5. $x^2 + y^2 = 20$
$x - 2y = 0$

6. $x^2 + y^2 = 25$
$x - y + 1 = 0$

7. $x^2 + y^2 = 9$
$x + y = 3$

8. $xy = 12$
$x + y = 7$

9. $y = x^2 - 6x + 5$
$y = x - 1$

10. $xy = 4$
$y = 2x + 2$

11. $y^2 = 4x$
$2x + y = 4$

12. $x^2 - y^2 = 24$
$x - 2y = 3$

13. Find the points of intersection of the line $y = 3 - 2x$ and the curve $y = x^2$.

14. Find the point(s) of intersection of the line $y = 2x - 1$ and the curve $y = x^2$. What can you say about the line as a result of your answer?

34

15. Find the points of intersection of the line and the curve in the given figure.

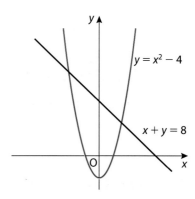

Section 2.6 Forming quadratic equations

Examine the quadratic equation $x^2 + x - 6 = 0$.

The factors of the left-hand side are $(x + 3)(x - 2)$

$$\Rightarrow (x + 3)(x - 2) = 0$$
$$\Rightarrow x = -3 \quad \text{or} \quad x = 2$$

i.e. -3 and 2 are the roots of the equation.

We can now use the reverse of this method to form a quadratic equation when we are given the roots.

Example 1

Form the quadratic equation with roots -4 and 5.

If the roots are -4 and 5, then

$$(x + 4)(x - 5) = 0$$
$$\Rightarrow x^2 - x - 20 = 0 \text{ is the equation}$$

If $x = \frac{1}{2}$ is a root of an equation, then

$$x = \frac{1}{2} \Rightarrow 2x = 1 \Rightarrow 2x - 1 = 0$$
$$\Rightarrow (2x - 1) \text{ is the factor which gives this root.}$$

Similarly if $x = -\frac{1}{3}$, then $3x = -1$ and so $(3x + 1)$ is the related factor.

Example 2

Form the equation whose roots are $-\frac{1}{4}$ and 3.

$x = -\frac{1}{4} \Rightarrow (4x + 1)$ is the related factor.

Roots $= -\frac{1}{4}, 3 \Rightarrow$ the equation is $(4x + 1)(x - 3) = 0$
$$\Rightarrow 4x^2 - 11x - 3 = 0 \text{ is the equation}$$

Exercise 2.6

Form the quadratic equation, given the two roots, in each of the following:

1. 2, 4	**2.** 5, 1	**3.** 3, 2	**4.** 3, -1
5. 4, -2	**6.** $-3, -4$	**7.** 6, -2	**8.** 5, 0
9. $-2, \frac{1}{2}$	**10.** $-5, -4$	**11.** $-\frac{1}{2}, 4$	**12.** $\frac{1}{4}, 8$
13. 0, -4	**14.** $\frac{1}{2}, -\frac{1}{2}$	**15.** ± 3	**16.** 0, $\frac{1}{4}$

17. If the roots of the equation $x^2 + ax + b = 0$ are 2 and -1, find the values of a and b.

Section 2.7 The laws of indices

$2^3 = 2 \times 2 \times 2 = 8$

2^3 is called '2 cubed' or '2 to the power of 3'.

3 is the **power** or **index** which tells us how many times the number 2 is multiplied by itself.

1. Multiplication

$4^2 \times 4^3 = (4 \times 4) \times (4 \times 4 \times 4)$
$\qquad = 4^5$

Similarly, $x^2 \times x^3 = (x \times x) \times (x \times x \times x) = x^5$

So $\qquad x^2 \times x^3 = x^{2+3} = x^5$

> To **multiply** powers of the same number **add** the indices.

2. Division

$\dfrac{3^5}{3^2} = \dfrac{\cancel{3} \times \cancel{3} \times 3 \times 3 \times 3}{\cancel{3} \times \cancel{3}} = 3^3$

Similarly, $\dfrac{x^5}{x^2} = \dfrac{\cancel{x} \times \cancel{x} \times x \times x \times x}{x \times x} = x^3$

Thus $\qquad \dfrac{x^5}{x^2} = x^{5-2} = x^3$

> To **divide** powers of the same number **subtract** the indices.

3. A power to a power

$(x^2)^3$ means $(x^2) \times (x^2) \times (x^2)$

$\Rightarrow (x^2)^3 = x^{2+2+2} = x^6$
$\qquad\qquad\quad = x^{2 \times 3}$

Similarly $(x^4)^3 = x^{4 \times 3} = x^{12}$

> To raise a power to a further power, multiply the indices.

4. A product raised to a power

$(ab)^n = a^n \times b^n$

5. Any number to the power of zero is 1

$a^0 = 1$ or $10^0 = 1$

6. Negative indices

$\dfrac{4^3}{4^5}$ can be written as

$$\dfrac{\cancel{4} \times \cancel{4} \times \cancel{4}}{\cancel{4} \times \cancel{4} \times \cancel{4} \times 4 \times 4} = \dfrac{1}{4^2}$$

Also $\dfrac{4^3}{4^5} = 4^{3-5} = 4^{-2} \Rightarrow \dfrac{1}{4^2} = 4^{-2}$

$$a^{-n} = \dfrac{1}{a^n}$$

$$\text{or } a^{-2} = \dfrac{1}{a^2}$$

7. Fractional indices

We use the rules of indices to show that $2^{\frac{1}{2}} = \sqrt{2}$.

$2^{\frac{1}{2}} \times 2^{\frac{1}{2}} = 2^{\frac{1}{2} + \frac{1}{2}} = 2^1 = 2$

Also $\sqrt{2} \times \sqrt{2} = 2$

$\therefore \ 2^{\frac{1}{2}} = \sqrt{2}$

Similarly $2^{\frac{1}{3}} = \sqrt[3]{2}$.

$$2^{\frac{1}{2}} = \sqrt{2}$$
$$2^{\frac{1}{3}} = \sqrt[3]{2}$$
$$\cdots\cdots$$
$$2^{\frac{1}{n}} = \sqrt[n]{2}$$

8. More fractional indices

One of the rules of indices is $(a^m)^n = a^{mn}$.

From this rule it follows that

$27^{\frac{2}{3}} = (27^{\frac{1}{3}})^2 = (\sqrt[3]{27})^2 = 3^2 = 9$

Note: $(\sqrt[3]{27})^2 = \sqrt[3]{27^2}$

$$8^{\frac{2}{3}} = \left(\sqrt[3]{8}\right)^2$$
$$16^{\frac{3}{4}} = \left(\sqrt[4]{16}\right)^3$$
$$\cdots\cdots$$
$$x^{\frac{m}{n}} = \left(\sqrt[n]{x}\right)^m$$

Example 1

Write each of these as whole numbers or fractions:

  (i) $\dfrac{3^4 \times 3^2}{3^5}$ (ii) $64^{\frac{1}{3}}$ (iii) $\dfrac{1}{4^{-2}}$ (iv) $8^{\frac{2}{3}}$

  (i) $\dfrac{3^4 \times 3^2}{3^5} = \dfrac{3^6}{3^5} = 3^1 = 3$ (ii) $64^{\frac{1}{3}} = \sqrt[3]{64} = 4$ $[\text{or } 64^{\frac{1}{3}} = (4^3)^{\frac{1}{3}} = 4]$

  (iii) $\dfrac{1}{4^{-2}} = 4^2 = 16$ (iv) $8^{\frac{2}{3}} = \sqrt[3]{8^2} = \sqrt[3]{64} = 4$

                     or $8^{\frac{2}{3}} = (8^{\frac{1}{3}})^2 = (\sqrt[3]{8})^2 = 2^2 = 4$

Example 2

  (i) Express $\left(\dfrac{8}{27}\right)^{\frac{2}{3}}$ in the form $\dfrac{a}{b}$, where $a, b \in N$.

  (ii) Express $\dfrac{125}{\sqrt{5}}$ as a power of 5.

(i) $\left(\dfrac{8}{27}\right)^{\frac{2}{3}} = \dfrac{8^{\frac{2}{3}}}{27^{\frac{2}{3}}} = \dfrac{(8^{\frac{1}{3}})^2}{(27^{\frac{1}{3}})^2} = \dfrac{(\sqrt[3]{8})^2}{(\sqrt[3]{27})^2} = \dfrac{2^2}{3^2} = \dfrac{4}{9}$

(ii) $\dfrac{125}{\sqrt{5}} = \dfrac{5^3}{5^{\frac{1}{2}}} = 5^{3-\frac{1}{2}} = 5^{2\frac{1}{2}} = 5^{\frac{5}{2}}$

Exercise 2.7

1. Simplify each of the following:

(i) $a^3 \times a^4$ (ii) $a \times a^5$ (iii) $a.a.a^2$ (iv) $2x^2 \times 3x$ (v) $a^3 \times 3a^2$

(vi) $\dfrac{x^5}{x^2}$ (vii) $\dfrac{a^4}{a}$ (viii) $\dfrac{6a^6}{2a^2}$ (ix) $(a^2)^3$ (x) a^0

2. Express each of the following in the form a^n where $a, n, \in N$:

(i) 25   (ii) 64   (iii) 27   (iv) 32   (v) 125   (vi) 81

3. What does the question mark (?) stand for in each of the following?

A $\quad 3^5 \times 3^{-2} = ?$

B $\quad \dfrac{3^3}{3^5} = ?$

C $\quad (2^3)^{-2} = ?$

D $\quad 6^{-1} \times 6^{-2} = ?$

E $\quad \dfrac{7^2}{7^2} = ?$

F $\quad 2^{-5} \times 2^3 = ?$

G $\quad (3^{-1})^{-2} = ?$

H $\quad \dfrac{5^3}{5^{-2}} = ?$

4. Copy and complete these.

(i) $2^{\blacksquare} \times 2^{-2} = 2^6$ (ii) $\dfrac{3^{-1}}{3^{\blacksquare}} = 3^{-5}$ (iii) $a^2 \times a^{\blacksquare} \times a^{-4} = a^{-3}$ (iv) $\dfrac{b^{\blacksquare}}{b^{-3}} = b^5$

(v) $(5^{\blacksquare})^3 = 5^{-12}$ (vi) $(2^{\blacksquare})^{-5} = 2^{10}$

5. Simplify these.

(i) $n^2 \times 5n^9$ (ii) $2n \times 3n^2$ (iii) $7n^5 \times 3n^8$ (iv) $5n^2 \times 2n^3 \times 3n^4$

(v) $(4n)^2$ (vi) $(2n)^3$ (vii) $(5n^2)^3$ (viii) $(2n^3)^5$

6. Simplify these.

(i) $\dfrac{6m^9}{3m^2}$ (ii) $\dfrac{2m^8}{10m^6}$ (iii) $\dfrac{2m^3}{m^7}$ (iv) $\dfrac{8m^6}{12m^3}$ (v) $\dfrac{15m^5}{10m^7}$

7. Find four pairs of equivalent expressions.

A $\dfrac{6x^8}{3x^2}$ **B** $\dfrac{x^6}{2}$ **C** $2x^4$ **D** $\dfrac{2}{x^4}$ **E** $2x^6$ **F** $\dfrac{12x^4}{6x^8}$ **G** $\dfrac{8x^9}{4x^5}$ **H** $\dfrac{5x^7}{10x}$

8. Find the value of each of these:

   (i) $\sqrt{25}$ (ii) $\sqrt[3]{27}$ (iii) $\sqrt[3]{64}$ (iv) $16^{\frac{1}{2}}$ (v) $36^{\frac{1}{2}}$ (vi) $125^{\frac{1}{3}}$

9. Express each of the following as a rational number:

   (i) $(2 \times 3)^2$ (ii) $\left(\frac{1}{2}\right)^3$ (iii) $\left(\frac{2}{3}\right)^2$ (iv) 3^{-2} (v) $\frac{3}{2^{-2}}$

10. Find four matching pairs.

$\textbf{A}$ 3^{-2} $\textbf{B}$ 2^{-3} $\textbf{C}$ 4^{-2} $\textbf{D}$ 6^{-1} $\textbf{E}$ -6 $\textbf{F}$ $\frac{1}{6}$ $\textbf{G}$ $\frac{1}{16}$ $\textbf{H}$ $\frac{1}{8}$ $\textbf{I}$ $\frac{1}{9}$

11. Express as rational numbers:

   (i) 2^{-2} (ii) $\frac{2^{-4}}{4^{-2}}$ (iii) $64^{\frac{1}{2}}$ (iv) $\left(\frac{9}{16}\right)^{\frac{1}{2}}$ (v) $\left(\frac{8}{27}\right)^{\frac{1}{3}}$

12. Write the following without using the $\sqrt{}$ sign:

   (i) $\sqrt{x}$ (ii) $\sqrt[3]{a}$ (iii) $\sqrt[4]{a}$ (iv) $\sqrt[3]{x^2}$ (v) $\sqrt[4]{a^3}$

13. Rewrite the following using the $\sqrt{}$ sign:

   (i) $x^{\frac{1}{2}}$ (ii) $a^{\frac{1}{4}}$ (iii) $x^{\frac{2}{3}}$ (iv) $a^{\frac{5}{2}}$ (v) $\left(\frac{a}{x}\right)^{\frac{1}{3}}$

14. Find the value of each of the following:

   (i) $4^{\frac{1}{2}}$ (ii) $8^{\frac{2}{3}}$ (iii) $16^{\frac{3}{4}}$ (iv) $4^{\frac{3}{2}}$ (v) $27^{\frac{2}{3}}$

   (vi) $16^{\frac{3}{2}}$ (vii) $64^{\frac{2}{3}}$ (viii) $100^{\frac{3}{2}}$ (ix) $81^{\frac{3}{4}}$ (x) $125^{\frac{2}{3}}$

15. Evaluate each of these:

   (i) 3^{-1} (ii) 4^{-2} (iii) $8^{-\frac{1}{3}}$ (iv) $\frac{1}{16^{-\frac{1}{4}}}$ (v) $64^{-\frac{1}{3}}$

16. Find the value of each of the following:

   (i) $16^{-\frac{1}{2}}$ (ii) $\frac{1}{8^{-\frac{2}{3}}}$ (iii) $16^{-\frac{3}{4}}$ (iv) $100^{-\frac{3}{2}}$ (v) $32^{-\frac{3}{5}}$

17. Express each of the following in the form 2^n:

   (i) 8 (ii) $\sqrt{2}$ (iii) $\sqrt{8}$ (iv) $\sqrt{32}$ (v) $\frac{\sqrt{8}}{2}$

18. Express each of the following in the form 5^n:

   (i) 25 (ii) $\sqrt{5}$ (iii) $\frac{25}{\sqrt{5}}$ (iv) $\sqrt{125}$ (v) $\frac{25}{\sqrt{125}}$

19. Express   (i) $8^{\frac{4}{3}}$ as a power of 2   (ii) $\frac{27}{\sqrt{3}}$ as a power of 3.

20. Evaluate $2a^{\frac{1}{2}}b^{-\frac{1}{3}}$ when $a = 100$ and $b = 64$.

Section 2.8 Equations involving indices

If $5^x = 5^2$, then $x = 2$.

Similarly, if $7^x = 7^{\frac{1}{2}}$, then $x = \frac{1}{2}$.

> In general, if $a^x = a^y$, then $x = y$.

If we are given the equation $25^x = 125$, we express each side as a power of the same base number. In this case the number is 5.

Thus
$$25^x = 125 \Rightarrow (5^2)^x = 5^3$$
$$\Rightarrow 5^{2x} = 5^3$$
$$\Rightarrow 2x = 3 \Rightarrow x = 1\tfrac{1}{2}$$

Example 1

Write each of these as whole numbers or fractions:

  (i) $4^x = 16$ (ii) $16^x = 64$ (iii) $3^x = \dfrac{1}{27}$ (iv) $25x = \dfrac{1}{125}$

(i)
$$4^x = 16$$
$$4^x = 4^2$$
$$\Rightarrow x = 2$$

(ii)
$$16^x = 64$$
$$\Rightarrow (4^2)^x = 4^3$$
$$\Rightarrow 4^{2x} = 4^3$$
$$\Rightarrow 2x = 3 \Rightarrow x = 1\tfrac{1}{2}$$

(iii)
$$3^x = \frac{1}{27}$$
$$\Rightarrow 3^x = \frac{1}{3^3}$$
$$\Rightarrow 3^x = 3^{-3}$$
$$\Rightarrow x = -3$$

(iv)
$$25x = \frac{1}{125}$$
$$\Rightarrow (5^2)^x = \frac{1}{5^3}$$
$$\Rightarrow 5^{2x} = 5^{-3}$$
$$\Rightarrow 2x = -3$$
$$\Rightarrow x = -1\tfrac{1}{2}$$

Example 2

Express $\dfrac{81}{\sqrt{3}}$ as a power of 3 and hence solve the equation $3^{x-2} = \left(\dfrac{81}{\sqrt{3}}\right)^2$.

$$\frac{81}{\sqrt{3}} = \frac{3^4}{3^{\frac{1}{2}}} = 3^{4-\frac{1}{2}} = 3^{3\frac{1}{2}} = 3^{\frac{7}{2}}.$$

$$3^{x-2} = \left(\frac{81}{\sqrt{3}}\right)^2 \Rightarrow 3^{x-2} = \left(3^{\frac{7}{2}}\right)^2$$
$$\Rightarrow 3^{x-2} = 3^{\frac{7}{2} \cdot \frac{2}{1}}$$
$$\Rightarrow 3^{x-2} = 3^7$$
$$\Rightarrow x - 2 = 7$$
$$\Rightarrow x = 9$$

Exercise 2.8

1. Express each of the following in the form 2^k, where k is an integer:
   (i) 8   (ii) 16   (iii) $\frac{1}{4}$ (iv) $\frac{1}{8}$ (v) $\frac{1}{32}$

2. Express each of the following in the form 3^k, where k is an integer:
   (i) 9   (ii) 27   (iii) 81   (iv) $\frac{1}{27}$ (v) $\frac{1}{81}$

Find the value of x in numbers (3–22).

3. $2^x = 8$ 4. $3^x = 27$ 5. $4^x = 32$ 6. $16^x = 64$

7. $25^x = 125$ 8. $9^x = 27$ 9. $8^x = 32$ 10. $16^x = 32$

11. $2^x = \frac{1}{4}$ 12. $3^x = \frac{1}{27}$ 13. $4^x = \frac{1}{8}$ 14. $5^x = \frac{1}{125}$

15. $9^x = \frac{1}{27}$ 16. $27^x = 81$ 17. $2^{-x} = 16$ 18. $\frac{1}{5^x} = 125$

19. $4^x = \frac{1}{32}$ 20. $2^{x+1} = 16$ 21. $3^{x+2} = 81$ 22. $4^{x-1} = 2^{x+1}$

23. Express each of the following in the form 2^k, where k is a rational number:
   (i) $\sqrt{2}$ (ii) $2\sqrt{2}$ (iii) $\sqrt{8}$
   (iv) $\frac{1}{2\sqrt{2}}$ (v) $\frac{1}{\sqrt{8}}$ (vi) $\frac{\sqrt{8}}{2}$

   > $\sqrt{8} = \sqrt{4} \times \sqrt{2} = 2\sqrt{2}$
   > $\sqrt{27} = \sqrt{9} \times \sqrt{3} = 3\sqrt{3}$

24. Find the value of x in each of the following:
   (i) $4^{x+1} = 32$ (ii) $2^x = \sqrt{8}$ (iii) $\frac{1}{2^x} = \sqrt{2}$ (iv) $8^x = \frac{1}{32}$

25. Solve each of these equations:
   (i) $2^x = \frac{\sqrt{2}}{2}$ (ii) $\frac{1}{9^x} = 27$ (iii) $3^{2x+1} = 243$ (iv) $25^x = \frac{125}{\sqrt{5}}$

26. Write $\frac{81}{\sqrt{3}}$ as a power of 3, and hence solve the equation $9^{x+1} = \frac{81}{\sqrt{3}}$.

27. Write $\sqrt[3]{16}$ as a power of 2, and hence solve the equation $2^x = \sqrt[3]{16}$.

28. Express $\frac{27}{\sqrt{3}}$ as a power of 3, and hence solve the equation $3^{2x+1} = \left(\frac{27}{\sqrt{3}}\right)^3$.

29. Express $\frac{16}{\sqrt{8}}$ as a power of 2, and hence solve the equation $2^{2x-2} = \frac{16}{\sqrt{8}}$.

30. Express $\frac{\sqrt{27}}{81}$ as a power of 3, and hence solve the equation $9^{3-x} = \frac{\sqrt{27}}{81}$.

31. Express (i) 16   (ii) $\sqrt{8}$ as a power of 2.
   Hence solve the equation $2^{2x-1} = \left(\frac{16}{\sqrt{8}}\right)^3$.

Section 2.9 Dealing with surds

1. Rational and irrational numbers

Any number which can be written in the form $\frac{a}{b}$, where a and b are integers, is called a rational number.

Examples of rational numbers are,

$$3 = \frac{3}{1}, \quad \frac{2}{3}, \quad 0.45 = \frac{45}{100}, \quad \frac{-3}{4}, \quad 1\frac{3}{8} = \frac{11}{8}$$

If you use your calculator to find $\sqrt{2}$, you will get 1.41421362…
This number is never-ending and non-repeating.
Such numbers are called **irrational numbers**.

The square root of any number that does not have an exact value is an irrational number.
Thus $\sqrt{3}, \sqrt{5}, \sqrt{15}, \ldots$ are irrational numbers.

2. Surds

Irrational numbers such as $\sqrt{5}, \sqrt{8}, \sqrt{13}, \ldots$ are generally called **surds**.

In this section we will show how to express a surd in its simplest form and perform simple operations on surds.

$\sqrt{100} = 10$.   Also $\sqrt{100} = \sqrt{25 \times 4} = \sqrt{25} \times \sqrt{4} = 5 \times 2 = 10$.
This illustrates a very important property of surds, as stated in the highlighted box.

$$\sqrt{ab} = \sqrt{a} \times \sqrt{b}$$
$$\sqrt{\frac{a}{b}} = \frac{\sqrt{a}}{\sqrt{b}}$$

We will now use the result $\sqrt{ab} = \sqrt{a} . \sqrt{b}$ to simplify surds, where possible.

(i) $\sqrt{8} = \sqrt{4} . \sqrt{2}$ (ii) $\sqrt{27} = \sqrt{9} . \sqrt{3}$ (iii) $\sqrt{48} = \sqrt{16} . \sqrt{3}$
   $= 2\sqrt{2}$ $= 3\sqrt{3}$ $= 4\sqrt{3}$

> $2\sqrt{2}$ is said to be the **simplest form** of $\sqrt{8}$.

3. Adding and subtracting surds

Surds may be added or subtracted only when they have the same irrational parts. If the irrational parts are not the same, we reduce each surd to its simplest form, where possible.

Example 1

Simplify $\sqrt{5} + \sqrt{45} - \sqrt{20}$.

We first express each surd in its simplest form:

$$\sqrt{5} + \sqrt{45} - \sqrt{20} = \sqrt{5} + \sqrt{9}\sqrt{5} - \sqrt{4}\sqrt{5}$$
$$= \sqrt{5} + 3\sqrt{5} - 2\sqrt{5}$$
$$= 4\sqrt{5} - 2\sqrt{5} = 2\sqrt{5}$$

42

4. Multiplying surds

When multiplying surds, multiply separately the rational factors and the irrational factors.

Examples (i) $\sqrt{6} \times \sqrt{2} = \sqrt{12} = \sqrt{4}.\sqrt{3} = 2\sqrt{3}$

(ii) $2\sqrt{3} \times 3\sqrt{5} = 2 \times 3 \times \sqrt{3} \times \sqrt{5} = 6\sqrt{15}$

(iii) $\sqrt{32} \times \sqrt{48} = \sqrt{16} \times \sqrt{2} \times \sqrt{16} \times \sqrt{3}$

$\qquad\qquad\qquad = 4\sqrt{2} \times 4\sqrt{3} = 16\sqrt{6}$

> **Remember**
> $\sqrt{6} \times \sqrt{6} = 6$

Example 2

Simplify $(2\sqrt{5} - 3)(2\sqrt{5} + 3)$.

$(2\sqrt{5} - 3)(2\sqrt{5} + 3) = (2\sqrt{5})(2\sqrt{5}) + (2\sqrt{5})(3) - (3)(2\sqrt{5}) - (3)(3)$

$\qquad\qquad\qquad\qquad = 4(5) + 6\sqrt{5} - 6\sqrt{5} - 9$

$\qquad\qquad\qquad\qquad = 20 - 9 = 11$

Exercise 2.9

1. Evaluate each of the following:

(i) $\sqrt{9}$ (ii) $(\sqrt{6})^2$ (iii) $(2\sqrt{3})^2$ (iv) $\left(\dfrac{5}{\sqrt{5}}\right)^2$ (v) $\left(\dfrac{\sqrt{8}}{\sqrt{2}}\right)^2$

2. Express each of these surds in its simplest form:

(i) $\sqrt{8}$ (ii) $\sqrt{12}$ (iii) $\sqrt{18}$ (iv) $\sqrt{27}$ (v) $\sqrt{45}$

3. Express these surds in their simplest forms:

(i) $\sqrt{75}$ (ii) $2\sqrt{18}$ (iii) $\sqrt{125}$ (iv) $4\sqrt{27}$ (v) $2\sqrt{48}$

4. Express each of the following in its simplest form:

(i) $5\sqrt{3} + 4\sqrt{3} - \sqrt{3}$ (ii) $2\sqrt{2} + 6\sqrt{2} - 3\sqrt{2}$ (iii) $2\sqrt{2} + \sqrt{18}$
(iv) $\sqrt{32} + \sqrt{18}$ (v) $\sqrt{27} + \sqrt{48} - 2\sqrt{3}$ (vi) $\sqrt{108} + \sqrt{12} - \sqrt{75}$

5. Express each of these products as a whole number:

(i) $\sqrt{5}.\sqrt{5}$ (ii) $2\sqrt{3} \times 3\sqrt{3}$ (iii) $3\sqrt{5} \times 4\sqrt{5}$ (iv) $3\sqrt{7} \times \sqrt{7}$

6. Simplify each of these:

(i) $\sqrt{5}(\sqrt{5} - 2)$ (ii) $2\sqrt{3}(\sqrt{3} - 2)$ (iii) $\sqrt{2}(3\sqrt{2} - \sqrt{3})$

7. Express the following products in their simplest forms:

(i) $2\sqrt{5}(\sqrt{2} - \sqrt{5})$ (ii) $(\sqrt{2} + 1)(\sqrt{2} - 1)$ (iii) $(5 + \sqrt{3})(5 - \sqrt{3})$
(iv) $(\sqrt{7} - 4)(\sqrt{7} + 4)$ (v) $(1 - 2\sqrt{3})(1 + 2\sqrt{3})$ (vi) $(\sqrt{2} + \sqrt{5})(\sqrt{2} - \sqrt{5})$

8. Simplify each of these:

    (i) $(2 - \sqrt{3})(4 + 2\sqrt{3})$ (ii) $(1 - 3\sqrt{2})(5 + 2\sqrt{2})$ (iii) $(3 + 2\sqrt{2})(3 - 2\sqrt{2})$

9. Write $(2 - 2\sqrt{5})^2$ in the form $a + b\sqrt{5}$, where $a, b \in Z$.

10. Given that $p = \sqrt{5} + \sqrt{3}$ and $q = \sqrt{5} - \sqrt{3}$, simplify $p^2 - q^2$.

Section 2.10 Equations involving surds

To solve the equation $\sqrt{x - 1} = 4$, we square both sides and thus eliminate the symbol.

i.e. $\sqrt{x - 1} = 4 \Rightarrow x - 1 = 16$

                 $\Rightarrow x = 17$

If the equation is in the form $4 + \sqrt{2x - 3} = 8$, we rearrange the equation so that the $\sqrt{}$ expression is isolated.

$\therefore$ $4 + \sqrt{2x - 3} = 8 \Rightarrow \sqrt{2x - 3} = 4$

We then square both sides and solve the equation.

When we solve an equation involving surds, it is important to check your solutions to verify that they are correct.

Example 1

Solve the equation $2 + \sqrt{4x - 3} = x$.

$2 + \sqrt{4x - 3} = x \Rightarrow \sqrt{4x - 3} = x - 2 \dots$ (isolate the $\sqrt{}$ term)

        $\Rightarrow$ $4x - 3 = (x - 2)^2$

        $\Rightarrow$ $4x - 3 = x^2 - 4x + 4$

        $\Rightarrow$ $x^2 - 8x + 7 = 0$

        $\Rightarrow (x - 7)(x - 1) = 0$

        $\Rightarrow x = 7$ or $x = 1$

Check: $x = 7$: $2 + \sqrt{25} = 7 \dots$ correct

        $x = 1$: $2 + \sqrt{1} = 1$ i.e. $2 + 1 \neq 1 \dots$ incorrect

        $\therefore$ the correct solution is $x = 7$

Note: The square root of a number is taken as the **positive** value only.

                Thus $\sqrt{25}$ is 5 (not ± 5).

                This fact is very important when checking your solutions.

Exercise 2.10

Solve the following equations and check your solutions in each case:

1. $\sqrt{x + 4} = 3$

2. $\sqrt{2x - 2} = 4$

3. $\sqrt{4x + 5} = 5$

4. $4 + \sqrt{x - 2} = 6$

5. $-3 + \sqrt{2x - 5} = 0$

6. $\sqrt{2x - 1} = \sqrt{x + 8}$

7. $2\sqrt{3x - 2} = 8$

8. $3\sqrt{8 - 2x} = 6$

9. $\sqrt{3x + 10} = x$

10. $x = \sqrt{12 - 4x}$

11. $x = \sqrt{5x - 4}$

12. $\sqrt{7x + 18} = x$

13. $2x = \sqrt{4x + 3}$

14. $2\sqrt{x - 6} = \sqrt{8 + x}$

15. $\sqrt{x + 1} = x - 1$

16. Simplify $(x + \sqrt{x})(x - \sqrt{x})$ when $x > 0$.

    Hence find the value of x for which $(x + \sqrt{x})(x - \sqrt{x}) = 6$.

17. Simplify $\left(\sqrt{x} - \dfrac{2}{\sqrt{x}}\right)\left(\sqrt{x} + \dfrac{2}{\sqrt{x}}\right)$.

    Hence solve the equation $\left(\sqrt{x} - \dfrac{2}{\sqrt{x}}\right)\left(\sqrt{x} + \dfrac{2}{\sqrt{x}}\right) = 3$, for $x > 0$.

18. Given that $t = k\sqrt{x + 5}$, find the value of k when $x = 1\frac{1}{4}$ and $t = \frac{1}{4}$, without using a calculator.

Test yourself 2

1. (i) Factorise $2x^2 + 5x - 3$.
    Hence solve the equation $2x^2 + 5x - 3 = 0$.
    (ii) Solve for x and y these simultaneous equations:
    $$y = 10 - 2x$$
    $$x^2 + y^2 = 25.$$
    (iii) Find the value of x in each of these equations:
    (a) $9^{2x-3} = \frac{1}{27}$
    (b) $3\sqrt{12} - \sqrt{27} = x\sqrt{3}$, where $x \in N$.

2. (i) Simplify $(2x - 3)^2 - (4x + 1)(x - 4)$.
    (ii) Solve the equation $x^2 - 7x - 6 = 0$, giving your answers correct to two decimal places.
    (iii) Express $\sqrt{50} - \sqrt{32} + 2\sqrt{8}$ in the form $k\sqrt{2}$, where $k \in N$.
    (iv) Solve the equation $3(3^x) = \sqrt{27}$.

3. (i) Given that $3a - 2b = 4$, find the value of b when $a = -2$.
    (ii) Solve for x and y the simultaneous equations
    $$x + 2y = 3$$
    $$x^2 - y^2 = 24.$$
    (iii) The area of this rectangle is 24 cm².

    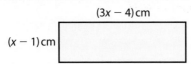
    $(3x - 4)$ cm
    $(x - 1)$ cm

    Find the length and width of the rectangle.

4. (i) Simplify $\dfrac{2x^4 \times 6x^3}{3x^5}$.

    (ii) Solve the equation $\dfrac{1}{x} + \dfrac{1}{x - 1} = \dfrac{3}{2}$.

    (iii) If $(n - 3)^2$ is a perfect square, which of the following expressions are perfect squares?

    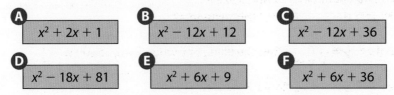

    A $x^2 + 2x + 1$ **B** $x^2 - 12x + 12$ **C** $x^2 - 12x + 36$

    D $x^2 - 18x + 81$ **E** $x^2 + 6x + 9$ **F** $x^2 + 6x + 36$

5. (i) If $x = 4$ is a root of the equation $2x^2 + kx - 20 = 0$, find the value of k.
    (ii) Solve these equations:
    (a) $4^x = 32$ (b) $4^x = \sqrt{2}$

(iii) Find the points of intersection of the line and the curve in the given figure.

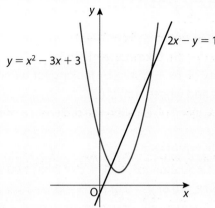

$2x - y = 1$

$y = x^2 - 3x + 3$

(iv) Solve for x the equation $\dfrac{3}{x+1} + \dfrac{1}{x-1} = 1$.

Give your answers in the form $a \pm \sqrt{b}$, where $a, b \in N$.

6. (i) Find the value of each of these:

    (a) $8^{\frac{2}{3}}$ (b) $25^{\frac{3}{2}}$ (c) $9^{-\frac{3}{2}}$

(ii) Solve for x and y these simultaneous equations:

$$x - 3y = 1$$
$$x^2 - y^2 = 0.$$

(iii) Express $\dfrac{2\sqrt{45}}{\sqrt{10}}$ in the form $k\sqrt{2}$, where $k \in N$.

(iv) If $3^{2x+1} = \dfrac{27}{\sqrt{3}}$, find the value of x.

7. The length of this rectangle is 7 cm longer than the width.
The width is x cm.
    (i) Write an expression for
        (a) the length of the rectangle
        (b) the area of the rectangle.
    (ii) The area of the rectangle is 44 cm².
        (a) Form an equation in x and solve it.
        (b) What is the perimeter of this rectangle?

x cm

8. (i) Given that $y = \dfrac{k}{k+w}$, find the value of y when $k = \frac{1}{2}$ and $w = \frac{1}{3}$.

(ii) Express $\dfrac{x}{x-1} - 1$ as a single fraction.

Hence solve the equation $\dfrac{x}{x-1} - 1 = \dfrac{x+1}{2}$, leaving your answers in $\sqrt{\ }$ form.

(iii) Solve the equation $4^{2x+1} = \sqrt{8}$.

(iv) Solve the equation $x - 3 = \sqrt{3x - 11}$ and verify your answer.

Summary of key points...

1. **Factorising quadratic expressions**

    (i) To factorise $3x^2 + 6x$, take out the HCF $3x$, i.e. $3x(x + 2)$.

    (ii) To factorise $ax^2 + bx + c$, start by looking for two numbers whose product is ac and whose sum is b.

    (iii) $x^2 - y^2 = (x - y)(x + y)$ is called the **difference of two squares**.

2. **Solving quadratic equations**

    (i) The quadratic equation $ax^2 + bx + c = 0$ has two solutions (or roots).

    (ii) If $xy = 0$, then $x = 0$ or $y = 0$ or both $= 0$.

    (iii) The roots of the quadratic equation $ax^2 + bx + c = 0$ are given by the formula
    $$x = \frac{-b \pm \sqrt{b^2 - 4ac}}{2a}.$$

3. **Simultaneous equations, one linear and one quadratic**

    The solutions of a pair of simultaneous equations, where one is linear and one is quadratic, are represented by the points of intersection of a straight line and a quadratic curve.

4. **Rules of indices**

    In the expression x^n, the number x is called the base and the number n is called the index or power.

    Here are the main rules of indices

    1. $x^1 = x$

    2. $x^m \times x^n = x^{m+n}$

    3. $(x^m)^n = x^{mn}$

    4. $x^m \div x^n = x^{m-n}$

    5. $x^0 = 1$

    6. $x^{-n} = \dfrac{1}{x^n}$

    7. $x^{\frac{1}{n}} = \sqrt[n]{x}$

    8. $x^{\frac{m}{n}} = (\sqrt[n]{x})^m$ or $x^{\frac{m}{n}} = \sqrt[n]{x^m}$

5. **Surds**

    (i) $\sqrt{ab} = \sqrt{a}.\sqrt{b}$

    (ii) $\sqrt{\dfrac{a}{b}} = \dfrac{\sqrt{a}}{\sqrt{b}}$

Coordinate Geometry – The Line

chapter 3

Key words

Cartesian plane   origin   axis   quadrant   vertex   horizontal
vertical   slope   parallel   perpendicular   positive   negative
linear equation   area   translation   intersection   collinear

Section 3.1 Coordinating the plane

The figure shows the coordinated plane and the location of the points A, B, C, D and E.

The horizontal line is called the **x-axis**.

The vertical line is called the **y-axis**.

The point (0, 0) is called the **origin** and is labelled O.

This coordinated plane is generally called the **Cartesian plane** in honour of the French mathematician, Rene Descartes (1596–1650).

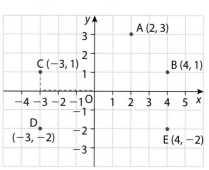

Example 1

Plot the points A(-1, 2), B(3, 2), C(3, -2) and D(-1, -2) on a coordinated plane.
  (i) Join the four points and name the figure you have drawn.
  (ii) Use the grid to write down the midpoint of [BC].

  (i) ABCD forms a square.
  (ii) The midpoint of [BC] is (3, 0).

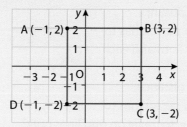

Exercise 3.1

1. Write down the coordinates of each of the points marked in the coordinated plane on the right:

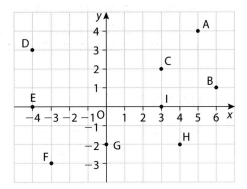

2. Draw a coordinated plane from −5 to 5 on the x-axis and from −4 to 4 on the y-axis. Now plot each of the following points:
   (i) A(3, 4)   (ii) B(−1, 3)   (iii) C(4, −3)   (iv) D(−4, −3)   (v) E(1, −3)

3. The four quadrants are shown on the right. In which quadrant does each of the following points lie?
   (i) (3, 5)
   (ii) (−2, −3)
   (iii) (1, −4)
   (iv) (−3, 1)
   (v) (3, −3)
   (vi) (−1, −3).

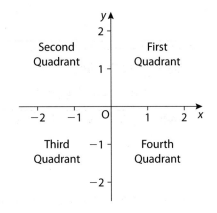

4. On which axis does each of the following points lie?
   (i) (4, 0)   (ii) (−3, 0)   (iii) (0, 4)   (iv) (0, −3)   (v) (0, 0).

5. (i) Write down the coordinates of the points A, B, C and D shown on the given grid.
   (ii) What is the shortest distance between A and C if a person has to travel along the grid lines and each unit is 100 metres?
   (iii) What is the shortest distance between B and D if a person has to go through A and has to travel on grid lines only? [1 unit = 100 metres].

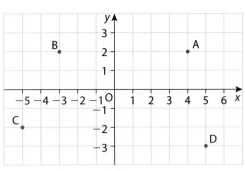

6. Look for a pattern in these coordinates. Use the pattern to find the missing coordinates.
   (i) $(3, 5)$, $(8, 0)$, $(2, 6)$, $(4, 4)$, ... $(0, ...)$, $(9, ...)$
   (ii) $(7, 8)$, $(5, 10)$, $(12, 3)$, $(2, 13)$, ... $(..., 11)$, $(0, ...)$
   (iii) $(4, 4)$, $(2, 6)$, $(5, 3)$, $(-1, 9)$, ... $(7, ...)$, $(-3, ...)$, $(..., -2)$.

Section 3.2 Distance between two points

The given diagram shows the points $A(x_1, y_1)$ and $B(x_2, y_2)$.

$|BC| = y_2 - y_1$ and $|AC| = x_2 - x_1$

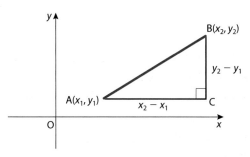

Using the Theorem of Pythagoras:

$|AB|^2 = |AC|^2 + |BC|^2$

$\qquad = (x_2 - x_1)^2 + (y_2 - y_1)^2$

$\therefore \qquad |AB| = \sqrt{(x_2 - x_1)^2 + (y_2 - y_1)^2}$

> The distance between $A(x_1, y_1)$ and $B(x_2, y_2)$ is
>
> $|AB| = \sqrt{(x_2 - x_1)^2 + (y_2 - y_1)^2}$

Example 1

Show that D(2, 4) is equidistant from
E(-5, 1) and F(5, -3).

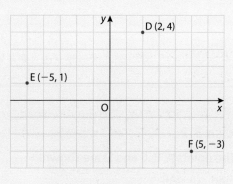

$|DE| = \sqrt{(x_2 - x_1)^2 + (y_2 - y_1)^2}$

$\qquad = \sqrt{(-5 - 2)^2 + (1 - 4)^2}$

$\qquad = \sqrt{(-7)^2 + (-3)^2}$

$\qquad = \sqrt{49 + 9} = \sqrt{58}$

$$\begin{array}{cc} D(2, 4) & E(-5, 1) \\ \downarrow & \downarrow \\ (x_1, y_1) & (x_2, y_2) \end{array}$$

Equidistant means the same distance.

$$|DF| = \sqrt{(x_2 - x_1)^2 + (y_2 - y_1)^2}$$

D(2, 4)   F(5, −3)

   ↓   ↓

(x_1, y_1) (x_2, y_2)

$$= \sqrt{(5 - 2)^2 + (-3 - 4)^2}$$

$$= \sqrt{(3)^2 + (-7)^2}$$

$$= \sqrt{9 + 49} = \sqrt{58}$$

Since $|DE| = |DF| = \sqrt{58}$, D is equidistant from E and F.

Example 2

If the distance between the points (2, 3) and (5, k) is $\sqrt{10}$, find two possible values of k.

$$\text{Distance} = \sqrt{(x_2 - x_1)^2 + (y_2 - y_1)^2}$$

(x_1, y_1) (x_2, y_2)

   ↓   ↓

(2, 3)   (5, k)

$$= \sqrt{(5 - 2)^2 + (k - 3)^2}$$

$$= \sqrt{9 + k^2 - 6k + 9}$$

$$= \sqrt{k^2 - 6k + 18}$$

$$\text{Distance} = \sqrt{10} \;\Rightarrow\; \sqrt{k^2 - 6k + 18} = \sqrt{10}$$

$$\Rightarrow\; k^2 - 6k + 18 = 10$$

$$\Rightarrow\; k^2 - 6k + 8 = 0$$

$$\Rightarrow\; (k - 2)(k - 4) = 0$$

$$\Rightarrow\; k = 2 \quad \text{or} \quad k = 4$$

Exercise 3.2

1. The points A, B, C and D are shown.

Find (i) $|AB|$

     (ii) $|AC|$

     (iii) $|AD|$.

Is $|DC| = |BC|$?

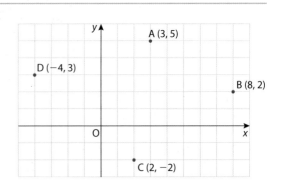

2. The given diagram shows the points D, E and F.

    (i) Write down the lengths of [FE] and [ED].

    (ii) Find $|DF|$.

Use the Theorem of Pythagoras to show that the triangle DEF is right-angled.

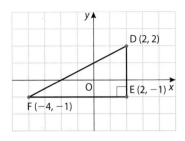

3. Find the distance between each of the following pairs of points:

    (i) (2, 1) and (3, 4)   (ii) (1, 5) and (2, 3)   (iii) $(-1, 4)$ and (2, 6)

    (iv) $(3, -2)$ and $(-5, 3)$ (v) $(-6, -1)$ and $(1, -3)$ (vi) $(4, -2)$ and $(0, -5)$

4. Find $|AB|$ in each of the following:

    (i) $A = (2, -4), B = (3, 1)$ (ii) $A = (0, 3), B = (-2, 5)$

    (iii) $A = (0, -2), B = (3, -1)$ (iv) $A = (5, -2), B = (3, -4)$

5. A(1, 1), B(3, 6) and C(5, 1) are the vertices of a triangle. Show that $|AB| = |BC|$.

6. X(1, 6), Y$(-3, -1)$ and Z$(2, -2)$ are the vertices of a triangle.

Find the lengths of the 3 sides and then state which two sides are equal in length.

Hence state what type of triangle is XYZ.

7. A wire ABC is used to support a flag pole [BD], as shown on the right.

Write down the coordinates of A, B, C and D.

Calculate the length of wire needed to support the pole.

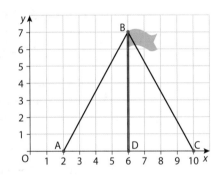

8. The centre of a circle is $(-3, 1)$ and (4, 3) is a point on the circle.

Find the length of the radius of the circle.

9. The points A(2, 1), B(6, 1), C(5, -2) and D(1, -2) are the vertices of a parallelogram.

Plot the parallelogram on a coordinated plane.

Find   (i) $|AC|$ (ii) $|BD|$.

Are the diagonals equal in length?

10. The distance between the points (5, 2) and (4, k) is $\sqrt{2}$.

Find two possible values for k.

11. X(3, k) and Y(-1, 2) are two points.

If $|XY| = 5$, find two possible values for k.

12. Jordan lives (3 km West, 4 km South) of the centre of the town marked O in the given diagram.

Michelle lives (2 km West, 3 km North) of Jordan's house.

How far does Michelle live from the centre of town?

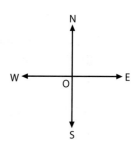

Section 3.3 The midpoint of a line segment

Here is a line segment [AB].

The coordinates of A are (1, 1).

The coordinates of B are (7, 5).

M is the **midpoint** of the line segment [AB].

The coordinates of M are (4, 3).

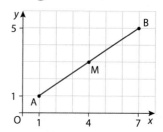

These coordinates are found as follows:

1. Add the x-coordinates of A and B and divide by 2, i.e. $\dfrac{1+7}{2} = 4$.

2. Add the y-coordinates of A and B and divide by 2, i.e. $\dfrac{1+5}{2} = 3$.

The midpoint of the line segment joining $A(x_1, y_1)$ and $B(x_2, y_2)$ is

$$\left(\frac{x_1 + x_2}{2}, \ \frac{y_1 + y_2}{2} \right)$$

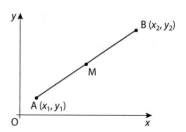

Example 1

Find the midpoint of the line segment joining A(−1, 3) and B(5, 7).

$$\text{Midpoint of [AB]} = \left(\frac{x_1 + x_2}{2}, \ \frac{y_1 + y_2}{2} \right)$$

$$= \left(\frac{-1 + 5}{2}, \ \frac{3 + 7}{2} \right)$$

$$= \left(\frac{4}{2}, \ \frac{10}{2} \right) = (2, 5).$$

$(-1, 3) \qquad (5, 7)$
$\downarrow \qquad\qquad \downarrow$
$(x_1, y_1) \qquad (x_2, y_2)$

Exercise 3.3

1. Find the midpoint of the line segment joining these points:
  (i) (2, 4) and (6, 2)   (ii) (2, 4) and (0, 2)   (iii) (2, −1) and (4, 3)
  (iv) (−2, 4) and (4, −2)   (v) (2, −3) and (0, −1)   (vi) (−3, 4) and (−1, −4).

2. Find the midpoint of the line segment joining (−3, 4) and (3, 7).
 On which axis does the midpoint lie?

3. The points (−2, 3) and (6, 5) are the end points of the diameter of a circle.
 Find the coordinates of the centre of the circle.

4. A(4, 3), B(1, −3), C(−2, −2) and D(1, 4) are the vertices of a parallelogram.
 Draw a sketch of this parallelogram.
 Find the midpoint of [AC].
 Verify that the midpoint of [AC] is also the midpoint of [BD].

5. Find M, the midpoint of the line segment joining A(−3, 4) and B(1, −6).
 Now show that $|AM| = |MB|$.

6. A(5, 2), and B(x_1, y_1) are two points.
 If M(2, 4) is the midpoint of [AB], find the coordinates of B.

Section 3.4 The slope of a line

The slope of the line AB is defined as

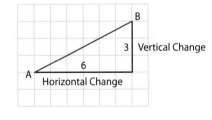

$$\frac{\text{the vertical change}}{\text{horizontal change}} \quad \text{or} \quad \frac{\text{rise}}{\text{run}}$$

The slope of AB $= \frac{3}{6} = \frac{1}{2}$.

In the diagram on the right, the slope
of AB is found by getting the

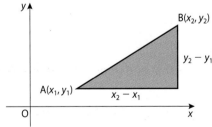

$$\frac{\text{vertical change}}{\text{horizontal change}} = \frac{y_2 - y_1}{x_2 - x_1}$$

Thus the slope, *m*, of AB is $= \dfrac{y_2 - y_1}{x_2 - x_1}$.

> The slope, *m*, of the line passing through (x_1, y_1) and (x_2, y_2) is
>
> $$m = \frac{y_2 - y_1}{x_2 - x_1}$$

Positive and negative slopes

As we go from left to right, the slope is positive if the line is rising and the slope is negative is the line is falling.

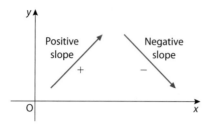

Parallel lines

The lines a and b in the diagram below both have the slope $\frac{3}{2}$.

These lines are parallel.

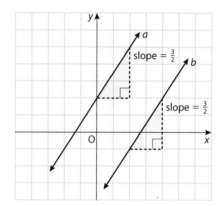

> Parallel lines have equal slopes

Perpendicular lines

The given lines a and b are perpendicular.

The slope of a is $\frac{3}{2}$.

The slope of $b = -\frac{2}{3}$.

Notice that one slope is minus the reciprocal of the other.

Notice also that the product of the two slopes is -1, i.e.,

$$-\frac{2}{3} \times \frac{3}{2} = -1$$

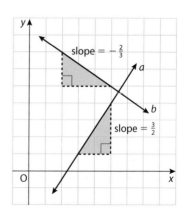

> If two lines are perpendicular, the product of their slopes is -1, i.e.,
> $$m_1 \times m_2 = -1$$

Example 1

If A = (3, −1) and B = (5, 2), find the slope of the line AB.

$$m = \frac{y_2 - y_1}{x_2 - x_1}$$

$$= \frac{2 + 1}{5 - 3} = \frac{3}{2}$$

$$
\begin{array}{cc}
(3, -1) & (5, 2) \\
\downarrow & \downarrow \\
(x_1, y_1) & (x_2, y_2)
\end{array}
$$

The slopes of AB = $\frac{3}{2}$.

Example 2

A(−1, 0), B(3, 2), C(−1, 4) and D(2, −2) are four points in the plane.
Show that AB is perpendicular to CD.

Let m_1 be the slope of AB and m_2 be the slope of CD.

$$
\begin{array}{cccc}
A(-1, 0) & B(3, 2) & \qquad\qquad & C(-1, 4) & D(2, -2) \\
\downarrow & \downarrow & & \downarrow & \downarrow \\
(x_1, y_1) & (x_2, y_2) & & (x_1, y_1) & (x_2, y_2)
\end{array}
$$

$$m_1 = \frac{y_2 - y_1}{x_2 - x_1} \qquad\qquad m_2 = \frac{y_2 - y_1}{x_2 - x_1}$$

$$= \frac{2 - 0}{3 + 1} \qquad\qquad = \frac{-2 - 4}{2 + 1} = \frac{-6}{3}$$

$$= \frac{2}{4} = \frac{1}{2} \qquad\qquad = \frac{-6}{3} = -2$$

$$m_1 \times m_2 = \frac{1}{2} \times (-2)$$

$$= -1$$

AB is perpendicular to CD as the product of the slopes is −1.

Exercise 3.4

1. The diagram shows four lines a, b, c and d.

   (i) Which lines have positive slopes?
   (ii) Which lines have negative slopes?

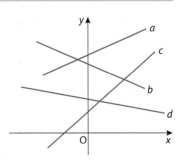

2. Three lines *a*, *b* and *c* are drawn on the grids below:

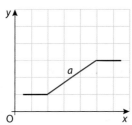 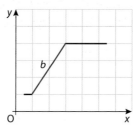 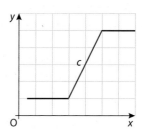

   (i) Which line has a slope of $\frac{3}{2}$?

   (ii) What is the slope of line *a*?

   (iii) What is the slope of line *c*?

3. Why is the slope of the given line negative?
Use the grid to work out the slope of the line.

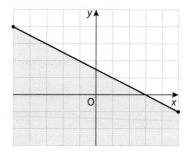

4. Find the slope of the line AB in each of the following:

   (i) A(3, 1) and B(5, 3)

   (ii) A(−1, 2) and B(3, −4)

   (iii) A(−1, −3) and B(0, 5)

   (iv) A(3, 0) and B(−1, −4)

   (v) A(−3, 2) and B(−5, 0)

   (vi) A(−5, 1) and B(−2, 3).

5. Show that the line passing through A(−1, −2) and B(3, 0) has the same slope as the line passing through C(2, 3) and D(−2, 1).
What can you say about the lines AB and CD?

6. ℓ contains the points (1, 1) and (2, 4).
m contains the points (4, 1) and (3, −2).
Investigate if ℓ is parallel to *m*.

7. A(−2, −4), B(5, −1), C(6, 4) and D(−1, 1) are the vertices of a quadrilateral.
Draw a rough sketch of the figure. Now verify that AB‖CD and AD‖BC.

8. The given diagram shows three lines *a*, *b*, and *c*.
Match the lines with these slopes:

    2, $\frac{1}{2}$,   1.

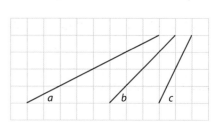

9. The slope of a line ℓ is $\frac{3}{4}$.

   (i) Write down the slope of a line m if m is parallel to ℓ.

   (ii) Write down the slope of a line n if n is perpendicular to ℓ.

10. The slopes of five lines are given below.

   Write down the slope of a line that is perpendicular to each of these lines:

   (i) $\frac{2}{3}$ (ii) $\frac{4}{5}$ (iii) $-\frac{3}{4}$ (iv) $-\frac{2}{5}$ (v) $-\frac{1}{2}$

11. A$(-1, 1)$, B$(1, 3)$, C$(6, 2)$ and D$(4, 4)$ are four points in the plane.

   Find the slope of   (i) AB   (ii) CD. Verify that AB $\perp$ CD.

12. The line m contains the points $(3, -1)$ and $(4, -2)$.

   (i) Find the slope of any line parallel to m.

   (ii) Find the slope of any line perpendicular to m.

13. If the slope of the line through the points $(3, 2)$ and $(8, k)$ is $\frac{3}{5}$, find the value of k.

14. The slope of the line through $(3, -2)$ and $(1, k)$ is $\frac{1}{3}$. Find the value of k.

15. The line ℓ contains the points $(-2, 0)$ and $(4, 3)$.

   The line m contains the points $(1, -1)$ and $(k, 1)$.

   (i) Find the slope of ℓ.   (ii) Find, in terms of k, the slope of m.

   (iii) If $\ell \| m$, find the value of k.

16. The diagram shows four lines ℓ, m, n and k.

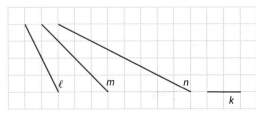

   (i) Explain why the slopes of ℓ, m, and n are negative.

   (ii) Match the lines with these slopes:

             $-\frac{1}{2}$,   0, -2, -1.

Section 3.5 The equation of a line

In the given line ℓ, the sum of the x and y values of each point is 5, e.g. $2 + 3 = 5$.

For this reason we say that the equation of the line ℓ is

   $x + y = 5$.

$x + y = 5$ is called the **equation of a line**,
or a **linear equation**.

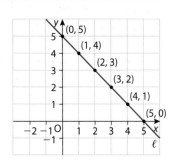

The equation was found by observing the relationship between the x and y values of each point and discovering that for all the points, $x + y = 5$.

We will now consider the figure on the right.

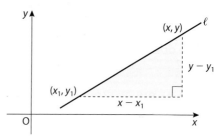

The line ℓ contains the point (x_1, y_1) and has slope m.

Let (x, y) be any other point on ℓ.

From the diagram, the slope of ℓ is $\dfrac{y - y_1}{x - x_1} = m$.

If we multiply both sides by $(x - x_1)$ we get,

$$y - y_1 = m(x - x_1)$$

> The equation of the line through (x_1, y_1) with slope m is found by using
> $$y - y_1 = m(x - x_1)$$

Example 1

Find the equation of the line containing the point $(-3, 2)$ and whose slope is $\frac{2}{3}$.

Equation of the line is: $y - y_1 = m(x - x_1)$ $m = \dfrac{2}{3}$

$$y - 2 = \frac{2}{3}(x + 3) \qquad\qquad (x_1, y_1) = (-3, 2)$$

$$y - 2 = \frac{2x}{3} + \frac{6}{3}$$

Multiply each term by 3: $3y - 6 = 2x + 6$

Bring all terms to right-hand side. $2x - 3y + 12 = 0$

∴   the equation of the line is: $2x - 3y + 12 = 0$

Equation of a line when given two points on the line

To find the equation of a line containing two points, we first find the slope of the line using the formula $\dfrac{y_2 - y_1}{x_2 - x_1}$.

We then use the formula $y - y_1 = m(x - x_1)$ to find the equation of the line.

You may use either of the two points as (x_1, y_1).

Example 2

Find the equation of the line containing the points $(-2, 3)$ and $(3, 1)$.

Slope of line: $m = \dfrac{y_2 - y_1}{x_2 - x_1}$

$\qquad\qquad = \dfrac{1 - 3}{3 + 2} = \dfrac{-2}{5}$

$$
\begin{array}{cc}
(-2, 3) & (3, 1) \\
\downarrow & \downarrow \\
(x_1, y_1) & (x_2, y_2)
\end{array}
$$

We now use the slope $-\dfrac{2}{5}$ and the point $(-2, 3)$... you may use either of the 2 points

Equation of line: $\quad y - y_1 = m(x - x_1)$

$\qquad\qquad\qquad y - 3 = -\dfrac{2}{5}(x + 2)$

$\qquad\qquad\qquad y - 3 = -\dfrac{2x}{5} - \dfrac{4}{5}$

$\qquad\qquad\quad 5y - 15 = -2x - 4$... multiply each term by 5.

$\Rightarrow \quad 2x + 5y - 11 = 0$ is the equation of the line.

Exercise 3.5

1. Find the equations of the following lines, given the slope and a point on the line in each case:
   (i) slope $= 2$; point $= (3, 4)$
   (ii) slope $= 4$; point $= (1, 5)$
   (iii) slope $= 5$; point $= (-2, 3)$
   (iv) slope $= -3$; point $= (-2, 0)$
   (v) slope $= -5$; point $= (-3, -2)$
   (vi) slope $= \frac{2}{3}$; point $= (3, -1)$.

2. Find the equations of the following lines, given the slope and a point on the line in each case:
   (i) slope $= \frac{3}{4}$; point $= (1, -4)$
   (ii) slope $= \frac{3}{5}$; point $= (-4, 2)$.

3. Find the equation of the line through $(-2, 3)$ with slope
   (i) 4
   (ii) -2
   (iii) $\frac{3}{4}$
   (iv) $-\frac{2}{3}$

4. Find the equation of the line through $(0, 0)$ and whose slope is -3.

5. Find the equation of the line through $(0, 0)$ and whose slope is
   (i) 3
   (ii) -5
   (iii) $\frac{1}{3}$
   (iv) $-\frac{3}{2}$
   What do you notice about the equation of each of these lines?

6. Find the slope of the line through $A(3, -4)$ and $B(1, 2)$.
   Hence find the equation of the line AB.

7. Find the equations of the lines through the following pairs of points:
   (i) $(2, 3)$ and $(4, 6)$
   (ii) $(-1, 2)$ and $(2, -4)$
   (iii) $(-5, 1)$ and $(1, 0)$
   (iv) $(-2, 3)$ and $(3, -1)$
   (v) $(2, 7)$ and $(0, 5)$
   (vi) $(-3, -5)$ and $(-1, -1)$.

8. Find the equation of the line through $(-2, 3)$ and the midpoint of the line segment joining $(1, -3)$ and $(3, -1)$.

9. The given diagram shows the gable-end of a house.

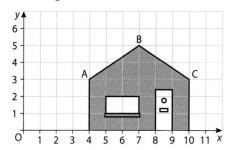

Use the grid to write down

   (i) the coordinates of the points marked A, B and C.

 (ii) the slope of AB

(iii) the equation of AB.

Section 3.6 The equation $y = mx + c$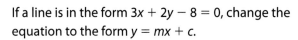

If the equation of a line is in the form

    $y = mx + c$, then

 (i) the slope is m

(ii) the line intersects the y-axis at $(0, c)$.

The point $(0, c)$ is called the **y-intercept**.

If a line is in the form $3x + 2y - 8 = 0$, change the equation to the form $y = mx + c$.

The slope is the value of m.

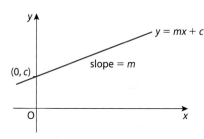

Example 1

Find the slope of the line $3x - 2y - 9 = 0$.

We write the equation in the form $y = mx + c$.

    $3x - 2y - 9 = 0$

$\Rightarrow$ $-2y = -3x + 9 \ldots$ leave the y term only on left-hand side

$\Rightarrow$ $2y = 3x - 9 \ldots$ multiply each term by -1

$\Rightarrow$ $y = \dfrac{3}{2}x - \dfrac{9}{2} \ldots$ divide each term by 2

$\therefore$ the slope of the line is $\dfrac{3}{2}$

Example 2

ℓ is the line $2x - 3y + 6 = 0$ and m is the line $3x + 2y - 4 = 0$.
Show that ℓ is perpendicular to m.

Slope of ℓ:

$$2x - 3y + 6 = 0$$
$$\Rightarrow \quad -3y = -2x - 6$$
$$\Rightarrow \quad 3y = 2x + 6$$
$$\Rightarrow \quad y = \frac{2}{3}x + 2$$
$$\Rightarrow \quad \text{slope of } \ell = \frac{2}{3}$$

Slope of m:

$$3x + 2y - 4 = 0$$
$$\Rightarrow \quad 2y = -3x + 4$$
$$\Rightarrow \quad y = -\frac{3}{2}x + 2$$
$$\Rightarrow \quad \text{slope of } m = -\frac{3}{2}$$

Slope of ℓ × slope of $m = \frac{2}{3} \times \left(-\frac{3}{2}\right)$

$$= \frac{-6}{6} = -1$$

Since the product of the two slopes $= -1$, the lines are perpendicular.

Exercise 3.6

1. Express each of the following lines in the form $y = mx + c$ and hence write down the slope of the line:
   (i) $x + y - 4 = 0$
   (ii) $3x + y - 5 = 0$
   (iii) $2x + 3y - 7 = 0$
   (iv) $5x - 2y + 3 = 0$
   (v) $3x + 4y - 2 = 0$
   (vi) $3x - 4y + 6 = 0$.

2. Express the line $\ell: 2x + 3y - 7 = 0$ in the form $y = mx + c$.
   (i)   Write down the slope of ℓ.
   (ii) What is the slope of any line parallel to ℓ?
   (iii) What is the slope of any line perpendicular to ℓ?

3. Show that the lines $x - 2y + 1 = 0$ and $3x - 6y - 7 = 0$ are parallel.
   What is the slope of any line perpendicular to these lines?

4. Show that the lines $2x + 3y - 4 = 0$ and $3x - 2y + 1 = 0$ are perpendicular to each other.

5. If the equation of the line ℓ is $y = 3x - 4$, write down the equation of any line, in the form $y = mx + c$, that is
   (i)   parallel to ℓ
   (ii) perpendicular to ℓ.

6. Investigate if the lines $y = \frac{2}{3}x + 4$ and $2x - 3y - 5 = 0$ are parallel.

7. The equation of the line m is $y = 3x - 2$.
   Find (i) the slope of m
        (ii) the point at which m intersects the y-axis.

8. The equations of six lines are given below:

a: $y = 2x - 3$
c: $y = x + 3$
e: $y = -\frac{1}{2}x + 4$

b: $y = \frac{1}{2}x + 5$
d: $y = -2x - 4$
f: $y = 2x - 2$

   (i) Name a pair of parallel lines.
   (ii) Name a pair of perpendicular lines.
   (iii) Which line crosses the y-axis at $(0, 4)$?
   (iv) Which line crosses the y-axis at $(0, -3)$?

9. By finding the slope and y-intercept, write down the equation of the given line.

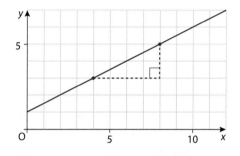

10. If the line $x + 2y - 6 = 0$ is parallel to the line $2x + ky - 5 = 0$, find the value of k.

11. If the line $2x - 3y + 7 = 0$ is perpendicular to the line $3x + ky - 4 = 0$, find the value of k.

12. For what value of k is the line $2x + ky - 4 = 0$ parallel to the line $x + 3y + 7 = 0$?

Section 3.7 Parallel and perpendicular lines

If we are given the equation of a line ℓ, such as $2x + 3y - 4 = 0$, we can find the slope of the line by expressing the equation in the form $y = mx + c$.

If we are also given a point (x_1, y_1), we can then find the equation of a line through (x_1, y_1) and which is parallel to or perpendicular to ℓ.

Example 1

Find the equation of the line through the point $(-2, 3)$ which is perpendicular to the line $2x - y + 5 = 0$.

To find the slope of $2x - y + 5 = 0$, we express it in the form $y = mx + c$.

$$2x - y + 5 = 0$$
$$\Rightarrow \quad -y = -2x - 5$$
$$\Rightarrow \quad\;\; y = 2x + 5... \qquad \text{multiply each term by } -1$$
$$\Rightarrow \quad \text{the slope is 2.}$$

The slope of the line perpendicular to this line is $-\frac{1}{2}$.

Equation of line through $(-2, 3)$ with slope $-\frac{1}{2}$ is:

$$y - y_1 = m(x - x_1) \qquad (x_1, y_1) = (-2, 3)$$

$$y - 3 = -\frac{1}{2}(x + 2) \qquad m = -\frac{1}{2}$$

$$y - 3 = \frac{-x}{2} - 1$$

$\Rightarrow \quad 2y - 6 = -x - 2\dots$ multiply each term by 2

$\Rightarrow \quad x + 2y - 4 = 0$ is the required equation.

Exercise 3.7

1. Find the slope of the line $2x + y - 4 = 0$.
   Now find the equation of the line through the point $(2, 4)$ and which is parallel to the line $2x + y - 4 = 0$.

2. Find the equation of the line through the point $(1, -6)$ and which is parallel to the line $3x - y + 4 = 0$.

3. Find the slope of the line $2x - 3y + 1 = 0$.
   What is the slope of any line perpendicular to $2x - 3y + 1 = 0$?
   Now find the equation of the line through the point $(4, -1)$ and which is perpendicular to the line $2x - 3y + 1 = 0$.

4. Find the equation of the line through $(-2, 1)$ and which is perpendicular to the line $3x + 2y - 4 = 0$.

5. Find the equation of the line through $(-4, 0)$ and which is parallel to the line $y = 3x - 5$.

6. A line passes through the origin and is perpendicular to the line whose equation is $3x - y - 2 = 0$. Find the equation of the line.

7. The point A has coordinates $(1, 7)$ and the point B has coordinates $(3, 1)$.
   The midpoint of [AB] is P.
   Find the coordinates of P.
   Now find the equation of the line which passes through P and which is perpendicular to the line $x + 5y - 7 = 0$.

8. The given diagram shows the points $A(-1, 5)$, $B(2, -1)$ and $C(0, 5)$.
   The line ℓ is parallel to AB and contains the point C.
   Find the equation of ℓ.

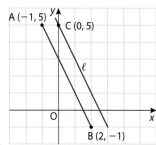

9. A line is perpendicular to the line whose equation is $y = 4x - 3$.
Find the equation of the line if it crosses the y-axis at $(0, 7)$.

10. Which one of the following lines is parallel to $3x + y - 4 = 0$?

A: $y = 3x - 2$ B: $y = \frac{1}{3}x + 4$ C: $6x + 2y + 7 = 0$ D: $x + 3y + 2 = 0$

11. The line $y = 2x + 5$ intersects the y-axis at the point P.
Find the equation of the line through P and which is perpendicular to $y = 2x + 5$.

12. The equation of the line AB is $5x - 3y = 26$.
    (i) Find the slope of AB.
    (ii) The point A has coordinates $(4, -2)$ and a point C has coordinates $(-6, 4)$.
        (a) Prove that AC is perpendicular to AB.
        (b) Find the equation of the line AC, expressing your answer in the form $ax + by = c$.

Section 3.8 Graphing lines

To draw a line such as $2x + 3y = 6$, we need to know at least two points on the line.

The easiest points to find are those at which the line crosses the x-axis and y-axis.

On the x-axis, $y = 0$; on the y-axis, $x = 0$.

Take the line $2x + 3y = 6$ Sketch of line $2x + 3y = 6$

When $x = 0$, then $2(0) + 3y = 6$
                                    $3y = 6$
                           $\Rightarrow$ $y = 2$

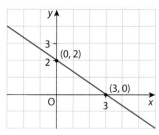

$\therefore$ $(0, 2)$ is one point on the line

When $y = 0$, then $2x + 3(0) = 6$
                              $2x = 6$
                            $x = 3$

$\therefore$ $(3, 0)$ is a second point on the line

A sketch of the line is shown on the right.

Lines parallel to the axes

The lines $x = 2$ and $x = 4$ are shown.

Notice that the x-value of all points on the line $x = 4$ is 4.

Similarly, the x-value of each point on the line $x = 2$ is 2.

All lines with equations of the form $x = a$ will be parallel
to the y-axis.

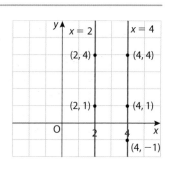

The diagram on the right shows the line $y = 2$.

Again notice that all the y-values of the points on this line are 2.

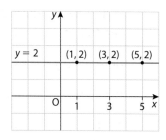

Lines containing the origin

A line such as $x + 2y = 0$, with no independent term, always contains the origin $(0, 0)$.

To plot the line $x + 2y = 0$, we know that it contains the origin.

To find a second point, we select a value for x and then find the corresponding y-value.

Let $x = 2$:
$$2 + 2y = 0$$
$$2y = -2$$
$$y = -1$$

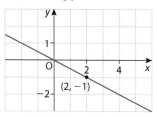

$\therefore$ $(2, -1)$ is a second point on the line.

A sketch of the line containing $(0, 0)$ and $(2, -1)$ is shown.

To verify that a point is on a given line

To investigate if the point $(3, -2)$ is on the line $x + 2y + 1 = 0$, we substitute 3 for x and -2 for y in the equation.

$$x + 2y + 1 = 0$$
$x = 3; y = -2$: $3 + 2(-2) + 1$
$$= 3 - 4 + 1$$
$$= 4 - 4 = 0$$

> If a point is on a line, then the coordinates of the point will satisfy the equation of the line.

Since $(3, -2)$ **satisfies** the equation $x + 2y + 1 = 0$, it shows that the point is on the line.

However $(-3, 4)$ is not on the line $x - 3y + 7 = 0$, since $-3 - 12 + 7 \neq 0$, i.e. it does not satisfy the equation.

Example 1

If the point $(k, 3)$ is on the line $4x - 3y + 1 = 0$, find the value of k.

We substitute k for x and 3 for y in the equation $4x - 3y + 1 = 0$.
$$\Rightarrow \quad 4k - 3(3) + 1 = 0$$
$$\Rightarrow \quad 4k - 9 + 1 = 0$$
$$\Rightarrow \quad 4k - 8 = 0$$
$$\Rightarrow \quad 4k = 8 \Rightarrow k = 2.$$

Exercise 3.8

1. Write down the equations of the lines a, b, c and
   d shown on the right.

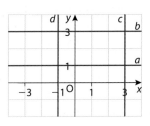

2. Draw a pair of axes and sketch these four lines:
   (i) $x = 4$ (ii) $y = 2$ (iii) $x = -2$ (iv) $y = -3$.

3. Use the graph of the line $2x + y = 6$ to write down
   (i) the value of x when $y = 0$
   (ii) the coordinates of the point where the line
       crosses the y-axis
   (iii) the value of y when $x = 1$
   (iv) the value of x when $y = 2$
   (v) the area of the triangle formed by the line,
       the x-axis and the y-axis.

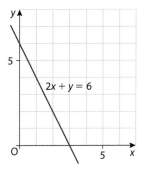

4. Find the coordinates of the points at which the line $x - 2y - 6 = 0$ intersects the
   x-axis and y-axis.
   Now use these points to draw a sketch of the line.

5. On separate diagrams, draw rough sketches of the following lines:
   (i) $x - y - 4 = 0$ (ii) $2x + y + 2 = 0$ (iii) $x - 2y + 4 = 0$

6. Find the coordinates of the points where the line $x - 2y = 5$ intersects the x-axis and
   y-axis. Hence draw a sketch of the line.

7. Draw a sketch of the line $2x - y + 6 = 0$.
   Hence write down the area of the triangle formed by the x-axis, the y-axis and the line.

8. On separate diagrams, draw rough sketches of the following lines:
   (i) $2x - y = 7$ (ii) $4x - y - 4 = 0$ (iii) $x - 3y - 6 = 0$

9. The equations of the lines A and B are:
   A: $y = \frac{2}{3}x + 2$
   B: $3x + 5y - 15 = 0$
   (i) Which line intersects the y-axis at $(0, 2)$?
   (ii) Which line intersects the x-axis at $(5, 0)$?
   (iii) Use the slopes of the two lines to investigate
       whether the lines are perpendicular to each other.
   (iv) Write down the area of the triangle formed by the line $3x + 5y - 15 = 0$, the x-axis
       and the y-axis.

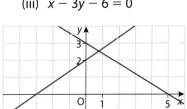

10. Each of the following lines contain the origin $(0, 0)$.

By taking a value for x and then finding the corresponding y-value, sketch each of the lines on separate diagrams:

    (i) $x - 2y = 0$ (ii) $x + 3y = 0$ (iii) $3x - y = 0$ (iv) $x - 4y = 0$.

11. The lines a, b, c and d are graphed in the given diagram.

Match each line with one of these equations:

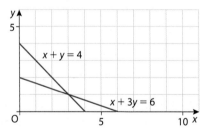

    (i) $x = -2$

    (ii) $x - y = 0$

    (iii) $2x + 5y = 10$

    (iv) $y = 4$

12.   (i) Verify that $(2, -5)$ is on the line $2x + y + 1 = 0$.

    (ii) Verify that $(2, -3)$ is on the line $y = x - 5$.

    (iii) Show that $(-3, 1)$ is not on the line $x - 3y + 1 = 0$.

    (iv) Investigate if $(2, 0)$ is on the line $2x - y + 3 = 0$.

13. Show that $(-3, 1)$ is on the line $2x + 4y + 2 = 0$.

14. If $(1, 4)$ is on the line $2x + y + k = 0$, find the value of k.

15. If $(2, -3)$ is on the line $x + ky + 7 = 0$, find the value of k.

16.   (i) Find the value of k if the line $2x + ky - 8 = 0$ contains the point $(3, 1)$.

    (ii) If $(1, t)$ lies on the line $y = 2x + 3$, find the value of t.

Section 3.9 Intersection of two lines

A sketch of the lines $x + y = 4$ and $x + 3y = 6$ is shown below.

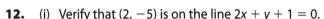

The point of intersection of the two lines can be read from the diagram.

This point is $(3, 1)$.

The point of intersection of any two lines can be found by sketching the lines on a grid and then reading their point of intersection from this grid.

However the point of intersection of two lines may be found more easily by using simultaneous equations, as shown in the following example.

> Simultaneous equations can be used to find the point of intersection of two lines.

Example 1

Use simultaneous equations to find the point of intersection of the lines
$$x + y = 5 \quad \text{and} \quad 2x - y = 4.$$

$$x + y = 5 \ldots ①$$
$$2x - y = 4 \ldots ②$$

Adding: $\quad 3x \quad = 9 \Rightarrow x = 3$

From ①: $\quad 3 + y = 5 \Rightarrow y = 2$

$\therefore$ the point of intersection is (3, 2).

Exercise 3.9

1. Using the one diagram, sketch the lines
$$x + y = 5 \quad \text{and} \quad x + 4y = 8.$$
Use your sketch to write down the point of intersection of the two lines.

2. A sketch of the lines $2x + y = 6$ and $x + y = 5$ is shown.

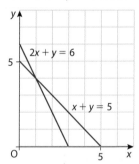

Use the sketch to write down the point of intersection of the two lines.
Now use simultaneous equations to verify your answer.

Use simultaneous equations to find the point of intersection of the following pairs of lines:

3. $x + y = 5$
$\quad 2x - y = 1$

4. $x - y = 2$
$\quad 2x + y = 7$

5. $2x + 5y = 1$
$\quad x - 3y = -5$

6. $x + 2y = -1$
$\quad 2x - 3y = -9$

7. $x + 3y = 7$
$\quad 2x - y = -7$

8. $x - 7y = 4$
$\quad 3x - y = -8$

9. $2x - 3y = 4$
$\quad 2x + 3y = -8$

10. $3x - 2y = 17$
$\quad 4x + 3y = 0$

11. $x + 3y = 13$
$\quad 2x + 5y = 21$

12. Use simultaneous equations to verify that the lines
$$2x + 3y = 12 \quad \text{and} \quad 3x - 4y = 1$$
intersect at the point (3, 2).

Section 3.10 Area of a triangle

The diagram below shows a triangle with vertices $(0, 0)$, (x_1, y_1) and (x_2, y_2).

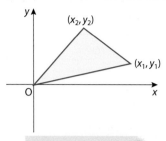

The area of this triangle is given by $\frac{1}{2}|x_1 y_2 - x_2 y_1|$

The two vertical lines $|\ \ |$ indicate that we take the positive value of the result.

Example 1

Find the area of the triangle with vertices $(0, 0)$, $(-2, 1)$ and $(3, 4)$.

$$\text{Area} = \frac{1}{2}|x_1 y_2 - x_2 y_1|$$
$$= \frac{1}{2}|(-2)(4) - (3)(1)|$$
$$= \frac{1}{2}|-8 - 3|$$
$$= \frac{1}{2}|-11|$$
$$= 5\frac{1}{2} \text{ square units}$$

$$
\begin{array}{cc}
(x_1, y_1) & (x_2, y_2) \\
\downarrow & \downarrow \\
(-2, 1) & (3, 4)
\end{array}
$$

Note: If none of the vertices of the triangle is at the origin, then the triangle has to be moved (translated) until one of the vertices is $(0, 0)$.

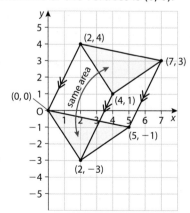

Let $(2, 4) \rightarrow (0, 0)$
$(7, 3) \rightarrow (5, -1)$
$(4, 1) \rightarrow (2, -3)$

Here we take 2 from each x-value and 4 from each y-value for each of the points.

Example 2

Find the area of the triangle with vertices $(2, 4)$, $(-3, 1)$ and $(3, -5)$.

Let
$$(2, 4) \rightarrow (0, 0)$$
$$(-3, 1) \rightarrow (-5, -3)$$
$$(3, -5) \rightarrow (1, -9)$$

Here we take 2 from each x-value and 4 from each y-value.

Area of triangle $= \frac{1}{2}|x_1 y_2 - x_2 y_1|$

$$= \frac{1}{2}|(-5)(-9) - (1)(-3)|$$

$$= \frac{1}{2}|45 + 3|$$

$$= \frac{1}{2}|48|$$

$$= 24 \text{ square units}$$

$$(x_1, y_1) \qquad (x_2, y_2)$$
$$\downarrow \qquad\qquad \downarrow$$
$$(-5, -3) \qquad (1, -9)$$

Exercise 3.10

1. Find the area of the triangle whose vertices are

   (i) $(0, 0)$, $(2, 1)$, $(3, 4)$ (ii) $(0, 0)$, $(5, 1)$, $(3, 6)$

   (iii) $(0, 0)$, $(-2, 3)$, $(1, -4)$ (iv) $(0, 0)$, $(3, 4)$, $(-2, -6)$

   (v) $(2, -1)$, $(-2, 4)$, $(0, 0)$ (vi) $(0, 0)$, $(6, 0)$, $(-2, 3)$.

2. $A(2, 3)$, $B(-5, 1)$ and $C(3, 1)$ are the vertices of a triangle.
   By using the translation $A(2, 3) \rightarrow (0, 0)$, find the images of B and C under this translation. Hence find the area of the triangle ABC.

3. By translating one of the vertices to $(0, 0)$, find the area of each of the triangles whose vertices are

   (i) $(2, 3)$, $(5, 1)$ and $(2, 0)$ (ii) $(-2, 3)$, $(4, 0)$ and $(1, -4)$

   (iii) $(-2, 1)$, $(3, 6)$ and $(0, -3)$ (iv) $(5, 1)$, $(2, -3)$ and $(7, 1)$.

4. The area of a triangle is *half length of base multiplied by perpendicular height.*
   Use this to write down the area of each of the triangles shown below.

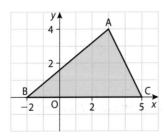
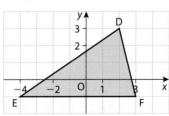

5. A(0, 0), B(4, −1), C(2, 3) and D(−2, 4) are the vertices of a quadrilateral.
Find the area of the quadrilateral by dividing it into the two triangles ABC and ACD.

6. Find the area of the quadrilateral with vertices A(0, 0), B(2, −3), C(4, 0) and D(0, 4).

7. The line $2x − y − 4 = 0$ intersects the x-axis at A and the y-axis at B.
Find the area of the $\triangle$OAB, where O is the origin.

8. Find the area of the triangle whose vertices are (0, 0), (1, 3) and (2, 6).
What conclusion can you draw from your answer?

9. Find the value of k if the area of the given triangle is
7 square units.

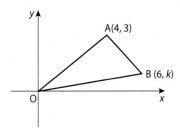

Test yourself 3

1. A(−1, 4) and B(2, 5) are two points in the plane.
Find (i) |AB| (ii) the slope of AB.

2. P is the point (1, 2) and Q is the point (−2, 6).
  (i)   Plot P and Q on graph paper.
  (ii) Find the slope of PQ.
  (iii) Find the equation of PQ.

3. The equation of a line is $y = 2x − 4$.
  (i)   Write down the slope of this line.
  (ii) At what point does the line intersect the y-axis?
  (iii) At what point does the line intersect the x-axis?
  (iv) What is the slope of any line that is perpendicular to $y = 2x − 4$?

4. (i) Verify that the point (2, 3) is on the line $2x − 3y + 5 = 0$.
  (ii) If the point (1, k) is on the line $2x − 3y + 7 = 0$, find the value of k.

5. A(−3, 1) and B(3, 9) are two points in the plane.
  (i)   Find M, the midpoint of [AB].
        On which axis does M lie?
  (ii) Find the slope of AB.
  (iii) Write down the slope of any line perpendicular to AB.
  (iv) Now find the equation of the line through the origin and which is perpendicular
        to AB.

6. Use the grid on the right to write down the slope of the line p.

   Now write down the equation of p in the form $y = mx + c$.

7. ℓ is the line $y - 6 = -2x - 2$.
   (i) Write down the slope of ℓ.
   (ii) Verify that $(1, 2)$ is a point on ℓ.
   (iii) ℓ intersects the y-axis at T.
        Find the coordinates of T.
   (iv) Show the line ℓ on a coordinate diagram.

8. The equation of the line k is $x - 2y + 10 = 0$.
   (i) Verify that $T(2, 6) \in k$.
   (ii) Find the slope of k.
   (iii) Find the equation of the line which contains T and is perpendicular to the line k.

9. (i) If the line $2x + y - 7 = 0$ is parallel to the line $4x + ky - 3 = 0$, find the value of k.
   (ii) The line $2x + 3y - 6 = 0$ intersects the x-axis at A and the y-axis at B.
        Find the coordinates of A and B and hence find the area of the triangle OAB, where O is the origin.

10. To clean the upstairs window on the side of a house, it is necessary to position the ladder so that it just touches the edge of the lean-to shed as shown in the diagram. The coordinates represent distances from O in metres, in the x and y directions shown.

    Find (i) the equation of the line of the ladder
         (ii) the height of the point A reached by the top of the ladder
         (iii) the length of the ladder in metres, correct to one decimal place.

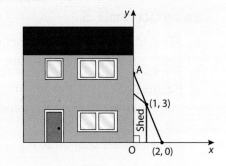

11. ℓ is the line $x - 2y + 2 = 0$.
    m is the line $3x + y - 8 = 0$.
    Use simultaneous equations to find the coordinates of P, the point of intersection of ℓ and m.

12. A line ℓ has slope -2 and passes through the point $(3, 6)$.
    (i) Find the equation of ℓ.
    (ii) Find the coordinates of the points at which the line intersects the x-axis and y-axis.
    (iii) Find the area of the triangle formed by ℓ, the x-axis and the y-axis.

13. (i) Find the equation of the straight line through $(0, 1)$ and $(3, 7)$.
    (ii) Another line has equation $y = 7 - 2x$.
         Without drawing the lines, explain how you can tell whether or not this line is perpendicular to the line in part (i).

14. The given graph shows three lines *a*, *b* and *c*.

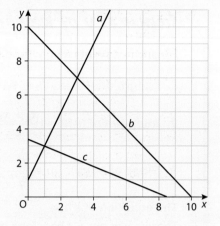

  (i)   Which line(s) have negative slopes?
  (ii) Use the grid to find the slope of the line *a*.
  (iii) Associate each of the lines with one of these equations:

        D: $y = 2x + 1$
        E: $x + y = 10$
        F: $2x + 5y = 17$.

15. *p* is the line $3x + 2y + c = 0$.
  (i) If $(3, -1)$ is a point on *p*, find the value of *c*.
  (ii) The line *q* is parallel to *p* and passes through the point $(-2, 5)$.
       Find the equation of *q*.

16. A(4, 2), B(−2, 0) and C(0, 4) are three points.
  (i)   Prove that AC is perpendicular to BC.
  (ii) Show that $|AC| = |BC|$.
  (iii) Find the area of the triangle ABC.

17. The linear graph below shows the relationship between degrees Celsius and degrees Fahrenheit.

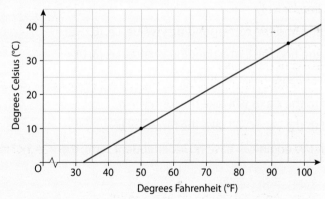

Use the graph to convert approximately

  (i)   35°C to Fahrenheit   (ii) 15°C to Fahrenheit
  (iii) 50°F to Celsius   (iv) 100°F to Celsius.

Use the two marked points on the graph to find the equation of the line in the form $ax + by + c = 0$.

Summary of key points...

For any two points A(x_1, y_1) and B(x_2, y_2):

1. Length of [AB] $= \sqrt{(x_2 - x_1)^2 + (y_2 - y_1)^2}$

2. Midpoint of [AB] $= \left(\dfrac{x_1 + x_2}{2}, \ \dfrac{y_1 + y_2}{2} \right)$

3. Slope of AB(m) $\quad m = \dfrac{y_2 - y_1}{x_2 - x_1} = \dfrac{\text{difference in } y\text{-values}}{\text{difference in } x\text{-values}}$

The equation of a line

The line $y = mx + c$ has slope m and intersects the y-axis at $(0, c)$.

The equation of the line which contains (x_1, y_1) and has slope m is

$$y - y_1 = m(x - x_1)$$

Parallel and perpendicular lines

If the line ℓ has slope m_1 and the line k has slope m_2, then

1. ℓ is parallel to k if $m_1 = m_2$.

2. ℓ is perpendicular to k if $m_1 \times m_2 = -1$.

If the slope of $\ell = \frac{3}{4}$ and $\ell \perp k$, then the slope of $k = -\frac{4}{3}$.

Graphing lines

To graph the line $2x - 3y = 6$:

1. Let $x = 0$ and find the corresponding y-value, i.e. $(0, -2)$.

2. Let $y = 0$ and find the corresponding x-value, i.e. $(3, 0)$.

3. Draw a line through $(0, -2)$ and $(3, 0)$.

Lines parallel to the x-axis will take the form $y = a$.

Lines parallel to the y-axis will take the form $x = b$.

Lines through the origin will have no independent term, e.g. $x = 2y$.

Point of intersection of two lines

The point of intersection of two lines is found by solving their simultaneous equations.

Area of a triangle

The area of the triangle with vertices $(0, 0)$, (x_1, y_1) and (x_2, y_2) is given by

$$\text{Area} = \tfrac{1}{2} |x_1 y_2 - x_2 y_1|.$$

Collecting Data and Sampling

Chapter 4

Key words

data	numerical	discrete	continuous	categorical data
ordinal	univariate	bivariate	primary data	secondary data
survey	experiment	data capture sheet	questionnaire	
respondent	bias	population	simple random sample	

Introduction

The charts and diagrams below can be seen regularly in newspapers, magazines and on television.

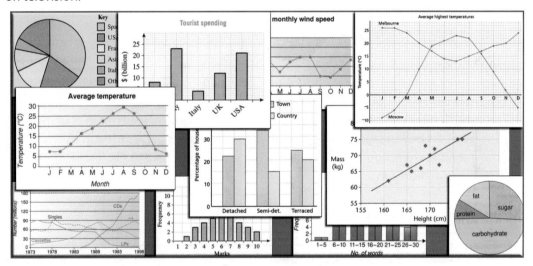

They are an attempt to present facts, figures and information in a way that is easy to understand. The information that is gathered is generally called **data**. The branch of mathematics that deals with collecting, presenting and analysing data is called **statistics**.

Statistics is generally concerned with

> collecting and recording data
> sorting and organising the data
> representing data in the form of charts and diagrams
> making calculations and choosing a suitable average
> interpreting the results and drawing conclusions from them.

This chapter introduces us to the different types of data and discusses some of the methods used to collect data.

Section 4.1 Types of data

Consider these questions:

> 'What is the most common shoe size in our class?'
> 'How many cars are there in the car park?'
> 'What were the times taken by a group of people to complete a crossword puzzle?'

To answer these questions we must either count or measure.

The answers to all three questions will be a number, e.g.,

    size 40 shoe;   134 cars;   26 minutes.

Data which can be counted or measured is called **numerical** data because the answer is a number. Numerical data can be either **discrete** or **continuous**.

Discrete data	**Continuous data**
Data which can take only certain individual values is called **discrete data**.	**Continuous data** is measured on some scale and can take any value on that scale.
Here are some examples of **discrete data**:	Here are some examples of **continuous data**:
> The number of goals scored by football teams on a Saturday > The numbers of desks in the classrooms of the school > The marks achieved in a test.	> The heights of students in your class > The speeds of cars passing a certain point on a road > The time taken to complete a 100-metre sprint

---

Example 1

For each of these types of data, write down whether it is discrete or continuous.
    (i)   the number of coins in your pocket
    (ii) the number of tickets sold for a concert
    (iii) the time taken to complete a sudoku puzzle
    (iv) the weights of students in your class
    (v) dress sizes.

    (i) discrete   (ii) discrete   (iii) continuous
    (iv) continuous   (v) discrete

Exercise 4.1

1. State if each of the following data is discrete or continuous:
    (i) The number of rooms in each of the houses on a road
    (ii) The number of CDs that have been sold
    (iii) The weights of the eggs in a carton
    (iv) Shoe sizes
    (v) The number of kilometres travelled on one litre of petrol.

2. Amy takes 22 minutes to complete a maths problem.
    Is the 22 minutes a discrete or continuous variable? Explain your answer.

    > A variable is something that is measured or observed.

3. A mechanic counts the number of spanners in his toolbox.
    Is this discrete or continuous data? Explain your answer.

4. Derek is examining a second-hand car.
    He is interested in
    (i) the number of doors in the car
    (ii) the number of seatbelts in the car
    (iii) the number of kilometres travelled.
    State if each of these three variables is discrete or continuous.

5. Sonia recorded how long it took her to run a cross-country race and the race-number on her bib.
    Say if each of these variables is discrete or continuous.

6. For each of these types of data, write down whether it is discrete or continuous.
    (i) The number of coins collected by a street performer.
    (ii) The length of a road.
    (iii) Shirt sizes.
    (iv) The midday temperature for each day in July.
    (v) The marks given by judges in a competition.
    (vi) The area of a field.
    (vii) The numbers of buttons on a selection of shirts.

    July Midday Temperatures

JULY						2011
SUN	MON	TUE	WED	THU	FRI	SAT
	1 17	2 16	3 18	4 18	5 18	6 17
7 19	8 20	9 22	10 22	11 21	12 21	13 22
14 22	15 23	16 24	17 23	18 23	19 23	20 24
21 24	22 23	23 23	24 24	25 25	26 23	27 23
28 25	29 25	30 24	31 25			

7. Emma says she is 16 years of age.
    Explain why this response is actually *continuous* but may appear to be *discrete*.

79

Section 4.2 Categorical data

The answer to the question, 'What colour is your car?' will not be a numerical value. Rather, it will fit into a group or category such as blue, red, black, white, …

Data which fits into a group or category is called **categorical data**.

Here are some examples of categorical data:

> gender (male, female)
> country of birth (Ireland, France, Spain, Nigeria,…)
> favourite sport (soccer, hurling, tennis, basketball…)

Categorical data in which the categories have an obvious order such as first division, second division, third division, etc, is called **ordinal data**.

Other examples of ordinal data are:

> type of house (1-bedroomed, 2-bedroomed, 3-bedroomed)
> attendance at football matches (never, sometimes, very often)
> opinion scales (strongly disagree, disagree, neutral, agree, strongly agree).

Univariate data

When **one item** of information is collected, for example, from each member of a group of people, the data collected is called **univariate data**.

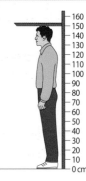

Examples of univariate data include:

> colour of eyes
> distance from school
> height in centimetres.

Bivariate data

Data that contains **two items** of information such as the height and weight of a person is generally called **paired data** or **bivariate data**.

Examples of bivariate data are:

> hours of study per week and marks scored in an examination
> the age of a car and the price of that car
> the engine sizes of cars and the number of kilometres travelled on a litre of diesel.

Colour of hair and gender is an example of **bivariate categorical data**.

The number of rooms in a house and the number of children in the house is an example of **bivariate discrete data**.

Example 1

For each of these sets of data, write down whether it is numerical or categorical:
  (i)   the sizes of shoes sold in a shop
  (ii)   the colours of shoes sold in a shop
  (iii) the subjects offered to Leaving Certificate students
  (iv)   the marks given by judges in a debating competition
  (v)   the crops grown on a village farm
  (vi)   the area of your sports hall.

(i)	numerical	(ii)	categorical	(iii)	categorical
(iv)	numerical	(v)	categorical	(vi)	numerical.

Exercise 4.2

1. State whether each of the following is categorical or numerical data:
  (i)   The number of bicycles sold by a shop in a particular week
  (ii)   The colours of cars sold by a garage last month
  (iii) The numbers of horses in the six races at a meeting
  (iv)   The favourite sports of all the students in a school.

2. Imelda bought a new dress.
  She wrote down   (i)   the colour of the dress
                     (ii) the number of buttons on the dress
                     (iii) the length of the dress.

For each of these data types, write down whether it is numerical or categorical.
Which of the three is discrete data?

3. State if each of the following is paired data:
  (i)   The colours of shirts on a stand
  (ii)   The blood-types and the heights of a group of students
  (iii) The number of brothers and their ages that each pupil in a class has.
  (iv)   The ages of all the people living on my street.

4. *The number of chairs in the classroom and the number of children in the class.*
  This is an example of discrete paired data.
  Write down two more examples of this type of data.

5. *The amount of flour and the number of eggs needed to make a cake.*
  (i)   Explain why this is paired data.
  (ii)   Which part of the data is discrete?
  (iii) Which part of the data is continuous?

6. All the football players in the premier league of a European country were categorised according to their ages and country of birth.

Copy and complete this sentence:

This is paired data; the first part is ……… data and the second part is ……… data.

7. A doctor records information about her patients.

The variables that she uses are described below:

   (i)   the colour of the patient's eyes

  (ii)   the patient's weight and height

 (iii)   the patient's shoe size

 (iv)   the patient's blood group.

State if each variable is   (a)   categorical   (b)   numerical.

Which of the four data types is discrete?

Describe in full the data type given in part (ii).

8. State whether each of the following statements is true or false.

Give a reason for your answer in each case.

    (i)   The number of pockets on a jacket is discrete data.

   (ii)   The types of trees in a forest is categorical data.

  (iii)   The countries in which people like to holiday is numerical data.

  (iv)   The number of receptions in each house on my street is categorical data.

   (v)   The age of a tree and the height of the tree is bivariate data.

  (vi)   The birth month of the students in your class is categorical data.

  (vii)   The number of matches played and the number of goals scored is bivariate and discrete data.

 (viii) The weights of horses in a race and the times taken by the horses to complete the race is bivariate and continuous data.

9. Cars are often categorised as small, economy, family, executive and luxury.

This is an example of **ordinal data**.

Give three more examples of ordinal data.

Section 4.3 Collecting data

Data is collected for a variety of reasons and from a variety of sources.

Companies do market research to find out what customers like or dislike about their products and to see whether or not they would like new products. The government carries out a census of every person in the country every five years. Local government, education authorities and other organisations use the information obtained for further planning.

Data can be collected by carrying out a survey, doing an experiment or by doing interviews and completing questionnaires.

Before you collect data, you need to have a clear aim in mind. You then need to decide what sort of data to collect and the most suitable and efficient method of collecting it.

The data you collect can be divided into two broad categories, namely, **primary data** and **secondary data**.

Primary data

Data that is collected by an organisation or an individual who is going to use it is called **primary data**.

Primary data is generally obtained

> by using a questionnaire
> by carrying out an experiment
> by investigations
> by making observations and recording the results.

Secondary data

Data which is already available or has been collected by somebody else for a different purpose is called **secondary data**.

Secondary data is obtained

> from the internet
> from published statistics and databases
> from tables and charts in newspapers and magazines.

The advantages and disadvantages of both types of data are given below.

Data	Advantages	Disadvantages
Primary data	> It is possible to collect exactly what your require > You know how it was collected > You know from whom it was collected	> Expensive > Time consuming
Secondary data	> Cheap to obtain > Easy to obtain	> Method of collection unknown > May be out of date > May not be exactly what is required

Surveys

Surveys are particularly useful for collecting data that is likely to be personal.

The main survey methods are:

> postal surveys in which people are asked questions
> personal interviews in which people are asked questions; this type of survey is very widely used in market research.
> telephone surveys; here the interview is conducted by phone
> **observation**, which involves monitoring behaviour or information

Survey method	Advantages	Disadvantages
Observation	Systematic and mechanical	Results are prone to chance
Personal interview and telephone survey	Many questions can be asked High response rate	Expensive Interviewer may influence responses
Postal survey	Relatively cheap Large amounts of data can be collected	Limited in the type of data that can be collected Poor response rate

Example 1

A businessman is considering building a leisure centre in the town centre. Which method of collecting primary data should he use to help him decide whether or not to build the leisure centre?

Data could be collected by using personal interviews or by doing a postal survey. The question 'Would you use a leisure centre if it was available?' should be included in any method used.

Experiments

Experiments are particularly useful for collecting scientific data. Drug companies carry out experiments to check if a new drug has any benefits or side-effects.

When you carry out an experiment you can use a **data capture sheet** to record your results.

The following example illustrates Derek's experiment to test whether or not a dice is fair:

Example 2

Derek has a six-sided dice. He throws it 60 times and records his results in a data capture sheet.

Derek 'expects' that each number on the dice should appear 10 times. He concludes that the dice is fair as all the frequencies are close enough to 10.

Score	Tally	Frequency
1	JHT IIII	9
2	JHT JHT I	11
3	JHT JHT II	12
4	JHT IIII	9
5	JHT JHT	10
6	JHT IIII	9

Exercise 4.3

1. Write down whether each of the following is an example of primary data or secondary data:
   (i) Alan counted the number of red vans passing the school gate.
   (ii) Helen examined records at a maternity hospital to find out how many babies were born each day in December.
   (iii) Robbie threw a dice 100 times and recorded the results to investigate if the dice was fair.
   (iv) Niamh used the internet to check the number of gold medals won by each competing country at the Beijing Olympics.

2. Roy and Damien want to predict next season's football league champions.
   Roy looks at the results for the last 5 years.
   Damien looks at the results for the 5 years before that.
   (i) What type of data are they using?
   (ii) Whose data is likely to be the more reliable and why?

3. A confectionery company wants to produce a new type of chocolate bar.
   Should they collect primary data or use secondary data if they wish to do market research?
   Give a reason for your answer.

4. A design company is given an assignment to design and market a new magazine aimed at younger women.
   (i) Explain how and why they could use both secondary and primary data.
   (ii) State one method of collecting primary data.

5. A government agency carried out a survey to find out what percentage of letters posted arrived at their destination on the following day. It surveyed ten businesses in Dublin city centre.
   (i) Do you think the results of this survey would match the results of the same survey if carried out in County Kerry?
   (ii) Would the information gathered be primary or secondary data?

Section 4.4 Questionnaires

A **questionnaire** is a set of questions designed to obtain data from individuals.

People who answer questionnaires are called **respondents**.

There are two ways in which the questions can be asked.

> An interviewer asks the questions and fills in the questionnaire

> People are given a questionnaire and asked to fill in the responses.

When you are writing questions for a questionnaire,

> be clear what you want to find out and what data you need

> ask short, simple questions

> start with simple questions to encourage the person who is giving the responses

> provide response boxes where possible: Yes ☐   No ☐

> avoid leading questions such as

       'Don't you agree that there is too much sport on television?'

  or   'Do you think that professional footballers are overpaid?'

> avoid personal questions such as those which involve name, exact age or weight.

Multiple-response questions

A choice of responses can be very useful in replying to the question, 'What age are you?'

Here is an example:

Tick your age in one of the boxes below:

☐	☐	☐	☐
Under 18 years	18–30	31–50	Over 50

Notice that there are no gaps in the ages and that only one response applies to each person.

Opinion scales

If you use an opinion scale, responses tend to cluster around the middle of the scale as often people do not want to appear extreme.

An opinion scale generally looks like this:

☐	☐	☐	☐	☐
strongly disagree	disagree	no opinion	agree	strongly agree

One way to avoid a middle cluster is to provide an even number of options so that there is no middle choice.

Sometimes respondents are asked to mark a point somewhere along a scale like that shown below.

disagree   agree

Again, there is a tendency to choose a point around the middle.

Avoiding bias

When you are collecting data, you need to make sure that your survey or experiment is **fair** and avoids **bias**. If bias exists, the data collected might be unrepresentative.

The boxes given below contain questions that should be avoided because they are too **vague**, too **personal**, or may **influence** the answer.

How often do you play tennis?

Sometimes ☐   Occasionally ☐   Often ☐

The three words *sometimes*, *occasionally* and *often* mean different things to different people.

Normal people enjoy swimming.
Do you enjoy swimming?

Yes ☐   No ☐

This is a leading question and may cause the result to be biased.
The first sentence should not be there.

Have you ever stolen goods from a supermarket?
Yes ☐   No ☐

Few people are likely to answer this question honestly if they have already stolen.

Do you agree that the EU is now big enough?
Yes ☐   No ☐

This question suggests that the right answer is yes.
It is **biased**.

Whenever you undertake a survey or experiment it is sensible to do a **pilot survey**. A pilot survey is one that is carried out on a very small scale to make sure the design and methods of the survey are likely to produce the information required.
It should identify any problems with the wording of questions and likely responses.

Avoid **personal** questions like 'Are you well educated?' or 'Where do you live?'

Exercise 4.4

1. Here is a list of questions and statements.
For each one, write down the letter of the style of response you would use.

(a) ☐ Yes   ☐ No   ☐ Don't know

(b) ☐ Agree   ☐ Disagree   ☐ Don't know

(c) ☐ 0   ☐ 1   ☐ 2   ☐ 3 or more

  (i)   How many children are there in your family?
 (ii)   Is Bulgaria is a member of the European Union?
(iii)   Smoking damages your health.
(iv)   Everybody should exercise for at least one hour each day.

2. Susan wants to find out what people think about the Green Party.
She is trying to decide between these two questions for her questionnaire.

(i) Do you like the Green Party?

Yes ☐   No ☐

(ii) Do you agree that the Green Party is the best party?

Yes ☐   No ☐

Which question should she use? Explain your answer.

3. Jack wants to find out what students think about the library service at his college.
Part of the questionnaire he has written is shown.

> **Q1.** What is your full name? ....
>
> **Q2.** How many times a week do you go to the library?
>
> ☐ Often   ☐ Sometimes   ☐ Never

(i) Why should Q1 not be asked?

(ii) What is wrong with the choices offered in Q2?

4. Terry is writing a questionnaire about people's ages. In it she asks the question:

> How old are you?   Young ☐   Middle-aged ☐   Elderly ☐

(i) What is wrong with the question and answers?

(ii) Rewrite the question and answers in a better way.

5. Carol wants to find out what people think of the HSE.
Part of the questionnaire she has written is shown.

> **Q1.** What is your date of birth? ....
>
> **Q2.** Don't you agree that waiting times for operations are too long?
>
> Yes ☐   No ☐
>
> **Q3.** How many times did you visit your doctor last year?
>
> ☐ less than 5   ☐ 5–10   ☐ 10 or more

(i) Why should Q1 not be asked?

(ii) Give a reason why Q2 is unsuitable.

(iii) (a) Explain why the responses to Q3 are unsuitable in their present form.

(b) Rewrite a more suitable question to be included in the questionnaire.

6. Which of the following questions do you think are biased?
Write down their letters and explain what makes them biased.

A: Did you go to a cinema in the last month?

B: It is important to eat fruit. Do you eat fruit?

C: How many hours of television do you watch each week?

D: In view of the huge numbers of road accidents outside this school, do you think the speed limit should be reduced?

7. Decide if the given question is suitable for use in a questionnaire. If it is not, give a reason why and rewrite the question to improve it.

> How much pocket money do you get?
>
> a little ☐   some ☐   a lot ☐

8. Angela is doing a questionnaire because she wants some information about the weights of people in her school. She asks them:
How much do you weigh?
  (i) Explain why that is not a good question to ask.
  (ii) Write a better question and give a set of response boxes with it.

9. Give a reason why questions A and B below should be re-worded before being included in a questionnaire.
Rewrite each one showing exactly how you would present it in a questionnaire.

Question A: Do you live in a working-class or middle-class area?

Question B: The new supermarket seems to be a great success. Do you agree?

10. Steve is doing a survey on football teams.
He writes a question and response boxes:
  (i) Give your reasons why Steve should not ask the question in such a way.
  (ii) Write a better question for Steve to use.

> How often do you watch a football match?
>
> Never ☐   Once a week ☐
>
> When I can ☐

11. In preparing questions for a survey on the use of a library, the following questions were considered. Explain why each question in its present form is unsuitable and rewrite the question.
  (i) Are you well educated or poorly educated?
  (ii) How often do you use the library?
  (iii) What type of books do you read?

12. A mobile phone company wants to carry out a survey.
It wants to find out the distribution of the age and sex of customers and the frequency with which they use their phones.
The company intends to use a questionnaire.
Write three questions and corresponding responses that will enable the company to carry out the survey.

13. A market research company is conducting a survey to find out whether most people had a holiday in Ireland, elsewhere in Europe or in the rest of the world, last year. It also wants to know if they stayed in self-catering accommodation, hotels or went camping.

Design **two** questions that could be used in a questionnaire to efficiently find out all this information.

14. Niamh has to carry out a survey into the part-time jobs of all the 16-year-olds in her school.

She has to find out:
> what proportion of these 16-year-olds have part-time jobs
> whether more girls than boys have part-time jobs.

Design **two** questions which she could include in her questionnaire.

15. Ian is writing a questionnaire.
These are two of his questions:
(a) Do you spend a lot of time surfing the Internet?
(b) What do you weigh?
    (i) What is wrong with each of these questions?
    (ii) Rewrite each question, showing exactly how Ian should present it in a questionnaire.

16. Grace and Gemma were carrying out a survey on the food people eat in the school canteen.

Grace wrote the question 'Which foods do you eat?'

Gemma said that this question was too vague.

Write down two ways in which this question could be improved.

17. Design a questionnaire consisting of six questions to find out about the kind of holidays people had last year.

18. A survey of reading habits is to be conducted.

Suggest five questions which could be included.

Section 4.5 Sampling

If you were asked to investigate the claim that

'14 year-old boys are taller than 14-year old girls in Ireland',

do you measure the heights of all 14-year olds in Ireland and compare the results for boys and girls? This could be an enormous task as there are about 60 000 14-year olds in this country.

In this study, we use the word **population** to describe all the 14-year old boys and girls in Ireland. In statistics a **population** is everything or everybody that could possibly be involved in a particular investigation or study.

When a population is too large for a study, we collect data or information from some of the population only.

In statistics this group is called **a sample**. The purpose of a sample is to collect data from some of the population and use it to draw conclusions about the whole population.

The **size** of a sample is important. If the sample is too small, the results may not be very reliable. If the sample is too large, the data may take a long time to collect and analyse.

Bias

The sample you select for your study is very important. If the sample is not properly selected, the results may be **biased**. If **bias** exists, the results will be distorted and so will not be representative of the population as a whole.

Bias in a sample may arise from any of the following:

> **Choosing a sample which is not representative**

    Example   Cara is doing a survey on people's attitude towards gambling. If she stands outside a casino and questions people as they enter or leave, the results will be biased as these people are already involved in gambling.

> **Not identifying the correct population**

    Example   The school principal wants to find out about students' attitudes to school uniforms. She questions 10 Leaving Certificate students only. This may lead to biased results as the opinions of the younger students (from 1st year to 5th year) are not included.

> **Failure to respond to a survey**
Many people do not fill in responses to questionnaires sent through the post. Those who do respond may not be representative of the population being surveyed.

> **Dishonest answers to questions**

Example 1

Conor carries out a survey to find out if people in his town enjoy watching sport. He stands outside a football ground and surveys people's opinions as they go in to watch a match.
Write two reasons why this is not a good sample to use.

(i) People who go to watch football matches usually enjoy sport; hence the sample may be biased.
(ii) Generally more men than women go to watch football, so the survey could be gender-biased.

Simple random sample

One of the ways to avoid bias in a survey is to take a **simple random sample** (or more commonly called a **random sample**).

In a random sample every member of the population being considered has an equal chance of being selected. Random samples need to be carefully chosen.

Methods for choosing a **simple random sample** could involve giving each member of the population a number and then selecting the numbers for the sample in one of these ways:

> putting the numbers into a hat and then selecting however many you need for the sample

> using a random number table

> using a random number generator on your calculator or computer

---

Example 2

A football club with 80 members has 5 tickets for an international match.
Describe two methods of choosing 5 members at random to receive these tickets.

Method 1 Each member is given a number and each number is written on a piece of paper.
The pieces of paper are put into a box and mixed up well and five pieces are chosen.
The members with the five numbers chosen receive the tickets.

Method 2 Below is an extract from a random number table:

526338	127642	463919	394821	563271
265389	276153	584326	427534	307263

We need to give each of the 80 members a two-digit number.
Start at 11 and end at 90.
We now have to select five two-digit numbers from the random numbers above. These numbers have to be between 11 and 90 inclusive.
If we start at the beginning of the first row and select two digit numbers we get:

52, 63, 38, 12, 76.

(Ignore any number over 90 or any repeated number.)
The members with the five selected numbers receive the tickets.

Electronic calculators are very useful for generating random numbers.

If you want to generate 3-digit numbers, press [SHIFT], and then press [Ran #].

Now press [=] and disregard the decimal point.

If the number displayed is 0.107, write 107.

Press [=] repeatedly to get more random numbers.

Exercise 4.5

1. Dara wants to find out how people get to work each day.
   Which of the following is the most appropriate group to question?
   A: Every fourth person at a bus stop.
   B: A group of people at lunch break.
   C: People arriving late for work.

2. Jennifer wants to investigate if people want longer prison sentences for criminals.
   Which of the following is the most appropriate group to question?
   A: Members of the gardaí.
   B: People at a football match.
   C: People who have been in prison.

3. Kate is doing a survey to find out how often people go to the cinema and how they travel to get there.
   She stands outside a cinema and questions people as they go in.
   Give a reason why this sample could be biased.

4. A county engineer is carrying out a traffic survey.
   He is trying to find out how busy a particular road is.
   Each day, he counts the numbers of cars passing a particular point between 2 p.m. and 3 p.m.
   He uses this information to write a report.
   State why his sample is likely to be biased.

5. Amy wants to find out how often people play sport.
   She went to a local sports shop and questioned the people she met.
   Explain why this sample is likely to be biased.

6. Trudy is investigating shopping habits.
   She interviews 50 women at her local supermarket on a Tuesday morning.
   Give three reasons why her sample may be biased.

7. Amanda wants to choose a sample of 500 adults from the town where she lives.
   She considers these methods of choosing her sample:

   Method 1: Choose people shopping in the town centre on Saturday mornings.
   Method 2: Choose names at random from the electoral register.
   Method 3: Choose people living in the streets near her house.

   Which method is most likely to produce an unbiased sample?
   Give a reason for your answer.

8. Below is an extract from a table of random numbers.
   Use these numbers to select a simple random sample of 5 from a population of 50:

88715	59454	76218	59364	20641
57169	94386	27856	10856	35728

9. The chart on the right gives the sex and height in metres of 30 children.
   (i) From this population of 30 children, choose a random sample of 5 children. Use the random number table below to do this.

55	18	62	23
10	83	12	22
55	23	52	11
27	19	29	43
93	86	46	14

Begin by using the first row. Write down the height and sex of each child in the chosen sample.

Child	Height	Sex	Child	Height	Sex
01	1.43	M	16	1.25	F
02	0.98	F	17	0.89	F
03	1.24	M	18	1.62	M
04	0.87	F	19	1.20	F
05	1.10	F	20	1.53	M
06	1.15	F	21	1.60	M
07	1.29	M	22	1.23	F
08	0.94	M	23	1.44	M
09	1.00	M	24	1.30	F
10	1.21	F	25	1.00	F
11	1.53	F	26	1.54	F
12	1.43	M	27	1.12	M
13	1.27	M	28	0.98	F
14	1.24	M	29	1.06	M
15	1.42	F	30	1.25	F

   (ii) Choose a second sample of 5 children.
   Use the same random number table, but begin by using the second line.
   Write down the height and sex of each child in the chosen sample.

10. Use the [Ran #] key on your calculator to choose another random sample of 5 children from the chart in question 9 above.

11. Paul needs to choose a sample of 100 members from his sports club.
   He writes down three possible methods of choosing his sample.
   (i) He chooses the names at random from the complete list of members on the club's database.
   (ii) He chooses the members who play in the club football teams.
   (iii) He asks people using the club on a Monday morning.

   For each of Paul's methods, state whether the sample is likely to be biased, explaining your answer.

12. Describe three ways of selecting a simple random sample of 10 pupils from a school of 100 pupils.

13. There are 1000 pupils in Alan's school.
   Alan samples 50 pupils at random and asks them to complete his survey.
   He finds that 15 of the pupils in the sample read comics.
   Estimate the number of pupils in the school who read comics.

Test yourself 4

1. State whether each of the following sets of data is numerical or categorical:
   (i) The circumference of trees in a wood.
   (ii) The types of vegetables grown on a farm.
   (iii) The favourite rugby team of the teachers in my school.
   (iv) The distance between home and school.
   (v) County of birth.
   (vi) Time taken to complete a cross-country race.
   (vii) The brands of toothpaste on sale in supermarkets.

2. Which of the following are discrete data and which are continuous data?
   (i) The numbers of windows in houses.
   (ii) The number of pupils who wear glasses.
   (iii) The weights of strawberries in a punnet.
   (iv) The time taken to complete a jigsaw puzzle.
   (v) The numbers of matches in a selection of match boxes.
   (vi) The lengths of material used to make curtains.

3. State whether each of the following is primary data or secondary data:
   (i) Counting the number of hatchback cars passing the school gate.
   (ii) Looking at records to see how many people passed through Shannon Airport each day in June one year.
   (iii) Phoning local supermarkets and stores to find the hourly pay rates for part-time work.
   (iv) Checking the internet to see how many medals each country won at the Vancouver Winter Olympics.
   (v) Examining tourist brochures to find the average midnight temperatures of selected cities for the month of June.

4. State whether each of the following is univariate data or bivariate data:
   (i) the shirt size of men
   (ii) hours of study and marks scored in a Science test
   (iii) midday temperature and number of ice-creams sold
   (iv) weekly pocket money of the students in your class
   (v) the weight of a parcel and the cost of posting that parcel.

5. For each of these questions or statements, what would be the best way to collect the data? Choose from the box.

   | A questionnaire or data collection sheet |
   | B experiment   C other source |

   (i) What sport do people in your class watch most often?
   (ii) How often do people go to the cinema? On which days?
   (iii) What percentage of motor vehicle accidents in Ireland occur between 6 p.m. and midnight?
   (iv) Eoin wants to find out if a dice is biased.

(v) Sarah wants to find out how many people in her class can run 100 metres in less than 15 seconds.

(vi) How people intend to vote in the next election?

(vii) The number of times a person scores a double in a game of darts.

(viii) What people think of the local bus service?

(ix) Where people go for their summer holidays.

(x) What percentage of accidents are caused by drunk drivers?

6. Pam writes a questionnaire to survey opinion on whether cars should be banned from the town centre.

   (i) Which two of the following points are important when she is deciding which people to ask?

   A   Ask people who look friendly.   B   Ask people at different times of the day.

   C   Ask some men and some women.   D   Ask the first people she sees.

   (ii) Which two of the following points are important when she is writing the questionnaire?

   A   Write polite questions.

   B   Write as many questions as she can think of.

   C   Write questions for car drivers only.

   D   Write questions that do not require long answers.

7. Katie is conducting a survey on television viewing habits.
   She thinks of two questions for the questionnaire.

   Question 1.   Do you consider yourself to be intelligent?

   Question 2.   When do you watch television?

   (i) Explain why each of these questions is unsuitable.

   (ii) Rewrite each of these questions so that she could include them in her questionnaire.

8. Write two questions for a questionnaire to test the truth of these statements:

   A: Most people choose to shop in a supermarket where it is easy to park a car.

   B: Children of school-going age watch more television than their parents.

9. This statement is made on a television programme about health.

   "Three in every eight pupils do not take any exercise out of school."

   (i) A school has 584 pupils. According to the television programme, how many of these pupils do not take any exercise outside school?

   (ii) Claire says, 'I go to the gym twice a week after school.' She decides to do a survey to investigate what exercise other pupils do outside of school.

   Write down **two** questions that she could ask.

Summary of key points...

Types of data

Primary data is information you collect yourself.

Secondary data is information that you get from existing records.

Numerical data is data that can be counted or measured.

Discrete data can only take particular values such as shoe sizes or goals scored in a match.

Continuous data can take any value in a particular range. Weight, temperature and length are all examples of continuous data.

Categorical data is described using words such as colour, favourite fruit or country of birth.

Univariate data consists of one item of information such as colour of hair.

Bivariate data contains two items of information such as the heights of children and their ages.

Questionnaires

A **survey** collects primary data.

One way of collecting primary data is to design and complete a **data collection sheet** or **questionnaire**.

When designing questions for a questionnaire:
- Be clear about what you want to find out.
- Keep each question as simple as possible.
- Never ask a leading question designed to get a particular response.
- Provide response boxes where possible.

Sampling

A **population** is everybody or everything that could be included in a particular survey or investigation.

A **sample** is a part of the population from which data is collected and then used to draw conclusions about the whole population.

In a **simple random sample** every member of the population has an equal chance of being chosen.

If data obtained from a sample does not properly represent the population as a whole, the results may well be **biased**.

5 Arithmetic

Key words

significant figures   percentage profit (or loss)   direct proportion
relative error   percentage error   tolerance   lower bound   upper bound
gross tax   tax credit   universal social charge (USC)   compound interest
principal   AER   depreciation   standard form

Section 5.1 Fractions – decimals – significant figures

1. Fractions

Here is a reminder of some of the work you will have done and the terms you will have met in your study of fractions so far.

$\div 4$

$\dfrac{12}{20} = \dfrac{3}{5}$

$\div 4$

$\dfrac{12}{20}$ and $\dfrac{3}{5}$ are called **equivalent** fractions.

$\dfrac{3}{5}$ is said to be the **simplest form** of the fraction $\dfrac{12}{20}$.

We can **order** fractions by rewriting them as equivalent fractions with a common denominator.

A fraction such as $\dfrac{3}{8}$ can be thought of as $3 \div 8$.

A calculator is very useful when changing fractions to decimals.

$$\dfrac{3}{8} = 3 \div 8 = 0.375$$

Example 1

(i) Express 125 metres as a fraction of 1 km.

(ii) $\dfrac{3}{7}$ of a sum of money is €360. Find the sum of money.

(i) There are 1000 metres in 1 km

∴   125 m as a fraction of 1 km $= \dfrac{125}{1000} = \dfrac{1}{8}$

(ii) $\dfrac{3}{7} = $ €360

$\dfrac{1}{7} = $ €120 … divide by 3

$\dfrac{7}{7} = $ €120 × 7 = €840

∴   the sum of money is €840.

2. Decimals

The decimal $2.347 = 2 + \frac{3}{10} + \frac{4}{100} + \frac{7}{1000}$.

Any decimal can be converted to a fraction as follows:

$$0.35 = \frac{35}{100} = \frac{7}{20}$$

0.35 and $\frac{7}{20}$ are equivalent values.

Not all fractions have an exact **decimal equivalent**.

The fraction $\frac{2}{3} = 0.66666 \ldots$

This is called a **recurring decimal** since one of the digits keeps recurring.

The decimal $0.6666\ldots$ is written as $0.\dot{6}$.

Similarly, $\frac{2}{11} = 0.181818 \ldots = 0.\dot{1}\dot{8}$.

The decimal $6.4837 = 6.484$, correct to 3 decimal places.
$= 6.48$ correct to 2 decimal places.
$= 6.5$, correct to 1 decimal place.

3. Significant figures

If the attendance at a football match was 34 176, it would be reasonable to write down 34 200 or 34 000.

34 200 is written correct to 3 significant figures.
34 000 is written correct to 2 significant figures.

When expressing a whole number correct to a given number of significant figures, zeros at the end of the number are not counted but must be included in the final result. All other zeros are significant.

Thus $52\,764 = 52\,760$ correct to 4 significant figures
$= 52\,800$ correct to 3 significant figures
$= 53\,000$ correct to 2 significant figures
$= 50\,000$ correct to 1 significant figure.

The number $70\,425 = 70\,400$ correct to 3 significant figures.
Notice here that the zero between the 7 and 4 is significant, but the two final zeros are not.

If a number is less than 1, then the zeros immediately after the decimal point are not significant.

Thus (i) $0.07406 = 0.0741$ correct to 3 significant figures
(ii) $0.00892 = 0.0089$ correct to 2 significant figures.

Exercise 5.1

1. Write each of these as a fraction in its simplest form:
   (i) 12 out of 20   (ii) 8 out of 30   (iii) 12 out of 16   (iv) 25 out of 40

2. Add each pair of fractions and simplify your answer:
   (i) $\frac{1}{4} + \frac{3}{8}$ (ii) $\frac{7}{12} + \frac{5}{8}$ (iii) $\frac{2}{7} + \frac{1}{6}$ (iv) $\frac{7}{9} + \frac{5}{6}$

3. Work out each of these:
   (i) $3\frac{3}{4} + 1\frac{1}{2}$ (ii) $2\frac{2}{3} + 1\frac{1}{4}$ (iii) $2\frac{4}{5} + 1\frac{1}{2}$ (iv) $5\frac{1}{2} + \frac{7}{10}$

4. Work these out:
   (i) $2\frac{4}{5} - 1\frac{1}{2}$ (ii) $4\frac{5}{6} - 2\frac{2}{3}$ (iii) $2\frac{2}{3} - \frac{3}{5}$ (iv) $4\frac{3}{8} - 2\frac{1}{6}$

5. Work these out:
   (i) $\frac{2}{3}$ of 15   (ii) $\frac{3}{4}$ of 28   (iii) $\frac{3}{5}$ of 65   (iv) $\frac{7}{8}$ of 56

6. Work out these multiplications:
   (i) $2\frac{1}{4} \times \frac{2}{3}$ (ii) $2\frac{1}{2} \times 1\frac{5}{7}$ (iii) $1\frac{2}{3} \div \frac{10}{9}$ (iv) $3\frac{3}{4} \div \frac{3}{8}$

7. Write each of these fractions in its simplest form.
   (i) The fraction of the circle that is red
   (ii) The fraction that is blue
   (iii) The fraction that is green
   (iv) The fraction that is yellow

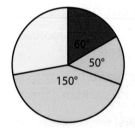

8. Change each of these fractions to a decimal:
   (i) $\frac{1}{8}$ (ii) $\frac{5}{8}$ (iii) $\frac{7}{8}$ (iv) $\frac{1}{16}$ (v) $\frac{7}{16}$

9. Write these lists in order, starting with the smallest:
   (i) $\frac{5}{8}$, 0.6, $\frac{13}{20}$, 0.58   (ii) $\frac{3}{10}$, 0.35, $\frac{9}{20}$, 0.4

10. Dawn and Eve run a race. After Dawn has covered $\frac{3}{5}$ of the distance, Eve has covered $\frac{2}{3}$ and is 50 metres ahead of Dawn.
    (i) How long is the race?
    (ii) How many metres does Eve still have to run?

11. Write 2.574 correct to
    (i) two decimal places   (ii) one decimal place.

12. Use your calculator to evaluate each of the following, correct to 1 decimal place:
    (i) $\frac{128.4 \times 46.9}{3.5}$ (ii) $\frac{18.2 \times 171}{384.6}$ (iii) $\frac{0.48 \times 536}{28.2}$

13. Evaluate the following, correct to one decimal place:
    (i) $\frac{1}{9} + \frac{3}{14}$ (ii) $\frac{6}{17.4} + \frac{1}{15}$ (iii) $\frac{6}{24} + \frac{0.4}{3.8}$

14. How many significant figures are there in each of these numbers?

    (i) 346   (ii) 1500   (iii) 780   (iv) 6080   (v) 150 900

    (vi) 1.27   (vii) 0.04   (viii) 0.607   (ix) 10.04   (x) 106 000

15. Write each of these numbers correct to two significant figures:

    (i) 3184   (ii) 648   (iii) 2916   (iv) 28 936   (v) 40 673

16. Write each of the following numbers correct to three significant figures:

    (i) 7516   (ii) 293.8   (iii) 14.27   (iv) 0.6274   (v) 1.0739

17. An oil tank is $\frac{7}{8}$ full and it contains 896 litres.

How many litres can the tank hold?

18. In a youth club, $\frac{3}{7}$ of the members are girls.

If there are 84 boys in the club, how many girls are in it?

19. Work out an estimate for $\dfrac{4.89 \times 0.087}{0.0053}$ by rounding each number correct to 1 significant figure.

Section 5.2 Ratio and proportion

1. Ratio

We use ratios to show how things are divided or shared.

The ratio $12:8 = \frac{12}{4}:\frac{8}{4} = 3:2$ ... divide each term by 4

$3:2$ is called the **simplest form of the ratio**.

A ratio is normally expressed in whole numbers.

The ratio $\frac{1}{3}:\frac{5}{6}$ can be expressed as whole numbers by multiplying each term by 6.

$$\therefore \frac{1}{3}:\frac{5}{6} = \frac{6}{3}:\frac{5\times 6}{6} = 2:5$$

Example 1

A sum of money is divided in the ratio $1:3:5$.
If the smallest part is €250, find the sum of money.

If a sum of money is divided in the ratio $1:3:5$, then the parts are

    $\frac{1}{9}, \frac{3}{9}, \frac{5}{9}$ ... nine parts in total

$\Rightarrow \frac{1}{9} = €250$

$\Rightarrow \frac{9}{9} = €250 \times 9 = €2250$

$\therefore$ the sum of money is €2250

---

2. Proportion

While ratios compare one part to another part, proportion compares a part to the total amount.

If there are 3 goalkeepers in a panel of 24 footballers, the proportion of goalkeepers in the panel is $\frac{3}{24} = \frac{1}{8}$.

If 1 litre of petrol costs €1.50, 2 litres cost €3.00 and 5 litres cost €7.50.

Here the cost of 1 litre, 2 litres, 5 litres are in **direct proportion**.

Example 2

The number of pages in a magazine increased from 64 to 80.
The original price of €4.40 increased in the same ratio.
What is the new price of the magazine?

(In this problem we are looking for **price**, so we keep price **last**.)

$$64 \text{ pages cost} \quad €4.40$$

$$1 \text{ page costs} \quad €\frac{4.40}{64}$$

$$80 \text{ pages cost} \quad €\frac{4.40}{64} \times \frac{80}{1} = €5.50$$

Therefore 80 pages cost €5.50.

Exercise 5.2

1. €80 is divided between two pupils in the ratio $7 : 3$.
   How much does each pupil get?

2. €572 is divided in the ratio $2 : 3 : 6$. Find the smallest share.

3. A prize fund is divided between A, B and C in the ratio $4 : 3 : 2$ respectively.
   If C's share is €1224, find the total fund.

4. In a school the ratio of girls to boys is $7 : 2$.
   If there are 735 girls in the school, how many boys are there?

5. An alloy consists of copper, zinc and tin in the ratio $1 : 3 : 5$.
   If there are 45 kg of tin in the alloy, find its total mass.

6. Express as a ratio in whole numbers: $\frac{1}{2} : \frac{1}{4} : \frac{1}{12}$.

7. €1575 was shared among three people in the ratio $1 : 2 : \frac{1}{2}$.
   Calculate the smallest share.

8. The perimeter of a rectangle is 200 cm.
   If length : breadth = 7 : 3, find the area of the rectangle.

9. A factory employs 360 unskilled workers, one skilled worker for every 5 unskilled workers and 1 foreman for every 12 skilled workers.
   Calculate the number of people employed in the factory.

10. Brass is made from copper and zinc in the ratio 5 : 3 by weight.
    (i) If there are 6 kg of zinc, work out the weight of copper.
    (ii) If there are 25 kg of copper, work out the weight of zinc.

11. In a school, the ratio of the number of students to the number of computers is $1 : \frac{2}{5}$.
    If there are 100 computers in the school, work out the number of students in the school.

12. Alice builds a model of a house. She uses a scale of 1 : 20.
    The height of the real house is 10 metres.
    (i) Work out the height of the model.

    The width of the model is 80 cm.
    (ii) Work out the width of the real house.

13. A map is drawn to a scale of 1 : 20 000.
    (i) Find the actual distance, in kilometres, between two points which are 15 cm apart on the map.
    (ii) Find the length on the map of a road which is 3.6 km in length.

14. The scale on a map is 1 : 25 000. The length of a wall on the map is 3.2 mm.
    Find the actual length in metres.

15. In the photograph John's height is 5 cm and his sisters's height is 4 cm.
    John's actual height is 1.5 m.
    What is his sister's actual height?

16. The number of pages in a comic book was increased from 48 to 80. If the price, which was previously €6.00, is increased in the same ratio, what should the new price be?

17. A petrol company carried out a fuel consumption test and found that the winter to summer ratio for the same car over the same test track was 3.5 : 4. The winter fuel consumption rate was 8.4 km per litre. Find the summer consumption rate.

18. In St Mark's School the ratio of pupils to teachers is 17.2 : 1.
    (i) Rewrite the ratio in the form m : n, where m and n are both whole numbers.
    (ii) What is the smallest possible number of pupils in the school?
    (iii) If the actual total of pupils and teachers is 1456, how many teachers are there?

19. The table opposite gives the relationship between some metric units and imperial units of measure.

Metric unit	Imperial unit
8 km	5 miles
30 cm	1 foot
1 kg	2.2 pounds
1 litre (ℓ)	1.75 pints
4.5 litres	1 gallon

Use the table to perform the following conversions:
  (i)   Convert 50 miles to kilometres.
  (ii) Convert 160 km to miles.
  (iii) Convert 900 cm to feet.
  (iv) Convert 12 feet to centimetres.
  (v)   Convert 40 kg to pounds.
  (vi) Convert 88 pounds to kilograms.
  (vii) Convert 40 litres to pints.
  (viii) Convert 84 pints to litres.

20. By how many metres is 15 miles greater than 23.5 km?
Use the table in question 19.

21. Tea served in a canteen is made from a mixture of two different types of tea, type A and type B. Type A costs €12.15 per kg. Type B costs €12.90 per kg.
The mixture costs €12.65 per kg.
If the mixture contains 7 kg of type A, how many kilograms of type B does it contain?

Section 5.3 Percentages

1. Revision: percentages and fractions

The word **per cent** means *per hundred* or *out of every hundred*.
The symbol **%** is used to represent *per cent*.
Thus 10% means 10 out of every hundred.

To change a percentage to a fraction, put the percentage over 100 and simplify the fraction.

Similarly, $20\% = \frac{20}{100} = \frac{1}{5}$

and $\quad 60\% = \frac{60}{100} = \frac{6}{10} = \frac{3}{5}.$

The fraction $\quad \frac{4}{5} = \frac{4}{5} \times \frac{100}{1}\%$

$\qquad\qquad = \frac{400}{5} = 80\%$

To change a fraction to a percentage, multiply it by 100 and add the % symbol.

2. Percentages and decimals

Examine the following to see the close connection between percentages and decimals:

  (i) $0.23 = \frac{23}{100} = 23\%$ (ii) $38\% = \frac{38}{100} = 0.38$ (iii) $0.04 = 4\%$

  (iv) $54\% = 0.54$ (v) $8\% = 0.08$ (vi) $3\frac{1}{2}\% = 0.035$

Rule

  (i) To change a decimal to a percentage multiply by 100 and add the % sign.
  (ii) To change a percentage to a decimal, divide by 100 and remove the % sign.

3. Finding the percentage of a quantity

To find 35% of €380, change 35% to a decimal, i.e. 0.35, and then multiply €380 by 0.35.
Thus 35% of €380 = €380 × 0.35 = €133.

Similarly, to increase 450 by 5%, we require 105% of 450.
105% of 450 = 450 × 1.05 = 472.5

Example 1

(i) 8% of a sum of money is €24.40. Find the sum of money.
(ii) A bill for €57.60 includes VAT at 20%.
    Find the amount of the bill before VAT is added.

(i)   8% = €24.40

$$1\% = € \frac{24.40}{8} = €3.05$$

100% = €3.05 × 100 = €305

(ii) €57.60 represents 120% of the bill ... 20% VAT is added

120% = €57.60

$$1\% = \frac{57.60}{120} = 0.48$$

100% = 0.48 × 100 = €48

4. Percentage profit and loss

When dealing with percentage profit or loss, we base this percentage on the **cost price** unless otherwise stated.

$$\text{Percentage profit} = \frac{\text{Profit}}{\text{Cost price}} \times \frac{100}{1}; \quad \text{Percentage loss} = \frac{\text{Loss}}{\text{Cost price}} \times \frac{100}{1}$$

Example 2

By selling a car for €14 400, a dealer would lose 4% on the purchase price.
(i) What did the dealer pay for the car?
(ii) Find his percentage profit if he had sold the car for €17 250.

(i) €14 400 represents 96% of the cost price.

        96% = €14 400

         1% = €150

     100% = €15 000, i.e., the cost price = €15 000.

(ii) Profit = €17 250 − €15 000 = €2250

$$\text{Percentage profit} = \frac{2250}{15\,000} \times \frac{100}{1} = 15\%$$

Exercise 5.3

1. Express each of these as a percentage:
   (i) 0.25   (ii) 0.34   (iii) $\frac{1}{4}$ (iv) $\frac{2}{5}$ (v) $\frac{3}{20}$

2. Express each of these percentages as a decimal:
   (i) 75%   (ii) 50%   (iii) 64%   (iv) 6%   (v) $2\frac{1}{2}$%

3. Work out each of these:
   (i) 15% of 75   (ii) 80% of 70   (iii) 45% of 120
   (iv) 9% of €350   (v) 26% of €850   (vi) 29% of 600 cm

4. Find (i) $2\frac{1}{2}$% of 300   (ii) $7\frac{1}{2}$% of €380   (iii) 120% of €400

5. Write these as percentages:
   (i) 20 out of 80   (ii) 30 out of 200   (iii) $2\frac{1}{2}$ out of 10

6. (i) Express 510 marks as a percentage of 600 marks.
   (ii) Express 50 ml as a percentage of 1 litre.

7. If 35% of a number is 297.5, find the number.

8. Work out each of these:
   (i) 30% of 150   (ii) 80% of 140   (iii) 35% of 140
   (iv) 32% of 180   (v) 16% of 200 kg   (vi) 69% of €88

9. (i) Increase 12 by 50%   (ii) Increase 140 by 15%
   (iii) Decrease 75 by 20%   (iv) Decrease 250 by 3%
   (v) Increase 120 by $12\frac{1}{2}$%   (vi) Decrease 45 by 5%

10. In a sale, the price of a piece of furniture was reduced by 15%.
    If the sale price was €1360, what was the price before the sale?

11. In a sale, the marked prices are reduced by 30%.
    (i) Calculate the sale price of a jacket if the marked price is €350.
    (ii) Find the marked price of a dress if the sale price is €168.

12. The price of a television set is €780.
    If this includes VAT at 20%, find the price before VAT is added.

13. By selling a jacket for €416, a store makes a profit of 30%.
    (i) Find the cost price of the jacket.
    (ii) If the jacket is reduced by 10% in a sale, calculate the percentage profit the store now has on the cost price.

14. An estate agent charges 0.75% fees on the sale price of a house.
 (i) Find his fees if a house is sold for €450 000 and VAT @ 20% on his fees is added on.
 (ii) Find the selling price of a house if the fees are €2775 before VAT is added.

15. Over a five-year period the population of a town increased from 145 000 to 205 000. What percentage increase is this, correct to the nearest whole number?

16. When an item is sold for €176, the profit is 10% on the cost price. When the selling price is increased to €192, calculate the percentage profit on the cost price.

17. A greengrocer buys 30 boxes of strawberries at €5.25 each and sells 28 of them at a profit of 30%. If the remaining two boxes are unsaleable, find his percentage profit on the deal.

18. By selling a laptop for €1150 a store makes a profit of 25%. At what price should the laptop be sold to make a profit of 20%?

19. (i) Express $\frac{2}{3}$ of 0.96 as a percentage of 5.12.
 (ii) $2\frac{1}{2}$% of the weight of sea water is made up of salt.
   What weight of sea water would be required to yield 100 kg of salt?

20. A boat salesman receives a commission on the price at which he sells a boat. The commission is calculated at the rate of 5% of the first €10 000 of the sale price of the boat plus 3% of the remainder.
 (i) Calculate his commission on a boat which he sells for €20 000.
 (ii) Find the sale price of a boat on which he gets a commission of €740.

21. $\frac{2}{9}$ of the girls in a school are over the age of 16.
 The school has 675 pupils of whom 56% are girls.
 How many girls in the school are over 16 years?

22. The price of a games console is €484 which includes VAT at 21%.
 Store A offers a discount of $22\frac{1}{2}$% on the selling price.
 Store B says that it will not charge VAT.
 In which store is the selling price the cheaper and by how much?

23. A petrol-engined car costs €28 600 and a diesel-engined model of the same car costs €31 500.
 Information on the running costs of the two cars is given in the table below:

	Cost of fuel per litre	No. of km/litre
Petrol car	€1.45	7
Diesel car	€1.36	9

If each car depreciates by 20% in the first year, calculate the difference in running costs (including depreciation) for the first year during which both cars travelled 18 900 km.

Section 5.4 Percentage error

When a land surveyor measures the length of a large field an error of 1 m may be relatively unimportant. But if a site engineer makes an error of 1 m in the length of a foundation wall for a house it may completely ruin his work. Thus we need to consider error in relation to the true value or true measurement.

The error in relation to the true value is called the **relative error**.

The value of the 'error' is always taken as positive.

If the relative error is multiplied by 100, we get the **percentage error**.

Remember

$$\text{Relative Error} = \frac{\text{Error}}{\text{True Value}}$$

$$\text{Percentage Error} = \frac{\text{Error}}{\text{True Value}} \times \frac{100}{1}\%$$

Example 1

To calculate the value of 121 + 46 + 37 + 26, Robbie made a rough estimate of the answer by rounding each number to the nearest 10 and adding the results. Calculate his percentage error.

Rough estimate = 120 + 50 + 40 + 30 = 240
True value = 121 + 46 + 37 + 26 = 230
Error = 240 − 230 = 10

$$\text{Percentage error} = \frac{\text{Error}}{\text{True value}} \times \frac{100}{1}\%$$

$$= \frac{10}{230} \times \frac{100}{1} = 4.347\%$$

$$= 4.3\%$$

Tolerance

When you put a plug in a sink bowl you assume it will fit. Plugs have to be made accurately so that you will not be disappointed.
The plug does not have to be exactly the right size.
There is a small error that is allowed.
This is called a **tolerance**.
A plug would probably fit if it is 0.5 mm too small. But it will not fit if it is 2 cm too small.

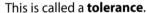

Ciara measures the width of a box to be 24 cm.
She has rounded the measurement to the nearest cm.

The measurement could be anywhere between 23.5 cm and 24.5 cm.
23.5 cm is called the **lower bound**; 24.5 cm is called the **upper bound**.

So the true length could be anywhere in the range between 0.5 cm below and 0.5 cm above the recorded value.

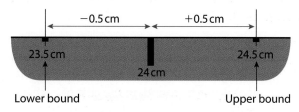

Remember

> The **lower bound** and the **upper bound** are the minimum and maximum values of a measurement or calculation.

Example 2

The length and breadth of this rectangle are measured to the nearest centimetre.

Find   (i) the maximum perimeter of the rectangle
       (ii) the minimum perimeter of the rectangle.

28 cm

16 cm

(i) To find the maximum perimeter you use the upper bounds.
     The upper bounds are 28.5 cm and 16.5 cm.
     Maximum perimeter = 2 (length + breadth)
                       = 2 (28.5 + 16.5) cm
                       = 90 cm

(ii) Minimum perimeter = 2 (27.5 + 15.5) cm
                       = 86 cm

Exercise 5.4

1. The length of a metal bar was estimated to be 50 cm.
   If the true length was 46 cm, calculate the percentage error, correct to one decimal place.

2. The estimate to repair a car was €600. If the final cost was €650, calculate the percentage error, correct to one decimal place.

3. The attendance at a football match was estimated to be 8000.
   If the true attendance was 7640, calculate the percentage error, correct to one decimal place.

4. The answer to 3.58 + 2.47 was given as 6.5.

What was the percentage error, correct to one decimal place?

5. A person used 300 as an approximation for $\dfrac{89.37 \times 3.05}{0.92}$.

Find the percentage error, correct to one decimal place.

6. Four items in a supermarket cost €3.70, €5.45, €7.40 and €12.10.
   (i) Barry estimates the total cost by ignoring the cent part in the cost of each item. Calculate the percentage error in his estimate, correct to one decimal place.
   (ii) Ann estimates the total cost by rounding the cost of each item to the nearest euro. Calculate the percentage error in her estimate, correct to one decimal place.

7. The area of a circle of diameter 14 cm is estimated to be 150 cm².

Taking $\pi = \frac{22}{7}$, find the true value of the area of the circle.

Hence find the percentage error in the estimate, correct to one decimal place.

8. A temperature can be measured as °Fahrenheit (F) or °Celsius (C).

The exact relationship between F and C is given by

$$F = \tfrac{9}{5}C + 32$$

An approximate relationship between F and C is given by the following rule:
'To find F, add 15 to C and double your answer.'

   (i) Find the value of F when C is 20 using the exact relationship formula.
   (ii) If the approximate relationship is used when C = 20, calculate the percentage error correct to one decimal place.

9. Garry measured the length of a basketball court to be 28 m and the width of the court to be 15 m, both correct to the nearest metre.
   (i) Write down the maximum length the court could be.
   (ii) Write down the minimum length the court could be.
   (iii) Calculate the maximum area the court could be.

10. Richard measured the length and breadth of his back garden, correct to the nearest metre.

He found the length was 27 metres and the breadth was 16 metres.
   (i) Find the maximum perimeter of the garden.
   (ii) Find the minimum area of the garden.

11. David picks strawberries at the rate of 2.8 kg per minute, correct to one decimal place.
   (i) Write down the maximum possible weight that David picks every minute.
   (ii) Find the minimum possible weight that David picks in one **hour**.
   (iii) One day David worked for 3 hours 15 minutes.
        Find the maximum possible weight of strawberries that David could have picked in that time.

12. The length, width and height of this box are measured to the nearest centimetre.

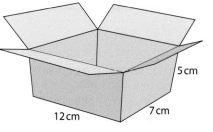

5 cm

7 cm

12 cm

   (i)   Write down the maximum length of the box.

  (ii)   Calculate the maximum volume of the box.

 (iii)   Calculate the difference between the maximum and minimum volumes of the box. Give your answer correct to the nearest cm³.

 (iv)   The correct volume of the box is 450 cm³. Find the percentage error in the volume of the box if the maximum possible volume is taken. Give your answer correct to 1 decimal place.

Section 5.5 Currency transactions

If we travel to a country not in the euro currency zone, we generally change our euro to the currency of that country.

If you see €1 = $1.35 displayed in a bank, how do you convert $100 to euro?

If we require euro in our answer, we put euro on the right-hand side of the 'equation'.

If €1 = $1.35, then

$$\$1.35 = €1 \text{ ... Reverse the order}$$

$$\$1 = €\frac{1}{1.35}$$

$$\$100 = €\frac{1}{1.35} \times \frac{100}{1} = €74.07$$

$$\therefore \ \$100 = €74.07$$

> Put the currency required on the right-hand side of the 'equation'.

Example 1

A US visitor exchanged $2000 for euro when the exchange rate was €1 = $1.36. A charge was made for this service. If the person received €1444.20, calculate the charge in euro.

We require euro in our answer, so we put euro on the right-hand side of the equation.

$$€1 = \$1.36$$

$$\Rightarrow \quad \$1.36 = €1$$

$$\$1 = €\frac{1}{1.36}$$

$$\$2000 = €\frac{1}{1.36} \times \frac{2000}{1}$$

$$\$2000 = €1470.59$$

The person received €1444.20.

$\Rightarrow$ the charge = €1470.59 − €1444.20 = €26.39

The charge is €26.39

Exercise 5.5

1. If €1 = $1.32,
    (i) what is the equivalent in euro of $1800
    (ii) what is the equivalent in dollars of €2800?

2. On a visit to Ireland a US tourist changed $3000 to euro when the rate was €1 = $1.36. How much, in euro, did she receive if the exchange bureau charged $2\frac{1}{2}$% commission?

3. If €1 = £0.85 sterling,
    (i) how many euro would you get for £1500?
    (ii) how much in sterling would you get for €2000?

4. Given that US$ = US Dollars, Y = Japanese Yen and F = Swiss Francs and €1 = US$1.4 = Y112 = F1.32.
    (i) How many US$ would you get for €1200?
    (ii) How many yen would you get for €2400?
    (iii) How many euro would you get for F4500?
    (iv) How many euro would you get for US$1350?
    (v) How many US dollars would you get for Y36 000?
    (vi) How many yen would you get for F7500?

5. A Swiss tourist paid 4600 francs to a travel agent for a holiday in Ireland.
    The cost to the travel agent of organising the holiday was €2860.
    Calculate in Swiss francs the profit made by the travel agent if €1 = 1.4 Swiss francs.

6. When the exchange rate was €1 = 9.8 South African Rand, a woman exchanged 12 000 South African Rand to euro at a bank. The bank charged a fee for this transaction. If the woman received €1166.60, find in euro the fee charged by the bank.

7. On a trip to Sweden a tourist exchanged €4500 for Swedish Krone when the exchange rate was €1 = 8.75 Krone. He spent 25 400 Krone and then on his return exchanged what he had left back into euro, when the exchange rate was now €1 = 8.60 Krone. How much did he receive in euro?

8. An Australian tourist exchanged $2500 for euro at an Irish bank.
    The bank charged a percentage commission for the transaction.
    If the exchange rate was €1 = $1.36 and the tourist received €1801.47, find the percentage commission charged by the bank.

9. A dealer bought Swiss francs when the exchange rate was €1 = 1.45 francs.
    If he received 43 400 francs, find how many euro he exchanged.
    Give your answer to the nearest euro.

    He sold the Swiss francs when the exchange rate was €1 = 1.28 francs.
    Find, correct to the nearest euro, how much the dealer lost or gained in the transaction.

Section 5.6 Income tax

Wage and salary earners pay income tax on all their incomes at one of two rates.
These rates are called the **Standard Rate** and the **Higher Rate**.
In 2011 the Standard Rate was 20% and the Higher Rate was 41%.
However these rates can change from year to year.

At the beginning of the year each employed person is given a **tax credit** and a **standard rate cut-off point**. If the standard rate cut-off point is €30 000, this means that the person pays income tax at the standard rate (say 20%) on the first €30 000 of income. Any income above €30 000 is taxed at the higher rate (say 41%). When this income tax has been calculated, it is called **gross tax**. The person's tax credit is then deducted from the gross tax to give the **tax payable**.

Tax payable

> Tax payable = Gross tax − tax credits

Example 1

A woman's income for the year is €45 000. She has a standard rate cut-off point of €28 000 and a tax credit of €4000. If the standard rate of income tax is 20% and the higher rate is 41%, how much income tax does she pay for the year?

Gross tax = 20% of €28 000 + 41% of the remainder of her salary

$\qquad$ = 20% of €28 000 + 41% of €17 000 ... Remainder = €17 000

$\qquad$ = (28 000 × 0.2) + (17 000 × 0.41)

$\qquad$ = 5600 + 6970 = €12 570

Tax payable = Gross tax − tax credit

$\qquad$ = €12 570 − €4000

∴ Tax payable = €8570

Example 2

A man pays €4500 income tax for the year and he has a tax credit of €2400. If he pays tax at the standard rate of 20% on all his income, calculate his gross income for the year.

Tax payable = Gross tax − tax credit

⇒ $\quad$ €4500 = Gross tax − €2400

⇒ Gross tax = €4500 + €2400 = €6900

Gross tax = 20% of gross income

$\Rightarrow$ 20% of gross income = €6900

$\qquad$ 1% of gross income = €$\dfrac{6900}{20}$

$\qquad$ 100% of gross income = €$\dfrac{6900}{20} \times \dfrac{100}{1}$

$\qquad\therefore$ gross income = €34 500

Example 3

A man paid €13 150 in income tax for the year.

He had a tax credit of €3500 and his standard rate cut-off point was €32 000.

The standard rate of income tax was 20% and the higher rate was 41%.

Calculate the man's gross income for the year.

Gross tax = tax payable + tax credit

$\qquad$ = €13 150 + €3500

Gross tax = €16 650

Tax payable on the first €32 000 = €32 000 × 0.2 ... 20% = 0.2

$\qquad\qquad\qquad\qquad\qquad\qquad$ = €6400

Therefore tax payable on income above €32 000 is

$\qquad$ €16 650 − €6400 = €10 250

€10 250 represents 41% of income above €32 000

$\therefore$ 41% of income above €32 000 is €10 250

$\qquad$ i.e. $\quad$ 41% = €10 250

$\qquad\qquad$ 1% = €$\dfrac{10\,250}{41}$

$\qquad\qquad$ 100% = €$\dfrac{10\,250}{41} \times \dfrac{100}{1}$ = €25 000

Therefore his income above €32 000 is €25 000.

Gross income = €32 000 + €25 000

$\qquad\qquad\quad$ = €57 000

Universal Social Charge (USC)

The Universal Social Charge (USC) came into effect on 1st January 2011. It replaced other levies which were abolished from that date.

The rates of USC per year and per week are given below:

Income thresholds		
Per year	**Rate of USC**	**Per week**
Up to €10 036	2%	Up to €193
From €10 036.01 to €16 016	4%	From €193.01 to €308
In excess of €16 016	7%	In excess of €308

Note: Disregard the 1 cent for calculation purposes.

Example 4

Conor has a weekly wage of €740.
Calculate the USC he has to pay each week.

His USC is calculated as follows:

€193 @ 2% + (€308 − €193) @ 4% + (740 − 308) @ 7%

= €193 @ 2% + €115 @ 4% + €432 @ 7%

= €38.70

He pays €38.70 in USC each week.

Exercise 5.6

1. Angela has an annual salary of €46 000.
    Her standard rate cut-off point is €28 000 and her tax credit is €3200.
    If the standard rate of income tax is 20% and the higher rate is 42%, find
    (i) the gross income tax for the year
    (ii) the amount of income tax paid for the year.

2. A printer has a weekly wage of €980.
    His standard rate cut-off point is €620 and his tax credits amount to €44. The standard rate of income tax is 20% and the higher rate is 42%.
    Find   (i) his gross tax for the week
            (ii) the amount of tax he pays each week.

3. Niamh has an annual salary of €48 000.
    She has a standard rate cut-off point of €34 000 and a tax credit of €4600.
    If the standard rate of income tax is 20% and the higher rate is 42%, find how much income tax she pays.

4. John has a weekly wage of €830 and a standard rate cut-off point of €635.
   His tax credits amount to €52 per week.
   If the standard rate of income tax is 20% and the higher rate is 42%, find how much income tax he pays each week.

5. Alan has an annual salary of €45 000.
   His tax credit is €4650 and his standard rate cut-off point is €31 000.
   If the standard rate of income tax is 20% and the higher rate is 45%, find how much income tax he pays for the year.

6. A salesperson has an annual salary of €43 000. Her tax credits amount to €3500 and she pays income tax on all her income at the standard rate of r%.
   If she pays €5960 in income tax for the year, find r.

7. A bus driver has a tax credit of €60 a week and pays income tax on all his wages at the standard rate of 20%. If he pays €140 in income tax for the week, find his gross weekly wage.

8. Linda has a gross annual salary of €48 000 and her standard rate cut-off point is €31 000. The standard rate of income tax is 20% and the higher rate is 35%.
   If she pays €7200 in income tax for the year, calculate her tax credit.

9. Helen paid €4400 in income tax for the year. Her tax credits amounted to €2600 and she paid income tax on all her salary at the standard rate of 20%.
   Find her gross salary for the year.

10. A man pays €6520 income tax for the year and he has a tax credit of €3600. He pays income tax on all his income at the standard rate of 22%.
    Calculate his gross annual salary.

11. The Universal Social Charge (USC) rates are given in the table below:

Per year	Rate of USC	Per week
Up to €10 036	2%	Up to €193
€10 036.01 to €16 016	4%	€193.01 to €308
In excess of €16 016	7%	In excess of €308

Note: Disregard the 1 cent for calculation purposes.
   (i) Aidan has an annual salary of €57 000.
       Calculate his USC for the year.
   (ii) Paula has a weekly wage of €950.
        Calculate her USC for the week.
   (iii) A salesperson has an annual salary of €63 000.
         Calculate her USC for the year.
   (iv) A plumber has a weekly wage of €1200.
        Calculate his USC for the week.

12. A woman paid €6600 in income tax for the year.
She had a tax credit of €4600 and her standard rate cut-off point was €28 000.
The standard rate of income tax was 20% and the higher rate was 40%.
  (i)   Calculate her gross tax for the year.
  (ii) How much income tax did she pay at the standard rate?
  (iii) How much income tax did she pay at the higher rate?
  (iv) How much income did she earn in excess of €28 000?
  (v)   What was the woman's gross income for the year?

13. Victor paid €7274 in income tax for the year.
He had a standard rate cut-off point of €31 000 and his tax credit was €6150.
The standard rate of income tax was 20% and the higher rate was 42%.
Calculate Victor's gross income for the year.

Section 5.7 Compound interest

If we invest €100 in a bank for one year at 5% per year (or per annum), we earn €5 interest.
We now have €105 in our account.

The €100 is called the **principal**.

5% is called the **rate** per annum.

The €105 is called the **amount** or **final amount**.

> The final amount is
> Principal + Interest

When dealing with compound interest, we work out the interest on a yearly basis and then add the interest to the principal to find the principal for the following year. The electronic calculator is particularly useful for finding the percentage of a sum of money.

If €500 is invested for one year at 4%, then the interest is 4% of €500.

The amount is 104% of €500.

104% = 1.04 and so 104% of €500 is $500 \times 1.04 = €520$.

Similarly if €600 is invested for one year at 3%, the amount is $€600 \times 1.03 = €618$.

Remember

> To find 104%, multiply by 1.04.
> To find $104\frac{1}{2}\%$, multiply by 1.045.
> To find 112%, multiply by 1.12.

If €300 is invested for 5 years at 4% per annum, the final amount (*F*) can be calculated like this:

$$300 \times \underbrace{1.04 \times 1.04 \times 1.04 \times 1.04 \times 1.04}_{} = 300\,(1.04)^5$$

For **5** years, you multiply by 1.04 **5** times, i.e., $(1.04)^5$.

The pattern shown on the previous page leads us to a formula for finding the final amount, F, when a sum of money P is invested at compound interest.

$$F = P(1 + i)^t$$

F = final amount
P = principal
i = interest expressed as a decimal
n = time in years

$1 + i$ is called the **multiplier**.

The formula given above may be stated in words as follows:

Amount after t years = original amount $\times$ (multiplier)^t

Example 1

Find the compound interest on €2800 for 3 years at 7.5% per annum.

Amount at end of year 1:   €2800 $\times$ 1.075 = €3010
Amount at end of year 2:   €3010 $\times$ 1.075 = €3235.75
Amount at end of year 3: €3235.75 $\times$ 1.075 = €3478.43

Interest = €3478.43 − €2800 = €678.43

Using the formula for the example above we get,

$F = P(1 + i)^t$

$F = €2800 \, (1.075)^3$ ... $i = 0.075$

$F = €3478.43$

Interest = €3478.43 − €2800 = €678.43 ... same answer

Finding the rate and the principal

If €300 is invested for 1 year at 6% per annum, then the interest is

€300 $\times$ 0.06 = €18

However, if we are given that €300 earns €18 in one year, how do we find the interest?
We could reason that if €300 earns €18, then €100 would earn €6, that is, a rate of 6%.

Thus the rate is $\dfrac{18}{\underset{3}{300}} \times \dfrac{\overset{1}{100}}{1} = \dfrac{18}{3} = 6\%$

$$\text{Rate} = \frac{\text{Interest}}{\text{Principal}} \times \frac{100}{1}\%$$

Example 2

If €650 amounts to €702 in one year, find the rate.

Interest = €702 − €650 = €52.

Rate = $\dfrac{\text{Interest}}{\text{Principal}} \times \dfrac{100}{1} = \dfrac{52}{650} \times \dfrac{100}{1} = 8$

∴ the rate = 8%

Example 3

A woman invested €6000 in a Building Society for two years.
The rate of interest for the first year was 3% per annum.
She did not withdraw any money at the end of the first year.
At the end of the second year her total investment was worth €6427.20.
What was the rate of interest for the second year?

Amount at the end of the first year = €6000 × 1.03

$$= €6180$$

Amount at the end of the second year = €6427.20
Therefore interest for second year = €6427.20 − €6180 = €247.20

Rate for the second year = $\dfrac{\text{Interest}}{\text{Principal}} \times \dfrac{100}{1}\%$

$$= \dfrac{247.20}{6180} = \dfrac{100}{1} = 4\%$$

The interest for the second year was 4%.

The compound interest formula can be used to find the principal, rate or time-period if sufficient information is given.

Example 4

What sum of money, invested at 4% per annum compound interest, will amount to €3149.62 after 3 years?

$F = P(1 + i)^t$

$3149.62 = P(1.04)^3$ ... here we are looking for the principal, P.

$P(1.04)^3 = 3149.62$

$P = \dfrac{3149.62}{(1.04)^3} = \dfrac{3149.62}{1.1249} = €2800$

The amount invested is €2800.

Annual equivalent rate

Some institutions, such as credit card companies, charge interest on a monthly basis. Generally these companies charge around 2% per month.

Let us see what happens if €100 is left unpaid for 12 months and **compound interest** at the rate of 2% is charged each month.
Amount at the end of 12 months is €100 $\times (1.02)^{12}$.

$$100(1.02)^{12} = 126.824$$

So at the end of the year €126.8 is owed.
This means that the interest for the year is €26.80.
Since the sum was €100, the interest charged is 26.8%.

Thus 2% compound interest per month is equivalent to an annual interest rate of 26.8%. This annual interest rate is generally called the **annual equivalent rate or AER**. It is the 'true' interest that you pay each year.

Example 5

An investment bond gives a 20% return when invested for 8 years.
Calculate the AER (annual equivalent rate) for this bond, correct to one decimal place.

If the return is 20%, this means that the amount is 1.20 times the sum invested.

$$\therefore \text{ (multiplier)}^8 = 1.2$$
$$\text{multiplier} = (1.2)^{\frac{1}{8}} \dots \text{ take the eighth root of both sides}$$
$$\text{multiplier} = 1.02305 \dots \text{ key in } 1.2 \boxed{x^y} (1 \boxed{\div} 8).$$

Therefore the rate is 2.3%.

Depreciation

If a car depreciates in value by 20% a year, then its value at the end of the first year will be 80% of its value at the beginning of the year.
To find 80% of a sum of money, multiply by 0.8 as 80% = 0.8.

· If a car cost €25 000 and depreciates in value by 15% each year, then its value
  (i) at the end of the first year = €25 000 $\times$ 0.85
  (ii) at the end of the second year = €25 000 $\times$ 0.85 $\times$ 0.85 = 25 000 $\times (0.85)^2$
  (iii) at the end of the third year = €25 000 $\times$ 0.85 $\times$ 0.85 $\times$ 0.85
$$= €25\,000 \times (0.85)^3$$

$$\dots\dots\dots\dots\dots\dots\dots\dots\dots$$

At the end of 8 years, its value is €25 000 $\times (0.85)^8$.

Example 6

A machine depreciates in value by 10% per annum.
If the machine is worth €58 320 at the end of 3 years, find its value when new.

Let P be the value of the machine when new.
Value of P at the end of 3 years $= P(0.9)^3$ ...

$$\therefore \quad P(0.9)^3 = 58\,320$$
$$P(0.729) = 58\,320$$
$$P = \frac{58\,320}{0.729} = 80\,000$$

> $100\% - 10\%$
> $= 90\% = 0.9$

The value of the machine when new is €80 000.

Exercise 5.7

1. Express each of these percentages as decimals:
   (i) 4%
   (ii) $5\frac{1}{2}\%$
   (iii) 12%
   (iv) $14\frac{1}{2}\%$
   (v) 112%

2. Write down the multiplier when you want to find these percentages of an amount:
   (i) 106%
   (ii) $105\frac{1}{2}\%$
   (iii) 110%
   (iv) 96%
   (v) $112\frac{1}{2}\%$

3. Calculate, to the nearest cent where necessary, the compound interest on
   (i) €600 for 2 years at 5%
   (ii) €1800 for 2 years at 9%
   (iii) €3500 for 3 years at $7\frac{1}{2}\%$
   (iv) €7800 for 3 years at $3\frac{1}{2}\%$.

4. €4600 was invested for 2 years at compound interest.
   If the rate for the first year was 4% and for the second year was 5%, find the total interest for the two years.

5. A company borrowed €12 000 from a bank at 11% per annum compound interest.
   The company repaid €5000 at the end of the first year.
   How much was owed to the bank at the end of the second year?

6. €2500 was invested in a building society.
   If it amounted to €2612.50 after one year, calculate the rate of interest.

7. A sum of money is invested at 7% per annum.
   If it amounts to €6848 after one year, find the sum invested.

8. €8000 is invested for 3 years at compound interest.
   The rate for the first year is 5% and for the second year is 6%.
   Find the amount of the investment at the end of two years.

   At the end of the third year, the money invested amounted to €9260.16.
   Calculate the rate of interest for the third year.

9. What sum of money invested for 3 years at 8% per annum compound interest would amount to €1007.77?

10. A person invested €10 000 in a building society.
The rate of interest for the first year was $2\frac{1}{2}$%.
At the end of the first year the person invested a further €1000.

The rate of interest for the second year was 2%.
Calculate the value of the investment at the end of the second year.

At the end of the third year the total investment amounted to €11 934.
Calculate the rate of interest for the third year.

11. What sum of money invested at 5% per annum compound interest would amount to €10 988.78 in 6 years?

12. A person borrows €15 000 for two years.
Interest for the first year is charged at 12% per annum.
The person repays €6000 at the end of the first year.
If the amount owed at the end of the second year is €12 042, find the rate of interest for the second year.

13. €5000 was invested for 3 years at compound interest.
The rate for the first year was 4%. The rate for the second year was $4\frac{1}{2}$%.
(i) Find the amount of the investment at the end of the second year.
(ii) At the beginning of the third year a further €4000 was invested.
The rate for the third year was r%.
The total investment at the end of the third year was €9811.36.
Calculate the value of r.

14. A sum of money was invested for 2 years.
The rate of interest for the first year was 4% and for the second year was 5%.
If the amount at the end of the second year was €9282, find the sum invested.

15. A sum of money invested at r% per annum compound interest amounts to €5175 after one year and to €5951.25 after two years.
Find   (i) the value of r (ii) the sum invested.

16. An investment bond gives 25% interest after 5 years.
Calculate the AER (annual equivalent rate) for this bond.
Give your answer correct to one decimal place.

17. A credit card company charges interest at a rate of 2.5% per month.
Calculate the overall percentage rate of interest for 12 months, to the nearest 0.1%.

18. Another credit card company's monthly interest rate is 1.5%.
Calculate the annual interest rate, to the nearest 0.1%.

19. Sean borrows €4000 from a bank on 1 January.

He agrees to pay back €1000 at the end of each month.

The bank charges interest at 2% per month on the outstanding amount of the loan.

(i) Continue the calculation until the loan is fully repaid. (The final repayment will be less than €1000.) When is it finally repaid?

(ii) How much is the last repayment?

Amount on 1 January		€4000
Interest, January	+	80
Repayment, 31 Jan	−	1000
Amount on 1 February		3080
Interest, February	+	61.60
Repayment, 28 Feb	−	1000
Amount on 1 March		2141.60

20. A sum of money invested at compound interest amounted to €4897.20 at the end of two years.

(i) The interest for the second year was 5%.
How much was the investment worth at the end of the first year?

(ii) The original sum invested was €4400.
What was the rate of interest for the first year?

21. A person invested €B in a building society at 4% per annum.

At the end of the first year the person invested a further €B, and left all the money in the society for a further year at 5% per annum.

If the total investment at the end of the second year amounted to €17 136, find the value of B.

22. The Sharks Loans Company is considering different ways of charging interest.

Option A   Charge 78% per year
Option B   78% ÷ 2 = 39%, so charge 39% per six months
Option C   78% ÷ 4 = 19.5%, so charge 19.5% per three months
Option D   78% ÷ 12 = 6.5%, so charge 6.5% per month

Calculate the AER, correct to one decimal place, for each option.

23. A woman invested €8000 in a bank at 7% per annum compound interest.
She withdrew €2000 at the end of the first year.
She left the remainder in the bank for a further year at r% interest. If her investment amounted to €6920.80 at the end of the year, find the value of r.

24. A machine cost €15 000.
If it depreciated in value by 15% per annum, find its value at the end of two years.

25. Vans depreciate in value by 20% per annum.
(i) If a van is bought for €23 000, find its value at the end of three years.
(ii) If the value of a van is €11 520 after two years, find its value when new.

26. A new car was bought for €24 000. It decreased in value by 20% in the first year.
If its value at the end of the second year was €16 128, by what percentage did its value decrease during the second year?

27. The value of a second-hand car decreases by 15% every year.
What is the percentage decrease in its value over a period of 3 years?
Give your answer correct to the nearest whole number.

28. The population of newts in a pond is decreasing by 8% a year.
There are 756 newts in the pond now.
How many will be there in 6 years time?

29. A car depreciates in value each year by 20% of its value at the beginning of that year.
If the value of the car at the end of its first three years is €14 336, find the value of the
car when new.

30. A hospital physiotherapy department gives
ultraviolet treatment.
Every patient having the treatment receives
a dose of 1 minute 9 seconds on day 1.
Each day the dose is increased by a
percentage which depends on the patient's
skin type, as shown in the table opposite.
(The dose is increased until it reaches a
maximum of 46 minutes 18 seconds, when it
is kept constant from then on.)

Skin type	Percentage increase per day
1. Always burns	10%
2. Tans with care but burns easily	15%
3. Tans easily and rarely burns	20%
4. Always tans, never burns	25%

   (i) Monica has skin of type 3. Calculate her dose on day 3.
   (ii) Karl has skin type 4. On which day will his dose first go above 3 minutes?
   (iii) Rita has skin type 2. On day 14 her dose is 4 minutes 0 seconds.
       What is her dose on day 16?

Section 5.8 Speed – distance – time

James travelled by car from Dublin to Cork,
a distance of 250 km, in $2\frac{1}{2}$ hours.

His average speed for the journey can be
found using this method:

$$\text{Average speed} = \frac{\text{distance travelled}}{\text{time taken}}$$

$$= \frac{250}{2.5} = 100 \text{ km/hr}$$

> Speed $= \dfrac{\text{Distance}}{\text{Time}}$
>
> Time $= \dfrac{\text{Distance}}{\text{Speed}}$
>
> Distance $=$ Time $\times$ Speed

You can use this triangle
to help you remember
the formulae.

Cover the value you wish
to find with your thumb:
e.g. to find speed cover S.
You are left with D over T,
that is

$$\frac{\text{distance}}{\text{time}}$$

Example 1

A motorist travelled 500 kilometres in 6 hours.
Her average speed for the first two hours was 100 km/hr.
Find her average speed in kilometres per hour for the last four hours.

Distance travelled in the first 2 hours is $100 \times 2 = 200$ km.
Therefore she travelled 300 km in the last 4 hours.

$$\text{Average speed} = \frac{\text{Distance}}{\text{Time}}$$

$$= \frac{300}{4} = 75$$

$\therefore$ average speed for last 4 hours = 75 km/hour.

Distance–time graphs

The distance–time graph below shows the journey of a cyclist who set out from town A.

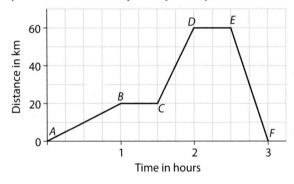

(i) From A to B he cycled a distance of 20 km in 1 hour.

(ii) At B he stopped for half an hour which is represented by $[BC]$.

(iii) At C he took a lift on a lorry and travelled to D, a distance of 40 km.
This part of the journey took half an hour.

(iv) He then rested for half an hour. This is represented by $[DE]$.

(v) He then took a train back to the town he originally left and completed the 60 km return journey in half an hour. This is represented by $[EF]$.
[In a distance–time graph the starting point and finishing point can be anywhere along the horizontal axis.]

Note **1.** In a distance–time graph, a slanted line represents a steady speed.

2. A horizontal line represents a rest period.

3. $\text{Speed} = \dfrac{\text{Distance travelled}}{\text{Time}}$

The speed from E to $F = \dfrac{60 \text{ km}}{\frac{1}{2} \text{ hour}} = \dfrac{120}{1} = 120 \text{ km/hr}$

Exercise 5.8

1. A train travels at 60 km/hr for two hours and then at 90 km/hr for one hour.
   Find its average speed over the three hours.

2. A journey takes 3 hours at an average speed of 120 km/hr.
   How long, in hours, will the journey take if the average speed is reduced to 80 km/hr?

3. Calculate the average speed, in km per hour, of a train that travels

   (i)   240 km in 2 hours
   (ii) 336 km in 3 hours
   (iii) 68 km in $\frac{1}{2}$ hour
   (iv) 392 km in $3\frac{1}{2}$ hours
   (v)   32 km in 15 minutes
   (vi) 90 km in 40 minutes.

4. The diagram shows a coach journey between Dublin and Tralee.

Dublin	190 km	Limerick	120 km	Tralee
08:30		11:00		13:15

   (i)   Calculate the average speed of the coach between Dublin and Limerick.
   (ii) Calculate the average speed between Limerick and Tralee.
   (iii) Calculate the average speed between Dublin and Tralee.
         Give your answer correct to the nearest whole number.

5. A journey of 276 km began at 1040 hrs and ended on the same day at 1430 hrs.
   Find the average speed in km/hour.

6. How far will a car travel
   (i)   in 3 hours at an average speed of 80 km/hr?
   (ii) in 4 hours at an average speed of 65 km/hr?
   (iii) in $2\frac{1}{4}$ hours at an average speed of 88 km/hr?

7. Find the time taken to travel
   (i)   210 km at an average speed of 70 km/hr
   (ii) 200 km at an average speed of 80 km/hr
   (iii) 20 km at an average speed of 60 km/hr.

8. It takes 4 hours and 20 minutes to travel a journey at an average speed of 120 km/hr.
   How many hours and minutes will it take to travel the same journey if the average
   speed is reduced to 100 km/hr?

9. A motorist travelled 320 km in five hours.
   Her average speed for the first 160 km was 80 km/hr.
   What was her average speed for the second 160 km?

10. A distance of 18 km is travelled in 25 minutes.
    Find the average speed in metres per second.

11. A train leaves Cork at 09:05 and arrives in Dublin at 12:25.
    The distance from Cork to Dublin is 250 km.
    Find the average speed of the train in km/h.

12. A hydrofoil travels a distance of 48 km at a speed of 36 km/h.
Calculate the journey time
(i) in hours, using fractions   (ii) in hours and minutes

13. A ferry travels a distance of 51.6 km at a speed of 24 km/h.
How long does the journey take, in hours and minutes?

14. A tiger runs at a speed of 50 kilometres per hour for 9 seconds.
How many metres does the tiger run?

15. Eamonn took 46 minutes to jog a distance of 6.4 km.
Calculate his average speed in km/hr, correct to 1 decimal place.

16. Anne walks a distance of 1.7 km to school from home.
She walks at an average speed of 5.1 km/hr.
What is the latest time she can leave home to be in school at 8.55 a.m.?

17. The distance–time graph given shows Emer's 3-hour journey.

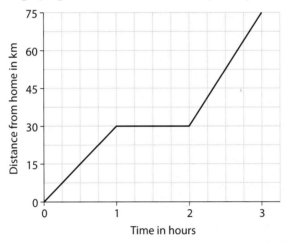

(i)   How far did she travel in the first hour?
(ii) For how long was she stopped?
(iii) How far did she travel in the third hour?
(iv) What was the total length of the journey?

18. This graph shows the journey of a tourist train running between two stations.
(i)   How far apart are the two stations?
(ii) What is the speed of the train, in km per minute, on the outward journey?
(iii) What is this speed in km per hour (km/h)?
(iv) What is the speed of the train, in km/h, on the return journey?

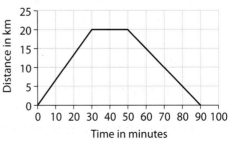

19. The graph below shows the distance travelled by a bus and also the time taken for a completed journey. The bus started the journey at 12.00 hours and finished the journey at 15.00 hours.

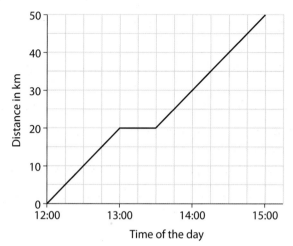

(i) How far did the bus travel in the first hour?
(ii) For how long did the bus stop?
(iii) How far did the bus travel between 13.30 and 15.00?
(iv) How much time passed when travelling from a point 10 km from the start to a point 40 km from the start?

20. The travel graph below shows Mr McLoone's journey by car from home to work.

   At *A*, he stops to buy a newspaper.
   At *B*, he stops to buy petrol.
   At *D*, he arrives at work.

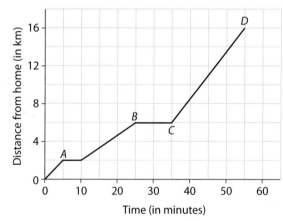

(i) How long does the journey take?
(ii) For how long does Mr McLoone stop to buy petrol?
(iii) What is the car's average speed from *C* to *D*?
(iv) Excluding the two stops, what was the car's average speed for the whole journey?

21. The solid line is the distance–time graph of a model car.

(i)   What is the speed, in metres per second, of the car during the first 2 seconds?

(ii) What happens to the speed of the car 2 seconds from the start?

(iii) What is the speed after that?

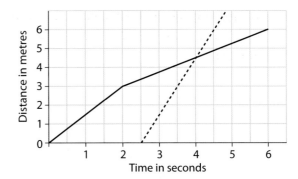

The dotted line is the distance–time graph of another model car.

(iv) What is the speed of the second car?

(v)   For how long is the second car travelling before it overtakes the first?

A third model car starts 4.5 seconds after the first and overtakes it 1.5 seconds later.

(vi) What is the speed of the third car?

Section 5.9 Working with numbers in standard form

If you use your calculator to perform the operation $60\,000 \times 4\,600\,000$, the screen will display the number 2.76×10^{11}.

This represents the number 2.76 multiplied by 10 eleven times.

The number 2.76×10^{11} is written in **scientific notation** or **standard form**.

Standard form is a convenient kind of shorthand for writing large and small numbers.

Definition

A number in the form $a \times 10^n$, where $1 \leqslant a < 10$, and n is an integer is said to be expressed in scientific notation or standard form.

Example

$$6.8 \times 10^4$$

| This part is written as a number between 1 and 10. | This part is written as a power of 10. |

Here are some numbers written in standard form:

(i) $4000 = 4 \times 1000 = 4 \times 10^3$

(ii) $64\,000 = 64 \times 1000 = 64 \times 10^3 = 6.4 \times 10^4$

(iii) $254\,000 = 2.54 \times 10^5$

Notice that if you move the decimal point

(i)   **1** place to the left, multiply by 10^1

(ii) **2** places to the left, multiply by 10^2

(iii) **3** places to the left, multiply by 10^3 …

Numbers less than 1

For a number less than 1, do the following:

(i) $0.04 = \dfrac{4}{100} = \dfrac{4}{10^2} = 4 \times 10^{-2}$

(ii) $0.007 = \dfrac{7}{1000} = \dfrac{7}{10^3} = 7 \times 10^{-3}$

(iii) $0.068 = \dfrac{6.8}{10^2} = 6.8 \times 10^{-2}$

On your calculator there is an $\boxed{\textbf{EXP}}$ or $\boxed{10^x}$ key which stands for 'exponential'.
To change the number 2.54×10^3 to decimal form, key in $2.54\,\boxed{10^x}\,3\,\boxed{=}$.
The calculator will display 2450.

Calculations in standard form

1. To add or subtract numbers expressed in standard form, convert each number to a decimal number and perform the addition or subtraction.

   Example $2.4 \times 10^2 + 1.68 \times 10^3$

   $= 2.4 \times 100 + 1.68 \times 1000$

   $= 240 + 1680 = 1920 = 1.92 \times 10^3$

2. To multiply (or divide) numbers expressed in standard form, first multiply the 'a' parts and then multiply the numbers expressed as powers of 10.
   The calculator is particularly useful in these operations.

   Thus $(3.8 \times 10^3)(9.4 \times 10^{-2}) = (3.8 \times 9.4) \times 10^3 \times 10^{-2}$

   $= 35.72 \times 10^1 \; ... \; 3 - 2 = 1$

   $= 3.572 \times 10^2$

Or using a calculator, key in

$$3.8\,\boxed{10^x}\,3\,\boxed{\times}\,9.4\,\boxed{10^x}\,\boxed{-2}\,\boxed{=}.$$

The result is 357.2.
$357.2 = 3.572 \times 10^2$.

Example 1

Express each of these in standard form:

(i) $2.76 \times 10^3 - 5.9 \times 10^2$

(ii) $\dfrac{(6 \times 10^3) \times (4.5 \times 10^4)}{1.2 \times 10^4}$

(i) $2.76 \times 10^3 - 5.9 \times 10^2 = 2760 - 590$

$= 2170 = 2.17 \times 10^3$

[or key in $2.76\,\boxed{10^x}\,3\,\boxed{-}\,5.9\,\boxed{10^x}\,2\,\boxed{=}$ The result is 2170]

(ii) $\dfrac{(6 \times 10^3) \times (4.5 \times 10^4)}{1.2 \times 10^4} = \dfrac{6 \times 4.5 \times 10^4 \times 10^3}{1.2 \times 10^4}$

$= \dfrac{27 \times 10^7}{1.2 \times 10^4}$

$\dfrac{27}{1.2} \times \dfrac{10^7}{10^4} = 22.5 \times 10^3$

$= 2.25 \times 10^4$

[or key in 6 $\boxed{10^x}$ 3 $\boxed{\times}$ 4.5 $\boxed{10^x}$ 4 $\boxed{\div}$ 1.2 $\boxed{10^x}$ 4 $\boxed{=}$

The result is 22 500.

This is then converted to 2.25×10^4]

Exercise 5.9

1. Write each of the following as a decimal number:
   (i) 6×10^2 (ii) 4.5×10^2 (iii) 6.8×10^3 (iv) 5.1×10^4
   (v) 6.7×10^4 (vi) 5.16×10^2 (vii) 7.05×10^3 (viii) 1.86×10^4

2. Write each of these numbers in standard form:
   (i) 400   (ii) 580   (iii) 6200   (iv) 5700
   (v) 60 000   (vi) 76 000   (vii) 92 000   (viii) 720 000

3. Change these numbers to decimal form:
   (i) 2.5×10^{-1} (ii) 6×10^{-2} (iii) 4.8×10^{-3} (iv) 9.2×10^{-4}

4. Write these numbers in standard form:
   (i) 0.04   (ii) 0.062   (iii) 0.007   (iv) 0.0065

5. Write these numbers in standard form:
   (i) 0.008   (ii) 0.0079   (iii) 0.0006   (iv) 0.00053

6. Which of these numbers are written in standard form?

A **B** **C**  **D** **E**

7. Work these out and express your answers as decimal numbers:
   (i) $3.8 \times 10^2 + 1.7 \times 10^3$ (ii) $1.76 \times 10 + 6.43 \times 10^2$
   (iii) $8.4 \times 10^3 - 1.7 \times 10^2$ (iv) $6.64 \times 10^2 - 9.4 \times 10$

8. Evaluate each of the following and give your answers in standard form:
   (i) $(3.6 \times 10^2) \times (1.5 \times 10^3)$ (ii) $(4.6 \times 10^2) \times (3.7 \times 10^{-1})$
   (iii) $(3.64 \times 10^{-2}) \times (9 \times 10^4)$ (iv) $(1.8 \times 10^{-4}) \times (8 \times 10^5)$

9. Write each of these in the form $a \times 10^n$, where $1 \leqslant a < 10$, $n \in Z$:

(i) $\dfrac{8.4 \times 10^5}{1.2 \times 10^2}$

(ii) $\dfrac{9 \times 10^4}{1.5 \times 10^2}$

(iii) $\dfrac{4.48 \times 10^3}{8 \times 10^{-1}}$

10. Write these in standard form:

(i) $\dfrac{1.4 \times 10^3 + 5.6 \times 10^2}{7 \times 10^{-1}}$

(ii) $\dfrac{(6.4 \times 10^2) + (8.2 \times 10^4)}{1.033 \times 10^2}$

11. Work out each of these without using a calculator.
Give your answer in standard form.

(i) $(5.4 \times 10^5) \times (3 \times 10^2)$

(ii) $\dfrac{4 \times 10^3}{8 \times 10^5}$

(iii) $\dfrac{4 \times 10^5}{5 \times 10^8}$

(iv) $\dfrac{1.6 \times 10^9}{8 \times 10^7}$

(v) $\dfrac{8 \times 10^4}{1.6 \times 10^5}$

(vi) $\dfrac{4.8 \times 10^{-2}}{3 \times 10^3}$

12. The Earth's diameter is 1.27×10^4 km and the diameter of Mars is 6.8×10^3 km.

(i) Which planet has the larger diameter?

(ii) What is the difference between their diameters?

(iii) What is the total if the two diameters are added?
Give your answer in standard form.

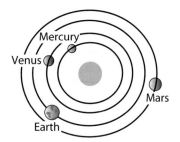

13. Express $\dfrac{1.2 \times 10^8 \times 3.6 \times 10^5}{1.8 \times 10^9}$ in standard form.

14. Calculate the value of $\dfrac{5.1 \times 10^8 + 19 \times 10^7}{1.4 \times 10^{12}}$ and write your answer as a decimal number.

15. This table shows the organised religions with most members in the year 2000.

(i) Write the number of Buddhists in decimal form.

(ii) Which religion had the most members?

(iii) Which religion had the fewest members?

(iv) The number of members of one religion is slightly more than half the number of members of another religion.
Which two religions are they?

Religion	Members
Buddhism	3.4×10^8
Christianity	1.92×10^9
Confucianism	6.37×10^6
Hinduism	7.67×10^8
Islam	1.04×10^9

16. Write each of these as decimal numbers:

(i) $\dfrac{6.8 \times 10^3 - 5.2 \times 10^2}{3.2 \times 10^2}$

(ii) $\dfrac{1.12 \times 10^{-2} \times 9.8 \times 10^5}{1.4 \times 10^2}$

Test yourself 5

1. (i)   A prize fund was divided between A, B and C in the ratio 5 : 2 : 1.
          If *B* received €520, find the total prize fund.
    (ii) During a sale all items of men's clothing are reduced by 20% of the marked price.
          (a) If the sale price of an overcoat is €336, what is the marked price?
          (b) If the store makes a profit of 5% on the cost price of the overcoat during the
              sale, what percentage profit did it make on the cost price before the sale?

    (iii) Denise has an annual salary of €47 500.
          She has a tax credit of €3600 and a standard rate cut-off point of €32 000.
          If the standard rate is 20% and the higher rate is 46%, find how much income tax
          she pays for the year.

2. (i)   Find four matching pairs.

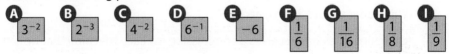

$$A \quad 3^{-2} \qquad B \quad 2^{-3} \qquad C \quad 4^{-2} \qquad D \quad 6^{-1} \qquad E \quad -6 \qquad F \quad \frac{1}{6} \qquad G \quad \frac{1}{16} \qquad H \quad \frac{1}{8} \qquad I \quad \frac{1}{9}$$

    (ii) A person invested €16 000 for two years.
          The interest for the first year was 7%.
          At the end of the second year the investment amounted to €18 061.60.
          Find the rate of interest for the second year.
    (iii) A large ball of wool is used to knit a scarf.
          The scarf is 40 stitches wide and 120 cm long.
          If the same size ball of wool is used to knit a scarf 25 stitches wide, work out the
          length of the new scarf.

3. (i)   The difference between $\frac{1}{6}$ of a number and $\frac{1}{7}$ of the number is 5.
          What is the number?
    (ii) The present reading on the electricity meter in Ann's house is 21 473 units.
          The previous reading was 20 649 units.
          (a) How many units of electricity were used since the previous reading?
          (b) What is the cost of the electricity used if each unit costs 20.5c?
          (c) A standing charge of €24.08 is added and VAT is then charged on the full
              amount. If Ann's bill is €233.53, calculate the rate at which VAT is charged.
    (iii) An Australian visitor to Ireland exchanged 2000 dollars for euro when the
          exchange rate was €1 = 1.6 Australian dollars. What was the percentage charge
          for the transaction if she received €1225?

4. (i)   The length and breadth of a rectangle are in the ratio 7 : 4.
          If the length of the rectangle is 21 cm, find its area.
    (ii) Sylvia has an annual salary of €42 800.
          Her tax credit is €3350 and her standard-rate cut off point is €31 000.
          If the standard rate of income tax is 20% and the higher rate is 42%, calculate how
          much income tax she pays for the year.

(iii) A sum of money invested at compound interest amounted to €5342.40 at the end of two years.
(a) If the interest rate for the second year was 6%, how much was the investment worth at the end of the first year?
(b) If the original sum invested was €4800, find the rate for the first year.

5. (i) A class of 36 students was asked how they travelled to school one morning. $\frac{1}{4}$ of the class travelled by bicycle, $\frac{2}{9}$ by bus, $\frac{1}{3}$ on foot, and the rest by car.
(a) What fraction of the students travelled by car?
(b) How many students travelled by bus?

(ii) Sophie is offered the following pay deals:
A: '5% increase this year, followed by a 4% increase next year'
B: '$4\frac{1}{2}$% increase this year, followed by a $4\frac{1}{2}$% increase next year'
Which offer should Sophie accept?

(iii) A machine salesman receives a commission for each machine that he sells.
The commission is calculated at the rate of 5% of the first €8000 of the sale price plus 2% commission of the remainder.
(a) Calculate his commission on a machine which he sells for €42 000.
(b) Find the sale price of a machine on which he gets a commission of €1360.

6. (i) Express $\dfrac{(7.2 \times 10^2) \times (6.2 \times 10^3)}{3.6 \times 10^4}$ as a decimal number.

(ii) (a) A sum of €6000 is invested in an eight-year government bond with an annual equivalent rate (AER) of 5%. What will be the value of the investment when it matures in eight years time?
(b) A different investment bond gives 25% interest after 8 years.
Calculate the AER for this bond.
Give your answer correct to 1 decimal place.

(iii) A plumber paid €240 income tax in a particular week.
He had a standard rate cut-off point of €600 and a tax credit of €80.
The standard rate of income tax was 20% and the higher rate was 40%.
Find (a) his gross income tax for the week
(b) the gross income tax he paid at 20%
(c) his gross wage for the week.

7. (i) A motorist travelled $\frac{2}{5}$ of his journey before stopping for petrol.
He then travelled a further 40 km before stopping again.
If he had then completed $\frac{2}{3}$ of the journey, find the total length of the journey.

(ii) A castle owner is thinking of increasing the entrance fee to his castle by 15%.
His advisors tell him that this will reduce the number of visitors by 14%.
Should he increase the fee? Explain your answer.

(iii) A sum of money was invested for two years at compound interest.
The rate for the first year was 6% and for the second year $5\frac{1}{2}$%.

If the value of the investment at the end of the two years was €6709.80, find the sum invested.

8. (i) Jean and Kevin shared €960 in the ratio 3 : 5.
Jean gave one third of her share to Michael.
Kevin gave half of his share to Michael.
What fraction of the original amount of money did Michael receive?
Give your fraction in its simplest form.

(ii) Bill buys a new lawn mower.
The value of the lawn mower depreciates by 20% each year.
(a) Bill says 'after 5 years the lawn mower will have no value'.
Bill is wrong. Explain why.

Bill wants to work out the value of the lawn mower after 2 years.
(b) By what single decimal number should Bill multiply the value of the lawn mower when new?

(iii) John has a tax credit of €3600 a year and his standard rate cut-off point is €30 000.
The standard rate of income tax is 20% and the higher rate is 35%.
If John pays €7650 income tax for the year, find
(a) the gross income tax he pays at the standard rate
(b) the gross income tax he pays at the higher rate
(c) the amount of income that he earned in excess of €30 000
(d) his gross salary for the year.

9. (i) A train left Tralee at 09.05 and arrived in Dublin at 12.50.
The distance from Tralee to Dublin is 315 km.
Find the average speed of the train for the journey.

(ii) (a) A map is drawn using a scale of 1 : 500 000. On the map, the distance between two towns is 21.7 cm.
Work out the real distance between the towns. Give your answer in kilometres.
(b) The answer to 10.25×3.84 was given as 40.
Calculate the percentage error, giving your answer correct to one decimal place.

(iii) A person invested €P in a savings bond at compound interest.
The rate for the first year was 4%.
At the end of the first year the person invested another €P in the bond.
The interest rate for the second year was $3\frac{1}{2}$% and for the third year was 3%.
If the total investment at the end of the third year amounted to €17 397.94, calculate the value of P.

summary of key points...

1. **Ratios**

   You can use **ratios** (such as 3 : 4 or 1 : 2 : 3) to show how things are divided or shared.

   Two quantities are in **direct proportion** if their ratios stay the same as the quantities increase or decrease.

2. **Percentages**

   (i)   To increase an amount by 4% multiply by 1.04.

   (ii) To decrease an amount by 4% multiply by 0.96.

   (iii) Percentage profit (or loss) $= \dfrac{\text{profit (or loss)}}{\text{original amount}} \times 100\%$

   (iv) Relative error $= \dfrac{\text{error}}{\text{true value}}$ Percentage error $= \dfrac{\text{error}}{\text{true value}} \times \dfrac{100}{1}\%$

   (v)   To calculate **compound interest**, find the multiplier.

   Amount after n years $=$ original amount $\times$ (multiplier)^n.

3. **Income tax**

   Tax payable $=$ Gross tax $-$ tax credits

   If the **standard rate cut-off point** is €30 000, this means that the person pays income tax at the **standard rate** on the first €30 000 of income.

4. **Currency transactions**

   When changing from one currency to another, put the currency required in your answer on the right-hand side of the equation.

5. **Speed–time–distance**

   Speed $= \dfrac{\text{Distance}}{\text{Time}}$;   Time $= \dfrac{\text{Distance}}{\text{Speed}}$;   Distance $=$ Time $\times$ Speed

6. **Numbers in standard form**

   Large and small numbers can conveniently be represented in **standard form**.

   A number is in standard form when:

   $$7.2 \times 10^6$$

   This part is written as a number between 1 and 10   This part is written as a power of 10

   To input numbers in standard form into your calculator, use the $\boxed{10^x}$ or $\boxed{\text{EXP}}$ key.

   To enter 4.5×10^7, press the keys $\boxed{4}$ $\boxed{\cdot}$ $\boxed{5}$ $\boxed{\times}$ $\boxed{10^x}$ $\boxed{7}$.

Probability

chapter 6

Key words

likelihood **impossible** **certain** **outcome** **event** **equally likely**
sample space **experiment** **relative frequency** **multiplication rule**
mutually exclusive **Venn diagrams** **Bernoulli trials** **permutation**
combination **expected value** **tree diagrams**

Section 6.1 Probability and chance

If you listen to weather forecasts you could hear expressions like these:

'There is a strong **likelihood** of rain tomorrow'.

'In the afternoon there is a **possibility** of thunder'.

'The rain will **probably** clear towards evening'.

Weather forecasts are made by studying charts and weather data to tell us how likely it is, for example, that it will rain tomorrow.

Probability uses numbers to tell us how likely something is to happen.

The **probability** or **chance** of something happening can be described by using words such as

Impossible   **Unlikely**   **Even Chance**   **Likely**   **Certain**

An event which is **certain to happen** has a **probability of 1**.

An event which **cannot happen** has a **probability of 0**.

All other probabilities will be a number greater than 0 and less than 1.

The more likely an event is to happen, the closer the probability is to 1.

The line shown below is called a **probability scale**.

There is an **even chance** that the next person you meet on the street will be a male.

It is **certain** that the sun will rise tomorrow.

It is **impossible** to get 7 when a normal dice is rolled.

Exercise 6.1

1. Describe the probability of each of the following events occurring as Impossible, Evens or Certain:
   (i) The sun will not set next week.
   (ii) The next baby born will be a boy.
   (iii) Christmas day will fall on 25th December this year.
   (iv) You draw a red card from a normal pack of cards.
   (v) A banana will grow on a pear tree.

2. There are seven labels on the probability scale below:

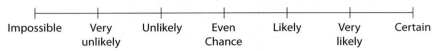

Impossible   Very unlikely   Unlikely   Even Chance   Likely   Very likely   Certain

   Which of these labels best describes the likelihood of each of these events occurring?
   (i) You will score 10 in a single throw of a normal dice.
   (ii) It will rain in Ireland sometime in the next week.
   (iii) You will win a prize in the club lottery with a single ticket.
   (iv) You will live to be 100 years old.
   (v) If I toss a coin it will show tails.
   (vi) A day of the week ending with the letter Y.
   (vii) You will draw an even number from these cards

3. David has these cards:
   He mixes the cards up
   and turns them face down.
   He turns one over. It has a 5 on it.
   He turns another card over.

   (i) Is it more likely he will get a number smaller than 5 or a number bigger than 5? Explain.
   (ii) Is it more likely that the card will show a circle rather than a triangle? Explain.

4. Make a copy of this probability scale.
   Put an arrow on the scale to show the probability of the events listed below occurring:

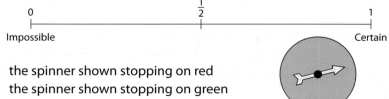

0        $\frac{1}{2}$ 1

Impossible   Certain

   (i) the spinner shown stopping on red
   (ii) the spinner shown stopping on green
   (iii) the next baby born being a girl
   (iv) a black bead being taken, without looking, from this bag
   (v) a red bead being taken, without looking, from this bag

5. Here are four spinners with different colours:

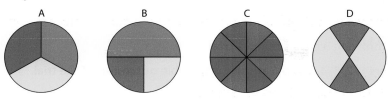

If the spinners are spun,
   (i)   Which spinner has an even chance of showing blue?
   (ii) Which spinner has an even chance of showing red?
   (iii) Which spinner has the least chance of showing yellow?
   (iv) Which spinner has one chance in three of showing yellow?
   (v)   Which spinner has one chance in four of showing red?
   (vi) Which spinner has the greatest chance of showing red?

6. Yoghurt is sold in packs of 12.
Robbie is going to take one without looking.

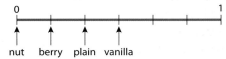

Use the probability scale to work out how many of these flavours are in a pack:
   (i)   vanilla   (ii)   plain   (iii)   nut   (iv)   berry.

7.

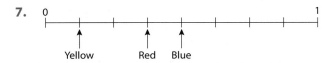

In a game Todd spins an arrow. The arrow stops on one of
sixteen equal sectors of a circle. Each sector of the circle is
coloured. The probability scale shows how likely it is for the
arrow to stop on any one colour. How many sectors are
   (i)   coloured red   (ii)   coloured blue   (iii)   coloured yellow?

8.

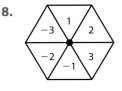

Maria uses a regular hexagon as a spinner for a game.
On a probability scale like this one below, draw an arrow to show
how likely Maria is to get these results when she spins the spinner:
   (i)   2
   (ii) a number less than zero   A hexagon is a six-sided figure.
   (iii) a number greater than 1.

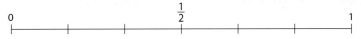

Section 6.2 Events and outcomes

Before you can start a certain game, you must throw a dice and get a six.

The act of throwing a dice is called a **trial**.

The numbers 1, 2, 3, 4, 5 and 6 are all the possible **outcomes** of the trial.

The required result is called an **event**.

If you require an even number when throwing a dice, then the **event** or **successful outcomes** are the numbers 2, 4 and 6.

> The result we want is called an **event**.

Equally likely outcomes

Two events are **equally likely** if they have the same chance of happening.

The chance of getting a red with this spinner is the same as the chance of getting a blue. Getting a red and getting a blue are **equally likely**.

The chance of getting a red with this spinner is not the same as the chance of getting a yellow. Getting a red and getting a yellow are not equally likely.

In general, if E represents an event, the probability of E occurring, denoted by $P(E)$, is given below:

$$P(E) = \frac{\text{number of successful outcomes in } E}{\text{number of possible outcomes}}$$

Note 1. The probability of any event E cannot be less than 0 or greater than 1, i.e., $0 \leqslant P(E) \leqslant 1$.

2. The probability of a certainty is 1.

3. The probability of an impossibility is 0.

For the spinner on the right,

$P(\text{green}) = \frac{1}{5}$, because 1 of the 5 sections is green

$P(\text{yellow}) = \frac{2}{5}$, because 2 of the 5 sections are yellow.

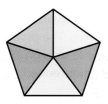

Example 1

Tickets numbered 1 to 12 are placed in a box.
If one ticket is drawn at random, find the probability of getting
  (i)   the number 4
  (ii) an even number
  (iii) a two-digit number
  (iv) a number divisible by 4

(i) There is one 4 in 12 equally likely numbers.

$\Rightarrow \quad P(4) = \frac{1}{12}$

(ii) The even numbers are 2, 4, 6, 8, 10, 12, i.e., 6 even numbers.

$\Rightarrow \quad P(\text{even number}) = \frac{6}{12} = \frac{1}{2}$

(iii) There are 3 two-digit numbers, i.e., 10, 11, 12.

$\Rightarrow \quad P(\text{two-digit number}) = \frac{3}{12} = \frac{1}{4}$

(iv) The numbers divisible by 4 are 4, 8, 12.

$\Rightarrow \quad P(\text{number divisible by 4}) = \frac{3}{12} = \frac{1}{4}$

Example 2

If a card is drawn from a pack of 52, find the probability that it is

(i) a king

(ii) a spade

(iii) a red card.

(i) There are 4 kings in the pack

$\Rightarrow \quad P(\text{king}) = \frac{4}{52} = \frac{1}{13}.$

(ii) There are 13 spades in the pack

$\Rightarrow \quad P(\text{spade}) = \frac{13}{52} = \frac{1}{4}.$

(iii) There are 26 red cards in the pack $\quad \Rightarrow \quad P(\text{red card}) = \frac{26}{52} = \frac{1}{2}.$

Example 3

A letter is selected at random from the letters of the word *COMPANION*.
Find the probability that the letter is

(i) P   (ii) N   (iii) a vowel   (iv) *M* or *N*.

(i) There is one *P* in nine letters $\Rightarrow \quad P(P) = \frac{1}{9}$

(ii) There are 2 *N*s in the word $\Rightarrow \quad P(N) = \frac{2}{9}$

(iii) There are 4 vowels in the word … [O, A, I, O] $\Rightarrow \quad P(\text{vowel}) = \frac{4}{9}$

(iv) There is one *M* and 2 *N*s in the word, i.e., 3 in total.

$\Rightarrow \quad P(M \text{ or } N) = \frac{3}{9} = \frac{1}{3}$

OO

Probability words

In many probability questions words such as **random** and **fair** are used.

These are ways of saying that all outcomes are equally likely.

If *A* is an event, it will either happen or not happen.
P(*A* happening) = 1 − P(*A* not happening)

For example:
A card is taken at **random** from a pack of cards.
This means that each card has an equal chance of being taken.
A **fair** dice is rolled.
This means that the outcomes 1, 2, 3, 4, 5 and 6 are equally likely.

Exercise 6.2

1. A fair dice is rolled.
   What is the probability of getting
   - (i)   a 5
   - (ii) a 1 or a 2
   - (iii) 4 or more
   - (iv) an odd number
   - (v)   less than 3
   - (vi) a prime number?

2. The fair spinner shown is spun. Work out the probability of the arrow pointing to:
   - (i)   yellow (Y),
   - (ii) green (G),
   - (iii) red (R),
   - (iv) blue (B),
   - (v)   red or blue (R or B).

   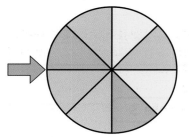

3. A letter is chosen at random from the word *GEOMETRY*.
   What is the probability that it is
   - (i)   the letter *R*
   - (ii) the letter *E*
   - (iii) a vowel?

4. What is the probability of getting a 4 on each of these spinners?
   - (i)
   - (ii)
   - (iii)

   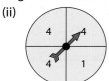
   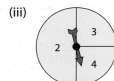

   What is the probability of getting a 2 or a 4 on spinner (iii)?

5. A card is drawn from a pack of
   52 playing cards.
   What is the probability that the
   card is
      (i) a red card
     (ii) a spade
    (iii) a king
    (iv) a red king?

   There are four suits in a pack of cards: hearts
   and diamonds which are red; clubs and
   spades which are black.
   Each suit contains 2, 3, 4, 5, 6, 7, 8, 9, 10, jack,
   queen, king and ace.
   The picture cards are jack, queen and king.

6. A bag contains 5 red beads, 4 black beads and 3 green beads.
   If a bead is drawn at random from the bag, find the probability that the bead is
      (i) red   (ii) green   (iii) red or black   (iv) not black.

7. In a casino, a pointer is spun and you win the amount shown
   in the sector where it comes to rest. Assuming that the
   pointer is equally likely to come to rest in any sector,
   what is the probability that you win
      (i) €5   (ii) no money
    (iii) some money   (iv) more than €5?

8. A letter is chosen at random from the letters of the word *DEDICATION*.
   What is the probability that the letter is
      (i) *D*   (ii) *I*   (iii) *D* or *I*   (iv) a vowel?

9. Megan has her birthday this week.
   What is the probability that her birthday falls on
      (i) Monday
     (ii) a day beginning with *T*
    (iii) a Saturday or a Sunday?

10. A dice has its faces numbered 2, 3, 3, 3, 4, 7.
    Find the probability of rolling
       (i) a '7'   (ii) an even number.

11. The 26 letters of the alphabet are written on discs.
    The five discs with vowels are put in bag A and
    the other discs are put in bag B.
    Find the probability of selecting
       (i) an 'o' from bag A
      (ii) a 'z' from bag B
     (iii) a 'w' from bag A.

    Vowels   Consonants

12. In an examination, each candidate is awarded one of the grades *A, B, C, D, E, F.*
Grade *A* is the highest and grade *F* is the lowest. The distribution of grades obtained by
the 30 pupils in a class is shown in the table below.

Grade	A	B	C	D	E	F
Number of pupils	4	9	7	5	3	2

If a candidate is chosen at random, what is the probability that he/she obtained
  (i) Grade *A*   (ii) Grade *C* or *D*   (iii) Grade *C* or higher?

13. A box contains 12 discs: 3 red, 2 yellow, 4 green and 3 white.
  (i) Find the probability of selecting
      (a) a red disc   (b) a yellow disc
  (ii) The 3 white discs are replaced by 3 yellow discs.
      Find the probability of selecting
      (a) a red disc   (b) a yellow disc.

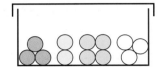

14. At the end of a Summer Camp 50 boys and girls were asked to name their favourite
game at the camp. The results are given in the table below:

	Tennis	**Basketball**	**Volleyball**
Girls	15	10	5
Boys	6	12	2

If a person was selected at random from the group of 50, find the probability that
the person
  (i) was a boy
  (ii) was a girl who named tennis as her favourite game
  (iii) named basketball as her/his favourite game.
If a girl was selected, find the probability that she had named volleyball as her favourite
game.

15. There are 6 counters in a box.
The probability of taking a green counter out of the box is $\frac{1}{2}$.
A green counter is taken out of the box and put to one side.
Gerry now takes a counter from the box at random.
What is the probability it is green?

16. This two-way table shows the numbers of males and females in a group of 50 who wear
or do not wear glasses.

	Male	**Female**	**Total**
Wearing glasses	16	18	34
Not wearing glasses	9	7	16
Total	25	25	50

Work out the probability that a person chosen at random is:

  (i) female,   (ii) not wearing glasses

 (iii) a male who wears glasses

17. This table shows the way that fifty red and blue counters are numbered either 1 or 2.
One of the counters is chosen at random.
What is the probability that the counter is:

	Red	Blue
1	12	8
2	8	22

  (i) a 1   (ii) blue   (iii) blue and a 1?

A blue counter is chosen at random.

 (iv) What is the probability that the counter is a 1?

A counter numbered 1 is chosen at random.

  (v) What is the probability that it is blue?

18. Mick put these numbered discs in a bag.

  (i) He shakes the bag and takes one disc without looking.
What is the probability of getting a 2?

 (ii) Mick wants to put more discs in the bag so that the chance of getting a 4 is twice the chance of getting a 3.
What discs should he put in the bag?

19. Mark played a card game with Paul. The cards were dealt so that both players received two cards. Mark's cards were a five and a four. Paul's first card was a six.

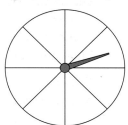

Mark   Paul

Find the probability that Paul's second card was

  (i) a five   (ii) a picture card [a King, Queen or Jack].

20. The circle on the right is divided into eight equal sectors.
Copy this diagram and in the sectors mark the letters R(red), G(green) or B(blue) so that when a spinner is spun, the probability of getting blue is $\frac{1}{4}$ and the probability of getting red will be twice the probability of getting green.

Section 6.3 Two events – Use of sample spaces

When two coins are tossed, the set of possible outcomes is

     {*HH, HT, TH, TT*}, where *H* = head and *T* = tail.

This set of possible outcomes is called a **sample space**.

By using this sample space, we can write down the probability of getting 2 heads, for example.

$P(HH) = \frac{1}{4}$

$P(\text{one head and one tail}) = \frac{2}{4} = \frac{1}{2}$

An experiment such as throwing two dice has a large number of possible outcomes, so we need to set out the sample space in an organised way, as shown in the following example.

Example 1

If two dice are thrown and the scores are added, set out a sample space giving all the possible outcomes. Find the probability that
  (i) the total is exactly 7
  (ii) the total is 4 or less
  (iii) the total is 11 or more
  (iv) the total is a multiple of 5.

The sample space is set out on the right.
There are 36 outcomes.

  (i) There are 6 totals of 7.
    $\Rightarrow$ $P(7) = \frac{6}{36} = \frac{1}{6}$

  (ii) There are 6 totals of 4 or less.
    $\Rightarrow$ $P(4 \text{ or less}) = \frac{6}{36} = \frac{1}{6}$

  (iii) There are 3 totals of 11 or more.
    $\Rightarrow$ $P(11 \text{ or more}) = \frac{3}{36} = \frac{1}{12}$

  (iv) The multiples of 5 are 5 and 10.
    There are 7 totals of 5 or 10.
    $\Rightarrow$ $P(\text{multiple of 5}) = \frac{7}{36}$

	1	2	3	4	5	6
1	2	3	4	5	6	7
2	3	4	5	6	7	8
3	4	5	6	7	8	9
4	5	6	7	8	9	10
5	6	7	8	9	10	11
6	7	8	9	10	11	12

Exercise 6.3

1. A fair coin is tossed and a fair dice is thrown.
   The table below shows all the possible outcomes.

		Dice					
		1	2	3	4	5	6
Coin	Head (*H*)	H, 1	H, 2	H, 3	H, 4	H, 5	H, 6
	Tail (*T*)	T, 1	T, 2	T, 3	T, 4	T, 5	T, 6

Write down the probability of getting each of these outcomes:
  (i) a head and a 5
  (ii) a tail and an even number
  (iii) a tail and 3 or greater
  (iv) a head and a multiple of 3.

2. Two dice are thrown and the scores obtained
are added. The resulting outcomes are
shown in the given sample space.
Find the probability that the sum of
the two numbers is

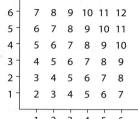

   (i) 9   (ii) 10

  (iii) 3 or less   (iv) 10 or 11.

3. Three coins are tossed, each toss resulting in a head (H) or a tail(T).
Make out a sample space for the possible results and write down the probability that
the coins show

   (i) *HHH*

  (ii) *HTH* in that order

 (iii) 2 heads and 1 tail in any order.

4. You play a game with two spinners, as shown.
They are spun at the same time and the scores are added.
Make out a sample space for the possible results and
write down the probability of getting a total of

   (i) 6   (ii) 10   (iii) an even number

Which score do you get most often?
Hence write down the probability of getting this score.

5. Of three cards, two are blue and one is red. The three cards are placed side by side,

in random order, on a table. One of these ways is   B   R   B

List all the other ways that the cards could be placed and write down the probability
that the two blue cards are next to each other.

6. The arrows on both these spinners are spun.

   (i) Make a list to show all the possible outcomes, e.g., (1, 5), (1, 6), …

  (ii) How many outcomes are there altogether?

 (iii) What is the probability that

     (a) both arrows point to an odd number

     (b) both point to an even number

     (c) the two numbers, to which the arrows are pointing, add up to 8?

7. *A*, *B* and *C* are horses equally likely to win a 3-horse race. List all the ways in which the horses can finish, assuming that all the horses finish the race and that there is no dead-heat.

   (i) What is the probability that the horses finish in the order *A*, *B* and *C*?

   (ii) What is the probability that *A* wins?

8. A blue spinner and a green spinner are spun together and the scores are multiplied.

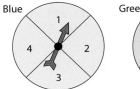 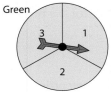

   Copy and complete the table of possible outcomes shown below.

	Blue			
Green	**1**	**2**	**3**	**4**
1				
2	2	4	6	8
3			9	

   Find the probability of getting
   (i) a score of 4   (ii) an even number   (iii) a score of 8 or more.

9. Three fair coins are tossed. Make out a sample space for all the possible outcomes.

   Now write down the probability that the outcome will be
   (i) three heads
   (iii) no heads
   (ii) two heads and one tail
   (iv) at least one head.

Section 6.4 Estimating probabilities from experiments

So far we have calculated probabilities on the basis that all outcomes are equally likely to happen. However, in real-life situations, events are not always equally likely and some other way must be found to make an estimate of the probability.

In such cases we carry out an experiment or survey to estimate the probability of an event happening.

Experiment

John suspects that a coin is biased.

In an experiment, he tosses the coin 200 times and records the number of heads after 10, 50, 100, 150 and 200 tosses.

The results are shown in the table on the right:

As the number of tosses increase, the number of heads divided by the number of tosses gets closer to 0.5, i.e., $\frac{1}{2}$.

This value is called **relative frequency** and it gives an **estimate of the probability** that the event will happen.

Number of tosses	Number of heads	Heads ÷ tosses
10	7	0.7
50	28	0.56
100	53	0.53
150	78	0.52
200	103	0.515

Thus an estimate of the probability that an event will occur by carrying out a survey or experiment is given by

$$\text{Relative frequency} = \frac{\text{Number of successful trials}}{\text{Total number of trials}}$$

In general, as the number of trials or experiments increases, the value of the relative frequency gets closer to the true or theoretical probability.

Example 1

Derek collects data on the colours of cars passing the school gate.
His results are shown in the table.

Colour	Tally	Frequency
White	卌 卌 卌 卌 IIII	24
Red	卌 卌 卌 卌 卌 卌 II	32
Black	卌 卌 IIII	14
Blue	卌 卌 卌 I	16
Green	卌 卌	10
Other	IIII	4

  (i) How many cars did Derek survey?
 (ii) What was the relative frequency of blue cars?
(iii) What was the relative frequency of red cars?
       Give your answer as a decimal.
 (iv) Write down an estimate of the probability that the next car passing the school gate will be green.
  (v) How can the estimate for the probability of green cars be made more reliable?

149

(i) The number of cars in the survey is the sum of the frequencies. This is 100 cars.

(ii) Relative frequency of blue cars $= \frac{16}{100} = \frac{4}{25}$.

(iii) Relative frequency of red cars $= \frac{32}{100} = 0.32$.

(iv) Probability of next car green $=$ relative frequency of green cars
$$= \frac{10}{100} = \frac{1}{10}$$

(v) The estimate for the probability of green cars can be made more reliable by increasing the number of cars observed. Five hundred cars would give a very accurate estimate of the true probability.

Expected frequency

A bag contains 3 red discs and 2 blue discs.

A disc is chosen at random from the bag and replaced.

The probability of getting a blue disc is $\frac{2}{5}$.

This means that, on average, you expect 2 blue discs in every 5 chosen or 20 blue discs in every 50 chosen.

To find the expected number of blue discs when you choose a disc 100 times,
(i) Work out the probability that the event happens once.
(ii) Multiply this probability by the number of times the experiment is carried out.

Thus the expected number of blue discs is
$$\frac{2}{5} \times \frac{100}{1} = 40.$$

> Expected frequency is probability $\times$ number of trials.

Example 2

The probability that a biased dice will land on each of the numbers 1 to 6 is given in the table on the right:

Number	1	2	3	4	5	6
Probability	0.1	0.1	0.2	a	0.2	0.3

(i) Write down the value of a.
(ii) If the dice is thrown 300 times, how many sixes would you expect?

(i) Since the dice must land on one of the numbers from 1 to 6, the sum of all the probabilities is 1.

> The sum of probabilities add up to 1.

$\therefore \qquad 0.1 + 0.1 + 0.2 + 0.2 + 0.3 + a = 1$
$\Rightarrow \qquad\qquad\qquad\qquad 0.9 + a = 1$
$\Rightarrow \qquad\qquad\qquad\qquad\qquad a = 1 - 0.9 \quad \Rightarrow \quad a = 0.1$

(ii) Expected number of sixes $=$ P(6) $\times$ number of trials
$$= 0.3 \times 300 = 90$$

Exercise 6.4

1. A fair coin is tossed 100 times.
   How many heads would you expect to get?

2. A fair six-sided dice is thrown 60 times.
   (i) How many sixes would you expect to get?
   (ii) How many twos would you expect to get?
   (iii) How many twos or sixes would you expect to get?

3. One ball is selected at random from the bag
   shown and then replaced. This procedure
   is done 400 times.
   How many times would you expect to select:
   (i) a blue ball,
   (ii) a white ball?

4. Joe thinks his coin is biased.
   He tosses it 200 times and gets 130 heads and 70 tails.
   (i) What is the experimental probability of getting a head with this coin?
   (ii) In 200 tosses, how many heads would you expect to get if the coin was fair?
   (iii) Do you think the coin is biased?
      Explain your answer.

5. A spinner, with 12 equal sectors, is spun 420 times.
   How often would you expect to spin:
   (i) an E
   (ii) an even number
   (iii) a vowel?

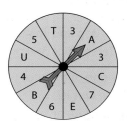

6. Helen wanted to find out if a dice was biased. She threw the dice 300 times.
   Her results are given in the table below.

Number on dice	1	2	3	4	5	6
Frequency	30	40	55	65	50	60

   (i) For this dice, calculate the experimental probability of obtaining
      (a) a 6   (b) a 2.
   (ii) For a fair dice, calculate the probability of scoring
      (a) a 6   (b) a 2.
   (iii) Do your answers suggest that the dice is fair?
      Give your reasons.

7. A spinner is labelled as shown.
   The results of the first 30 spins are given below.

   | 1 | 2 | 3 | 3 | 5 | 1 | 3 | 2 | 2 | 4 | 5 | 3 | 2 | 1 | 2 |
   | 5 | 2 | 4 | 1 | 5 | 1 | 5 | 2 | 2 | 4 | 2 | 5 | 4 | 2 | 3 |

   Construct a table showing the number of ones, twos, etc. scored.
   If the spinner was fair, how many times would you expect each number to appear?
   Do you think this spinner is fair? Give a reason for your answer.

8. Gemma keeps a record of her chess games with Helen.
   Out of the first 10 games, Gemma wins 6.
   Out of the first 30 games, Gemma wins 21.
   Based on these results, estimate the probability that Gemma will win her next game of chess with Helen.

9. This spinner is biased.
   The probability that the spinner will land on each of
   the numbers 1 to 4 is given in the table below.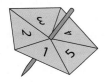

Number	1	2	3	4	5
Probability	0.35	0.1	0.25	0.15	

   The spinner is spun once.
   (i) Work out the probability that the spinner will land on 5.
   (ii) Write down the number on which the spinner is most likely to land.
   (iii) If the spinner is spun 200 times, how many times would you expect it to land on 3?

10. Olivia, Ben and Joe each rolled a different dice 360 times.

Number	Olivia	Ben	Joe
1	27	58	141
2	69	62	52
3	78	63	56
4	43	57	53
5	76	56	53
6	67	64	5

    Only one of the dice was fair.
    Whose was it?
    Explain your answer.
    Whose dice is the most biased?
    Explain your answer.

11. The probability that a biased dice will land on each of the numbers 1 to 6 is given in the table below:

Number	1	2	3	4	5	6
Probability	x	0.2	0.1	0.3	0.1	0.2

    (i) Calculate the value of x.
    (ii) If the dice is thrown once, find the probability that the dice will show a number higher than 3.
    (iii) If the dice is thrown 1000 times, estimate the number of times it will show a 6.

12. A four-sided dice has faces numbered 1, 2, 3 and 4.
The 'score' is the number on which it lands. Five pupils throw the dice to see if it is biased. They each throw it a different number of times. Their results are shown in the table.

Pupil	Total number of throws	Score			
		1	2	3	4
Andy	20	7	6	3	4
Brian	50	19	16	8	7
Ciara	250	102	76	42	30
Dara	80	25	25	12	18
Emma	150	61	46	26	17

(i) Which pupil will have the most reliable set of results? Why?

(ii) Add up all the score columns and work out the relative frequency of each score. Give your answers to one decimal place.

(iii) Is the dice biased? Explain your answer.

13. A red and blue dice were each tossed 100 times.

This bar chart shows the results.
One of the dice is fair and the other unfair. Which do you think is the fair dice? Why?

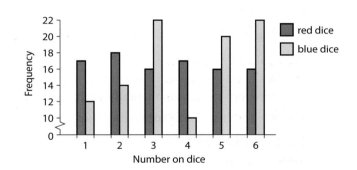

14. Four friends are using a spinner for a game and they wonder if it is perfectly fair. They each spin the spinner several times and record the results.

Name	Number of spins	Results		
		0	1	2
Alan	30	12	12	6
Keith	100	31	49	20
Bill	300	99	133	68
Ann	150	45	73	32

(i) Whose results are most likely to give the best estimate of the probability of getting each number?

(ii) Make a table by adding together all the results.
Use the table to decide whether you think the spinner is biased or unbiased.

(iii) Use the results to work out the probability of the spinner getting a '2'.

15. There are 100 sweets in a box.
Eric takes a sweet without looking.
He writes down what sort it is and then **puts it back**.
He does this 100 times. This chart shows Eric's results.

toffee	20
mint	38
jelly	14
choco	25
caramel	3

  (i) Eric thought there must be exactly 20 toffees in the box.
Explain why he is wrong.
 (ii) What is the smallest number of caramels that could be in the box?
(iii) Is it possible there is any other sort of sweet in the box? Explain.
(iv) Eric starts again and does the same thing another 100 times.
Will his chart have exactly the same numbers on it?
 (v) Eric's friend takes a sweet. What sort is he most likely to get?

Section 6.5 Mutually exclusive events – the addition rule

Seven cards with different numbers and colours are shown:

Consider these two events:

 (i) drawing a red card   (ii) drawing an even number.

These two outcomes cannot happen together as there is no red card with an even
number on it.

These outcomes are said to be **mutually exclusive**.

If the events A and B cannot happen together, then

> **P(A or B) = P(A) + P(B)**

> Outcomes are mutually exclusive if they cannot happen at the same time.

This is called the **addition law** for mutually exclusive events.

Using the cards above,

$$P(\text{red card or even number}) = P(\text{red card}) + P(\text{even number})$$
$$= \tfrac{3}{7} + \tfrac{2}{7} = \tfrac{5}{7}$$

> The addition law is sometimes called the **OR** Rule

When events are not mutually exclusive

Now consider these cards:

What is the probability of a red card or an even number?
There are 3 red cards and 3 even numbers.

The probability is not $P(\text{red card}) + P(\text{even number})$
i.e., not $\tfrac{3}{8} + \tfrac{3}{8}$ as the number 4 is counted twice.

There are only 5 red cards or even numbers.

> $\therefore$ $P(\text{red card or even number}) = \tfrac{5}{8}$

For the cards on the previous page,

P(red or even number) $= P$(red) $+ P$(even number) $- P$(red and even number)

$$= \tfrac{3}{8} + \tfrac{3}{8} - \tfrac{1}{8}$$
$$= \tfrac{6}{8} - \tfrac{1}{8} = \tfrac{5}{8}$$

In general when two events A and B can occur at the same time,

P(A or B) $= P$(A) $+ P$(B) $- P$(A and B)

Example 1

A number is to be selected at random from the integers 1 to 30 inclusive. Find the probability that the number is
 (i)   a multiple of 3
 (ii) a multiple of 5
 (iii) a multiple of 3 or a multiple of 5.

 (i)   The multiples of 3 are: 3, 6, 9, 12, 15, 18, 21, 24, 27, 30.
    $\Rightarrow$ P(multiple of 3) $= \tfrac{10}{30} = \tfrac{1}{3}$

 (ii) The multiples of 5 are: 5, 10, 15, 20, 25, 30.
    $\Rightarrow$ P(multiple of 5) $= \tfrac{6}{30} = \tfrac{1}{5}$

 (iii) The numbers 15 and 30 are each multiples of both 3 and 5.
    $\Rightarrow$ P(multiple of 3 or 5) $= P$(multiple of 3) $+ P$(multiple of 5)
                $- P$(multiple of 3 and 5)
        $= \tfrac{10}{30} + \tfrac{6}{30} - \tfrac{2}{30} = \tfrac{14}{30} = \tfrac{7}{15}$

Exercise 6.5

1. An unbiased dice is thrown.
   Find the probability that the number showing is
     (i) 3   (ii) an even number   (iii) a 3 or an even number.

2. A box contains discs numbered 1 to 16.
   If a disc is selected at random, what is the probability that it is
     (i)   an odd number   (ii) a multiple of 4
   (iii) an odd number or a multiple of 4?

3. A bag contains 4 red, 3 blue and 2 green marbles.
   If a marble is selected at random, what is the probability that it is
     (i) a red marble   (ii) a green marble   (iii) a red or a green marble?

4. A card is selected at random from a pack of 52 playing cards.
What is the probability that it is
   (i) a spade   (ii) a red picture card
(iii) a spade or a red picture card?

5. A number is selected at random from the integers 1 to 12 inclusive.
Find the probability that the number is
   (i) even   (ii) a multiple of 3   (iii) even or a multiple of 3.

6. A card is drawn at random from a pack of 52.
What is the probability that the card is
   (i) a club   (ii) a king   (iii) a club or a king
  (iv) a red card   (v) a queen   (vi) a red card or a queen?

7. A pair of dice are thrown. What is the probability of getting
   (i) a total of 12
  (ii) the same number on both dice
 (iii) a total of 12 or the same number on both dice?

8. Martin picks a card at random from this set.
Martin says

> The probability of picking a yellow card is $\frac{2}{5}$.
>
> The probability of picking a 3 is $\frac{2}{5}$.
>
> So the probability of picking a yellow card or a 3
> is $\frac{2}{5} + \frac{2}{5} = \frac{4}{5}$.

   (i) Explain why Martin is wrong.
  (ii) What is the correct probability of picking a yellow card or a 3?

9. An ordinary dice is rolled.
Explain whether or not these pairs of outcomes are mutually exclusive.
The first one is done for you.

	First outcome	Second outcome
(i)	The score is 5.	The score is 3.
	These outcomes are mutually exclusive. A dice cannot show a score of 3 and a score of 5 at the same time.	
(ii)	The score is 3.	The score is an even number.
(iii)	The score is an even number.	The score is greater than 4.
(iv)	The score is a prime number.	The score is an even number.
(v)	The score is a multiple of 5.	The score is a multiple of 3.

Section 6.6 Use of Venn diagrams

The Venn diagram on the right shows two sets, A and B, in the universal set U.

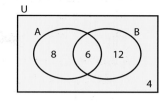

The number of elements in each region is also shown.
8 is the number of elements in A but not in B.
12 is the number of elements in B but not in A.
6 is the number of elements in both A and B.
4 is the number of elements that are in neither A nor B.

If information is presented in the form of a Venn diagram, it is easy to write down the probability of different events occurring.

In the diagram above, the total number of elements is

$$8 + 6 + 12 + 4 = 30.$$

Probability of both A and B is written is P(A and B).

From the Venn diagram, $P(\text{A and B}) = \dfrac{6}{30} = \dfrac{1}{5}$

$P(\text{B only}) = \dfrac{12}{30} = \dfrac{2}{5}$

$P(\text{neither A nor B}) = \dfrac{4}{30} = \dfrac{2}{15}$

$P(\text{A or B}) = \dfrac{8 + 6 + 12}{30} = \dfrac{26}{30} = \dfrac{13}{15}.$

In the diagram below, the sets A and B do not intersect.

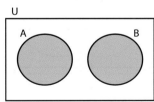

Thus A and B are **mutually exclusive** events as they cannot happen at the same time.

In this case, **P(A or B) = P(A) + P(B)**.

Example 1

The Venn diagram shows the sports played by members of a club.
How many members played
  (i)   both football and tennis
  (ii) tennis but not football
  (iii) neither of these two games
  (iv) football or tennis?
Now write down the probability of each of the above.

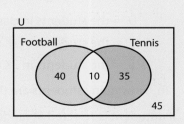

(i) Both football and tennis = 10
(ii) Tennis but not football = 35
(iii) Neither of these two games = 45
(iv) Football or tennis = 40 + 10 + 35 = 85

$$P(i) = \frac{10}{\text{total membership}} = \frac{10}{130} = \frac{1}{13}$$

$$P(ii) = \frac{35}{130} = \frac{7}{26}$$

$$P(iii) = \frac{45}{130} = \frac{9}{26}$$

$$P(iv) = \frac{85}{130} = \frac{17}{26}$$

Exercise 6.6

1. The given Venn diagram shows the numbers of students who took History and Geography in a class of 40.

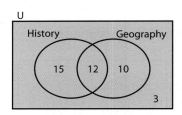

   If a student is selected at random, find the probability that the student
   (i) took Geography
   (ii) took both History and Geography
   (iii) took neither of these subjects
   (iv) took History but not Geography.

2. In the given Venn diagram,

   U = the students in class 2K

   F = the students in 2K who play football

   B = the students in 2K who play basketball.

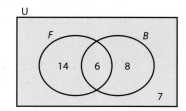

   (i) How many students are there in the class?

   If a student is selected at random, find the probability that the student
   (ii) plays football
   (iii) plays basketball but not football
   (iv) plays neither of these two games
   (v) plays both football and basketball
   (vi) plays football or basketball.

3. In the given Venn diagram,

   U represents the houses in a given street,

   C represents those which have a cat and

   D represents those which have a dog.

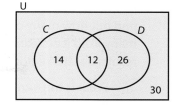

If a household is selected at random,
what is the probability that it has
   (i)   a cat
   (iii) a dog but not a cat
   (v)   neither a cat nor a dog
   (ii) a cat and a dog
   (iv) a cat or a dog

4. The given Venn diagram shows the languages taken by a group of 50 students.

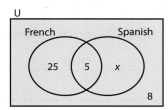

   (i)   Find the value of *x*.

   If a student is selected at random, find the probability that the student takes
   (ii)   French
   (iv)   French or Spanish
   (iii) both French and Spanish
   (v)   one of these languages only.

5. In a class of 30 students, 8 study music (M),
   14 study art (A) while 6 study both music and art.
   (i)   Represent this information on a copy of the
         given Venn diagram.

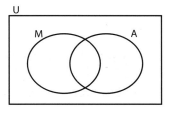

   If a student is selected at random, what is the
   probability that the student studies
   (ii)   both music and art
   (iv)   neither music nor art
   (iii) art but not music
   (v)   music or art?

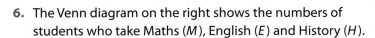

6. The Venn diagram on the right shows the numbers of
   students who take Maths (*M*), English (*E*) and History (*H*).

   If a student is selected at random, find the probability
   that the student takes
   (i)   English
   (iii) Maths or English
   (v)   all three subjects
   (ii) both Maths and History
   (iv) Maths only
   (vi) English or History.

7. In a class of 40 children, a survey was carried out to find out how many children liked chocolate and how many liked ice-cream. The Venn diagram shows the results but the region marked A is not filled in.

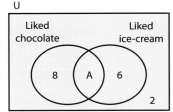

   (i)   What is the number in region A?
   (ii) What can you say about the children in region A?
   (iii) If one child is chosen at random, what is the probability that the child liked ice-cream but not chocolate?
   (iv) One of the children who liked chocolate is chosen at random. What is the probability that the child also liked ice-cream?

SECTION 6.7 The multiplication rule – Bernoulli trials

We show below the sample space for tossing a coin and throwing a dice.

		Dice				
	1	2	3	4	5	6
H	H1	H2	H3	H4	H5	H6
T	T1	T2	T3	T4	T5	T6

From the sample space, we can see that

$$P(\text{H}, 6) = \tfrac{1}{12}.$$

Whether or not the coin lands on 'head' has no effect on whether the dice shows a 6 or any other score. The two events, 'getting a head' and 'scoring a 6', are independent.

Now the probability of getting a head when tossing a coin is $\frac{1}{2}$.

The probability of getting a 2 on the dice is $\frac{1}{6}$.

If we multiply the two probabilities $\frac{1}{2}$ and $\frac{1}{6}$ we get $\frac{1}{12}$, as found above.

This illustrates the **multiplication rule** of probability which is given below.

> **Multiplication Rule:** $P(\text{A and B}) = P(\text{A}) \times P(\text{B})$

The multiplication rule is particularly useful when dealing with two or more events where each event is independent of the other. It provides an alternative approach to problems such as throwing two dice, already dealt with in Section 6.3.

> The multiplication rule is generally referred to as the **AND** rule.

Example 1

Amanda throws an ordinary dice and spins the spinner shown. Each colour is equally likely. Find the probability that she gets a red and an even number.

$P(\text{red}) = \frac{1}{3}$ $P(\text{even number}) = \frac{3}{6} = \frac{1}{2}$

$\therefore$ $P(\text{red and even number}) = \frac{1}{3} \times \frac{1}{2} = \frac{1}{6}$

Note: You can also get this result by using a sample space.

Example 2

Mary and John have their birthdays in the same week.
Find the probability that
  (i)   Mary's birthday falls on Monday
  (ii) both have their birthdays on Monday
  (iii) both have their birthdays on either Saturday or Sunday.

  (i) $P(\text{Mary's birthday on Monday}) = \frac{1}{7}$

  (ii) $P(\text{both birthdays on Monday})$ $= P(M, \text{Mon}) \times P(J, \text{Mon})$
          $= \frac{1}{7} \times \frac{1}{7} = \frac{1}{49}$

  (iii) $P(\text{both birthdays on Sat or Sun})$ $= \frac{2}{7} \times \frac{2}{7}$
          $= \frac{4}{49}$

Bernoulli trials

Consider the experiment of throwing a dice and requiring a 6 to start a game.

If a 6 is thrown it can be regarded as a 'success'. Any other number thrown is a 'failure'.

If each throw of the dice is regarded as a **trial**, then
- for each trial there are two possible outcomes, 'success' and 'failure'
- the probability of success (getting a 6) is the same for each trial
- each trial is independent of the outcomes of other trials.

When an experiment consists of repeated trials and the conditions listed above exist, such trials are known as **Bernoulli trials**, named after James Bernoulli.

James Bernoulli (1654–1705) was a Swiss mathematician who did pioneering work in probability and calculus.

In the experiment above, if a 6 is thrown for the first time on the third trial, we say that 'the first success occurs on the third trial'.

For our course, we will deal with problems that involve up to three Bernoulli trials only.

Example 3

A fair coin is tossed until a head occurs.
Find the probability that the first head occurs on the third toss.

If the first head occurs on the 3rd toss, then the first two tosses show tails, i.e., TTH

$P(H) = \frac{1}{2}$ and $P(T) = \frac{1}{2}$

$P(TTH) = \frac{1}{2} \times \frac{1}{2} \times \frac{1}{2} = \frac{1}{8}$

T = tail
H = head

$\therefore$ the probability that a head occurs on the 3rd toss is $\frac{1}{8}$.

Example 4

A fair dice is rolled repeatedly.
Find the probability that a 5 or a 6 first appears on the third throw.

Let a 5 or a 6 represent 'success' (S) and 1, 2, 3, 4 represent 'failure' (F).

$P(\text{success}) = \frac{2}{6} = \frac{1}{3}$ and $P(\text{failure}) = \frac{4}{6} = \frac{2}{3}$

If the first 'success' is on the 3rd throw, the sequence is FFS.

$P(FFS) = \frac{2}{3} \times \frac{2}{3} \times \frac{1}{3} = \frac{4}{27}$

$\therefore$ probability that 5 or 6 first appears on 3rd throw is $\frac{4}{27}$.

Example 5

A candidate takes a 3-question multiple choice test.
There are four choices in each question.
If she guesses on each question, what is the probability that
 (i) she gets all three answers correct
 (ii) she gets the first two answers wrong but the third correct?

 (i) There are 4 choices;
   so $P(\text{correct answer}) = \frac{1}{4}$ and $P(\text{wrong answer}) = \frac{3}{4}$.

   $P(\text{all three correct}) = \frac{1}{4} \times \frac{1}{4} \times \frac{1}{4} = \frac{1}{64}$

 (ii) $P(\text{first 2 wrong and 3rd correct}) = P(\text{wrong}) \times P(\text{wrong}) \times P(\text{correct})$
   $= \frac{3}{4} \times \frac{3}{4} \times \frac{1}{4} = \frac{9}{64}$

Note: If S stands for 'success' and F stands for 'failure' in Bernoulli trials, then the probability of only one 'success' in three trials is the sum of these three probabilities:

$P(FFS) + P(FSF) + P(SFF)$

Exercise 6.7

1. A coin is tossed twice. What is the probability of getting
   (i) 2 heads
   (ii) a head on the first toss and a tail on the second?

2. A coin is tossed and a dice is thrown.
   What is the probability of getting
   (i) a head and a 6
   (ii) a tail and an even number
   (iii) a head and a multiple of 3?

3. Two dice are thrown. Find the probability of getting
   (i) 2 fives
   (ii) 2 even numbers
   (iii) both dice showing a number less than 3.

4. A bag contains 5 red discs and 4 blue discs. A disc is selected
   at random and then replaced. A second disc is then selected.
   Find the probability that
   (i) both discs are red
   (ii) the first is red and the second is blue
   (iii) the first is blue and the second is red.

5. In an experiment, a card is drawn from a pack of 52 and a dice is thrown.
   Find the probability of obtaining
   (i) a diamond and a 6 on the dice
   (ii) a black card and an even number on the dice
   (iii) a heart and a multiple of 3 on the dice.

   > There are 13 diamonds,
   > 26 black cards and 13 hearts
   > in a pack of playing cards.

6. The letters of the word ALGEBRA are written on individual cards and the cards are then
   put into a box. A card is selected at random and then replaced. A second card is then
   selected.
   Find the probability of obtaining
   (i) the letter A twice
   (ii) the letters G and E in that order
   (iii) the letter R twice
   (iv) two vowels.

7. When a tennis ball is dropped into the device shown, it is equally
   likely to come out any of the holes marked A, B, C and D.
   If a tennis ball is dropped in, find the probability that it
   will come out of the hole marked
   (i) A
   (ii) A or C.
   If two other balls are dropped in one after the other, find the
   probability that
   (iii) both will come out the hole marked A
   (iv) both will come out the hole marked A or both will come out the hole marked C.

   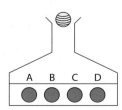

8. There are three tame mice, Sam, Pam and Ham in an enclosure.
    They can choose to eat at five containers (A, B, C, D and E).
    The choice is totally random.

    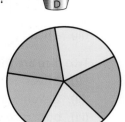

    (i)   What is the probability that Sam will eat from
          container A?
    (ii) What is the probability that Sam and Pam will both eat
          (a)   from container A   (b)   from the same container?

9. This spinner is spun twice. Each sector is equally likely.
    Find the probability that
    (i)   the first colour is yellow
    (ii) the first two colours are red and green in that order
    (iii) the first two colours are red
    (iv) the first two colours are both red or both yellow.

10. Ann and Barry celebrate their birthdays in a particular week.
    Assuming that the birthdays are equally likely to fall on any day of the week, what is the
    probability that
    (i)   Ann's birthday is on Wednesday
    (ii) both birthdays are on Monday
    (iii) both birthdays are on a day beginning with T?

11. James tosses a fair coin several times.
    Find the probability for each of these events:
    (i)   the first head occurs on the second toss
    (ii) the first head occurs on the third toss.

12. Katie throws a fair dice until she gets a 6.
    Calculate the probability that she gets
    (i)   6 on the first throw
    (ii) the first 6 on the third throw.

13. The probability of getting a head with a biased coin is $\frac{2}{3}$.
    Jack tosses the coin three times.
    (i)   Calculate the probability that he gets heads on all three throws.
    (ii) Calculate the probability that he gets the first head on
          (a)   the second throw   (b)   the third throw.

14. 25% of pupils in a school travel to school by bus.
    Three pupils in the school are selected at random.
    Find the probability that
    (i)   all three travel by bus
    (ii) the first two pupils selected do not travel by bus
    (iii) the first two pupils do not travel by bus but the third one does.

15. A bag contains 3 red beads and 2 green beads. A bead is selected
    from the bag and then replaced. This process is repeated.
    Find the probability that
    (i)   the first bead selected is green
    (ii) the first green bead selected is at the third attempt.

16. Andy plays a series of tennis matches against the same opponent.
    The probability that he wins any match is $\frac{4}{5}$.
    Calculate the probability that
    (i)   Andy has his first win in his second match
    (ii) Andy has his first win in his third match
    (iii) Andy loses all three matches.

17. The probability that it will rain on any given day in May is 0.3.
    If three days in May are selected at random, find the probability that
    (i)   the first day has no rain   (ii) the first two days will have rain
    (iii) the third day is the first day to have rain.

18. A cube has the letter 'A' on four faces and the letter 'B' on the remaining two faces.
    It is thrown three times.
    Calculate the probability of obtaining
    (i)   B on the first throw   (ii) the first B on the second throw
    (iii) the first A on the third throw.

19. Shane draws a card from a normal pack of playing cards and then replaces it.
    He does this three times.
    Calculate the probability that he selects
    (i)   a diamond on the first draw   (ii) the first diamond on the third draw
    (iii) only one diamond in the three draws.

20. A fair coin is tossed at the start of each match in a 3-match series.
    One captain tosses and the other calls 'Heads' or 'Tails'.
    Find the probability that the toss is called correctly
    (i)   three times   (ii) exactly once   (iii) exactly twice.

21. Andy is playing football and tennis.
    He has one match in each sport to play.
    The probability that he wins the football match is 0.3.
    The probability that he will draw is 0.5.

    He has a 0.6 chance of winning the tennis match, otherwise he will lose.
    Find the probability that
    (i)   Andy loses the football match
    (ii) Andy wins both matches
    (iii) Andy loses both matches
    (iv) Andy wins the football match and loses the tennis match.

22. In a board game, a counter is moved along the squares by an amount equal to the number thrown on a fair dice. If you land on a square at the bottom of a ladder you move the counter to the square at the top of that ladder.

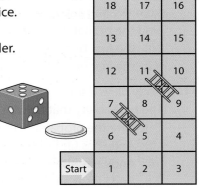

(i) What is the probability that a player reaches square 4 with one throw of the dice?

(ii) What is the probability that a player can reach square 7 with one throw of the dice?

(iii) What is the probability of taking two throws to get to square 2?

(iv) List the three possible ways to land on square 18 with exactly three throws of the dice.

(v) Calculate the probability of landing on square 18 with exactly three throws of the dice.

Section 6.8 **Tree diagrams**

The possible outcomes of two or more events can be shown in a particular type of diagram called a **tree diagram**.

In a tree diagram
  (i) write the outcomes at the end of each branch
  (ii) write the probabilities on each branch.

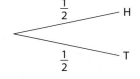

In this tree diagram representing the outcomes when a coin is tossed, there are two branches (or two outcomes).

The probability, $\frac{1}{2}$, is written on each branch.

The possible outcomes when these two spinners are spun can be shown in a tree diagram.

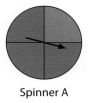

Spinner A

Spinner B

Probabilities along the branches are found by multiplying.

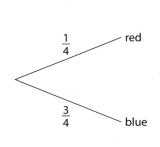

$\frac{1}{4}$ red

$\frac{3}{4}$ blue

$\frac{3}{5}$ red   probability of (A red, B red) $= \frac{1}{4} \times \frac{3}{5} = \frac{3}{20}$

$\frac{2}{5}$ blue   probability of (A red, B blue) $= \frac{1}{4} \times \frac{2}{5} = \frac{2}{20}$

$\frac{3}{5}$ red   probability of (A blue, B red) $= \frac{3}{4} \times \frac{3}{5} = \frac{9}{20}$

$\frac{2}{5}$ blue   probability of (A blue, B blue) $= \frac{3}{4} \times \frac{2}{5} = \frac{6}{20}$

The probability that both spinners give the same colour is found as follows:

probability of same colour = probability of (A red, B red) + probability of (A blue, B blue)

$$= \frac{3}{20} + \frac{6}{20} = \frac{9}{20}$$

It is better not to simplify the fractions: it makes them easier to compare and add.

Notice that the sum of the probabilities at the end of the four branches add up to 1.

Example 1

Box A contains 3 red beads and 4 blue beads
Box B contains 2 red beads and 3 blue beads
One bead is taken at random from each box.
  (i) Draw a tree diagram to show all the outcomes.
  (ii) Work out the probability that they both will have the same colour.

  (i) The tree diagram below shows all the possible outcomes.
       Taking a red bead from box A and taking a red bead from box B are
       independent events.
       So P(red, red) = P(red) × P(red)
       $$= \frac{3}{7} \times \frac{2}{5} = \frac{6}{35}$$

Box A	Box B	Outcome	Probability
	$\frac{2}{5}$ R	R R	$\frac{3}{7} \times \frac{2}{5} = \frac{6}{35}$
$\frac{3}{7}$ R			
	$\frac{3}{5}$ B	R B	$\frac{3}{7} \times \frac{3}{5} = \frac{9}{35}$
	$\frac{2}{5}$ R	B R	$\frac{4}{7} \times \frac{2}{5} = \frac{8}{35}$
$\frac{4}{7}$ B			
	$\frac{3}{5}$ B	B B	$\frac{4}{7} \times \frac{3}{5} = \frac{12}{35}$

  (ii) P(same colour) = P(both red or both blue)
        = P(R, R) + P(B, B)
        $$= \frac{6}{35} + \frac{12}{35} = \frac{18}{35}$$

Exercise 6.8

1. A coin is tossed twice.
    Copy and complete the tree diagram
    to show all the outcomes.
      (i) How many outcomes are there?
      (ii) What is the probability of two heads?

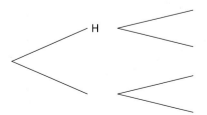

---

2. Copy and complete the tree diagram for these two spinners.

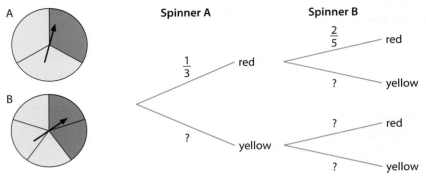

What is the probability that A and B show
  (i)   the same colour   (ii) different colours?

3. A bag contains 4 **red** beads and 3 **blue** beads.
A second bag contains 2 **red** beads and 8 **blue** beads.
Jack takes one bead at random from each bag.
  (i)   Complete the probability tree diagram.
  (ii) Find the probability that Jack takes
      (a)   2 red beads
      (b)   red and blue in that order
      (c)   red and blue in any order.

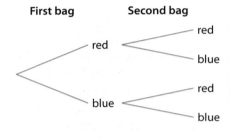

4. Paula has a dice with 5 red faces and 1 green face.
She rolls the dice twice.
  (i)   Copy and complete the tree diagram.
  (ii) Find the probability that the dice shows the same colour each time.
  (iii) Find the probability that the dice shows green and red in that order.

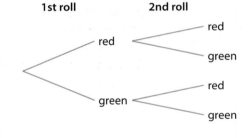

5. Fabio has a coin which is weighted so that the probability that it lands 'head' is $\frac{3}{5}$ and 'tail' is $\frac{2}{5}$.
  (i)   Copy and complete the tree diagram for two throws of the weighted coin.
  (ii) What is the probability of two heads?
  (iii) Find the probability of getting one 'head' and one 'tail' (in either order).

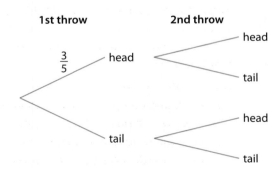

6. Bag A contains 2 blue counters and 3 white counters.
Bag B contains 3 blue counters and 4 white counters.
A counter is taken at random from each bag.

Copy and complete the tree diagram to show all the possible outcomes.
Work out the probability that the counters will both be:
  (i) white
  (ii) blue
  (iii) the same colour.

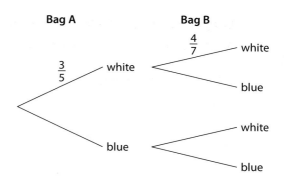

7. A bag contains 3 green and 4 white marbles. A marble is chosen at random from the bag, its colour noted and then it is replaced in the bag. The bag is shaken and a second marble is chosen at random. The tree diagram shows all the possible outcomes.

Use the tree diagram to find the probability of choosing
  (i) two green marbles
  (ii) two white marbles
  (iii) a white marble and then a green marble in that order.

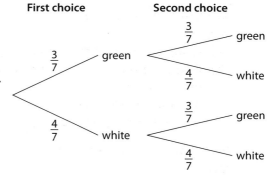

8. Bag A contains 5 red counters and 7 black counters.
Bag B contains 2 yellow counters and 8 red counters.

A counter is chosen from each bag.
  (i) Copy and complete the tree diagram to show the possible outcomes.
  (ii) Find the probability of choosing
       (a) a black and a yellow counter
       (b) two red counters.

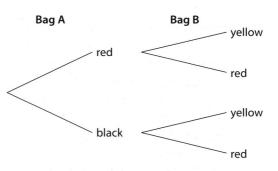

9. On his way to work, Nick goes through a set of traffic lights and then passes over a level crossing.

   Over a period of time, Nick has estimated the probability of stopping at each of these.

   The probability that he has to stop at the traffic lights is $\frac{2}{3}$.

   The probability that he has to stop at the level crossing is $\frac{1}{5}$.

   These probabilities are independent.
   - (i) Construct a tree diagram to show this information.
   - (ii) Calculate the probability that Nick will not have to stop at either the lights or the level crossing on his way to work.

10. An ordinary coin is tossed three times.

    Draw a tree diagram to show all the possible outcomes.

    Work out the probability of getting
    - (i) 3 heads
    - (ii) 2 heads and a tail in any order.

11. A bag contains 20 coins.

    There are 6 gold coins and the rest are silver.

    A coin is taken at random from the bag.

    The type of coin is recorded and the coin is then returned to the bag.

    A second coin is then taken at random from the bag.

    - (i) The tree diagram shows all the ways in which two coins can be taken from the bag.
      Copy the diagram and write the probabilities on it.
    - (ii) Use your tree diagram to calculate the probability that one coin is gold and one coin is silver.

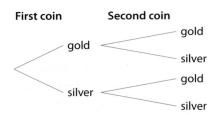

Section 6.9 Expected value

The circle shown is divided into 3 sectors.

When the spinner is spun it will land on 10, 6 or 4.

If the spinner is spun twice and we get 10 and 6, then the average of the two spins is $\frac{10 + 6}{2}$ i.e. 8.

If the spinner is spun 100 times, is there a quick way of finding the 'average' value of these spins?

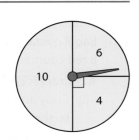

This average or **expected value** is found by multiplying each number by its probability and adding the results.

This is set out in the table below.

Outcome (x)	Probability (P)	x × P
10	$\frac{1}{2}$	5
6	$\frac{1}{4}$	$1\frac{1}{2}$
4	$\frac{1}{4}$	1

When each outcome is multiplied by the corresponding probability, we get 5, $1\frac{1}{2}$ and 1.
The sum of these results is $7\frac{1}{2}$.

The number $7\frac{1}{2}$ is the **expected value**.

If the spinner above is spun a large number of times, the mean value of the outcomes approaches the expected value $7\frac{1}{2}$. Statisticians call this fact the **law of large numbers**.

Notice that the expected value $7\frac{1}{2}$ is not one of the outcomes 4, 6 and 10.

> In general, the expected value need not be one of the given outcomes.

The expected value of the outcome of an experiment is denoted by **E(x)**.
When all the outcomes are multiplied by their corresponding probabilities and the results added, the operation can be expressed in a concise way as follows:

$$E(x) = \Sigma x.P(x), \text{ where } \Sigma \text{ represents 'the sum of'.}$$

The expected value is widely used in the insurance industry and in the operation of casino games. If you would like to know whether or not a casino game is fair, you would need to know what the payout is and the probability of getting that payout. In simple terms, you need to know the expected value of the payouts.

Let us consider this fun-park spinning-wheel on the right.
It costs €8 to spin the wheel and you win the amount to which the arrow is pointing.
Is this a "fair game?"

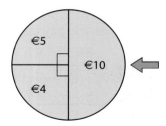

First we calculate the expected value of the payout.

Outcome (x)	Probability (P)	x × P
€10	$\frac{1}{2}$	€5
€5	$\frac{1}{4}$	€1.25
€4	$\frac{1}{4}$	€1

$\Sigma x.P(x) = €5 + €1.25 + €1 = €7.25$

The expected value of the payout is €7.25.

But it costs €8 to spin the wheel.

The expected payout now is €7.25 − €8, i.e., −€0.75

Thus if the wheel is spun a large number of times you could expect to lose €0.75 on average on each spin.

To determine whether or not a game is fair, we need to take into account

  (i) the expected value of the payout

 (ii) the cost of playing the game.

Then   (a)   if the expected payout is zero, the game is fair

           (b)   if the expected payout is greater than zero, you will win in the long-run

           (c)   if the expected payout is less than zero, you will lose in the long-run.

Example 1

This circle is divided into 6 equal sectors.

You pay €8 to spin the arrow and you win the amount in the sector in which the arrow stops.

What is the expected amount you win or lose in this game?

We find the expected value of the payout as follows:

Payout (x)	Probability (P)	Payout × Probability
0	$\frac{2}{6}$	0
6	$\frac{2}{6}$	€2
12	$\frac{1}{6}$	€2
15	$\frac{1}{6}$	€2.50

$\Sigma x.P(x) = €0 + €2 + €2 + €2.50 = €6.50$

The expected payout is €6.50.

When you pay the €8 to play, the expected payout is

    €6.50 − €8 = −€1.50

So you can expect to lose €1.50 if you play the game.

Exercise 6.9

1. The table on the right shows the outcomes and their probabilities when a fair dice is thrown.
Copy and complete the table and show that the expected value is 3.5.

Outcome (x)	Probability (P)	x × P
1	$\frac{1}{6}$	$\frac{1}{6}$
2	$\frac{1}{6}$	
3	$\frac{1}{6}$	
4	$\frac{1}{6}$	
5	$\frac{1}{6}$	$\frac{5}{6}$
6	$\frac{1}{6}$	

2. Find the expected value when this spinner is spun a large number of times.

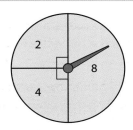

3. When this spinner is spun the amount in the sector in which the arrow stops is paid out.
What is the expected value of the payout?

4. A card is selected at random from the cards shown and then replaced. The process is repeated several times.
Find the expected value of the number selected.

5. In the given wheel, you win the amount in the sector in which the arrow stops.
It costs €10 to play the game. How much could you expect to win or lose if you play this game?
Explain why the game is not fair.

6. In a casino, it costs €6 to throw a dice.
If you roll a 3, you win €12.
If you roll an even number, you win €6.
For the remaining numbers, you don't win anything.
How much can you expect to win or lose if you play this game?

7. A card is drawn from a normal pack of cards.
    If a king is drawn you win €50.
    If a diamond is drawn you win €8.
    If a Jack is drawn you lose €5.
    If you draw any other card, you neither win nor lose.
    If it costs €10 to play this game, how much can you expect to win or lose?
    Give your answer correct to the nearest 10c.

8. A sports club sells 1000 tickets for a confined draw.
    There is one prize of €100, five prizes of €50 and ten prizes of €20.
    Find the expected value of a prize.

9. Here is the sample space when two dice are
    thrown and the scores are added.
    (i) What is the probability of getting a total
         of 9?

    In a casino, a game consists of throwing two
    dice and adding the scores.
    If you score a total of 7, you win €24.
    If you score 9, you lose €27.
    For all other scores you neither win nor lose.
    If you play this game, what do you expect to
    win or lose?
    If you pay €2 to play this game, could you say
    it was a fair game? Explain you answer.

	1	2	3	4	5	6
1	2	3	4	5	6	7
2	3	4	5	6	7	8
3	4	5	6	7	8	9
4	5	6	7	8	9	10
5	6	7	8	9	10	11
6	7	8	9	10	11	12

10. Make out a sample space for all the outcomes when three coins are tossed.
    A game consists of tossing three coins and counting the number of heads obtained.
    If you get exactly two heads you win €20.
    For any other result you lose €5.
    If you pay €2 to play this game, how much can you expect to win or lose?
    Use your answer to state whether or not the game is fair.

Section 6.10 The fundamental principle of counting ———

A make of car comes in four different models as shown below:

Standard (S)

Classic (C)

Elegant (E)

Diamond (D)

Each model comes in three different colours: silver(*s*), red(*r*), and black(*b*).
Here are the choices a customer has:

(S, s), (S, r), (S, b), (C, s), (C, r), (C, b), (E, s), (E, r), (E, b), (D, s), (D, r), (D, b).

There are 12 choices listed.
For each of the **4** models, there are **3** colours.

The number of choices is found by multiplying the number of models by the number of colours,

   i.e. $4 \times 3 = 12$.

This example illustrates the **Fundamental Principle of Counting** which is given on the right.

> If one task can be done in x ways, **and** following this, a second task can be done in y ways, then the first task followed by the second task can be done in xy ways.

Example 1

A team consists of 11 players.
In how many ways can a captain and vice-captain be chosen?

Captain	**and**	Vice-captain	
11	$\times$	10	= 110

and indicates **multiplication**

$\therefore$ there are 110 ways of selecting a captain and vice-captain.

When dealing with two or more operations, it can be convenient to use 'boxes' for the selection, as shown on the right.

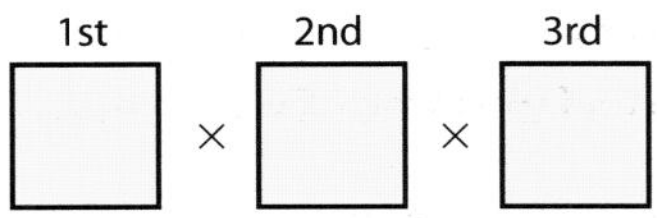

1st $\times$ 2nd $\times$ 3rd

Example 2

A code consists of a letter of the alphabet followed by two different digits from 1 to 9 inclusive. How many codes are possible?

There are 26 letters and 9 digits.
We use three 'boxes' as each code consists of 1 letter and 2 digits.

26	9	8

The first box can be filled in 26 ways......
The second box can be filled in 9 ways......   9 digits
The third box can be filled in 8 ways......   1 digit used

There are 26 letters in the alphabet.

$\therefore$ Number of Codes $= 26 \times 9 \times 8$
                              $= 1872$

Exercise 6.10

1. A dice is thrown and a coin is tossed.
   How many different outcomes are possible?
   List these outcomes.

2. A lunch menu has 3 starters and 4 main courses.
   How many different two-course meals are possible?

3. A code consists of three different digits from 1 to 9.
   How many codes are possible?

4. There are four roads from *A* to *B* and
   five roads from *B* to *C*.
   In how many different ways can
   a person travel from *A* to *C*?

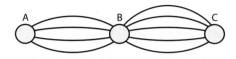

5. A pupil must choose one subject out of each of the following subject groups:
   Group A has 3 modern language subjects.
   Group B has 2 science subjects.
   Group C has 2 business subjects.
   How many different subject selections are possible?

6. A code consists of one of the letters *A, B, C, D, E* and *F* and one digit from 1 to 9.
   How many different codes are possible?

7. A coin is tossed and a digit from 0 to 9 is selected. How many different outcomes are possible?

8. A car manufacturer produces different types of cars as follows:
   - the model can be Saloon, Estate or Hatchback
   - the colours can be silver, black or red
   - the style can be Standard, Deluxe or Premium.
   How many different choices of car does a buyer have?

9. A committee consists of 10 people.
   In how many ways can a chairperson and secretary be chosen?

10. How many different 3-digit numbers can be formed from the digits 4, 5, 6, 7, 8, 9 if each digit is used once only in a number?

11. There are eight horses in a race.
    In how many ways can the first three places be filled?

Section 6.11 Arrangements (permutations)

The letters A, B and C can be arranged in a line in the following ways:

    ABC   ACB   BAC   BCA   CAB   CBA

There are six different arrangements.

Using boxes for the number of choices for each letter, we have

3	2	1

> The first box can be filled in 3 ways; the 2nd box in 2 ways; the third box in 1 way.

$3 \times 2 \times 1 = 6$, as found above.

We use the notation **3!**, pronounced '3 factorial', to represent $3 \times 2 \times 1$.

Similarly, $4! = 4 \times 3 \times 2 \times 1 = 24$

    and $5! = 5 \times 4 \times 3 \times 2 \times 1 = 120$

In general $n! = n(n-1)(n-2) \dots 3.2.1$

> The number of arrangements (or permutations) of n different objects is $n!$, where
> $$n! = n(n-1)(n-2) \dots 3.2.1.$$

Permutation is another word for an 'arrangement'.

Example 1

How many different six-digit numbers can be formed from the digits 1, 2, 3, 4, 5, 6 using all the digits in each number?

The six digits can be arranged in 6! ways.
$$6! = 6 \times 5 \times 4 \times 3 \times 2 \times 1$$
$$= 720 \text{ numbers}$$

Permutations with restrictions

The letters of the word *LEAVING* can be arranged in 7! ways.
How many of these arrangements begin with the letter *L*?

In this type of problem we use 'boxes' into which we write the number of choices.
The first box we fill is the one containing the restriction.

In this example, the first box can be filled in one way only, i.e., *L*.

    L

1	6	5	4	3	2	1

The remaining boxes can be filled in 6, 5, 4, 3, 2 and 1 ways.

Therefore the number of arrangements beginning with *L* is

    $1 \times 6 \times 5 \times 4 \times 3 \times 2 \times 1 = 720$

If there are two restrictions, fill in the boxes that relate to these restrictions first.

Example 2

The letters of the word *TUESDAY* are arranged in a line.
  (i)   How many different arrangements are possible?
  (ii) How many of these arrangements begin with *T* and end with a vowel?

  (i)   There are 7 different letters in the word *TUESDAY*.
        ∴   the number of arrangements is 7!
              7! = 7 × 6 × 5 × 4 × 3 × 2 × 1
                 = 5040

  (ii) Using 'boxes' for arrangements beginning with *T* and ending in a vowel, we have:

        T   Vowels

        | 1 | 5 | 4 | 3 | 2 | 1 | 3 |

        The first box can be filled in 1 way only, i.e., with *T*.
        The last box can be filled in 3 ways as there are 3 vowels; *U*, *E*, *A*.
        There are 5 letters remaining; so the remaining boxes can be filled in 5, 4, 3, 2, 1 ways.
        Therefore the number of arrangements is
              1 × 5 × 4 × 3 × 2 × 1 × 3
              = 360

Example 3

  (i)   In how many ways can the letters of the word *NUMBERS* be arranged?
  (ii) In how many of these arrangements are the letters *M* and *B* always together?

  (i)   There are seven letters in the word *NUMBERS*.
        Therefore the number of arrangements is 7!
              7! = 7 × 6 × 5 × 4 × 3 × 2 × 1
                 = 5040

  (ii) If *M* and *B* come together, we treat them as one unit or box.

        | | | | MB | | |

        There are now six boxes to be arranged.
        This is done in 6! ways.
        For each of these arrangements, | MB | can be arranged in 2! ways.
        ∴   the number of arrangements is 6! × 2!
              6! × 2! = 720 × 2
                      = 1440

Exercise 6.11

1. In how many ways can the letters of the word *EIGHT* be arranged if all the letters are taken each time?

2. How many different arrangements can be made using all of the letters of the word *RECANT*?
   (i) How many of these arrangements begin with *R*?
   (ii) How many of the arrangements begin with *R* and end with *T*?

3. How many different four-digit numbers can be formed using the digits 3, 4, 5, 6 if no digit can be repeated in a number?

4. How many three-digit numbers can be formed with the digits 1, 2, 3, 4, 5?
   (i) How many of these numbers begin with 5?
   (ii) How many of these numbers are greater than 400?

5. How many different arrangements can be made using all of the letters of the word *POLAND*?
   (i) How many of these arrangements begin with a vowel?
   (ii) How many of the arrangements begin with *P* and end with *D*?
   (iii) How many of the arrangements begin with *P* and end with a vowel?

6. How many arrangements of three letters can be made using the letters *A, B, C, D, E, F* if no letter can be repeated in an arrangement?

7. Six horses run in a race. Assuming that all the horses finish and that there is no dead-heat,
   (i) in how many ways can the horses finish the race?
   (ii) in how many ways can the first three places be filled?

8. How many arrangements can be made using the letters of the word *ORANGE*?
   (i) How many of these arrangements begin with *O*?
   (ii) How many of the arrangements begin with a vowel?
   (iii) How many arrangements begin with a vowel and end with a vowel?

9. In how many ways can the letters *A, B, C, D*, and *E* be arranged in a line if *D* is never first?

10. In how many different ways can the five letters of the word *ANGLE* be arranged?
    In how many of these arrangements do the two vowels come together?

    See Worked Example 3.

11. In how many ways can the letters of the word *CARPET* be arranged?
    In how many of these arrangements are the letters *P* and *T* together?

12. How many 4-digit numbers can be formed using the digits 4, 5, 6 and 7, if no digit can be repeated in a number?
   (i)   How many of these numbers are greater than 6000?
   (ii) Find the probability that a number is greater than 6000?

13. Two women, *A* and *B*, and two men, *C* and *D*, sit in a row for a photograph.
   (i)   How many different arrangements of the four people are possible?
   (ii)   Write out the four possible arrangements that have the two women in the middle.
   (iii) If an arrangement of the four people is chosen at random from all of the possible arrangements, what is the probability that the two women will be in the middle?

14. Shauna has five counters and she places them in a straight line.
   They are of five different colours: red, white, green, blue and yellow.
   (i)   How many different arrangements are possible?
   (ii)   In how many arrangements is the first counter blue?
   (iii) In how many arrangements is the first counter blue and the fifth counter green?

15. Evaluate each of the following:
   (i) 5!   (ii) 7!   (iii) $\dfrac{6!}{3!}$ (iv) $4! \times 3!$

16. (i) Is $7! = 4! \times 3!$?   (ii) Is $8! = 5! + 3!$?

17. Express 8! in the form
   (i) $p(7!)$ (ii) $q(6!)$

18. If $10! + 9! = k(9!)$, find the value of *k*.

Test yourself 6

1. The spinner has 8 equal sectors. Find the probability of
   (i) spinning a 5
   (ii) not spinning a 5
   (iii) spinning a 2
   (iv) spinning a 7
   (v) not spinning a 7.

2. Ben rolls a fair dice 300 times.
   How many times would you expect him to roll
   (i) a 6
   (ii) an even number?

3. One letter is chosen at random from the letters of the word *DEALING*.
   (i) Find the probability that the letter chosen is *G*.
   (ii) Find the probability that the letter chosen is a vowel or *G*.

4. A bag contains 6 red beads, 4 blue beads and 2 green beads. If a bead is drawn at random from the bag, what is the probability that it is
   (i) green
   (ii) blue
   (iii) green or blue
   (iv) not red?

5. There are four possible results in a fairground game. The table shows the probability of each result.
   (i) What is the probability of getting your money back?
   (ii) What is the most likely result?
   (iii) What is the probability of not winning the top prize?
   (iv) How many times would you expect to lose if you played the game 100 times?

Result	Probability
Top prize	$\frac{1}{20}$
Consolation prize	$\frac{1}{10}$
Your money back	?
Lose	$\frac{3}{5}$

6. James takes a book from a shelf at random.
   The table shows the probability of getting different types of book.

Subject	Hardback	Paperback
Fiction	0.1	0.3
Sport	0.2	0
Computers	0.1	0.15
Animals	0.05	0.1

   What is the probability that the book chosen will be
   (i) a paperback
   (ii) a book about computers?
   If there are 120 books on the shelf altogether,
   (iii) how many of them are about animals?

7. A school snack bar offers a choice of four snacks.

The four snacks are burgers, pizza, pasta and salad.

Students can choose **one** of these four snacks.

The table shows the probability that a student will choose burger or pizza or salad.

Snack	burger	pizza	pasta	salad
Probability	0.35	0.15		0.2

300 students availed of the snack bar on Tuesday.

Work out an estimate for the number of students who chose pasta.

8. Jane throws a red dice and a blue dice at the same time.

Show all the possible outcomes in a sample space.

Find the probability that Jane obtains

  (i) a total of 10

  (ii) a total of 12

  (iii) a total less than 6

  (iv) the same number on both dice.

9.  Cliona picks two cards at random from the 3, 4, 5 and 6 of hearts.

Find the probability that the sum of the numbers on the two cards is more than 9.

10. Four friends, Ava, Brian, Cloe and Dara, each write their name on a card and the four cards are placed in a hat.

Ava chooses two cards to decide who does the maths homework that night.

List all the possible combinations.

What is the probability that Cloe and Dara have to do the homework?

11. These number cards are shuffled and put into a row.

John picks one card at random and does not replace it. He then picks a second card.

  (i) If the first card was the '11', find the probability that John selects an even number with the second draw.

  (ii) If the first card was the '8', find the probability that he selects a number higher than 9 with the second draw.

12. In a small school, a class consists of children of a variety of ages as given in the table.

5-year-old girls	5-year-old boys	6-year-old girls	6-year-old boys	7-year-old girls	7-year-old boys
3	4	6	8	5	2

A pupil is selected at random.
What is the probability that the pupil is
   (i) a 6-year-old boy   (ii) a girl
   (iii) a 6 or 7-year-old child   (iv) a boy or a 6-year-old child?

13. (i) Aidan has a dice with 3 red faces, 2 blue faces and 1 green face.
         He throws the dice 300 times.
         The results are shown in the following table.

Red	Blue	Green
156	98	46

   (a) What is the relative frequency of getting a red face?
   (b) Do you think the dice is fair?
        Explain your answer.
   (ii) Emma has a dice with 4 red faces and 2 blue faces.
        She throws the dice 10 times and gets 2 reds.
        Emma says the dice is **not** fair.
        Explain why Emma could be wrong.

14. A coin is biased so that the probability of a head is $\frac{2}{3}$.
The coin is thrown three times.
Find the probability of obtaining
   (i) tails on each of the first two throws   (ii) the first head on the third throw.

15. Bag A contains 2 blue beads and 3 red beads.
Bag B contains 3 blue beads and 6 red beads.
A bead is picked at random from each bag.
Draw a tree diagram to show all the possible outcomes.
   (i)   What is the probability that both discs are blue?
   (ii) What is the probability that both discs are red?
   (iii) What is the probability that both discs are the same colour?
   (iv) What is the probability that the discs are of different colours?

16. A game consists of rolling a fair dice.
If the outcome is 1, you win €1; if the outcome is 2 you win €2; for 3, 4, 5 and 6 you win
€3, €4, €5 and €6 respectively.
It costs €4 to roll the dice once.
Find the expected amount you could win or lose if you played this game.
Do you think the game is fair? Explain your answer.

17. Here is a 4-sided spinner.

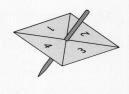

The sides of the spinner are labelled 1, 2, 3 and 4.
The spinner is biased.
The probability that the spinner will land on each of
the numbers 2 and 3 is given in the table below.

Number	1	2	3	4
Probability	x	0.3	0.2	x

The probability that the spinner will land on 1 is equal to the probability that it will
land on 4.
  (i) Work out the value of x.

Sarah is going to spin the spinner 200 times.
  (ii) Work out an estimate for the number of times it will land on 2.

18. Thirty students were asked to state the activities they
enjoyed from swimming (S), tennis (T) and hockey (H).
The numbers in each set are shown.
One student is randomly selected.
  (i) Which of these pairs of events are mutually
     exclusive?
    (a) 'selecting a student from S', 'selecting a student from H'
    (b) 'selecting a student from S', 'selecting a student from T'.

  (ii) What is the probability of selecting a student who enjoyed either hockey or tennis?

19. A dice has the numbers 1, 1, 1, 2, 2, 3 on its faces.
  (i) What is the probability of scoring 2?

The dice is thrown three times.
  (ii) What is the probability of getting a 2 on each
     of the first two throws?
  (iii) What is the probability of getting the first 2 on the third throw?

20. Adam and Mandy are playing a game in which three coins are tossed.
Adam wins if there are no heads or one head.
Mandy wins if there are either two or three heads.
Is the game fair to both players? Explain your answer.

21. How many different 3-digit numbers can be formed using the digits 1, 2, 3, 4, 5 if no
digit is repeated in the number?
  (i) How many of these numbers begin with 3?
  (ii) How many of these numbers are greater than 300

Summary of key points...

Probability scale

The **probability** of an event is expressed as a number from 0 to 1 inclusive.

- If an event is **impossible**, its probability is 0.
- If an event is **certain**, its probability is 1.

Theoretical probability

$$P(\text{event}) = \frac{\text{the number of ways the event can occur}}{\text{the total number of possible outcomes}}$$

Mutually exclusive events

If two events cannot occur at the same time, they are **mutually exclusive**.

When events A and B are mutually exclusive, **P(A or B) = P(A) + P(B)**

The probability of outcome A not happening is given by $P(\text{not A})$:

P(not A) = 1 − P(A)

Relative frequency

$$\text{Relative frequency} = \frac{\text{number of successful trials}}{\text{total number of trial}}$$

Expected frequency = probability $\times$ number of trials

Independent events – The Multiplication Rule

Two events are independent if one does not affect the outcome of the other.

If events A and B are independent, then **P(A and B) = P(A) × P(B)**

Bernoulli trials

A **Bernoulli trial** is an experiment that consists of repeated trials satisfying these conditions:

- there are two possible outcomes, 'success' and 'failure'
- the probability of success is the same for each trial
- each outcome is independent of the outcomes of other trials.

The Fundamental Principle of Counting

If one task can be done in x ways, and following this, a second task can be done in y ways, then the first task followed by the second task can be done in xy ways.

Arrangements (Permutations)

The number of arrangements of n different objects is n!, where

n! = n(n − 1)(n − 2) ... 3.2.1

7 Complex Numbers

Key words

natural numbers   integers   rational number   irrational number
terminating decimals   recurring decimals   real numbers
imaginary number   complex number   real part   imaginary part
conjugate   Argand diagram   modulus   equality   translation   rotation

Section 7.1 Number systems

In your study of maths so far you will have dealt with natural numbers, integers, fractions and decimals.

Here is a reminder of these number systems:

N = **natural numbers** = 1, 2, 3, 4, 5, ...

Z = **integers** = ... −3, −2, −1, 0, 1, 2, 3, ...

Q = **rational numbers (or fractions)** which are numbers that
can be written in the form $\frac{a}{b}$, where $a, b \in$ Z.

$\frac{1}{2}, \frac{3}{4}, -\frac{2}{3}, -\frac{5}{2}, \frac{10}{1}$ are examples of rational numbers.

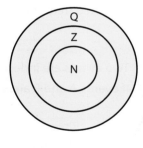

If these numbers are represented by a Venn diagram,
it can be seen that N $\subset$ Z and Z $\subset$ Q.

We have used these number systems to solve equations such as

(i)	(ii)	(iii)
$x - 5 = 3$	$x + 5 = 3$	$3x + 5 = 3$
$x - 5 + 5 = 3 + 5$	$x + 5 - 5 = 3 - 5$	$3x + 5 - 5 = 3 - 5$
$x = 8, \in$ N	$x = -2, \in$ Z	$3x = -2$
		$x = -\frac{2}{3}, \in$ Q

Now we will solve the equation,

$$x^2 = 2$$
$$x = \pm\sqrt{2}$$

Using a calculator, $\sqrt{2} = 1.4142135...$

This is a non-repeating, non-terminating (ending) decimal.

Because $\sqrt{2}$ cannot be written as a ratio (rational number), it is said to be **irrational**.

$\sqrt{2}, \sqrt{3}$ and $\sqrt{5}$ are examples of irrational numbers.

Since $\sqrt{4} = 2$ and $\sqrt{16} = 4$, it can be seen that not all square roots are irrational numbers.

One of the best known irrational numbers is $\pi = 3.141592\ldots$

It cannot be written as a fraction.

However $\frac{22}{7}$ is a close approximation to its value.

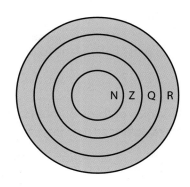

The numbers we have met so far include

  (i)   natural numbers

 (ii)   integers

(iii)   rational numbers

(iv)   irrational numbers.

All these numbers combined are called **real numbers**.

The set of real numbers is denoted by the letter R.

Example 1

Show that each of these are rational numbers:

  (i)   5.2   (ii)   0.3333…   (iii) $\sqrt{\dfrac{16}{9}}$

(i) $5.2 = 5 + \frac{2}{10} = 5 + \frac{1}{5} = 5\frac{1}{5} = \frac{26}{5}$, a rational number.

(ii)   0.3333…   Let $x = 0.3333\ldots$

$\qquad\qquad\qquad\qquad 10x = 3.3333$

$\qquad\qquad\qquad\qquad\ \ x = 0.3333$

Subtract:$\qquad\qquad 9x = 3$

$\qquad\qquad\qquad\qquad\ \ x = \frac{3}{9} = \frac{1}{3} \ldots$ a rational number

(iii) $\sqrt{\dfrac{16}{9}} = \dfrac{\sqrt{16}}{\sqrt{9}} = \dfrac{4}{3}$, a rational number

---

Note: The example above illustrates that terminating decimals and recurring decimals can be written as fractions (rational numbers). All rational numbers are also real numbers.

Exercise 7.1

1. Describe in words each of the following sets:

  (i)   natural numbers   (ii)   integers

(iii)   rational numbers   (iv)   irrational numbers.

2. Write down an example of each of the following:

  (i)   a natural number which is greater than 10

 (ii)   an integer that is not a natural number

(iii)   a positive rational number that is not an integer

(iv)   a rational number that is also an integer.

3. Say whether each of the following is true or false:
   (i) $3 \in N$ (ii) $5 \in Z$ (iii) $-4 \in N$ (iv) $\frac{2}{3} \in Q$
   (v) $-\frac{3}{4} \in Z$ (vi) $1.3 \in Q$ (vii) $2.4 \in Z$ (viii) $8 \in Q$

4. Express each of the following in the form $\frac{a}{b}$, $a, b, \in N$:
   (i) 0.7   (ii) 1.2   (iii) 2.6   (iv) 8.2   (v) 0.05

5. Which of these numbers are irrational?
   (i) $\sqrt{8}$ (ii) $\sqrt{16}$ (iii) $4\sqrt{7}$ (iv) π (v) $\sqrt{24}$

6. By simplifying first, determine whether or not each of the following is a natural number:
   (i) $\frac{16}{4}$ (ii) $\frac{18}{4}$ (iii) $\sqrt{81}$ (iv) $\sqrt{\frac{48}{3}}$ (v) $\frac{25}{10}$

7. Describe the type of number that is needed to solve each of these equations. Select from natural numbers, integers, rational numbers and irrational numbers.
   (i) $x + 4 = 9$ (ii) $3x - 2 = 7$ (iii) $4x + 14 = 2$
   (iv) $3x - 4 = 7$ (v) $3x - \sqrt{5} = 0$ (vi) $x^2 = 17$

8. Copy and complete the work on the right to express 0.4444… as a fraction.

   Let $x = 0.4444\ldots$
   $10x = 4.444\ldots$
   $x = 0.444$
   $9x = \ldots\ldots\ldots$
   $x = \ldots\ldots\ldots$

9. Change each of these recurring decimals into rational numbers:
   (i) 0.7777…   (ii) 1.7777…   (iii) 0.1555…

10. Which of these numbers are between 2 and 3?
    (i) $\sqrt{5}$ (ii) $\sqrt{7}$ (iii) $\sqrt{11}$ (iv) $\sqrt{12} - 1$ (v) $\pi - 1$

11. Write down an irrational number between
    (i) 4 and 5   (ii) 6 and 7   (iii) 0 and 1   (iv) 10 and 11

12. Which of these numbers are rational?
    (i) $3\frac{1}{2}$ (ii) $\sqrt{5}$ (iii) $(\sqrt{5})^2$ (iv) $2\sqrt{10}$ (v) $\pi + 3$

13. In each of the following, write down two integers which satisfy the given conditions:
    (i) when the integers are multiplied, the result is a natural number
    (ii) when the integers are divided, the result is a negative rational number
    (iii) the square root of the sum of the two integers is a natural number
    (iv) the square root of the difference between the integers is an irrational number.

Section 7.2 Complex numbers

$\sqrt{25} = 5$ because $5 \times 5 = 25$.

Similarly $\sqrt{36} = 6$ and $\sqrt{100} = 10$.

But what is $\sqrt{-4}$?, that is, what number multiplied by itself is -4?

The answer is not 2 or -2 since $2^2 = 4$ and $(-2)^2 = 4$.

When all real numbers, whether positive or negative, are squared, the result is always positive.

$\therefore \quad \sqrt{-4}$ is not a *real number*.

Numbers such as $\sqrt{-1}$, $\sqrt{-4}$ and $\sqrt{-25}$ are called **imaginary numbers**.

We use the symbol ***i*** to represent the imaginary number $\sqrt{-1}$.

Since $\quad i = \sqrt{-1}$,

$\qquad i^2 = -1 \ldots$ square both sides

Imaginary numbers $\qquad \boxed{i = \sqrt{-1} \ \text{and} \ i^2 = -1}$

Here are some imaginary numbers written using *i* instead of $\sqrt{-1}$.

  (i) $\quad \sqrt{-9} = \sqrt{9}. \ \sqrt{-1} = 3i$

 (ii) $\quad \sqrt{-25} = \sqrt{25}. \ \sqrt{-1} = 5i$

(iii) $\quad \sqrt{-18} = \sqrt{18}. \ \sqrt{-1} = \sqrt{9}. \ \sqrt{2}.i = 3\sqrt{2}i$

Complex numbers

A number such as $3 + 4i$ is called a **complex number**.

It consists of a **real** part and an **imaginary** part.

3 is called the **real** part

4 is called the **imaginary** part.

> A complex number is a number of the form $a + bi$, where $i = \sqrt{-1}$.

The real number 5 may be written in the form $5 + 0i$.

The real part is 5 and the imaginary part is 0.

The imaginary number $-6i$ may be written in the form $0 - 6i$.

The real part is 0 and the imaginary part is -6.

We use the capital letter **C** to represent the set of complex numbers.

The lower case letter *z* is generally used to represent a complex number, e.g.,

$\qquad z_1 = 2 + 3i \quad \text{or} \quad z_2 = -2 + 5i.$

Example 1

Find the real part and imaginary part of each of these:

(i) $2 - 5i$ (ii) $-1 + 2i$ (iii) 6 (iv) $-2i$

	Real part	Imaginary part
(i) $2 - 5i$	2	−5
(ii) $-1 + 2i$	−1	2
(iii) $6 = 6 + 0i$	6	0
(iv) $-2i = 0 - 2i$	0	−2

Exercise 7.2

1. Simplify each of the following using the i symbol:

(i) $\sqrt{-4}$ (ii) $\sqrt{-100}$ (iii) $\sqrt{-64}$ (iv) $\sqrt{-49}$ (v) $\sqrt{-1}$

2. Write down the real part and the imaginary part of each of these complex numbers:

(i) $2 + 5i$ (ii) $6 - 2i$ (iii) $-1 + 9i$ (iv) $-3 + i$ (v) $a + bi$
(vi) $\frac{1}{2} - 3i$ (vii) -4 (viii) $-3i$ (ix) i (x) $(x - 2) + 6i$

3. Write each of these in the form $a + bi$:

(i) $6 + \sqrt{-16}$ (ii) $\sqrt{-121}$ (iii) $-2 - \sqrt{-100}$ (iv) $2 + \sqrt{-8}$

Section 7.3 Adding and subtracting complex numbers

To add or subtract two complex numbers, add or subtract the real parts and the imaginary parts separately.

Example 1

Express each of the following in the form $a + bi$:

(i) $(3 + 2i) + (4 - 3i)$ (ii) $(-5 + 3i) + (-1 - 7i)$
(iii) $(-6 + 3i) - (5 - 2i)$ (iv) $(a + bi) + (c + di)$

(i) $(3 + 2i) + (4 - 3i) = 3 + 2i + 4 - 3i = 7 - i$
(ii) $(-5 + 3i) + (-1 - 7i) = -5 + 3i - 1 - 7i = -6 - 4i$
(iii) $(-6 + 3i) - (5 - 2i) = -6 + 3i - 5 + 2i = -11 + 5i$
(iv) $(a + bi) + (c + di) = a + bi + c + di = (a + c) + (b + d)i$

Multiplying by a real number

We simplify $3(2 - 4i)$ by multiplying each term inside the bracket by 3.
Thus $3(2 - 4i) = 6 - 12i$ and $-3(-4 + 3i) = 12 - 9i$.

Example 2

If $z_1 = 1 + 2i$ and $z_2 = 5 - 2i$, express in the form $a + bi$:

   (i) $3z_1$ (ii) $z_1 + z_2$ (iii) $2z_1 - z_2$ (iv) $z_1 - 3z_2$

$$
\begin{aligned}
\text{(i)} \quad 3z_1 &= 3(1 + 2i) \\
&= 3 + 6i
\end{aligned}
\qquad
\begin{aligned}
\text{(ii)} \quad z_1 + z_2 &= (1 + 2i) + (5 - 2i) \\
&= 1 + 2i + 5 - 2i \\
&= 6 + 0i
\end{aligned}
$$

$$
\begin{aligned}
\text{(iii)} \quad 2z_1 - z_2 &= 2(1 + 2i) - (5 - 2i) \\
&= 2 + 4i - 5 + 2i \\
&= -3 + 6i
\end{aligned}
\qquad
\begin{aligned}
\text{(iv)} \quad z_1 - 3z_2 &= (1 + 2i) - 3(5 - 2i) \\
&= 1 + 2i - 15 + 6i \\
&= -14 + 8i
\end{aligned}
$$

Exercise 7.3

1. Write each of the following complex numbers in the form $a + bi$:

   (i) $(3 + 4i) + (5 + i)$ (ii) $(3 - 4i) + (2 - 6i)$

  (iii) $(5 - i) + (-2 - 3i)$ (iv) $(-3 + 6i) + (4 - 2i)$

   (v) $(2 - 6i) + (-4 - i)$ (vi) $(-3 - 2i) + (6 - 2i)$

 (vii) $(3 - 6i) + 5$ (viii) $3i + (-2 - 4i)$

  (ix) $(a + bi) + (3 + 2i)$ (x) $(a + bi) + (x + yi)$

2. Write each of the following in the form $a + bi$:

   (i) $(2 + 5i) - (1 + 2i)$ (ii) $(3 - 2i) - (5 + 4i)$

  (iii) $(-2 + i) - (3 - 5i)$ (iv) $(-3 - 4i) - (-2 + 6i)$

   (v) $(4 - 2i) - (3 - 7i)$ (vi) $(-6 - 2i) - (5 - i)$

 (vii) $(3 - 4i) - 6$ (viii) $5i - (3 + 2i)$

  (ix) $(a + bi) - (5 - 2i)$ (x) $(x + yi) - (p - qi)$

3. If $z_1 = 2 + 3i$ and $z_2 = 5 - i$, express each of the following in the form $a + bi$:

   (i) $3z_1$ (ii) $3z_1 + z_2$

  (iii) $z_1 + 3z_2$ (iv) $2z_1 + 4z_2$

   (v) $4z_1 - 3z_2$ (vi) $2z_1 - 4z_2$

4. If $z_1 = 1 - 2i$, $z_2 = 3 + 2i$ and $z_3 = 1 - 3i$, express in the form $a + bi$:

   (i) $z_1 + z_3$ (ii) $2z_2 - z_3$

  (iii) $z_1 + z_2 - z_3$ (iv) $2z_3 - 3z_1$

   (v) $z_1 - (z_2 + z_3)$ (vi) $z_1 - z_2 - 2z_3$

5. Express $3(4 + i) - 2(2 - 5i)$ in the form $a + bi$.

6. Find a complex number z_1 to satisfy each of the following equations:

   (i) $(3 + 4i) + z_1 = 7 + 5i$ (ii) $z_1 + (5 + 2i) = 6 - 4i$

  (iii) $(8 - 3i) - z_1 = 3 + 2i$ (iv) $(8 + 6i) - (4 - 3i) = z_1$

Section 7.4 Multiplying complex numbers

We have already learned how to multiply two algebraic expressions such as $(2x + 4)(x - 3)$,

i.e.
$$(2x + 4)(x - 3) = 2x^2 - 6x + 4x - 12$$
$$= 2x^2 - 2x - 12$$

We multiply two complex numbers in the same way, replacing i^2 with -1.

> Remember $i^2 = -1$

Example 1

Express each of the following in the form $a + bi$:
  (i) $i(3 - 2i)$ (ii) $(2 + 3i)(-4 + 5i)$ (iii) $(3 - 2i)(5 + 3i)$

  (i) $i(3 - 2i) = 3i - 2i^2 = 3i - 2(-1) = 3i + 2 = 2 + 3i$
  (ii) $(2 + 3i)(-4 + 5i) = 2(-4 + 5i) + 3i(-4 + 5i)$
  $= -8 + 10i - 12i + 15i^2$
  $= -8 - 2i + 15(-1) \ldots \quad i^2 = -1$
  $= -8 - 2i - 15$
  $= -23 - 2i$
  (iii) $(3 - 2i)(5 + 3i) = 3(5 + 3i) - 2i(5 + 3i)$
  $= 15 + 9i - 10i - 6i^2$
  $= 15 - i - 6(-1) \ldots \quad i^2 = -1$
  $= 15 - i + 6 = 21 - i$

Exercise 7.4

Express each of the following in the form $a + bi$:

1. $i(3 + 2i)$

2. $3i(1 - 5i)$

3. $-2i(4 - 3i)$

4. $(2 - 3i)(4 + i)$

5. $(2 + i)(3 - 2i)$

6. $(-1 + i)(3 + 2i)$

7. $(1 - 3i)(4 + 2i)$

8. $(1 - 4i)(1 + i)$

9. $(2 - 3i)(2 + 3i)$

10. $(-3 + 4i)(2 - i)$

11. $(3 - 2i)^2$

12. $(4 + 2i)^2$

13. If $z_1 = 3 - 2i, z_2 = 5 + i$ and $z_3 = -1 + 3i$, express in the form $a + bi$,
  (i) $z_1 . z_3$ (ii) $z_2 . z_3$ (iii) $z_1(z_2 - z_3)$ (iv) $iz_1 z_2$

14. Copy and complete this table:

$i \times i$	=		=	
$i \times i \times i$	=	$i \times i^2$	=	
$i \times i \times i \times i$	=		=	
$i \times i \times i \times i \times i$	=		=	
$i \times i \times i \times i \times i \times i$	=		=	

Section 7.5 Dividing complex numbers

1. The conjugate of a complex number

If $z = a + bi$ is a complex number, then $a - bi$ is called the **complex conjugate** of z, or simply the **conjugate** of z.

The conjugate of z is written as $\bar{z}$.

Thus to find the conjugate of a complex number, change the sign of the imaginary part only.

The conjugate of   (i) $3 - 4i$ is $3 + 4i$

                   (ii) $-2 + 6i$ is $-2 - 6i$.

Example 1

If $z = 3 - 4i$,   find in the form $a + bi$

  (i) $z + \bar{z}$ (ii) $z . \bar{z}$.

$$
\begin{aligned}
\text{(i)} \quad z + \bar{z} &= (3 - 4i) + (3 + 4i) \\
&= 3 - 4i + 3 + 4i \\
&= 6 + 0i \\
\text{i.e.} \quad & \quad 6
\end{aligned}
$$

$$
\begin{aligned}
\text{(ii)} \quad z . \bar{z} &= (3 - 4i)(3 + 4i) \\
&= 9 + 12i - 12i - 16i^2 \\
&= 9 + 0i + 16 \\
&= 25 + 0i \\
\text{i.e.} \quad & \quad 25
\end{aligned}
$$

Notice that the results of (i) and (ii) are both real numbers.

Remember   When a complex number and its conjugate are added or multiplied, the result is always a real number.

2. Dividing complex numbers

To express $\dfrac{4 + 10i}{5}$ in the form $a + bi$, we divide each term of the numerator by 5.

Thus $\dfrac{4 + 10i}{5} = \dfrac{4}{5} + \dfrac{10}{5}i = \dfrac{4}{5} + 2i$.

To express $\dfrac{2 - 3i}{4 + 2i}$ in the form $a + bi$, we multiply the numerator and denominator by the conjugate of the denominator.

This will result in a real number below the line.

The steps involved are illustrated in the following example.

Example 2

Express $\dfrac{6 + 2i}{2 - 3i}$ in the form $a + bi$.

$$\frac{6 + 2i}{2 - 3i} = \frac{6 + 2i}{2 - 3i} \times \frac{2 + 3i}{2 + 3i}$$

$$= \frac{(6 + 2i)(2 + 3i)}{(2 - 3i)(2 + 3i)}$$

$$= \frac{12 + 18i + 4i + 6i^2}{4 + 6i - 6i - 9i^2}$$

$$= \frac{12 + 22i - 6}{4 + 9}$$

$$= \frac{6 + 22i}{13} = \frac{6}{13} + \frac{22}{13}i$$

Exercise 7.5

1. Write down the conjugate of each of these complex numbers:
   (i) $2 + 3i$ (ii) $-3 - 4i$ (iii) $4 - 6i$ (iv) $(x + 2) + yi$

2. If $z_1 = 2 + 3i$ and $z_2 = 3 - 4i$, express in the form $a + bi$:
   (i) $\bar{z}_1$ (ii) $2\bar{z}_2$ (iii) $z_1 + \bar{z}_2$ (iv) $\bar{z}_1 . \bar{z}_2$ (v) $\bar{z}_1 . z_2$

3. Write each of these complex numbers in the form $a + bi$:
   (i) $\dfrac{6 + 4i}{2}$ (ii) $\dfrac{3 - 2i}{2}$ (iii) $\dfrac{7 + 3i}{4}$ (iv) $\dfrac{-2 + 6i}{3}$

4. Express each of the following in the form $a + bi$:
   (i) $\dfrac{2}{3 - 2i}$ (ii) $\dfrac{5}{3 - 4i}$ (iii) $\dfrac{3}{6 - i}$ (iv) $\dfrac{2 + 3i}{1 - 2i}$

   (v) $\dfrac{4 - 3i}{3 + 2i}$ (vi) $\dfrac{-2 + 3i}{5 - i}$ (vii) $\dfrac{6 + 5i}{2 - 3i}$ (viii) $\dfrac{6 - 2i}{i}$

5. If $z_1 = 3 - 4i, z_2 = 5 + i$ and $z_3 = -2 + i$, express in the form $x + yi$:
   (i) $z_1 . \bar{z}_1$ (ii) $\dfrac{z_1}{z_3}$ (iii) $\bar{z}_2 . z_1$ (iv) $\dfrac{z_3}{\bar{z}_1}$ (v) $\dfrac{z_1 - z_2}{\bar{z}_3}$

6. If $z_1 = 1 + 2i$ and $z_2 = 3 - 2i$, express in the form $a + bi$:
   (i) $2iz_2$ (ii) $iz_1 - iz_2$ (iii) $\dfrac{i}{z_1}$ (iv) $\dfrac{z_2}{i}$ (v) $\dfrac{iz_1}{iz_2}$

7. If $z_1 = 3 + 4i$ and $z_2 = 12 - 5i$, show that $z_1 . \bar{z}_2 + \bar{z}_1 . z_2$ is a real number.

8. If $z = 5 + 4i$,   (i) calculate $z . \bar{z}$ (ii) express $\dfrac{z}{\bar{z}}$ in the form $a + bi$.

9. Let $w = (1 - 3i)(2 + i)$. Express w in the form $p + qi$, $p, q \in R$.

   For what value of a is $\dfrac{\bar{w}}{2i} = aw$, where $a \in R$?

10. Given $u = 3 - 6i$.
    (i) Express iu in the form $a + bi$.   (ii) Show that $iu + \dfrac{u}{i} = 0$.

194

Section 7.6 The Argand diagram

To represent a complex number on a graph, we construct a horizontal axis and vertical axis similar to the x and y axes.
The horizontal axis is called the **real axis (Re)**.
The vertical axis is called the **imaginary axis (Im)**.

Complex numbers are then plotted in the same way as points on the coordinated plane.
For example, the complex number $3 + 2i$ is represented by the point $(3, 2)$.
A diagram on which complex numbers are illustrated is called an **Argand Diagram**.

Some complex numbers are illustrated in the Argand diagram below.

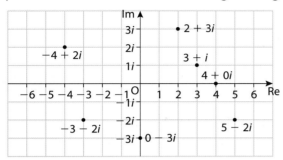

Note: The number 4 is $4 + 0i$ and $-3i = 0 - 3i$.

Exercise 7.6

1. Draw an Argand diagram and on it represent the following complex numbers:
   (i) $4 + i$ (ii) $3 + 3i$ (iii) $4 - 2i$ (iv) $1 - i$ (v) $-4 + i$
   (vi) $-3 + 2i$ (vii) $-3 - 2i$ (viii) $5 - 2i$ (ix) -4 (x) $3i$

2. Write each of the following complex numbers in the form $a + bi$ and then plot them on an Argand diagram:
   (i) $(3 - 2i) + (-1 + 4i)$ (ii) $2(1 - 2i) + 3i$
   (iii) $3(2 - i) - (6 - 6i)$ (iv) $(2 + i)(-1 - i)$

3. $z_1 = 2 - i$ and $z_2 = 1 + 3i$ are two complex numbers.
   Write each of the following in the form $a + bi$ and then plot the number on an Argand diagram.
   (i) z_1 (ii) $z_1 + z_2$ (iii) $z_1 . z_2$ (iv) iz_2

4. Express each of the following in the form $a + bi$ and then illustrate your result on an Argand diagram:
   (i) $2(3 - 2i)$ (ii) $3(1 - 2i) + 4i$ (iii) $(3 + 4i) - (2 - i)$

5. Plot each of the following on an Argand diagram:
   (i) i (ii) i^2 (iii) i^3 (iv) i^4

6. If $z_1 = 4 + 2i$ and $z_2 = -1 + 2i$, plot each of the following on the same Argand diagram.
   (i) z_1 (ii) $\bar{z}_2$ (iii) $z_1 + \bar{z}_1$ (iv) $z_2 . \bar{z}_2$

Section 7.7 The modulus of a complex number

The **modulus** (or length) of a complex number is the distance from the origin to the point representing the complex number on an Argand diagram.

The modulus of the complex number

$a + bi$ is $\sqrt{a^2 + b^2}$.

The modulus of $a + bi$ is written as $|a + bi|$

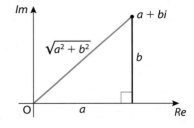

Modulus

> The modulus of the complex number,
> $z = a + bi$ is
> $$|z| = |a + bi| = \sqrt{a^2 + b^2}.$$

Example 1

If $z_1 = -2 + 3i$ and $z_2 = 3 + 4i$, find

(i) $|z_1|$ (ii) $|z_2|$ (iii) $|z_1 + z_2|$

Verify that $|z_1| + |z_2| > |z_1 + z_2|$.

(i) $|z_1| = |-2 + 3i| = \sqrt{(-2)^2 + (3)^2}$
$$= \sqrt{4 + 9} = \sqrt{13}$$

(ii) $|z_2| = |3 + 4i| = \sqrt{(3)^2 + (4)^2}$
$$= \sqrt{9 + 16}$$
$$= \sqrt{25} = 5$$

(iii) $z_1 + z_2 = -2 + 3i + 3 + 4i$
$$= 1 + 7i$$
$$|z_1 + z_2| = |1 + 7i| = \sqrt{1^2 + 7^2}$$
$$= \sqrt{1 + 49}$$
$$= \sqrt{50} = \sqrt{25}.\sqrt{2} = 5\sqrt{2}$$

$$|z_1| + |z_2| = \sqrt{13} + 5 \approx 3.6 + 5$$
$$\approx 8.6$$
$$|z_1 + z_2| = 5\sqrt{2} \qquad \approx 5(1.4)$$
$$\approx 7$$

Since $8.6 > 7 \Rightarrow |z_1| + |z_2| > |z_1 + z_2|$.

Note: $\approx$ means 'approximately equal to'.

Exercise 7.7

Evaluate each of these:

1. $|-3 + 4i|$ **2.** $|8 + 6i|$ **3.** $|2 + 3i|$ **4.** $|-1 + 2i|$

5. $|3 - 2i|$ **6.** $|5 + i|$ **7.** $|-3 + i|$ **8.** $|6 - i|$

9. $|4 + 0i|$ **10.** $|5|$ **11.** $|0 - 3i|$ **12.** $|5i|$

13. Evaluate each of these:
    (i) $|2(1 - 2i)|$ (ii) $|\sqrt{3} + i|$ (iii) $|3 + 4i - (1 - 2i)|$

14. Write down four complex numbers each having the same modulus as $3 + 4i$.

15. If $z_1 = -3 - 2i$ and $z_2 = 1 - 3i$, evaluate each of the following:
    (i) $|z_1|$ (ii) $|z_2|$ (iii) $|z_1 - z_2|$ (iv) $|z_1 . z_2|$

16. If $z_1 = 5 + 3i$ and $z_2 = 2 - i$, find
    (i) $|z_1|$ (ii) $|z_2|$ (iii) $|z_1 + z_2|$
    Now show that $|z_1| + |z_2| > |z_1 + z_2|$.

17. If $z_1 = 2 - 3i$ and $z_2 = 1 + 2i$, find
    (i) $|z_1|$ (ii) $|z_2|$ (iii) $z_1 . z_2$ (iv) $|z_1 . z_2|$
    Now show that $|z_1| . |z_2| = |z_1 . z_2|$.

18. If $z = 3 + 2i$, find $z . \bar{z}$, where $\bar{z}$ is the conjugate of z.
    Hence find $|z . \bar{z}|$.

19. Given $z_1 = -2 + i$ and $z_2 = -3 - 4i$.
    Evaluate   (i) $|z_1|$ (ii) $|z_2|$ (iii) $|z_1 - z_2|$
    Investigate if $|z_1| - |z_2| = |z_1 - z_2|$.

20. Let $w = 3 - i$.
    (i) Express $w + 6i$ in the form $a + bi$.
    (ii) Find the value of $|w + 6i|$.

21. Express $|a + 8i|$ in terms of a.
    Hence find the two values of a for which $|a + 8i| = 10$.

22. Let $w = 3 - 4i$.
    Verify that $|w|^2 = w . \bar{w}$, where $\bar{w}$ is the conjugate of w.

23. If $z_1 = 5 + i$ and $z_2 = -2 + 3i$, find $|z_1|$ and $|z_2|$.
    Now show that $|z_1|^2 = 2|z_2|^2$.

24. If $z_1 = 2 + 3i$ and $z_2 = 2 - 3i$, express $\dfrac{z_1}{z_2}$ in the form $a + bi$.
    Now find the value of $k \in R$ such that $|z_1| = k\left|\dfrac{z_1}{z_2}\right|$.

Section 7.8 Equality of complex numbers ─────────────

If two complex numbers are equal, then the real parts are equal and the imaginary parts are equal.

> If $a + bi = c + di$,
>
> then $a = c$ and $b = d$.

Example 1

If $5 - i = x + (5 - 2y)i$, find the values of x and y.

$$5 - i = x + (5 - 2y)i$$

Equating the real parts we get: $5 = x$ i.e. $x = 5$

Equating the imaginary parts:

$$-i = (5 - 2y)i$$
$$\Rightarrow \quad -1 = 5 - 2y \dots \quad \text{the coefficient of } -i \text{ is } -1$$
$$\Rightarrow \quad 2y = 6 \Rightarrow y = 3$$
$$\therefore \quad x = 5 \quad \text{and} \quad y = 3$$

Example 2

a and b are real numbers such that

$$a(2 + i) + 8 - bi = 5b - 3 - i.$$

Find the value of a and the value of b.

$$a(2 + i) + 8 - bi = 5b - 3 - i$$
$$\Rightarrow \quad 2a + ai + 8 - bi = (5b - 3) - i$$
$$\Rightarrow \quad (2a + 8) + i(a - b) = (5b - 3) + i(-1)$$

Equating the real parts we get:

$$2a + 8 = 5b - 3 \quad \Rightarrow \quad 2a - 5b = -11 \dots \quad \text{①}$$

Equating the imaginary parts we get:

$$a - b = -1 \dots \quad \text{②}$$

Solving equations ① and ②:

$$\text{①} \quad : \quad 2a - 5b = -11$$
$$\text{②} \times 2: \quad 2a - 2b = -2$$
$$\phantom{\text{②} \times 2: \quad 2a} -3b = -9 \quad \Rightarrow \quad b = 3$$

From ②: $a - 3 = -1 \quad \Rightarrow \quad a = 2$

$\therefore \quad a = 2 \quad \text{and} \quad b = 3$

Exercise 7.8

Find the values of x and y in numbers (1–10).

1. $(x + 3) + i(y - 1) = 6 + 2i$

2. $(2x + 1) + i(1 - y) = 5 - 3i$

3. $x + iy + 6 - 9i = 6 - 10i$

4. $3(2x + 3yi) + 4 - 6i = 2 - 5i$

5. $(2x - 4) + 5i = (x - 3) + yi$

6. $2(x + yi) + 3(4 - 6i) = 7 - 3i$

7. $x(2 + 3i) - 2y = 3 + 6i$

8. $6 - 9i - 2(x + yi) = 8 - 3i$

9. $2x + (x + y)i = 4 - 5i$

10. $(x - iy) + (y + xi) = 1 - 5i$

11. Find a and b if $3(a + bi) - 4(ai - b) = 6 - 3i$.

12. Find the value of a and b if $(4a - 2) + (a - 4)i = (4 - 2b) + 2bi$.

13. Find a and b if $(a + bi)(5 + i) = 3 - 2i$.

14. Find the value of x and the value of y if $x(3 + 4i) + 5 = y(1 + 2i)$.

15. Solve for x and y in each of the following equations:
    (i) $(2x - 1) + (x + y)i = (y - 6) + (2y - 4)i$
    (ii) $2(x + yi) = 4(2 + 3i) - 2(1 - 2i)$

Section 7.9 Quadratic equations with complex roots

To solve a quadratic equation of the form $ax^2 + bx + c = 0$, we generally use factors.
However if $ax^2 + bx + c$ cannot be factorised, we use the formula

$$x = \frac{-b \pm \sqrt{b^2 - 4ac}}{2a} \quad \text{to solve the equation.}$$

If $b^2 - 4ac$ is negative, i.e., less than zero, then the roots will be complex numbers.
If an equation has complex roots, we generally use z for the variable.

Example 1

Solve the equation $z^2 + 6z + 10 = 0$, expressing your answers in the form $a \pm bi$.

Using the formula $z = \dfrac{-b \pm \sqrt{b^2 - 4ac}}{2a}$ we have $\begin{cases} a = 1 \\ b = 6 \\ c = 10 \end{cases}$

$$\Rightarrow \quad z = \frac{-6 \pm \sqrt{36 - 4(1)(10)}}{2(1)}$$

$$= \frac{-6 \pm \sqrt{-4}}{2}$$

$$= \frac{-6 \pm 2i}{2} \quad \dots \sqrt{-4} = \sqrt{4}. \ \sqrt{-1} = 2i$$

$$= -3 \pm i$$

$$\therefore \quad z = -3 + i \text{ or } -3 - i$$

Note: The complex roots in Example 1 are a conjugate pair, i.e., each root is the conjugate of the other.

Thus if $2 + 3i$ is a root of a quadratic equation, then $2 - 3i$ is also a root.

> ## Example 2
>
> If $z = 3 + i$ is a root of the equation $z^2 - 6z + k = 0$, find the value of k and write down the other root in the form $a + bi$.
>
> If $z = 3 + i$ is a root of the equation $z^2 - 6z + k = 0$, it satisfies the equation.
>
> We now substitute $(3 + i)$ for z in the equation $z^2 - 6z + k = 0$.
>
> Thus $\quad (3 + i)^2 - 6(3 + i) + k = 0$
> $\Rightarrow \quad 9 + 6i + i^2 - 18 - 6i + k = 0$
> $\Rightarrow \quad 9 + 6i - 1 - 18 - 6i + k = 0$
> $\Rightarrow \quad -10 + k = 0 \quad \Rightarrow \quad k = 10$
>
> The other root is the conjugate of $3 + i$, i.e., $3 - i$.

Exercise 7.9

1. Solve each of the following equations, giving your answers in the form $a + bi$:
   (i) $z^2 + 4z + 5 = 0$ (ii) $z^2 + 6z + 13 = 0$ (iii) $z^2 + 2z + 10 = 0$
   (iv) $z^2 - 6z + 34 = 0$ (v) $z^2 - 10z + 29 = 0$ (vi) $z^2 - 2z + 17 = 0$

2. Show that $2 + 5i$ is a root of the equation $z^2 - 4z + 29 = 0$ and write down the other root.

3. Show that $4 - 3i$ is a root of the equation $z^2 - 8z + 25 = 0$ and write down the other root.

4. Show that $6 + i$ is a root of the equation $z^2 - 12z + 37 = 0$ and write down the other root.

5. If $-5 + i$ is a root of the equation $z^2 + kz + 26 = 0$, find the value of k.

6. If $5 - 3i$ is a root of the equation $z^2 - 10z + k = 0$, find the value of k.

7. If $4 + i$ and $4 - i$ are roots of the equation $z^2 + az + b = 0$, find the value of a and the value of b.

Section 7.10 Complex numbers and transformations

In this section we will use the Argand diagram to show graphically the effect of some operations on complex numbers.

1. Multiplying a complex number by a real number

If a complex number $z_1 = 3 + 2i$ is multiplied by the real number 2, we get
$2z_1 = 2(3 + 2i) = 6 + 4i$

The real part is increased by a factor of 2 and the imaginary part is also increased by a factor of 2.

Similarly $3z_1 = 3(3 + 2i) = 9 + 6i$.

z_1, $2z_1$ and $3z_1$ are shown on the Argand diagram below:

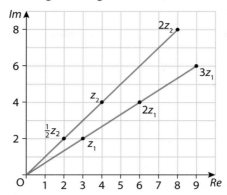

The diagram above also shows $z_2 = 4 + 4i$.

$2z_2 = 2(4 + 4i) = 8 + 8i$ and $\frac{1}{2}z_2 = \frac{1}{2}(4 + 4i) = 2 + 2i$ are also shown.

Notice that when the complex number z_1 is multiplied by 2, the modulus of $2z_1$ is twice the modulus of z_1.

Similarly the modulus of $3z_1$ is three times the modulus of z_1.

The diagram also shows that $\left|\frac{1}{2}z_2\right| = \frac{1}{2}|z_2|$.

2. Adding the same complex number to different complex numbers

The diagram below shows the complex numbers

$$0 = 0 + 0i, \qquad z_1 = 2 + 3i, \qquad z_2 = -3 + 2i \quad \text{and} \quad z_3 = 1 + 3i$$

If we add $4 + 2i$ to each of these numbers we get:

$$4 + 2i, \qquad 6 + 5i, \qquad 1 + 4i \quad \text{and} \quad 5 + 5i.$$

These numbers are illustrated in the Argand diagram below:

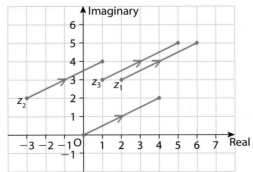

When the complex number $4 + 2i$ is added to $0, z_1, z_2$ and z_3, the diagram above illustrates that the result is a translation.

All the numbers are moved a given distance in the same direction.

3. Multiplying a complex number by i

If a complex number $z = 4 + i$ is multiplied by i we get,

$$i(4 + i) = 4i + i^2 = -1 + 4i$$

If we multiply $z = 4 + i$ by i, i^2 and i^3, we get

$$iz = -1 + 4i \dots \text{ as found above}$$

$$i^2(z) = -1(4 + i) = -4 - i$$

$$i^3(z) = i^2 \cdot i(z) = -i(4 + i)$$
$$= -4i - i^2$$
$$= 1 - 4i$$

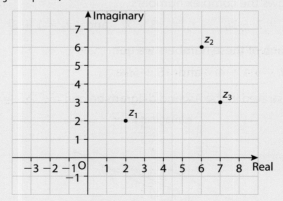

From the diagram we can see that when a complex number is multiplied by i, the result is a rotation through 90° in an anticlockwise direction each time it is multiplied by i.

Remember

> $z \times i$, z rotates through 90°
> $z \times i^2$, z rotates through 180°
> $z \times i^3$, z rotates through 270°

Example 1

Using the Argand diagram below, write down the complex numbers z_1, z_2 and z_3.
  (i)   Given that $z_2 = a \cdot z_1$, find a.
  (ii)   Given that $z_3 = z_1 + z$, find z.

From the diagram, $z_1 = 2 + 2i$, $z_2 = 6 + 6i$ and $z_3 = 7 + 3i$.

  (i)   If $z_2 = a \cdot z_1$, then $6 + 6i = a(2 + 2i)$
  $$\therefore \quad a = 3$$

  (ii)   If $z_3 = z_1 + z$, then $7 + 3i = 2 + 2i + z$
  $$\therefore \quad z = 7 + 3i - 2 - 2i$$
  $$z = 5 + i$$

Exercise 7.10

1. Plot the complex number $z = 4 + 2i$ on an Argand diagram.

On the same diagram plot the complex numbers $2z$ and $\frac{1}{2}z$.

Verify (i) $|2z| = 2|z|$ (ii) $|\frac{1}{2}z| = \frac{1}{2}|z|$.

2. Given $z_1 = 2 - i$.

Plot on an Argand diagram the complex numbers $z_1, 3z_1, 4z_1$ and $-2z_1$.

Use the diagram to describe the relationship between the numbers $z_1, 3z_1, 4z_1$ and $-2z_1$.

3. Using the Argand diagram below, write down the complex numbers z_1 and z_2.

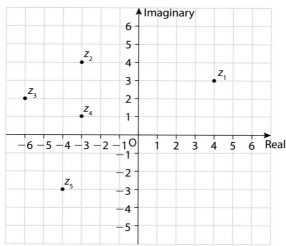

(i) Show that $z_2 = iz_1$.

(ii) Which of the points z_3, z_4 or z_5 represents i^2z_1?

(iii) If $z_6 = i^3(z_2)$, find z_6 in the form $a + bi$.

4. The complex numbers z_1, z_2 and z_4 are plotted on an Argand diagram.

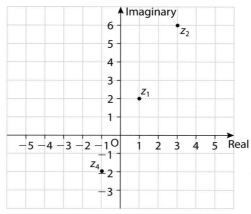

(i) Given $z_2 = az_1$, find a.   (ii) Given $z_4 = bz_1$, find b.

5. Plot the complex number $z = 6 + 2i$ on an Argand diagram.

On the same diagram plot the complex numbers

   (i) iz (ii) i^2z (iii) i^3z.

6. Plot on an Argand diagram the complex numbers

$$z_1 = 4 + i, \quad z_2 = 7 + 2i \quad \text{and} \quad z_3 = 5 + 5i.$$

Join the three points and shade in the triangle formed.

If $z_4 = -3 - 4i$, plot these complex numbers on the same Argand diagram:

$$z_1 + z_4, \quad z_2 + z_4 \quad \text{and} \quad z_3 + z_4.$$

Join the resulting points and shade in the new triangle.

Describe the transformation that results from adding $-3 - 4i$ to z_1, z_2 and z_3.

7. Write down any complex number z.

Show that $i^4z = z$.

Explain, in terms of rotation, the effect of multiplying a complex number by i^4.

8. Given, $z = 3 - 2i$.

Plot z, iz, i^2z and i^3z on an Argand diagram.

Using a compass and with the origin as centre, verify that a circle can be drawn through z, iz, i^2z and i^3z.

9. Plot the point $z_1 = 3 + i$ and $z_2 = 1 + 2i$ on an Argand diagram.

If $z_3 = z_1 . z_2$, find z_3 and plot it on the same diagram.

Join z_1, z_2 and z_3 to the origin.

Use a protractor to measure the angle that each of the points z_1, z_2 and z_3 makes with the real axis.

Use your results to show that the sum of the first two angles is equal in measure to the third angle.

Test yourself 7

1. (i) Write down one example of each of the following:
    (a) A natural number that is greater than 25 and less than 40
    (b) An integer which is less than -5 and a multiple of 2
    (c) A rational number between 1 and 2
    (d) An irrational number between 8 and 9.

    (ii) Given that $z_1 = 3 + 4i$ and $z_2 = -1 + 2i$,
    (a) express $2z_1 - 3z_2$ in the form $a + bi$
    (b) express $\dfrac{1}{z_1}$ in the form $a + bi$.
    (c) If $z_1 + kz_2 = 6 - 2i$, find the value of k, where $k \in R$.

    (iii) Find x and y if
    $$x(3 - 2i) + y(-2 + i) = 5 - 4i, \text{ where } x, y \in R.$$

2. (i) Simplify $3(1 + 5i) + i(3 - 2i)$ and express your answer in the form $p + qi$, where $p, q \in R$.

    (ii) Let $z_1 = 10 - 2i$ and $z_2 = 2 - 3i$.
    Show that $\dfrac{z_1}{z_2}$ can be written in the form $k(1 + i)$, where $k \in N$ and hence write down the value of k.

    (iii) Write $\dfrac{3 + 2i}{2 - i}$ in the form $x + yi, x, y \in R$.
    Hence find $|x + yi|$.

3. (i) Write each of the following in the form $a + bi$:
    (a) $3 + \sqrt{-16}$ 　　　(b) $2 - \sqrt{-9}$ 　　　(c) $\dfrac{-10 + \sqrt{-100}}{5}$

    (ii) Let $z = 1 - 4i$, where $i^2 = -1$.
    Plot z and iz on an Argand diagram.

    (iii) If $|2 + ki| = \sqrt{29}$, find the two values of $k \in R$.

4. (i) Write down an irrational number that has a value between 6 and 7.

    (ii) Express each of the following in the form $a + bi$:
    (a) $3(2 + 3i) - i(2 - 3i)$ 　　　(b) $\dfrac{2}{1 - 2i}$

    (iii) If $z_1 = 3 - 4i$ and $z_2 = 2 + 3i$, express z_1z_2 in the form $a + bi$.
    Verify that $|z_1z_2| = |z_1||z_2|$.

5. (i) State whether each of the following is true or false:
    (a) $-2 \in N$ 　　　(b) $4 \in Z$ 　　　(c) $\frac{2}{3} \in Q$ 　　　(d) $\sqrt{16}$ is irrational

(ii) Solve the equation $z^2 - 4z + 13 = 0$.
Express the roots in the form $a + bi$.

(iii) Plot $z_1 = 2 - 4i$ and $z_2 = -4 + 2i$ on an Argand diagram.
Find $|z_1|$ and $|z_2|$.
Write down two other complex numbers that have the same moduli as z_1.

6. (i) Simplify $7(2 + i) + i(11 + 9i)$ and express your answer in the form $a + bi$,
where $a, b \in R$ and $i^2 = -1$.

(ii) If $z_1 = 2 + 3i$ and $z_2 = 5 - i$, find
(a) $z_1 + z_2$
(b) $z_1 - z_2$.
Now investigate if $|z_1 + z_2| > |z_1 - z_2|$.

(iii) Let $w = 3 - 4i$
Solve the equation $x + w = 3yi$, for $x, y \in R$.

7. (i) If $z = 2i$, plot (a) z^2 and (b) iz on an Argand diagram.

(ii) Write down, in the form $a + bi$, the complex number z_1 shown on the Argand diagram below.

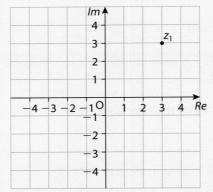

Now find the complex numbers iz_1, i^2z_1 and i^3z_1 and plot them on a copy of the Argand diagram above.
By examining the diagram, describe the geometrical transformation that has taken place.

(iii) If $z_1 = -4 + i$ is a root of the equation $z^2 + 8z + k = 0$, find the value of k and hence write down z_2, the other root of the equation.
Find z_1z_2 and hence find t, if $|z_1z_2| = t|z_1|$, for $t \in R$.

8. (i) If $w = 3 - i$, plot $w + 4i$ on an Argand diagram.
Now find $|w + 4i|$.

(ii) If $z = -2 + i$, express z^2 in the form $a + bi$, where $a, b \in R$.
Hence solve the equation
$$kz^2 = 2z + t \quad \text{for real } k \text{ and real } t.$$

(iii) If $2 - i$ is a root of the equation $z^2 + pz + q = 0$, write down the other root.
Hence find the value of p and the value of q.

206

Summary of key points...

1. **Number systems**

    N = **natural numbers** = 1, 2, 3, 4 ...

    Z = **integers** = ... $-3, -2, -1, 0, 1, 2, 3, ...$

    Q = **rational numbers** = numbers in the
    form $\frac{a}{b}$, where a and b are integers.

    Numbers such as $\sqrt{2}$, π or non-repeating
    and non-recurring decimals are called
    irrational numbers.

    All the numbers above are **real numbers (R)**

    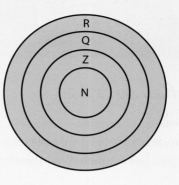

2. **Complex numbers**

    (i) A **complex number** is a number in the form $a + bi$ where $i = \sqrt{-1}$
         and $\boldsymbol{i^2 = -1}$.

    (ii) The **complex conjugate** of $3 + 4i$ is $3 - 4i$.
          When a complex number and its conjugate are added or
          multiplied, the result is always a real number.

    (iii) To express $\dfrac{2 + 3i}{4 + 2i}$ in the form $a + bi$, multiply above and below

           by $4 - 2i$, the conjugate of the denominator.

    (iv) If $z = a + bi$, then the modulus of z is $|a + bi| = \sqrt{a^2 + b^2}$.

    (v) If $a + bi = c + di$, then $a = c$ and $b = d$.

    (vi) A complex number can be represented on an **Argand diagram**.
          The horizontal axis is called the **real axis**.
          The vertical axis is called the **imaginary axis**.

    (viii) The equation $ax^2 + bx + c = 0$ will have complex roots if
            $b^2 - 4ac < 0$.

3. **Transforming complex numbers**

    When a complex number z is multiplied
    by i, the result is a rotation through 90°
    in an anticlockwise direction.

$z \times i$,	z rotates through 90°
$z \times i^2$,	z rotates through 180°
$z \times i^3$,	z rotates through 270°

8 Measures of Location and Spread

Key words

mode   median   mean   range   variability   consistent   empirical rule
quartile   inter-quartile range   outlier   frequency distributions
grouped frequency distributions   mid-interval value   standard deviation

Section 8.1 Mode – Median – Mean

Average is a word that is frequently used in everyday language. For example, we refer to the average weekly wage, the average daily temperature, the average score in a golf competition or the average mark in an examination.

In each of the above examples, we are representing all the values in a set of data by a **single value** or **typical value** which we call the **average**.

The idea of an average is extremely useful because it enables us to compare one set of data with another by comparing just two values, namely their averages.

There are several ways of expressing an average, but the most commonly used averages are the **mode**, the **median** and the **mean**.

1. The Mode

The **mode** is the most common value in a set of data. The mode is very useful when one value appears much more often than any other. It is easy to find and can be used for non-numerical data such as the colours of cars sold by a garage.

Example 1

The ages of students on a school bus are:

$$12, \ 15, \ 12, \ 13, \ 14, \ 16, \ 15, \ 11, \ 12$$
$$16, \ 15, \ 16, \ 14, \ 10, \ 13, \ 17, \ 15, \ 17$$

Placing these in order we get:

$$10, \ 11, \ 12, \ 12, \ 12, \ 13, \ 13, \ 14, \ 14, \ 15, \ 15, \ 15, \ 15, \ 16, \ 16, \ 16, \ 17, \ 17$$

The number in this list with the greatest frequency is 15.

$$\therefore \quad \text{the mode} = 15$$

---

2. The Median

To find the median of a list of numbers, put the numbers in order of size, starting with the smallest. The **median** is the middle number.

If there are 11 numbers in the list, the middle number is $\frac{1}{2}(11 + 1)$, i.e., the 6th number.

If there are 10 numbers in the list, the middle number is $\frac{1}{2}(10 + 1)$, i.e., the $5\frac{1}{2}$th number.

This value is half the sum of the 5th and 6th numbers.

> If there are n numbers in a list, the middle term is $\frac{1}{2}(n + 1)$.
> If $\frac{1}{2}(n + 1) = 4$, then the 4th number is the median.

Example 2

Find the median of these numbers: 5, 8, 12, 4, 9, 3, 7, 2.

Writing the numbers in order of size we get:

$$2, 3, 4, 5, 7, 8, 9, 12$$

The median is $\frac{1}{2}(5 + 7) = \frac{5 + 7}{2} = \frac{12}{2} = 6$

> Write the numbers in order of size to find the median.

$\therefore$ the median $= 6$

3. The Mean

To find the mean of a set of numbers,

1. Find the sum of all the numbers.
2. Divide this sum by the number of numbers.

The mean is the most frequently used 'average'.

It is important because it considers every piece of data. However it can be affected by extreme values.

> The mean is $= \dfrac{\text{sum of the numbers}}{\text{number of numbers}}$

Example 3

Find the mean of these numbers:

$$12, 14, 10, 17, 21, 22$$

$$\text{Mean} = \frac{12 + 14 + 10 + 17 + 21 + 22}{6} = \frac{96}{6} = 16$$

Example 4

Five girls and three boys took part in a quiz.

The mean mark for the girls was 54.

The mean mark for the boys was 62.

Find the mean mark for the whole group.

To find the mean, add the total of the marks for the girls to the total of the marks for the boys and divide the result by 8.

$$\text{Total of the marks for the girls} = 54 \times 5 = 270$$
$$\text{Total of the marks for the boys} = 62 \times 3 = 186$$

Total for all 8 = 270 + 186 = 456

$$\text{Mean for the whole group} = \frac{456}{8} = 57$$

Exercise 8.1

1. Find the mean of each of these arrays of numbers:

    (i) 2, 6, 10, 14, 18   (ii) 0, 2, 8, 16, 6, 22

    (iii) 3, 7, 8, 13, 4, 12, 9   (iv) 5, 12, 3, 4, 3, 6, 9

2. Rewrite each of the following arrays of numbers in order of size and then write down

    (i) the mode   (ii) the median.

      (a) 8, 11, 2, 5, 8, 7, 8, 2, 5   (b) 3, 3, 7, 8, 7, 9, 8, 5, 7, 11, 12

3. The speeds, in kilometres per hour, of 11 cars travelling on a road are shown:

        41, 42, 31, 36, 42, 43, 42, 34, 41, 37, 45

    (i) Find the median speed.   (ii) Find the mean speed.

4. A rugby team played 10 games.

    Here are the numbers of points the team scored.

        12, 22, 14, 11, 7, 18, 22, 14, 36, 14

    (i) Write down the mode.

    (ii) What is the median number of points scored?

   (iii) Find the mean number of points scored.

5. Rearrange the following marks in order and then write down the median in each case.

    (i) 9, 5, 8, 3, 2, 7, 6   (ii) 8, 12, 18, 9, 14, 7, 10, 6

6. Write down seven different numbers with a median of 12.

7. The mean of four numbers is 7 and three of these numbers are 5, 12 and 9.
   (i) Find the sum of the four numbers.   (ii) Find the fourth number.

8. The mean of four numbers is 19. Three of them are 21, 25 and 16.
   Find the fourth number.

9. The mean of four sums of money is €4.90. When a fifth sum is added, the mean of the five sums is €5.34. Find the fifth sum of money.

10. Write five numbers so that
   the mode is 4
   the mean is 6
   the median is 5.

11. (i) The mean of 3, 7, 8, 10 and x is 6. Find x.
   (ii) The mean of 1, k, 3, 6 and 8 is 7. Find k.

12. The mean of 5 numbers is 11.
   When a sixth number is included the mean of the six numbers is 12.
   Find the sixth number.

13. The mean weight of five dates was 50 g.
   Kate ate one and the mean weight of the
   four remaining dates was 40 g.
   What was the weight of the date that Kate ate?

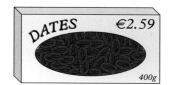

14. Nicky's marks in four tests were:

   8, 4, 5, 3

   What mark did she get in her fifth and sixth tests if her modal mark was 4 and her mean mark was 5 after the six tests?

15. Matthew's marks in eight tests are shown below.
   What mark did he score in the ninth test if his median mark was 6?

   5   9   7   3   7   4   5   8

16. In a survey, a group of boys and girls wrote down how many hours of television they watched one week.

Boys	17	22	21	23	16	12	**Girls**	9	13	15	19	10	12
	0	5	13	15	13	14		9	8	12	14	15	11

   (i) Find the mean time for the boys.
   (ii) Find the mean time for the girls.
   (iii) Find the median time for each group.
   (iv) Do the boys spend more time watching television than the girls? Explain your answer.

17. The numbers 4, 8, 12, 17, x are arranged in order of size.
If the mean of the numbers is equal to the median, find x.

18. The mean height of a group of eight students is 165 cm.
   (i) What is the total height of all eight students?

A ninth student joins the group. He is 168 cm tall.
   (ii) What is the mean height of all nine students?

19. The mean of five numbers is 39.
Two of the numbers are 103 and 35 and each of the other three numbers is equal to x.
Find   (i)   the total of the five numbers
        (ii) the value of x.

20. On four tests, each marked out of 100, my average was 85.
What is the lowest mark I could have scored on any one test?
A 0   B 40   C 60   D 81   E 85
Explain your answer.

21. Fred went fishing each week.
Each week he recorded the number of fish caught.
After several weeks he calculated the following averages.

| The **mean** number of fish caught per week was 9.3. |
| The **modal** number of fish caught per week was 12. |
| The **median** number of fish caught per week was 10. |

The next week he did not catch any fish.
This had never happened before.
Fred recalculated his averages.

   (i) Which of these averages could not have been affected?
        Give a reason for your answer.
   (ii) Which of the averages was certainly affected?
        Explain your answer.

Section 8.2 Range and variability

The **range** for a set of data is the highest value of the set minus the lowest value.

The range is not an average.

It shows the **spread** of the data.
It is very useful when comparing two sets of data.

The range is a crude measure of spread because it uses
only the largest and the smallest values of the data.

> The range of a set of data is the largest value minus the smallest value.

Example 1

Jane's marks, out of 20, in ten maths tests were as follows:

$$8, \ 8, \ 14, \ 12, \ 12, \ 10, \ 14, \ 12, \ 18, \ 12$$

Conor's marks in the same tests were

$$12, \ 14, \ 12, \ 16, \ 10, \ 12, \ 10, \ 12, \ 10, \ 12$$

Find   (i) the mean   (ii) the range

of Jane's marks and Conor's marks and comment on the results.

For Jane: (i)   the mean $= \dfrac{8 + 8 + 14 + 12 + 12 + 10 + 14 + 12 + 18 + 12}{10}$

$$= \frac{120}{10} = 12$$

(ii)   the range $=$ highest mark $-$ lowest mark

$$= 18 - 8$$
$$= 10$$

For Conor: (i)   the mean $= \dfrac{12 + 14 + 12 + 16 + 10 + 12 + 10 + 12 + 10 + 12}{10}$

$$= \frac{120}{10} = 12$$

(ii)   the range $= 16 - 10$
$$= 6$$

Comment: Although the means are the same, Conor's marks have a smaller range. This shows that Conor's results are **more consistent** than Jane's.

The more spread-out nature of Jane's marks compared to Conor's, in Example 1 above, illustrates the **variability** of data and how important it can be.

The **range** is often used as a measure of variability because it is easy to calculate and easy to understand.

Quartiles and Interquartile range

When data is arranged in order of size, we have already learned that the **median** is the value half-way into the data.

So we can say that the median divides the data into two halves.

The data can also be divided into four quarters.

When the data is arranged in ascending order of size:

> the **lower quartile** is the value one quarter of the way into the data
> the **upper quartile** is the value three quarters of the way into the data
> the upper quartile minus the lower quartile is called the **interquartile range**.

Consider the following data which is arranged in order of size. It contains 15 numbers.

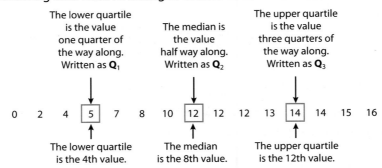

The lower quartile $Q_1 = 5$.

The median $Q_2 = 12$.

The upper quartile $Q_3 = 14$.

The interquartile range $= Q_3 - Q_1$

$\qquad = 14 - 5$

$\qquad = 9$

> The interquartile range is
> upper quartile − lower quartile
> $= Q_3 - Q_1$

Example 2

These are the test marks of 11 students:

$\qquad$ 52, 78, 61, 49, 79, 47, 54, 58, 72, 62, 73

Find $\qquad$ (i) $\quad$ the median $\qquad$ (ii) $\quad$ the lower quartile

$\qquad$ (iii) $\quad$ the upper quartile $\qquad$ (iv) $\quad$ the interquartile range.

We first rewrite the numbers in order, starting with the smallest:

$\qquad$ 47, 49, 52, 54, 58, 61, 62, 72, 73, 78, 79

(i) The median is the middle value of the list.

$\quad$ Since there are 11 values, the middle value is

$\quad \frac{1}{2}(11 + 1)$ i.e. the 6th value.

$\quad$ The 6th value is 61 $\Rightarrow$ the median = 61.

(ii) The lower quartile is the value that is $\frac{1}{4}$ way through the distribution.

$\quad$ This value is found by getting $\frac{1}{4}(11 + 1) =$ the 3rd value.

$\quad$ The 3rd value is 52 $\Rightarrow$ the lower quartile $(Q_1) = 52$.

(iii) The upper quartile is the value that is $\frac{3}{4}$ way through the distribution.

$\quad$ This value is found by getting $\frac{3}{4}(11 + 1) =$ 9th value.

$\quad$ This ninth value is 73 $\Rightarrow$ the upper quartile $(Q_3) = 73$.

(iv) The interquartile range $= Q_3 - Q_1$

$\qquad\qquad\qquad\qquad\quad = 73 - 52$

$\qquad\qquad\qquad\qquad\quad = 21$

Note: If there is an even number of values in a distribution, e.g.,

$$2, \quad 5, \quad 6, \quad 8, \quad \boxed{9, \quad 12,} \quad 15, \quad 17, \quad 20, \quad 25$$

The middle value is $\frac{1}{2}(10 + 1) = \frac{1}{2}(11) = 5\frac{1}{2}$th value

This is the average of the 5th and 6th values.

The median is $\frac{1}{2}(9 + 12) = \frac{1}{2}(21) = 10\frac{1}{2}$.

Exercise 8.2

1. Find the range for each of the following sets of data:
   - (i) 6, 3, 8, 2, 9, 5, 10
   - (ii) 21, 16, 72, 40, 67, 65, 55, 34, 17, 48, 32, 19, 44, 61, 73
   - (iii) 8, 2, 9, 6, 7, 10, 12, 13, 5, 12, 10, 8, 10, 4

2. Miss Moore gave her class a maths test.
   Here are the marks for the girls:

   7, 5, 8, 5, 2, 8, 7, 4, 7, 10, 3, 7, 4, 3, 6

   What is   (i)   the median mark   (ii)   the range of marks?

   The median mark for the boys in her class was 7 and the range of marks for the boys was 4.
   By comparing the results, explain whether the boys or girls did better in the test.

3. Nine students submitted their assignments which were marked out of 40.
   The marks obtained were:

   37, 34, 34, 29, 27, 27, 10, 4, 34

   - (i) Write down the range of marks.   (ii) Write down the median mark.
   - (iii) Find   (a)   the lower quartile
               (b)   the upper quartile
               (c)   the interquartile range.

4. Find   (i)   the lower quartile
            (ii)   the upper quartile
            (iii) the interquartile range
   for this set of data:

   4, 12, 7, 6, 10, 5, 11, 14, 2, 3, 9

5. Here are the times, in minutes, for a bus journey:

   15, 7, 9, 12, 9, 19, 6, 11, 9, 16, 8

   - (i)   Find the range of these times.   (ii)   Find the lower quartile.
   - (iii) Find the upper quartile.   (iv)   Write down the interquartile range.

6. A group of boys and girls took a French test. These are the marks which the boys got:

13, 14, 14, 15, 14, 14, 15, 17, 16, 14, 16, 12

(i) Find the range of the boys' marks.

(ii) Calculate the mean mark of the boys.

The mean mark for the girls in the class was 13.2 and the girls' marks had a range of 7.

(iii) Make two statements about the differences between the boys' and girls' marks in the French test.

7. Conor played nine rounds of crazy golf. Here are his scores:

51, 53, 50, 41, 59, 64, 66, 65, 50

Find   (i)   the range   (ii)   the lower quartile

              (iii)   the upper quartile   (iv)   the interquartile range.

8. A greengrocer sold bags of apples from different countries.
A bag contained 9 French apples.

The weight of each apple is given below, in grams.

101, 107, 98, 109, 115, 103, 96, 112, 104

(i) Calculate the mean weight of a French apple.

(ii) Find the range of the weights of the French apples.

Another bag contained 9 South African apples.
Their mean weight was 107 g and their range was 19 g.

(iii) Make two comments on the weights of the apples in the two bags.

9. A set of cards has these numbers on them

(i) Find five cards from this set with median 6 and range 4.

(ii) Find four cards with median 6 and range 3.

10. Solve these two problems:

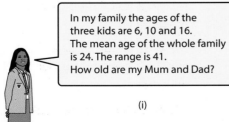

In my family the ages of the three kids are 6, 10 and 16.
The mean age of the whole family is 24. The range is 41.
How old are my Mum and Dad?

(i)

There are 5 children in my family.
The youngest is 8 and I am 15.
The median child's age is 13.
The range of childrens' ages is 17.
The mean of our ages is 14.
How old are we?

(ii)

11. The PE teacher in a school measures the time, in seconds, it takes the members of the football team and the hockey team to run 100 metres.

Football team

13   14   15   11   14   12   12   13   11   13   15

Hockey team

12   13   14   11   14   16   15   13   15   17   11

  (i) Calculate the mean, median and range for each team.
 (ii) Which group do you think is the faster?
        Give a reason for your answer.

Section 8.3 Deciding which average to use ———————

The three averages, the **mean**, the **mode** and the **median** are all useful but one may be more appropriate than the others in different situations.

The **mode** is useful when you want to know, for example, which shoe size is the most common.

The **mean** is useful for finding a 'typical' value when most of the data is closely grouped. The mean may not give a typical value if the data is very spread out or if it includes a few values that are very different from the rest. These values are known as **outliers**.

Take, for example, a small company where the chief executive earns €12 100 a month and the other eleven employees earn €2500 each a month.

Here the mean monthly salary is €3300 which is not typical of the monthly salaries.

In situations like this, the **median** or middle value may be more typical.

The table below, which compares the advantages and disadvantages of each type of average, should help you make the correct decision.

Average	Advantages	Disadvantages
Mode	› Easy to find › Not influenced by extreme values	› May not exist › Not very useful for further analysis
Median	› Unaffected by extremes › Easy to calculate if data is ordered	› Not always a given data value › Not very useful for further analysis
Mean	› Uses all the data › Easy to calculate › Very useful for further analysis	› Distorted by extreme results › Mean is not always a given data value

Example 1

There are 10 apartments in a block.
On a particular day the number of letters delivered to each of the
apartments is
$$2, 0, 5, 3, 4, 0, 1, 0, 3, 15$$
Calculate the mean, mode and median number of letters.
Which of these averages is the most suitable to represent this data?
Give a reason for your answer.

$$\text{Mean} = \frac{2 + 0 + 5 + 3 + 4 + 0 + 1 + 0 + 3 + 15}{10} = \frac{33}{10} = 3.3$$

Mode $= 0$

Median: 0, 0, 0, 1, 2, 3, 3, 4, 5, 15

$$\text{Median} = \frac{2 + 3}{2} = \frac{5}{2} = 2\frac{1}{2}$$

Here the mean has been distorted by the large number of letters delivered to one
apartment. It is, therefore, not a good measure of the 'typical' number of letters
delivered.
Neither is the mode a good measure of the 'typical' number of letters,
since 7 out of 10 apartments do receive some letters.
The median is the best measure of the 'typical' number of letters delivered since
half of the apartments receive more than the median and half receive less than
the median.

Exercise 8.3

1. Decide which average you would use for each of the following.
   Give a reason for your answer.
   (i) The average mark in an examination.
   (ii) The average uniform size for all the pupils in a class.
   (iii) The average height of the players in a basketball team.
   (iv) The colours of the cars sold by a garage.
   (v) The average salary of seven people who work for a small company.

2. The weights, in kilograms, of a boat crew are:

   96, 86, 94, 96, 91, 95, 90, 96, 43

   Calculate (i) their median weight
   (ii) their mean weight.

   Which of these two averages best describes the data above?
   Give a reason for your answer.

3. Find   (i) the mean   (ii) the median   of these numbers:

      9, 11, 11, 15, 17, 18, 100

Which of these two averages would you chose to best describe these numbers?

4. Shane recorded the midday temperatures for one week during his holiday in Spain.

Day	1	2	3	4	5	6	7
Midday temperature (°C)	32	30	30	28	33	31	30

   (i) Find the mean midday temperature.
  (ii) Give a reason why the mean is appropriate for this data.

5.   (i) Find the mean of this set of numbers:

      37, 26, 37, 18, 18, 20, 26, 18, 37, 37, 18.

  (ii) Why is the mode a bad choice of average in this case?

6. Find   (i) the mean   (ii) the median   for the following set of data:

      3, 5, 4, 7, 29, 9, 2, 4, 10, 8

Which of these two averages is the more suitable to represent the data?
Give a reason for your answer.

7. Katie is word processing her college assignment. She records the number of errors she makes on each page. These are the numbers of errors she recorded:

      6, 19, 14, 17, 51, 16, 20, 13, 16

   (i) Write down the modal number of errors.
  (ii) Find the median number of errors.
 (iii) Calculate the mean number of errors, correct to one decimal place.
 (iv) Write down the average which best represents this data.
      Explain your answer.

8. The annual salaries of the employees in a small company are listed below:

      €30,000, €25,000, €24,000, €22,000, €20,000, €105,000

Find   (i) the mean salary
       (ii) the median salary.
     (iii) Why can't you find the mode?
Which of the averages, mean or median, best represents the 'typical' salary?

9. A youth club leader gets a discount on cans of drinks if she buys one size only.
She took a vote on which size people wanted. The results were as follows:

Size of can (ml)	100	200	330	500
Number of votes	9	12	19	1

Mode = 330 ml
Median = 200 ml
Mean = 245.6 ml, correct to one decimal place.

Which size can should she buy?
Explain your answer.

Section 8.4 Frequency distributions

The table below shows the numbers of emails received in a day by 31 people in an office.

Number of emails	0	1	2	3	4	5	6	7
Frequency (number of people)	4	11	8	6	1	0	0	1

This table is called a **frequency distribution table**.
From the table we can see that the number of people who received 3 emails is 6.

We will now show how to find the **mode**, **median** and **mean** of a frequency distribution.
The frequency table below shows the numbers of letters in the answers to a crossword.

No. of letters in word	3	4	5	6	7
Frequency	3	4	9	5	2

The **mode** is the number of letters (in the word) that occurs most frequently.
Thus the mode is 5 as it occurs more often than any other number.

The **median** is the middle number in the distribution.

The total frequency is $3 + 4 + 9 + 5 + 2$, i.e., 23.

The middle value of 23 values is $\frac{1}{2}(23 + 1)$, i.e., the 12th value.

The 23 values could be listed like this:

$$3 \quad 3 \quad 3 \quad 4 \quad 4 \quad 4 \quad 4 \quad 5 \quad 5 \quad 5 \quad 5 \quad \boxed{5} \quad 5 \quad 5 \quad 5 \quad 5 \quad 6 \quad 6 \quad 6 \quad 6 \quad 6 \quad 7 \quad 7$$

middle value

The middle number in this list is the 12th number.
This number is 5.
∴   the median = 5

Note: The median can be read from the table without listing all the numbers.
We take the frequency row and find the column that contains the 12th number.
The sum of the first two frequencies is $3 + 4 = 7$.
The sum of the first three frequencies is $3 + 4 + 9 = 16$.
Thus the 12th value occurs in the third column, where the number of letters in the word is 5.
∴   the median = 5

The mean of a frequency distribution

The table below shows the marks (from 1 to 10) scored by the 20 pupils in a class.

Marks	1	2	3	4	5	6	7	8	9	10
No. of pupils	1	1	1	3	5	3	2	2	1	1

The average or mean mark of this distribution is found by dividing the total number of marks by the total number of pupils.

To find the total number of marks we multiply each mark (or *variable*) by the number of pupils (*frequency*) who received that mark.

$\therefore$ the mean $= \dfrac{1(1) + 2(1) + 3(1) + 4(3) + 5(5) + 6(3) + 7(2) + 8(2) + 9(1) + 10(1)}{1 + 1 + 1 + 3 + 5 + 3 + 2 + 2 + 1 + 1}$

$= \dfrac{110}{20} = 5.5$ marks

If x stands for the variable and f stands for the frequency, then

$$\text{mean} = \frac{\Sigma fx}{\Sigma f}$$

$$\boxed{\text{Mean} = \frac{\Sigma fx}{\Sigma f}}$$

where Σfx is the sum of all the variables multiplied by the corresponding frequencies and Σf is the sum of the frequencies.

Example 1

If the mean of the frequency distribution below is 3, find the value of x.
Write down the mode of the distribution.

Goals scored	1	2	3	4	5	6
Number of matches	7	8	4	4	3	x

Mean $= \dfrac{7(1) + 8(2) + 4(3) + 4(4) + 3(5) + x(6)}{7 + 8 + 4 + 4 + 3 + x}$

$= \dfrac{7 + 16 + 12 + 16 + 15 + 6x}{26 + x} = \dfrac{66 + 6x}{26 + x}$

Since the mean $= 3$ $\Rightarrow$ $\dfrac{66 + 6x}{26 + x} = 3$

$\Rightarrow \quad 66 + 6x = 3(26 + x)$

$\Rightarrow \quad 66 + 6x = 78 + 3x$

$\Rightarrow \quad 3x = 12$

$\Rightarrow \quad x = 4$

The mode $= 2$, as 2 occurs with the greatest frequency.

Exercise 8.4

1. The following table gives the numbers of goals scored in 60 matches on a particular weekend:

Goals scored	1	2	3	4	5	6
No. of matches	12	16	10	8	6	8

(i) Write down the mode of the distribution.

(ii) Find the median number of goals scored.

2. Calculate the mean of this frequency distribution:

Variable (x)	1	2	3	4	5	6
Frequency (f)	9	9	6	4	7	3

3. A test consisted of 10 questions, 1 mark per question, and 0 for an incorrect solution. The following table shows how a class of students scored in the test:

Marks	3	4	5	6	7	8	9
No. of students	3	2	6	10	0	3	1

   (i) How many students were in the class?
   (ii) Write down the mode of the data.
   (iii) Calculate the mean mark per student.
   (iv) How many students scored better than the mean mark?
   (v) Find the median mark.

4. Paula has 6 people in her family. She wonders how many people are in her friends' families. She asks each of her friends and records the information in a table.

Number in family	2	3	4	5	6	7	8
Frequency	2	4	6	5	2	0	1

   (i) Write down the modal number of people in the family.
   (ii) Find the median number of persons per family.
   (iii) Calculate the mean of the distribution.

5. Carol is trying to estimate how many words she has written in an essay. She records the number of words she wrote on each line of one page. Her results are given in the table below.

Words per line	10	11	12	13	14	15
No. of lines	1	3	6	9	7	4

   (i) How many lines in total were there on the page?
   (ii) How many lines contained 14 words?
   (iii) What was the modal number of words per line?
   (iv) Find the median number of words per line.
   (v) Calculate the mean of the distribution.

6. The table below shows the number of goals scored in 100 hockey matches on a particular Saturday.

Goals scored	0	1	2	3	4	5
No. of matches	10	25	30	25	10	0

   (i) Write down the modal number of goals scored.
   (ii) Calculate the mean of the distribution.
   (iii) Find the greatest number of matches that could have ended in a draw.
   (iv) How many matches could have ended in a two-all draw?

7. If the mean of the frequency distribution below is 2, find the value of x.

Variable	0	2	3	4
Frequency	4	3	x	3

8. The mean mark from the following frequency distribution table was found to be 6. Calculate the value of y.

Marks	3	5	8
No. of students	3	y	7

9. The frequency table below has two missing values.

Variable (x)	1	3	4	6	
Frequency (f)	2	4	6		3

(i) The range of x is 7 and the sum of the frequencies is 20.
Use this information to complete the table.
(ii) What is the modal value of x?
(iii) Find the mean value of x.

Section 8.5 Grouped frequency distributions ———————

1. The Mean

When dealing with a large number of variables, such as the ages of people in a certain district, it is often convenient to arrange the data in **groups** or **classes**.
Thus, when recording the ages of people, the results could be grouped (0–9) years, (10–19) years … etc.

The grouped frequency distribution table below shows the marks (out of 25) achieved by 50 students in a test.

Marks achieved	1–5	6–10	11–15	16–20	21–25
No. of students	11	12	15	9	3

While it is not possible to find the exact mean of a grouped frequency distribution, we can find an estimate of the mean by taking the **mid-interval value** of each class.
The mid-interval value in the (1–5) class is found by adding 1 and 5 and dividing by 2,

i.e., $\dfrac{1 + 5}{2} = 3$

Similarly, the mid-interval value of the (6–10) class is $\dfrac{6 + 10}{2} = 8$.

The table given above is reproduced again with the mid-interval values written in smaller size over each class interval.

	3	8	13	18	23
Marks achieved	1–5	6–10	11–15	16–20	21–25
No. of students	11	12	15	9	3

$$\text{Mean} = \frac{\Sigma fx}{\Sigma f} = \frac{11(3) + 12(8) + 15(13) + 9(18) + 3(23)}{11 + 12 + 15 + 9 + 3} = \frac{555}{50} = 11.1$$

2. The Mode and the Median

The table below gives the daily sales of mobile phones in a local shop.

No. of phones	0–4	5–9	10–14	15–19	20–24
Frequency	5	8	4	9	3

From this **grouped** table we cannot give the exact mode, but we can say that the **modal class** is the interval (15–19) because this interval contains the greatest frequency.

When you are dealing with grouped data, you will never be able to state what the median is, but you can identify the class interval in which the median lies.

In the table above, the total frequency is 5 + 8 + 4 + 9 + 3, i.e., 29.

The middle value of this distribution is $\frac{1}{2}(29 + 1)$, i.e., the 15th value.

The sum of the first two frequencies is 5 + 8 = 13.

The sum of the first three frequencies is 5 + 8 + 4 = 17.

Thus the 15th value lies in the class interval (10–14).

∴ the median lies in the (10–14) class interval.

Exercise 8.5

1. People attending a course were asked to choose one of the whole numbers from 1 to 12. The results were recorded as follows:

Number	1–3	4–6	7–9	10–12
No. of people	3	17	2	8

   (i) Write down the modal class of the distribution.
   (ii) Use the mid-interval value of each class to estimate the mean of the distribution.
   (iii) In which interval does the median lie?

2. The ages of children in a youth-club are given in the following table:

Ages (in years)	10–12	12–14	14–16	16–18	18–20
No. of children	12	24	18	12	4

   (i) What is the modal age group?
   (ii) Use the mid-interval value of each class to estimate the mean of the distribution, giving your answer to the nearest half year.
   (iii) In which interval does the median lie?

3. Use the mid-interval values to estimate the mean of the following frequency distribution:

Class	14–16	16–18	18–20	20–22	22–24
Frequency	1	5	12	3	0

Give your answer correct to one decimal place.

4. The time taken by 20 students to run a cross-country course were noted, to the nearest minute, and the results are given in the following table:

Time (in minutes)	12–14	15–17	18–20	21–23
No. of students	3	5	8	4

    (i) Use the mid-interval value of each class to estimate the mean of the distribution, giving your answer correct to the nearest minute.
   (ii) In which interval does the median lie?

5. The ages of some people watching a film are given in this frequency table:

Age (in years)	10–20	20–30	30–40	40–50
No. of people	4	15	11	10

    (i) Use the mid-interval value of each class to estimate the mean of the distribution, giving your answer correct to the nearest year.
   (ii) In which interval does the median lie?

6. One hundred people were asked to record the number of mobile phonecalls they received on a particular day. The results are shown in the table below.

No. of calls	0–4	5–9	10–14	15–19	20–24
Frequency	45	29	17	8	1

    (i) In which interval does the median lie?
   (ii) What is the modal group?
  (iii) Use the mid-interval values to estimate the mean number of calls. Give your answer correct to the nearest whole number.

Section 8.6 Standard deviation

Consider the marks scored in two tests shown below:

English	46	48	51	53	64	67	70
Mathematics	14	38	49	58	67	84	89

The mean in each test is 57, but the spread of marks in the tests is quite different.
While the mean gives an indication of the central or typical value, very often the spread or **dispersion** of the marks about the mean is more important.

One of the most important and frequently-used measures of spread is called **standard deviation**. It shows how much variation there is from the average (mean). It may be thought of as the average difference of the scores from the mean, that is, how far they are away from the mean. A low standard deviation indicates that the data points tend to be very close to the mean; a high standard deviation indicates that the data is spread out over a large range of values.

> The Greek letter σ is used to denote standard deviation.

Take, for example, all adult men in Ireland. The average height is about 177 cm with a standard deviation of about 8 cm.
For this large population, about 68% of the men have a height within 8 cm of the mean.

For any large population we can make the following much stronger statement which is generally called the **Empirical Rule**.

The Empirical Rule

> For any large population with mean $\bar{x}$ and standard deviation σ
> (i)   about 68% of the values will lie within one standard deviation of the mean, that is, between $\bar{x} + \sigma$ and $\bar{x} - \sigma$
> (ii) about 95% of the values will lie within two standard deviations of the mean
> (iii) almost all (99.7%) will lie within three standard deviations of the mean.

Procedure for finding the standard deviation

The steps used to find the standard deviation of a set of numbers are as follows:

1. Calculate the mean of the numbers. This is written $\bar{x}$.

2. Find the deviation (or difference) of each variable, x, from the mean. This is denoted by $(x - \bar{x})$.

3. Square each of these deviations, i.e., find $(x - \bar{x})^2$.

4. Find the sum (Σ) of these values, i.e., find $\Sigma(x - \bar{x})^2$.

5. Divide this result by n, the number of numbers.
   This gives $\dfrac{\Sigma(x - \bar{x})^2}{n}$.

6. Finally, get the square root of the result in **5**.

   There is no need to use this formula if you can remember the steps listed above.
   Alternatively, you may use a calculator.

> Standard deviation
> $$\sigma = \sqrt{\dfrac{\Sigma(x - \bar{x})^2}{n}}$$

Example 1

Find the standard deviation of the numbers 6, 9, 10, 12, 13.

The mean $= \dfrac{6 + 9 + 10 + 12 + 13}{5} = \dfrac{50}{5} = 10.$

$$\sigma = \sqrt{\dfrac{(6 - 10)^2 + (9 - 10)^2 + (10 - 10)^2 + (12 - 10)^2 + (13 - 10)^2}{5}}$$

$$= \sqrt{\dfrac{(-4)^2 + (-1)^2 + (0)^2 + (2)^2 + (3)^2}{5}}$$

$$= \sqrt{\dfrac{16 + 1 + 0 + 4 + 9}{5}} = \sqrt{\dfrac{30}{5}} = \sqrt{6} = 2.45$$

∴   the standard deviation is 2.45

Finding the Standard Deviation of a Frequency Distribution

When finding the standard deviation from a frequency distribution, the deviation of each variable from the mean is squared and then multiplied by the frequency (f) of that variable. The result is then divided by the sum of the frequencies.
Finally, we get the square root of the result.

This procedure can be represented by the formula

$$\sqrt{\dfrac{\Sigma f(x - \bar{x})^2}{\Sigma f}}$$ where $\Sigma f(x - \bar{x})^2$ is the sum of the $f(x - \bar{x})^2$ column and Σf is the sum of the frequencies.

The worked example below will show how to lay out your work when finding the standard deviation of a frequency distribution.

Example 2

Find the standard deviation of the following frequency distribution:

Variable (x)	1	2	3	4	5	6
Frequency (f)	9	9	6	4	7	3

First find the mean of the distribution.

The mean $= \dfrac{(9 \times 1) + (9 \times 2) + (6 \times 3) + (4 \times 4) + (7 \times 5) + (3 \times 6)}{9 + 9 + 6 + 4 + 7 + 3}$

$\Rightarrow \quad \bar{x} = \dfrac{114}{38} = 3$

Now set out a table like this.

x	f	$x - \bar{x}$	$(x - \bar{x})^2$	$f(x - \bar{x})^2$
1	9	−2	4	36
2	9	−1	1	9
3	6	0	0	0
4	4	1	1	4
5	7	2	4	28
6	3	3	9	27

$$\downarrow \qquad\qquad\qquad\qquad\qquad\qquad\qquad\qquad \downarrow$$
$$\Sigma f = 38 \qquad\qquad\qquad\qquad\qquad\qquad \Sigma f(x - \bar{x})^2 = 104$$

$$\sigma = \sqrt{\frac{\Sigma f(x - \bar{x})^2}{\Sigma f}} = \sqrt{\frac{104}{38}} = 1.65$$

Note: To calculate the standard deviation of a grouped frequency distribution, take the mid-interval values of the variables and proceed as in Example 2 above.

Use of calculator to find standard deviation

The tedious work involved in calculating the standard deviation of a large set of data can be substantially reduced by using a scientific calculator.

In the following examples, we will use the **Casio fx-83ES** calculator to illustrate the keys and steps involved in finding standard deviation.

Example 3

Find (a) the mean (b) the standard deviation of the following sets of numbers:
(i) 5, 3, 1, 8, 2   (ii) 10, 6, 2, 16, 4

(i) Key in ⌊MODE⌋ and select ⌊2⌋ for statistics mode.

Then select ⌊1⌋ for 1 − VAR.

Now input the numbers ⌊5⌋ ⌊=⌋
⌊3⌋ ⌊=⌋
⌊1⌋ ⌊=⌋
⌊8⌋ ⌊=⌋
⌊2⌋ ⌊=⌋

CASIO		*fx-83ES*
	X	FREQ
1	5	1
2	3	1
3	1	1
4	8	1
5	2	1

To get your answers, key in [AC] to clear, and [SHIFT] [1] to go to menu.

Now select [5] to get statistics on variables.

Then select [2] for $\bar{x}$ (the mean), then [=]

The mean $\bar{x}$ is 3.8.

To proceed to get the standard deviation, key in [AC] to clear.

Now key in [SHIFT] [1] to go to menu and select [5] to get statistics on variables.

Now key in [3] for $x\,\sigma\,n$ (standard deviation) [=]

The result is 2.4819… = 2.5

∴   standard deviation = 2.5

(ii)   10, 6, 2, 16, 4.

Here are the sequence of keys to find the mean and standard deviation.

[MODE] [2] [1]

[10] [=] [6] [=] [2] [=] [16] [=] [4] [=]

[AC] [SHIFT] [1] [5] [2] [=]   7.6 = mean

[AC] [SHIFT] [1] [5] [3] [=]   4.963869… = 5.0 = standard deviation

Example 4

The following frequency distribution table shows the number of birdies scored per round of golf.

No. of birdies	0	1	2	3	4	5	6
Frequency	5	6	4	6	3	1	0

Find the mean and standard deviation, correct to one decimal place.

Key in [MODE] and select [2] for statistics mode.

The select [1] for 1 − VAR and input variables.

[0] [=]   [5] [=]
[1] [=]   ◄ REPLAY ►   [6] [=]
[2] [=]   [4] [=]
[3] [=]   [6] [=]
[4] [=]   [3] [=]
[5] [=]   [1] [=]
[6] [=]   [0] [=]

CASIO		fx-83ES
	X	FREQ
1	0	5
2	1	6
3	2	4
4	3	6
5	4	3
6	5	1
7	6	0

For answers key in

AC SHIFT 1 5 2 = 1.96 = 2.0 = mean (birdies per round)

AC SHIFT 1 5 3 = 1.4554... = 1.5 = standard deviation

∴ Mean = 2.0 and standard deviation = 1.5

Exercise 8.6

1. Calculate the standard deviation of each of the following arrays of numbers, giving your answer correct to one decimal place:
   (i) 2, 5, 6, 7
   (ii) 3, 6, 7, 9, 10
   (iii) 2, 4, 6, 8, 10
   (iv) 1, 3, 7, 9, 10
   (v) 8, 12, 15, 9
   (vi) 1, 3, 4, 6, 10, 12

   Use your calculator to verify your answer in each case.

2. Show that the following sets of numbers have the same standard deviation:
   (a) 2, 3, 5, 7, 8
   (b) 6, 7, 9, 11, 12

3. Find the standard deviation of the numbers

   2, 3, 4, 5, 6.

   Now find the standard deviation of these numbers

   12, 13, 14, 15, 16.

   (i) What is the relationship between the two sets of numbers?
   (ii) What is the relationship between their standard deviations?
   (iii) What conclusion can you draw from the results?

4. Verify that 2 is the mean of this distribution. Hence calculate the standard deviation, correct to 1 decimal place.

Variable	0	2	3	4
Frequency	4	3	2	3

5. Show that the mean of the given frequency distribution is 3 and hence find the standard deviation, correct to 2 decimal places.

Variable	1	2	3	4
Frequency	1	4	9	6

6. Calculate the standard deviation of the following frequency distribution, correct to 1 decimal place.

Variable	2	4	6	8
Frequency	4	3	0	2

7. Calculate the mean and hence the standard deviation of the following frequency distribution.

Variable	0	4	6	8
Frequency	4	3	2	3

8. Ms Byrne gave the 30 students in her class a quick spelling test.
   The marks obtained are presented in the table below.

Mark	0	1	2	3	4	5
Number of students	3	3	3	6	12	3

Calculate the mean and standard deviation of the distribution, correct to one decimal place.

9. The number of letters delivered to a business premises on each day of the 5-day working week were as follows:

   18, 26, 22, 34, 25

   (i) Calculate the mean number of letters delivered.
   (ii) Calculate the standard deviation, correct to one decimal place.
   (iii) If $\bar{x}$ is the mean and σ is the standard deviation, find the values of $\bar{x} + \sigma$ and $\bar{x} - \sigma$.
   (iv) On how many days is the number of letters delivered within one standard deviation of the mean?

10. The data below gives the number of books read in the last month by a class of 20 students.

Number of books, x	0	1	2	3	4
Number of students, f	2	5	6	5	2

Find the mean and standard deviation of the number of books.

11. Using the mid-interval values, find the standard deviation of the given grouped frequency distribution. Give your answer correct to 1 decimal place.

Class interval	1–3	3–5	5–7	7–9
Frequency	4	3	0	2

12. The following table shows the times taken by 15 pupils to solve a problem.

Time (in minutes)	2–4	4–6	6–10
No. of students	3	5	7

By taking mid-interval values, calculate
   (i) the mean
   (ii) the standard deviation.

13. There are two routes for a worker to get to his office. Both the routes involve delays due to traffic lights. He records the time it takes over a series of six journeys for each route. The results are shown in the table.

Route 1	15	15	11	17	14	12
Route 2	12	15	18	16	17	12

   (i) Work out the mean time taken for each route.
   (ii) Calculate the standard deviation of each of the two routes.
   (iii) Using your answers to (i) and (ii), suggest which route you would recommend. State your reason clearly.

Test yourself 8

1. (i) The mean of 3, 7, 8, 10, x is 6. Find x.
    (ii) The mean of 3, 3, y, 7, 8, 10, y is 7. Find y.

2. The number of goals scored by the 11 members of a hockey team in 2009 were as follows:

    6   0   8   12   2   1   2   9   1   0   11

    (i)   Find the median.
    (ii) Find the upper and lower quartiles.
    (iii) Find the interquartile range.

3. Jenny obtained these scores for the first eight modules of her course.

    63   49   51   52   70   67   52   76

    (i) Find her mean score.
    (ii) She needs a mean score of 62 over 9 modules to pass her course.
         What does she need to score in her ninth module?

4. The range for the eight numbers shown is 40.
    Find **two** possible values for the missing number.

5. These are the salaries of five employees in a small business.

    Mr A: €45 000   Mr B: €35 800   Mr C: €42 800
    Mr D: €45 000   Mr E: €170 600

    (i) Find the mean, median and mode of their salaries.
    (ii) Which does not give a fair average?
         Explain why in one sentence.

6. The mean of five numbers is 15.
    The numbers are in the ratio 1 : 2 : 3 : 4 : 5.
    Find the smallest number.

7. Find (i) the median (ii) the upper quartile (iii) the lower quartile for these numbers

    12   6   4   9   8   4   9   8   5   9   10

8. Ten men travelled to watch a rugby match.
    The mean age of the men was 25 years and
    the range of their ages was 6.
    Write each statement below and then write
    next to it whether it is
    (i) true   (ii) could be true   or (iii) false.

    (a) The youngest man was 18 years old.
    (b) All the men were at least 20 years old.
    (c) The oldest person was 4 years older than
         the youngest.
    (d) Every man was between 20 and 26 years old.

9. Ian had 16 boxes of matches.
He counted the number of matches in each box.
The table below gives his results.

No of matches per box	41	42	43	44
No. of boxes	2	7	4	3

(i) Write down the modal number of matches per box.
(ii) What is the median number of matches per box?
(iii) Calculate the mean number of matches per box.

10. Alan has six different trees in his small garden. He is a keen gardener and wishes to know how many trees his neighbours have. He records the number of trees in each garden on his road.

No. of trees	3–7	8–12	13–17	18–22
No. of gardens	4	9	5	3

(i) What is the modal group?
(ii) In which interval does the median lie?
(iii) Estimate the mean number of trees per garden, correct to one decimal place.

11. Find (i) the mean (ii) the standard deviation for these numbers:

   7, 11, 6, 8, 13

Give your answer to (ii) correct to one decimal place.

12. The times taken by a group of 16 students to run 100 metres are shown below:

Time (in seconds)	11	12	13	14
No. of students	2	5	6	3

Work out the mean and standard deviation of this data, correct to one decimal place in each case.

13. These are the scores of two players over six rounds of golf.

Rory	87	69	80	86	84	80
Darren	77	91	90	85	67	70

(i) Calculate the mean score for each player.
(ii) Use your calculator or otherwise to find the standard deviation of the scores for each player, correct to 1 decimal place.
Use the data to state whom you think is the better player.
Give a reason for your answer.

Summary of key points...

Averages

The **mode** is the value that occurs most often.

The **median** is the middle number in a list of numbers after they have been put in order.

The **mean** is found by adding up all the numbers and dividing by the number of numbers.

The mean of a frequency distribution is:

$$\text{Mean} = \frac{\Sigma fx}{\Sigma f}$$

Range and quartiles

Range	Largest value minus smallest value
Lower quartile, Q_1	The lower quartile is the value one-quarter of the way through the data.
Upper quartile, Q_3	The upper quartile is the value three-quarters of the way through the data.
Interquartile range	The interquartile range = upper quartile − lower quartile, i.e., $Q_3 - Q_1$

If there are n values in a data set,
$$Q_1 = \tfrac{1}{4}(n + 1)\text{th value}$$
$$Q_3 = \tfrac{3}{4}(n + 1)\text{th value}$$

Weighted mean

The weighted mean $= \dfrac{\Sigma wx}{\Sigma w}$, where w is the weight given to each value of x.

Which average to use

The **mode** is useful when we need the most frequent value.
It is the only average for categorical data.

The **median** gives the middle value and is useful when the data is very spread out.

The **mean** is useful when we need a 'typical' value when most of the data is fairly closely grouped. It may not be a good average if the data contains a few values very different from the rest.

Standard deviation

The standard deviation, σ, of a set of data is given by the formula on the right.

$$\sigma = \sqrt{\frac{\Sigma(x - \bar{x})^2}{n}}$$

The bigger the standard deviation the more spread out the data is.

When using a **calculator** to find the standard deviation of 10, 6, 2, 16, 4 use the following sequence of keys:

MODE 2 1

10 = 6 = 2 = 16 = 4 =

AC SHIFT 1 5 2 =   7.6 = mean

AC SHIFT 1 5 3 =   4.963869... = 5.0 = standard deviation

Area and Volume

chapter 9

Key words

perimeter	quadrilateral	parallelogram	trapezium	net
sector	circumference	arc	prism	cylinder	sphere
hemisphere	cone	Trapezoidal Rule	cross-section	ordinates

Section 9.1 Perimeter and area of triangles and quadrilaterals

The box below contains formulas for the areas and perimeters of some regular figures.

1. Rectangle

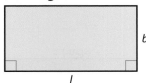

Area = $l \times b$
Perimeter = $2(l + b)$

2. Square

Area = x^2
Perimeter = $4x$

3. Triangle

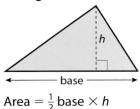

Area = $\frac{1}{2}$ base $\times h$

4. Parallelogram

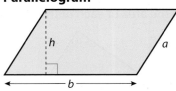

Area = $b \times h$
Perimeter = $2(a + b)$

5. Trapezium

A trapezium is a quadrilateral with two parallel sides.
Perimeter = sum of the lengths of the four sides
Area = $\frac{1}{2}(a + b) \times h$ or $\frac{1}{2}(a + b)h$

In words: Area is half the sum of the lengths
of the parallel sides multiplied by
the perpendicular height.

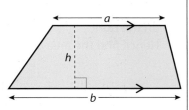

The theorem of Pythagoras

Many of the problems dealing with perimeter and area will involve the use of the theorem of Pythagoras which states that

$$x^2 = y^2 + z^2$$

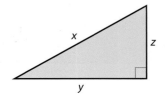

Example 1

Find the area of the given trapezium.

$$\text{Area} = \tfrac{1}{2}(a + b) \times h \text{ cm}^2$$
$$= \tfrac{1}{2}(20 + 12) \times 11$$
$$= \tfrac{1}{2}(32) \times 11$$
$$= 176 \text{ cm}^2$$

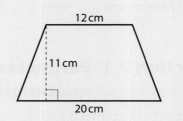

Exercise 9.1

1. The figure shows a rectangle 8 cm by 6 cm.
   Find   (i) its area
         (ii) its perimeter
         (iii) the length of the diagonal of the rectangle.

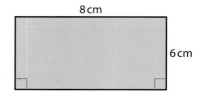

2. Find the area of each of the triangles shown below:

   (i) 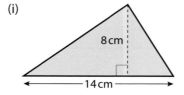   (ii) 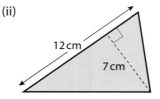   (iii)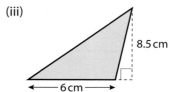

3. Find the area of the shaded portions of the diagram on the right.
   Hence find the area of the unshaded part.

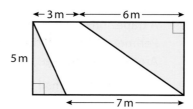

4. Find the value of x in each of these triangles:

(i)

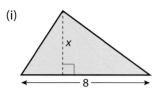

Area = 24 sq. units

(ii)

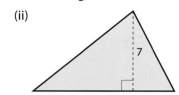

Area = 42 sq. units

(iii)

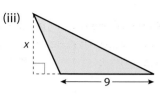

Area = 36 sq. units

5. (i) Write down the area of each triangle shown below.
   (ii) Use your answers in (i) above to find the value of h in each triangle.

(a)

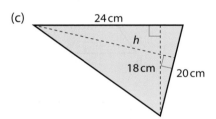

(b)

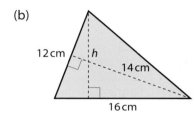

(c)

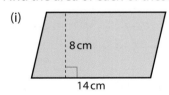

6. Find the area of each of these parallelograms:

(i)

(ii)

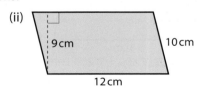

(iii)

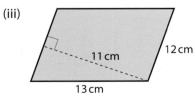

7. The perimeter of the given rectangle is 52 cm.

Find (i) its breadth
     (ii) its area.

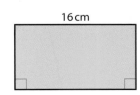

8. Find the area of each of the following figures:

(i)

(ii)

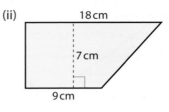

(iii)

9. ABCD is a parallelogram, as shown.

  (i) Calculate the area of the parallelogram.

  (ii) Work out the perpendicular distance from A to DC.

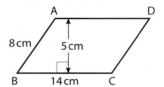

10. Work out the area of each of these trapeziums:

(i)

(ii)

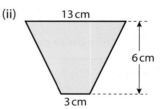

(iii)

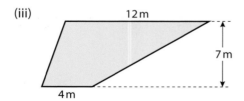

11. Calculate the area of each of these trapeziums:

(i)

(ii)

(iii)

12. (i) Write down an expression for the perimeter of the triangle in terms of x.
   (ii) If the perimeter of the triangle is 29, calculate the value of x.

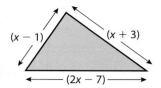

13. The area of each figure below is given.
   Find the perpendicular height, h, in each case.

   (i)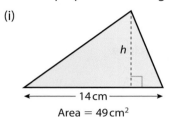
   14 cm
   Area = 49 cm²

   (ii)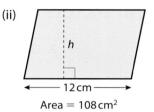
   12 cm
   Area = 108 cm²

   (iii)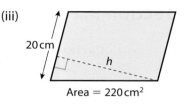
   20 cm
   Area = 220 cm²

14. James thinks that there is not enough information to find the perimeter of each of these shapes.
   Explain why James is wrong and find the perimeter of each shape.

   (i)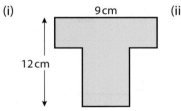
   9 cm
   12 cm

   (ii)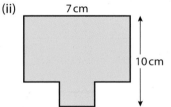
   7 cm
   10 cm

   (iii)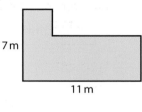
   7 m
   11 m

15. Dillon has five square tiles, each with side 1 cm. The tiles must be laid edge to edge.

   Where should he put the last tile to make a shape that has the largest perimeter?
   Where should he put the last tile to make a shape that has the smallest perimeter?

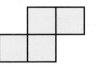

16. The area of the square ABCD is 36 cm².

   Find the area of the shaded square constructed with [AC] as one of its sides.

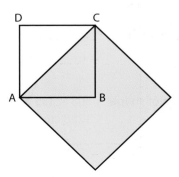

239

17. ABCD is a trapezium with [AB] parallel to [DC].
The lengths of [AB] and [CD] are in the ratio 1 : 2.
The perpendicular distance between [AB] and [DC] = 12 cm.
The area of ABCD = 72 cm².

Calculate the length of [AB].

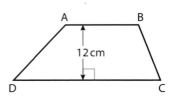

Section 9.2 Circles and sectors

1. Circle

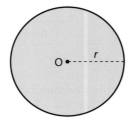

Area = πr^2

Circumference = $2\pi r$

2. Sector of a circle

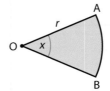

Area of OAB = $\dfrac{x}{360} \times \pi r^2$

Length of arc AB = $\dfrac{x}{360} \times 2\pi r$

Example 1

Work out the perimeter and area of the given figure.

Perimeter of semi-circle = πr
$= \pi \times 14$
$= 43.98 \dots$ using the π key
$= 44$ cm

Perimeter of shape $= 44 + 28 + (2 \times 35)$
$= 142$ cm

Area of semi-circle $= \dfrac{\pi r^2}{2}$

$= \dfrac{\pi \times 14^2}{2} = 307.87$ cm²
$= 308$ cm²

Area of shape $= 308 + (35 \times 28)$
$= 1288$ cm²

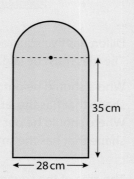

Example 2

Find (i) the area of the sector AOB
(ii) the length of the arc AB.

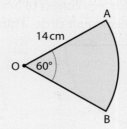

(i) Area of sector AOB

$= \dfrac{60°}{360°} \times \pi r^2$

$= \dfrac{1}{6} \times \pi \times 14^2$

$= \dfrac{\pi \times 14^2}{6}$

$= 102.6 \text{ cm}^2$

(ii) Length of arc AB

$= \dfrac{60°}{360°} \times 2\pi r$

$= \dfrac{1}{6} \times 2 \times \pi \times 14$

$= \dfrac{2 \times \pi \times 14}{6}$

$= 14.66 \text{ cm}^2$

$= 14.7 \text{ cm}^2$

Example 3

The area of a circle is 803.84 cm².
Find the length of the radius of the circle, using the π key on your calculator.

Area of circle $= \pi r^2$

$\Rightarrow \pi r^2 = 803.84$

$\Rightarrow r^2 = \dfrac{803.84}{\pi} = 255.87$

$r^2 = 255.87 \Rightarrow r = \sqrt{255.87} = 16 \text{ cm}$

Exercise 9.2

1. Use the π key on your calculator to find the circumference of each of these circles, correct to one decimal place.

(i)

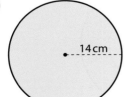

14 cm

(ii)

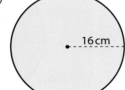

16 cm

(iii)

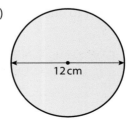

12 cm

2. Find the area of each of the circles in Question 1 in cm², correct to 1 decimal place.

3. Calculate each area correct to one decimal place.
They are either a semi-circle, a quarter circle or three-quarters of a circle.

(i)

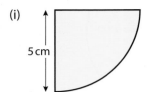

5 cm

(ii)

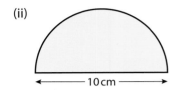

10 cm

(iii)

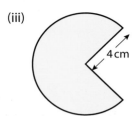

4 cm

4. Find the length of the arc AB in each of the sectors shown below.
Give each answer in cm, correct to 1 decimal place.

(i)

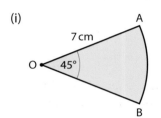

A
7 cm
O   45°
B

(ii)

O
30°
12 cm
A   B

(iii)

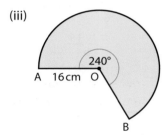

A   16 cm   O   240°
B

5. The diagram shows a sector of a circle, centre O.
The radius of the circle is 6 cm.
Angle AOB = 120°.

Work out the perimeter of the sector.
Give your answer in terms of π in its simplest form.

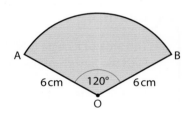

A   B
6 cm   120°   6 cm
O

6. The diagram on the right shows a rectangular
garden 35 m by 14 m. There is a semi-circular
flowerbed at each end. The shaded area is put
down to lawn. Find, correct to the nearest
whole number,

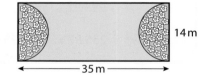

14 m

35 m

 (i) the combined area of the two flower beds
(ii) the perimeter of the lawn.

7. Calculate the area coloured blue,
correct to one decimal place.

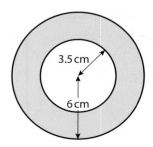

3.5 cm

6 cm

8. Calculate the area of the shaded segment of this quarter circle.
Give your answer in cm², correct to 1 decimal place.

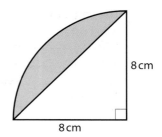

8 cm

8 cm

9. The diagram shows a star made by removing four identical quarter circles from the corners of a square of side 30 cm.
Find the area of the star in cm², correct to the nearest whole number.

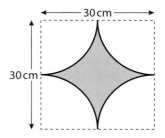

30 cm

30 cm

10. The diagram represents the plan of a sports field. The field is a rectangle with semicircular ends. The rectangle has length 100 m and width 70 m. The semicircles have diameter 70 m.

 (i) Work out the area of the field in m², correct to the nearest whole number

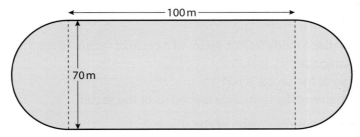

100 m

70 m

The field is to be covered in fertiliser that costs 5 cent per square metre.
(ii) Work out the cost of the fertiliser required for the field.

11. The area of a circle is 616 cm².
Find the length of the radius of the circle, correct to the nearest whole number.

12. Anto buys a pizza and shares it evenly among his six friends and himself.
If the pizza has a radius of 20 cm, what is the area of each slice, correct to the nearest cm².

13. The Dublin Eye has a radius of 30 m.
    A full rotation lasts 13 minutes.
    (i) How far do you travel in that 13 minutes
         on the wheel, correct to the nearest whole
         number?
    (ii) What is the speed of the wheel in metres
         per second, correct to two decimal places?

14. A piece of wire 72 cm in length is bent into a semicircle
    and diameter, as shown.
    Find the length of the diameter, correct to the nearest cm.

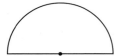

15. Kate is waiting for a train.
    It's 3 o'clock and her train is due at twenty-five to four.
    If the train is on time and the minute hand of the
    station clock is 20 cm long, what area will the minute
    hand sweep through before Kate catches her train?
    Give your answer to the nearest whole number.

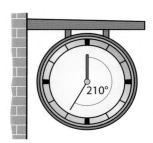

16. Here is a shape made from a sector of a circle of radius 16 cm
    and a semicircle.
    The angle of the sector is 60°.
    The diameter of the semicircle is a radius of the sector.

    (i) Work out the perimeter of the shape.
    (ii) Work out the area of the shape.
    Give each answer correct to the nearest whole number.

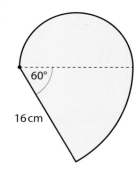

Section 9.3 Rectangular solids – prisms

1. Rectangular solid

Volume $= l \times b \times h$

Surface area $= 2lb + 2lh + 2bh$

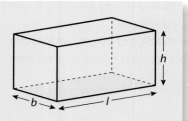

2. Right prisms

A **prism** is an object with a uniform **cross-section**.

 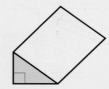

Volume of a prism = area of cross-section × length

$$= A \times l$$

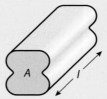

Example 1

Find the volume of the prism shown on
the right.

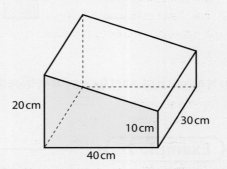

Volume = area of shaded cross-section × length

Area of cross-section consists of a rectangle
and a triangle, as shown.

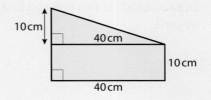

Area of cross-section $= (40 \times 10) + \frac{1}{2}(40 \times 10)$

$$= 400 + 200$$

$$= 600 \text{ cm}^2$$

Volume of prism = Area of cross-section × length

$$= (600 \times 30) \text{ cm}^3$$

$$= 18\,000 \text{ cm}^3$$

3. Nets and 3-D shapes

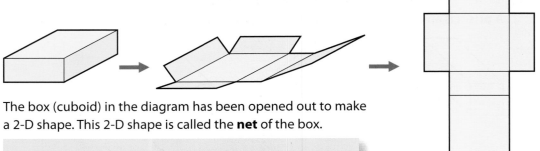

The box (cuboid) in the diagram has been opened out to make a 2-D shape. This 2-D shape is called the **net** of the box.

> A net is a 2-D shape that can be folded into a 3-D shape.

Here are two possible nets for a cube.

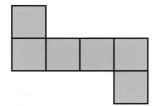 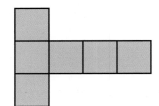

> There are 12 possible different nets of a cube.

This is a sketch of a net for a square-based pyramid.

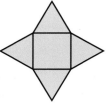

Example 2

The net of a rectangular box is shown. Draw a sketch of this box and find its volume.

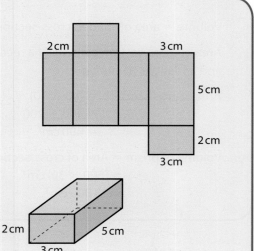

A sketch of the box is shown

Volume = length × breadth × height
= 5 cm × 3 cm × 2 cm
= 30 cm³

Exercise 9.3

1. Find the volume of each of these rectangular solids:

(i)

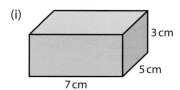

3 cm
5 cm
7 cm

(ii)

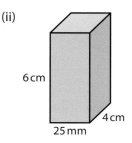

6 cm
4 cm
25 mm

(iii)

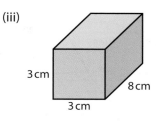

3 cm
3 cm
8 cm

2. Calculate (i) the volume
          (ii) the surface area
of the rectangular solid shown on the right.

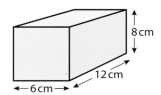

8 cm
12 cm
6 cm

3. The volume of the given rectangular solid is 2040 cm³.

Find the value of the height, h, in cm.

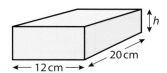

h
20 cm
12 cm

4. Find the missing side x in each case. All lengths are in cm.

(i)

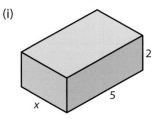

2
5
x

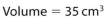

Volume = 35 cm³

(ii)

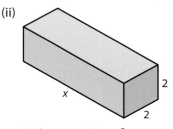

2
x
2

Volume = 24 cm³

(iii)

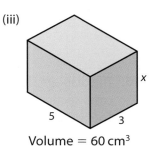

x
5
3

Volume = 60 cm³

5. Find the volume of each of these prisms:

(i)

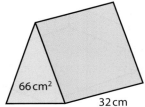

66 cm²
32 cm

(ii)

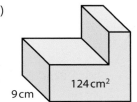

124 cm²
9 cm

(iii)

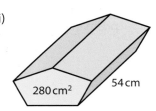

280 cm²
54 cm

247

6. Find the volume of each of these prisms:

(i)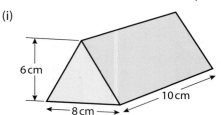

(ii)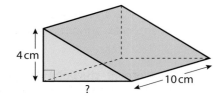

7. This triangular prism has a volume of 140 cm³.
Work out the length of the base of its
cross-section.

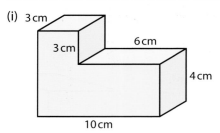

8. Work out the volume of each of these prisms:

(i)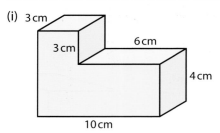

(ii)

9. The cross-section of this prism is a trapezium.
 (i) Find the area of this trapezium.
 (ii) Work out the volume of the prism.

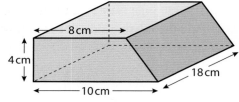

10. The diagram shows the
cross-section of a swimming pool.
The width of the swimming pool
is 6 m.
Work out the volume of water in
the pool.

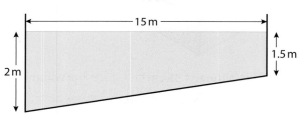

11. Work out the volume of this
prism in cm³.

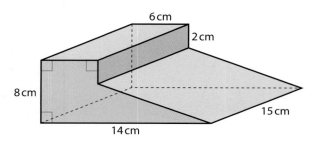

12. Here are nets of a cube.

A
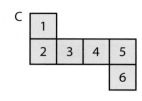

B
```
    5
4 1 2 3
    6
```

C
```
1
2 3 4 5
        6
```

Imagine that each of these nets is folded to make a cube.
For each net, which face could be opposite face 1 when folded?

13. This net is folded to make a cube.

   (i)   Which vertex will join to N?
  (ii)   Which line will join to [CD]?
 (iii)   Which line will join to [IH]?

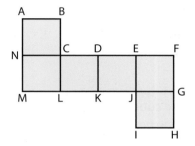

14. This net for a cube is to be made into a dice.
Copy this net and insert dots on the remaining
squares so that dots on opposite faces add up to 7.

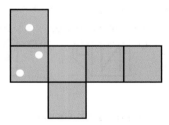

15. This is the net of a rectangular box.

Find (i) the surface area of the box
        (ii) the volume of the box.

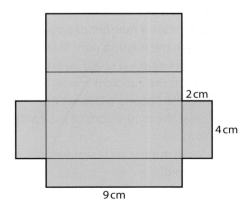

16. Here are the nets of some 3-D shapes. Identify the shapes.

(i)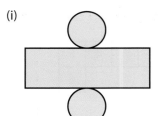

(ii)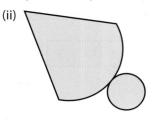

(iii)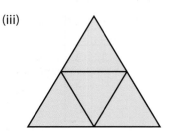

17. Draw the net of this triangular prism.

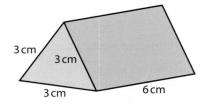

3 cm
3 cm
3 cm
6 cm

18. Which of the cubes below could have been made by folding the net on the right?

A

B

C

D

E

19. The diagram shows a partly-completed net for a cuboid drawn on a grid of 1 cm squares.

(i) What shape is needed to complete the net? Include its size.

(ii) There are a number of options for where to place the missing part. Make a list of the edges where it could be attached.

(iii) When the cuboid is made, which of the labelled points will meet A?

(iv) Give the dimensions of the completed cuboid.

(v) Work out the total surface area of the cuboid.

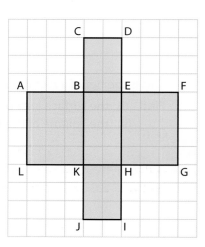

Section 9.4 Cylinders and spheres

Given below are the formulae you will need when dealing with cylinders, spheres and hemispheres.

---

1. The cylinder

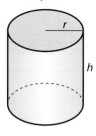 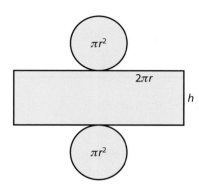

Volume $= \pi r^2 h$

Curved surface area $= 2\pi rh$

Total surface area of solid cylinder
$$= 2\pi rh + 2\pi r^2$$
$$= 2\pi r(h + r)$$

2. The sphere
Volume $= \frac{4}{3}\pi r^3$
Surface area $= 4\pi r^2$

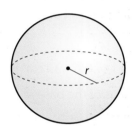

3. The hemisphere
Volume $= \frac{2}{3}\pi r^3$
Surface area of solid hemisphere $= 3\pi r^2$.

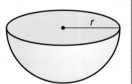

Example 1

Find (i) the volume
     (ii) the total surface area
of the solid cylinder shown.
Give your answer in terms of π.

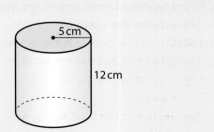

(i) Volume $= \pi r^2 h$

$= \pi \times 5^2 \times 12$

$= 300\pi \ \text{cm}^3$

(ii) Total surface area $= 2\pi r h + 2\pi r^2$

$= (2 \times \pi \times 5 \times 12) + (2 \times \pi \times 5^2)$

$= 120\pi + 50\pi$

$= 170\pi \ \text{cm}^2$

Example 2

The volume of a cylinder is $15\,840 \ \text{cm}^3$.
If the height is 35 cm, find the length of the radius of the base.

Volume $= 15\,840 \ \text{cm}^3$

$\Rightarrow \pi r^2 h = 15\,840$

$\Rightarrow \pi \times r^2 \times 35 = 15\,840$

$\Rightarrow r^2 = \dfrac{15\,840}{\pi \times 35}$

$\Rightarrow r^2 = 144.06$

$\Rightarrow r = \sqrt{144.06} = 12 \ \text{cm}$

The radius of the base $= 12$ cm

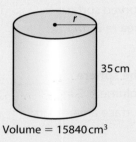

35 cm

Volume $= 15840 \ \text{cm}^3$

Equal volumes

If the volumes of two different shapes are equal, we write down the formula for the volume of each shape and then equate the two volumes. This enables us to get an unknown dimension in one of the two shapes.

Here are some examples of equal volumes:

> If liquid is poured from one shape into a container of a different shape, the volume of the liquid remains the same.
> If a solid object is immersed in liquid in a container, the volume of displaced water is equal to the volume of the immersed object.

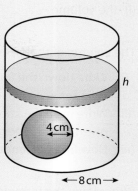

Example 3

A sphere of radius 4 cm is dropped into a cylinder partly filled with water. When the sphere is completely submerged, the level of water rises h cm.
If the radius of the cylinder is 8 cm, find the value of h.

In the given diagram, the volume of the sphere is equal to the volume of the shaded cylinder of height h.
Volume of sphere = Volume of cylinder

$$\Rightarrow \quad \tfrac{4}{3}\pi r^3 = \pi r^2 h$$
$$\Rightarrow \tfrac{4}{3}\pi(4)^3 = \pi(8)^2.h$$
$$\Rightarrow \tfrac{4}{3} \times 64 = 64h \; \dots \text{ divide both sides by } \pi$$
$$\Rightarrow \qquad\qquad \tfrac{4}{3} = h \; \dots \text{ divide both sides by } 64$$
$$\therefore h = \tfrac{4}{3} = 1\tfrac{1}{3}\,\text{cm}$$

Note: In example 3 above, we are given two solids of equal volume, i.e., the volume of the sphere equals the volume of the cylinder.

$$\Rightarrow \tfrac{4}{3}\pi(4)^3 = \pi(8)^2 h.$$

Here both sides of the equation contain π.
When this occurs, we divide both sides by π and so there is no need to substitute a value for π.

Exercise 9.4

1. Use the π key on your calculator to find the volume of each of these cylinders. Give your answers in cm³, correct to one decimal place.

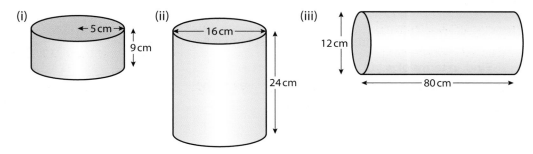

2. Find the total surface area of each of the solid cylinders shown in question 1. Give each answer correct to the nearest whole number.

3. A solid cylinder has radius 7 cm and height 10 cm. Taking $\pi = \frac{22}{7}$, find

    (i) the volume   (ii) the total surface area of the cylinder.

4. The volume of the given cylinder is 350π cm³.

    (i) Write down the formula for the volume of a
        cylinder.
    (ii) Write in all the known values in the formula,
         given that the height is 14 cm.
    (iii) Now find the length of the radius of the cylinder.

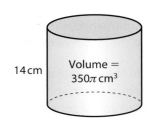

14 cm   Volume = 350π cm³

5. Write down the formula for the curved surface area of a cylinder.
The curved surface area of a cylinder is 110 cm².
If the height of the cylinder is 5 cm, find the length of the radius correct
to 1 decimal place.

6. The total surface area of a solid cylinder is 252π cm².
If the length of the radius of the base is 6 cm, find the height of the cylinder.

7. Find the volume of each of the following spheres, giving your answers correct to one
decimal place:

(i)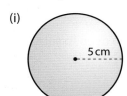
5 cm

(ii)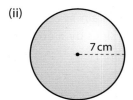
7 cm

(iii)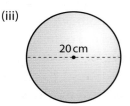
20 cm

8. Find the surface area of each of the spheres in Question 7.
Give each answer correct to the nearest whole number.

9. The length of the radius of a solid hemisphere is 5 cm.

    Find, in terms of π, (i) the volume
                      (ii) the total surface area of the
                         hemisphere.

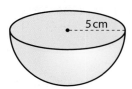
5 cm

10. The volume of a sphere is 288π cm³.

    (i) Find the length of the radius of the sphere.
    (ii) Find, in terms of π, its total surface area.

11. A container is in the shape of a cylinder on top of a hemisphere as shown. The cylinder has a radius of length 3 cm and the container has a total height of 15 cm.

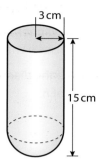

Calculate the volume of the container in cm³, correct to the nearest whole number.

12. The cylinder and the sphere shown on the right have equal volumes.

Find the length of the radius of the cylinder, correct to the nearest centimetre.

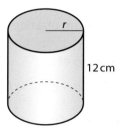
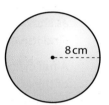

13. A cylinder has height $4\frac{1}{2}$ cm and radius length 2 cm.
This cylinder has the same volume as a hemisphere.
Find the radius of the hemisphere.

14. The diagram on the right shows a sphere of radius 7 cm fitting exactly into a cylinder, i.e., the sphere touches the cylinder at the top, bottom and sides.

  (i) Find the volume of the cylinder in cm³, correct to the nearest whole number.
 (ii) Show that the surface area of the sphere is equal to the curved surface area of the cylinder.
(iii) Find the radio:
       Volume of sphere : Volume of cylinder.

15. A sphere with radius of length 3 cm has a volume equal to eight times the volume of a sphere with radius of length r cm. Calculate r.

16. The height of a cylinder is equal to the length of its diameter.
The curved surface area of the cylinder is 100π cm². Calculate the height.

17. When a solid sphere of radius 6 cm is dropped into a cylinder partly filled with water, the level of the water rises h cm, as shown on the right.

   If the diameter of the cylinder is 16 cm, find the value of h.

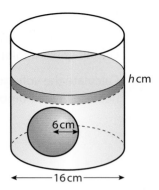
h cm

6 cm

16 cm

18. A wine glass is in the form of a hemisphere of radius 4 cm, as shown.
   Find its volume in terms of π.

4 cm

   A full cylindrical container of wine is just sufficient to fill 21 of these wine glasses.
   If the radius of the base of the cylinder is 8 cm, find its height.

19. Nine solid metal spheres, each of radius 2 cm, are dropped into a cylinder partly filled with water. If the spheres are totally immersed, find the increase in the height of the water if the radius of the cylinder is 3 cm.

20. Three tennis balls, each of diameter 7 cm, are sold in a cylindrical container. The internal diameter of the container is equal to the diameter of a tennis ball, and the height of the container is such that the tennis balls cannot move about. What fraction of the space within the container is occupied by the tennis balls?

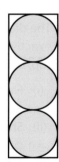

Section 9.5 The cone

The cone on the right is called a *right circular cone* as its vertex is directly above the centre of the base.
The perpendicular height $= h$.
The slant height $= l$.
The radius of the base $= r$.
By the *Theorem of Pythagoras* $l^2 = h^2 + r^2$.

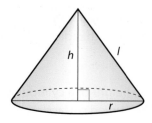
h l

r

The Cone

Volume of a cone $= \frac{1}{3}\pi r^2 h$

Curved surface area $= \pi r l$

Total surface area of solid cone $= \pi r l + \pi r^2$

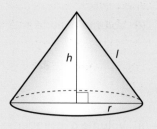

Example 1

The height of a cone is 12 cm and the radius of the base is 5 cm.
Using the π key on your calculator, find correct to 1 decimal place
(i) the volume   (ii) the curved surface area of the cone.

By the Theorem of Pythagoras
$$l^2 = 12^2 + 5^2$$
$$= 144 + 25 = 169$$
$$\therefore \quad l = \sqrt{169} = 13 \text{ cm}$$

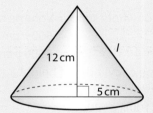

Volume of cone $= \frac{1}{3}\pi r^2 h$

$\qquad = \frac{1}{3} \times \pi \times 5^2 \times 12$

$\qquad = 314.2 \text{ cm}^3$

Curved Surface Area $= \pi r l$

$\qquad = \pi \times 5 \times 13$

$\qquad = 204.2 \text{ cm}^2$

Example 2

The diagram on the right represents the model of a
rocket ship. The model is made from a solid cylinder
and a solid cone. Both have a circular base of diameter
20 cm. The height of the cone is 24 cm.

  (i) Calculate the volume of the cone in terms of π.
 (ii) Find the height of the cylinder if the volume of
     the cylinder is 4 times the volume of the cone.
(iii) Find the value of k if the volume of the cylinder
     of height k is half the volume of the whole solid
     model.

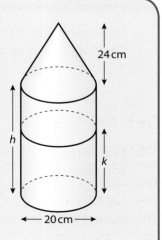

(i) Volume of cone $= \frac{1}{3}\pi r^2 h$

$$= \frac{1}{3}\pi(10^2)24 \ldots r = 10\text{ cm}$$

$$= \frac{2400\pi}{3} = 800\pi\text{ cm}^3$$

(ii) Volume of cylinder $= 4(800\pi)$

$$= 3200\pi\text{ cm}^3$$

$$\Rightarrow \pi r^2 h = 3200\pi$$

$$\Rightarrow \pi(100)(h) = 3200\pi \ldots r = 10\text{ cm}$$

$$100h = 3200 \ldots \text{divide both sides by } \pi$$

$$h = \frac{3200}{100}$$

$$\therefore h = 32\text{ cm}$$

(iii) Volume of whole solid $=$ Volume of cone $+$ Volume of cylinder

$$= 800\pi\text{ cm}^3 + 3200\pi\text{ cm}^3$$

$$= 4000\pi\text{ cm}^3$$

$\therefore$ Volume of cylinder of height $k = 2000\pi\text{ cm}^3 \ldots$ half volume of whole solid

$$\pi r^2 k = 2000\pi$$

$$\pi(100)k = 2000\pi$$

$$\Rightarrow 100k = 2000 \ldots \text{divide both sides by } \pi$$

$$\Rightarrow k = \frac{2000}{100} = 20\text{ cm}$$

Exercise 9.5

(In the following questions, use the π key on your calculator.)

1. Find the volume of the cone shown on the right.
    Give your answer in cm³, correct to 1 decimal place.

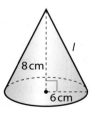

2. Find, correct to the nearest whole number, the volume of a cone of base radius 8 cm
    and height 21 cm.

3. The given solid cone has base radius 5 cm and slant height 13 cm.

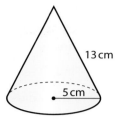

   Find (i) the curved surface area
        (ii) the total surface area
        (iii) the height of the cone
        (iv) the volume of the cone.
   Give each answer in terms of π.

4. The volume of a cone is 360π cm³.
   If the height of the cone is 30 cm, find the length of the radius of the base.

5. The curved surface area of a cone is 112π cm².
   If the slant height of the cone is 14 cm, find the length of the base radius.

6. A cone is attached to a hemisphere of radius 4 cm, as shown.
   If the total height of the object is 10 cm, find

   (i) the height of the cone
   (ii) the volume of the object in cm³, correct to
        one decimal place.

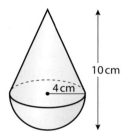

7. The given shape consists of a cylinder and cone.

   (i) Find the volume of the cylinder in terms of π.
   (ii) Find the volume of the cone in terms of π

   Hence find the volume of the shape, correct to the
   nearest cm³.

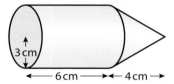

8. A solid metal cylinder of radius 5 cm and height 12 cm is melted down and recast into a
   cone of base radius 10 cm.
   Calculate the height of the cone.

9. The radius of the base of a cone and the radius of a sphere are each 6 cm in length.
   If the volume of the cone is equal to the volume of the sphere, find the height of the
   cone.

10. Express, in terms of π, the volume of a cylinder of height 12 cm and radius 4 cm.

    A cone of base radius 4 cm and height h cm has the same volume as the cylinder.
    Calculate the value of h.

11. A right circular cone of radius 6 cm and height 12 cm is totally immersed in a cylinder partly filled with water, as shown.

Find, in terms of π, the volume of the cone.

If the radius of the cylinder is 8 cm, find the value of h, the increase in the height of the water.

12. The volume of a cone is $\dfrac{512\pi}{3}$ cm³.

The cone's height and radius length are equal.
Calculate the length of the radius.

13. A toy is made of a cone which fits exactly on top of a hemisphere, as shown in the diagram.
The radius length of the hemisphere is 6 cm and the volume of the cone is half the volume of the hemisphere.
 (i) Find the volume of the cone in terms of π.
 (ii) Find the height of the cone.

14. Wax in the shape of a cylinder with radius of length 4 cm and height 36 cm is melted down. The resulting wax is formed into cone-shaped candles.
Each candle has height 6 cm and base of radius length 2 cm.
 (i) Calculate the number of candles that can be made, assuming that no wax is lost.
 (ii) The candles are placed, base down and in rows of six, in the smallest possible rectangular box.
      Calculate, in cm³, the volume (internal capacity) of the box.

15. Work out the volume of this shape.
Give your answer in cm³, correct to
1 decimal place.

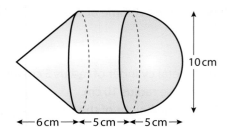

16. The diagram shows a cone cut into two parts, part A and part B. Work out the volume of part B, correct to the nearest whole number.

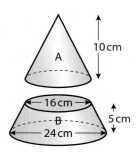

17. A device is made of a cone which fits exactly on top of a hemisphere, as shown in the diagram.
The radius length of the hemisphere is 6 cm and the total height of the device is 21 cm.

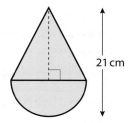

(i) Write down the height of the cone and hence find the volume of the cone in terms of π.
(ii) Find the volume of the hemisphere in terms of π.
(iii) Express as a ratio in its simplest form,
Volume of cone : Volume of hemisphere.

Section 9.6 More difficult problems

1. Water flowing through a pipe

If water flows through a cylindrical pipe at the rate of 10 cm/sec, then the volume of water that passes through the pipe each second is the same as the volume of a portion of the pipe of length 10 cm, as shown.

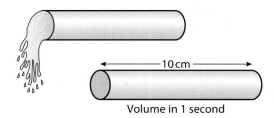

Volume in 1 second

Example 1

Water flows through a cylindrical pipe of internal diameter 3 cm at the rate of 14 cm/sec. How long will it take to fill a cylinder of base diameter 14 cm and height 45 cm?

Volume of water that flows in 1 sec is the same as the volume of the cylinder shown on the right.

Vol. of water $= \pi r^2 h$

$$\pi \times \left(\frac{3}{2}\right)^2 \times 14 \ldots r = \tfrac{3}{2}\,cm$$

$$= \frac{63\pi}{2}\,cm^3 \ldots \text{leave your answer in terms of } \pi$$

Volume of the cylinder $= \pi(7)^2.45$
$$= 2205\pi\,cm^3 \ldots \text{again in terms of } \pi$$

Time taken (in secs.) to fill cylinder $= 2205\pi \div \dfrac{63\pi}{2}$

$$= \frac{2205\pi \times 2}{63\pi}$$

$$= 70 \text{ seconds}$$

2. Ratios when dimensions are not given

In some figures we are not given dimensions but if we know the ratios of two corresponding lengths we can compare the volumes of the two figures. This is illustrated in the following example.

Example 2

A cylinder and a cone have radii of equal lengths.
If the height of the cone is twice the height of the cylinder, find the ratio,
Volume of cylinder : Volume of cone.

Let the radius of each figure be r.
Height of cylinder $= h$; Height of cone $= 2h$.

Volume of cylinder $= \pi r^2 h$ ... radius $= r$, height $= h$

Volume of cone $= \frac{1}{3} \pi r^2 h$

$$= \frac{1}{3} \pi r^2 (2h) = \frac{2\pi r^2 h}{3}$$

Volume of cylinder : Volume of cone $= \pi r^2 h : \frac{2\pi r^2 h}{3}$

$$= h : \frac{2h}{3} \text{ ... divide both sides by } \pi r^2$$

$$= 3h : 2h \text{ ... multiply both sides by 3}$$

$$= 3 : 2$$

Exercise 9.6

1. Cone A has radius r cm and height h cm.
   Cone B has radius $2r$ cm and height $2h$ cm.
   Find the ratio, Volume of cone A : Volume of cone B.

2. Two solid cones of equal height have the lengths of the radii of their bases in the ratio $1 : 2$.
   Calculate the ratio of their volumes.

3. The diagram on the right shows 2 solid cylinders A and B.
   Express the volume of each cylinder in terms of π.

   Now find in the form $1 : n$, the ratio
   (i) Volume of A : Volume of B
   (ii) Curved surface area of A : Curved surface area of B.

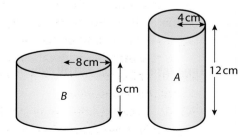

4. Water flows along a circular pipe of internal radius 1 cm at the rate of 35 cm/sec. Calculate
   (i) the volume of water that flows through the pipe in 1 minute
   (ii) the number of litres that flow through the pipe in one hour.
      (Take $\pi = \frac{22}{7}$ and 1 litre $= 1000$ cm³)

5. Calculate the volume of a cylinder of height 7 cm and of radius 2 cm.
   Water flows through a circular pipe of internal radius 2 cm at a rate of 7 cm/sec into an empty rectangular tank that is 1.2 m long, 1.1 m wide and 30 cm high.
   How long, in minutes, will it take to fill the tank?
   Give your answer correct to the nearest minute.

6. Oil flows through a circular pipeline of radius 4 cm at the rate of 20 cm/sec.
   How long will it take to fill a cylindrical tank of diameter 1.2 metres and height 3 metres?
   Give your answer in minutes.

7. A buoy consists of a cone attached to a hemisphere, as shown.
   The radius of the base of the cone is 7 cm.
   If the volume of the hemisphere is equal to the volume of the cone, calculate the height of the cone in centimetres.

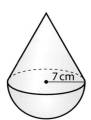

8. A cylinder of radius 3 cm and height 20 cm is full of water.
   This water is just sufficient to fill a right circular cone of radius 6 cm and height h cm and a hemispherical bowl of radius 3 cm.

   Find, in terms of π,
   (i) the volume of the cylinder,
   (ii) the volume of the hemisphere,
   (iii) the height, h, of the cone.

9. A solid is in the shape of a hemisphere surmounted by a cone, as in the diagram.
   (i) The volume of the hemisphere is 18π cm³.
      Find the radius of the hemisphere.
   (ii) The slant height of the cone is $3\sqrt{5}$ cm.
      Show that the vertical height of the cone is 6 cm.
   (iii) Show that the volume of the cone equals the volume of the hemisphere.
   (iv) This solid is melted down and recast in the shape of a solid cylinder. The height of the cylinder is 9 cm.
      Calculate its radius.

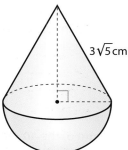

10. (i) Write down, in terms of π and r, the volume of a hemisphere with radius of length r.

(ii) A fuel storage tank is in the shape of a cylinder with a hemisphere at each end, as shown.

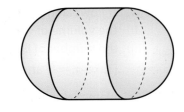

The capacity (internal volume) of the tank is $81\,\pi\,\text{m}^3$.

The ratio of the capacity of the cylindrical section to the sum of the capacities of the hemispherical ends is $5:4$.

Calculate the internal radius length of the tank.

Section 9.7 The Trapezoidal Rule

Engineers and surveyors often have to calculate the area of shapes which have irregular boundaries. Many methods of obtaining approximations for the areas of such shapes have been used throughout the ages. These methods generally involve the division of the area into strips of equal width and then adding the areas of the strips to find the total area. An example of this is shown in the figure below.

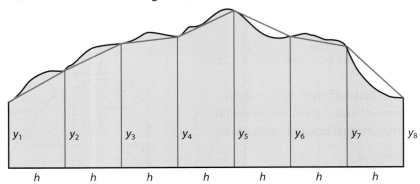

In the figure above, a line is drawn across the top of each strip to give a number of trapeziums. The sum of the areas of these trapeziums is then found. This sum is approximately equal to the required area.

Earlier in this chapter we dealt with the area of a trapezium which is given by the formula

$$\text{Area} = \frac{h}{2}(a + b)$$

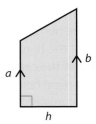

The sum of the areas in the first figure above is given by

$$\text{Area} \approx \left[\frac{h}{2}(y_1 + y_2) + \frac{h}{2}(y_2 + y_3) + \frac{h}{2}(y_3 + y_4) + \dots + \frac{h}{2}(y_7 + y_8)\right]$$

This simplifies to: Area $\approx \dfrac{h}{2}[y_1 + 2(y_2 + y_3 + y_4 + y_5 + y_6 + y_7) + y_8]$.

This method of approximating the area of an irregular figure is known as the **Trapezoidal Rule**.

The Trapezoidal Rule may be memorised more easily by expressing it in words as follows:

Trapezoidal Rule:

$$\text{Area} \approx \frac{h}{2}[\text{first height} + \text{last height} + 2(\text{remaining heights})]$$

In the given figure, the vertical lines $y_1, y_2, \ldots y_6$ are generally called **offsets** or **ordinates**.
Notice that there are 6 ordinates for 5 strips.
Similarly, there are 7 ordinates for 6 strips.

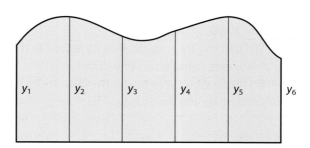

y_1 is called the **first** ordinate and y_6 is called the **last** ordinate.
y_2, y_3, y_4 and y_5 are called the middle or **remaining** ordinates or heights.

Example 1

Find the area of the shape shown in the diagram below, given that the width of each strip is 10 m. The lengths of the ordinates are given.

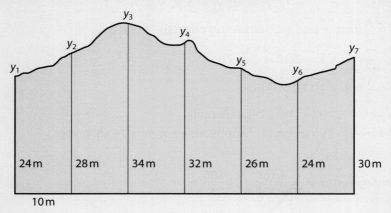

For convenience, we will label the offsets $y_1, y_2, y_3 \ldots y_7$

$\Rightarrow y_1 = 24,\ y_2 = 28,\ y_3 = 34,\ y_4 = 32,\ y_5 = 26,\ y_6 = 24,\ y_7 = 30.$

$$\text{Area} \approx \frac{h}{2}[\text{first} + \text{last} + 2(\text{remaining offsets})]$$

$$= \frac{10}{2}[24 + 30 + 2(28 + 34 + 32 + 26 + 24)]$$

$$= 5[54 + 2(144)]$$

$$\text{Area} = 1710 \text{ m}^2$$

Example 2

The diagram below is a graph of the function $f(x) = x^2 - 8x + 17$ in the domain $0 \leqslant x \leqslant 4$.

(i) Use the Trapezoidal Rule to estimate the area between the curve and the x-axis, using strips of width 1 unit.

(ii) If the exact area under the curve is $25\frac{1}{3}$ square units, find the percentage error using the Trapezoidal Rule.

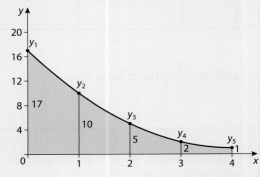

$f(x) = x^2 - 8x + 17$

$f(0) = 0 - 0 + 17 = 17$

$f(1) = 1^2 - 8(1) + 17 = 10$

$f(2) = 2^2 - 8(2) + 17 = 5$

$f(3) = 3^2 - 8(3) + 17 = 2$

$f(4) = 4^2 - 8(4) + 17 = 1$

The offsets are: $y_1 = 17, y_2 = 10, y_3 = 5, y_4 = 2, y_5 = 1$

(i) $\text{Area} = \frac{h}{2}[\text{first} + \text{last} + 2(\text{remaining offsets})]$

$$= \frac{1}{2}[17 + 1 + 2(10 + 5 + 2)]$$

$$= \frac{1}{2}[18 + 2(17)] = \frac{1}{2}[52]$$

$$= 26 \text{ square units}$$

(ii) Actual area $= 25\frac{1}{3}$ sq. units   Approximate area $= 26$ sq. units

Error $= 26 - 25\frac{1}{3} = \frac{2}{3}$

$$\text{Percentage error} = \frac{\text{error}}{\text{true value}} \times \frac{100}{1}\%$$

$$= \frac{\frac{2}{3}}{25\frac{1}{3}} \times \frac{100}{1}\% = \frac{2}{76} \times \frac{100}{1} = 2.63\%$$

Percentage error $= 2.63\%$

Note: If a shape consists of two areas above and below a horizontal line, as shown, we add the offsets above and below the line.

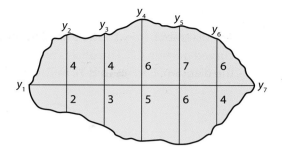

For example $y_2 = 4 + 2 = 6$
$\quad\quad\quad\quad y_3 = 4 + 3 = 7$, etc. ...

Also, $y_1 = 0$ and $y_7 = 0$.
That is the first and last heights are both zero.

Example 3

A surveyor is estimating the area of the plot of land shown below.
A base line [AB] is drawn and offsets are measured at intervals of x metres.
Using the Trapezoidal Rule, the surveyor estimated the area to be 612 m². Find x.

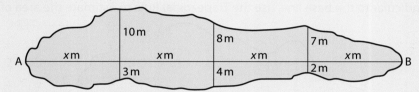

We label the offsets y_1, y_2, y_3, y_4 and y_5.
$y_1 = 0, y_2 = 13, y_3 = 12, y_4 = 9, y_5 = 0$.

Area $\approx \dfrac{h}{2}$ [first + last + 2(remaining offsets)]

$\therefore 612 = \dfrac{x}{2}[0 + 0 + 2(13 + 12 + 9)]$

$\quad 612 = \dfrac{x}{2}[68]$

$\quad 612 = 34x$

$\quad\quad x = \dfrac{612}{34}$

$\quad\quad x = 18$ m

Exercise 9.7

1. The diagram below shows the figure ABCD bounded by three straight lines and the curved portion CD. The offsets are perpendicular to [AB] and their lengths are shown on the diagram. Each strip is 10 m wide.

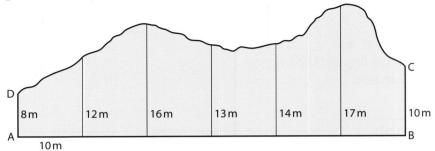

Use the Trapezoidal Rule to find an estimate for the area of ABCD.

2. An engineer has to estimate the area of the site shown below. He divides the site into 8 strips, as shown. Given that the width of each strip is 12 m and that the offsets are perpendicular to the base line, use the Trapezoidal Rule to estimate the area of the site.

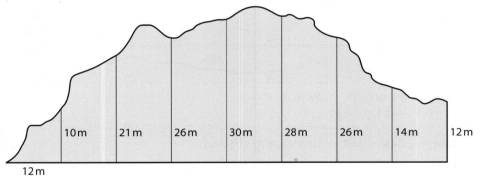

3. Use the Trapezoidal Rule to estimate the area of the region shown below. All measurements are in metres.

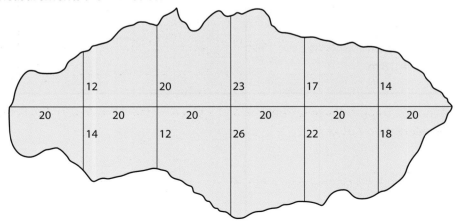

4. In the figure below, all the measurements are in metres.
Use the Trapezoidal Rule to find an approximate area of the figure.

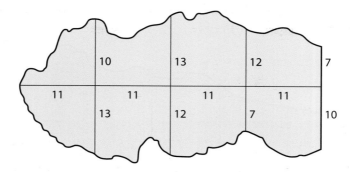

5. Using the Trapezoidal Rule, the estimate of the area of the figure ABCD shown below is 656 m². Calculate the length of the line segment marked *x*.

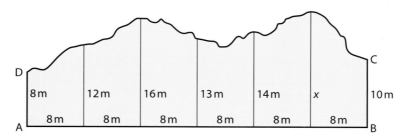

6. The diagram below shows a sketch of a piece of paper ABCD with one jagged side.
At equal intervals of *h* cm along [BC], perpendicular measurements of 12 cm, 8 cm, 9 cm 6 cm, 5 cm, 7 cm and 11 cm are made to the top edge.

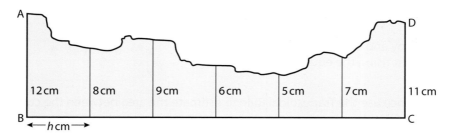

Using the Trapezoidal Rule, the area of the piece of paper is calculated to be 325.5 cm². Calculate the value of *h*.

7. The sketch shows a field ABCD which has one uneven edge.
At equal intervals of 6 m along [BC], perpendicular measurements of 7 m, 8 m, 10 m, 11 m, 13 m, 15 m and x m are made to the top of the field.

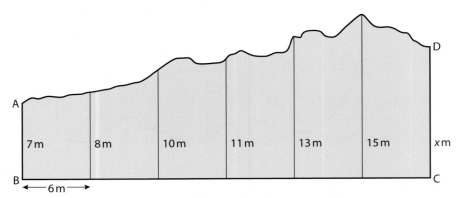

A

7m   8m   10m   11m   13m   15m x m

B

←—6 m—→

C

D

Using the Trapezoidal Rule, the area of the field is calculated to be 399 m². Calculate the value of x.

8. The diagram shows the curve $y = x^2 + 3$ in the domain $0 \leqslant x \leqslant 4$.

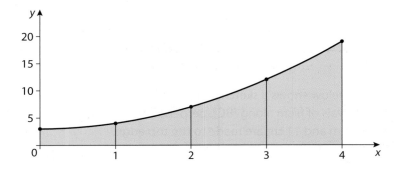

(i) Copy and complete the table on the right using the equation of the curve.

x	0	1	2	3	4
y					

(ii) Hence use the Trapezoidal Rule to estimate the area between the curve and the x-axis.

(iii) If the exact area is $33\frac{1}{3}$ square units, find the percentage error in using the Trapezoidal Rule.

Test yourself 9

1. (i) Work out the area of this trapezium.

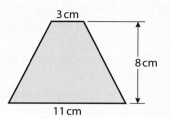

(ii) *Cleano* soap powder is sold in cubical boxes. The small size has a side of 10 cm and contains 600 grams. The large size has a side of 15 cm. Calculate the weight of powder contained in the large size.

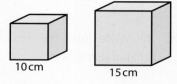

(iii) The cylinder and the cone shown below have equal volumes.

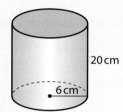 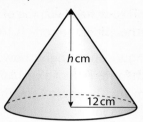

(a) Find the volume of the cylinder in terms of π.

(b) Calculate h, the vertical height of the cone.

2. (i) The volume of the rectangular block shown is 384 cm³.
Find the length of the side marked a.

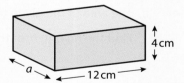

(ii) Use the Trapezoidal Rule to estimate the area of the figure ABCD shown below.

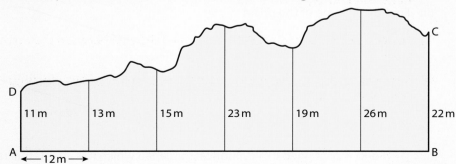

(iii) A cylindrical water tank has internal diameter 40 cm and height 50 cm.
A cylindrical mug has internal diameter 8 cm and height 10 cm.

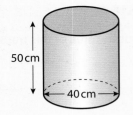

    (a) Find the volume of the tank, in terms of π.

    (b) Find the volume of the mug, in terms of π.

    (c) How many mugs can be filled from a full tank?

3. (i) Write down the area of this parallelogram.

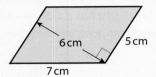

(ii) A solid cone has a volume of 192π cm³.
If the height of the cone is 16 cm, find the radius of the base.

(iii) The figure on the right shows a wedge of cheese which forms part of a circular cylinder of radius 14 cm and thickness 4 cm. The angle in the sector is 45°, as shown.
Find, in cm³, the volume of the wedge, correct to the nearest whole number.

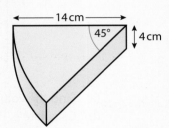

4. (i) The area of the given triangle is 68 cm².

Find the height, h, of the triangle in centimetres.

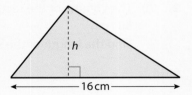

(ii) Find the volume of the prism shown here.

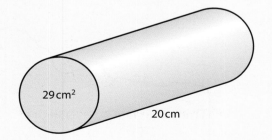

(iii) (a) Soup is contained in a cylindrical saucepan which has an internal radius of length 12 cm. The depth of the soup is 18 cm.
Calculate, in terms of π, the volume of soup in the saucepan.

(b) A ladle, in the shape of a hemisphere with internal
radius of length 6 cm, is used to serve the soup.
Calculate, in terms of π, the volume of soup
contained in one full ladle.

(c) How many full ladles of soup does the saucepan
contain?

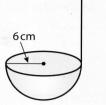

6 cm

5. (i) Calculate the area of the sector shown
on the right.
Give your answer to the nearest cm².

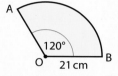

(ii) The diagram below shows a solid rectangular block of metal 75 cm by 11 cm by
6 cm. It is melted down and recast into cylindrical rods of length 25 cm and radius
of length 1 cm, as shown.
Calculate the number of complete rods that can be made from the block.

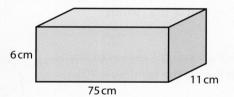

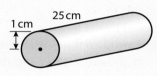

(iii) Using the Trapezoidal Rule, an estimate for the area of the figure shown below is
1087.5 m².

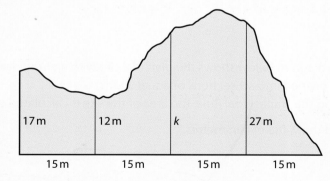

Find the length of the offset marked k, in metres.

6. (i) The circle on the right has a radius of 7 cm.
Find the area of the shaded portion correct
to the nearest cm².

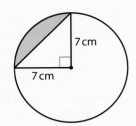

(ii) Calculate the volume of the given prism.

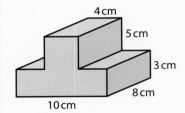

(iii) A salt cellar is in the shape of a cylinder and hemisphere,
as shown. The radius of the hemisphere is 2 cm.

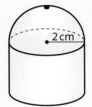

(a) Express, in terms of π, the volume of the hemisphere.

(b) If the volume of the hemisphere is $\frac{1}{2}$ the volume of the
cylinder, calculate the height of the cylinder.

7. (i) A window is in the shape of a rectangle and a semicircle,
as shown. The rectangular part of the window is 70 cm
wide and 90 cm high.
Find the area of the window in cm², correct to the
nearest cm².

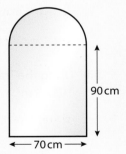

(ii) The diagram below shows the plan of a site with an irregular boundary.
It is divided into six sections of equal width.
Using the Trapezoidal Rule, the area of the site is calculated to be 3156 m².

Find the value of *h* in metres.

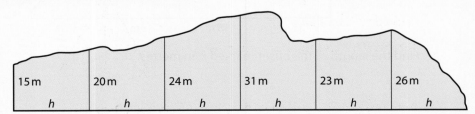

Summary of key points...

1. **Trapezium**

   Area of a trapezium $= \frac{1}{2}(a + b) \times h$

   In words: Half the sum of the parallel sides
   multiplied by the perpendicular height.

   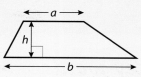

2. **Circles – sectors – arcs**

   Area of circle $= \pi r^2$

   Circumference of circle $= 2\pi r$

   Length of arc $= 2\pi r \times \frac{\theta}{360}$.

   Area of sector $= \pi r^2 \times \frac{\theta}{360}$.

   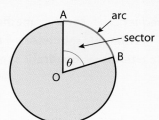

3. **Prism**

   A prism is a 3-D shape with the same
   cross-section all along its length.

   Volume of a prism =
   area of cross-section $\times$ length

   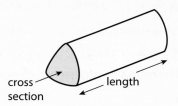

4. **Cylinder**

   Volume $= \pi r^2 h$

   Total surface area of solid cylinder $= 2\pi r^2 + 2\pi rh$

   Curved surface area $= 2\pi rh$

   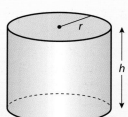

5. **Sphere**

   Volume of sphere $= \frac{4}{3}\pi r^3$

   Surface area $= 4\pi r^2$

   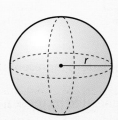

6. **The cone**

   Volume of cone $= \frac{1}{3}\pi r^2 h$

   Curved surface area $= \pi rl$

   Total surface area of solid cone $= \pi rl + \pi r^2$

   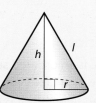

7. **Trapezoidal Rule**

   Area $\approx \frac{h}{2}$ [first height + last height + 2(remaining heights)]

Patterns and Sequences

Key words

> pattern   sequence   term   **method of difference**   *n*th term
> **coefficient**   **arithmetic sequence**   **common difference**   **arithmetic series**
> **S_n, the sum to *n* terms**   **quadratic sequence**

Section 10.1 Patterns in number

The ability to see patterns or sequences is very important in mathematics.
We meet number patterns such as 1, 3, 5, 7, … or 5, 10, 15, 20, … on a regular basis.

We see **patterns** in designs such as tiling and mosaics.

Here is a growth pattern of squares made from matchsticks.

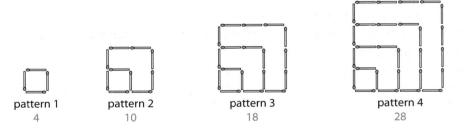

pattern 1   pattern 2   pattern 3   pattern 4
   4   10   18   28

The numbers in red below each pattern represent the numbers of matches used
in each shape.
The numbers 4, 10, 18, 28, … generated by these patterns form a sequence that is a little
more complex than the sequences 1, 3, 5, 7, … or 5, 10, 15, 20, … .

Number sequences

A number sequence is an ordered set of numbers with a rule to find every number in the
sequence. The rule which takes you from one number to the next could be a simple addition
or multiplication, but generally it is more tricky than that. In more difficult sequences you
need to examine them carefully to identify the pattern.

Each number in a sequence is called a **term**.
The first term is written as T_1 ;   the 4th term is T_4.

Look at these sequences and their rules.

> 4, 8, 16, 32, … doubling the preceding term each time … 64, 128, …
> 4, 7, 10, 13, … adding 3 to the preceding term each time … 16, 19, …
> 36, 32, 28, 24, … subtracting 4 from the preceding term each time … 20, 16, …

These sequences are all quite straightforward once you have found the link from one term to the next.

Method of differences

For some sequences that are not immediately obvious, we need to look at the difference between consecutive terms to determine the pattern.

Consider the sequence: 3   6   11   18   27

Difference between terms: 3   5   7   9

Here the differences form a sequence of their own.
The pattern is much easier to detect in this sequence.
The next difference is 11.
We now find the next term of the first sequence by adding 11 to 27.
The next term is $27 + 11$, i.e., 38.

Exercise 10.1

1. Look at the following number sequences.
   Write down the next three terms in each and explain how the sequence is found.
   (i)   2, 4, 6, 8, …   (ii)   1, 3, 5, 7, …
   (iii)   1, 4, 7, 10, …   (iv)   1, 2, 4, 8, …
   (v)   3, 9, 27, …   (vi)   16, 8, 4, …
   (vii)   20, 18, 16, …   (viii)   2, 6, 18, …

2. By considering the differences in the following sequences, write down the next two terms in each case:
   (i)   2, 4, 7, 11, …   (ii)   1, 2, 5, 10, …
   (iii)   2, 6, 12, 20, …   (iv)   2, 3, 6, 11, 18, …
   (v)   1, 4, 10, 19, …   (vi)   2, 7, 14, 23, …

3. Look carefully at each number sequence below.
   Find the next two terms in the sequence and try to explain the pattern.
   (i)   1, 1, 2, 3, 5, 8, 13, …   (ii)   3, 4, 7, 11, 18, 29, …
   (iii)   1, 8, 27, 64, …   (iv) $1, \frac{1}{3}, \frac{1}{9}, \frac{1}{27}, \ldots$

4. Examine these number patterns:
Write down the next line in each pattern without using a calculator.
Now use a calculator to check that you are correct.

(i)	$6 \times 9 = 54$	(ii) $\quad 9 \times 1 = 9$	(iii) $\qquad 7 \times 7 = 49$
	$66 \times 9 = 594$	$9 \times 12 = 108$	$67 \times 67 = 4489$
	$666 \times 9 = 5994$	$9 \times 123 = 1107$	$667 \times 667 = 444889$
	$= = = = = =$	$9 \times 1234 = 11106$	$6667 \times 6667 = 44448889$
		$= = = = = = = =$	$= = = = = = = = = =$

Section 10.2 The *n*th term of a sequence

When using a number sequence, we sometimes need to know, for example, the 50th or 100th term without having to write out all 50 or 100 terms. To do this we need to find the rule which generates the sequence.

This rule is generally called the **nth** term or T_n.
If $T_n = 2n + 3$, then $T_1 = 2(1) + 3 = 5$
$$T_2 = 2(2) + 3 = 7$$
$$T_3 = 2(3) + 3 = 9$$

....

From this we can see that $T_n = 2n + 3$ generates the sequence 5, 7, 9, ...
The rule, $T_n = 2n + 3$, allows us to find any term of the sequence.

Example 1

The *n*th term of a sequence is $4n - 3$.
Write down the first five terms of the sequence.

$T_n = 4n - 3$
$T_1 = 4(1) - 3 = 1$
$T_2 = 4(2) - 3 = 5$
$T_3 = 4(3) - 3 = 9$
$T_4 = 4(4) - 3 = 13$
$T_5 = 4(5) - 3 = 17$

The first 5 terms are: 1, 5, 9, 13, 17.

Finding the *n*th term of a sequence

Consider the sequence   2, 5, 8, 11, ...
Here we have the **same difference** between any term and the next.
This difference is **3**.
The nth term of the sequence will be $3n \pm$ a number.
$3n$ will generate the sequence   3, 6, 9, 12.

Compare the new sequence with the original one and see what number you need to add to or subtract from each term to get the original pattern.

-1 ↱ 2, 5, 8, 11   Here we subtract one from each term
    ↳ 3, 6, 9, 12   to get the original term.

So the nth term is $3n - 1$;

$\therefore\ T_n = 3n - 1$

In the sequence 6, 10, 14, 18, … the difference is **4**.
The nth term will be $T_n = \mathbf{4}n \pm$ a number.
$4n$ generates the sequence 4, 8, 12, …
Comparing the original sequence with the new sequence we have:

$+2$ ↱ 6, 10, 14, 18, …   Here we add 2 to each term to get the
    ↳ 4, 8, 12, 16, …   corresponding term of the original sequence.

The nth term is $T_n = 4n + 2$

Example 2

Find the nth term of the sequence 3, 7, 11, 15, … .

In the sequence 3, 7, 11, 15, …, the difference between the terms is 4.
So the first part of the nth term is $4n$.
This would generate the sequence 4, 8, 12, 16, …
Comparing the sequences we have: 3, 7, 11, 15 ⌉
                        4, 8, 12, 16 ⌋ -1

Here we subtract 1 from each term to get the original sequence.

$\therefore\ T_n = 4n - 1$

Example 3

Find the nth term and the 20th term of the sequence 4, 7, 10, 13, 16, …

In the sequence 4, 7, 10, 13, …, the difference between the terms is **3**.

$T_n = 3n \pm$ a number

$3n$ generates the sequence 3, 6, 9, 12, …

Comparing: $+1$ ↱ 4, 7, 10, 13, …
                ↳ 3, 6, 9, 12, …

Here we add 1 to each term of the second sequence to get the first sequence.

$\therefore\ T_n = 3n + 1$

$T_{20} = 3(20) + 1$ … substitute 20 for n
$T_{20} = 61$

Exercise 10.2

1. Use each of the following rules to write down the first three terms of the sequence:
   (i) $n + 4$ for $n = 1, 2, 3$
   (ii) $2n + 1$ for $n = 1, 2, 3$
   (iii) $4n + 3$ for $n = 1, 2, 3$
   (iv) $3n - 2$ for $n = 1, 2, 3$.

2. In each of the following sequences the nth term, T_n, is given.
   Write down the first four terms of each sequence:
   (i) $T_n = 3n$
   (ii) $T_n = 2n + 3$
   (iii) $T_n = 3n - 2$

3. If $T_n = 3n - 4$, find T_1, T_3 and T_{10}.

4. Write down the first three terms of each of these sequences where the nth term is given.
   (i) $T_n = n^2$
   (ii) $T_n = n^2 + 3$
   (iii) $T_n = 2n^2 + 1$

5. If $T_n = 2n^2 - 1$, work out
   (i) T_1
   (ii) T_2
   (iii) T_5
   (iv) T_{10}.

6. If $T_n = 2n - 6$, show that $T_1 + T_5 = 0$.

7. Find the next two terms and the nth term of each of the following sequences:
   (i) $3, 5, 7, 9, 11, \ldots$
   (ii) $4, 7, 10, 13, \ldots$
   (iii) $2, 6, 10, 14, 18, \ldots$
   (iv) $5, 9, 13, 17, \ldots$

8. Find the nth term and the 20th term of each of these sequences:
   (i) $2, 5, 8, 11, \ldots$
   (ii) $6, 8, 10, 12, \ldots$
   (iii) $4, 9, 14, 19, \ldots$
   (iv) $2, 7, 12, 17, \ldots$

9. For the sequence $6, 11, 16, 21, \ldots$
   find (i) T_n
   (ii) T_{20}
   (iii) T_{100}

10. The nth term of a sequence is given by $T_n = 3n - 4$.
    Which term of the sequence is 23?

    [Hint: Let $3n - 4 = 23$.]

Section 10.3 Sequences from shapes

These designs are made by arranging counters in squares.

Design 1   Design 2   Design 3   Design 4   Design 5

The number of counters in each design is shown in this table.

Design number	1	2	3	4	5
Number of counters	1	4	9	16	25

The numbers in the sequence   1, 4, 9, 16, 25 … are called **square numbers**.

From the sequence, it can be seen that the number of counters required for design 6 is 6^2, i.e. 36, and for design n, it is n^2.

Example 1

These designs are made by arranging counters in L-shapes.

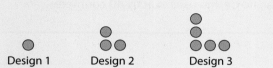

Design 1   Design 2   Design 3   Design 4   Design 5

(i)   Copy and complete this table for these designs.

Design number	1	2	3	4	5
Number of counters	1				

(ii)   How many counters are in the 6th design?

(iii) How many counters are needed to make the 15th design? Explain how you worked out your answer.

(iv) Which design uses 99 counters?

(v)   Is it possible to make one of these designs with exactly 40 counters. Explain your answer.

(i)   Here is the table:

Design number	1	2	3	4	5
Number of counters	1	3	5	7	9

(ii)   There will be   9 + 2, i.e. 11, counters in the 6th design.

(iii) To find the number of counters in the 15th design we need to find the nth term.

   1, 3, 5, 7, 9, … . Here the difference is 2.

So the nth term will be $2n \pm$ a number.

$2n$ generates   2, 4, 6, 8, … so we need to take 1 from each term of this sequence to get the first sequence.

$$\therefore\ T_n = 2n - 1$$

The 15th design is represented by T_{15}.

$$T_n = 2n - 1 \Rightarrow T_{15} = 2(15) - 1 = 29$$

So 29 counters are needed for the 15th design.

(iv) To find which design uses 99 counters, we let $T_n = 99$.

$$T_n = 99 \Rightarrow 2n - 1 = 99$$
$$\Rightarrow \quad 2n = 100$$
$$\Rightarrow \quad n = 50$$

Design number 50 uses 99 counters.

(v) Let $\quad T_n = 40$
$$2n - 1 = 40$$
$$2n = 41$$
$$n = 20\tfrac{1}{2}$$

Since n is not a whole number, no design uses exactly 40 counters.

Exercise 10.3

1. A pattern of triangles is built up from matchsticks.

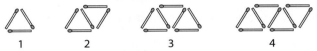

1   2   3   4

(i) Draw the 5th set of triangles in this pattern.
(ii) Write down the sequence of numbers generated by the matchsticks in the first six patterns.
(iii) Find an expression in n for the number of matches in the nth set of triangles.
(iv) How many matches are needed for the 50th set of triangles?

2. Here is a pattern sequence

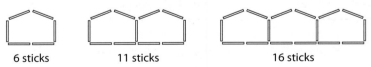

6 sticks   11 sticks   16 sticks

(i) Draw the 4th pattern in this sequence.
(ii) Write down the sequence of numbers generated by the sticks in the first six patterns.
(iii) Show that the number of sticks in the nth pattern is given by $T_n = 5n + 1$.
(iv) How many sticks are required for the 20th pattern?
(v) For which pattern are 51 sticks required?

3. Complete the table of values for this sequence of matchstick patterns.

Number of squares	1	2	3	4	5
Number of matchsticks	4	7			

(i) How many matchsticks are required for the 6th pattern?

(ii) Find an expression in *n* for the *n*th pattern.

(iii) Use the expression found to find the number of matchsticks required for the 50th pattern.

4. A pattern of squares is built up from matchsticks as shown.

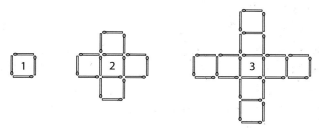

(i) Draw the 4th pattern.

(ii) Find an expression in *n* for the number of squares in the *n*th pattern.

(iii) How many squares are there in the 30th pattern?

(iv) Which pattern contains exactly 77 squares?

5. Look at these matchstick shapes.

  5 matchsticks   9 matchsticks

(i) Copy and complete the table below:

Shape number	1	2	3	4	5
Number of matchsticks	5	9	...	...	...

(ii) How many matchsticks are there in Shape 7?

(iii) Find an expression for the number of matchsticks in Shape *n*.

(iv) Which shape contains exactly 101 matchsticks?

6. (i) Find the eighth term of the sequence whose *n*th term is $4n - 1$.

(ii) Find the *n*th term of the sequence whose first four terms are

  2   8   14   20

7. Each of these patterns uses black tiles.

(i) How many black tiles will be in pattern 5?

(ii) How many black tiles will be in pattern 10?

Pattern 1   Pattern 2   Pattern 3   Pattern 4

(iii) Find an expression for the number of black tiles in pattern *n*.

(iv) How many tiles will be in pattern 100?

(v) Which pattern will have exactly 101 tiles?

8. A conference centre had tables each of which could sit six people.
When put together, the tables could seat people as shown.

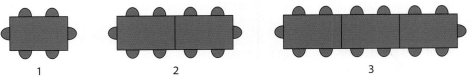

1   2   3

   (i)   How many people could be seated at 4 tables?
  (ii)   How many people could be seated at *n* tables put together in this way?
(iii)   A conference had 90 people who wished to use the tables in this way.
        How many tables would they need?

9. Regular pentagons of side length 1 cm are joined together to make a pattern
as shown.

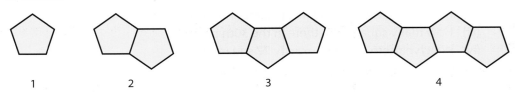

1   2   3   4

   (i)   Write down the perimeter of each of the first 4 shapes.
        (Do not include internal lines.)
  (ii)   What is the perimeter of the 5th and 6th shapes?
(iii)   Find an expression for the perimeter of the *n*th shape.
(iv)   Find the length of the perimeter of the 50th shape.
 (v)   Which shape has a perimeter of length 92 cm?

Section 10.4 Arithmetic sequences ───────────────

Consider these sequences: (i)   2, 4, 6, 8, 10, …
                                (ii)   3, 7, 11, 15, 19, …
In (i)   each term is found by adding 2 to the preceding term.
In (ii)   each term is found by adding 4 to the preceding term.
These are examples of **arithmetic sequences**.

Arithmetic sequence

> A sequence, in which any term after the first can
> be obtained by adding a fixed number to the term
> before it, is called an arithmetic sequence.

The first term is denoted by **a**.
The fixed number is called the **common difference** and is denoted by the letter **d**.

Here are some examples of arithmetic sequences:

	First term (a)	Common difference (d)
(i) 5, 8, 11, …	5	3
(ii) 6, 3, 0, …	6	−3
(iii) −4, 0, 4, …	−4	4

The common difference d = **any term − previous term**.

In the sequence   12, 7, 2, …

$$d = 7 - 12 = -5.$$

Since d is negative, the sequence is decreasing.

Finding the nth term of an arithmetic sequence

If a is the first term of an arithmetic sequence and d is the common difference, the sequence may be written as follows:

$$a, \quad a + d, \quad a + 2d, \quad a + 3d, \quad \ldots \quad a + (n - 1)d$$
$$T_1 \qquad T_2 \qquad T_3 \qquad T_4 \quad \ldots \qquad T_n$$

> The nth term of an arithmetic sequence is given by $T_n = a + (n - 1)d$

Example 1

In the arithmetic sequence   3, 8, 13, …, find
(i) a (ii) d (iii) T_n (iv) T_{20}

(i) a, the first term = 3

(ii) d, the common difference = any term − previous term = 8 − 3 = 5

(iii) $T_n = a + (n - 1)d$ (iv) $T_n = 5n - 2$
$ = 3 + (n - 1)5$ $ T_{20} = 5(20) - 2$
$ = 3 + 5n - 5$ $\phantom{(iv) T_{20}} = 98$
$ = 5n - 2$

Example 2

(i) Find the nth term of the arithmetic sequence   7, 10, 13, 16, …
(ii) Which term of the sequence is 97?
(iii) Show that 168 is not a term of the sequence.

(i) 7, 10, 13, 16, ... $\qquad$ $a = 7$ and $d = 3$

$$T_n = a + (n-1)d$$
$$= 7 + (n-1)3$$
$$= 7 + 3n - 3$$
$$T_n = 3n + 4$$

(ii) Let $T_n = 97 \Rightarrow 3n + 4 = 97$
$$3n = 97 - 4 = 93$$
$$n = 31$$

The 31st term is 97.

(iii) Let $T_n = 168$
$$3n + 4 = 168 \Rightarrow 3n = 168 - 4$$
$$3n = 164$$
$$n = \frac{164}{3} = 54\frac{2}{3}$$

Since n is not a whole number, 168 is not a term of the sequence.

Exercise 10.4

1. Find a and d for each of the following arithmetic sequences:
   (i) 2, 5, 8, ...
   (ii) 7, 12, 17, ...
   (iii) 0, 3, 6, 9, ...
   (iv) −2, 1, 4, ...
   (v) 60, 55, 50, ...
   (vi) 6, 1, −4, ...

2. Write out the next three terms of the following arithmetic sequences:
   (i) 2, 6, 10, ...
   (ii) 8, 4, 0, ...
   (iii) −6, −3, 0, ...

3. In the arithmetic sequence 2, 6, 10, 14, ... write down
   (i) a, the first term
   (ii) d, the common difference
   (iii) T_n and hence the value of T_{20}

4. Find T_n, the nth term of each of the following sequences:
   (i) 1, 5, 9, 13, ...
   (ii) 6, 8, 10, 12, ...
   (iii) −5, 0, 5, 10, ...

5. If T_n of a sequence is $3n - 4$, write down the value of
   (i) T_1
   (ii) T_2
   (iii) T_{14}
   (iv) d, the common difference.

6. Find T_n of the arithmetic sequence 12, 15, 18, ...
   Hence write down the value of (i) T_{10} (ii) T_{40}.

7. In an arithmetic sequence $T_n = 5n - 1$.
   Find T_1, T_2, and T_3.
   Hence write down the value of a and the value of d.

8. In the sequence 4, 7, 10, ..., write down the value of a and the value of d.
   Find an expression for T_n and hence write down T_{20}.

9. The nth term of an arithmetic sequence is given by $T_n = 4n - 1$.
   Write down the first three terms of this sequence.
   Hence find the value of a and the value of d.

10. Find an expression for T_n of the arithmetic sequence
    2, 6, 10, ...
    For what value of n is $T_n = 46$?

11. Find T_n of the arithmetic sequence 1, 3, 5, ...
    For what value of n is $T_n = 87$?

12. These designs are made by
    arranging counters in
    triangles.

    Triangle 1   Triangle 2   Triangle 3   Triangle 4
    (i) Draw the 5th
        triangle.
    (ii) How many counters are there in triangle 6?
    (iii) Write down the number sequence formed by the first six triangles.
          Explain why this is not an arithmetic sequence.

13. Complete the table of values for this
    sequence of matchstick patterns.

Number of triangles	1	2	3	4	5
Number of matchsticks	3				

    (i) Explain why the sequence generated by the numbers of matchsticks is an
        arithmetic sequence.
    (ii) Write an expression for the nth term of the sequence.
    (iii) How many matchsticks are needed for the 30th term of the sequence?
    (iv) Which term of the pattern has 81 matchsticks?

14. Find T_n of the arithmetic sequence 8, 5, 2, ...
    For what value of n is $T_n = -34$?

15. If T_n of the arithmetic sequence 4, 7, 10, 13, ... is 127, find the value of n.

16. Which term of the arithmetic sequence 6, 11, 16, ... is 186?

17. Which term of the arithmetic sequence $-8, -6, -4, ...$ is 38?

18. In the sequence 15, 20, 25, 30, ..., $T_n = 215$. Find n.

287

19. Here is a pattern made from sticks.

 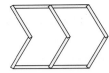 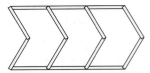

| Pattern number 1 | Pattern number 2 | Pattern number 3 |

   (i)   How many sticks are there in the 5th pattern?

   (ii) Find, in terms of n, the number of sticks needed for the nth pattern.

  (iii) How many sticks are needed for the 20th pattern?

  (iv) Which pattern has 122 sticks?

20. T_n of a sequence is $T_n = n^2 + 4$.
Find T_1, T_2 and T_3 and hence state if the sequence is arithmetic.

Section 10.5 Finding the values of a and d

If we are given any two terms of an arithmetic progression, we can use simultaneous equations to find the values of a and d. We can then find any other term of the sequence.

Example 1

T_4 of an arithmetic sequence is 11   and $T_9 = 21$.
Find the values of a and d and hence find T_{50}.

$$T_n = a + (n - 1)d$$
$$T_4 = 11 \Rightarrow a + 3d = 11 \ldots ①$$
$$T_9 = 21 \Rightarrow \underline{a + 8d = 21} \ldots ②$$
Subtracting: $-5d = -10$
$$\Rightarrow d = 2$$

Substituting   2 for d in ① we get $T_{50} = a + 49d$
           $a + 3(2) = 11$ $= 5 + 49(2) = 5 + 98$
         $\Rightarrow a + 6 = 11 \Rightarrow a = 5$ $= 103$
         $\therefore a = 5$ and $d = 2$

Example 2

If $x + 1$, $2x - 2$, and $2x + 1$ are three consecutive terms of an arithmetic sequence, find the value of x.
Hence write down T_n and T_{100} of the sequence.

If $x + 1, 2x - 2$ and $2x + 1$ are in arithmetic sequence, then

$$T_2 - T_1 = T_3 - T_2$$
$$\Rightarrow \quad (2x - 2) - (x + 1) = (2x + 1) - (2x - 2)$$
$$\Rightarrow \quad 2x - 2 - x - 1 = 2x + 1 - 2x + 2$$
$$\Rightarrow \qquad\qquad x - 3 = 3$$
$$\Rightarrow \qquad\qquad\qquad x = 6$$

The first three terms are: 7, 10, 13.
$$\Rightarrow a = 7 \text{ and } d = 3$$
$$\begin{aligned} T_n &= a + (n - 1)d \\ &= 7 + (n - 1)3 \\ &= 7 + 3n - 3 \end{aligned}$$
$$\Rightarrow \quad T_n = 3n + 4$$
$$\Rightarrow \quad T_{100} = 3(100) + 4 = 304$$

Exercise 10.5

1. The first term of an arithmetic sequence is 5.
   If the fifth term is 33, find d, the common difference.
   Hence find T_n and T_{20}.

2. In an arithmetic sequence, $T_4 = 14$ and $T_9 = 34$.
   Find the values of a and d and hence write down the value of T_{13}.

3. In an arithmetic sequence, $T_5 = 21$ and $T_{10} = 41$.
   Find the values of a and d.
   Hence find T_n and T_{60}.

4. In an arithmetic sequence, the eighth term is -18 and the third term is 12.
   Find the values of a and d.
   Hence find T_{100}.

5. In an arithmetic sequence, $T_3 = 4$ and $T_{10} = -17$.
   Find the values of a and d.
   Write down T_n of the sequence and find the value of n for which $T_n = -47$.

6. In an arithmetic sequence, the first term is 3 and $T_6 = 2T_3$.
   (i) Find the value of the common difference, d.
   (ii) Find T_n, the nth term.

7. In an arithmetic sequence, $T_1 + T_5 = 0$ and $T_{13} = 20$.
   (i) Find the value of a and the value of d.
   (ii) Show that the seventh term is twice the fifth term.

8. In an arithmetic sequence, $T_4 = -9$ and $T_{15} = -31$.
Find the values of a and d.
Write down T_n of the sequence and hence find which term is equal to -81.

9. Lamp-posts are put at the end of every 100 m stretch of a motorway, as shown,

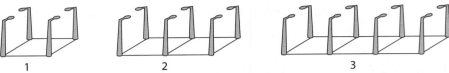

1   2   3

   (i)   How many lamp-posts are needed for 500 m of motorway?
  (ii) Write down, as a number sequence, the number of lamp-posts required for 100 m,
       200 m, 300 m, 400 m, ...
 (iii) Find an expression in n for the nth term of this sequence.
 (iv) Use the expression found in (iii) to write down the number of lamp-posts needed
       for 8 km of motorway.
  (v) The M51 is a motorway being built.
       The contractor has ordered 2402 lamp-posts.
       How long is this motorway?

10. In an arithmetic sequence, $T_1 + T_3 = 12$ and $T_4 + T_6 = 24$.
Find the values of a and d.

11. In an arithmetic sequence, the sixth term is 20 and the tenth term is four times the
second term.
Find the values of a and d. Hence calculate T_{100}.

12. If $x, 2x + 3$ and $4x + 5$ form three consecutive terms of an arithmetic sequence, find
the value of x.

13. Find the value of x in each of the following arithmetic sequences:
   (i) $x - 1, x + 1, 3x - 3$
  (ii) $x + 4, 3 - x, x + 10$.

14. Tommy builds fences of different lengths using pieces of wood.

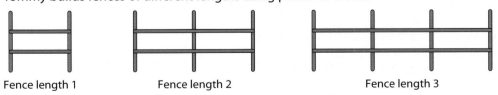

Fence length 1   Fence length 2   Fence length 3

   (i) Sketch fence length 5.
      Tommy counted how many pieces he needed to make each fence length.
      He then drew up the table below.

Fence length	1	2	3	4	5	6
Number of pieces	4	7	10			

(ii) Complete the table to show how many pieces of wood he would use for fence lengths 4, 5 and 6.

(iii) Write down, in terms of n, an expression for the number of pieces of wood needed for fence length n.

(iv) How many pieces of wood are needed for fence length 40?

(v) If 91 pieces of wood are needed, what is the number of the fence length?

Section 10.6 Arithmetic series

When the terms of an arithmetic sequence are added, they form an **arithmetic series**.

For example, 1, 3, 5, 7, ... is an arithmetic sequence

but 1 + 3 + 5 + 7 ... is an arithmetic series.

> The + sign between the terms changes a sequence to a series.

We use the notation S_n to denote the sum of the first n terms of a series.

Thus S_1 = sum of one term, i.e., $S_1 = T_1$

$S_2 = T_1 + T_2$

$S_3 = T_1 + T_2 + T_3$

The formula for S_n of an arithmetic series is given on the right.

> The sum to n terms of an arithmetic series is given by the formula
>
> $$S_n = \frac{n}{2}\{2a + (n-1)d\}.$$

Example 1

Find S_n and hence S_{20} of the series   5 + 8 + 11 + 14 + ...

In the series   5 + 8 + 11 + 14 + ..., $a = 5$ and $d = 3$.

$$S_n = \frac{n}{2}\{2a + (n-1)d\}$$

$$= \frac{n}{2}\{2(5) + (n-1)(3)\} \ldots \ (a = 5, d = 3)$$

$$= \frac{n}{2}\{10 + 3n - 3\}$$

$$S_n = \frac{n}{2}\{3n + 7\}$$

$$S_{20} = \frac{20}{2}\{60 + 7\}$$

$$= 10(67)$$

$$= 670$$

Example 2

Given the arithmetic series $5 + 7 + 9 + \ldots$.
If $S_n = 192$, find the value of n.

$$S_n = 192$$

$$\frac{n}{2}\{2a + (n-1)d\} = 192$$

$$\frac{n}{2}\{10 + (n-1)2\} = 192 \ldots (a = 5 \text{ and } d = 2)$$

$$\frac{n}{2}\{10 + 2n - 2\} = 192$$

$$\frac{n}{2}\{2n + 8\} = 192$$

$$\frac{2n^2}{2} + \frac{8n}{2} = 192$$

$$n^2 + 4n - 192 = 0$$

$$(n - 12)(n + 16) = 0$$

$$n = 12 \ldots \text{disregard the negative answer} -16$$

$$\therefore S_{12} = 192$$

Note:
$$S_4 = T_1 + T_2 + T_3 + T_4$$
$$S_5 = T_1 + T_2 + T_3 + T_4 + T_5$$

Subtracting: $S_5 - S_4 = \qquad\qquad T_5$

Similarly $S_n - S_{n-1} = T_n$

Remember:
$T_n = S_n - S_{n-1}$

Example 3

In an arithmetic series, $S_n = n^2 + 2n$.
Find S_1, S_2 and S_3 and hence write down T_1, T_2 and T_3.

$$S_n = n^2 + 2n \Rightarrow S_1 = 1^2 + 2(1) = 3 \Rightarrow T_1 = 3$$
$$S_2 = 2^2 + 2(2) = 8 \Rightarrow T_1 + T_2 = 8 \Rightarrow T_2 = 5$$
$$S_3 = 3^2 + 2(3) = 15 \Rightarrow T_1 + T_2 + T_3 = 15$$
$$\Rightarrow 3 + 5 + T_3 = 15$$
$$\Rightarrow T_3 = 7$$

$\therefore$ the first three terms are $3, 5, 7$.

Exercise 10.6

1. For the arithmetic series $2 + 5 + 8 + \ldots$,
   (i) find the value of a and d
   (ii) find the sum of the first 12 terms.

2. Find the sum of the first 20 terms of the series
   $$3 + 7 + 11 + 15 + \ldots$$

3. Find S_n and hence S_{16} of the arithmetic series
   $$1 + 4 + 7 + 10 + \ldots$$

4. The first four terms of a series are $7 + 10 + 13 + 16 + \ldots$
   Find S_8, the sum of the first eight terms.

5. Write down the value of a and the value of d for the series
   $$16 + 12 + 8 + 4 + \ldots$$
   Hence find S_{24} of the series.

6. In an arithmetic series the nth term, $T_n = 5n - 2$.
   Find the values of a and d and hence find S_{16} of the series.

7. Show that S_n of the series $1 + 2 + 3 + \ldots$ is $\frac{n}{2}(n + 1)$.

   Hence find the sum of the series $1 + 2 + 3 + \ldots + 100$.

8. S_n of the series $-4 - 2 + 0 + 2 + \ldots$ is 84.
   (i) Write down the value of a and the value of d.
   (ii) Find the value of n.

9. Here are some patterns made of squares.

 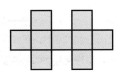 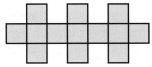

   Pattern number 1   Pattern number 2   Pattern number 3

   The diagram on the right shows part of Pattern number 4.

   (i) Copy and complete Pattern number 4.
   (ii) How many squares are there in Pattern 6?
   (iii) Find an expression for the number of squares in Pattern n.
   (iv) How many squares are there in total in the first 20 Patterns?

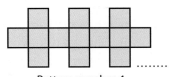

   Pattern number 4

10. In an arithmetic series, $T_5 = 9$ and $T_8 = 27$.
    (i) Find the values of a and d.   (ii) Find S_{10} of the series.

293

11. In an arithmetic series, $T_3 = 0$ and $T_8 = 10$.
Find the values of a and d and hence find S_n of the series.
How many terms of the series must be added so that their sum is 36?

12. Find S_n of the series $5 + 8 + 11 + 14 + \ldots$.
If $S_n = 98$, find the value of n.

13. A student made tile designs using red and blue tiles, as shown.

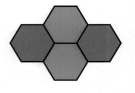  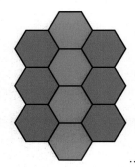

....

    (i) Find an expression in n for the total number of
        (a) red tiles used in the nth design
        (b) blue tiles used in the nth design.
   (ii) Find, in terms of n, an expression for the total number of tiles used in
        the nth design.
  (iii) How many tiles in total are needed to complete 10 designs using the same pattern?

14. Which term of the series $3 + 8 + 13 \ldots$ is 98?
Now find the sum of these terms.

15. S_n of an arithmetic series is given by $S_n = n^2 + 6n$.
Find S_1 and S_2 and hence write down the values of T_1 and T_2.

16.   (i) Write down the 10th term of the sequence which begins $3, 7, 11, 15, \ldots$
   (ii) Write down an expression for the nth term of this sequence.
  (iii) Show that 1997 cannot be a term in this sequence.
  (iv) Calculate the number of terms in the sequence $3, 7, 11, 15, \ldots, 399$.
   (v) Hence find the sum of the series $3 + 7 + 11 + 15 + \ldots + 399$.

17. The nth term of an arithmetic series is $T_n = 52 - 4n$.
    (i) Find the values of a and d.
   (ii) Find which term is zero.
  (iii) Find the sum of the terms which are positive.

18. The sum of the first n terms of an arithmetic series is given by
$$S_n = 4n^2 - 8n.$$
    (i) Use S_1 and S_2 to find the first term and the common difference.
   (ii) How many terms of the series must be added to give a sum of 252?

19. In an arithmetic series, $T_5 = 21$ and $T_{10} = 11$.

    (i) Find the first term and the common difference.

    (ii) Find the sum of the first 20 terms.

    (iii) For what value of n is $S_n = 0$?

20. The first three patterns of a tiling sequence are shown below.
The sequence continues in the same way.

1st pattern

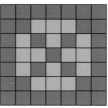

2nd pattern

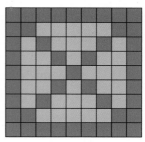

3rd pattern

In each pattern, the tiles form a square of blue and green tiles.

    (i) In the table below, write down the number of blue tiles needed for each of the first five patterns.

Pattern	1	2	3	4	5
Number of blue tiles	21	33			

    (ii) Find, in terms of n, an expression for the number of blue tiles needed for the nth pattern.

    (iii) Use the formula for T_n, found in (ii) above, to find the number of blue tiles in the 10th pattern.

    (iv) Find, in terms of n, a formula for the total number of blue tiles in the first n patterns.

    (v) How many patterns can be made with 399 blue tiles?

Section 10.7 Quadratic sequences

$1, 4, 9, 16, 25, \ldots$ is the sequence of square numbers.
Since $T_1 = 1^2, T_2 = 2^2, T_3 = 3^2, \ldots T_n = n^2$.

Sequences that have an nth term containing n^2 as the highest power are called quadratic sequences.

Let us examine the first seven terms of the sequence $T_n = n^2$.

$$
\begin{array}{ccccccc}
1 & \quad 4 & \quad 9 & \quad 16 & \quad 25 & \quad 36 & \quad 49 \\
& 3 & 5 & 7 & 9 & 11 & 13 \\
& & 2 & 2 & 2 & 2 & 2
\end{array}
$$

first difference

second difference

Notice that the second differences are all the same, i.e., 2.

Now let us look at the sequence with nth term $= 2n^2 - n$.
The first five terms of this sequence are

		1		6		15		28		45	
			5		9		13		17		first difference
				4		4		4			second difference

Here the second differences are all the same, i.e., 4.

Notice that in each of the quadratic sequences above the coefficient of n^2 in the nth term is half the second difference.

Remember

> In a quadratic sequence, the coefficient of n^2 in the nth term is half the second difference.

Investigation

Write out the first five terms of the sequence with $T_n = 2n^2 + 3$.
Write out the first differences and the second differences between consecutive terms.
Investigate if the coefficient of n^2 in the nth term is half the value of the second difference.

Finding the nth term of a quadratic sequence

The nth term of a quadratic sequence will always be of the form

$$T_n = an^2 + bn + c$$

We now use a difference table to find the values of a, b and c as shown in the following example.

Example 1

Find the nth term of the sequence   3, 10, 21, 36

The terms and the 1st and 2nd differences are shown on the right.

Terms	3		10		21		36
1st differences		7		11		15	
2nd differences			4		4		

T_n will be of the form $T_n = an^2 + bn + c$
$a = 2$ ... half the value of the second difference

$\therefore T_n = 2n^2 + bn + c$

296

We now express T_1 and T_2 in terms of b and c.

$T_n = 2n^2 + bn + c \Rightarrow T_1 = 2 + b + c$

But $\qquad T_1 = 3 \Rightarrow 2 + b + c = 3 \Rightarrow b + c = 1 \dots \textcircled{1}$

$T_2 = 8 + 2b + c$

But $\quad T_2 = 10 \Rightarrow 8 + 2b + c = 10 \Rightarrow 2b + c = 2 \dots \textcircled{2}$

We now solve the simultaneous equations $\textcircled{1}$ and $\textcircled{2}$

$$
\begin{array}{l|l}
b + c = 1 \dots \textcircled{1} & b + c = 1 \\
2b + c = 2 \dots \textcircled{2} & \Rightarrow 1 + c = 1 \\
\quad -b = -1 \Rightarrow b = 1 & \Rightarrow c = 0
\end{array}
$$

$\therefore \; T_n = 2n^2 + n \dots a = 2, b = 1, c = 0$

Exercise 10.7

1. Find the next two terms of these quadratic sequences by finding the first and second differences:

   (i) $3, 4, 6, 9, 13, \dots$ (ii) $3, 6, 11, 18, 27, \dots$ (iii) $2, 7, 14, 23, 34, \dots$

2. Which of these sequences are quadratic?

   (i) $6, 8, 12, 18, 26, 36, \dots$ (ii) $6, 8, 10, 12, 14, 16, \dots$

   (iii) $3, 4, 7, 12, 19, 28, \dots$ (iv) $0, 3, 8, 15, 24, \dots$

3. Find the first 5 terms of the sequences with these nth terms:

   (i) $T_n = n^2 + 4$ (ii) $T_n = n^2 - 1$ (iii) $T_n = 2n^2 + n + 1$

4. Find the 10th term of the sequence with $T_n = n^2 + 2n - 4$.

5. Write the sequence $4, 7, 12, 19, 28, \dots$ as follows

$$
\begin{array}{ccccc}
4 & 7 & 12 & 19 & 28
\end{array}
$$

       $-$ $-$ $-$ $-$ first difference

         $-$ $-$ $-$ second difference

   If $T_n = an^2 + bn + c$, use the second difference to write down the value of a.

6. Find an expression for the nth term of each of these quadratic sequences:

   (i) $5, 8, 13, 20, 29, \dots$ (ii) $2, 8, 18, 32, 50, \dots$

7. Find an expression for the nth term of the sequence

   $7, 10, 15, 22, 31, \dots$

8. Show that the nth term of the quadratic sequence $8, 15, 26, 41, 60, \ldots$ is $2n^2 + n + 5$.

9. Use a difference table to work out the nth term of this sequence:

$3, 8, 15, 24, 35, \ldots$

10. Each layer of cubes in these designs forms a square.

   (i) How many cubes will be in Model 4?

   (ii) Use the pattern to write down the number of cubes in Model 5.

  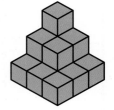

Model 1   Model 2   Model 3

   (iii) Show that the expression $\dfrac{n}{6}(n + 1)(2n + 1)$

gives the correct number of cubes in Model 3 and Model 4.

   (iv) Use the expression for the nth term to find how many cubes in Model 10.

11. Here are some rugs stacked in a carpet showroom.

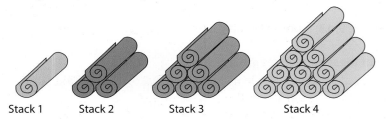

Stack 1   Stack 2   Stack 3   Stack 4

   (i) Copy and complete the table on the right.

Stack number	1	2	3	4	5	...
Number of rugs	1	3				...

   (ii) Draw a difference table for the sequence for the number of rugs.

   (iii) Use the differences to find an expression for the nth term of this sequence.

   (iv) Use the nth term to find the number of rugs in Stack 20.

Test yourself 10

1. (i) The first three terms of an arithmetic sequence are   5, 8, 11, ...
        (a) Write down the first term and the common difference.
        (b) Find an expression in n for the nth term of the sequence.
        (c) Which term of the sequence is 62?
    (ii) In an arithmetic sequence, $T_3 = 11$ and $T_7 = 27$.
        (a) Find the value of the first term and the common difference.
        (b) Find the sum of the first 10 terms of the series.

2. (i) The first two terms of an arithmetic sequence are   5, 0, ...
        (a) Find d, the common difference.
        (b) Find T_n and hence T_{10} of the sequence.

    (ii) Look at these shapes made with sticks.

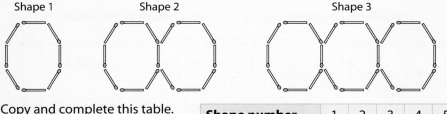

Shape 1   Shape 2   Shape 3

        (a) Copy and complete this table.

Shape number	1	2	3	4	5
Number of sticks	8				

        (b) Find an expression in n for the number of sticks in the nth shape.
        (c) How many sticks are there in shape 12?
        (d) Find the sum of all the sticks used in the first 20 shapes.

3. (i) An arithmetic sequence is   8, 6, 4, ...
        (a) Write down the value of a, the first term and d, the common difference.
        (b) Find an expression in n for the nth term of the sequence.
        (c) Which term of the sequence is -20?
    (ii) Write down the formula for S_n, the sum to n terms of an arithmetic series.
        The common difference of the series is 3 and $S_8 = 132$.
        Find the first 3 terms of the series and hence find the value of T_{24}.

4. (i) The nth term of an arithmetic sequence is given by $T_n = 12 - 4n$.
        (a) Find the first term and the common difference.
        (b) Which term of the sequence is -64?
    (ii) A pattern of shapes is shown below.

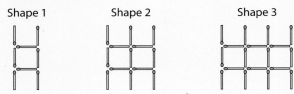

Shape 1   Shape 2   Shape 3

(a) Copy and complete this table for the shapes above.

Shape	1	2	3	4	5
Number of matches	8				

(b) Find an expression in n for the nth term of the sequence formed by the numbers of matches required for successive patterns.

(c) How many matches would there be in Shape 20?

(d) Find the sum of all the matches used in the first 12 shapes.

5. (i) Which *one* of the following sequences is arithmetic?

    (a) 6, 4, 0, ...   (b) 3, −1, 3, −...   (c) −5, −3, −1, 1, ...

    Now find T_n of this arithmetic sequence.

  (ii) Write down the first differences and second difference between the terms of the quadratic sequence

$$8, 15, 26, 41, 60, \ldots$$

    Hence find an expression in n for the nth term of the sequence.

6. (i) In an arithmetic sequence, the first term is 9 and the common difference is 4. Find T_n, the nth term, and hence write down the value of T_{10}.

  (ii) In an arithmetic series $T_{10} = 19$ and $S_{10} = 55$.

    (a) Write down the formula for T_n and S_n of an arithmetic series.

    (b) Find the first term and common difference of the sequence above.

7. (i) The first three terms of an arithmetic series are $2 + 8 + 14 \ldots$

    (a) Find d, the common difference.

    (b) Find T_n, the nth term of the series.

    (c) Find the value of n such that $T_n = 200$.

    (d) Find the sum of the first 20 terms.

  (ii) Here are the first 3 diagrams of a matchstick pattern.

    (a) How many matchsticks will be in Diagram 4?

    (b) Using the sequence formed, write down the number of matchsticks in Diagram 5.

Diagram 1   Diagram 2   Diagram 3

    (c) Explain why the sequence is quadratic.

    (d) Find an expression for the nth term of the sequence.

    (e) Use the nth term to find the number of matchsticks in Diagram 10.

Summary of key points...

1. **Generating a sequence when given T_n**

   If you know the formula for T_n, the nth term of a sequence, you can find any term of the sequence by substituting a value for n.

   $n = 1, 2, 3, \ldots$ gives the first three terms.

2. **Finding the nth term**

   For the sequence   5, 8, 11, ... we find the nth term as follows

   (i) The common difference between the terms is 3, so the nth term will be $3n \pm$ a number.

   (ii) To find this number, we find what we add to 3 to get the first term 5. This number is 2.

   $\therefore T_n = 3n + 2$.

3. **Arithmetic sequences**

   For the arithmetic sequence $a, a + d, a + 2d, a + 3d, \ldots$

   $$T_n = a + (n - 1)d \qquad S_n = \frac{n}{2}\{2a + (n - 1)d\}$$

   In an arithmetic sequence, the common difference d is

   $d =$ **any term − previous term**

4. **Finding T_n from consecutive sums**

   $S_6 - S_5 = T_6$

   In general $T_n = S_n - S_{n-1}$.

5. **Quadratic sequences**

   The nth term of a quadratic sequence will contain a term in n^2.

   The coefficient of n^2 is half the value of the second difference.

Key words

parallelogram   perpendicular height   equilateral   theorem
converse   axiom   congruent   similar   equiangular
corresponding sides   tangent   point of contact   chord   transversal

Section 11.1 Revision of angles and triangles

The diagrams shown below will remind us of some of the results we have encountered in our study of Geometry so far.

Names and types of angles

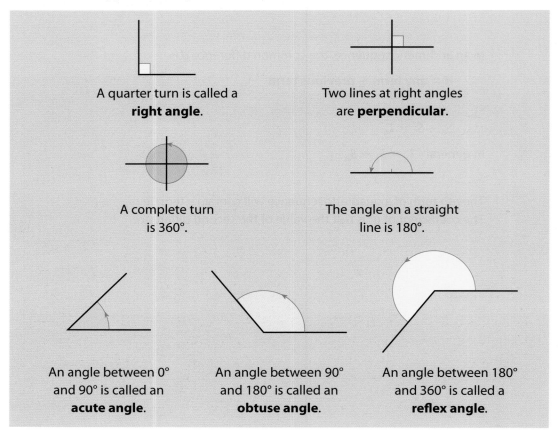

A quarter turn is called a **right angle**.

Two lines at right angles are **perpendicular**.

A complete turn is 360°.

The angle on a straight line is 180°.

An angle between 0° and 90° is called an **acute angle**.

An angle between 90° and 180° is called an **obtuse angle**.

An angle between 180° and 360° is called a **reflex angle**.

Properties of angles

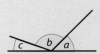
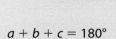

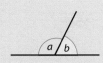

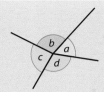

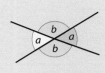

$a + b + c = 180°$

Angles which meet at a point on a straight line add up to 180°.

$a + b = 180°$

A pair of angles that add together to make 180° are called **supplementary angles.**

$a + b + c + d = 360°$

Angles which meet at a point add up to 360°.

Two straight lines which cross at a point form two pairs of **vertically opposite angles**. Vertically opposite angles are **equal**.

Angles formed when a straight line crosses a pair of parallel lines have the following properties:

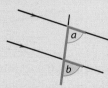

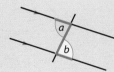

Corresponding angles are equal. So $a = b$. You can find them by looking for an F shape.

Alternate angles are equal. So $a = b$. Look for a Z shape.

The **interior angles** x and y sum to 180°.
$x + y = 180°$.

Triangles and their properties

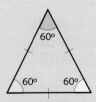

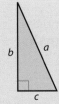

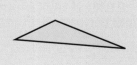

An **equilateral triangle** has:
3 sides equal
3 interior angles equal (60°)

An **isosceles triangle** has:
2 sides equal
base angles equal

A **right-angled triangle** has:
1 angle of 90°
$a^2 = b^2 + c^2$

Triangles without any of these properties are called **scalene triangles**.

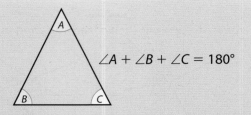

$\angle A + \angle B + \angle C = 180°$

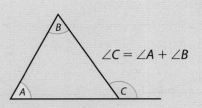

$\angle C = \angle A + \angle B$

The angles of a triangle sum to 180°.

The **exterior angle** of a triangle is equal to the sum of the interior opposite angles.

Congruent triangles

Triangles are congruent if one of these conditions is true:

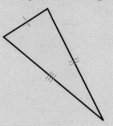 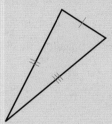

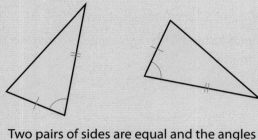

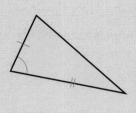

Three pairs of sides are equal (**SSS**).

Two pairs of sides are equal and the angles between them (the included angle) are equal (**SAS**).

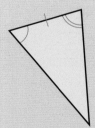 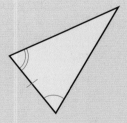

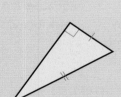

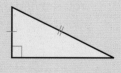

Two pairs of angles are equal and the sides between them are equal (**ASA**).

Both triangles have a right angle, the hypotenuses are equal and one pair of corresponding sides is equal (**RHS**).

Exercise 11.1

1. Write down the size of the angles marked with letters in each of the following diagrams where arrows indicate parallel lines.

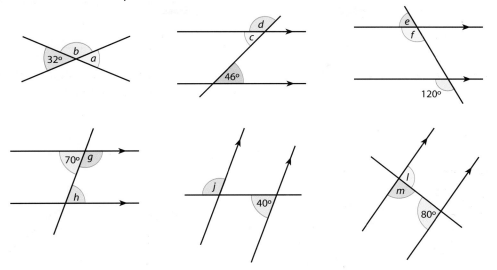

2. Find the size of the angle marked with a letter in each of the following triangles:

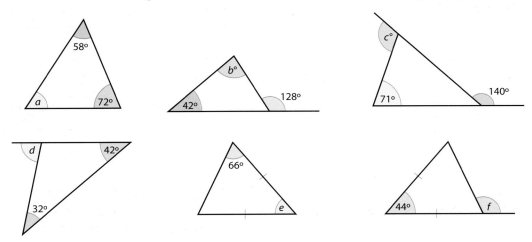

3. Find the size of the angle marked with a letter in the following figures:

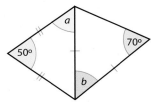
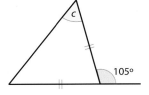
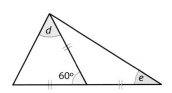

4. Find the measure of the angles marked x and y in the given diagram if the line ℓ is parallel to the line m.

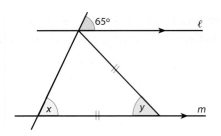

5. Find the values of a, b, c and d in the following triangles:

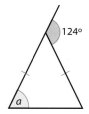 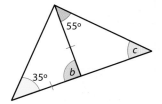 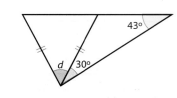

6. In the given triangle, BC∥DEF. Find |∠DAE|.

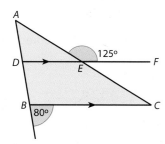

7. In the given diagram, AC is parallel to BE. If |∠BCA| = 80° and |∠CAB| = 55°, find
  (i) x
  (ii) y.

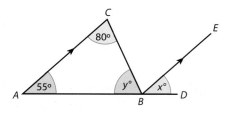

8. In the given diagram, |AB| = |AC| and |∠BAD| = 104°.

  (i) Find |∠CAB|.
  (ii) Find |∠ABC|.

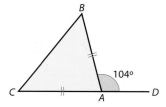

9. Find the measure of the angle marked with a letter in each of the following diagrams, where the arrows indicate parallel lines:

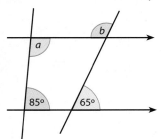 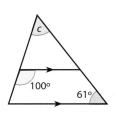 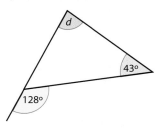

10. Find the values of x and y in the following triangles:

(i)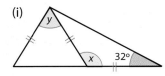

(ii)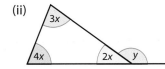

(iii)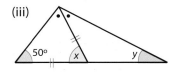

11. Use the *Theorem of Pythagoras* to find the length of the side marked with a letter in each of these triangles:

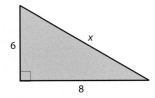 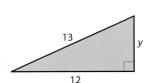 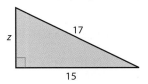

12. Find $|AB|$ in the given right-angled triangle.

Now find the area of the triangle ABC.

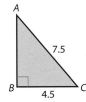

13. In the given figure, the angles ACB and ABD are both right angles.
If $|AC| = 3$, $|CB| = 4$ and $|BD| = 12$, find

(i) $|AB|$

(ii) $|AD|$.

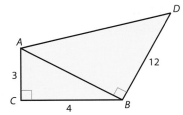

14. Find the length of the side marked *x* in each of the following right-angled triangles:

(i)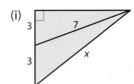

(ii)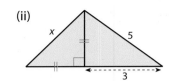

(iii)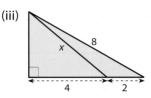

15. Find the values of *x* and *y* in the given diagram.
[Remember: $(\sqrt{5})^2 = 5.$]

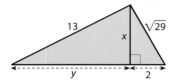

16. Explain why the two triangles below are congruent.

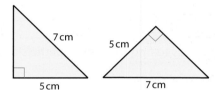

17. ABCD is a parallelogram.

Explain why the triangles ABD and
BCD are congruent.

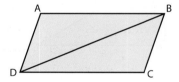

18. In the given diagram, $|AC| = |AD|$ and $|BD| = |CE|$.

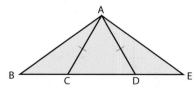

Prove that the triangles ABC and ADE are congruent.

19. In the given figure, $|\angle ACB| = |\angle CDB| = 90°$.
Find the lengths of the sides marked *x* and *y*.

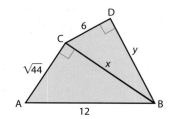

Section 11.2 Area of triangles and parallelograms

The diagrams below show two identical triangles.

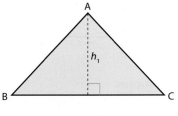

Area $= \frac{1}{2}|BC| \times h_1$

In this triangle, the base is [BC] and the perpendicular height is h_1.

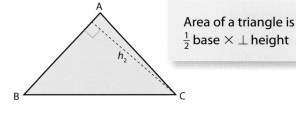

Area of a triangle is $\frac{1}{2}$ base $\times \perp$ height

Area $= \frac{1}{2}|AB| \times h_2$

In this triangle, the base is [AB] and the perpendicular height is h_2.

Since both triangles are identical, their areas are equal.

The areas were found by using different bases and different perpendicular heights.

This illustrates an important theorem about the area of a triangle, as given on the right.

Theorem
For any triangle, base times height does not depend on the choice of the base.

Example 1

In the given triangle, $|BC| = 16$ cm, $|AB| = 12$ cm and $|AD| = 10$ cm.

Find (i) the area of $\triangle ABC$

(ii) $|EC|$.

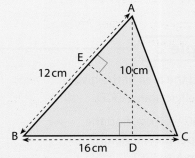

(i) Area of $\triangle ABC = \frac{1}{2}$ base $\times$ perpendicular height

$= \frac{1}{2} \times 16$ cm $\times 10$ cm   ... base is [BC]

$= 80$ cm^2

(ii) Area is also $\frac{1}{2}|AB| \times |EC|$.

$\therefore \quad \frac{1}{2}|AB| \times |EC| = 80$ cm^2

$\frac{1}{2}(12) \times |EC| = 80$

$6|EC| = 80$

$|EC| = \frac{80}{6} = \frac{40}{3} = 13\frac{1}{3}$

$|EC| = 13\frac{1}{3}$ cm

Area of a parallelogram

The figure on the right shows a parallelogram ABCD. In a parallelogram, the opposite sides are parallel and equal in length.

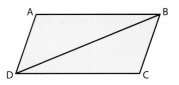

The diagonal [DB] divides the parallelogram into two triangles, ABD and BCD.

These triangles are congruent because the three sides in △ABD are equal in length to the three sides in △BCD.

Since the triangles are congruent, they are equal in area.

Theorem
A diagonal of a parallelogram bisects the area.

This shows that the diagonal [DB] bisects the area of the parallelogram ABCD.

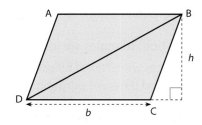

In the given parallelogram,

$$\text{area of } \triangle DCB = \frac{1}{2} \times \text{base} \times \text{height}$$
$$= \frac{1}{2} \times |DC| \times h$$
$$= \frac{1}{2} b \times h$$

Area of ABCD = twice area of △DCB.

∴ $\text{Area of ABCD} = 2\left[\frac{1}{2}b \times h\right]$
$$= b \times h$$

Theorem
The area of a parallelogram is the base multiplied by the perpendicular height.

Example 2

(i) Find the area of the given parallelogram ABCD.

(ii) If $|BC| = 9$ cm, find the perpendicular height, h, from A to [BC].

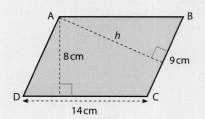

(i) Area of ABCD = base × perpendicular height
$$= 14 \times 8$$
$$= 112 \text{ cm}^2$$

(ii) Area of ABCD is also $|BC| \times h$
$$= 9 \text{ cm} \times h$$
$$= 9h \text{ cm}^2$$

But area of ABCD $= 112 \text{ cm}^2$ ... from (i) above

∴ $9h = 112$
$$h = \frac{112}{9} = 12\frac{4}{9} \text{ cm}$$

Exercise 11.2

1. Write down the area of each of these triangles:

(i)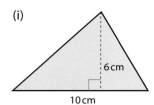

(ii)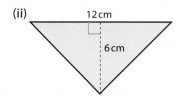

(iii)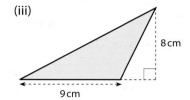

2. In the given triangle, |AB| = 9 cm, |BC| = 12 cm and the perpendicular height from C to [AB] is 8 cm.

   Find   (i) the area of the triangle ABC

          (ii) the perpendicular distance from A to [BC].

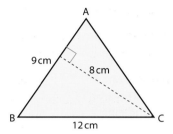

3. Find the value of x in each of these triangles:

(i)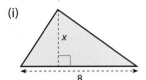

Area = 16 sq. units

(ii)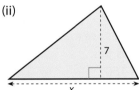

Area = 35 sq. units

(iii)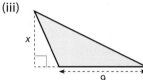

Area = 27 sq. units

4. Find the value of h in each of these triangles:

(i)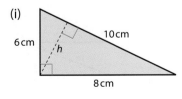

(ii)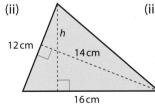

(iii)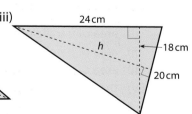

5. Find the area of each of these parallelograms:

(i)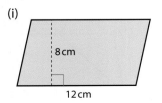

(ii)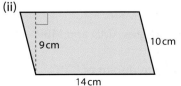

(iii)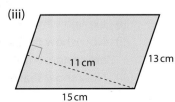

6. Find the area of the given parallelogram ABCD.
Now find the length of the side [BC].

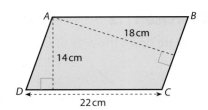

7. ABCD and DCEF are parallelograms.
Use the diagram to explain why the two
parallelograms are equal in area.

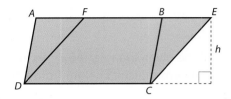

8. The area of the parallelogram ABCD is 40 cm².
If |DB| = 15 cm, find |AE|, where AE ⊥ DB.

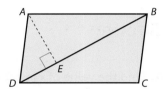

9. ABCD is a parallelogram and angles are marked 1 to 5.
   (i) Name three pairs of equal angles.
  (ii) Explain why $|\angle 1| + |\angle 2| = 180°$.

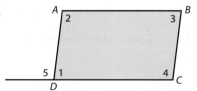

10. ABCD and ADBE are both parallelograms.
If the area of the triangle DCB = 15 cm², find
   (i) area of parallelogram ABCD
  (ii) area of parallelogram ADBE
 (iii) area of the figure ADCE
 (iv) the perpendicular height from A to [DC],
       if |DC| = 7.5 cm.

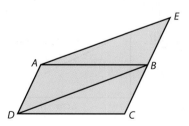

11. ABCD is a parallelogram and M is the midpoint of [AB].
   (i) Explain why $|\angle DAM| = |\angle MBP|$.
  (ii) Now show that the triangles AMD and MBP
      are congruent.
 (iii) Now show that B is the midpoint of [CP].

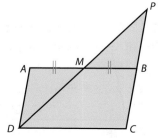

12. In the given parallelogram, DE ⊥ AC and BF ⊥ AC. The area of ABCD is 80 cm².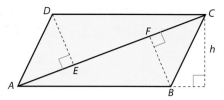

   (i) If |AC| = 16 cm, find |DE|.

   (ii) Explain why |DE| = |BF|.

   (iii) If |AB| = 10 cm, find the length of the perpendicular height, h.

13. ABCD is a parallelogram and E is a point on [AB].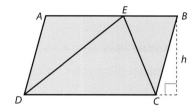

   (i) Explain why the area of △DCE is equal to half the area of ABCD.

   (ii) If the area of ABCD is 60 cm² and the area of △ADE is 20 cm², find the area of △ECB.

Section 11.3 Triangles and ratios

Angles and sides

The triangle ABC on the right is drawn to scale.

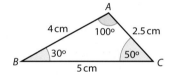

Notice   (i)   the largest angle is opposite the longest side

         (ii)   the smallest angle is opposite the shortest side.

These properties will hold for all triangles and are stated in the theorem below.

> **Theorem**
> The angle opposite the greater of two sides is greater than the angle opposite the lesser side.

In the given triangle ABC, we are given the measures of the three angles.

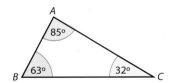

> **Converse** means opposite or reversed.

The converse of the theorem above states that [BC] is the longest side because it is opposite the greatest angle and [AB] is the shortest side because it is opposite the smallest angle.

> **Converse of theorem:**
> The side opposite the greater of two angles is longer than the side opposite the lesser angle.

Triangle inequality

The shortest distance between two points is the line that joins these points.

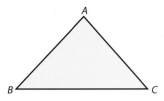

It follows from this that

$$|BA| + |AC| > |BC|$$

Similarly $|AB| + |BC| > |AC|$

and $|BC| + |CA| > |AB|$.

Theorem
Two sides of a triangle are together greater than the third side.

Transversals

In the given diagram, ℓ, m and n are parallel lines.

The lines p and q are called **transversals**.

For the transversal p, $|AB| = |BC|$.

In this case we say that the parallel lines cut off **equal segments** on the transversal.

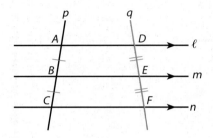

The line q is another transversal.
It can be shown that the line segments [DE] and [EF] are also equal in length.

The same property also holds for all other transversals.

> **Theorem**
> If three parallel lines cut off equal segments on some transversal line, then they will cut off equal segments on any other transversal.

Example 1

The diagram shows three parallel lines and two transversals, x and y.

$$|AB| = |BC|.$$

If $|DE| = 6$ cm, find $|EF|$.

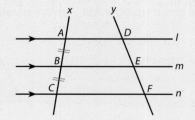

Since the parallel lines cut equal segments on the transversal x, they will also cut equal segments on the transversal y.

∴ $|DE| = |EF|$
∴ $|EF| = 6$ cm

Line parallel to a side of a triangle

The diagram on the right shows the side [AB] of the triangle divided into three equal parts. If lines are drawn through D and E parallel to BC, then the points X and Y will divide the side [AC] into three equal parts also.

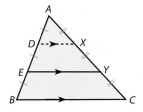

In the given triangle, X divides the side [AB] in the ratio $s : t$.

If XY is parallel to BC, then Y will divide [AC] also in the ratio $s : t$, as shown.

This diagram illustrates a very important and useful geometric result which is given on the right.

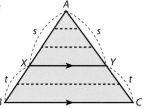

Theorem
A line drawn parallel to one side of a triangle divides the other two sides in the same ratio.

Example 2

In the given triangle, the arrows indicate that the lines are parallel. Find the length of the side marked x.

$$\frac{3}{4} = \frac{2}{x}$$

$3x = 8$ ...multiply both sides by $4x$

$x = \frac{8}{3} = 2\frac{2}{3}$

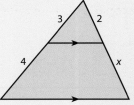

Similar triangles

The triangles ABC and DEF shown below have equal angles.

Notice that the triangles have the same shape but different sizes.
These triangles are said to be **similar** or **equiangular** triangles.

The sides [AB] and [DE] are said to be **corresponding sides**, as they are both opposite the 60° angle.

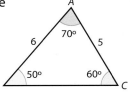

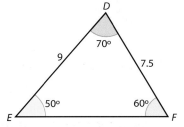

Notice that $|DE| = 1\frac{1}{2}|AB|$ and $|DF| = 1\frac{1}{2}|AC|$.

Similarly $|EF|$ is $1\frac{1}{2}|BC|$.

This illustrates that $\dfrac{|AB|}{|DE|} = \dfrac{|AC|}{|DF|} = \dfrac{|BC|}{|EF|} = \dfrac{6}{9} = \dfrac{2}{3}$.

This important result for similar triangles is stated in the theorem on the right.

Theorem

If two triangles ABC and DEF are similar, then their sides are proportional, in order

$$\frac{|AB|}{|DE|} = \frac{|BC|}{|EF|} = \frac{|AC|}{|DF|}$$

> **Example 3**

(i) Explain why the two given triangles are similar.
(ii) Find the length of the side marked x.

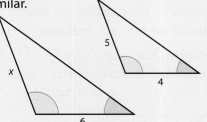

(i) Two angles in one triangle are equal to two angles in the other triangle. Thus the third angles in the triangles are equal.

(ii) $\frac{x}{5} = \frac{6}{4}$

$4x = 30$

$x = \frac{30}{4} = 7\frac{2}{4} = 7\frac{1}{2}$

> Two triangles will be similar if 2 angles in one triangle are equal to 2 angles in the other triangle.

Exercise 11.3

1. (i) Which is the longest side in the given triangle ABC?
   (ii) Which is the shortest side?
   (iii) Explain why $|BA| + |AC| > |BC|$.

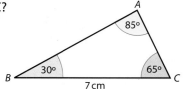

2. In the given triangle XYZ, $|XY| = 7$ cm and $|YZ| = 10$ cm.
   Say if each of the following
   (i) could be true
   (ii) is false
       (a) $|XZ| = 2$ cm
       (b) $|XZ| = 6$ cm
       (c) $|XZ| = 18$ cm.

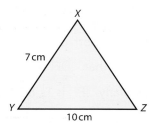

3. In the given triangle, $|AB| = 5$ cm, $|BC| = 10$ cm and $|AC| = 8$ cm.

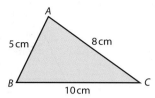

   (i) Name the largest angle in this triangle. Give a reason for your answer.
   (ii) Name the smallest angle.

4. a, b and c are parallel lines.
   p, q and r are three transversals intersecting a, b and c.
   $|DE| = |EF|$, $|GH| = 8$ cm and $|JK| = 7$ cm.

   Find   (i) $|HI|$ (ii) $|GJ|$.

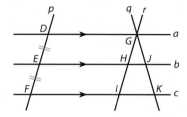

5. In the diagram, ℓ, m and n are parallel lines.
   They make intercepts of the indicated lengths
   on the lines j and k.
   AB is parallel to j.

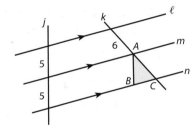

   (i) Write down the length of [AB].
   (ii) Write down the length of [AC].

6. In each of the following triangles, the arrows indicate that the lines are parallel.
   Find the length of the line segment marked x in each triangle:

   (i)

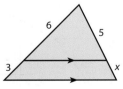

   (ii)

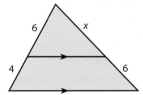

   (iii)

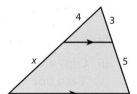

7. Find the length of the line segment marked a in each of the following triangles, where
   the arrows indicate parallel lines:

   (i)

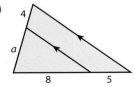

   (ii)

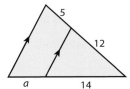

   (iii)

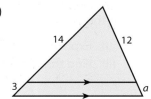

8. In the given diagram, DE‖BC.

   If $\dfrac{|AD|}{|DB|} = \dfrac{2}{1}$ and $|AE| = 14$ cm,

   find $|EC|$.

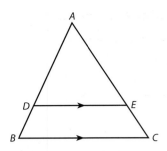

9. In the given diagram, PQ‖YZ and $\dfrac{|XQ|}{|QZ|} = \dfrac{5}{3}$.

   If $|PY| = 4$ cm, find $|PX|$.

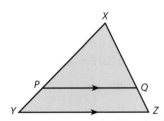

10.

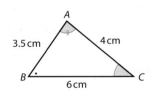

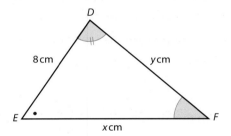

   (i)   Explain why the triangles ABC and DEF are similar.
   (ii) Which side of the triangle DEF corresponds to the side [AC]?
   (iii) Find the values of x and y.

11. The two given triangles are similar.

   (i) Copy and complete this statement:
        'Each side of the bigger triangle is… times
        the length of the corresponding side of
        the smaller triangle'.
   (ii) Find the values of x and y.

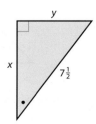

12. In the given triangles, the marked angles are equal.

   (i) Explain why the two triangles are similar.
   (ii) Find the values of x and y.

13. The triangles ABC and XYZ are similar.

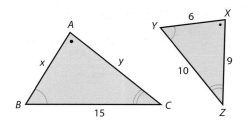

    (i) Which side of the triangle XYZ corresponds to [AB]? Explain your answer.

   (ii) Find the values of x and y.

14. Find the value of x and the value of y in the given similar triangles.

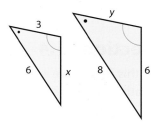

15. In the given figure, BC∥DE.
Draw the triangles ABC and ADE as separate diagrams.
Mark in the lengths of the known sides in each triangle.

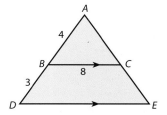

    (i) Explain why the triangles ABC and ADE are similar.

   (ii) Now find |DE|.

16. ABCD is a quadrilateral in which AB∥DC and $|\angle DAB| = |\angle DBC|$.

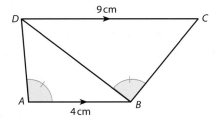

    (i) Name two other equal angles in this figure.

   (ii) Now explain why the triangles ABD and DCB are similar.

  (iii) Which side in △DCB corresponds to [DB] in △ABD?

  (iv) Which side in △ABD corresponds to [BC] in △BCD?

17. In the given triangle, DE∥BC.
$|AD| = 8$,
$|DB| = 4$ and
$|AC| = 9$.
Find |AE|.
[Hint: Let $|AE| = x$ $\Rightarrow$ $|EC| = 9 - x$.]

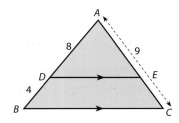

319

18. Explain why the triangles ABC and ADE are similar.

    (i) Fill in the missing parts in these ratios:

$$\frac{|AD|}{|AB|} = \frac{|AE|}{\boxed{}} = \frac{|DE|}{\boxed{}}.$$

    (ii) Use these ratios to find the values of x and y.

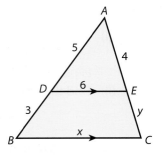

Section 11.4 Circle theorems

In this section we will deal with the geometry of the circle and look at some important mathematical results known as **circle theorems**.

You will have already learned that the angle in a semicircle is a right angle.

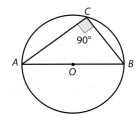

In this circle, $|\angle ACB| = 90°$.

Tangents and chords

A tangent to a circle is a straight line which meets the circle at one point only.

In the given diagram, ℓ is a tangent to the circle.

T is called the **point of contact**.

[AB] and [CD] are **chords** of the circle.

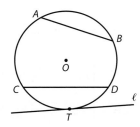

In the given diagram, [OM] is perpendicular to the chord [AB].

    $\therefore \quad |AM| = |MB|$

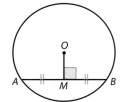

> **Theorem**
> The perpendicular from the centre of a circle to a chord bisects the chord.

Example 1

In the given diagram, O is the centre of the circle and [OM] is perpendicular to [AB]. If $|OM| = 5$ and $|OB| = 13$, find $|AB|$.

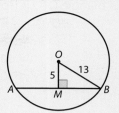

The triangle OBM is right-angled.

$$\therefore \quad |OB|^2 = |OM|^2 + |MB|^2$$
$$13^2 = 5^2 + |MB|^2$$
$$169 = 25 + |MB|^2$$
$$|MB|^2 + 25 = 169$$
$$|MB|^2 = 169 - 25$$
$$= 144$$
$$|MB| = 12$$

Since M is the midpoint of [AB], $|AM| = |MB|$.
$$|AB| = |AM| + |MB|$$
$$= 12 + 12$$
$$|AB| = 24$$

The diagram below shows a tangent PT to the circle k with centre O.

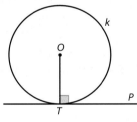

Theorem (1)
A tangent is perpendicular to the radius that goes to the point of contact.

T is the point of contact and [OT] is a radius. $OT \perp TP$

Theorem (2)
If a point P lies on a circle k, and a line ℓ is perpendicular to the radius to P, then ℓ is a tangent to k.

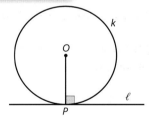

Example 2

In the given diagram, PT is a tangent to the circle and [OT] is a radius.

If $|\angle TOQ| = 120°$, find the measures of the angles marked x and y.

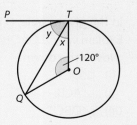

The triangle OTQ is isosceles as $|OT| = |OQ| = $ radius

$\therefore \quad |\angle OTQ| = |\angle OQT| = x$

$\therefore \qquad 2x = 180° - 120°$

$\qquad\qquad = 60$

$\qquad\quad x = 30°$

Since $OT \perp PT \implies |\angle OTP| = 90°$

$\therefore \quad x + y = 90°$

$\qquad 30 + y = 90° \qquad \ldots x = 30°$

$\qquad\qquad y = 90° - 30°$

$\qquad\qquad y = 60°$

Corollary

If two circles intersect at one point only, then the two centres and the point of contact are collinear.

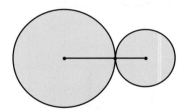 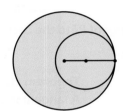

A **corollary** is a statement attached to a theorem which has been proven and follows obviously from it.

Exercise 11.4

1. Find the measure of the angles marked with letters in the following circles with O as centre:

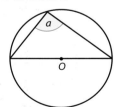 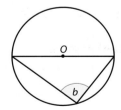 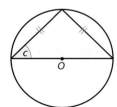

2. In the given circle, O is the centre.
   Explain why △OAC is isosceles.
   Now write down
   (i) $|\angle OCA|$
   (ii) $|\angle ACB|$
   (iii) $|\angle OBC|$

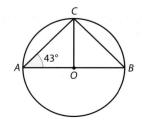

322

3. Find the measure of the angles marked with letters in the following diagrams, where O is the centre of the circles.

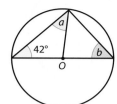 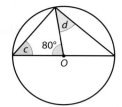 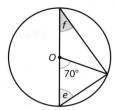

4. In the given diagram, O is the centre of the circle, $|AB| = 6$ and $|OB| = 5$.
   (i)   Name the right-angled triangle.
   (ii) $|OB| = 5$.
         Name two other line segments that are 5 units in length.
   (iii) Find $|AC|$.
   (iv) Find $|BC|$.
   (v)   Find the area of $\triangle ABC$.

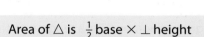

Area of $\triangle$ is $\frac{1}{2}$ base $\times \perp$ height

5. In the given figure, O is the centre of the circle and OM $\perp$ AB.
   If $|OM| = 5\,cm$ and $|AB| = 12\,cm$, find
   (i) $|AM|$
   (ii) the length of the radius of the circle.

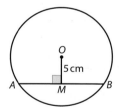

6. In the given diagram, O is the centre of the circle of radius 26 cm.
   OX is perpendicular to CD and $|OX| = 10\,cm$.
   Find $|CD|$.

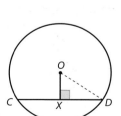

7. ST is a tangent to the given circle with O as centre.
   If $|\angle PST| = 40°$, find
   (i) $|\angle OST|$
   (ii) $|\angle OSP|$
   (iii) $|\angle OPS|$
   (iv) $|\angle SOP|$

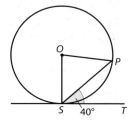

8. In the given diagram, PT is a tangent to the circle of centre O and $|\angle BPE| = 55°$.

Find   (i) $|\angle EPO|$
         (ii) $|\angle BPO|$
         (iii) $|\angle ABP|$
         (iv) $|\angle BAP|$.

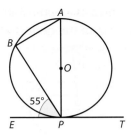

9. In the given figure, BX is a tangent to the circle with centre O.

If $|\angle XOD| = 120°$, find $|\angle OBX|$.

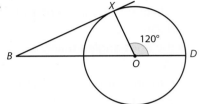

10. In the given diagram, PT is a tangent to the circle of centre O and radius length 5 cm.

If $|PQ| = 8$ cm, find $|PT|$.

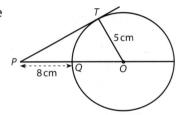

11. In the given diagram, PQ is a tangent to the circle of centre O.

If $|\angle TPO| = 30°$, find
   (i) $|\angle POT|$
   (ii) $|\angle TOR|$
   (iii) $|\angle ORT|$
   (iv) $|\angle RTO|$.

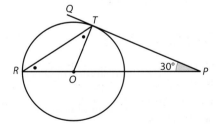

12. PT is a tangent to the circle of centre O.

If $|\angle POT| = 70°$ and $|\angle PAO| = 40°$,
find   (i) $|\angle OPT|$
         (ii) $|\angle OPA|$.

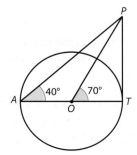

13. In the given diagram, O is the centre of the circle.
    PA and PB are tangents to the circle.
    (i) Explain why the triangles AOP and BOP
        are congruent.
    (ii) Hence show that |PA| = |PB|.

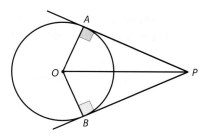

> The lengths of two tangents from a
> point to a circle are equal.

14. In the given diagram, PA and PT are tangents to the circle of centre O.

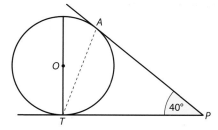

    If |∠APT| = 40°, find |∠ATO|.

15. In the given diagram, AB is a tangent to the
    circle and [AD] is a diameter.
    If |∠ABD| = 70° and |AB| = |AE|,
    find   (i) |∠EAB|
            (ii) |∠DAE|
            (iii) |∠ADE|.

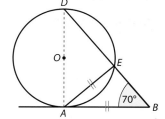

Section 11.5 Formal proofs of theorems

Geometry results or **theorems** are proved in a
formal or structured way by using previously
established results and axioms to explain the
steps that we take. This method of proving
geometric results was first used by a Greek
mathematician named Euclid about 300 BC.

> An **axiom** is a statement
> accepted without proof. The
> angles in a straight line add to
> 180° is an example of an axiom.

The proofs of numerous theorems are contained
in his famous book on geometry called *Elements*.
Today, over 2000 years later, we still use Euclid's
approach to solve many problems in geometry.

> A **theorem** is a statement
> that can be shown to be true
> through the use of axioms and
> logical argument.

In this section formal proofs of the ten theorems on your course are given. You will not be
asked to reproduce these proofs in your examination. They are given here to illustrate the
formal steps that are followed in the proof of a geometric theorem.

You will be familiar with the results of these theorems from the earlier sections of this chapter.
The various geometric problems that you solved used the results established in these theorems.

Theorem 1 The angle opposite the longer of two sides is greater than the angle opposite the shorter side.

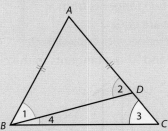

Given: The triangle ABC in which $|AC| > |AB|$

To Prove: $|\angle ABC| > |\angle ACB|$.

Construction: Take the point D on [AC] such that $|AD| = |AB|$. Join BD. Name the angles 1, 2, 3 and 4, as shown.

Proof:
$|\angle 1| = |\angle 2|$ …isosceles triangle
$|\angle 2| > |\angle 3|$ …exterior angle > interior angle
$\Rightarrow\ |\angle 1| > |\angle 3|$
$\Rightarrow\ |\angle 1| + |\angle 4| > |\angle 3|$
$\Rightarrow\ |\angle ABC| > |\angle ACB|$

Theorem 2 The sum of the lengths of any two sides of a triangle is greater than that of the third side.

Given: The triangle ABC.

To Prove: $|BA| + |AC| > |BC|$

Construction: Produce BA to D such that $|AD| = |AC|$. Join DC.

Proof:
$|\angle ACD| = |\angle ADC|$ …($|AD| = |AC|$)
But $|\angle BCD| > |\angle ACD|$
$\Rightarrow\ |\angle BCD| > |\angle ADC|$
In the triangle BCD, $|BD| > |BC|$ …side opposite greater angle
But $|BD| = |BA| + |AC|$
$\Rightarrow\ |BA| + |AC| > |BC|$.

| **Theorem 3** | If three parallel lines make segments of equal length on a transversal, then they will also make segments of equal length on any other transversal. |

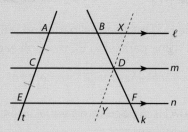

| *Given:* | Three parallel lines ℓ, m and n intersecting the transversal t at the points A, C and E such that $|AC| = |CE|$. |
| | Another transversal k intersects the lines at B, D and F. |

| *To prove:* | $|BD| = |DF|$. |

| *Construction:* | Through D draw a line parallel to t intersecting ℓ at X and n at Y. |

| *Proof:* | ACDX and CEYD are parallelograms. |

$\Rightarrow$ $|AC| = |XD|$ and $|CE| = |DY|$ ...opposite sides

But $|AC| = |CE|$.

$\Rightarrow$ $|XD| = |DY|$

In the triangles BDX and YDF,

$\qquad |XD| = |DY|$

$\quad |\angle BDX| = |\angle YDF|$ ...vertically opposite

$\quad |\angle DBX| = |\angle DFY|$ ...alternate angles

$\Rightarrow$ the triangles BDX and YDF are congruent

$\Rightarrow$ $|BD| = |DF|$ ...corresponding sides

| **Theorem 4** | Let ABC be a triangle. If a line XY is parallel to BC and cuts [AB] in the ratio $s : t$, then it cuts [AC] also in the same ratio. |

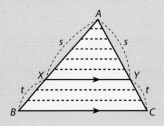

Given:	The triangle ABC with XY parallel to BC.

To Prove:	$\dfrac{|AX|}{|XB|} = \dfrac{|AY|}{|YC|}$

Construction:	Divide [AX] into s equal parts and [XB] into t equal parts. Draw a line parallel to BC through each point of the division.

Proof: The parallel lines make intercepts of equal length along the line [AC].

∴   [AY] is divided into s equal intercepts and [YC] is divided into t equal intercepts.

∴ $\dfrac{|AY|}{|YC|} = \dfrac{s}{t}$

But $\dfrac{|AX|}{|XB|} = \dfrac{s}{t}$ $\Rightarrow$ $\dfrac{|AX|}{|XB|} = \dfrac{|AY|}{|YC|}$

Theorem 5   If two triangles ABC and DEF are similar, then their sides are proportional in order:

$$\frac{|AB|}{|DE|} = \frac{|BC|}{|EF|} = \frac{|AC|}{|DF|}$$

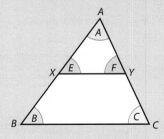

Given:	The triangles ABC and DEF in which $|\angle A| = |\angle D|, |\angle B| = |\angle E|$ and $|\angle C| = |\angle F|$.

To Prove:	$\dfrac{|AB|}{|DE|} = \dfrac{|BC|}{|EF|} = \dfrac{|AC|}{|DF|}.$

Construction:	Mark the point X on [AB] such that $|AX| = |DE|$. Mark the point Y on [AC] such that $|AY| = |DF|$. Join XY.

Proof: The triangles AXY and DEF are congruent   ...(SAS)

∴ $|\angle AXY| = |\angle DEF| = E$ ...corresponding angles

∴ $|\angle AXY| = |\angle ABC|$

∴   XY||BC

∴ $\dfrac{|AB|}{|AX|} = \dfrac{|AC|}{|AY|}$ ...a line parallel to one side divides the other side in the same ratio

∴ $\dfrac{|AB|}{|DE|} = \dfrac{|AC|}{|DF|}$

Similarly it can be proved that $\dfrac{|AB|}{|DE|} = \dfrac{|BC|}{|EF|}$.

∴ $\dfrac{|AB|}{|DE|} = \dfrac{|BC|}{|EF|} = \dfrac{|AC|}{|DF|}$.

Theorem 6   For a triangle, base times height does not depend on the choice of base.

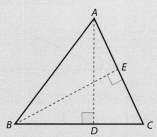

Given: The triangle ABC with AD ⊥ BC and BE ⊥ AC.

To prove: $|BC|\cdot|AD| = |AC|\cdot|BE|$.

Proof: In the triangles ADC and BEC

$|\angle ADC| = |\angle BEC| = 90°$

∠ACD is common to both

⇒ $|\angle CAD| = |\angle EBC|$

⇒   the triangles ADC and BEC are similar

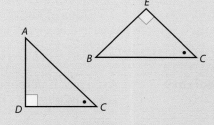

Since the corresponding sides are in the same ratio,

⇒ $\dfrac{|AD|}{|BE|} = \dfrac{|AC|}{|BC|}$

⇒ $|BC|\cdot|AD| = |AC|\cdot|BE|$.

Theorem 7

Given:

To prove:

Proof:

A diagonal bisects the area of a parallelogram.

The parallelogram ABCD and the diagonal [AC].

The diagonal [AC] bisects the area of ABCD.

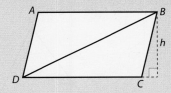

In the triangles ABC and ADC,

|AB| = |DC| ...opposite sides

|BC| = |AD| ...opposite sides

|AC| = |AC|

∴   the triangles ABC and ADC are congruent   ...(SSS)

∴   the area of △ABC = area of △ADC

∴   the diagonal [AC] bisects the area of ABCD.

Theorem 8

The area of a parallelogram is the base by the height.

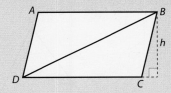

Given:

To Prove:

Proof:

The parallelogram ABCD with perpendicular height, h.

The area of ABCD = |DC| × h.

Area of △BCD = $\frac{1}{2}$ base × perpendicular height

= $\frac{1}{2}$|DC| × h

Area of △ABD = area of △BCD   ...diagonal bisects area of a parallelogram

⇒   Area ABCD = $2\left[\frac{1}{2}|DC| \times h\right]$

Area of ABCD = |DC| × h

Theorem 9

Given:

A tangent is perpendicular to the radius that goes to the point of contact.

A tangent t to a circle of centre O. P is the point of contact of the tangent and circle and [OP] is the radius to the point of contact.

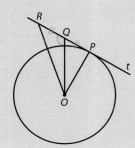

To prove:	OP $\perp$ t
Construction:	Let the perpendicular to the tangent from the centre O meet it at Q. Pick another point R on t such that $\lvert PQ \rvert = \lvert QR \rvert$. Join OQ and OR.
Proof:	In the triangles OPQ and OQR,

$$\lvert OQ \rvert = \lvert OQ \rvert \quad \text{...common side}$$
$$\lvert PQ \rvert = \lvert QR \rvert \quad \text{...given}$$
$$\lvert \angle OQP \rvert = \lvert \angle OQR \rvert \quad \text{...both 90°}$$

$\therefore$ the triangles OPQ and OQR are congruent   ...(RHS)

$\therefore$ $\lvert OR \rvert = \lvert OP \rvert$ ...both hypotenuses

So R is a second point where t meets the circle.

This contradicts the given fact that t is a tangent.

Thus t must be perpendicular to [OP], i.e., OP $\perp$ t.

Note: The proof above is an example of proof by contradiction.

Theorem 10	The perpendicular from the centre of a circle to a chord bisects the chord.
Given:	A circle k with centre O and a chord [AB]. OM $\perp$ AB.
To Prove:	$\lvert AM \rvert = \lvert MB \rvert$
Construction:	Join OA and OB.
Proof:	In the triangles AOM and BOM,

$$\lvert OA \rvert = \lvert OB \rvert \quad \text{... = radius}$$
$$\lvert OM \rvert = \lvert OM \rvert \quad \text{...common side}$$
$$\lvert \angle OMA \rvert = \lvert \angle OMB \rvert \quad \text{...both = 90°}$$

$\therefore$ the triangles AOM and BOM are congruent   ...(RHS)

$\therefore$ $\lvert AM \rvert = \lvert MB \rvert$.

Test yourself 11

1. In the given triangle, marked sides are equal and $|\angle CAE| = 124°$.
   (i) What sort of triangle is ABC?
   (ii) Name two equal angles.
   (iii) Find $|\angle ABC|$.

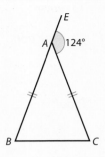

2. ABCD is a parallelogram.
   If $|\angle CAB| = 25°$ and $|\angle BDC| = 55°$, find $|\angle AOD|$.

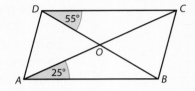

3. Find the area of each of the parallelograms shown below:

   (i)
   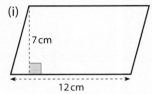

   (ii)
   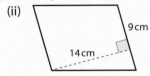

   (iii)
   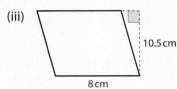

4. The area of the given parallelogram is $280\ cm^2$.
   (i) Find the value of h.
   (ii) If $|AB| = 28\ cm$, find the perpendicular height from A to DC.

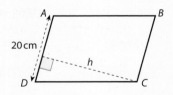

5. ABCD and ABDE are both parallelograms.
   (i) Explain why ABCD and ABDE are equal in area.
   (ii) If the area of $\triangle ABC = 24\ cm^2$, find the area of the figure ABCE.

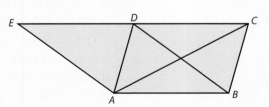

6. In the given figure, BC is a tangent to the circle at B and O is the centre of the circle.
   (i) Explain why $OB \perp BC$.
   (ii) Name two line segments that are equal in length.
   (iii) Find $|\angle BOA|$.

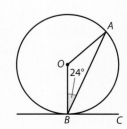

7. In the given diagram PT is a tangent to the circle of centre O and radius 7 cm.

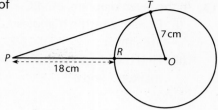

    (i) What is |∠PTO|?
        Explain your answer.
   (ii) Write down |PO|.
  (iii) Find |PT|.

8. In the given circle, O is the centre, |∠ACD| = 65° and |AB| = |BC|.

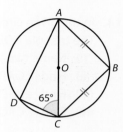

    (i) Name two right angles in the figure.
   (ii) Find |∠BAD|.

9. In the given circle, O is the centre and the angles x and y are marked.

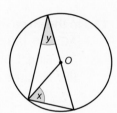

    (i) Copy this figure and mark in another angle x
        and another angle y.
   (ii) Explain why $x + y = 90°$.

10. PT is a tangent to the circle at T.
The centre of the circle is O.
|PT| = 6 cm and |ON| = |NP|.

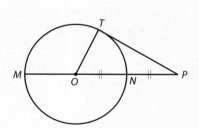

    (i) What is |∠OTP|?
   (ii) Find the length of the radius of the circle.

11. In the given triangle , $\ell \| k$.
Calculate the value of x.

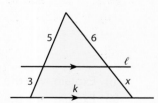

12. In the given triangle, XY||BC and |AX| : |XB| = 3 : 2.
If |YC| = 10 cm, find |AY|.

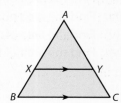

13. In the given diagram, DE∥BC.

   (i) Explain why the triangles ADE and ABC are similar.

   (ii) Find the length of the line segments marked x and a.

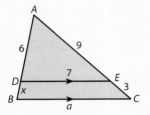

14. In the given circle, O is the centre and AD is a tangent at A. The triangle AOB is equilateral.

   (i) Name two right angles in the figure.

   (ii) Find $|\angle OAB|$

   (iii) Find $|\angle BAD|$

   (iv) Find $|\angle CAO|$.

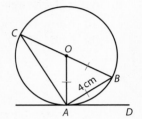

15. In the given figure, $\angle CAB$ and $\angle ABD$ are both right angles. $|AC| = 6$, $|AB| = 8$ and $|AD| = 17$.

   (i) Find $|DB|$.

   (ii) Find the area of ACBD.

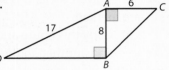

16. ABCD, AEBD and AEFC are parallelograms. The area of △ABE = 12 square units.

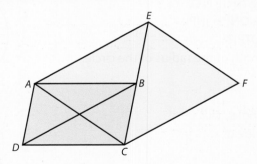

   (i) Explain why the area of △ABD is also 12 square units.

   (ii) Explain why the parallelograms ABCD and AEBD are equal in area.

   (iii) Find the area of the figure ADCE.

   (iv) Find the area of △ABC.

   (v) Find the area of △ACE.

   (vi) Find the area of the figure ADCFE.

Summary of key points...

1. The sum of the lengths of any two sides of a triangle is greater than the length of the third side.

2. The angle opposite the longer of two sides is greater than the angle opposite the shorter side.

3. For any triangle, base times height does not depend on the choice of base.

4. A diagonal of a parallelogram bisects the area.

5. The area of a parallelogram is the base multiplied by the perpendicular height.

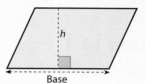

6. If three parallel lines cut off equal segments on some transversal line, then they will cut off equal segments on any other transversal.

7. A line drawn parallel to one side of a triangle divides the other two sides in the same ratio.

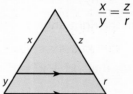

$$\frac{x}{y} = \frac{z}{r}$$

8.

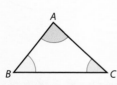
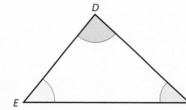

If two triangles ABC and DEF are similar, then their sides are proportional in order,

$$\frac{|AB|}{|DE|} = \frac{|BC|}{|EF|} = \frac{|AC|}{|DF|}.$$

9. The perpendicular from the centre of a circle bisects the chord.

10. A tangent is perpendicular to the radius that goes to the point of contact.

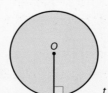

Key words

centre   radius   diameter   equation   inside   outside   element of
intersection   tangent   horizontal   perpendicular

Section 12.1 Equation of a circle with centre (0, 0)

The diagram opposite shows a circle with centre (0, 0)
and radius r.

$P(x, y)$ is any point on the circle.

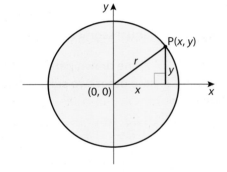

From the right-angled triangle, we see that

$$x^2 + y^2 = r^2$$

We say that $\mathbf{x^2 + y^2 = r^2}$ is the equation of the circle.

To find the equation of a circle, we need to know
  (i)   the centre of the circle
  (ii)   the length of the radius.

> The equation of the circle with centre (0, 0) and radius r is $x^2 + y^2 = r^2$.

Example 1

Find the equation of the circle with centre (0, 0) and radius
  (i)   3   (ii) $1\frac{1}{4}$.

(i)   The equation is $x^2 + y^2 = r^2$
                      $\Rightarrow$ $x^2 + y^2 = 9 \dots$ (r = 3)

(ii)   Here $r = 1\frac{1}{4} = \frac{5}{4}$

              $\Rightarrow$ $x^2 + y^2 = \left(\frac{5}{4}\right)^2$

              $\Rightarrow$ $x^2 + y^2 = \frac{25}{16}$

              $\Rightarrow$ $16x^2 + 16y^2 = 25 \dots$ multiply both sides by 16

Example 2

Find the equation of the circle with centre $(0, 0)$ and
which contains the point $(4, -1)$.

The radius of the circle is the distance from $(0, 0)$ to $(4, -1)$.

$\Rightarrow \quad r = \sqrt{(4 - 0)^2 + (-1 - 0)^2}$ $\qquad (x_1, y_1) \qquad (x_2, y_2)$

$\qquad = \sqrt{16 + 1} = \sqrt{17}$ $\qquad\qquad \downarrow \qquad\qquad \downarrow$

$\qquad\qquad\qquad\qquad\qquad\qquad\qquad (0, 0) \qquad (4, -1)$

Equation is $\quad x^2 + y^2 = r^2$

$\qquad \Rightarrow \quad x^2 + y^2 = (\sqrt{17})^2$ $\qquad\qquad (\sqrt{8})^2 = 8$

$\qquad \text{i.e.} \quad x^2 + y^2 = 17$ $\qquad\qquad (\sqrt{a})^2 = a$

Finding the radius when given the equation

The circle whose equation is $x^2 + y^2 = r^2$ has centre $(0, 0)$ and radius $= r$.

$\Rightarrow \quad$ the circle $x^2 + y^2 = 16$ has $\quad$ (i) centre at $(0, 0)$ $\qquad$ (ii) radius $= \sqrt{16} = 4$

However, if the equation of the circle is $4x^2 + 4y^2 = 9$, first divide each term by 4 so that the
equation is in the form $x^2 + y^2 = r^2$.

$\qquad \Rightarrow \quad 4x^2 + 4y^2 = 9 \quad \Rightarrow \quad x^2 + y^2 = \dfrac{9}{4}$

$\Rightarrow \quad$ the length of the radius $= \sqrt{\dfrac{9}{4}} = \dfrac{\sqrt{9}}{\sqrt{4}} = \dfrac{3}{2}$

Example 3

Find the length of the radius of these circles:
  (i) $x^2 + y^2 = 8$ $\qquad\qquad\qquad$ (ii) $\quad 9x^2 + 9y^2 = 16$

  (i) $x^2 + y^2 = 8$ $\qquad\qquad\qquad$ (ii) $\quad 9x^2 + 9y^2 = 16$

  $\Rightarrow \quad r = \sqrt{8}$ $\qquad\qquad\qquad\qquad \Rightarrow \quad x^2 + y^2 = \dfrac{16}{9}$ ... divide both sides by 9

  $\qquad = \sqrt{4}.\sqrt{2}$ $\qquad\qquad\qquad\qquad\qquad \Rightarrow \quad r = \sqrt{\dfrac{16}{9}}$

  $\Rightarrow \quad r = 2\sqrt{2}$ $\qquad\qquad\qquad\qquad\qquad \Rightarrow \quad r = \dfrac{4}{3}$

Exercise 12.1

1. Write down the equation of the circle with centre $(0, 0)$ and radius:
   (i) 2 $\qquad\qquad$ (ii) 3 $\qquad\qquad$ (iii) 1 $\qquad\qquad$ (iv) 5 $\qquad\qquad$ (v) $\sqrt{2}$

2. Write down the equation of the circle with centre $(0, 0)$ and radius:
   (i) $\sqrt{8}$ $\qquad\qquad$ (ii) $2\sqrt{2}$ $\qquad\qquad$ (iii) $3\sqrt{2}$ $\qquad\qquad$ (iv) $\dfrac{2}{3}$ $\qquad\qquad$ (v) $\dfrac{4}{3}$

3. Find the distance from $(0, 0)$ to $(-3, 4)$.

   Hence write down the equation of the circle with centre $(0, 0)$ and which contains the point $(-3, 4)$.

4. Find the equation of the circle with centre $(0, 0)$ and which passes through the point
       (i) $(2, 3)$ (ii) $(-1, 2)$ (iii) $(4, -3)$ (iv) $(4, 0)$

5. The given diagram shows two circles a and b, both with centres $(0, 0)$.

   a contains the point $(5, 0)$.

   b contains the point $(3, 0)$.
       (i) Write down the equation of circle a.
       (ii) Write down the equation of circle b.
       (iii) Write down the coordinates of the points where circle a intersects the y-axis.
       (iv) Write down the coordinates of the points where circle b intersects the x-axis.

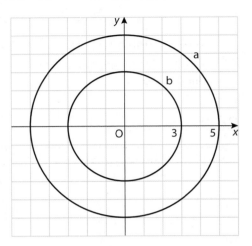

6. Draw a sketch of the circle $x^2 + y^2 = 16$. Mark on it the coordinates of the points where it crosses the x-axis and y-axis.

7. Express, in terms of π, the area of the circle $x^2 + y^2 = 36$.

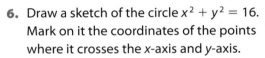

Area of circle $= \pi r^2$

8. Write down the radius of each of these circles:
       (i) $x^2 + y^2 = 9$ (ii) $x^2 + y^2 = 49$ (iii) $x^2 + y^2 = 1$
       (iv) $x^2 + y^2 = 12$ (v) $x^2 + y^2 = 27$ (vi) $x^2 + y^2 = 5$

9. Express each of the following circles in the form $x^2 + y^2 = k$.

   Hence write down the length of the radius of each circle:
       (i) $4x^2 + 4y^2 = 9$ (ii) $9x^2 + 9y^2 = 25$ (iii) $4x^2 + 4y^2 = 49$

10. The points $(4, 3)$ and $(-4, -3)$ are the end points of the diameter of a circle.

   Find
       (i) the coordinates of the centre of the circle
       (ii) the length of the radius
       (iii) the equation of the circle.

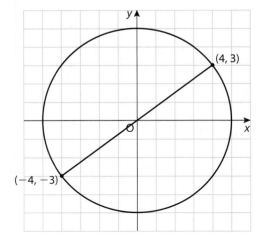

11. Find the length of the diameter of the circle $x^2 + y^2 = 81$.

12. Verify that $(2\sqrt{5})^2 = 20$.
Hence write down the equation of the circle with centre $(0, 0)$ and radius $= 2\sqrt{5}$.

13. Write down the equation of the circle with centre $(0, 0)$ and radius of length

    (i) $\sqrt{6}$ (ii) $2\sqrt{6}$ (iii) $3\sqrt{2}$ (iv) $2\sqrt{3}$ (v) $3\sqrt{5}$.

14. The equation of a circle, c, is $x^2 + y^2 = 9$.
Find the equation of the circle, d, with centre $(0, 0)$ and radius equal in length to the diameter of c.

Section 12.2 Points and Circles

A given point may be inside, on or outside a circle.

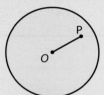 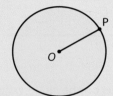 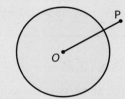

A point P is **inside** a circle if the distance from the centre of the circle to the point P is **less** than the radius.

A point P is **on a circle** if the distance from the centre of the circle to the point P is **equal** to the radius.

A point P is **outside** a circle if the distance from the centre of the circle to the point P is **greater than** the radius.

Example 1

Are the points
    (i) $(1, -3)$ and   (ii) $(3, -2)$ inside, outside or on the circle $x^2 + y^2 = 13$?

The length of the radius of the circle is $\sqrt{13}$.

(i) The distance from the centre $(0, 0)$ to $(1, -3)$ is
$$\sqrt{(1 - 0)^2 + (-3 - 0)^2} = \sqrt{1 + 9} = \sqrt{10}$$
Since $\sqrt{10} < \sqrt{13} \Rightarrow (1, -3)$ is inside the circle.

(ii) The distance from $(0, 0)$ to $(3, -2)$ is
$$\sqrt{(3 - 0)^2 + (-2 - 0)^2} = \sqrt{9 + 4} = \sqrt{13}$$
Since $\sqrt{13}$ is equal to the length of the radius of the circle,
$\Rightarrow$ $(3, -2)$ is on the circle.

Another method

Another method of determining whether a point is inside, on or outside a circle is to substitute the coordinates of the point into the given equation of the circle.

If $x^2 + y^2 < r^2$, the point is **inside** the circle.
If $x^2 + y^2 = r^2$, the point is **on** the circle.
If $x^2 + y^2 > r^2$, the point is **outside** the circle.

Example 2

Investigate if the point $(-3, 4)$ is inside, on or outside the circle $x^2 + y^2 = 16$.

Substituting -3 for x and 4 for y in the equation $x^2 + y^2 = 16$, we get

Is $(-3)^2 + (4)^2 = 16$?

$9 + 16 > 16$

i.e. $25 > 16$ ... (greater than r^2)

$\therefore$ $(-3, 4)$ is outside the circle.

Exercise 12.2

1. (i) Show that the point $(3, -1)$ is on the circle $x^2 + y^2 = 10$.
   (ii) Show that the point $(5, -1)$ is outside the circle $x^2 + y^2 = 20$.
   (iii) Show that the point $(1, 2)$ is inside the circle $x^2 + y^2 = 8$.

2. Investigate whether the point $(3, 2)$ is inside, on or outside the circle $x^2 + y^2 = 10$.

3. Verify that the point $(3, 4)$ is on the circle $x^2 + y^2 = 25$.
   Write down the coordinates of the four points at which this circle intersects the x-axis and y-axis.

4. Show that the following points are on the given circles:
   (i) $(2, 1)$: $x^2 + y^2 = 5$ (ii) $(-2, 5)$: $x^2 + y^2 = 29$
   (iii) $(-4, 0)$: $x^2 + y^2 = 16$ (iv) $(\sqrt{5}, \sqrt{5})$: $x^2 + y^2 = 10$

5. Investigate if each of the following points is inside, outside or on the given circle:
   (i) $(1, -4)$: $x^2 + y^2 = 16$ (ii) $(-2, 3)$: $x^2 + y^2 = 13$
   (iii) $(-5, 2)$: $x^2 + y^2 = 26$ (iv) $(-3, 1)$: $x^2 + y^2 = 12$

6. Which one of the following points is outside the circle $x^2 + y^2 = 34$?
   (i) $(5, -2)$ (ii) $(-5, 3)$ (iii) $(-4, 5)$

7. Draw a sketch of the circle $x^2 + y^2 = 16$.
   The circle intersects the y-axis at the points P and Q.
   (i) Find the coordinates of P and Q.   (ii) Find $|PQ|$.

8. $x^2 + y^2 = 18$.
   The point $(4, k)$ is outside the circle. Find the least possible value of k, if $k \in N$.

Section 12.3 The equation of a circle with centre (h, k) and radius r

The diagram below shows a circle with centre $C(h, k)$ and radius r.

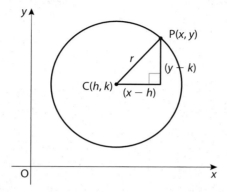

Let $P(x, y)$ be any point on the circle. The distance from C to P is equal to the radius.

Using the distance formula we have:

$$|CP| = \sqrt{(x - h)^2 + (y - k)^2} = r \quad \Rightarrow \quad (x - h)^2 + (y - k)^2 = r^2$$

This is the equation of the circle of centre (h, k) and radius r.

To use the formula above to find the equation of a circle, we need
  (i) the centre of the circle, (h, k) (ii) the radius of the circle, r.

> The equation of the circle with centre (h, k) and radius r is
> $$(x - h)^2 + (y - k)^2 = r^2.$$

Example 1

Find the equation of the circle with centre $(2, -3)$ and radius 5.

The equation is (h, k) $r = 5$

        $(x - h)^2 + (y - k)^2 = r^2$ $\downarrow$

$\Rightarrow$ $(x - 2)^2 + (y + 3)^2 = (5)^2$ $(2, -3)$

$\Rightarrow$ $(x - 2)^2 + (y + 3)^2 = 25$ is the equation

Finding the centre and radius when given the equation

In the equation $(x - h)^2 + (y - k)^2 = r^2$, centre $= (h, k)$ and radius $= r$.

In the equation $(x - 2)^2 + (y + 3)^2 = 16$,

we can see that $h = 2$ and $k = -3$;   also $r = \sqrt{16} = 4$.

$\Rightarrow$ centre $= (2, -3)$ and radius $= 4$.

Example 2

Find the centre and radius of the circle $(x + 3)^2 + (y - 4)^2 = 8$.

Comparing the equations $(x - h)^2 + (y - k)^2 = r^2$
and $(x + 3)^2 + (y - 4)^2 = 8$

we have $h = -3, k = 4$ and $r^2 = 8$
$$\Rightarrow \quad r = \sqrt{8}$$

$\therefore$ the centre $= (-3, 4)$ and radius $= \sqrt{8}$

Example 3

The circle with centre $(1, 3)$ passes through the
point $(3, 5)$.
Find the equation of the circle.

The radius is the distance from $(1, 3)$ to $(3, 5)$.

$$\text{Radius} = \sqrt{(x_2 - x_1)^2 + (y_2 - y_1)^2}$$
$$= \sqrt{(3 - 1)^2 + (5 - 3)^2}$$
$$= \sqrt{4 + 4} = \sqrt{8}$$

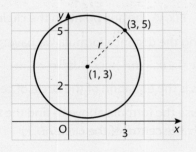

Equation of circle is: $(x - h)^2 + (y - k)^2 = r^2$ (h, k) $r = \sqrt{8}$
$$\Rightarrow \quad (x - 1)^2 + (y - 3)^2 = (\sqrt{8})^2 \qquad \downarrow$$
$$\Rightarrow \quad (x - 1)^2 + (y - 3)^2 = 8 \qquad\qquad (1, 3)$$

Exercise 12.3

1. Find the equations of the following circles, given the centre and radius in each case:
   - (i) centre $= (3, 1)$; radius $= 2$
   - (ii) centre $= (3, 4)$; radius $= 3$
   - (iii) centre $= (1, -4)$; radius $= 5$
   - (iv) centre $= (-3, 5)$; radius $= 4$
   - (v) centre $= (-3, -2)$; radius $= 1$
   - (vi) centre $= (3, 0)$; radius $= 6$
   - (vii) centre $= (-3, -5)$; radius $= \sqrt{10}$
   - (viii) centre $= (0, -2)$; radius $= 2\sqrt{2}$

2. The centre of a circle is $(2, 4)$ and it contains the point $(-1, 3)$.
   Find   (i) the length of the radius   (ii) the equation of the circle.

3. Find the equation of the circle which passes through the point $(-1, 5)$ and whose
   centre is $(5, -2)$.

4. The given circle has centre (2, 2).
   If the circle contains the point (5, 1),
   find its equation.

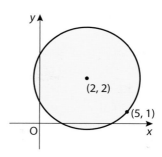

5. The line segment joining (3, 5) and (−1, 1) is the diameter of a circle.
   Find (i) the centre of the circle
      (ii) the length of the radius of the circle
      (iii) the equation of the circle.

Find the centre and radius of each of the following circles:

6. $(x − 2)^2 + (y − 3)^2 = 16$

7. $(x − 4)^2 + (y + 3)^2 = 9$

8. $(x + 2)^2 + (y + 5)^2 = 64$

9. $(x + 5)^2 + (y − 1)^2 = 81$

10. $x^2 + (y − 4)^2 = 25$

11. $(x − 3)^2 + y^2 = 9$

12. $(x − 1)^2 + (y + 5)^2 = \frac{16}{9}$

12. $x^2 + (y − 2)^2 = 12$

14. The given circle touches both the x-axis and y-axis.
    If the radius of the circle is 3, write down the
    coordinates of C, the centre.
    Hence write down the equation of the circle.

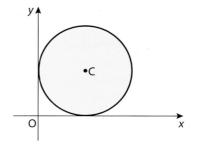

15. The diagram shows two circles C_1 and C_2.
    The centre of C_1 is on the x-axis and its
    radius is 4.
    (i) Write down the coordinates of the
        centre of C_1.
    (ii) Write down the equation of C_1.
    (iii) What is the length of the radius of C_2?
    (iv) Find the coordinates of the centre of C_2.
    (v) Write down the equation of C_2.
    (vi) Write down the coordinates of the point
        that is common to C_1 and C_2.

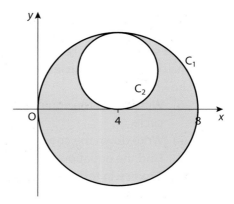

16. The diagram shows four circles of equal radius length.
The circles are touching as shown.
The equation of k_1 is $x^2 + y^2 = 4$.

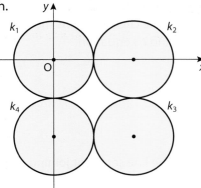

    (i) Write down the radius of k_1.

    (ii) Write down the coordinates of the centre of k_3.

    (iii) Write down the equation of k_3.

    (iv) Is $x^2 + (y + 4)^2 = 4$ the equation of k_2 or k_4? Explain your answer.

17. A$(-1, 2)$ and B$(5, 4)$ are the end points of the diameter of a circle k.
Find the coordinates of the centre of k and hence write down its equation.

18. The point $(4, 3)$ is the centre of a circle c. If the x-axis is a tangent to c find

    (i) the length of the radius of c (ii) the equation of c.

19. The given diagram shows four semicircles.
The centres all lie on the x-axis.
The radius length of the three smaller semicircles is 2.

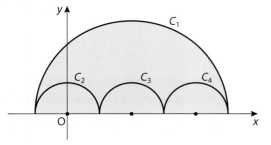

    (i) Find the coordinates of the centre of C_3.

    (ii) Write down the equation of C_3.

    (iii) Find the equation of C_1.

    (iv) Investigate whether the circumference of the semicircle C_1 is equal to the sum of the circumferences of the three smaller semicircles.

> You are finding the equation of the full circle in each case.

20. The diagram shows three semicircles C_1, C_2 and C_3.
Each semicircle has radius length 1 unit.
The centres of the circles are P, Q and R, as shown.

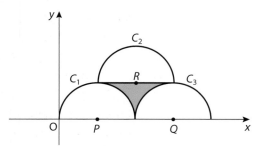

    (i) Write down the equation of the circle, C_1.

    (ii) Write down the coordinates of R.

    (iii) Find the equation of the circle, C_2.

    (iv) Express, in terms, of π the area of the shaded region in the diagram.

> Area of circle is πr^2.

Section 12.4 Intersection of a line and a circle

The diagram below shows a line ℓ intersecting a circle at the points A and B.

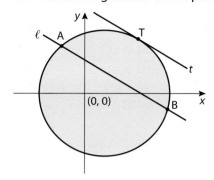

The line t intersects the circle at one point only. This line is said to be a **tangent** to the circle.

To find the point(s) of intersection of a line and circle, we express the line in the form

$$y = \ldots \qquad \text{or} \qquad x = \ldots$$

When selecting $y = \ldots$ or $x = \ldots$, avoid fractions if possible.

We then use simultaneous equations to find the point(s) of intersection of the line and circle.

> If a line is a tangent to a circle, it will intersect the circle at one point only.

Example 1

Find the points of intersection of the line $x + 3y - 5 = 0$ and the circle $x^2 + y^2 = 5$.

Step 1   Express x in terms of y in the equation of the line.
$$x + 3y - 5 = 0 \quad \Rightarrow \quad x = -3y + 5 \ldots \text{①}$$

Step 2   Substitute $(-3y + 5)$ for x in the equation of the circle.

$\Rightarrow \quad x^2 + y^2 = 5$ now becomes
$$(-3y + 5)^2 + y^2 = 5$$
$$\Rightarrow \quad 9y^2 - 30y + 25 + y^2 = 5$$
$$\Rightarrow \quad 10y^2 - 30y + 20 = 0$$
$$\Rightarrow \quad y^2 - 3y + 2 = 0 \ldots \text{ divide each term by 10.}$$
$$\Rightarrow \quad (y - 2)(y - 1) = 0$$
$$\Rightarrow \quad y = 2 \quad \text{or} \quad y = 1$$

Substituting these values for y in equation ① we get:
$$y = 2 \Rightarrow x = -3(2) + 5 \Rightarrow x = -1 \qquad \text{i.e. the point } (-1, 2)$$
$$y = 1 \Rightarrow x = -3(1) + 5 \Rightarrow x = 2 \qquad \text{i.e. the point } (2, 1)$$

Thus the two points of intersection are $(-1, 2)$ and $(2, 1)$.

Example 2

Show that the line $3x + y + 10 = 0$ is a tangent to the circle $x^2 + y^2 = 10$ and find the point of contact.

If $3x + y + 10 = 0 \Rightarrow y = -3x - 10$ ... ①

> Here we express y in terms of x to avoid fractions.

Substituting $(-3x - 10)$ for y in the equation of the circle we get:

$$x^2 + (-3x - 10)^2 = 10$$
$$\Rightarrow \quad x^2 + 9x^2 + 60x + 100 = 10$$
$$\Rightarrow \quad 10x^2 + 60x + 90 = 0$$
$$\Rightarrow \quad x^2 + 6x + 9 = 0 \text{ ...} \qquad \text{divide each term by 10}$$
$$\Rightarrow \quad (x + 3)(x + 3) = 0$$
$$\Rightarrow \quad x = -3 \text{ ...} \qquad \text{notice that there is only one value for } x$$

We now substitute -3 for x in equation ①

$$x = -3 \Rightarrow y = -3(-3) - 10$$
$$= 9 - 10 = -1 \qquad \text{i.e. the point } (-3, -1)$$

Therefore the point of intersection is $(-3, -1)$.
Since there is only one point of contact, the line is a tangent to the circle.

Exercise 12.4

1. Find the points of intersection of the line ℓ and the circle c in each of the following:
   (i) $\ell: x - y = 1$; $c: x^2 + y^2 = 13$
   (ii) $\ell: x + y - 4 = 0$; $c: x^2 + y^2 = 10$
   (iii) $\ell: x - 2y - 5 = 0$; $c: x^2 + y^2 = 25$
   (iv) $\ell: x + 3y - 10 = 0$; $c: x^2 + y^2 = 20$

2. Find the point of intersection of the line $2x - y - 5 = 0$ and the circle $x^2 + y^2 = 5$.

3. Show that the line ℓ is a tangent to the circle k in each of the following.
   Find the point of contact in each case:
   (i) $\ell: x + y - 2 = 0$; $k: x^2 + y^2 = 2$
   (ii) $\ell: x - 3y - 10 = 0$; $k: x^2 + y^2 = 10$
   (iii) $\ell: x - y - 4 = 0$; $k: x^2 + y^2 = 8$

4. Find the point(s) of intersection of the line $x - y - 3 = 0$ and the circle $x^2 + y^2 = 9$.
   Is the line a tangent to the circle? Explain your answer.

5. Find the points of intersection of the line $x - 2y = 0$ and $x^2 + y^2 = 20$.

6. Find the equation of the circle of centre $(0, 0)$ and which contains the point $(3, 1)$.
Find the coordinates of the points of intersection of this circle and the line $x + y + 4 = 0$.

7. A$(4, -1)$ and B$(-1, 4)$ are two points.
Find the equation of AB.
Now find the coordinates of the points of intersection of the line AB and the circle $x^2 + y^2 = 5$.

8. Show that the line $x - 2y + 10 = 0$ is a tangent to the circle $x^2 + y^2 = 20$ by finding the point of contact.

9. The diagram shows a circle of centre C and radius length 3.
The circle touches the x-axis and y-axis.

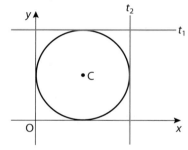

(i) Write down the coordinates of C.
(ii) Write down the equation of the circle.
(iii) The line t_1 is a tangent to the circle and is parallel to the x-axis.
Write down the equation of t_1.
(iv) The line t_2 is also a tangent to the circle and is parallel to the y-axis.
Find the equation of t_2.
(v) Write down the coordinates of the point of intersection of t_1 and t_2.

Section 12.5 A circle intersecting the axes

The circle shown intersects the x-axis at $(-1, 0)$ and $(4, 0)$.

In each of the points, the y-value is zero.

In general, when any line or circle intersects the x-axis, the y-values of the points of intersection will be zero.

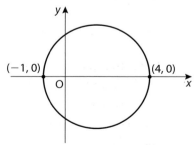

Similarly, a line or circle intersects the y-axis at the points where $x = 0$.

Example 1

Find the coordinates of the points at which
(i) the circle $x^2 + y^2 = 16$ intersects the x-axis
(ii) the circle $(x + 3)^2 + (y - 2)^2 = 10$ intersects the y-axis.

(i) $x^2 + y^2 = 16$ intersects the x-axis at the points where $y = 0$.

$$y = 0 \Rightarrow x^2 + 0 = 16$$
$$\Rightarrow x^2 = 16 \Rightarrow x = \pm 4$$
$$\Rightarrow x^2 + y^2 = 16 \text{ intersects the } x\text{-axis at } (4, 0) \text{ and } (-4, 0).$$

(ii) $(x + 3)^2 + (y - 2)^2 = 10$ intersects the y-axis at the points where $x = 0$.

$$x = 0 \Rightarrow (0 + 3)^2 + (y - 2)^2 = 10$$
$$\Rightarrow \quad 9 + y^2 - 4y + 4 = 10$$
$$\Rightarrow \quad \quad y^2 - 4y + 3 = 0$$
$$\Rightarrow \quad \quad (y - 1)(y - 3) = 0$$
$$\Rightarrow \quad \quad \quad y = 1 \quad \text{or} \quad y = 3$$
$$\Rightarrow \quad (x + 3)^2 + (y - 2)^2 = 10 \text{ intersects the } y\text{-axis at } (0, 1) \text{ and } (0, 3).$$

Exercise 12.5

1. Find the coordinates of the points where each of these circles intersect the x-axis:

(i) $x^2 + y^2 = 4$ 　　　　　(ii) $x^2 + y^2 = 25$ 　　　　　(iii) $x^2 + y^2 = 81$.

2. Find the coordinates of the points where the circle $x^2 + y^2 = 49$ intersects the y-axis.

3. Find the coordinates of the points where each of these circles intersect the x-axis:

(i) $(x - 5)^2 + (y + 4)^2 = 25$ 　　　　　(ii) $(x - 2)^2 + (y - 3)^2 = 25$

4. Find the coordinates of the points where the circle $(x - 2)^2 + (y + 3)^2 = 20$ intersects the y-axis.

5. Show that the point $(3, 2)$ is on the circle $(x - 6)^2 + (y - 6)^2 = 25$.

6. Write down the centre and radius length of the circle

$$(x + 4)^2 + (y - 1)^2 = 9.$$

Now show that the point $(-3, 0)$ is inside the circle.

7. Investigate if the point $(3, 2)$ is inside, on or outside the circle

$$(x - 2)^2 + (y + 1)^2 = 4.$$

8. The end points of a diameter of a circle are $(-2, -3)$ and $(-4, 3)$.
Find the equation of the circle.
The circle cuts the y-axis at the points A and B.
Find $|AB|$.

9. The x-axis is a tangent to the circle with centre $(-2, 4)$.
(i) What is the length of the radius of the circle?
(ii) Write down the equation of the circle.

Test yourself 12

1. The circle c has equation $x^2 + y^2 = 49$.
   (i) Write down the centre and radius of c.
   (ii) Verify that the point $(5, -5)$ is outside the circle c.

2. A circle k has centre $(0, 0)$ and it contains the point $(3, 4)$.
   Find the equation of k.
   Now write down the coordinates of the points where the circle k intersects the x-axis.

3. The circle c has equation $x^2 + y^2 = 36$.
   (i) Write down the length of the radius of c.
   (ii) Another circle has centre $(0, 0)$ and a radius that is twice the length of the radius of c.
   Write down the equation of this circle.

4. Find the equation of the circle with centre $(2, -3)$ and radius 4.

5. The equation of the circle c is $(x - 3)^2 + (y - 4)^2 = 25$.
   (i) Write down the centre and radius length of c. ·
   (ii) Show that the point $(6, 0)$ lies on the circle c.

6. Show that the line $x - 3y = 10$ is a tangent to the circle $x^2 + y^2 = 10$ by finding the point of intersection.

7. The equation of a circle is $x^2 + y^2 = 36$.
   (i) Find the length of the radius of the circle.
   (ii) Show, by calculation, that the point $(7, 1)$ is outside the circle.
   (iii) Find the coordinates of the points where the circle intersects the y-axis.

8. The diagram below shows three circles a, b and c with centres A, O and C respectively on the x-axis.

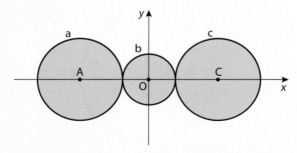

The radius of circle a and the radius of circle c are both equal to the diameter of circle b.
Circles a and c touch circle b, as shown.
If the equation of b is $x^2 + y^2 = 9$, find
   (i) the coordinates of A and C.
   (ii) the equations of the circles a and c
   (iii) the equations of the two tangents common to a and c but which do not touch b.

9. The line $y = 10 - 2x$ intersects the circle $x^2 + y^2 = 40$ at the points A and B.
    (i) Find the coordinates of A and the coordinates of B.
    (ii) Show the line, the circle and the points of intersection on a coordinate diagram.

10. The points $(-1, -1)$ and $(3, -3)$ are the end points of a diameter of a circle, s.
    (i) Find the centre and radius length of s.
    (ii) Find the equation of s.
    (iii) Show, by calculation, that the point $(1, -1)$ lies inside the circle.

11. A$(-1, 0)$ and B$(5, 0)$ are the end points of a diameter of the circle k with C as centre, as shown.
    (i) Write down the coordinates of C and the radius length of k.
    (ii) Find the equation of k.
    (iii) The lines t_1 and t_2 are tangents to the circle k and are parallel to the x-axis.
    Write down the equations of t_1 and t_2.

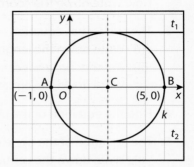

12. The line $x - 3y = 0$ intersects the circle $x^2 + y^2 = 10$ at the points A and B.
    (i) Find the coordinates of A and the coordinates of B.
    (ii) Show that [AB] is a diameter of the circle.

13. Write down the centre and radius length of the circle
$$(x - 3)^2 + (y - 4)^2 = 20.$$
The circle intersects the x-axis at A and B.
Find the coordinates of A and B.
Hence write down $|AB|$.

14. A$(0, -1)$ and B$(8, -1)$ is a diameter of a circle, as shown.

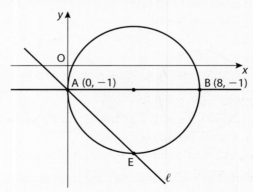

    (i) Find the centre and radius length of the circle.
    (ii) Write down the equation of the circle.

The line ℓ intersects the circle at A and E. The slope of ℓ is $-\frac{4}{5}$.
    (iii) Write down the slope of EB. Explain your answer.

15. The circle k has equation $(x + 2)^2 + (y - 3)^2 = 25$.

P and Q are the endpoints of a diameter of k and PQ is horizontal.

   (i) Write down the coordinates of the centre of k and its radius length.

  (ii) Draw a sketch of k on the coordinate plane.

 (iii) Find the coordinates of P and the coordinates of Q.

 (iv) Write down the equations of two vertical tangents to k.

  (v) Another circle also has these two vertical lines as tangents.

      The centre of this circle is on the x-axis.

      Find the equation of this circle.

16. A circle has equation $x^2 + y^2 = 13$.

The points A$(2, -3)$, B$(-2, 3)$ and C$(3, 2)$ are on the circle.

   (i) Verify that [AB] is a diameter of the circle.

  (ii) Verify that $|\angle ACB|$ is a right angle.

17. In the given diagram, k_1 is the circle of centre A$(0, 2)$ and radius 2.

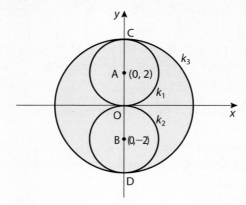

k_2 is the circle of centre B$(0, -2)$ and radius 2.

Write down the equations of k_1 and k_2.

k_3 is the circle of centre $(0, 0)$ which touches k_1 at C and k_2 at D.

Write down the equation of k_3.

Write down also the equation of the tangent common to k_1 and k_3 at the point C.

18. The circle k has equation $(x + 4)^2 + (y - 3)^2 = 36$.

   (i) Write down the coordinates of the centre of k and its radius length.

  (ii) Draw a sketch of k on a coordinate plane.

 (iii) The point $(2, 3)$ is one end-point of a diameter of k.

      Find the coordinates of the other end-point.

19. c is the circle with centre $(-1, 2)$ and radius 5.

Write down the equation of c.

The circle k has equation $(x - 8)^2 + (y - 14)^2 = 100$.

Show that P$(2, 6)$ is on the circle k.

Show also that P$(2, 6)$ is on the line which joins the centres of the two circles.

Summary of key points...

The equation of a circle

The equation of the circle with centre (0, 0) and radius r is

$$x^2 + y^2 = r^2$$

The equation of the circle with centre (h, k) and radius r is

$$(x - h)^2 + (y - k)^2 = r^2$$

Finding the centre and radius from the equation

For the circle $x^2 + y^2 = a^2$, centre = (0, 0), radius = a.

For the circle $(x - h)^2 + (y - k)^2 = a^2$, centre = (h, k), radius = a.

Points and circles

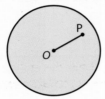
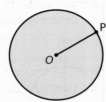
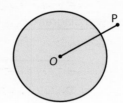

Point inside if   Point on if   Point outside if
$|OP| <$ radius $|OP| =$ radius $|OP| >$ radius

Intersection of a line and a circle

Simultaneous equations are used to find the point(s) of intersection of a line and a circle.

To find the points of intersection of the line $x + 3y - 5 = 0$ and the circle $x^2 + y^2 = 5$,

 (i)   express x in terms of y in the equation of the line,

       i.e. $x = -3y + 5$

 (ii) substitute this value for x into the equation of the circle,

       i.e. $(-3y + 5)^2 + y^2 = 5$

(iii) solve this equation to find two values for y

(iv)   find the two corresponding values for x.

A circle intersecting axes

A circle intersects the x-axis at the points where $y = 0$.

A circle intersects the y-axis at the points where $x = 0$.

Proving a line is a tangent to a circle

A line is a tangent to a circle if there is only one point of intersection.

Representing Data

chapter 13

Key words

bar chart   line plot   pie chart   histogram   equal class intervals
shape   continuous data   symmetrical distribution   positive skew
negative skew   stem and leaf diagram   back-to-back stem and leaf diagram
bivariate data   scatter graph   correlation   causal relationship

Section 13.1 Bar charts and Pie charts

1. Bar charts

Bar charts are a simple but effective way of displaying data.

A bar chart consists of a series of bars of the same width, drawn either vertically or horizontally from an axis.

The heights (or lengths) of the bars always represent the frequencies.

The bars are generally separated by narrow gaps of equal width.

Example 1

The frequency table shows the numbers of text messages received by a group of students on a particular Sunday.
Illustrate the information by a bar chart.

No. of messages	0	1	2	3	4	5	6	7	8	9
Frequency	0	1	2	4	6	9	11	14	9	4

The bar chart is shown below.

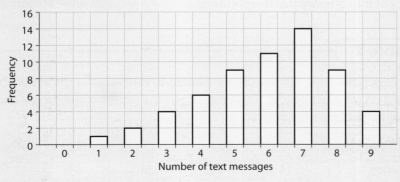

2. Line plots

A **line plot** is used to display small sets of discrete or categorical data. It is similar to a bar chart with dots (•) or crosses (×) used instead of a bar. Each dot represents one unit of the variable.

The line plot opposite shows the sales of the different-sized shoes by a shoe shop on a particular day.

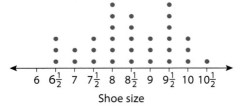

The number of pairs sold was

$$3 + 2 + 3 + 6 + 5 + 3 + 6 + 3 + 1 = 32$$

3. Pie charts

A **pie chart** is a good way of displaying data when you want to show how something is shared or divided. It is particularly suitable for displaying categorical data.

The pie chart below shows how Shane spent the last 24 hours.

The pie chart is divided up into sectors.

The whole circle represents the 24 hours.

We can see that Shane spent roughly the same time sleeping as he did at school.

The angle of each sector is proportional to the frequency of the category that it represents.

> Pie charts are particularly suitable for displaying categorical data.

Example 2

In a survey on holidays, 120 people were asked to state which type of transport they used on their last holiday. This table shows the results of the survey. Draw a pie chart to illustrate the data.

Type of transport	Train	Coach	Car	Ship	Plane
Frequency	24	12	59	11	14

We need to find the fraction of 360° which represents each type of transport.
This is usually done in a table, as shown below.

Type of transport	Frequency	Calculation
Train	24	$\frac{24}{120} \times 360 = 72°$
Coach	12	$\frac{12}{120} \times 360 = 36°$
Car	59	$\frac{59}{120} \times 360 = 177°$
Ship	11	$\frac{11}{120} \times 360 = 33°$
Plane	14	$\frac{14}{120} \times 360 = 42°$
Totals	120	360°

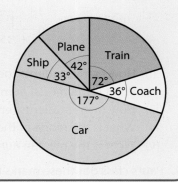

The pie chart is shown on the right.
A protractor was used to measure the angles.

This pie chart gives information about the medals won by an Athletics Club at a sports meeting.

If a total of 24 medals were won, we find the number of each
type as follows:

(i)   Gold medals: $\frac{75°}{360°} \times \frac{24}{1} = 5$

(ii) Silver medals: $\frac{150°}{360°} \times \frac{24}{1} = 10$

(iii) The angle in the bronze sector is $360° - 150° - 75° = 135°$.

Bronze medals: $\frac{135°}{360°} \times \frac{24}{1} = 9$

Exercise 13.1

1. The hair colours of all the students
   in a class are recorded.
   The bar chart on the right shows
   the results.

   (i)   How many students have
         black hair?
   (ii) Which hair colour is
         the mode?
   (iii) How many students are
         there in the class?

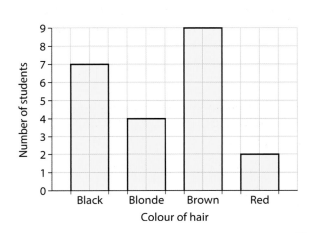

2. This bar chart shows the number of pictures remembered by each student in a memory experiment.

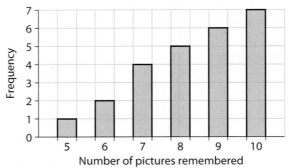

(i) How many students took part in the experiment?
(ii) What is the modal number of pictures remembered?
(iii) How many students remembered less than 7 pictures?
(iv) What is the range of the number of pictures remembered?
(v) What is the median number of pictures remembered?

3. Paul's class got these marks for a project.

19	16	45	43	40	39	36	30	28	42	35	40
32	38	41	48	27	18	29	38	42	26	41	35

(i) Use a copy of this table. Fill it in.

Mark	11–20	21–30	31–40	41–50
Tally				
Frequency				

(ii) Draw a bar chart for this data.

4.

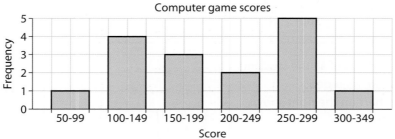

This graph shows scores in a computer game.
(i) Scores of 250 or more won a prize. How many people won a prize?
(ii) How many people played altogether?
(iii) A paper said that *'Five people scored between 270 and 299 points.'*
   Is this correct?
   Choose one of these answers.
   (a) Yes   (b) No   (c) Can't tell

5. This bar chart shows the numbers who attended five first-aid training sessions and the months during which these sessions took place.

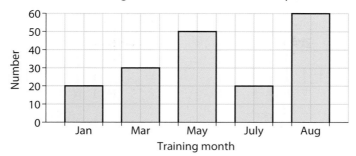

  (i) Find the total number who attended the five sessions.
 (ii) Which two months accounted for half the total that attended?
(iii) What was the mean number of people who attended each session?

6. This bar chart shows the average monthly temperature at noon for each of four months.
Brenda says 'the dotted line shows the mean for the four months'.
Use the bar chart to explain why Brenda cannot be correct.

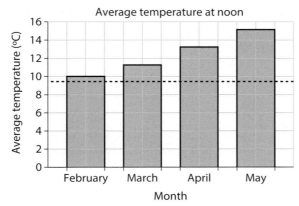

7. The line plot below illustrates the number of goals scored per match by a hockey team.

  (i) How many matches have the team played?
 (ii) Which number of goals scored is the mode?
(iii) What is the range of the number of goals scored?
(iv) What percentage of their matches were scoreless?

8. These bar charts show the number of hours of TV watched by four boys in one week.

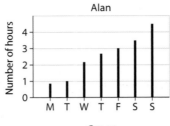

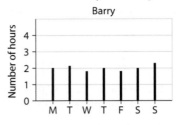

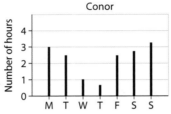

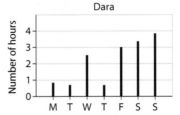

Whose graph matches these comments?
  (i)   I watched most TV at the beginning and end of the week.
  (ii) I watched about the same amount of TV each day.
  (iii) I watched quite a lot of TV on four days and not much on the other three days.
  (iv) Each day I watched more TV than the day before.

9. The bar chart below is called a dual bar chart. It compares two sets of data. It gives the number of patients attending surgeries in the mornings and evenings for six days.

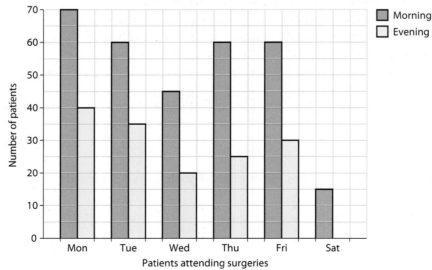

  (i)   On which day did most patients attend?
  (ii) On which day did fewest patients attend?
  (iii) On which day was there no evening surgery?
  (iv) On which day did 90 patients attend?
  (v)   How many more patients attended on Tuesday morning than on Tuesday evening?

10. The sizes of dresses sold in a shop during one week are given in the table below:

Size	8	10	12	14	16	18
Frequency	3	7	10	12	6	2

Draw a pie chart to illustrate this data.

11. The pie chart on the right illustrates the grades achieved by a group of 264 students.

Find the number of students that achieved grade E.

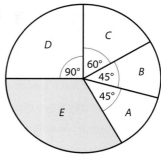

12. The given pie chart illustrates the favourite lessons of 120 Junior Cert students in a Cork school.
How many pupils named each of these as their favourite lessons?

  (i) maths   (ii) PE

What percentage of pupils chose science as their favourite lesson?

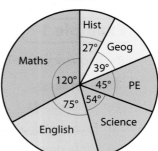

13. An ice cream stall sells vanilla, strawberry and chocolate ice creams. The pie chart illustrates the sales of ice cream for last Saturday. The number of vanilla and the number of chocolate ice creams sold were the same. The stall sold 60 strawberry ice creams. How many chocolate ice creams were sold?

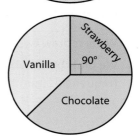

14. In a survey, 320 people on an aircraft and 800 people on a ferry were asked to state their nationality.

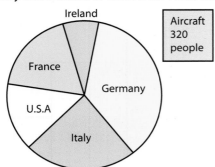

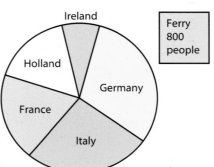

Jane looked at the charts and said 'There were about the same number of people from Italy on the aircraft and on the ferry'.
Explain why Jane is wrong.

Section 13.2 Histograms

One of the most common ways of representing a frequency distribution is by means of a **histogram**.

Histograms are very similar to bar charts but there are some important differences:
> there are no gaps between the bars in a histogram
> histograms are used to show **continuous data**
> the data is always **grouped**; the groups are called classes
> the **area** of each bar or rectangle represents the frequency.

Histograms may have equal or unequal class intervals.

For our course we will confine our study to histograms with **equal class intervals**.

When the class intervals are equal, drawing a histogram is very similar to drawing a bar chart.

Example 1

The frequency table below shows the times taken by 32 students to solve a problem.

Time (in secs)	0–10	10–20	20–30	30–40	40–50	50–60
No. of students	1	2	8	12	6	3

(i)   Draw a histogram to represent this data.
(ii) Write down the modal class.
(iii) In which interval does the median lie?

We first draw two axes at right angles to each other.

We plot the variables (time in this case) on the horizontal axis and plot the frequencies (number of students) on the vertical axis.

(i) The histogram is shown.

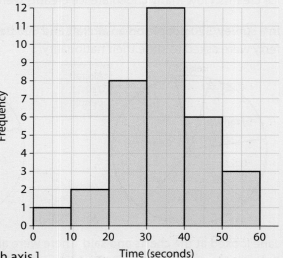

[NOTE: It is important to label each axis.]

(ii) The modal class is the class with the highest frequency.
This is the (30–40) second class.

∴   the modal class is (30–40) seconds.

(iii) The median is the value halfway through the distribution.

There are 32 students altogether; so the middle students are the 16th and 17th students.

The sum of the numbers of students in the first three intervals is

1 + 2 + 8 i.e. 11

The 16th and 17th students will lie in the next interval, (30–40) seconds.

Thus, the median lies in the (30–40) second interval.

Exercise 13.2

1. At the end of their journeys, 30 motorists were asked how many kilometres they had travelled. Their responses are shown in the table below:

Distance (in km)	0–20	20–40	40–60	60–80	80–100
Frequency	6	12	7	4	1

[0–20 means ⩾0 and <20]

   (i)   Draw a histogram to illustrate this data.

   (ii) How many motorists had travelled 40 km or more?

   (iii) What is the modal class?

   (iv) What percentage of the motorists travelled between 20 km and 40 km?

2. The histogram below shows the ages of people living in a village.

   (i)   How many people were aged between 30 years and 40 years?

   (ii) Which is the modal class?

   (iii) How many people were aged under 30 years?

   (iv) How many people lived in the village?

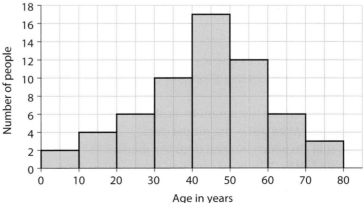

   (v)   Which interval contains 20% of the people surveyed?

   (vi) In which interval does the median age lie?

3. The frequency table on the right gives the waiting times of a group of patients at a doctor's surgery.
  (i) Draw a histogram to illustrate this data.
  (ii) How many patients were included in the survey?
  (iii) Which is the modal class?
  (iv) In which interval does the median lie?
  (v) What is the greatest number of patients who could have waited longer than 10 minutes?

Waiting time (in mins)	No. of patients
0–4	2
4–8	6
8–12	10
12–16	12
16–20	8

4. The histogram below shows the times taken, in seconds, for a group of pupils to solve a puzzle.

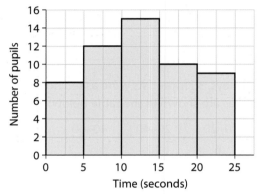

  (i) How many pupils took 15 seconds or longer to solve the puzzle?
  (ii) How many pupils took part in the test?
  (iii) Which is the modal class?
  (iv) In which interval does the median lie?
  (v) What is the greatest number of pupils who could have solved the puzzle in less than 8 seconds?
  (vi) What is the least number of pupils who could have solved the puzzle in less than 12 seconds?

5. The grouped frequency table opposite shows the minutes spent in a shopping complex by a number of people:
  (i) Draw a histogram to illustrate the data.
  (ii) Write down the modal class.
  (iii) In which interval does the median lie?
  (iv) Which interval contains exactly 20% of the people?
  (v) What is the greatest number of people who could have spent more than 30 minutes in the shopping complex?
  (vi) Use the mid-interval values to calculate the mean time spent in the shopping complex, correct to the nearest minute.

Minutes	Number of people
5–15	8
15–25	14
25–35	28
35–45	20

Section 13.3 The shape of a distribution

In the previous section we encountered histograms of various shapes.

The diagrams below show four histograms, all with different shapes.

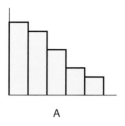 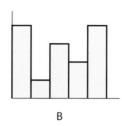 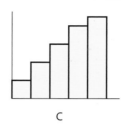 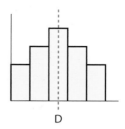

| A | B | C | D |

Only histogram D appears balanced or symmetrical as it has an axis of symmetry.
The other three histograms are less balanced or **skewed** in some way.

Histograms are very useful when you want to see where the data lies and so get a clear
picture of the shape of the distribution. For example, in histogram A above, we can see that
most of the data is concentrated at the lower values. In histogram C the data is concentrated
at the higher values.

There are some shapes that occur frequently in distributions and you should be able to
recognize and name them. The most common and frequently occurring shapes follow.

1. Symmetrical distributions

- This distribution has an axis of symmetry down the middle.
  It is called a **symmetrical distribution**.

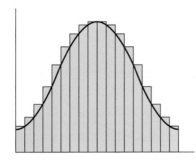 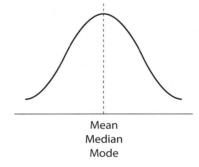

Mean
Median
Mode

Mean = Median = Mode

> It is one of the most common and most important distributions in statistics.
> It is generally referred to as the **normal distribution**.

> Real-life examples of a symmetrical (or normal) distribution are
>   (i) the heights of a random sample of people
>   (ii) the intelligence quotient (IQ) of a population

2. Positive skew

> When a distribution has most of the data at the lower values, we say it has a **positive skew**. The following histogram shows a positive skew as most of the data, represented by the higher bars, are mainly to the left.

If there is a positive skew, most of the data is to the left.

Notice that there is a long tail to the right of the distribution.

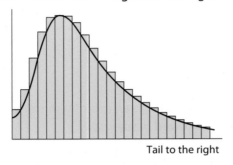

Tail to the right

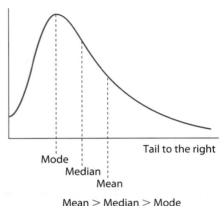

Tail to the right

Mode
Median
Mean

Mean > Median > Mode

> Real-life examples of a distribution with a positive skew are
>   (i)   the number of children in a family
>   (ii) the age at which people first learn to ride a bicycle
>   (iii) the age at which people marry.

3. Negative skew

> When a distribution has most of the data at the higher values, we say that the distribution has a **negative skew**.
>
> When a distribution has a negative skew the tail will be to the left.

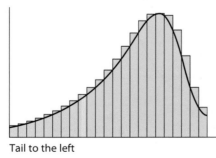

Tail to the left

Mode
Median
Mean

Mean < Median < Mode

In a distribution with a **positive** skew, the tail is to the **right**; with a **negative** skew, the tail is to the **left**.

> Real-life examples of a distribution with a negative skew are
>   (i) the ages at which people have to get their first pair of reading glasses
>   (ii) the heights of players playing in a basketball league.

Exercise 13.3

1. Describe the distribution shown on the right.

   (i) What is this distribution commonly known as?
   (ii) Give one real-life example of this distribution.

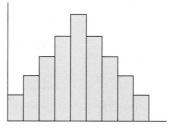

2. Describe the distribution shown on the right.
   Give one real-life example of this distribution.

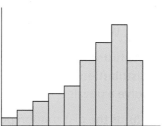

3. Is this distribution positively or negatively skewed?
   You will notice that most of the values are
   at the lower end of the distribution.
   Give one real-life situation that is an example
   of this type of distribution.

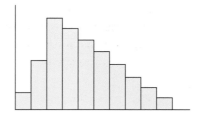

4. Here are three distributions:

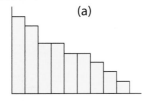
(a)

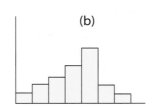
(b)

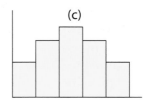
(c)

   (i) Which of these distributions is symmetrical?
   (ii) Which distribution is positively skewed?
   (iii) Which distribution is negatively skewed?
   (iv) Which distribution is the most likely to be represented by this data?
       'The weights of international rugby players'.
   (v) Which distribution best describes this data?
       'The intelligence quotients (IQ) of a large number of second-level students.'

5. Describe the distribution shown.

   Which of the three averages, the mode,
   the mean or the median is the most suitable
   average to describe this data?

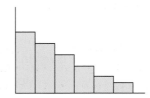

6. Two distributions (A) and (B) are shown below:

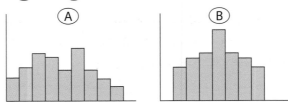

Name the distribution that is likely to represent each of these situations.
   (i)   'The marks achieved in maths by all the leaving certificate students last year'.
   (ii) 'The marks achieved in biology by a class of 30 students'.
   (iii) What is distribution (B) generally known as?

7. The histogram opposite shows the distribution of the times taken to solve a puzzle.

   (i) Is the distribution positively or negatively skewed?
   (ii) Explain why the mode is higher than the mean in this distribution.

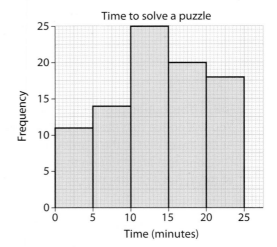

Time to solve a puzzle

8. Describe the distribution illustrated on the right. For the mode, mean and median of this distribution,
   (i) state which of the three is the smallest
   (ii) state which of the three is the largest.

9. A safety officer records the speeds of cars passing a school. The table shows the speeds that he recorded.

Speed (km/hr)	25–30	30–35	35–40	40–45	45–50
Frequency	25	20	10	5	3

   (i)   Draw a histogram to show this data.
   (ii) Is the distribution positively skewed or negatively skewed? Explain your answer.
   (iii) Copy the statement below and place the symbols > or < in the boxes in relation to the data given in the table above.

   Mode ☐ Median ☐ Mean

Section 13.4 Stem and leaf diagrams

A **stem and leaf diagram** is a very useful way of presenting data. It is useful because it shows all the original data and also gives you the overall picture or shape of the distribution.

It is similar to a horizontal bar chart, with the numbers themselves forming the bars.

Stem and leaf diagrams are suitable only for small amounts of data.

Often the stem shows the tens digit of the values and the leaves show the units digit. If you put them together you get the original value.

For example, 4|2 represents 42.

A typical stem and leaf diagram is shown below.

```
0 | 6  9
1 | 2  5  (7) ←──────── This represents 17.
2 | 3  3  6  8
3 | 0  2  7
4 | 1  2  6
5 | 3                    Key: 3|2 = 32
```

You must always add a key to show how the stem and leaf combine.

The data represented above is:

6, 9, 12, 15, 17, 23, 23, 26, 28, 30, 32, 37, 41, 42, 46, 53

Example 1

Here are the marks gained by a class of students in a science test.

58	65	40	59	68	63	81	76	63	57	44	47	53	70	80
68	81	61	57	49	70	54	75	69	65	59	52	63	63	74

(i) Construct a stem and leaf diagram to represent this data.

(ii) What is the mode of the data?

(iii) What is the median?

(iv) What is the range of the data?

(i) First draw the stem of the diagram.

```
4 |
5 |
6 |
7 |
8 |
```

The smallest value in the list is 40 and the largest is 81.

The stem of the diagram will be the tens digits from 4 to 8.

Now work through the data values and put the second digit on the appropriate row.

For the first value, 58, the 8 will go on the row starting with 5.

```
4 | 0  4  7  9
5 | 8  9  7  3  7  4  9  2
6 | 5  8  3  3  8  1  9  5  3  3
7 | 6  0  0  5  4
8 | 1  0  1
```

The numbers on the right of the diagram are the leaves.

Finally rewrite the diagram with all the leaves in order, with the smallest nearest to the stem.

Remember to include a key.

```
4 | 0  4  7  9
5 | 2  3  4  7  7  8  9  9
6 | 1  3  3  3  3  5  5  8  8  9
7 | 0  0  4  5  6
8 | 0  1  1
```
Key: $6|3 = 63$

(ii) The mode is 63 as this is the value that occurs most often.

(iii) As there are 30 values, the median will be the mean of the 15th and 16th values.

Count the values in the stem and leaf diagram to find the 15th and 16th values.

Since these are both 63, the median is 63.

> If there are 30 values, the middle value is $\frac{1}{2}(30 + 1)$ i.e. $15\frac{1}{2}$.
>
> This will be half the sum of the 15th and 16th values.

(iv) The range is the highest value minus the lowest value.

$= 81 - 40$

$= 41$

Different values for the stems

Here are the times, in seconds, for the contestants in a 60-metre race.

6.6   4.9   5.7   7.6   8.2   6.3   6.5   7.4   5.1   5.3   6.2   7.8

This time we will use the units as the stems.

Step 1   Draw the first diagram.
The units are the stems.
The tenths are the leaves.

```
4 | 9
5 | 7  1  3
6 | 6  3  5  2
7 | 6  4  8
8 | 2                    Key: 6|3 = 6.3 seconds
```

Step 2   Put the leaves in numerical order.

```
4 | 9
5 | 1  3  7
6 | 2  3  5  6
7 | 4  6  8
8 | 2
```

Back-to-back stem and leaf diagrams

Two stem and leaf diagrams can be drawn using the same stem.

These are known as back-to-back stem and leaf diagrams.

The leaves of one set of data are put to the right of the stem.

The leaves of the other set of data are put on the left.

A back-to-back stem and leaf diagram is very useful to compare two sets of data.

Jack and Ciara compared the length of time they spent each evening on their homework.

Their times are shown in the back-to-back stem and leaf diagram.

```
                Jack    |    Ciara
      6   5   5   3   2 | 2 |
              8   6   5 | 3 | 6  7
                  3   2 | 4 | 4  6  6
                      1 | 5 | 2  3  4  5
                        | 6 | 4  8
```

Key: 5|3 = 35 minutes   Key: 4|6 = 46 minutes

We read Jack's times from the stem to the left.

Thus Jack's times are:

22, 23, 25, 25, 26, 35, 36, …

Ciara's times are:

36, 37, 44, 46, 46, 52, …

> Sometimes the key is given as 5|3|6.
> This means 36 for Ciara and 35 for Jack.

The following example shows how a back-to-back stem and leaf diagram can be used to compare two sets of data.

Example 2

Robert and Jane compared the lengths of time they spent each evening watching television.

Their times are shown in the following back-to-back stem and leaf diagram.

Robert		Jane
7 4 4 2 3	2	
9 6 ④	3	4 6
5 3	4	5 7 7
2	5	③ 3 4 6
	6	5 7

Key: 3|4 = 43 minutes   Key: 4|5 = 45 minutes

(i)   What does the diagram show about the lengths of time Robert and Jane spent watching television?

(ii) What was Jane's median time spent watching television?

(iii) What was Robert's median time?

(iv) Do these median times support your conclusion in (i) above?

(i)   By looking at the diagram, we can see that most of Robert's times are between 23 and 39 minutes.
      Most of Jane's times are between 45 and 67 minutes.
      This shows that Jane spends more time watching television than Robert does.

(ii) For Jane, the value that is halfway through the distribution is 53.
      Thus her median time spent watching television is 53 minutes.

(iii) Robert's median time is 34 minutes.

(iv) Because Jane's median time is greater than Robert's, it supports the view expressed in (i) above that she spends more time than Robert watching television.

Finding the interquartile range from a stem and leaf diagram

In Chapter 8, we found that the lower quartile is the value in the data that is one quarter way through the distribution. The upper quartile is the value that is three quarters way through the distribution. The difference between the upper quartile and the lower quartile is the **interquartile range**.

We will now show how to find the two quartiles and the interquartile range of a distribution presented as a stem and leaf diagram.

Example 3

The stem and leaf diagram on the right shows the marks, out of 50, obtained in a maths test.

Find
  (i)   the median mark
  (ii)   the lower quartile
  (iii)   the upper quartile
  (iv)   the interquartile range.

Marks obtained

1	2	8			
2	1	4	7	7	8
3	1	4	5	7	
4	1	2	8		
5	0				

Key: $2|1 = 21$

(i) The median mark is the mark that is halfway through the distribution.
There are 15 data values.
The halfway value is $\frac{1}{2}(15 + 1)$ i.e. the 8th value.
Starting at the lowest value, the 8th value is 31
∴ the median = 31

(ii) The lower quartile is the value that is one quarter way through the distribution.
This value is $\frac{1}{4}(15 + 1)$ i.e. the 4th value
This value is 24.
∴ the lower quartile = 24

(iii) The upper quartile is the value that is three quarters of the way through the distribution.
This value is $\frac{3}{4}(15 + 1)$ i.e. the 12th value.
This value is 41.
∴ the upper quartile = 41

(iv) The interquartile range = upper quartile minus lower quartile
$$= 41 - 24$$
$$= 17$$

Exercise 13.4

1. The stem and leaf diagram on the right shows the marks obtained by a group of students in a Spanish test.
  (i)   How many students took this test?
  (ii)   How many students got between 70 and 79 marks?
  (iii)   What was the highest mark achieved?
  (iv)   What was the lowest mark?
  (v)   How many students got 80 marks or more?

stem	leaf				
5	1	4	6		
6	2	3	3	6	
7	2	3	5	7	8
8	0	0	2	4	6	6
9	3	4			

Key: $7|3$ means 73 marks

2. The stem and leaf diagram below shows the ages, in years, of 25 people who wished to enter a 10 km walking competition.

```
1 | 4  4  6  9
2 | 1  3  7  7  7  8
3 | 3  6  6  7  9
4 | 0  2  3  3  8  8
5 | 1  3  4  7          Key: 1|6 means 16 years old
```

   (i) How many people were less than 20 years old?
  (ii) Write down the modal age.
 (iii) How many people were between 35 and 45 years old?
 (iv) What was the median age?

3. The amount of petrol, in litres, bought by 20 motorists is shown.

16	23	27	10	35	42	26	25	24	17
23	41	33	35	25	19	16	31	12	29

Construct a stem and leaf diagram to represent this information.

4. Twenty four pupils were asked how many CDs they had in their collection.
The results are shown below:

23	2	18	14	7	4	25	21	32	26	31	6
17	6	18	19	31	21	12	1	0	8	14	15

   (i) Draw a stem and leaf diagram to represent this information.
  (ii) How many pupils had more than 20 CDs?
 (iii) What is the median number of CDs per pupil?

5. The times, in seconds, taken to answer 24 telephone calls are shown.

3.2	5.6	2.4	3.5	4.3	3.6	2.8	5.8	3.3	2.6	3.5	2.8
5.6	3.5	4.2	1.5	2.7	2.5	3.7	3.1	2.9	4.2	2.4	3.0

Copy and complete the stem and leaf diagram to represent this information.

```
1 |
2 |
3 | 2
4 |
5 |          Key: 3|2 means 3.2 seconds
```

   (i) How many of the calls took longer than 4 seconds to answer?
  (ii) What is the difference, in seconds, between the shortest and the longest times to answer the calls?
 (iii) What is the median length of time taken to answer the calls?
 (iv) What is the modal length of time?

6. The stem and leaf diagram below shows the marks achieved by 19 students in a test.

stem	leaf
2	2
3	4 6
4	2 7 9
5	3 4 5 8 9
6	0 2 6 7
7	2 6
8	1 4

Key: 4|2 = 42 marks

  (i) Write down the range of the marks.
 (ii) Find the value of the lower quartile.
(iii) What is the upper quartile?
(iv) What is the interquartile range?

7. These are the ages, in years, of the members of a table tennis club.

| 15 | 17 | 12 | 16 | 24 | 29 | 36 | 25 | 38 | 42 | 17 |
| 53 | 44 | 49 | 53 | 29 | 21 | 11 | 38 | 14 | 29 | |

  (i) Draw a stem and leaf diagram to show these ages.
 (ii) What is the lower quartile?
(iii) Find the upper quartile.
(iv) What is the interquartile range?

8. The results for examinations in Science and French for a class of students are shown in the back-to-back stem and leaf diagram below:

Science		French
7 5	2	
8 0	3	6
5 5	4	0 5 7 8
9 5 4 3 2	5	1 5 8
9 7 5	6	2 4 4 5 7
3 1	7	2 4 5 6
6 3	8	3 5
1	9	

Key: 1|7 = 71 marks   Key: 3|6 = 36 marks

  (i) How many students took the examinations?
 (ii) What is the range of marks in
      (a) Science   (b) French?
(iii) What is the median mark in Science?
(iv) What is the interquartile range of the French marks?

9. Brian and Martin played ten rounds on a 9-hole golf course.
The stem and leaf diagram shows the number of strokes they took for each round.

	Brian		Martin
	9 7	3	
9 5 5 3 1 0		4	5 9
3 2		5	0 2 3 5 7
		6	2 4
		7	1

Key: 2|5 = 52 strokes   Key: 4|5 = 45 strokes

Write down   (i)   Brian's lowest score   (ii)   Brian's median score

       (iii)   Martin's median score   (iv)   the range of Brian's scores

       (v)   the range of Martin's scores.

Which of the two players is the better golfer?

Explain your answer.

10. The back-to-back stem and leaf diagram below shows the pulse rates of a group of college students in Galway. They are split into those who smoked and those who didn't.

Smoke		Do not smoke
	5	0 8 9
9 8 5	6	0 4 4 5 6 6 6 8 8
6 6 5 0 0	7	0 1 1 8 9
8 8 6 3 0	8	0 1 6 8 8
2 0	9	

Key: 5|6 = 65   Key: 5|8 = 58

(i)   Find the median and range of the pulse rates of the group who smoked.

(ii)   Find the median and range of the pulse rates of the group who did not smoke.

(iii)   If a lower pulse rate indicates a higher level of fitness, which of the two groups is the fitter? Explain your answer.

11. Ten men and ten women were asked how much television they watched the previous weekend. Their times, in minutes, were as follows:

Men	40	41	42	52	52	52	64	65	65	71
Women	40	41	51	62	63	75	87	88	93	95

Copy and complete the back-to-back stem and leaf diagram opposite.

Men		Women
	4	0
	5	
4	6	
	7	
	8	
	9	

Key: 4|6 = 64 mins   Key: 4|0 = 40 mins

(i)   What is the modal time for men?

(ii)   What is the median time for

       (a) men   (b) women?

(iii)   What is the range of times for

       (a) men   (b) women?

(iv)   Use the results in (ii) and (iii) to show that women spend more time watching television than men do.

12. Ann and Conor played nine rounds of crazy golf during their summer holidays. Their scores are shown in the back-to-back stem and leaf diagram below.

			Ann					Conor			
					3	0	0	2			
				1	4	1	1	1	2		
9	3	1	0	0	5	2					
		6	5	4	6	8					

Key: 1|4 = 41   Key: 4|1 = 41

(i) Conor's lowest score was 30. What was Ann's lowest score?

(ii) What was Conor's modal score?

(iii) What was Ann's median score?

In crazy golf, the player with the lowest score wins. Conor actually shot the highest score that summer but was still chosen as the better player.

(iv) Give a reason for this choice.

13. The table below gives the examination marks in French and English for a class of 20 pupils.

French	75	69	58	58	46	44	32	50	53	78
	81	61	61	45	31	44	53	66	47	57
English	52	58	68	77	38	85	43	44	56	65
	65	79	44	71	84	72	63	69	72	79

(i) Construct a back-to-back stem and leaf diagram to represent these results.

(ii) What is the median mark in French?

(iii) What is the median mark in English?

(iv) In which subject did the pupils perform better? Explain your answer.

Section 13.5 Scatter graphs

Statements such as 'Drink driving causes accidents' or 'Obesity can cause heart-attacks' are often made in the media. The Road Safety Authority, for example, might produce data to show that there is a relationship between drink driving and having a car accident.

This section shows you how to compare two sets of data to find out if a relationship exists between them. For example, you could expect that a relationship exists between the number of ice-creams sold in a seaside shop and the average daytime temperatures.

Jane and her friend collected the following data to find out.

Average temperature (°C)	10	12	16	20	13	16	14	17	19	20	21	16
No. of ice-creams sold	1	5	20	50	15	25	14	30	32	42	50	30

They plotted each pair of values, (10, 1), (12, 5), (13, 15) and so on, on graph paper.

They used the horizontal axis for the temperature and the vertical axis for the numbers of ice-creams sold.

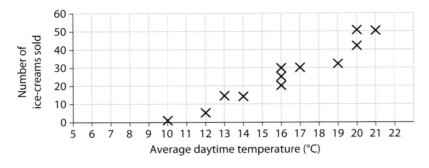

Data such as (10, 1) and (12, 5) which comes in pairs is called **bivariate data**.

The points plotted above are called a **scatter diagram** or **scatter graph**.

The diagram shows that the number of ice-creams sold increases as the temperature increases. This indicates that there is an association or relationship between the temperature and the number of ice-creams sold.

If the points on a scatter graph lie approximately on a straight line, we say that there is a linear relationship between the two sets of data. The closer the points are to a straight line, the stronger the relationship will be.

Example 1

On a journey between two towns, Andrew wrote down the number of kilometres that were left on the journey. He did this every ten minutes.
The table below shows the data he recorded

Time (mins)	10	20	30	40	50	60	70	80	90	100
Kilometres to go	72	60	50	42	40	32	25	18	10	0

Draw a scatter graph to illustrate this data.

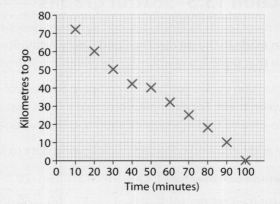

The scatter graph shows that there is a linear relationship between the two sets of data. The greater the time spent travelling, the fewer kilometres there are to go.

Sometimes there is no relationship between two sets of data.

The table below shows the relationship between temperature and rainfall every Sunday over an 11-week period.

Temperature (in °C)	20	21	24	26	30	33	34	35	38	40	44
Rainfall (mm)	12	4	22	8	16	4	2	10	14	0	2

This is the scatter graph of the data.

There does not appear to be any relationship between the two sets of data as the points are well scattered and there is no indication of a linear pattern.

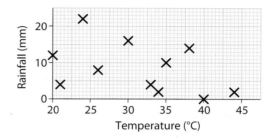

Correlation

The strength of the relationship between two sets of data is known as **correlation**. If the points on a scatter graph lie on or close to a straight line, a **strong correlation** is said to exist.

The three scatter graphs below show some different types of relationships between two sets of data.

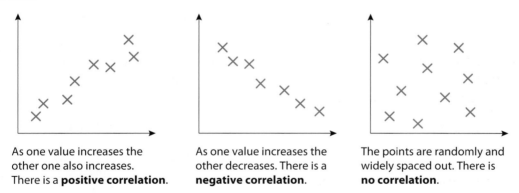

As one value increases the other one also increases. There is a **positive correlation**.

As one value increases the other decreases. There is a **negative correlation**.

The points are randomly and widely spaced out. There is **no correlation**.

We could have strong or weak positive correlation, and strong or weak negative correlation.

The scatter diagrams below illustrate different types of correlation.

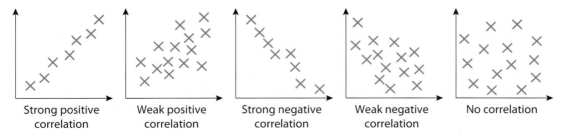

Strong positive correlation

Weak positive correlation

Strong negative correlation

Weak negative correlation

No correlation

Example 2

The table shows the weights and heights of 12 people.

Height (cm)	150	152	155	158	158	160	163	165	170	175	178	180
Weight (kg)	57	62	63	64	58	62	65	66	65	70	66	67

(i) Draw a scatter graph to show this data.

(ii) Describe the strength and type of correlation between these heights and weights.

(i) We draw two axes at right angles.
We put the heights on the horizontal axis.
We start with 140 cm and go up to 180 cm.
We put the weights on the vertical axis, starting at 55 kg and going up to 70 kg.
We then plot the points (150, 57), (152, 62), ... etc.
The scatter graph is shown below.

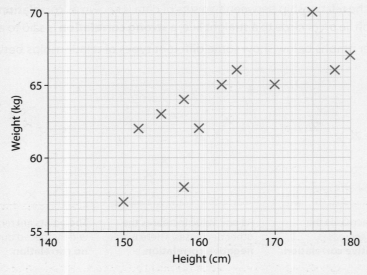

(ii) The correlation is weak positive as the points do not lie very close to a straight line. The correlation is positive because the weight generally increases as the height increases.

Exercise 13.5

1. Four scatter graphs are shown below.

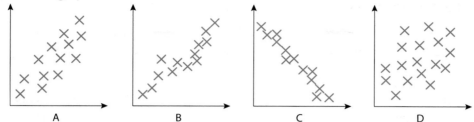

(i)   Which of these graphs shows the strongest positive correlation?

(ii) Which of these graphs shows negative correlation?

(iii) Which of these graphs shows the weakest correlation?

2. Here are sketches of six scatter graphs:

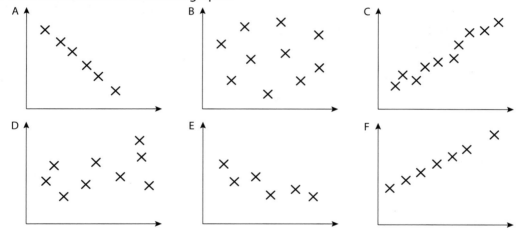

Which diagram(s) show

(i)   positive correlation

(ii) negative correlation

(iii) no correlation

(iv) strong negative correlation?

Describe the correlation in graph F.

3. This scatter graph shows the number of books read by some children and the reading ages of these children.

(i)   How many children have read more than 100 books?

(ii) One of these children has read 50 books. What is the reading age of this child?

(iii) Describe the relationship shown by the scatter graph.

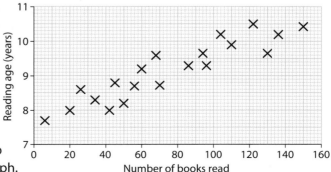

4. The examination marks of a sample number of
students in both their mock and final examinations
are shown in the given scatter graph.

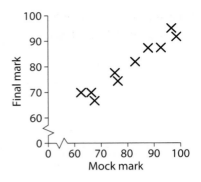

(i) Describe the correlation shown in the graph.
(ii) What can you say about the relationship
between the mock and final marks of
the students?

5. This scatter diagram shows the weights, in kg, and the heights, in cm, of 20 male
members of a basketball club.

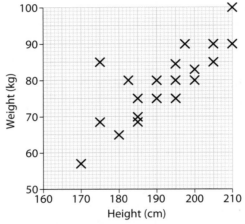

(i) Write down the weight of the heaviest member.
(ii) Write down the height of the shortest member.
(iii) One member is particularly heavy for his height.
Write down the height and weight of this member.
(iv) Describe the correlation shown in this graph.

6. Ten children are given two tests to complete. One test involves some number puzzles.
The other test involves spotting mistakes in pictures.
The table shows the scores in the tests for these children.

Child	A	B	C	D	E	F	G	H	I	J
Number puzzle score	12	7	10	3	7	10	5	5	12	14
Picture puzzle score	3	12	7	16	10	5	14	12	5	1

(i) Draw a scatter graph to show this data.
(Put the number score on the horizontal axis.)
(ii) Describe the strength and type of correlation between these scores.
Does the type of correlation surprise you? Explain.

7. Ben wants to buy a secondhand bike.

He records the age and price of the type he wants from a website.

Age (years)	6	3	2	4	6	1	4	8	2	7
Price (€)	60	180	240	120	100	280	160	40	200	50

   (i) Draw a scatter graph of this information on graph paper, putting age on the horizontal axis.

   (ii) What does the scatter graph tell you about the connection between the ages of these bikes and their prices?

   (iii) Describe, in two words, the correlation that exists.

8. The table shows the marks of 15 students taking Paper 1 and Paper 2 of a maths exam. Both papers were marked out of 40.

Paper 1	36	34	23	24	30	40	25	35	20	15	35	34	23	35	27
Paper 2	39	36	27	20	33	35	27	32	28	20	37	35	25	33	30

   (i) Draw a scatter diagram to show this information.

   (ii) Describe the correlation shown in the scatter diagram.

9.

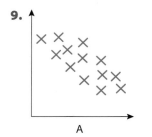 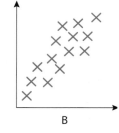 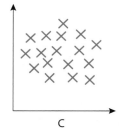 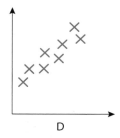

A   B   C   D

Four scatter graphs are shown above. For each of the following situations, choose the most appropriate of the scatter graphs. Explain your choice in each case.

   (i) Boys' heights and their shoe sizes.

   (ii) Men's weights and the times taken by them to complete a crossword puzzle.

   (iii) Ages of cars and their selling prices.

   (iv) Marks achieved in Maths Paper 1 and Maths Paper 2.

10. Describe the type of correlation you would expect between:

   (i) the age of a boat and its secondhand selling price,

   (ii) the heights of children and their ages,

   (iii) the shoe sizes of children and the distances they travel to school,

   (iv) time spent watching television and time spent studying,

   (v) the number of cars on the road and the number of accidents.

Section 13.6 Measuring correlation

The points on the scatter graph on the right are in a straight line.

In this case we say that there is **perfect positive correlation** between the two variables.

If we use the letter r to represent the correlation and if perfect positive correlation exists, we say that $r = 1$.

In the diagram below, **perfect negative correlation** exists and $r = -1$.

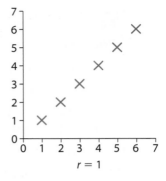

$r = 1$

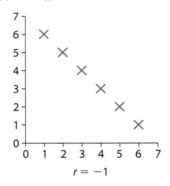

$r = -1$

All other correlations will have values between 1 and -1.

If there is no correlation, $r = 0$.

The value of r is called the **correlation coefficient**.

The scatter diagrams below give examples of some values of r.

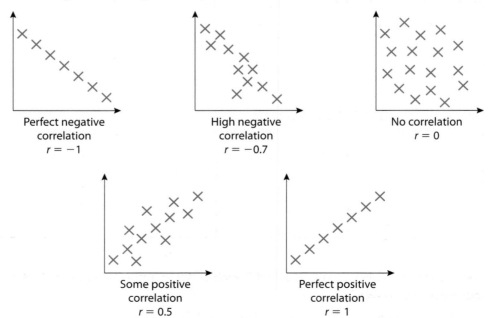

Perfect negative
correlation
$r = -1$

High negative
correlation
$r = -0.7$

No correlation
$r = 0$

Some positive
correlation
$r = 0.5$

Perfect positive
correlation
$r = 1$

Example 1

Shown below are four scatter graphs A, B, C and D.

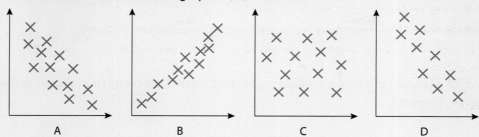

A   B   C   D

Here are six correlation coefficients (i.e. values for r)

0.2,   −0.8,   −0.2,   0,   0.9,   −0.6

Choose the most likely correlation coefficient from these to match the scatter graphs A, B, C and D above.

A: −0.6   B: 0.9   C: 0   D: −0.8

Exercise 13.6

1. Describe in two words the correlation shown opposite.

   Which of these numbers is the most likely to represent this correlation?

   −0.8,   0.9,   0,   0.1,   0.7

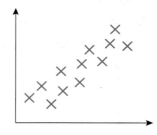

2. Four scatter graphs A, B, C and D are shown below.

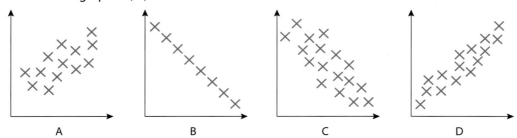

A   B   C   D

   Match one of the following numbers with each of the graphs above so that it best represents the correlation:

   0.1,   −0.4,   1,   −1,   0.6   −0.8,   0.8

3. Draw a separate scatter graph that might represent each of the following correlation coefficients:

    (i) 1   (ii) −0.9   (iii) 0.5   (iv) 0

4. Which one of these numbers represents 'strong negative correlation'?

    (i) 0.3   (ii) −0.1   (iii) 1   (iv) −0.9   (v) −0.5

5. Which of these correlation coefficients best represents the correlation shown in the given diagram?

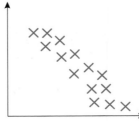

    (i) 0.8   (ii) −0.8   (iii) −1   (iv) 0.5

6. Which of these correlation coefficients shows the strongest correlation?

    (i) 0.7   (ii) −0.2   (iii) −1   (iv) 0.9

7. Which of these correlation coefficients shows the weakest correlation?

    (i) −0.8   (ii) 0.1   (iii) −1   (iv) 0.9

8. Match one of these correlation coefficients to each of the descriptions below:

        0.9,   −0.1,   −1,   −0.8   0,   0.2

    (i)   Strong positive correlation
    (ii) Strong negative correlation
    (iii) No correlation
    (iv) Perfect negative correlation
    (v)   Very weak negative correlation
    (vi) Very weak positive correlation

Section 13.7 Causal relationships and correlation

The price of a used car depends, among other things, on the age of the car. The age of the car **causes** the price of the car to decrease. We say that there is a **causal relationship** between the price of the car and the age of the car.

Definition

> When a change in one variable causes a change in another variable, we say that there is a causal relationship between them.

The scatter graph below shows the relationship between the sales of iced drinks and temperature. The correlation is strong and positive. You would expect this as the rise in temperature would tend to result in an increase in the sales of iced drinks.

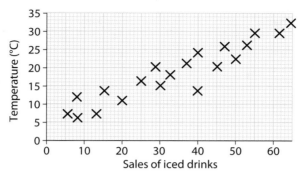

So it would be reasonable to conclude that there is a causal relationship between the sales of iced drinks and an increase in temperature.

The scatter diagram below shows the number of laptops and the number of fridges sold by an electrical shop over a ten-month period.

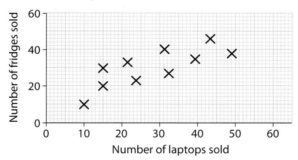

The graph shows that there is a reasonably strong positive correlation between the number of laptops sold and the number of fridges sold. However, this does not mean that there is a causal relationship between them; buying a laptop does not cause you to buy a fridge.

> Correlation does not necessarily mean that there is a causal relationship.

Exercise 13.7

1. Which of the following pairs of variables are likely to have a causal relationship?
   (i) Sales of television sets and sales of DVD recorders.
   (ii) A car's engine-size and its petrol consumption.
   (iii) Marks in your maths test and the distance you live from your school in kilometres.
   (iv) Sales of vegetables and sales of chocolate.
   (v) Sales of computers and sales of software.
   (vi) Outside temperature and the amount of gas used for central heating.

2. The scatter graph shows the age of cars and the number of kilometres travelled.

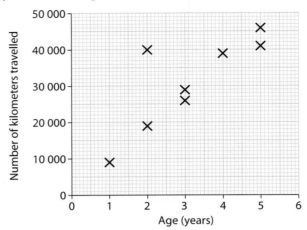

(i) One of these cars is 4 years old.
How many kilometres has this car travelled?

(ii) Describe the relationship shown by this scatter graph.

(iii) Is there a causal relationship between these variables?
Explain your answer.

(iv) The age and number of kilometres travelled by one of these cars looks out of place.
(a) What is the age of this car and how many kilometres has it travelled?
(b) Give a possible reason why the results for this car are different from the rest of the cars.

3. The scatter graph below shows the relationship between the ages and prices of used motorcycles.

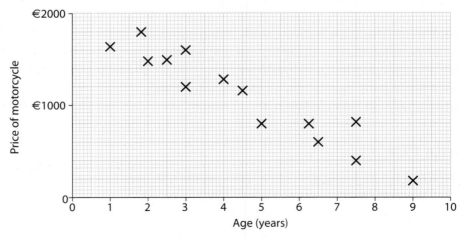

(i) Describe the correlation shown in this scatter graph.

(ii) Is there a causal relationship between the variables?
Explain your answer.

4. The number of hours of sunshine and the maximum temperature at a seaside resort were measured on seven days in June.

Hours of sunshine	5	9	8	6	5	2	4
Temperature (°C)	26	30	29	26	24	19	23

(i) Plot this data on a scatter graph.
   Use the scales shown below.

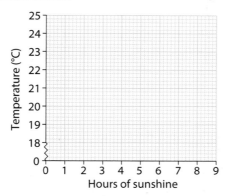

(ii) Describe the relationship shown by your scatter graph.

(iii) Is there a causal relationship between the hours of sunshine and the maximum temperature at the resort?
   Explain your answer.

5. A small electrical shop recorded the yearly sales of radio sets and television sets over a period of 10 years.
   The results are shown in the table below.

Year	1	2	3	4	5	6	7	8	9	10
No. of televisions sold	60	68	73	80	85	88	90	96	105	110
No. of radios sold	80	60	72	65	60	55	52	44	42	36

(i) Using scales going from 50 to 120 for the sales of televisions and 30 to 90 for the sales of radios, draw a scatter graph.

(ii) What sort of correlation does the scatter graph suggest?

(iii) Is there a causal relationship between the television sales and radio sales?
   Explain your answer.

Test yourself 13

1. The number of laptops sold by a store was recorded each month for a period of 23 months. The results are shown in the stem and leaf diagram below.

stem	leaf						
1	8	9					
2	3	6	7	9			
3	2	6	6	6	7	8	
4	4	5	5	7	7	7	7
5	2	7	8	9			

Key: 1|8 means 18 laptops

   (i) Write down the modal number of laptops sold.
   (ii) Write down the median.
   (iii) Find the lower quartile.
   (iv) Find the upper quartile.
   (v) Work out the interquartile range.

2. Here are the marks scored by 19 girls in a science test.

54	42	61	47	24	43	55	62	30	27
28	43	54	46	25	32	49	73	50	

   (i) Construct a stem and leaf diagram to show these results.
   (ii) Write down the range of the marks.
   (iii) What is the lower quartile?
   (iv) What is the upper quartile?
   (v) Write down the interquartile range.

3. The following stem and leaf diagram shows the amounts of money spent on a Friday night by a group of college students.

Males							Females					
					8	0	6					
			7	6	5	1	0	5	5	5	8	8
9	9	9	8	6	6	2	5	5	8	8	9	
		8	8	5	5	3	5	5				
				8	5	4	0					

Key: 5|4 = €45   Key: 3|5 = €35

   (i) How many students were in the group?
   (ii) Write down the largest amount of money spent by the males.
   (iii) What is the median amount of money spent by the females?
   (iv) What is the median amount of money spent by the males?
   (v) Comment on whether males or females spent the most money.

4. The total cost of a holiday was €1800.
The pie chart shows how this cost was made up.

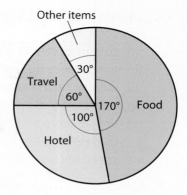

- (i)   How much was spent on food?
- (ii) How much was spent on travel?
- (iii) How much was spent on the hotel?
- (iv) How much was spent on other items?

5. The table shows the temperature of water as it cools in a freezer.

Time (minutes)	5	10	15	20	25	30
Temperature (°C)	36	29	25	20	15	8

- (i) Draw a scatter diagram to illustrate this information.
      Keep temperature on the horizontal axis.
- (ii) What type of correlation is shown?

6. Four scatter diagrams A, B, C and D are shown below.

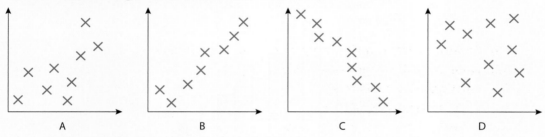

- (i)   Which diagram shows no correlation?
- (ii) Which diagram shows negative correlation?
- (iii) Which diagram shows weak positive correlation?
- (iv) Associate one of these correlation coefficients with each of the diagrams above:
    - (a) 0.8
    - (b) 0
    - (c) −0.7
    - (d) 0.3

7. What type of correlation could you expect if you took readings of these variables and drew a scatter diagram?

Describe each correlation as
- (a) positive
- (b) negative
- (c) no correlation
- (i)   number of people in a shop; goods sold
- (ii) sales of perfume; amount spent on advertising perfume
- (iii) birth rate; rate of inflation
- (iv) outside temperature; sales of sun cream
- (v)   distance (north) from equator; winter daylight hours.

8. Suggest the type of diagram that would be suitable to represent each of the following types of data:
   (i) colours of sweaters in a store
   (ii) the distance from school and the time taken to travel to school
   (iii) comparing the results of a maths test for the boys and girls in a class of 30
   (iv) the country of origin of a group of immigrants to Ireland
   (v) the percentage share of the grocery market in Ireland of six leading supermarket chains
   (vi) speed of cars and the number of traffic accidents.

9. A distribution is represented by the histogram shown on the right.

   (i) Describe this distribution.
   (ii) Give two real-life examples of distributions of this type.

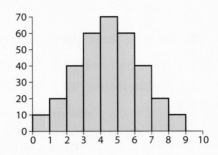

10. The histogram below represents a distribution.

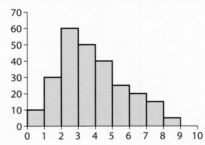

   (i) Explain why the distribution is skewed.
   (ii) Is it positively or negatively skewed?
   (iii) Give one example from everyday life of this type of distribution.

11. (i) Describe the distribution shown below.

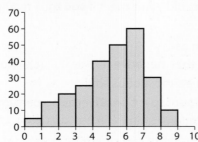

   (ii) Give an example of a distribution from real-life that is skewed in this way.

Summary of key points...

Bar charts and pie charts

1. Bar charts can be used to show patterns or trends in the data.
   The bars are of equal width and there are gaps between the bars.
2. Pie charts show how a quantity is shared or divided.
   All the sector angles in a pie chart add to 360°.

Stem and leaf diagrams

1. A stem and leaf diagram keeps all the data values and shows the shape of a distribution.
2. A back-to-back stem and leaf diagram allows us to compare two sets of data by using the spread of the data and some other measure such as the median.

Shape of a distribution

Histograms show the spread of the data and the shape of a distribution.
Three of the more common shapes are shown below.

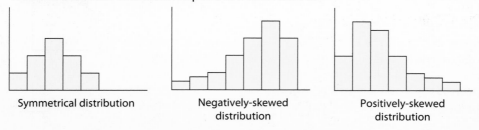

Symmetrical distribution   Negatively-skewed distribution   Positively-skewed distribution

Scatter graphs and correlation

1. Scatter graphs are used to show whether two sets of data are related.
2. Correlation is a measure of the strength of the relationship between two variables.
3. The closer the points on a scatter graph are to a straight line, the stronger the relationship.

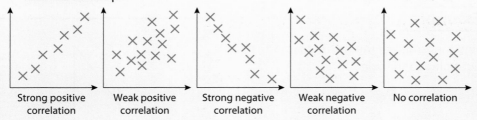

Strong positive correlation   Weak positive correlation   Strong negative correlation   Weak negative correlation   No correlation

4. When a change in one variable directly causes a change in another variable, there is said to be a causal relationship between them.
5. Correlation does not necessarily mean there is a causal relationship.

Key words

Pythagoras   right-angled triangle   sine   cosine   tangent
opposite side   adjacent side   hypotenuse   sine rule   cosine rule
compass   sector   arc   quadrants   reference angle   surd form

Section 14.1 The Theorem of Pythagoras

The given figure shows a right-angled triangle.

The side opposite the right angle is called the **hypotenuse**.

A Greek mathematician named Pythagoras is credited with the proof of a very important theorem involving right-angled triangles.

It is known as the **Theorem of Pythagoras** and is given below.

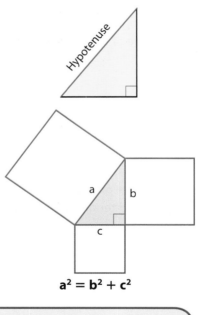

Theorem of Pythagoras
In a right-angled triangle, the area of the square drawn on the hypotenuse is equal to the sum of the areas of the squares drawn on the other two sides.

$$a^2 = b^2 + c^2$$

> **Example 1**
>
> Find the length of the side marked x in this right-angled triangle.
>
> $x^2 = 8^2 + 5^2$
> $x^2 = 64 + 25$
> $x^2 = 89$
> $x = \sqrt{89}$
> $x \approx 9.4$ cm, correct to one decimal place.

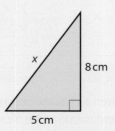

Exercise 14.1

1. The area of square A is 23 cm² and the area of
   square C is 35 cm².
   Find the area of square B.

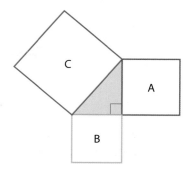

2. Use the figure in Question 1 to find the area of square C if square A is 17 cm² and
   square B is 14 cm².

3. Three squares have areas of 18 cm², 21 cm² and 39 cm².
   Will the squares fit exactly along the sides of a right-angled triangle?
   Explain your answer.

4. Calculate the length of the side marked with a letter in each of the following triangles:
   (Give answer correct to one decimal place where necessary.)

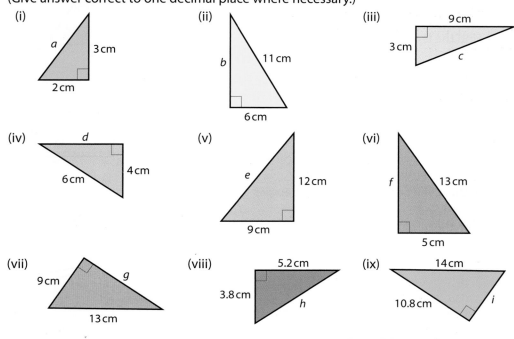

5. A rectangle is 10 cm long and 8 cm wide.
   Calculate the length of the diagonal.
   Give your answer in centimetres, correct to
   one decimal place.

6. Use the given grid to write down the lengths of [PR] and [QR].
   Hence find the length of [PQ], correct to one decimal place.

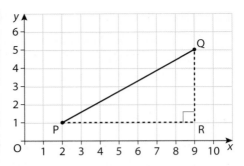

7. A golf flag casts a shadow 3 m long.
   If the distance from the top of the flag pole to the end of the shadow is 4 m, find the height, f, in metres, correct to one decimal place.

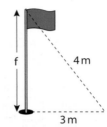

8. In the given figure, |AB| = 10 cm, |AD| = 5 cm and |DC| = 6 cm.
   The angles at A and D are right angles.
   Find the length of [BC].

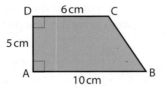

9. The diagram shows a right-angled triangle ABC.
   (i) Find the length of [BD].
   (ii) Find the length [AD] in centimetres, correct to one decimal place.

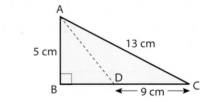

10. In the given figure, the two right angles are marked.
    Find the lengths of c and d.

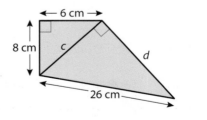

11. The diagram shows a horizontal shelf [AB].
    The shelf is fixed to a vertical wall at A.
    The support [CD] is fixed to the wall at C and to the shelf at D.
    |AB| = 23 cm, |AC| = 20 cm and |BD| = 8 cm.
    Calculate the length of [CD].

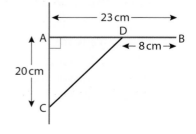

12. Find the missing dimension required to work out the perimeter
of the room shown.

Give your answer in metres, correct to one decimal place.

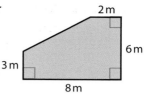

Section 14.2 Sine, Cosine and Tangent ratios _____

One of the most common uses of trigonometry is in working out lengths and angles in right-angled triangles. Three very special ratios connecting angles and sides are given below.

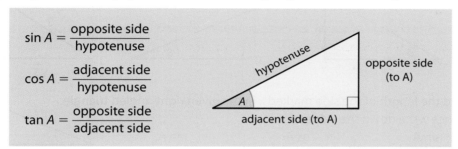

$$\sin A = \frac{\text{opposite side}}{\text{hypotenuse}}$$

$$\cos A = \frac{\text{adjacent side}}{\text{hypotenuse}}$$

$$\tan A = \frac{\text{opposite side}}{\text{adjacent side}}$$

A useful memory aid is SOHCAHTOA.

If we are given $\cos A = \frac{3}{4}$, we can draw a sketch
of a right-angled triangle in which the side
adjacent to A is 3 and the hypotenuse is 4.

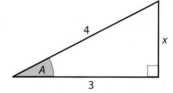

We now find the third side by using the
Theorem of Pythagoras.

Let the third side $= x$.
$$x^2 + 3^2 = 4^2$$
$$x^2 + 9 = 16$$
$$x^2 = 7$$
$$x = \sqrt{7}$$

Example 1

If $\tan B = \frac{\sqrt{5}}{2}$, find the value of $\sin B$ and $\cos B$.

$\tan B = \frac{\sqrt{5}}{2} \Rightarrow$ opposite side to B is $\sqrt{5}$ and adjacent side is 2.

Now draw a rough sketch of a right-angled triangle.
Let x be the length of the hypotenuse.
$$x^2 = 2^2 + (\sqrt{5})^2 \dots (\sqrt{5})^2 = 5$$
$$x^2 = 4 + 5$$
$$x^2 = 9 \Rightarrow x = 3$$

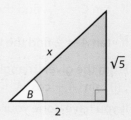

From the triangle: $\sin B = \frac{\sqrt{5}}{3}$ and $\cos B = \frac{2}{3}$.

Exercise 14.2

1. In the given triangle, state which of the ratios sine, cosine or tangent
      (i)   connects 3, 4 and the angle A
      (ii) connects 4, 5 and the angle A
      (iii) connects 3, 5 and the angle A.

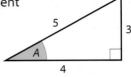

2. Find the sin, cos and tan of the angle marked with a capital letter in each of the
following triangles:

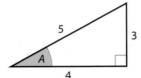 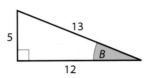 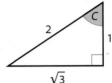

3. Find the length of the side marked x in the given right-angled triangle.
Hence write down the value of
      (i) $\sin A$ (ii) $\cos A$ (iii) $\tan A$.

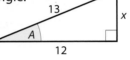

4. Find the value of a in the given right-angled triangle.
Hence write down the value of
      (i) $\sin B$ (ii) $\cos B$ (iii) $\tan B$.

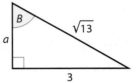

5. The angle θ and three sides of a right-angled triangle are shown in
the given diagram.
State whether each of these ratios represent $\sin\theta$, $\cos\theta$ or $\tan\theta$.

      (i) $\dfrac{4}{5}$ (ii) $\dfrac{4}{\sqrt{41}}$ (iii) $\dfrac{5}{\sqrt{41}}$.

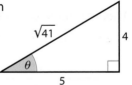

6. Given that $\cos B = \frac{5}{13}$, draw a rough sketch of a right-angled triangle and use it to write
down the ratios, $\sin B$ and $\tan B$.

7. (i) If $\tan A = \frac{1}{2}$, find $\sin A$.   (ii) If $\cos B = \frac{2}{5}$, find $\tan B$.

8. If $\tan C = \dfrac{1}{\sqrt{3}}$, find the values of $\sin C$ and $\cos C$.

9. If $\tan A = \frac{3}{4}$, find the value of $(\sin^2 A + \cos^2 A)$.

10. From the given triangle, write down the value of
      (i) $\sin^2 A + \cos^2 A$ (ii) $\sin^2 B + \cos^2 B$.

If you have done your calculations
correctly, you have verified a very
important fact about any angle, i.e.,
        $\sin^2 A + \cos^2 A = 1.$

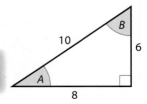

Section 14.3 Using a calculator

We use the $\boxed{\text{sin}}$, $\boxed{\text{cos}}$ and $\boxed{\text{tan}}$ keys on an electronic calculator to find the sine, cosine and tangent of any angle.

To find sin 35°, key in $\boxed{\text{sin}}$ 35 $\boxed{=}$.

The result is 0.573576… = 0.5736, correct to 4 decimal places.

Parts of a degree

A degree can be divided into 60 parts.

Each part is called 1 **minute**, written 1′.

$$1° = 60'$$

To find tan 34.5° or 34°30′ on your calculator, you may use either of these methods

Thus   34.5° = 34°30′.

1. For tan 34.5°

key in $\boxed{\text{tan}}$ 34.5 $\boxed{=}$

Result = 0.6873

2. For tan 34°30′

key in $\boxed{\text{tan}}$ 34 $\boxed{\circ'''}$ 30 $\boxed{\circ'''}$ $\boxed{=}$

Result = 0.6873

Using the $\boxed{\text{sin}^{-1}}$ $\boxed{\text{cos}^{-1}}$ and $\boxed{\text{tan}^{-1}}$ keys

If we are given that sin A = 0.8661, we can find the angle A by using the $\boxed{\text{sin}^{-1}}$ key.

The $\boxed{\text{sin}^{-1}}$ key is got by keying in $\boxed{\text{SHIFT}}$ $\boxed{\text{sin}}$.

Thus if sin A = 0.8661, we find A by keying in $\boxed{\text{SHIFT}}$ $\boxed{\text{sin}}$ 0.8661 $\boxed{=}$.

The result is 60.008° = 60°.

Similarly, if tan B = 1.2734, we find the angle B by keying in $\boxed{\text{SHIFT}}$ $\boxed{\text{tan}}$ 1.2734 $\boxed{=}$.

The result is 51.86°… correct to 2 decimal places.

Example 1

(i) Find cos 72°18′, correct to 4 decimal places.

(ii) If sin A = 0.5216, find A correct to the nearest degree.

(i) To find cos 72°18′, key in $\boxed{\text{cos}}$ 72 $\boxed{\circ'''}$ 18 $\boxed{\circ'''}$ $\boxed{=}$

The result is 0.3040.

> Notice that the $\boxed{\circ'''}$ key is used twice.

Or 18′ = $\frac{18°}{60}$ = 0.3° ⇒ 72°18′ = 72.3°

Thus to find 72.3°, key in $\boxed{\text{cos}}$ 72.3 $\boxed{=}$

(ii) If sin A = 0.5216, we find A by keying in

$\boxed{\text{SHIFT}}$ $\boxed{\text{sin}}$ 0.5216 $\boxed{=}$

The result is 31.44°.   ⇒ A = 31°, to the nearest degree.

Note: If you are given $\sin A = \frac{4}{7}$, you can find the angle A by keying in

$$\boxed{\text{SHIFT}}\ \boxed{\sin}\ 4\ \boxed{\div}\ 7\ \boxed{=}$$

The result is 34.8°.

Exercise 14.3

1. Use your calculator to evaluate each of the following, correct to 4 decimal places:
   (i) sin 48°   (ii) cos 74°   (iii) tan 15°   (iv) sin 72°   (v) cos 28.5°

2. Use your calculator to evaluate the following, correct to 4 decimal places:
   (i) sin 32°18'   (ii) cos 43°24'   (iii) tan 30°36'   (iv) cos 73°54'

3. Use your calculator to find the measure of each of these angles, correct to the nearest degree:
   (i) $\sin A = 0.7453$ (ii) $\cos B = 0.3521$ (iii) $\tan C = 1.4538$
   (iv) $\cos A = 0.2154$ (v) $\tan B = 0.8923$ (vi) $\sin C = 0.2132$

4. Find the value of A in each of the following.
   Give your answer in degrees, correct to one decimal place.
   (i) $\sin A = 0.6$ (ii) $\cos A = 0.7534$
   (iii) $\tan A = 3.84$ (iv) $\cos A = 0.2715$

5. Find the measure of the angle θ, correct to the nearest degree, in each of the following:
   (i) $\sin \theta = \frac{2}{3}$ (ii) $\cos \theta = \frac{3}{5}$ (iii) $\tan \theta = \frac{7}{8}$ (iv) $\sin \theta = \frac{2}{5}$
   (v) $\tan \theta = \frac{6}{11}$ (vi) $\sin \theta = \frac{1}{5}$ (vii) $\cos \theta = \frac{9}{11}$ (viii) $\tan \theta = 1\frac{3}{5}$

6. If $\cos A = 0.5484$ and $A < 90°$, find A and hence find the value of $\sin A$, correct to 2 decimal places.

7. Find, correct to the nearest degree, the size of the angles marked A, B and C in the triangles below:

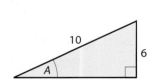

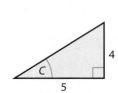

Section 14.4 Solving right-angled triangles

In this section we will use the sine, cosine and tangent ratios to find an unknown side or an unknown angle in a right-angled triangle.

When using your calculator to find the sine, cosine or tangent of an angle, write the value correct to 4 decimal places.

Example 1

Find the length of the side marked *x* in the given triangle.

$$\tan 32° = \frac{x}{14}$$

$$x = 14 \times \tan 32°$$

$$x = 14 \times 0.6249$$

$$x = 8.75, \text{ correct to two decimal places.}$$

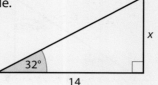

Example 2

In the given triangle, $|AB| = 9$ and $|BC| = 13$.
Find $|\angle ACB|$, correct to the nearest degree.

$$\tan \angle ACB = \frac{9}{13}$$

$$|\angle ACB| = \tan^{-1} \frac{9}{13}$$

$$|\angle ACB| = 34.695° \qquad \text{Key in } \boxed{\text{SHIFT}}\ \boxed{\text{tan}}\ 9\ \boxed{÷}\ 13\ \boxed{=}$$

$$= 35°, \text{ correct to the nearest degree.}$$

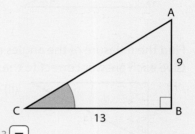

Exercise 14.4

1. Write down which trigonometric ratio is needed to calculate the length of the side marked *x* in each of these triangles:

(i)

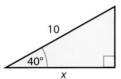

(ii)

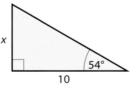

(iii)

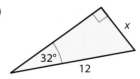

2. In each of the following triangles, work out the length of the side marked with a letter. Give each answer correct to 1 decimal place.

(i)

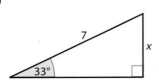

(ii)

(iii)

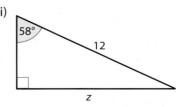

3. Find the length of the side marked x in these triangles:
Give your answers correct to one decimal place.

(i)

(ii)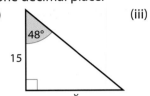

(iii)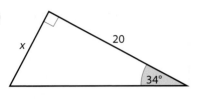

4. Find the size of the angle marked A in each of these triangles:
Give your answers correct to the nearest degree.

(i)

(ii)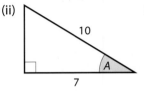

(iii)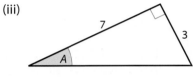

5. Find the measure of the angles marked p, q and r in each of these triangles:
Give each answer correct to the nearest degree.

(i)

(ii)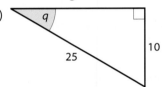

(iii)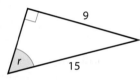

6. Copy and complete the following to find the length of the side marked x.

$$\frac{8}{x} = \cos 32°$$

$$x \times \cos 32° = 8$$

$$x = \frac{8}{\cos 32°}$$

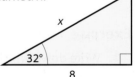

7. Find the length of the hypotenuse marked x in each of these triangles:

(i)

(ii)

(iii)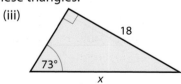

Give each answer correct to 1 decimal place.

8. Find the values of x and y, correct to the nearest
whole number in the given triangle.

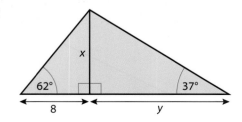

9. In the given triangle, find
    (i)   x, correct to 1 decimal place
    (ii) the angle A, correct to the nearest degree.

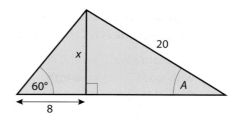

10. ABCD is a rectangle as shown.
    If |DC| = 11 cm and |∠BDC| = 28°, find the length
    of the diagonal [DB].
    Give your answer in centimetres, correct to
    one decimal place.

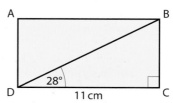

11. In the given triangle ABC, |AB| = 5 cm and |∠ABC| = 90°.
    D is a point on [CB] and |AD| = |CD|.
    If |DB| = 12 cm, find
    (i) |AD|
    (ii) |∠ACB|, correct to the nearest degree.

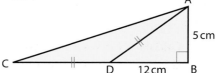

12. In the given diagram, |AD| = 6 cm, |DB| = 9 cm,
    |∠CAD| = 35° and CD⊥AB.
    Find
    (i) |CD|, correct to 1 decimal place
    (ii) |∠CBD|, correct to the nearest degree.

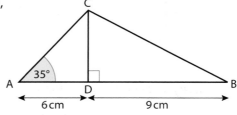

13. Paula stands at point P on the bank of a river.
    Vertically across from her on the other bank
    is a tree, T.
    She walks 25 metres along the bank to a point Q.
    She measures the angle between QT and QP
    and finds that it is 38°.
    Find the width of the river, correct to the
    nearest metre.

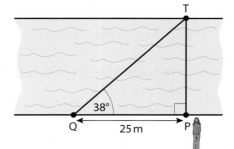

14. From a point on the ground 20 m from the base of a tree,
    the angle of elevation to the top of the tree is 47°.
    Calculate the height of the tree, correct to the
    nearest metre.

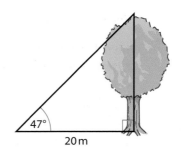

15. From a point on the ground 10 m from a block of flats, the angle of elevation to the top of the block is 76°. Calculate the height of the block of flats, correct to the nearest metre.

16. The diagram shows the cross-section of a roof with sides 7.5 m in length.
Both sides are inclined at an angle of 32° to the horizontal.
(i) Find the height marked h.
(ii) Find the width, w, of the roof support.
Give each answer in metres, correct to 1 decimal place.

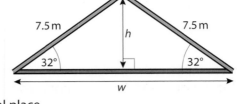

17. The diagram below shows the cross-section ABCD of a valley.

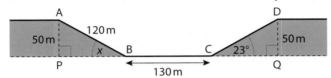

Calculate   (i) the angle x, correct to the nearest degree
(ii) $|PB|$, in metres, correct to the nearest metre
(iii) $|CQ|$, correct to the nearest metre
(iv) the distance straight across the valley from A to D, correct to the nearest metre.

18. Ryan and Emily are estimating the height of a phone mast.
Ryan stands 15 m from the mast and measures the angle of elevation to the top as 60°.
Emily stands 25 m from the mast and measures the angle of elevation to the top as 46°.
Can they both be correct? Discuss.

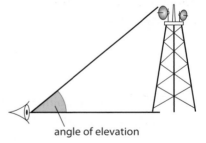

angle of elevation

19. In the given triangle, $|AB| = 10$ m, $|BD| = 2$ m and $|\angle ABC| = 53°$.
(i) Write down $|\angle BAC|$.
(ii) Find $|BC|$ and hence find $|DC|$.

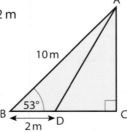

20. The total angle of swing of a particular pendulum is 44° (22° each way).
Work out the difference in height of the bottom of the pendulum at the lowest and highest point in the swing.
Give your answer correct to the nearest centimetre.

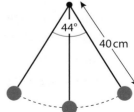

Section 14.5 The area of a triangle

The diagram shows a triangle ABC.

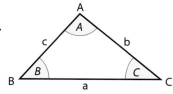

We use capital letters to denote the angles at the vertices A, B and C.

We use the lower-case letters a, b and c to represent the sides opposite the angles A, B and C.

The area of the given triangle is $\frac{1}{2} \times$ base $\times$ perpendicular height

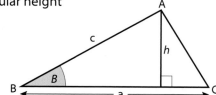

$$= \tfrac{1}{2} \times a \times h$$

But $\dfrac{h}{c} = \sin B$

$\Rightarrow \quad h = c \times \sin B$

Now area $\frac{1}{2} \times a \times h$ becomes $\frac{1}{2} \times a \times c \times \sin B$

Area $= \frac{1}{2}ac \sin B$

This is a very useful formula for finding the area of a triangle if we know two sides and the angle between these sides.

Area of a triangle

Area $= \frac{1}{2}ab \sin C$

In words: Area = Half the product of any two sides
multiplied by the sine of the angle
between them.

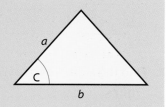

Example 1

Find the area of the triangle shown on the right.

Here we have 2 sides and the angle between them.

Area $= \frac{1}{2}(7)(8) \sin 46°$

$\qquad = (0.5)(7)(8) \sin 46°$

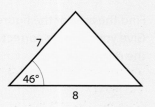

Using a calculator, key in $0.5 \times 7 \times 8 \times \boxed{\sin}\, 46 \boxed{=}$.

The answer is   20.14 sq. units, correct to 2 decimal places.

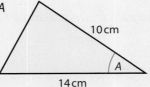

Example 2

If the area of the given triangle is 40 cm², find the angle A correct to the nearest degree.

Area of $\triangle = \frac{1}{2}(10)(14) \sin A$

$\Rightarrow \quad \frac{1}{2}(10)(14) \sin A = 40$

$\Rightarrow \quad 70 \sin A = 40$

$\Rightarrow \quad \sin A = \frac{40}{70}$

$\Rightarrow \quad A = \sin^{-1} \frac{40}{70}$

To find A, key in [SHIFT] [sin] 40 [÷] 70 [=]

The result is 34.85°

$\therefore \quad A = 35°$, correct to the nearest degree.

Exercise 14.5

1. Find the area of each of the triangles shown below.
   Give your answers in cm², correct to one decimal place.

   (i)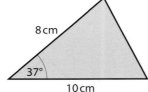

   (ii)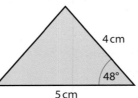

   (ii)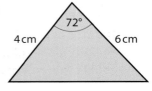

2. Find the area of each of these triangles in cm², correct to the nearest whole number.

   (i)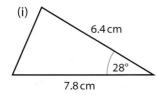

   (ii)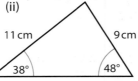

   (iii)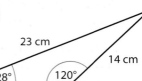

3. Find the area of the figure ABCD.
   Give your answer correct to
   the nearest integer.

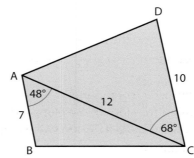

4. Find the area of this parallelogram, correct to the nearest cm².

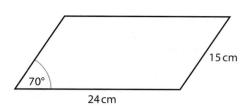

15 cm

70°

24 cm

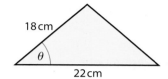

A parallelogram can be treated as two equal triangles.

5. Find the area of the given triangle if sin θ = 0.7.
Give your answer to the nearest cm².

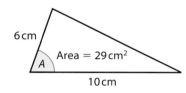

18 cm

θ

22 cm

6. The area of each of the triangles below is given.
Find the measure of the angle marked with a letter.
Give your answer correct to the nearest degree in each case.

6 cm

Area = 29 cm²

A

10 cm

18 cm

Area = 47 cm²

B

14 cm

7. The area of the triangle shown is 30 square units.
Find the length of the side marked x,
correct to 1 decimal place.

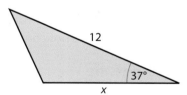

12

37°

x

8. The area of an equilateral triangle is 43.3 cm².
Find the length of the side of the triangle.

9. In the given triangle, cos A = $\frac{4}{5}$.
Without using a calculator, find the value of sin A.
Hence find the area of the triangle.

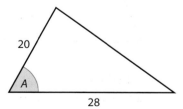

20

A

28

10. RST is a triangular plot of land in which |RT| = 18 m and |TS| = 23 m.
The area of the plot is 207 m².
  (i) Draw a rough sketch of this plot.   (ii) Find |∠RTS|.
  (iii) If the lengths of the sides of the plot are doubled but the measure of ∠RTS remains
      unchanged, investigate if the area of the plot is also doubled.
      Explain your answer.

11. A farmer wants to give a triangular plot of land
to his daughter on which she can build a house.
The plot is bounded on two sides by a hedge
and a road.
The hedge makes an angle of 78° with
the road.
If the road frontage of the plot is
20 metres, how far along the hedge
should the plot extend if the
area of the plot is 1500 m²?
Give your answer correct
to the nearest metre.

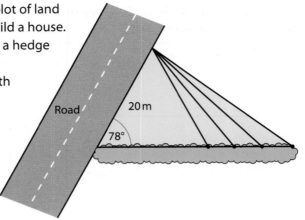

12. In the given triangle ABC, cos ∠BAC = $\frac{1}{5}$.
  (i) Find sin ∠BAC in surd form.
  (ii) Show that the area of the triangle ABC
       can be written in the form $k\sqrt{k}$, $k \in$ N.
       Hence write down the value of k.

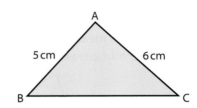

Section 14.6 The Sine Rule

In our study of trigonometry so far we have dealt mainly with right-angled triangles.

In this section we will deal with the Sine Rule which enables us to find sides and angles of a
triangle which does not contain a right angle.

The Sine Rule

For any triangle *ABC*,

$$\frac{a}{\sin A} = \frac{b}{\sin B} = \frac{c}{\sin C}$$

or $\quad\frac{\sin A}{a} = \frac{\sin B}{b} = \frac{\sin C}{c}$

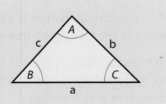

The Sine Rule may also be stated in words, as shown.

$$\frac{\text{Any side}}{\text{sine of opposite angle}} = \frac{\text{Any other side}}{\text{sine of its opposite angle}}$$

To use the Sine Rule to solve a triangle, we need to
know one side and the angle opposite this side
as well as one other angle or side.

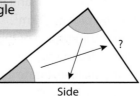

In practice, two parts of the Sine Rule only are used when solving problems, i.e.,

$$\frac{a}{\sin A} = \frac{b}{\sin B} \quad \text{or} \quad \frac{\sin A}{a} = \frac{\sin B}{b}$$

To find a side, have the sides on top.
To find an angle, have the angles on top.

Example 1

Find, correct to the nearest whole number, the length of the side marked x in the given triangle.

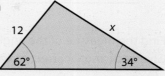

Here we have a side of length 12 and the opposite angle is 34°.

Using the Sine Rule we have: $\dfrac{x}{\sin 62°} = \dfrac{12}{\sin 34°}$

$\Rightarrow \dfrac{x}{0.8829} = \dfrac{12}{0.5592}$ key in sin 62 and sin 34

$\Rightarrow x(0.5592) = 12(0.8829)$

$\Rightarrow x = \dfrac{12(0.8829)}{0.5592} = 18.946 \Rightarrow x = 19$

Example 2

Find the measure of the angle A, correct to the nearest degree. Hence find the area of the triangle ABC.

$$\frac{12}{\sin 53°} = \frac{14}{\sin A}$$

$\Rightarrow \dfrac{12}{0.7986} = \dfrac{14}{\sin A}$

$\Rightarrow 12 \sin A = 14(0.7986)$

$\Rightarrow \sin A = \dfrac{14(0.7986)}{12} = 0.9317$

$\Rightarrow A = \sin^{-1} 0.9317$

To find A key in SHIFT sin 0.9317 = .

The result is 68.70°

$\therefore A = 69°$, correct to the nearest degree

We now find the angle B to get the area of $\triangle$ABC.

$$B = 180° - 53° - 69° \Rightarrow B = 58°$$

Area of $\triangle$ABC $= \frac{1}{2}|AB|.|BC| \sin B$

$\qquad = (0.5)(12)(14) \sin 58°$

$\qquad = 71.236$

$\qquad$ Area $= 71.2 \text{ cm}^2$

Exercise 14.6

1. Find, correct to 1 decimal place, the length of the side marked *x* in each of these triangles.

(i)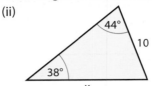

(ii)

(iii)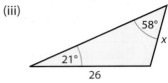

2. Find the measure of the angle marked with a letter in each of these triangles.
Give each angle correct to the nearest degree.

(i)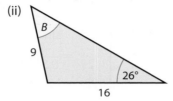

(ii)

(iii)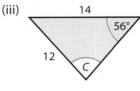

3. In the given triangle, $|\angle BAC| = 71°$, $|BC| = 22$ cm and $|AC| = 15$ cm.

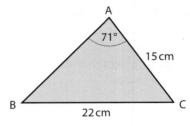

Find   (i) $|\angle ABC|$, correct to the nearest degree
         (ii) $|AB|$, correct to the nearest cm.

4. In the given triangle, $|AB| = 22$, $|\angle BAC| = 65°$
and $|\angle ABC| = 71°$.
Find, correct to the nearest integer,
  (i) $|BC|$
  (ii)   the area of the triangle ABC.

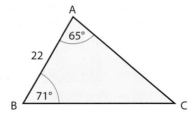

5. In the given triangle, $|CD| = 15$ m, $|\angle ADC| = 30°$,
$|\angle CAD| = 23°$ and $|\angle ABC| = 90°$.
Find, in metres, correct to 1 decimal place,
  (i) $|AC|$
  (ii) $|AB|$.

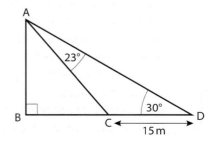

6. From a point A on level ground, the angle of elevation of the top of a tower [BC] is 40°. On walking 50 m towards the tower, the angle of elevation is now 60°. Find, correct to the nearest metre
  (i) |CD|
  (ii) the height of the tower [BC].

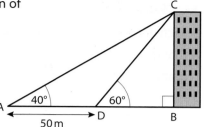

7. Two lighthouses P and Q are 73 km apart. Another lighthouse, R, is situated 52 km from Q. If |∠RPQ| = 31.5°, find
  (i) |∠PRQ|, correct to the nearest degree
  (ii) |PR|, correct to the nearest kilometre.

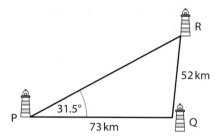

8. ABC is a triangle and D is on the line BC. If |BD| = 4 cm, |AC| = 6 cm, |∠ACD| = 65° and |∠DAC| = 70°, find
  (i) |DC|, correct to the nearest cm
  (ii) the area of △ABC, correct to the nearest cm².

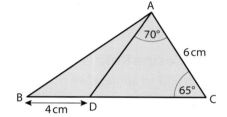

9. The diagram shows two parallel banks of a river. The angles from two points R and S on one bank to a tree on the opposite bank are 38° and 47°, as shown. Find, correct to the nearest metre
  (i) the distance from R to the tree
  (ii) the width, w, of the river.

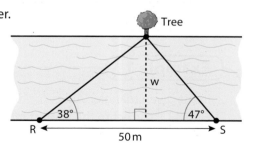

10. A farmer makes a triangular pen bounded by a fence 59 metres long, a hedge 68 metres long and a wall. The angle between the wall and the hedge is 49°. Draw a rough sketch of the triangle.
  (i) Find the measure of the angle between the fence and the wall, correct to the nearest degree.
  (ii) Find the length of the wall, correct to the nearest metre.
  (iii) Find the area of the pen, correct to the nearest m².

Section 14.7 The Cosine Rule

In each of the triangles shown below, we are given 3 pieces of information.

In triangle **A**, we are given two sides and the included angle (i.e. the angle between them).

In triangle **B**, we are given the lengths of the three sides.

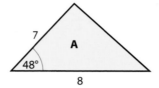 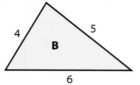

In neither of these triangles can the Sine Rule be used to find the remaining sides and angles.

To solve these triangles we use another rule, called the **Cosine Rule**, which is given below.

For any triangle, ABC

$$a^2 = b^2 + c^2 - 2bc \cos A$$
or $\quad b^2 = c^2 + a^2 - 2ca \cos B$
or $\quad c^2 = a^2 + b^2 - 2ab \cos C$

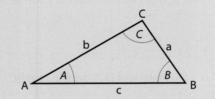

The Cosine Rule is used

1. to find an angle when three sides are given.

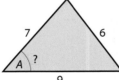

2. to find the third side when two sides and the included angle are given.

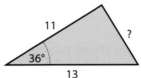

> ### Example 1
>
> In the given triangle, $|AB| = 6$, $|AC| = 8$ and $|\angle BAC| = 48°$.
> Find $|BC|$, correct to the nearest integer.
>
>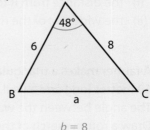
>
> Let $[BC] = a$.
> To find the side **a**, we use the *Cosine Rule*
> beginning with a^2.
> $$a^2 = b^2 + c^2 - 2bc \cos A \dots (b = 8 \text{ and } c = 6)$$
> $$= 8^2 + 6^2 - 2.8.6 \cos 48°$$
> $$= 64 + 36 - 96(0.6691)$$
> $$= 35.77$$
> $\Rightarrow \quad a = 5.98$ i.e. $|BC| = 5.98 = 6$, correct to the nearest integer.

Example 2

Find $|\angle ABC|$, in the given triangle.

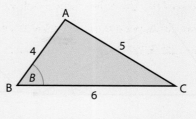

$\angle ABC = B$

To find the angle **B** we use the Cosine Rule beginning with **b²**.

$$b^2 = c^2 + a^2 - 2ca \cos B$$
$$\Rightarrow \quad 25 = 16 + 36 - 2(4)(6) \cos B$$
$$25 = 52 - 48 \cos B$$
$$25 - 52 = -48 \cos B$$
$$-27 = -48 \cos B$$
$$48 \cos B = 27$$
$$\cos B = \tfrac{27}{48}$$
$$B = \cos^{-1} \tfrac{27}{48} \dots \text{[key in } \boxed{\text{SHIFT}}\ \boxed{\text{cos}}\ 27\ \boxed{\div}\ 48\ \boxed{=}\ ]$$
$$B = 55.77°$$

$\therefore \quad |\angle ABC| = 56°$, correct to the nearest degree.

$a = 6$
$b = 5$
$c = 4$

Note: **1.** When solving a triangle, we generally try to use the *Sine Rule* first. If the *Sine Rule* cannot be used, we then use the *Cosine Rule*.

   2. If the cosine of an angle in a triangle is negative, the angle will lie between 90° and 180°.

Compass Directions

The diagram on the right shows some compass directions.

Compass directions begin with N (for North) or S (for South) and then a given number of degrees East or West.

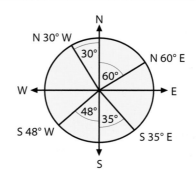

Exercise 14.7

1. Find the length, correct to one decimal place, of the side marked with a letter in each of the following triangles:

(i)

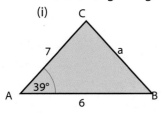

(ii)

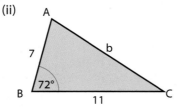

(iii)

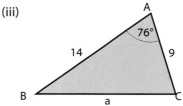

2. Find, correct to the nearest whole number, the length of the side marked with a letter in each of these triangles:

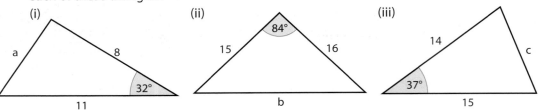

(i)

a, 8, 11, 32°

(ii)

84°, 15, 16, b

(iii)

14, 37°, c, 15

3. Find the measure of the angle marked with a letter in each of the following triangles. Give each angle correct to the nearest degree.

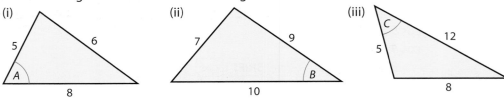

(i)

5, 6, A, 8

(ii)

7, 9, B, 10

(iii)

C, 5, 12, 8

4. Find the measure of the smallest angle in the given triangle. Give your answer correct to the nearest degree.

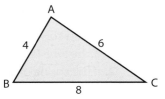

A, 4, 6, B, 8, C

5. In the given triangle, |PQ| = 15 cm, |PR| = 12 cm and |RQ| = 5 cm.

Find |∠PQR|, correct to the nearest degree.

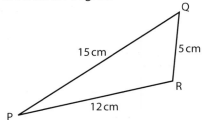

Q, 15 cm, 5 cm, R, 12 cm, P

6. The distance from the tee to the pin on the green is 190 metres.
A golfer hits a shot at an angle of 20° away from the direct line to the hole.
If the ball travels 170 m, find the distance between the ball and the hole.
Give your answer correct to the nearest metre.

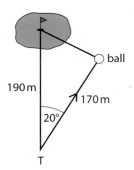

ball, 190 m, 170 m, 20°, T

7. Use the information in the given figure to find
  (i) |AC|, correct to the nearest metre.
  (ii) Use this length of [AC] to find |∠ABC|, correct to the nearest degree.

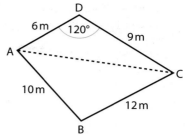

8. On a snooker table, the cue ball and black ball are situated as shown in the diagram.
Find the distance the cue ball has to travel before hitting the black ball.
Give your answer correct to the nearest centimetre.

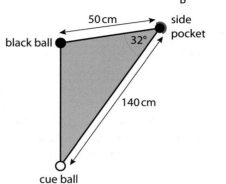

9. Two ships, R and T, leave a port P at the same time.
R travels in a direction N 80° E at a speed of 24 km/hr.
T travels in a direction S 60° E at a speed of 32 km/hr.
How far apart are the ships one hour after leaving port?
Give your answer correct to the nearest kilometre.

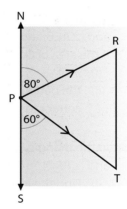

The following problems may involve the use of the *Sine Rule* as well as the *Cosine Rule*.

10. In the given triangle ABC, D is a point on [BC].
|BD| = 6 cm, |AC| = 9 cm, |∠DCA| = 80° and |∠CAD| = 50°.

  (i) Find |DC|
  (ii) Find |AB|, correct to the nearest cm.

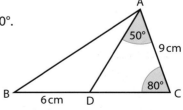

11. In the triangle XYZ, |XY| = 22 cm, |YZ| = 15 cm and |∠XYZ| = 74°.

  Find (i) |XZ|, correct to the nearest cm.
       (ii) |∠YXZ|, correct to the nearest degree.

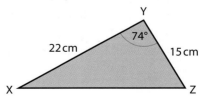

12. In the quadrilateral ABCD, $|AC| = 5$, $|BC| = 4$, $|\angle BCA| = 110°$,
$|\angle ACD| = 33°$ and $|\angle CDA| = 23°$.
Find, correct to two decimal places,

   (i) $|AB|$

   (ii) $|CD|$.

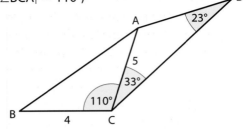

13. The diagram shows wires attached to a
communications antenna.
Find the length h, correct to the nearest metre.

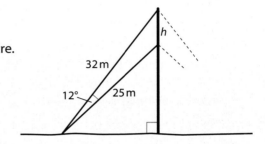

14. In the given triangle ABC, $|BC| = 60$ m
and $|\angle ACB| = 150°$.
If the area of $\triangle ABC = 450$ m², find

   (i) $|AC|$

   (ii) the perimeter of the triangle ABC,
correct to the nearest metre.

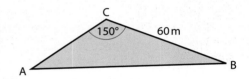

15. In the triangle PQR, $|PR| = 7$ cm, QR = 13 cm
and $|\angle PRQ| = 80°$.

   (i) Find the length of [PQ] in centimetres,
correct to one decimal place.

   (ii) Find $|\angle QPR|$, correct to the nearest degree.

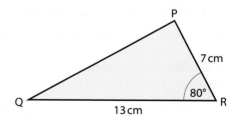

16. S and T are two points 300 metres apart on a
straight path due north.
A pillar, P, is N 40° E of S.
The pillar is N 70° E of T.

   (i) Find the distance from T to the pillar,
correct to the nearest metre.

   (ii) Find the shortest distance, d, from the path to
the pillar, correct to the nearest metre.

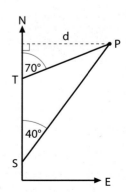

17. From a point A on the same level as the base of a radio mast, the angle of elevation of the top of the mast is 25°. From a point B, 20 metres closer to the mast, and on the same level, the angle of elevation is 32°. Find the height of the radio mast in metres, correct to the nearest metre.

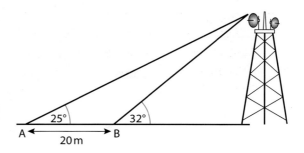

18. The diagram shows a point A, which lies 10 km due south of a point B.
A straight road AD is such that D is N 43° E of A.
P and Q are two points on this road which are both 8 km from B.

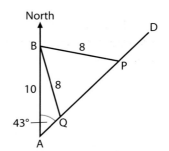

  (i) Find $|\angle BPA|$, correct to the nearest degree.
  (ii) Find $|\angle ABP|$, correct to the nearest degree.

Section 14.8 The angles 30°, 45° and 60°

The angles 30°, 45° and 60° are used very frequently and we will use triangles to express the sine, cosine and tangent ratios of these angles as fractions or surds.

The 45° angle

The triangle on the right is isosceles where the equal sides are 1 unit in length.

The hypotenuse is $\sqrt{2}$ units in length.

The sine, cosine and tangent ratios can be read from the triangle.

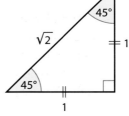

$$\sin 45° = \frac{1}{\sqrt{2}} \qquad \cos 45° = \frac{1}{\sqrt{2}} \qquad \tan 45° = 1$$

The angles 30° and 60°

The given right-angled triangle has angles of 60° and 30°.

We can use this triangle to write down the trigonometric ratios of these two angles.

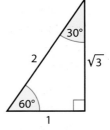

$$\sin 60° = \frac{\sqrt{3}}{2} \qquad \cos 60° = \frac{1}{2} \qquad \tan 60° = \sqrt{3}$$

$$\sin 30° = \frac{1}{2} \qquad \cos 30° = \frac{\sqrt{3}}{2} \qquad \tan 30° = \frac{1}{\sqrt{3}}$$

Note: The sine, cosine and tangent ratios for 30°, 45° and 60° are given on page 13 of *Formulae and Tables*.

Example 1

Without using a calculator, find the values of x and y in the given right-angled triangle.

$$\frac{x}{4} = \tan 60°$$

$$\Rightarrow \quad \frac{x}{4} = \frac{\sqrt{3}}{1}$$

$$\Rightarrow \quad x = 4\sqrt{3}$$

$$\frac{4}{y} = \cos 60°$$

$$\Rightarrow \quad \frac{4}{y} = \frac{1}{2}$$

$$\Rightarrow \quad y = 8$$

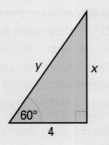

Exercise 14.8

Without using a calculator, write the value of each of the following as a simple fraction or as a surd:

1. $\cos 60°$ 2. $\tan 45°$ 3. $\sin 30°$ 4. $\cos 45°$ 5. $\sin^2 30°$

6. $\cos 30°$ 7. $\sin 60°$ 8. $\cos^2 45°$ 9. $\sin^2 60°$ 10. $\tan^2 30°$

11. Show that   (i) $1 - \sin^2 30° = \cos^2 30°$ (ii) $\sin 60° = 2 \sin 30° \cos 30°$

12. Without using a calculator, find the values of x and y in the given triangle.

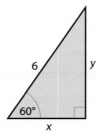

13. Find the values of x and y in the given triangle, without using a calculator.

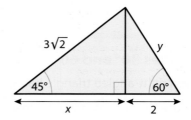

14. Find the values of x, y and z in the given diagram, without using a calculator.

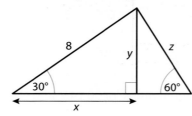

15. A field is in the shape of an equilateral triangle, as shown.
Each side is 40 m in length.
Suggest two methods of finding the area of this field
without using a calculator.
Find the area using each of these methods.
Give your answer in surd form.

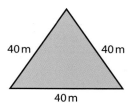

Section 14.9 Area of sector – Length of arc

You will have already learned how to find the circumference and area of a circle.

The formulae for these are given below.

> **Circumference** of a circle $= 2\pi r$
>
> **Area** of a circle $= \pi r^2$

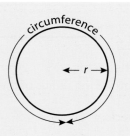

In this section we will learn how to find
  (i) the length of an arc of a circle
 (ii) the area of a sector of a circle.

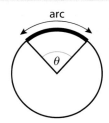
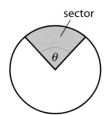

The diagram below shows a circle with O as centre.

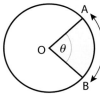

OAB is a sector of the circle, where $|\angle AOB| = \theta$.

AB is called the **minor arc**.

> Area of sector AOB $= \dfrac{\theta}{360°} \times \pi r^2$
>
> Length of minor arc AB $= \dfrac{\theta}{360°} \times 2\pi r$

(**Example 1**)

The given circle has radius 9 cm, and $|\angle AOB| = 120°$.
Taking $\pi = \frac{22}{7}$, find

  (i) the length of the minor arc AB
 (ii) the area of the shaded sector AOB.

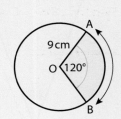

417

(i) Length of arc AB $= \dfrac{120°}{360°} \times 2\pi r$

$$= \dfrac{120}{360} \times \dfrac{2}{1} \times \dfrac{22}{7} \times \dfrac{9}{1}$$

$$= 18.86 \text{ cm}$$

(ii) Area of sector AOB $= \dfrac{120°}{360°} \times \pi r^2$

$$= \dfrac{120}{360} \times \dfrac{22}{7} \times \dfrac{9^2}{1} = 84.86 \text{ cm}^2$$

Example 2

The area of the sector AOB = 205 cm².
Find the length of the radius of the circle.

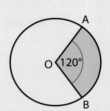

Let r be the radius.

$$\text{Area of AOB} = \dfrac{120}{360} \times \pi r^2 = 205 \text{ cm}^2$$

$$\Rightarrow \quad \dfrac{\pi r^2}{3} = 205$$

$$\Rightarrow \quad \pi r^2 = 205 \times 3 \dots \quad \text{multiply both sides by 3}$$

$$\Rightarrow \quad r^2 = \dfrac{205 \times 3}{\pi}$$

$$= 195.76 \dots \quad \text{use } \pi \text{ key on your calculator}$$

$$\Rightarrow \quad r = \sqrt{195.76} = 13.99$$

$$\Rightarrow \quad \text{radius} = 14 \text{ cm, correct to the nearest cm.}$$

Exercise 14.9

1. Find the area of each of these sectors, correct to the nearest cm²:

(i)

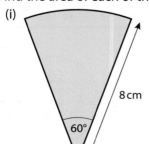

(ii)

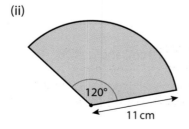

(iii)

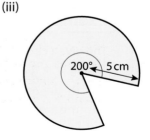

2. Find the length of the arc in each of the sectors in question 1 on the previous page. Give your answer in centimetres, correct to one decimal place.

3. Find, correct to one decimal place,
    (i) the area of the sector AOB
    (ii) the length of the arc AB in the given diagram.

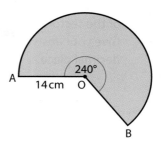

4. The radius of the given circle is 18 cm.
    The measure of ∠AOB = 75°.
    (i) Find the length of the arc AB, correct to the nearest centimetre.
    (ii) Find the area of the sector AOB, correct to the nearest cm^2.

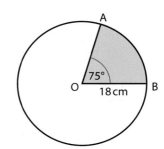

5. Find the length of the radius of this circle if the area of the given sector is 77 cm^2.

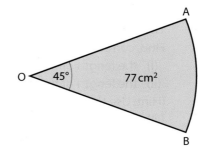

6. In the given sector, |∠AOB| = 140° and its area is 276 cm^2.
    Find the length of the radius of the circle, correct to the nearest cm.

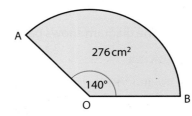

7. A golfer can hit a ball 220 m with an accuracy of 15° either side of his intended direction. Find the length of the arc along which he might find his ball, correct to the nearest metre.

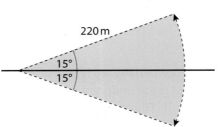

8. A coastguard radar makes a sweep of 55° from
   its base, B.
   If the range of the radar is 3.5 km, find the area
   of the sector swept by the radar.
   Give your answer in km², correct to one
   decimal place.

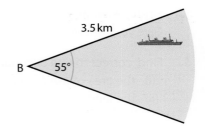

9. *OPQ* is a sector of a circle with radius 20 cm.
   X is the midpoint of [*OP*] and *Y* is the midpoint of [*OQ*].
   Angle *POQ* = 65°.
   Calculate
   (i) the area *XPQY*
   (ii) the perimeter of *XPQY*.
       Give each answer correct to the nearest whole number.

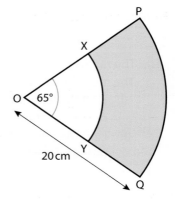

10. The given sector has a radius of 18 cm.
    The angle in the sector is 80°.
    Find, correct to the nearest whole number in each case,
    (i)   the length of the arc AB
    (ii) the length of the chord [AB]
    (Hint: Use the Cosine Rule)
    (iii) the area of the sector OAB
    (iv) the area of the triangle OAB
    (v)   the area of the shaded region.

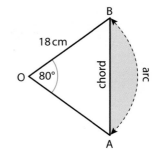

11. The diagram shows part of a football pitch.

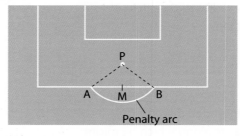

   The penalty arc is part of a circle, radius 10 metres, with centre P.
   M is the midpoint of [AB] and |PM| = 6 metres.
   (i) Find the measure of the ∠APB, correct to the nearest degree.
   (ii) Calculate the length of the penalty arc, correct to one decimal place.

Section 14.10 Ratios of angles greater than 90°

1. The Unit Circle

The circle on the right has centre at (0, 0) and radius
1 unit in length.
It is generally referred to as the unit circle.

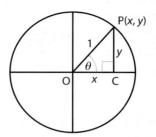

Let P(x, y) be any point on the circle, as shown.

From the triangle OPC,

$$\frac{x}{1} = \cos\theta \qquad\qquad \frac{y}{1} = \sin\theta$$

$$\Rightarrow \quad x = \cos\theta \qquad \Rightarrow \quad y = \sin\theta$$

∴   the coordinates of P are **(cos θ, sin θ)**

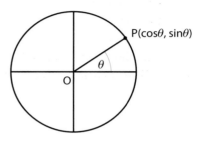

> The coordinates of any point on
> the unit circle are **P(cos θ, sin θ)**.

The unit circle shown crosses the x-axis and y-axis at the indicated points.

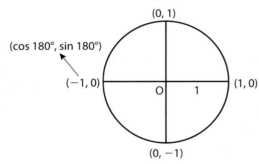

We can use these points to write down the value of sin θ and cos θ for the angles 0°, 90°, 180°, 270° and 360°.

Thus (−1, 0) gives the values of cos 180° and sin 180°,

i.e.   cos 180° = −1 and sin 180° = 0.

2. The Four Quadrants

The x-axis and y-axis divide a full rotation of 360°
into 4 quadrants as shown on the right.

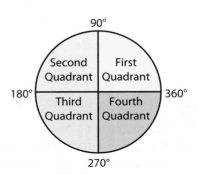

The unit circle on the right shows an angle, θ, in each of the four quadrants. The signs shown in each triangle determine whether a ratio is positive or negative.

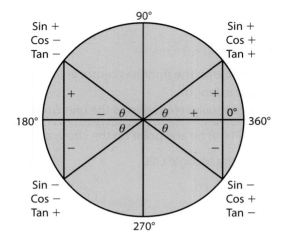

The positive ratios in the four quadrants are shown in the highlighted section below.

(i)   In the 1st quadrant, all (A) positive
(ii) In the 2nd quadrant, sin(S) only positive
(iii) In the 3rd quadrant, tan(T) only positive
(iv) In the 4th quadrant, cos(C) only positive

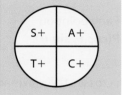

3. Finding the ratio of an angle between 90° and 360°

An electronic calculator will give the sine, cosine and tangent of any angle, including the negative sign, if it exists. However, if we need the ratio of a certain angle as a fraction or as a surd, the following steps must be followed:

1. Make a rough sketch of the angle to determine in which quadrant it lies.

2. Use 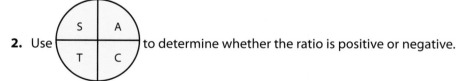 to determine whether the ratio is positive or negative.

3. Determine the angle ($<90°$) between the rotated line and the **x-axis**.
This angle is known as the **reference angle**.

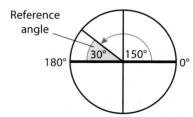

4. Use a calculator or the 30°, 45° and 60° triangles to find the required ratio.
Use the diagram in **2** above to determine the sign of the ratio.

Example 1

Find in surd form   (i)   sin 120°   (ii)   cos 225°

(i)   sin 120°:

120° is in the second quadrant

$\Rightarrow$ the sine ratio is positive

The reference angle is 180° − 120° = 60°.

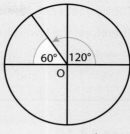

Using the triangle shown,

$$\sin 60° = \frac{\sqrt{3}}{2} \quad \Rightarrow \quad \sin 120° = \frac{\sqrt{3}}{2}$$

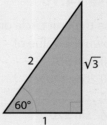

(ii)   cos 225°:

225° is in the third quadrant

$\Rightarrow$ the cosine ratio is negative

The reference angle is 225° − 180° = 45°.

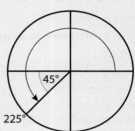

Using the 45° triangle shown,

$$\cos 45° = \frac{1}{\sqrt{2}} \quad \Rightarrow \quad \cos 225° = -\frac{1}{\sqrt{2}}.$$

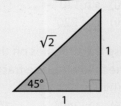

Example 2

Given   cos A = −0.4153 and 0° ⩽ A ⩽ 360°.
Use your calculator to find the values of A in degrees, correct to one decimal place.

cos A = −0.4153

Disregard the negative sign and find the reference angle.

To find this reference angle, key in $\boxed{\text{SHIFT}}$ $\boxed{\text{cos}}$ 0.4153 $\boxed{=}$

The result is 65.46°

    = 65.5°, correct to one decimal place.

The cosine is negative in the second and third quadrants.

Therefore, the two values of A are,

      180° − 65.5° and 180° + 65.5°

∴ A = 114.5° and 245.5°

Exercise 14.10

1. Use the unit circle on the right to write
down the value of

    (i) sin 50°

    (ii) cos 220°

    (iii) cos 50°

    (iv) sin 220°

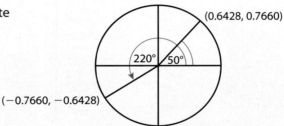

2. Use a calculator to write down, correct to four decimal places, the value of each of these
ratios:

    (i) sin 138°   (ii) cos 212°   (iii) tan 318°   (iv) cos 159°

    (v) tan 193°   (vi) sin 236°   (vii) cos 317°   (viii) tan 254°

3. If cos 120° = −cos 60°, copy and complete the following in the same way:

    (i) sin 130° = ...   (ii) cos 115° = ...   (iii) tan 160° = ...

    (iv) cos 220° = ...   (v) sin 250° = ...   (vi) tan 300° = ...

4. Use the triangles on the right to express each of
the following as a fraction or as a surd:

    (i) sin 120°   (ii) cos 135°

    (iii) sin 240°   (iv) sin 210°

    (v) cos 330°   (vi) tan 225°

    (vii) cos 150°   (viii) sin 300°

    (ix) tan 150°

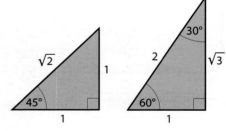

5. Find, correct to the nearest degree, the two values of A if sin A = 0.2167 and 0° ⩽ A ⩽ 360°.

6. Find, correct to the nearest degree, the two values of B for 0° ⩽ B ⩽ 360°, given that

    (i) cos B = −0.8428   (ii) tan B = −1.2464.

7. If $\sin \theta = \frac{1}{2}$, find 2 values for θ, if 0° ⩽ θ ⩽ 360°.

8. If $\cos \theta = \frac{1}{\sqrt{2}}$, find 2 values for tan θ, if 0° ⩽ θ ⩽ 360°.

9. If $\tan A = \dfrac{1}{\sqrt{3}}$, find 2 values for $\cos A$, if $0° \leqslant A \leqslant 360°$.

10. If $\sin \theta = -\dfrac{\sqrt{3}}{2}$, find two values for $\cos \theta$ without using a calculator if $0° \leqslant \theta \leqslant 360°$.

11. Find A, correct to the nearest degree, if $\sin A = -\frac{4}{5}$ and $\cos A = -\frac{3}{5}$ for $A \leqslant 360°$.

12. If $\sin B = \frac{3}{5}$ and $\cos B = -\frac{4}{5}$, find the value of $\tan B$ without using a calculator if $0° \leqslant B \leqslant 360°$.

13. If $\tan B = \dfrac{1}{\sqrt{3}}$ and $\sin B = -\frac{1}{2}$, express $\cos B$ as a surd.

14. If $\tan A = \frac{1}{2}$ and $180° < A < 270°$, find $\sin A$ in surd form.

Test yourself 14

1. Use the given right-angled triangle to write down
    (i) $\sin A$ (ii) $\tan A$
Now find the measure of the angle A,
correct to the nearest degree.

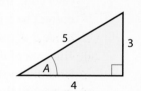

2. Find the length of the side marked x in the given triangle.
Hence write down as fractions
    (i) $\tan A$ (ii) $\cos A$.

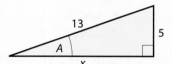

3. In the given triangle, $|\angle ACB| = 34°$, $|\angle ABC| = 90°$, and $|AB| = 12\,\text{cm}$.
Find $|BC|$, in cm, correct to one decimal place.

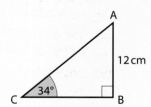

4. In the given triangle, $|AB| = 12\,\text{cm}$, $|CD| = 20\,\text{cm}$, $|\angle ABC| = 43°$ and $|\angle ACD| = 90°$.

    (i) Find $|AC|$, correct to the nearest cm.
    (ii) Find $|\angle ADC|$, correct to the nearest degree.

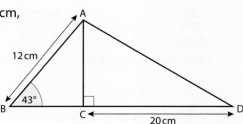

5. In the given triangle ABC, |AB| = 5 cm, |AC| = 8 cm and |∠BAC| = 52°.
Find, correct to the nearest whole number in each case,
   (i) the area of the triangle ABC
   (ii) the length of [BC]
   (iii) |∠BCA|.

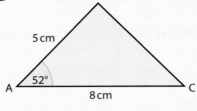

6. In the given diagram, |AD| = 6 cm, |DB| = 9 cm, |∠CAD| = 35° and CD is perpendicular to AB.

   (i) Find |CD|, in cm, correct to one decimal place.
   (ii) Find |∠CBD|, correct to the nearest degree.

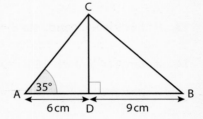

7. (i) Find the measure of the angle A in the given figure.
   Give your answer in degrees, correct to one decimal place.

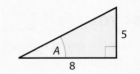

   (ii) The area of the given triangle is 51 cm².
   Find the the measure of the angle A, correct to the nearest degree.

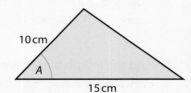

8. The radius of the given circle is 7 cm and |∠AOB| = 95°.
   (i) Find the area of the sector AOB in cm², correct to the nearest whole number.
   (ii) Find the length of the arc AB in centimetres, correct to one decimal place.

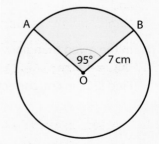

9. In the given figure, |YZ| = 15 m, |∠XYW| = 40°, |∠YZW| = 20° and |∠WXY| = 90°.
   Find, in metres, correct to one decimal place,
   (i) |WY|
   (ii) |WX|.

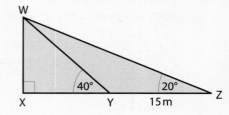

10. In the given figure, OAB is a sector of radius 8 cm and $|\angle AOB| = 40°$.
Find, in cm², correct to one decimal place
  (i) the area of the sector OAB
  (ii) the area of the shaded region.

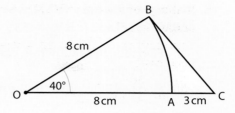

11. In the triangle PQR, $|PQ| = |PR|$, $|QR| = 15$ cm and $|\angle RPQ| = 40°$.
  (i) Find $|PR|$, correct to the nearest centimetre.
  (ii) S is a point on the line QR such that $|RS| = 10$ cm. Find $|PS|$, correct to the nearest centimetre.

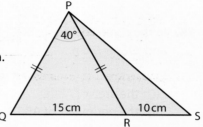

12. (i) If $\sin A = -0.8660$, find two values for A, for $0° \leqslant A \leqslant 360°$.
  (ii) Use the triangle on the right to write the value of $\sin^2 60° + \cos^2 30°$ in the form $\dfrac{a}{b}$, $a, b \in \mathbb{N}$.

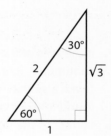

13. In the quadrilateral ABCD, $|\angle BAD| = 90°$, $|\angle BDC| = 63°$, $|AB| = 12$ cm, $|AD| = 9$ cm and $|DC| = 14$ cm.
Find, correct to the nearest integer,

  (i) the length of [BD]
  (ii) the area of ABCD.

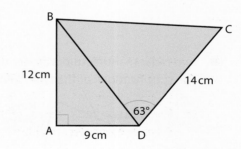

14. The diagram shows a tower.
At A, the angle of elevation to the top of the tower is 43°.
At B, the angle of elevation to the top of the tower is 74°.
The distance $|AB|$ is 10 m.
Calculate the height of the tower, in metres, correct to one decimal place.

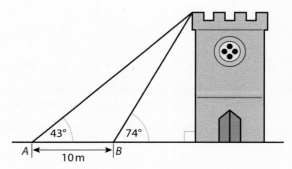

15. The area of the triangle ABC is 66 cm².
|AB| = 16 cm and |∠BAC| = 55°.

    (i) Find |BC|, in centimetres, correct to one decimal place.

    (ii) Find |∠ABC|, correct to the nearest degree.

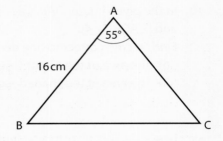

16. In the given sectors, |∠BOC| = 40°, |OD| = 5 cm and |OC| = 9 cm.

Find, correct to the nearest whole number,
    (i) the area of ABCD
    (ii) the perimeter of ABCD.

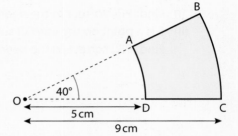

17. If the area of the triangle PQR is 42 cm², find |PR|, in centimetres, correct to one decimal place.
Given also that |RQ| = 11 cm, use the value you have found for |PR| to find the measure of the angle RQP, correct to the nearest degree.

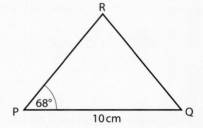

18. Two radar manufacturers are trying to sell their products to the coastguard. The specifications of the two different products, A and B, are given below:

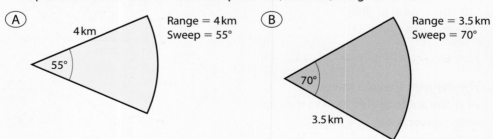

    (i) If the most important feature is the area of the sector covered by the radar, which radar should be chosen? Explain your answer.

    (ii) If radar A costs €75 000 and radar B costs €73 500, which radar gives the best value for money?
Explain your answer.

Summary of key points...

The Theorem of Pythagoras

In a right-angled triangle, the square on the hypotenuse is equal to the sum of the squares on the other two sides.

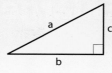

$$a^2 = b^2 + c^2$$

Sine, cosine and tangent ratios

$$\sin \theta = \frac{\text{opposite}}{\text{hypotenuse}} \qquad \tan \theta = \frac{\text{opposite}}{\text{adjacent}}$$

$$\cos \theta = \frac{\text{adjacent}}{\text{hypotenuse}}$$

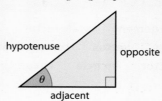

Area of a triangle

The area of the triangle ABC:

$$\text{Area} = \tfrac{1}{2} ab \sin C$$

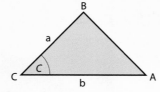

The Sine Rule

$$\frac{a}{\sin A} = \frac{b}{\sin B} = \frac{c}{\sin C}$$

or

$$\frac{\sin A}{a} = \frac{\sin B}{b} = \frac{\sin C}{c}$$

The Cosine Rule

$$a^2 = b^2 + c^2 - 2bc \cos A$$

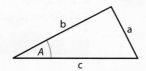

Ratios of 30°, 45° and 60°

The values of the trigonometric ratios for the angles 30°, 45° and 60° can be found from the triangles on the right.

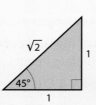 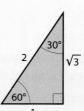

Sector of a circle

$$\text{Area of sector AOB} = \frac{\theta}{360°} \times \pi r^2$$

$$\text{Length of arc AB} = \frac{\theta}{360°} \times 2\pi r$$

Ratios of angles greater than 90°

The diagram shows the positive ratios in the four quadrants.

   (i)   In the first quadrant, all (A) positive
   (ii) In the second quadrant, sin(S) only positive
  (iii) In the third quadrant, tan(T) only positive
  (iv) In the fourth quadrant, cos(C) only positive.

Geometry 2 –
Enlargements & Constructions

Key words

enlargement   scale factor   centre of enlargement   object
image   vertex   corresponding sides   construct   tangent
bisector   incircle   circumcircle   median   centroid   scale drawing

Section 15.1 Enlargements

Here are two photographs.

They are both printed from the
same negative.

The dimensions of the photo on the right are twice the dimensions of the photo on the left.

We say that one photo is an **enlargement** of the other.

Since the length and width of the larger photo are twice those of the smaller photo, we say
that the **scale factor** of the enlargement is **2**.

In this diagram the rectangle A′B′C′D′ is an enlargement of the rectangle ABCD.

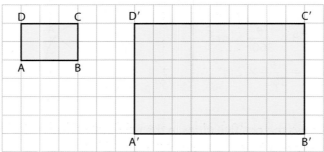

Here $|AB| = 3$ and $|A'B'| = 9$ $|AD| = 2$ and $|A'D'| = 6$

The sides of the rectangle A′B′C′D′ are three times as long as the sides of the rectangle
ABCD. Here the **scale factor** is **3**.

Now consider the two triangles ABC and A'B'C', shown below.

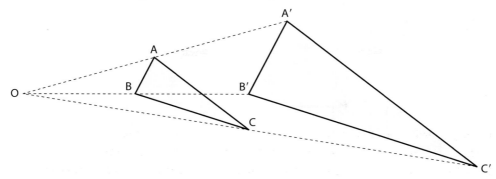

The triangle A'B'C' is an enlargement of the triangle ABC.

The point O is called the **centre of enlargement**.

Since $|OA'| = 2|OA|$, the scale factor is 2.

Since the scale factor is 2, $|A'B'| = 2|AB|$, $|A'C'| = 2|AC|$ and $|B'C'| = 2|BC|$.

The given triangle ABC is called the **object**.

The triangle A'B'C' is called the **image**.

The dotted lines are called guidelines or **rays**.

Drawing enlargements

To construct the image of a given figure under an enlargement, we need
  (i)   the centre of enlargement
  (ii) the scale factor of the enlargement.

The diagram below shows a square ABCD and a centre of enlargement O.

We will now enlarge ABCD with O as centre of enlargement and scale factor 3.

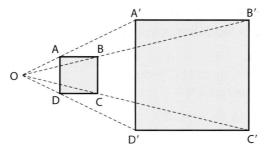

To find the image of A, we join O to A and continue to A' so that $|OA'| = 3|OA|$.

Similarly, join O to B and continue to B' so that $|OB'| = 3|OB|$.

Repeat the process for the points C and D.

The square A'B'C'D' is the image of the square ABCD.

Since the scale factor is 3, $|A'B'| = 3|AB|$ and $|A'D'| = 3|AD|$.

When a vertex is the centre of enlargement

The diagrams below show how to enlarge the shape ABCD by a scale factor of 2, using A as the centre of enlargement.

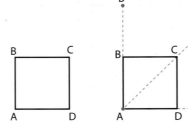 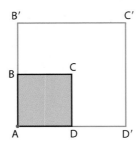

Notice that the centre of enlargement, A, does not move.

In the final figure, $|AB'| = 2|AB|$, $|AD'| = 2|AD|$ and $|AC'| = 2|AC|$.

The diagram on the right shows an enlargement where the centre of enlargement, X, is inside the figure.

In this enlargement, the scale factor is 2.

Draw the line [XA] and extend it so that $|XA'| = 2|XA|$.

Extend [XB] so that $|XB'| = 2|XB|$.

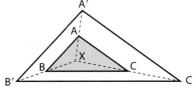

Repeat for [XC].

Each side of the enlarged triangle A'B'C' is twice the length of the corresponding side in △ABC.

For any enlargement, the scale factor is found by dividing the length of the image side by the length of the corresponding object side.

The scale factor is $\dfrac{\text{length of image side}}{\text{length of corresponding object side}}$

Enlargements with a Scale Factor less than 1

An enlargement with a scale factor less than 1 produces a smaller figure nearer to the centre of enlargement.

In this figure, A'B'C' is the image of ABC under an enlargement where the scale factor is $\frac{1}{2}$.

Thus $|OA'| = \frac{1}{2}|OA|$ and $|A'B'| = \frac{1}{2}|AB|$.

When the scale factor is a positive fraction less than 1, the result is a reduction of the given figure.

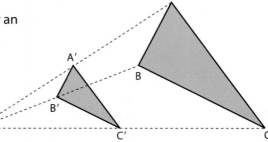

If the scale factor is k, then

   (i) if $k > 1$, the figure is enlarged   (ii) if $k < 1$, the figure is reduced.

Finding the centre of enlargement

When a figure and its enlargement are given, then the centre of enlargement is found by joining two sets of corresponding points and continuing the lines until the meet.

In the diagram below, A'A and C'C meet at O. The centre of enlargement is this point, O.

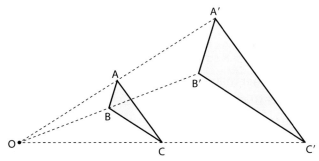

Example 1

In the given figure, AB'C' is an enlargement of the triangle ABC where A is the centre of enlargement.
If $|AC| = 6$, $|CC'| = 9$ and $|B'C'| = 12.5$, find

  (i) the scale factor of the enlargement

 (ii) $|BC|$

(iii) the ratio $|AB| : |AB'|$.

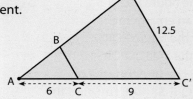

  (i) It may simplify your work if you draw the two triangles separately.

$$\text{The scale factor} = \frac{\text{image length}}{\text{object length}}$$

$$= \frac{|AC'|}{|AC|}$$

$$= \frac{15}{6} = 2.5$$

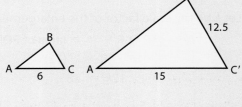

 (ii) Since the scale factor is $2\frac{1}{2}$, $|B'C'| = 2\frac{1}{2}|BC|$

$$|B'C'| = 2\frac{1}{2}|BC| \quad \Rightarrow \quad |BC| = \frac{|B'C'|}{2\frac{1}{2}} = \frac{12.5}{2.5} = 5$$

$$\therefore \quad |BC| = 5$$

(iii) $|AB'| = 2\frac{1}{2}|AB|$

$$\therefore \quad \frac{|AB'|}{|AB|} = 2\frac{1}{2} = \frac{5}{2}$$

$$\therefore \quad |AB'| : |AB| = 5 : 2$$

$$\Rightarrow \quad |AB| : |AB'| = 2 : 5$$

$$\frac{x}{y} = \frac{3}{4}$$
$$\Rightarrow \quad x : y = 3 : 4$$

Enlargement and area

The given grid shows that one triangle is an enlargement of the other. The scale factor is 2.

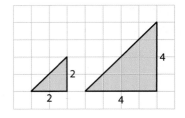

$$\text{Area of smaller triangle} = \tfrac{1}{2}(2)(2)$$
$$= 2 \text{ square units}$$
$$\text{Area of larger triangle} = \tfrac{1}{2}(4)(4)$$
$$= 8 \text{ square units}$$

Notice that the area of the larger triangle is four times the area of the smaller triangle.

Notice also that 4 is (scale factor)^2.

If the scale factor is k, then

$$\text{Area of image} = k^2 \text{ (Area of object)}.$$

> When a figure is enlarged by a scale factor k, the area of the image figure is increased by a scale factor k^2.

Example 2

The figure P'Q'R'S' is an enlargement of the figure PQRS. If the area of PQRS is 12 cm^2 and the area of P'Q'R'S' = 48 cm^2, find the scale factor of the enlargement.

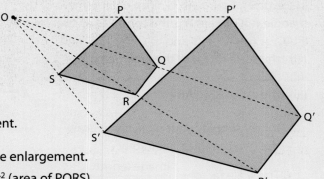

Let k be the scale factor of the enlargement.

$$\text{Area of P'Q'R'S'} = k^2 \text{ (area of PQRS)}$$
$$\Rightarrow \quad 48 = k^2 (12)$$
$$12k^2 = 48$$
$$k^2 = 4$$
$$k = 2$$

∴   the scale factor of the enlargement is 2.

In example 2 above, the figure PQRS is enlarged by a scale factor of 2.

If we start with the figure P'Q'R'S' and enlarge it to get the image PQRS, it is clear that the scale factor is $\frac{1}{2}$.

That is, each side in PQRS will be half the corresponding side in P'Q'R'S'.

> If a figure is enlarged by a scale factor k, then the scale factor for the inverse enlargement is $\frac{1}{k}$.

Going from the image figure back to the original figure is generally called the **inverse enlargement**.

In the given figure, A is an enlargement of B.
The scale factor, k, is $1\frac{1}{2}$.

Now if B is an enlargement of A, the scale factor is $\frac{1}{k}$.

$$\frac{1}{k} = \frac{1}{1\frac{1}{2}} = \frac{2}{3}$$

$\therefore$ the inverse scale factor $= \frac{2}{3}$.

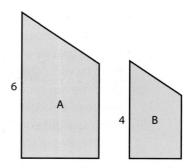

Exercise 15.1

1. The diagram on the right shows a figure
and its enlargement.

    (i)   Use the grid to write down the
scale factor of the enlargement.

    (ii) The lengths of two sides are given.
Find the lengths of the sides
marked
x and y.

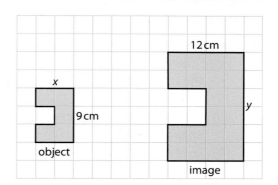

2. In the given diagram, the triangle A′B′C′
is the image of the triangle ABC under an
enlargement with centre O and scale factor 2.
If $|BC| = 4$, $|AC| = 6$ and $|A′B′| = 10$, find

    (i) $|B′C′|$

    (ii) $|A′C′|$

    (iii) $|AB|$.

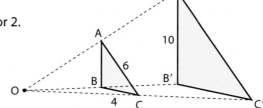

3. Make a copy of the rectangle ABCD, as shown.
Draw an enlargement of ABCD with A as centre
of enlargement and scale factor 2.
Label the image AB′C′D′.
Which point of the given rectangle remains in its
original position?

4. Make a copy of this triangle.
Now draw an enlargement of this triangle with Z
as centre of enlargement and scale factor 3.
Label the image figure X′Y′Z.
Write down the length of

    (i) [ZY′]   (ii) [ZX′]

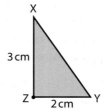

5. The given diagram shows the figure ABCD and its enlargement PQRS.
   (i) Use the grid to write down the scale factor of the enlargement.
   (ii) Describe how you would find the centre of enlargement.
   (iii) Use a straight edge to find the coordinates of the centre of enlargement.

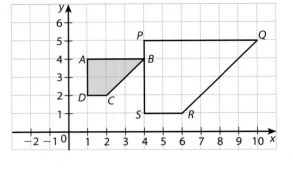

6. In the given figure, the triangle marked B is an enlargement of the triangle marked A. Use the grid to write down
   (i) the scale factor of the enlargement
   (ii) the coordinates of the centre of enlargement.
   (iii) Use the grid to write down the area of triangle A and triangle B.
   (iv) If the scale factor is k, verify that area of triangle B = k^2 times area of triangle A.

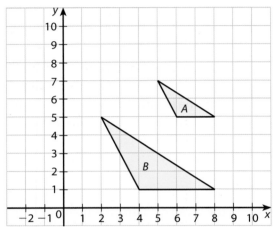

Area of a triangle is half base multiplied by perpendicular height.

7. In the given diagram, the triangle ORS is the image of the triangle OPQ under an enlargement with O as centre.
   $|OP| = 4$, $|PR| = 6$ and $|SR| = 8$.
   Draw OPQ and ORS as separate triangles and use these triangles to write down
   (i) the scale factor of the enlargement
   (ii) $|PQ|$
   (iii) the ratio $|OQ| : |OS|$.
   If the area of $\triangle OPQ = 4$ square units, find the area of $\triangle ORS$.

8. Make a copy of the given triangle PQR. Now draw an enlargement of the triangle with A as centre and scale factor 2.

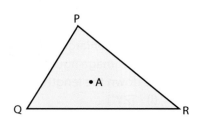

9. The triangles A′B′C′ and $A_2B_2C_2$ are enlargements of the triangle ABC.

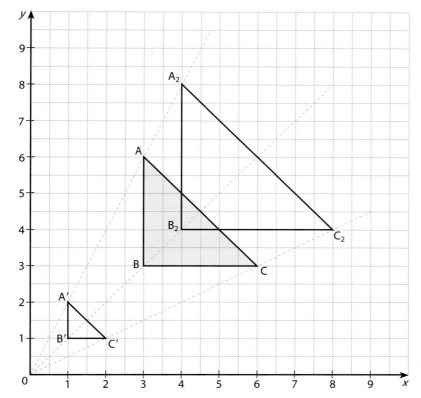

(i) Which triangle is the result of an enlargement with a scale factor less than 1?

(ii) Write down the scale factor for
    (a) △A′B′C′   (b) $\triangle A_2B_2C_2$.

(iii) If |BC| = 12 cm, find
    (a) |B′C′| (b) $|B_2C_2|$.

10. For each of these pairs of shapes, state whether the larger shape is an enlargement of the smaller shape.
Explain your answer in each case.

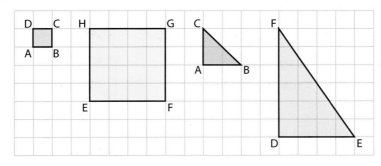

11. In the given diagram, one figure is an enlargement of the other.

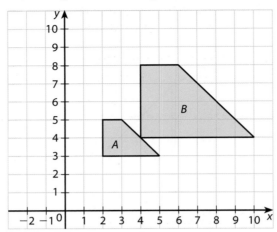

(i) Use the grid and a straight edge to write down the coordinates of the centre of enlargement.

(ii) If B is an enlargement of A, write down the scale factor.

(iii) If A is an enlargement of B, write down the scale factor.

(iv) If the area of A = 15 square units, find the area of B.

12. In the given figure, AB'C' is an enlargement of the triangle ABC, where A is the centre of enlargement. If $|AC| = 8$, $|CC'| = 12$ and $|B'C'| = 25$, find

(i) the scale factor of the enlargement

(ii) $|BC|$ (iii) the ratio $|AB| : |AB'|$

(iv) the area of the $\triangle AB'C'$ if the area of $\triangle ABC$ is 16 square units.

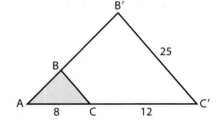

13. This diagram is reduced on a photocopier to $\frac{2}{3}$ of its original size.

(i) If the height of the original diagram is 156 mm, how high will the reduced diagram be?

(ii) If the label on the reduced diagram is 28 mm in height, find the height of the label on the original diagram.

14. In the given figure, box B is an enlargement of box A.

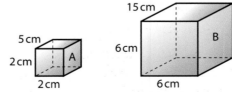

(i) Write down the value of k, the scale factor of the enlargement.

(ii) What is the relationship between k and the scale factor for volume?

15. The design on a hardcover book is to be used on the paperback version.
To do this, the design is reduced to $\frac{3}{5}$ of its original size.
How high will the design be on the paperback cover if it is 18 cm high on the hardcover?

16. Darren enlarged a diagram by scale factor 2 for a science project. He decided it still wasn't large enough, so he enlarged his enlargement by scale factor 1.5.

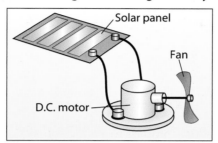

   (i) What single scale factor could he have used to get the final diagram from the original?

   (ii) If the dimensions of the double enlargement were 42 cm by 28 cm, what were the dimensions of the original diagram?

17. The scale on a map is 1 : 1000.
Anna enlarges the map by a scale factor 2.

   (i) What is the scale for the enlarged map?

   (ii) On the original map, Anna's street is 6 cm long.
What is the actual length of the street in real life?
Give your answer in metres.

Sean borrowed Anna's original map and he enlarged it by a scale factor $\frac{1}{2}$.

   (iii) What is the scale on Sean's enlarged map?

   (iv) If the distance between two railway stations is 1 km, how far are they apart on Sean's enlarged map?

Section 15.2 Constructions

In your study of constructions for your Junior Certificate you will have learned:

> How to bisect a line segment
> How to bisect an angle
> How to construct various triangles
> How to draw parallel and perpendicular lines

In this section we will deal with six new constructions that are on the Leaving Certificate course as well as the application of these constructions to real-life situations. For these constructions you will need a compass, straight edge and protractor.

> When you use a compass you must leave the construction arcs as evidence that you have used the correct method.

1. Constructing an angle of 60°

Each angle in an equilateral triangle is 60°.

We will now use this information to draw an angle of 60°.

> In an equilateral triangle, all the sides are equal in length.

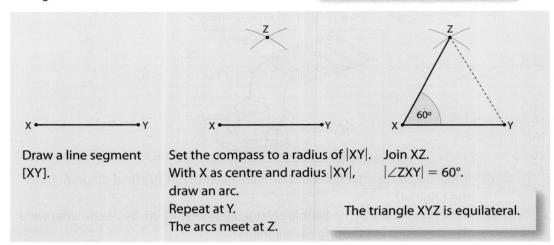

Draw a line segment [XY].

Set the compass to a radius of |XY|. With X as centre and radius |XY|, draw an arc. Repeat at Y. The arcs meet at Z.

Join XZ. |∠ZXY| = 60°.

> The triangle XYZ is equilateral.

2. How to construct a tangent to a circle at a given point on it

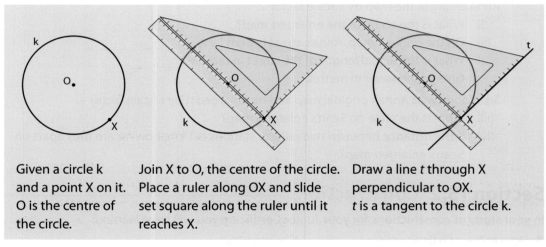

Given a circle k and a point X on it. O is the centre of the circle.

Join X to O, the centre of the circle. Place a ruler along OX and slide set square along the ruler until it reaches X.

Draw a line t through X perpendicular to OX. t is a tangent to the circle k.

3. How to construct a parallelogram, given the lengths of the sides and the measures of the angles

The instructions on the following page show how to construct a parallelogram ABCD where |AB| = 3.5 cm, |AD| = 4 cm and |∠DAB| = 55°.

We first draw a rough sketch of ABCD.

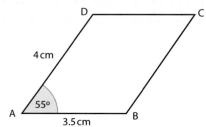

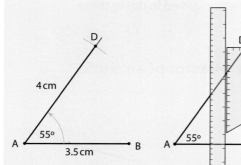

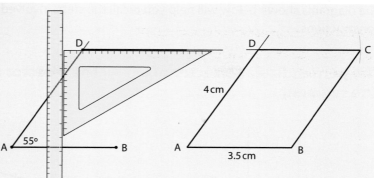

| Draw a horizontal line [AB] = 3.5 cm. Use a protractor to measure an angle of 55° at A. Draw a line through A and measure \|AD\| = 4 cm. | Place set square along the line AB. Use a ruler to slide the set square up to the point D. Draw a line through D parallel to AB. | Use a compass with a radius of 3.5 cm (the same as \|AB\|) to draw an arc on the line. \|DC\| = 3.5 cm. Join BC. ABCD is the required parallelogram. |

Circles and triangles

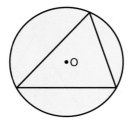

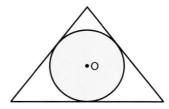

The **circumcircle** of a triangle is the circle which passes through the three vertices, as shown.
The centre, O, of this circle is called the **circumcentre** of the triangle.

A circle inscribed in a triangle such that all three sides touch the circle is called the **incircle** of the triangle. The centre of the incircle is called the **incentre** of the triangle. In the figure above, O is the incentre.

The construction of the circumcircle and incircle of a triangle will involve two constructions that you studied for your Junior Certificate examination.

The diagrams shown below will help you recall the steps involved in doing these constructions.

The perpendicular bisector of a line segment

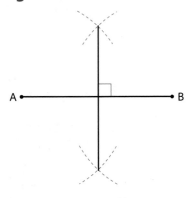

The bisector of an angle

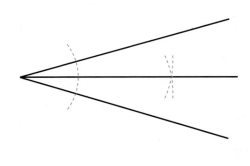

You should practise these constructions before attempting to draw the circumcircle and incircle of a triangle.

4. How to construct the circumcircle of a given triangle

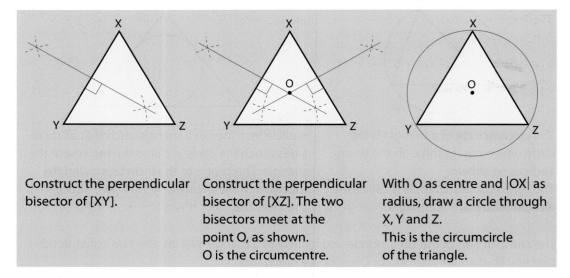

Construct the perpendicular bisector of [XY].

Construct the perpendicular bisector of [XZ]. The two bisectors meet at the point O, as shown. O is the circumcentre.

With O as centre and |OX| as radius, draw a circle through X, Y and Z. This is the circumcircle of the triangle.

5. How to construct the incircle of a given triangle

The construction of the incircle of a triangle involves constructing the bisector of an angle which is given on the previous page.

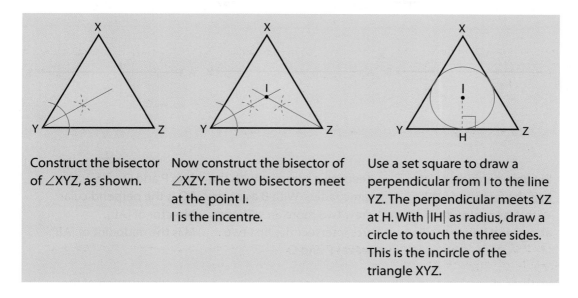

Construct the bisector of ∠XYZ, as shown.

Now construct the bisector of ∠XZY. The two bisectors meet at the point I.
I is the incentre.

Use a set square to draw a perpendicular from I to the line YZ. The perpendicular meets YZ at H. With |IH| as radius, draw a circle to touch the three sides. This is the incircle of the triangle XYZ.

6. How to construct the centroid of a triangle

The line segment joining the vertex of a triangle to the midpoint of the opposite side is called a **median**.

In the given triangle [XM] is a median.
|ZM| = |MY|, as shown.

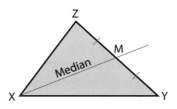

The point of intersection of the three medians of a triangle is called the **centroid** of the triangle.

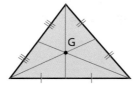

G is the centroid.

To find the midpoint of any line segment, we construct the perpendicular bisector of that line segment, as shown below.

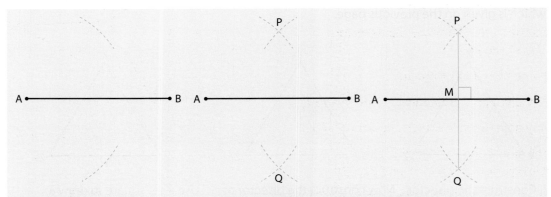

Set your compass to over half the length of [AB]. With A as centre draw an arc above and below the line.

Keep your compass with the same radius. With B as centre draw two more arcs. These arcs intersect the first two arcs at P and Q.

Join P and Q. PQ is the perpendicular bisector of [AB]. M is the midpoint of [AB].

The three diagrams below illustrate the steps to be followed in the construction of the centroid of a triangle.

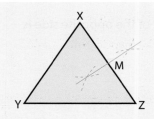 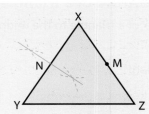 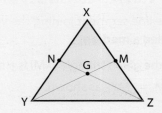

Construct the perpendicular bisector of [XZ], as shown. M is the midpoint of [XZ].

Now construct the perpendicular bisector of [XY]. N is the midpoint of [XY].

Join YM and ZN. They meet at the point G. G is the centroid of the triangle.

Applications of the given constructions

In the given diagram, the line ℓ is the perpendicular bisector of [AB].

Any point on this bisector is the same distance from A and B.

Thus |AX| = |XB|.

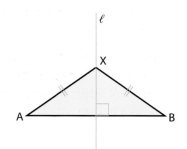

444

Take any three points X, Y and Z.
How do we find a point that is the same distance from all three points?

Construct the perpendicular bisectors of [XY] and [YZ].

Name these lines ℓ and m.

Any point on ℓ is equidistant from X and Y.

Any point on m is equidistant from Y and Z.

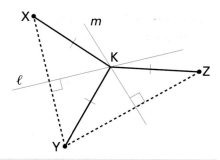

The lines ℓ and m intersect at K.
K is equidistant from X, Y and Z.

Equidistant means 'the same distance'.

The **largest circle** that can be drawn inside a triangle is the **incircle**, that is, the circle that touches all three sides.

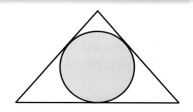

Exercise 15.2

1. Draw a line 5 cm in length.
   Using a compass and ruler only, construct the perpendicular bisector of the line.

2. Use your protractor to draw an angle of 70°.
   Now use your compass and ruler to construct the bisector of the angle.

3. Construct the triangle ABC with base |BC| = 6 cm, |AB| = 4.5 cm and |∠ABC| = 60°.

4. Using a compass and ruler only, construct an angle of 60°.

5. Construct the parallelogram shown on the right.

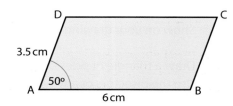

6. Construct a rectangle of length 6 cm and breadth 4 cm.

7. Construct the parallelogram PQRS so that |PQ| = 7 cm, |PS| = 5 cm and |∠QPS| = 55°.
   Measure |PR|.

8. The diagram on the right shows a rough sketch of the parallelogram ABCD.
   Construct this parallelogram if its perpendicular height is 4 cm.

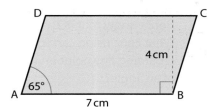

9. Draw the parallelogram ABCD in which the base |AB| = 4.5 cm, |BC| = 3 cm and |AC| = 6 cm. Measure ∠ABC.

10. Draw a triangle of sides 6 cm, 5 cm and 4 cm.
Now construct the circumcircle of this triangle.
Show all construction lines.

11. Draw the right-angled triangle, as shown on the right.
Now construct the circumcircle of this triangle.
What do you notice about the circumcentre of the triangle?
Now draw any other right-angled triangle and construct the circumcircle.
Did you get the same result as you got for the first triangle?
What conclusion is suggested regarding the circumcentre of a right-angled triangle?

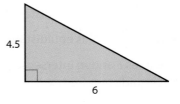
4.5
6

12. The diagram shows three villages, Drum, Moore and Tubber.
The distances between the villages are shown.

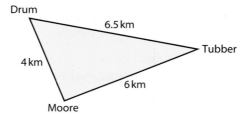
Drum
6.5 km
Tubber
4 km
6 km
Moore

Using the scale 1 cm = 1 km, draw an accurate drawing of the diagram above.
It is planned to build a school that is equidistant from the three villages.
Show on your drawing where the school should be built.

13. Draw a triangle of sides 6.5 cm, 5 cm and 4 cm.
Use the bisectors of any two angles of the triangle to find the centre of its incircle.
Now draw the incircle.

14. The line XD is the bisector of ∠AXB.
K is a point on XD, KZ ⊥ AX and KY ⊥ XB.
Show that the triangles XKZ and XKY
are congruent.
Hence show that |KZ| = |KY|.
What conclusion can you come to
regarding any point on the bisector
of an angle?

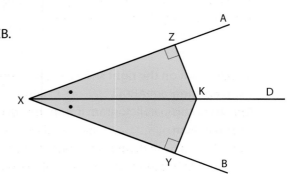
A
Z
K
D
X
Y
B

15. Construct the triangle shown.
Now construct the medians [AM] and [BN].
The medians intersect at the point G.
Measure |AG| and |GM|.
Now find the ratio $\dfrac{|AG|}{|GM|}$. Find also the ratio $\dfrac{|BG|}{|GN|}$.
Based on the answers you have found, complete this statement:
'The medians of a triangle divide one another in the ratio ... : ....'

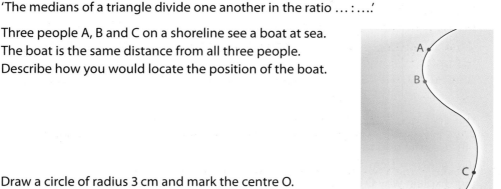

16. Three people A, B and C on a shoreline see a boat at sea.
The boat is the same distance from all three people.
Describe how you would locate the position of the boat.

17. Draw a circle of radius 3 cm and mark the centre O.
Mark a point X on this circle.
Now use a ruler and set square to draw a tangent to this circle at the point X.

18. The given figure shows a circle and two chords [AB] and [CD].
What can you say about the perpendicular bisector of [AB]?
Now describe how these two chords can be used to find
the centre of the circle.

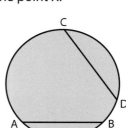

19. Draw a circle of radius 3.5 cm. [Do not mark the centre.]
Draw any two chords similar to those in Q18 above.
Use these two chords to locate the centre of the circle.

20. In Q19 we used two chords to find the centre of a circle.
The given diagram shows a circle and two points on
the circle.
Describe another way of finding the centre of
this circle using the points X and Y.

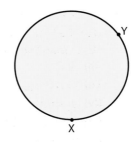

21. A campsite is in the shape of a triangle with busy roads
running along all three sides of the site.
The sides of the site are 110 m, 150 m and 170 m in length.
   (i) Using 10 m = 1 cm, draw a scaled diagram of this site.
   (ii) Show on the diagram the best position to pitch a tent
       so that it is as far away as possible from all three roads.

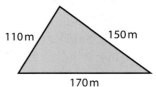

Test yourself 15

1. In the given diagram, K′L′M′N′ is an enlargement of KLMN.

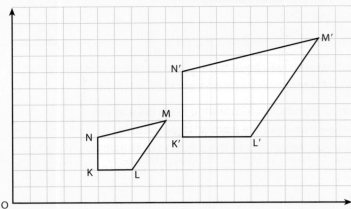

(i) Use the grid to find the scale factor of the enlargement.
(ii) If |KN| = 5 cm, find |K′N′|.
(iii) If |N′M′| = 21 cm, find |NM|.
(iv) Explain why O is the centre of enlargement.
(v) If |ON| = 16 cm, find |ON′|.

2. The diagram shows two figures P and Q where one is an enlargement of the other.

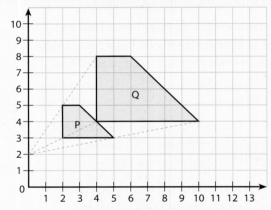

(i) Write down the coordinates of the centre of enlargement.
(ii) If Q is an enlargement of P, find the scale factor.
(iii) If P is an enlargement of Q, find the scale factor.
(iv) If the area of P is 24 cm², find the area of Q.

3. In the given figure, AB′C′D′ is an enlargement of ABCD.
(i) Name the centre of enlargement.
(ii) Find the scale factor of the enlargement.
(iii) Find |D′C′|.
(iv) If |AC| = 9.4 m, find |AC′|.
(v) If ABCD is an enlargement of AB′C′D′, what is the scale factor of the enlargement?

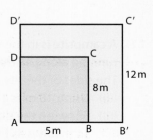

4. The triangle AB'C' is an enlargement of the triangle ABC with A as centre and scale factor 1.5.
   If |AC| = 8, |B'C'| = 9 and |BB'| = 3, find
   (i) |AC'|
   (ii) |BC|
   (iii) |AB|.
   If the area of △ABC = 20 square units, find the area of △AB'C'.

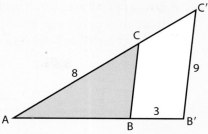

5. Construct a triangle of sides 5 cm, 4 cm and 3.5 cm. Now construct the circumcircle of this triangle.

6. Make an accurate construction of the parallelogram given on the right.
   Measure |AC|.

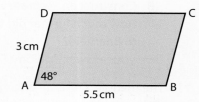

7. X, Y and Z are three schools.
   The distance from X to Y is 15 km; the distance from Y to Z is 12 km and the distance from X to Z is 18 km.
   Make a scale drawing of these distances, using 1 cm = 3 km.
   Now construct the location of a sportsfield that is equidistant from all three schools.

8. This diagram was made by enlarging a triangle by a scale factor of 2.5.
   (i) Which is the original triangle?
   (ii) If |BE| = 4.5 cm, find |CD|.
   (iii) If the triangle ABE is the image of the triangle ACD under an enlargement, what is the scale factor?
   (iv) If |∠AEB| = 28°, find the size of the angle ADC.
   (v) If the area of △ABE = 4.2 cm², find the area of △ACD.

9. Shape C has been enlarged to shape C'.

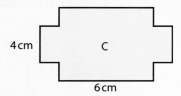
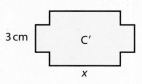

   (i) What scale factor was used?
   (ii) What is the length of the side marked x in shape C'?
   (iii) If the area of C' is 18 cm², find the area of C.

10. A group of walkers cannot walk straight from Ashfield to Briarfield, as they usually do. Instead they have to go through Caim to avoid a conservation area.
Caim is 7.2 km from Ashfield and 5.4 km from Briarfield.

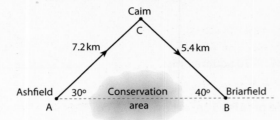

  (i) Construct an accurate scale drawing of the route using 1 cm = 1 km.
 (ii) How much further did the group walk, compared to the direct route from Ashfield to Briarfield?
Give your answer in kilometres, correct to one decimal place.

11. The triangle XYZ is an enlargement of the triangle DHG with O as centre.
$|DG| = 8$, $|XZ| = 12$ and $|XY| = 9$.

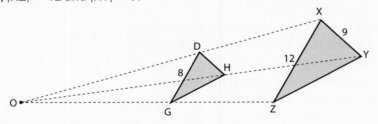

  (i) Find the scale factor of the enlargement.
 (ii) Find $|DH|$.
(iii) The area of the triangle XYZ is 27 square units. Find the area of the triangle DHG.

12. In each of the two pairs of diagrams shown, shape Q is an enlargement of shape P.

For each pair of diagrams, write down
  (i) the scale factor of the enlargement
 (ii) the value of x.

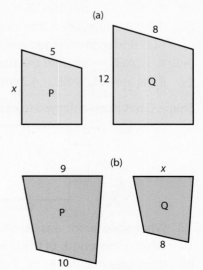

Summary of key points...

Enlargements

When a shape is enlarged

> the object and its image are similar; the size changes but not the shape

> the **scale factor** gives the number of times the length of any line segment has been increased

> if the scale factor k is greater than 1 ($k > 1$), the image is larger than the original

> if the scale factor k is less than 1 ($k < 1$), the image is smaller than the original

> if a figure is enlarged by a scale factor k, its area will be increased by a scale factor of k^2

> the centre of enlargement is found by drawing lines through two sets of corresponding points. The centre is the point of intersection of these lines.

> if the scale factor for an enlargement is k, the scale factor for the inverse enlargement is $\frac{1}{k}$.

Constructions

Circumcircle

The centre of the circumcircle is the point of intersection of the perpendicular bisectors of the sides

Incircle

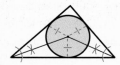

The centre of the incircle is the point of intersection of the bisectors of the angles.

Centroid

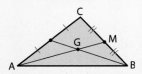

The line AM is called a **median**.
The point G, where the medians meet, is called the **centroid** of the triangle.

An angle of 60°

Tangent to a circle

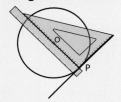

Parallelograms

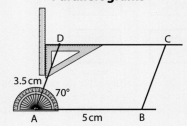

Key words

input	output	rule	function machine	mapping diagrams
domain	range	function	codomain	couples	ordered pairs
parabola	coefficient	composite function	quadratic function	

Section 16.1 **Functions**

Consider what happens to the number 7 in the two operations below:

$$7 \longrightarrow \boxed{\begin{array}{c}\text{multiply}\\\text{by 4}\end{array}} \longrightarrow \boxed{\begin{array}{c}\text{add}\\1\end{array}} \longrightarrow 29$$

The number 7 is first multiplied by 4 and then 1 is added to the result to get 29.
In this operation, 7 is called the **input** number and 29 is called the **output** number.
The **rule** for the operation is 'multiply by 4 and add 1'.
The operation shown in the diagram above is generally referred to as a **function machine** or **flow chart**.

If we call the input number x and the output number y, we can then write the 'rule' in terms of x and y.

$$x \longrightarrow \boxed{\begin{array}{c}\text{multiply}\\\text{by 3}\end{array}} \longrightarrow \boxed{\begin{array}{c}\text{add}\\2\end{array}} \longrightarrow y$$

The rule for this function machine is 'multiply by 3, then add 2'.
We can write this as $x \times 3 + 2 = y$ or $y = 3x + 2$.

Here are the rules for these function machines:

(i)
$$x \longrightarrow \boxed{\begin{array}{c}\text{multiply}\\\text{by 2}\end{array}} \longrightarrow \boxed{\begin{array}{c}\text{add}\\4\end{array}} \longrightarrow y \qquad \text{Rule: } y = 2x + 4$$

(ii)
$$x \longrightarrow \boxed{\begin{array}{c}\text{multiply}\\\text{by 8}\end{array}} \longrightarrow \boxed{\begin{array}{c}\text{subtract}\\7\end{array}} \longrightarrow y \qquad \text{Rule: } y = 8x - 7$$

The rule $y = 2x + 4$ may also be written as $x \to 2x + 4$.

Examples of inputs and corresponding outputs are common in everyday life.
An electronic calculator is an example of a function machine.

If you input 6 and press the x^2 key, the output is 36.

If the barcode on the cover of your book is scanned, the price of the book will appear on the screen of the scanner.

When a farmer applies fertilizer (input) to his crops, the yield (output) will be increased.

Domain, range and mapping diagrams

Consider the function machine: → [multiply by 5] → [subtract 4] →

We will input all the numbers from the set {1, 2, 3, 4, 5, 6}.
The output numbers are: {1, 6, 11, 16, 21, 26}.
The set of input numbers is called the **domain**.
The set of output numbers is called the **range**.

The input numbers and the output numbers can be represented by a special type of diagram called a **mapping diagram**.
Each input number is mapped onto its output number.

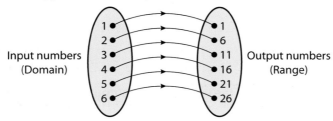

In the mapping diagram above, notice that there is one and only one output number for each input number.

> In mathematics, we use the word **function** for any rule that produces one output value only for each input value.

Identifying functions

When a function is represented by a mapping diagram, each element of the domain maps onto **one and only one** element of the range.

Consider these two mapping diagrams:

(i)
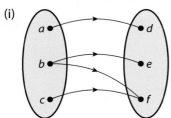

(ii)
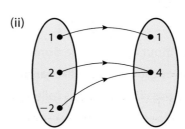

453

Diagram (i) is not a function since the element *b* is paired with 2 different elements in the range.

Diagram (ii) is a function since each element in the domain is mapped onto *one and only one* element in the range.

Couples

From the mapping diagram above, it can be seen that a function may be written as a set of **couples** or **ordered pairs**, i.e. (input, output).

When a function is written as a set of couples, no two distinct couples will have the same input.

> {(1, 4), (2, 5), (3, 6), (4, 7)} is a function as no two couples have the same input.
> {(2, 7), (3, 8), (3, 9), (4, 12)} is **not** a function as the input 3 has two different outputs.

Notation for a function

Consider this rule for a function: "Double the number and add 4."
If we input *x*, the output will be $2x + 4$.
The rule for this function may be written in any one of these three ways:

    (i) $f(x) = 2x + 4$
    (ii) $f: x \rightarrow 2x + 4$
    (iii) $y = 2x + 4$.

These three notations tell us that if the input is 3, the output $(2x + 4)$ is $[(2 \times 3) + 4]$, i.e. 10. This can be written as $f(3) = \mathbf{10}$.

The codomain

Take the two sets $A = \{1, 2, 3\}$ and $B = \{1, 3, 5, 7, 9, 11\}$.
If we are asked to list the couples of the function $f: x \rightarrow 2x - 1$, where the input numbers come from set A and the output numbers come from set B, we could set up a mapping diagram as follows:

The couples are (1, 1), (2, 3) and (3, 5).

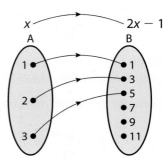

The set A is the **domain**, i.e. {1, 2, 3}.
The **range** is {1, 3, 5}.
The set B is called the **codomain**, that is, the set of allowable outputs.
∴ the codomain = {1, 3, 5, 7, 9, 11}.

> The set of inputs is called the **domain**.
>
> The set of outputs is called the **range**.
>
> The set of possible outputs is called the **codomain**.

Example 1

A function is defined as $f: x \rightarrow 3x - 2$.
The domain of f is $\{0, 1, 2, 3, 4\}$.
Represent f on a mapping diagram and write out the couples generated.
What is the range of f?

x	$3x - 2$	$f(x)$
0	$0 - 2$	-2
1	$3 - 2$	1
2	$6 - 2$	4
3	$9 - 2$	7
4	$12 - 2$	10

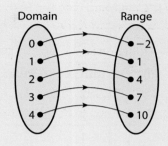

The couples are: $\{(0, -2), (1, 1), (2, 4), (3, 7), (4, 10)\}$.
The range is $\{-2, 1, 4, 7, 10)$.

Exercise 16.1

1. Find the outputs for these:

(i)
$3 \rightarrow$, $7 \rightarrow$, $8 \rightarrow$ [multiply by 2] $\rightarrow$ [subtract 4] $\rightarrow$ ... ...

(ii)
$2 \rightarrow$, $1 \rightarrow$, $0 \rightarrow$ [add 4] $\rightarrow$ [multiply by 2] $\rightarrow$ ... ...

2. Write the rules for these function machines as $y = \ldots$.

(i)
$x \rightarrow$ [multiply by 2] $\rightarrow$ [add 4] $\rightarrow y$

(ii)
$x \rightarrow$ [multiply by 8] $\rightarrow$ [subtract 7] $\rightarrow y$

(iii)
$x \rightarrow$ [divide by 4] $\rightarrow$ [subtract 3] $\rightarrow y$

(iv)
$x \rightarrow$ [add 3] $\rightarrow$ [multiply by 4] $\rightarrow y$

3. Write the rules for these function machines in the form $x \rightarrow \ldots$

(i)
$x \rightarrow$ [multiply by 3] $\rightarrow$ [add 2] $\rightarrow y$

(ii)
$x \rightarrow$ [multiply by 5] $\rightarrow$ [subtract 2] $\rightarrow y$

(iii)
$x \rightarrow$ [divide by 3] $\rightarrow$ [add 2] $\rightarrow y$

(iv)
$x \rightarrow$ [add 2] $\rightarrow$ [multiply by 7] $\rightarrow y$

4. Copy and complete the following tables:

(i)

Input: x	Rule: $x^2 + 4$	Output: y	Couples
-2	$(-2)^2 + 4$	8	$(-2, 8)$
-1			
0			
1			
2			

(ii)

Input: x	Rule: $3 - 2x$	Output: y	Couples
-3			
-2			
-1			
0			
1			
2			

5. Find the missing operations in these function machines:

(i)

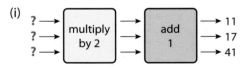

(ii)

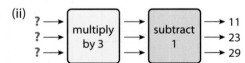

6. What numbers went into each of these function machines?

(i)

```
? →  multiply  →  add  → 11
? →  by 2      →  1    → 17
? →           →       → 41
```

(ii)

```
? →  multiply  →  subtract  → 11
? →  by 3      →  1         → 23
? →           →            → 29
```

7. Use the given mapping diagram to write down
   (i)   the domain
   (ii) the range
   (iii) the set of couples formed
   (iv) the rule that gives the outputs.

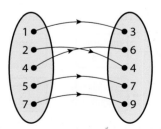

8. State whether each of the following mapping diagrams is a function.
Give a reason for your answer in each case.

(i)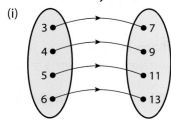

(ii)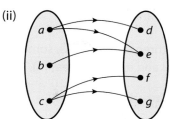

(iii)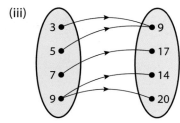

(iv)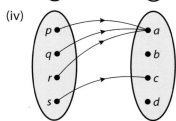

9. Say why the following set of couples is a function:

{(1, 4), (2, 5), (3, 6), (4, 7)}.

10. Say why the following set of couples is not a function:

{(2, 5), (3, 6), (5, 8), (2, 10)}.

11. Investigate if each of these sets of couples represents a function.
If it is not a function, state the reason why.

(i) {(0, 0), (1, 1), (2, 4), (3, 9), (4, 16)}
(ii) {(−2, 1), (−1, 3), (−2, 5), (1, 6), (2, 9)}
(iii) {(−3, 4), (0, 11), (2, 9), (4, 11)}.

12. For each of the mapping diagrams below, write down

(i) the domain   (ii) the range   (iii) the codomain.

(a)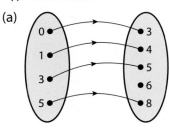

(b)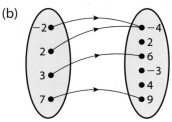

13.

$x \longrightarrow$ [multiply by 2] $\longrightarrow$ [add 4] $\longrightarrow y$ describes a function.

Copy the table on the right and fill in the
missing input and output numbers.

Input	Output
3	
−2	
	8
	−8

14. $f: x \rightarrow 6x - 2$ defines a function.

If the couples $(2, a)$, $(-4, b)$, $(c, 16)$ and $(d, -14)$ are couples of f, work out the values of a, b, c and d.

15. In the three tables below, some input and output numbers are given.

By 'trial and error' or guessing, find the rule for each function in the form $y = \dots$.

(i)

Input	Output
3	2
7	10
5	6
11	18

(ii)

Input	Output
1	5
3	11
5	17
10	32

(iii)

Input	Output
1	4
3	10
6	19
8	25

Section 16.2 Operations involving functions

1. Notation

We have already seen that a function may be written in any of these ways:

(i) $f(x) = 3x - 2$ (ii) $f: x \rightarrow 3x - 2$ (iii) $y = 3x - 2$

In each case, the output is $(3x - 2)$ when the input is x.

The notation $f(3)$ is used to represent the output number when the input number is 3.
Thus, $f(3) = 3(3) - 2 = 7$.

While $f(x)$ is generally used to describe a function, other letters such as $g(x)$ and $h(x)$ are used when we are dealing with more than one function.

Example 1

The functions f and g are defined on R such that

$$f: x \rightarrow x + 5 \quad \text{and} \quad g: x \rightarrow x^2 - 1.$$

Find   (i) $f(3)$ (ii) $g(-3)$ (iii) $f(2k)$ (iv) $f(k + 1)$ (v) $g(3k)$ (vi) $g(k + 1)$

(i) $f(x) = x + 5$ (ii) $g(x) = x^2 - 1$ (iii) $f(x) = x + 5$
     $f(3) = 3 + 5$ $g(-3) = (-3)^2 - 1$ $f(2k) = 2k + 5$
        $= 8$ $= 9 - 1$
                                  $= 8$

(iv) $f(x) = x + 5$ (v) $g(x) = x^2 - 1$ (vi) $g(x) = x^2 - 1$
    $f(k + 1) = (k + 1) + 5$ $g(3k) = (3k)^2 - 1$ $g(k + 1) = (k + 1)^2 - 1$
            $= k + 6$ $= 9k^2 - 1$ $= k^2 + 2k + 1 - 1$
                                           $= k^2 + 2k$

---

2. Composite functions

The diagram below shows a function *f* illustrated by the mapping diagram from A to B, and the function *g* illustrated by the mapping diagram from B to C.

The red arrows represent the couples of a new function combining *f* and *g*.

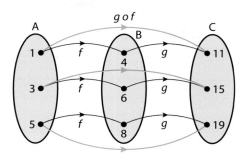

It is called the **composite function** *g* after *f*.
It is written as **gof**, or simply **gf**.

The couples of *gf* from the diagram are {(1, 11), (3, 15), (5, 19)}.

We will now consider two functions:
$f(x) = 2x + 5$ and $g(x) = x - 3$ to find the rule for the composite function $gf(x)$.

> *gof* is read '*g* after *f*'

These functions are illustrated on the right.

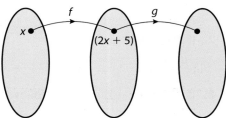

In *f*, the output is $(2x + 5)$ when the input is *x*.

We will now use $(2x + 5)$ as the input for the function *g*.

Since $g(x) = x - 3$, then $gf(x) = g(2x + 5)$
$$= (2x + 5) - 3 \dots \text{replacing } x \text{ with } (2x + 5).$$
$$gf(x) = 2x + 2$$

We will now consider what happens when the order is changed.

$$fg(x) = f(x - 3)$$
$$= 2(x - 3) + 5 \dots \text{replacing } x \text{ with } (x - 3).$$
$$fg(x) = 2x - 1$$

> If *f* and *g* are two functions, then $fg(x) \neq gf(x)$.

Since $2x + 2 \neq 2x - 1$, this shows that $gf(x) \neq fg(x)$.

Example 1

Given that $f(x) = x + 3$ and $g(x) = x^2 - 1$, find

(i) $fg(2)$ (ii) $gf(-1)$ (iii) $fg(x)$ (iv) $gf(x)$.

Find also the value of *x* for which $fg(x) = gf(x)$.

459

(i) $fg(2) = f(3) = 6 \dots$ $g(2) = 2^2 - 1 = 3$

(ii) $gf(-1) = g(2) = 3$

(iii) $fg(x) = f(x^2 - 1) = (x^2 - 1) + 3 = x^2 + 2$

(iv) $gf(x) = g(x + 3) = (x + 3)^2 - 1 = x^2 + 6x + 9 - 1$
$$= x^2 + 6x + 8$$

$$fg(x) = gf(x) \Rightarrow x^2 + 2 = x^2 + 6x + 8$$
$$0 = 6x + 6$$
$$\text{i.e.} \quad 6x + 6 = 0$$
$$6x = -6 \Rightarrow x = -1$$

Exercise 16.2

1. If $f(x) = 2x - 3$, find
   (i) $f(1)$ (ii) $f(0)$ (iii) $f(2)$ (iv) $f(-1)$ (v) $f(-3)$

2. If $f(x) = x^2 - 3$, find
   (i) $f(0)$ (ii) $f(1)$ (iii) $f(2)$ (iv) $f(-2)$ (v) $f(-4)$

3. If $f(x) = 5x - 2$, solve the following equations:
   (i) $f(x) = 8$ (ii) $f(x) = 3$ (iii) $f(k) = -12$

4. If $f(x) = 3x - 2$ and $g(x) = 2 - 4x$, solve these equations:
   (i) $f(x) = 4$ (ii) $g(x) = -10$ (iii) $g(x) = f(4)$

5. Given $f(x) = 5x - 1$, find
   (i) $f(-3)$ (ii) $f(\frac{1}{5})$ (iii) $f(k)$ (iv) $f(2k)$ (v) $f(2k - 1)$

6. The function f is defined as $f: x \rightarrow 2 - 3x$.
   Find the value of the number k if $kf(3) = 7f(2)$.

7. The function f is defined by $f: R \rightarrow R: x \rightarrow 3x - 4$.
   For what value of k is $f(k) + f(2k) = 0$?

8. $f: x \rightarrow 4x$ and $g: x \rightarrow x + 1$ define two functions.
   If $g(3) + k[f(3)] = 8$, find the value of k.

9. $f(x) = 2x^2 - 1$ and $g(x) = x + 2$ define two functions.
   Solve these equations:
   (i) $f(x) = 3$ (ii) $g(x) = f(3)$ (iii) $f(x) = g(x)$

10. A function $f(x)$ is defined by $f(x) = 1 + \dfrac{2}{x}$.

    (i) Evaluate $f(-4)$ and $f\left(\tfrac{1}{5}\right)$.

    (ii) Find the value of x for which $f(x) = 2$.

    (iii) Find the value of k if $kf(2) = f\left(\tfrac{1}{2}\right)$.

11. $g(x) = 1 - 4x$ defines a function.

    (i) Find $g(k + 1)$.

    (ii) Solve the equation $g(k + 1) = g(-3)$.

12. $f(x) = 2x - 3$ and $g(x) = x + 5$ are two functions.

    Find (i) $f(2)$ (ii) $g(-2)$ (iii) $fg(2)$ (iv) $gf(-2)$.

    Now find an expression for $fg(x)$.

13. The arrow diagram on the right shows two functions

$$f(x) = 2x + 1 \text{ and } g(x) = 3x - 2.$$

Copy and complete this double arrow diagram.

Now write down the three couples of the function $gf(x)$.

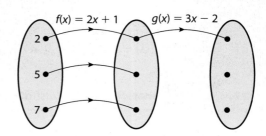

14. $f: x \rightarrow 2x + 1$ and $g: x \rightarrow 4x - 3$ are two functions.

    Find (i) $f(3)$ (ii) $gf(3)$ (iii) $fg(-2)$ (iv) $gf(x)$.

    For what value of x is $fg(x) = 19$?

15. $f: x \rightarrow 2x + 1$ and $g: x \rightarrow x^2$ are two functions.

    What is (i) $f(4)$ (ii) $g(-3)$ (iii) $fg(2)$ (iv) $gf(4)$?

16. f and g are two functions such that

    $f(x) = 2x - 1$ and $g(x) = 3x + 2$.

    Find (i) $fg(1)$ (ii) $gf(-3)$ (iii) $gf(x)$ (iv) $fg(x)$.

17. The functions f and g are defined as follows:

$$f: x \rightarrow 2x - 1 \quad \text{and} \quad g: x \rightarrow x^2 + 2.$$

    Find (i) $fg(-2)$ (ii) $gf\left(\tfrac{1}{2}\right)$ (iii) $fg(x)$ (iv) $gf(x)$.

    For what values of x is $gf(x) = fg(x)$?

18. The function $f(x) = gh(x)$, where $g(x) = 2x$ and $h(x) = x + 3$.
Using the domain $\{1, 2, 3, 4\}$, find

    (i)   the range of the function h

    (ii) an expression for $f(x)$

    (iii) the range of the function f.

19. The functions f and g are defined as follows:

$$f(x) = 1 - 3x \quad \text{and} \quad g(x) = x^2 - 1.$$

    (i) Find $fg(3)$.

    (ii) If $fg(x) = -8$, find the value(s) of x.

20. Given that $f(x) = \sqrt{x^2 + 8}$, evaluate $f(2)$ and $f(8)$.
Given that $f(2) \times f(8) = k\sqrt{6}$, find k, where $k \in \mathbb{N}$.

21. Given that $f(x) = \dfrac{k}{x^2} + 1, x \neq 0$ and $f(3) = 5$, find the value of k.

22.   (i) Given that $f(x) = 3x + 2$, show that $f(x) + f(y) = f(x + y) + 2$.

    (ii) $f(x) = 2x^2$ and $g(x) = 3x - 1$ are two functions.

        (a) Find $fg(x)$ and $gf(x)$.

        (b) For what value(s) of x is $fg(x) = gf(x)$?

Section 16.3 Finding unknown coefficients

You will already have learned how to draw the graphs of functions
such as $f(x) = 2x + 4$ or $f(x) = x^2 + 2x - 4$.

The function $f(x) = 2x + 4$ represents a **straight line**.

The function $f(x) = x^2 + 2x - 4$ represents a shape like that
shown on the right.
This smooth curve is called a **parabola**.

Consider the function $f(x) = ax + b$.
If we are told that $(2, 4)$ is on this line, this is another
way of saying that $f(2) = 4$.
Similarly, if $(3, 0)$ is on the line, then $f(3) = 0$.

The following example illustrates how to find unknown coefficients of a function when given
some couples of the function.

Example 1

The given diagram shows part of the graph of the function

$$y = ax + b.$$

Find the values of a and b.

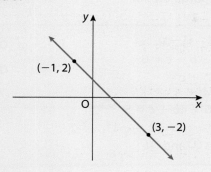

$(3, -2) \in y = ax + b$
$\Rightarrow \quad -2 = 3a + b$ i.e. $3a + b = -2$ ...①
$(-1, 2) \in y = ax + b$ i.e. $-a + b = 2$ ...②
$\Rightarrow \quad 2 = -a + b$ subtracting: $\underline{4a \qquad = -4}$
                                       $\Rightarrow a = -1$

From ①: $3(-1) + b = -2$
$\Rightarrow \quad -3 + b = -2 \Rightarrow b = 1$
$\therefore \quad a = -1 \quad$ and $\quad b = 1$

Quadratic functions

A function such as $f(x) = x^2 - 3x + 2$, which contains a term in x^2, is called a **quadratic function**.

The diagram on the right shows a curve crossing the x-axis at the points where $x = -1$ and $x = 4$.

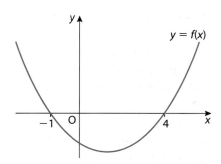

These numbers are the roots of the equation.

$$(x + 1)(x - 4) = 0$$
i.e. $x^2 - 3x - 4 = 0.$

Thus, the equation of the curve is

$$f(x) = x^2 - 3x - 4.$$

Example 2

The graph of the quadratic function
$f(x) = x^2 + bx + c$ is shown.
Find the values of b and c.
Hence write down the coordinates of
P and Q.

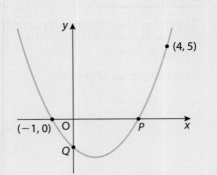

$(-1, 0) \in$ the curve $\rightarrow f(-1) = 0$.
$f(-1) = 1 - b + c \Rightarrow 1 - b + c = 0$
$\qquad\qquad \Rightarrow -b + c = -1 \dots \text{①}$
$(4, 5) \in$ the curve $\Rightarrow f(4) = 5$.
$f(4) = 16 + 4b + c \Rightarrow 16 + 4b + c = 5$
$\qquad\qquad \Rightarrow \qquad 4b + c = -11 \dots \text{②}$
We now solve equations ① and ②.
①: $-b + c = -1$
②: $4b + c = -11$
$\quad -5b \quad = 10 \quad \Rightarrow b = -2$
From ①: $2 + c = -1 \Rightarrow c = -3$
$\therefore b = -2$ and $c = -3$ i.e. $f(x) = x^2 - 2x - 3$.

To find the coordinates of P, we solve the equation $f(x) = 0$.
$f(x) = 0 \Rightarrow x^2 - 2x - 3 = 0$
$\qquad\quad \Rightarrow (x - 3)(x + 1) = 0$
$\qquad\quad \Rightarrow x = 3 \quad \text{or} \quad x = -1$
$\therefore$ the coordinates of P are $(3, 0)$.

To find the coordinates of the point where a curve crosses the y-axis, we let $x = 0$.
$x = 0 \Rightarrow f(x) = 0 - 0 - 3$ i.e. $f(x) = -3 \Rightarrow y = -3$
$\therefore$ the coordinates of Q are $(0, -3)$.

Exercise 16.3

1. $f(x) = ax - 6$ defines a function.
   If $f(2) = -2$, find the value of a.

2. If $(1, 5)$ is a couple of the function $f(x) = kx + 4$, find the value of k.

3. $g(x) = 3x + k$ defines a function.
   If $g(4) = 10$, find the value of k.

4. If $(-3, 2)$ is a point on the line $y = kx + 11$, find the value of k.

5. $f(x) = ax^2 + 3$ is a function.
   If $(-1, -1)$ is a couple of this function, find the value of a.

6. $g(x)$ is a function such that $g(x) = x^2 - 2x + p$, where $p \in R$.
   If $(1, 2)$ is a couple of this function, find the value of p.

7. The graph of the linear function $f(x) = ax + b$
   is shown.

   Find the values of a and b.

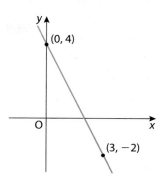

8. A function f is defined as $f: x \rightarrow 2x - 1$.
   If the mapping diagram on the right represents f,
   find the values of a, b and c.

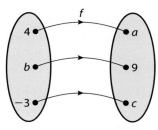

9. $g: x \rightarrow ax^2 + bx + 1$ is a function defined on R.
   If $g(1) = 0$ and $g(2) = 3$, write down two equations in a and b.
   Solve these equations to find the values of a and b.

10. A function is defined by $f: x \rightarrow ax^2 + bx + 1$.
    If $f(1) = 0$ and $f(-1) = 0$, find the value of a and the value of b.

11. $f: x \rightarrow x^2 + px + q$ defines a function.
    Given that $f(3) = 4$ and $f(-1) = 4$, find the values of p and q.
    Using these values for p and q, solve the equation $x^2 + px + q = 0$.

12. The diagram shows part of the graph of
    the function

    $\qquad f: x \rightarrow x^2 + bx + c.$

    The named couples are elements of the function.

    (i) Find the values of b and c.
    (ii) If $(2, y)$ is a point on the graph, find the
         value of y.

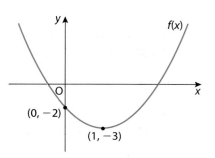

13. Functions f and g are defined as follows:
    $f: x \rightarrow x^2 + 1$ and $g: x \rightarrow ax + b$, where a and b are constants.
    If $f(0) = g(0)$ and $g(2) = 15$, find the values of a and b.

14. The function $f(x) = x^2 + bx + c$ is graphed on
the right.

   (i) Use the graph to find two equations in
b and c.

   (ii) Solve the equations to find the value of
b and the value of c.

   (iii) Using these values for b and c, solve the
equation $x^2 + bx + c = 0$ to find the
coordinates of the point D.

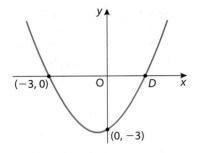

15. The graph of the function $f(x) = x^2 + kx + p$ is shown
on the right.

Use the information given to find the values of
k and p.

Hence find the coordinates of the point A.

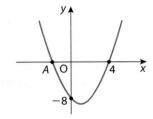

Test yourself 16

1. (a) A function is defined by $f: x \rightarrow 4x - 5$.

(i) Find $f(3)$.

(ii) Find the value of k for which $kf(3) = f(10)$.

(b) The function $h: x \rightarrow 10x - 1$ is shown on the given arrow diagram.
Find the numbers represented by a, b, c and d.

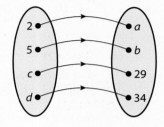

(c) $f: x \rightarrow 3x - 1$ and $g: x \rightarrow 5x + 2$ define two functions.
Find (i) $fg(2)$ (ii) $gf(-2)$ (iii) $gf(x)$ (iv) $fg(x)$.

Use your results to (iii) and (iv) to solve the equation $2[gf(x)] = fg(x)$.

2. (a) (i) What operation does the question mark stand for in the given function machine?

(ii) $f(x) = 3x - 4$ defines a function.
If the domain of $f(x)$ is $\{-3, -2, -1, 0\}$, what is the range of $f(x)$?

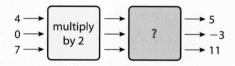

(b) The function f is defined on R such that $f: x \rightarrow 3x - 1$.
Find (i) $f(2)$ (ii) $f\left(\frac{1}{2}\right)$.
Find the value of k such that $f(2) = kf\left(\frac{1}{2}\right)$.
For what values of h is $f(h) = kf\left(\frac{1}{h}\right)$?

(c) A straight line has equation $y = mx + c$, where m and c are constants.

(i) The point $(2, 7)$ lies on this line.
Write down an equation in m and c to illustrate this information.

(ii) A second point $(4, 17)$ also lies on this line.
Write down another equation in m and c to illustrate this information.

(iii) Hence calculate the values of m and c.

(iv) Write down the slope of the line.

3. (a) $f(x) = 7x - 6$ defines a function.

(i) Find $f\left(\frac{1}{7}\right)$.

(ii) Find the value of x for which $f(x) = 71$.

(b) $f: x \rightarrow x^2$ and $g: x \rightarrow 2x + 3$ define two functions.
Find (i) $fg(2)$ (ii) $gf(-3)$.
Find $gf(x)$ and $fg(x)$ and hence solve the equation $gf(x) + 6 = fg(x)$.

(c) The graph shown is defined by the function
$$f(x) = -x^2 + kx + \ell.$$

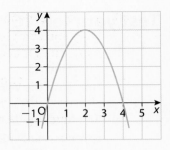

(i) What is $f(0)$?
Hence write down the value of ℓ.

(ii) Use another point on the curve to find the value of k.

4. (a) $h: x \rightarrow 2x + a$ and $k: x \rightarrow b - 5x$ are two functions where a and b are real numbers.
If $h(1) = -5$ and $k(-1) = 4$, find the value of a and the value of b.

(b) $f(x) = 2x^2$ and $g(x) = 3x - 1$ are two functions.
Find   (i) $f(3)$ (ii) $g(1)$ (iii) $g\left(\frac{1}{3}\right)$.
If $f(3) = kg(1)$, find k.

(c) The curve on the right is the graph of the function
$$f(x) = 10 - 3x - x^2.$$

Find the coordinates of the points marked A, B and C.

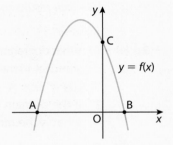

5. (a) State whether each of these mapping diagrams represents a function, giving a reason for your answers:

(i)

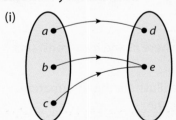

(ii)

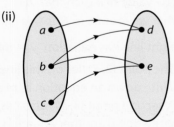

(b) $f(x) = 2x^2$ and $g(x) = 3x - 1$ are two functions.
Evaluate   (i) $fg\left(\frac{1}{3}\right)$ (ii) $gf(-2)$.
For what values of x is $f(x) = g(x)$?

(c) The curve on the right is the graph of the function
$$f(x) = 8 - 2x - x^2.$$

Find the coordinates of the points marked A, B and C.

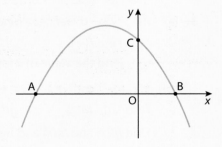

6. (a) $y = 3x - 2$ defines a function.
Copy and complete the given table
for this function and hence draw its graph.

x	−1	0	1	2
y				

(b) $f: x \rightarrow x^2 + 1$ and $g: x \rightarrow 2x$ define two functions.

    (i) Verify that $g(h + k) = g(h) + g(k)$.

    (ii) Investigate if $f(h + k) = f(h) + f(k)$.

    (iii) For what value of x is $f(x) = g(x)$?

    (iv) There was only one value of x in part (iii) above.
Explain what this single value for x means in the context of the graphs of the
two functions.

(c) The function $f(x) = x^2 + bx + c$ is graphed
on the right. The curve crosses the x-axis at
$(-1, 0)$ and it contains the point $(3, -4)$.

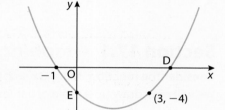

    (i) Write down two equations in b and c.

    (ii) Solve these equations to find the
values of b and c.

    (iii) Use these values for b and c to write
down the function $f(x)$.

    (iv) Use this function to find the coordinates of D and E.

Summary of key points...

Graphing Functions

Key words

> linear function   intercept method   proportional graphs
> quadratic function   parabola   second difference   maximum value
> minimum value   increasing   decreasing   exponential function

Section 17.1 Graphing linear functions

Consider the function $f(x) = 3x + 2$, where $0 \leqslant x \leqslant 4$.
We will now draw up a table of values for x and find the corresponding values for $f(x)$ or y.

Inputs	Rule	Outputs	Couples (input, output)
x	$3x + 2$	y	
0	$3(0) + 2$	2	(0, 2)
1	$3(1) + 2$	5	(1, 5)
2	$3(2) + 2$	8	(2, 8)
3	$3(3) + 2$	11	(3, 11)
4	$3(4) + 2$	14	(4, 14)

Note: The set of outputs 2, 5, 8, 11, 14   has a linear pattern

                  +3 +3 +3 +3   ... first difference is a constant

The graph of $f(x) = 3x + 2$ is plotted on the right.

From the line we can see that the slope is $\frac{6}{2} = 3$.

This is the same as the constant difference between the outputs.

From this we can see that the constant difference represents the slope.

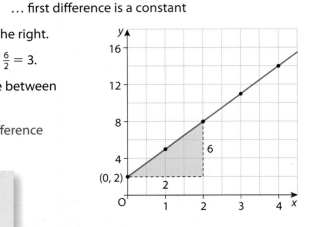

> For the line $y = 3x + 2$, 3 is the slope
> of the line and the line intersects the
> y-axis at (0, 2).

The line also shows that the function is **increasing**, as the y-value is constantly increasing by 3 for each unit increase in the x-values.

Example 1

Graph the function $f(x) = 2x - 4$ in the domain $-1 \leqslant x \leqslant 4$.
Use your graph to find

(i) $f(3)$ (ii) the value of x for which $f(x) = -2$ (iii) the slope of the line.

To find three points, we select the smallest and largest x-values in the given domain and one value for x in between those two.

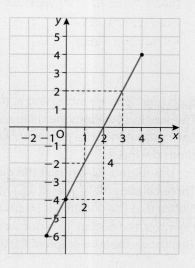

x	2x − 4	y
−1	−2 − 4	−6
0	0 − 4	−4
4	8 − 4	4

The three points are $(-1, -6)$, $(0, -4)$
and $(4, 4)$.
Join these points to give a line.

(i) $f(3)$ represents the y-value when $x = 3$.
From the graph, this is 2, i.e. $f(3) = 2$.

(ii) $f(x) = -2 \Rightarrow y = -2$.
The value of x in the graph when $y = -2$ is $x = 1$.

(iii) From the yellow triangle, the slope is $\frac{4}{2} = 2$.

The intercept method for drawing a line

If the equation of a line is in a form such as $3x - 4y = 12$, it is more convenient to find the two points where the line intersects the x-axis and the y-axis.

$$3x - 4y = 12$$

$$x = 0 \Rightarrow 0 - 4y = 12 \Rightarrow y = -3$$

∴ $(0, -3)$ is one point on the line.

$$y = 0 \Rightarrow 3x = 12 \Rightarrow x = 4$$

∴ $(4, 0)$ is a second point on the line.

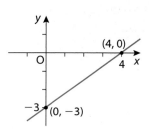

These points are joined to give the required line.

This method is generally called the **intercept method**.

Proportional and non-proportional graphs

Graphed below are two functions $f(x) = 4x + 2$ and $g(x) = 4x$.
Three points on each line are shown.

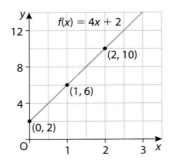 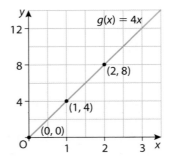

> Both functions are increasing at the same rate (both slopes = 4).
> The starting positions are different.
> Each output in $g(x)$ is proportional to the input, i.e., (1, 4), (2, 8) ... each output is four times the input.
  For this reason, we say that the graph of $y = g(x)$ is a **directly proportional graph**.
> Three couples of $f(x)$ are (0, 2), (1, 6) and (2, 10).
  Notice that the output 6 is six times the input 1.
  However, the output 10 is not six times the input 2.
  This shows that the graph of $f(x)$ is **not** directly proportional.

Proportional graphs

A directly proportional graph will

(i) contain the origin (0, 0)
(ii) be linear.

Here are three graphs A, B and C.

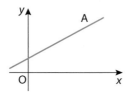 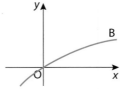 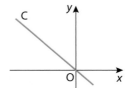

A is not directly
proportional
as it does not go
through (0, 0).

B is not proportional
as it is cuved, i.e.,
not linear.

C is directly
proportional as
it is linear and
contains (0, 0).

Exercise 17.1

1. Copy and complete the table on the right and use the table to draw a graph of the line $y = 2x - 3$ in the domain $-1 \leqslant x \leqslant 4$.

x	2x − 3	y
−1		
0		
1		
2		
3		
4		

2. Draw the graph of $f(x) = 2x - 5$ in the domain $0 \leqslant x \leqslant 5$.

3. Copy and complete the table on the right and hence draw a graph of the function $f(x) = 3x - 4$ in the domain $-1 \leqslant x \leqslant 3$.

x	3x − 4	y
−1		
0		
3		

4. Draw the graph of the function $f(x) = 6 - x$ in the domain $0 \leqslant x \leqslant 6$ by finding only three points on the line.

5. Draw the graph of the function $f(x) = 2x - 2$ in the domain $-2 \leqslant x \leqslant 3$.

6. Drawn on the right is the graph of a function $y = f(x)$.

   Use the graph to write down
   (i) $f(3)$ (ii) $f(0)$ (iii) $f(-4)$
   (iv) the value of x when $f(x) = -2$
   (v) The value of x when $f(x) = 6$.

   Use the grid to write down the slope of the line.
   Is the function $y = f(x)$ increasing or decreasing?
   Explain your answer.

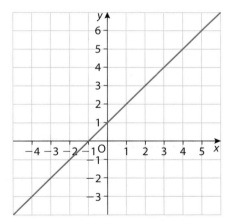

7. Use the grid in the given diagram to write down the slope of the line.
   Now express the equation of the line in the form $y = mx + c$.

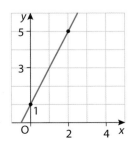

8. The given diagram shows the graphs of two
lines, $f(x) = x + 1$ and $g(x) = 2x - 2$.

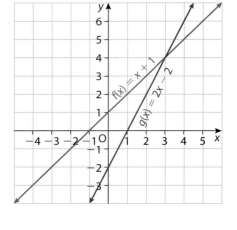

   (i) Write down the point of intersection
   of the two lines.
   (ii) What is the meaning of the equation
   $f(x) = g(x)$ in this situation?
   (iii) Solve the equation $x + 1 = 2x - 2$.
   Is there any connection between the
   value you found for x and the point of
   intersection of the two lines?
   (iv) Is there another way of finding the point
   of intersection of two lines besides drawing
   their graphs?
   (v) If $f(k)$ has the same value as $g(k)$, write down the value of k.

9. On the same diagram, draw the lines $y = 5 - x$ and $y = 2x - 4$, in the domain $0 \leqslant x \leqslant 4$.
   Use your graph to write down the point of intersection of the two lines.

10. By finding the couples $(*, 0)$ and $(0, *)$, draw a graph of the line $y = 4 - 2x$.

11. Use the intercept method to draw the graph of the line $3x + 2y = 6$.

12. A car uses petrol at the rate of 1 litre per 10 km.
    Copy and complete the table below to show the petrol consumption of the car over a
    journey of 50 km.

Distance	0	10	20	30	40	50
Petrol consumption	0					

   (i) Draw the graph to show this information.
   (ii) Is the graph directly proportional? Explain your answer.
   (iii) By taking two (input, output) values, find the equation of the line.
   (iv) Use the equation you have found to find the petrol consumption for a journey of 75 km.

13. The lines $y = x + 2$, $y = -x + 2$ and
    $y = 2x + 2$ have been graphed on the
    same axes on the right.

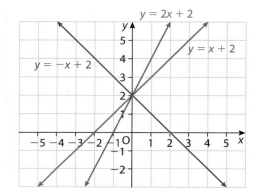

   (i) How are the lines similar?
   (ii) How are the linear equations similar?
   (iii) How are the lines different?
   (iv) How are the linear equations different?
   (v) Which function is decreasing?
   (vi) Which function is increasing at the
   faster rate?

14. $f(x) = 4x - 3$ defines a function.

Make out a table of inputs and outputs for $f(x)$ from $x = -2$ to $x = 4$.

Are the first differences between the outputs constant?

Explain why the function is linear.

15. Penguins survive in freezing climates.

The temperature $T°C$ at a penguin colony, t hours after midnight, is given by the rule $T = -0.5t - 1$.

t	0	1	2	3	4	5	6
T	0						

  (i)   Complete the table, which gives the temperature up to 6 a.m..
 (ii)   Plot the points whose coordinates are given by the values in the table on a set of axes of your own.
(iii)   Join the plotted points with a straight line. Do not extend the line.
 (iv)   From your graph, read off the temperature at 5.30 a.m..
  (v)   Use the rule that relates T to t to find the exact temperature at 5.30 a.m..

16. John is given two sunflower plants. One plant is 16 cm high and the other is 24 cm high. John measures the height of each plant at the same time every day for a week. He notes that the 16 cm plant grows 4 cm each day, and the 24 cm plant grows 3.5 cm each day.

  (i)   Draw up a table showing the heights of the two plants each day for the week, starting on the day that John got them.

 (ii)   By taking two inputs and outputs, write two equations – one for each plant – in the form $k = \boxed{}d + \boxed{}$, where k is the height in cm and d is the day of the week (1 to 7).

(iii)   John assumes that the plants will continue to grow at the same rate.
        Draw graphs to represent the heights of the two plants over the first 28 days.
        (Take 1 unit = 5 days on x-axis.)

 (iv)   (a) From your diagram, write down the point of intersection of the two graphs.
        (b) Explain what the point of intersection means with respect to the two plants.

  (v)   The point of intersection can be found either by reading the graph or by using algebra.
        State one advantage of finding it using algebra.

 (vi)   John's model for the growth of the plants might not be correct.
        State one limitation of the model that might affect the point of intersection and its interpretation.

Section 17.2 Graphs of quadratic functions

A **quadratic function** is a function such as $f(x) = x^2 - 3x + 4$, where the highest power of x is 2.

The simplest quadratic function is $f(x) = x^2$.
If we use input values from -3 to 3, we can get the output values shown in the table below.

x	-3	-2	-1	0	1	2	3
y	9	4	1	0	1	4	9

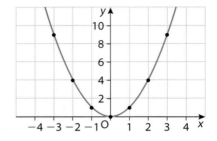

The points shown on this curve are:
$(-3, 9), (-2, 4), (-1, 1), (0, 0), (1, 1), (2, 4), (3, 9)$.

When these points are joined, a smooth curve
called a **parabola** is formed.
The graph above is symmetrical about the y-axis.
For this reason, the y-axis is called the **axis of symmetry**.

Drawing the graph of a quadratic function

To draw the graph of a quadratic function, we take a given number of x-values and find the corresponding $f(x)$ values (or y-values) and plot the resulting points.

When asked to draw the graph of a function, we are usually given the x-values we are to use. The values of x from -2 to 3 is written as $-2 \leqslant x \leqslant 3$.

The steps used in drawing a quadratic graph are given in the following example.

Example 1

Draw the graph of the function $f(x) = x^2 - 2x - 3$ in the domain $-2 \leqslant x \leqslant 4$.
We set out a table of ordered pairs as follows:

x	x² − 2x − 3	y
-2	$4 + 4 - 3$	5
-1	$1 + 2 - 3$	0
0	$0 + 0 - 3$	-3
1	$1 - 2 - 3$	-4
2	$4 - 4 - 3$	-3
3	$9 - 6 - 3$	0
4	$16 - 8 - 3$	5

Plotting these ordered pairs,
we get the following curve:

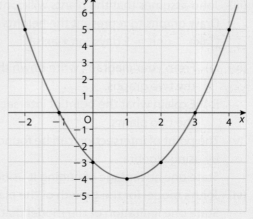

The ordered pairs found are:
$(-2, 5), (-1, 0), (0, -3), (1, -4),$
$(2, -3), (3, 0), (4, 5)$.

Graphing functions when the coefficient of x^2 is negative

If the coefficient of x^2 is negative in a quadratic function, e.g. $f(x) = -3x^2 + 4$, then the graph of the function will take the shape shown on the right.

x^2 negative

Example 2

Draw the graph of the function $f(x) = -x^2 + 3x + 4$ in the domain $-2 \leqslant x \leqslant 5$ by setting out a table of values.

Use your table to show that the second differences between the outputs are constant and write down the value of this constant.

The table of values, and the first and second differences between the outputs, are shown below.

x	$-x^2 + 3x + 4$	y	1st difference	2nd difference
-2	$-4 - 6 + 4$	-6	6	2
-1	$-1 - 3 + 4$	0	4	2
0	$0 + 0 + 4$	4	2	2
1	$-1 + 3 + 4$	6	0	2
2	$-4 + 6 + 4$	6	2	2
3	$-9 + 9 + 4$	4	4	2
4	$-16 + 12 + 4$	0	6	2
5	$-25 + 15 + 4$	-6		

The required points are:
$(-2, -6), (-1, 0), (0, 4), (1, 6),$
$(2, 6), (3, 4), (4, 0), (5, -6).$

The graph of the function is shown.

From the table above, the second differences are constant. This constant is 2.

In a quadratic function, the second difference between the output values is always constant.

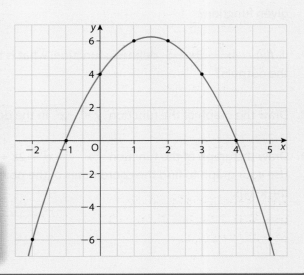

Exercise 17.2

1. Complete the table on the right and hence draw a graph of the function $f(x) = x^2 - 4$ in the domain $-3 \leqslant x \leqslant 3$.

x	x² – 4	y
−3		
−2		
−1		
0		
1		
2		
3		

2. Draw the graph of the function $f: x \rightarrow x^2 - 4x$ in the domain $-1 \leqslant x \leqslant 4$.

3. Draw the graph of the function $f(x) = x^2 + x - 2$ in the domain $-3 \leqslant x \leqslant 3$.

4. Draw the graph of the function $f(x) = 2x^2 - x - 3$ in the domain $-2 \leqslant x \leqslant 3$.

5. Draw the graph of the function $f(x) = 2x^2 + 3x - 4$ in the domain $-3 \leqslant x \leqslant 2$.

6. $f(x) = 2x^2 - 5x - 3$ defines a function.

   Draw up a table of input and output values for $x = -2$ to $x = 4$.
   Write down the first differences and second differences between the output values.
   Write down the value of the second difference.
   What is the connection between this second difference and the coefficient of x^2 in the given function?

7. If $f(x) = 4x^2 - 3x + 5$ defines a function, what is the second difference between the outputs?

8. Draw the graph of the function $y = -x^2$ in the domain $-2 \leqslant x \leqslant 2$.

9. Draw the graph of the function $f: x \rightarrow -x^2 + 2x + 3$ in the domain $-2 \leqslant x \leqslant 4$.
   Use your graph to find the coordinates of the points where the graph crosses the x-axis.

Section 17.3 Using and interpreting quadratic graphs

1. The meaning of the equation $f(x) = 0$

The graph on the right shows the curve
$f(x) = x^2 - 2x - 3$ intersecting the x-axis at a and b.

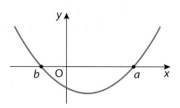

The x-values of these points are the roots of the
associated quadratic equation $x^2 - 2x - 3 = 0$.
Why is this?

$f(x) = x^2 - 2x - 3$ may also be written as $y = x^2 - 2x - 3$.
When $y = 0$, then $x^2 - 2x - 3 = 0$.
$y = 0$ is another name for the x-axis.
Thus, the solution of the equation $x^2 - 2x - 3 = 0$ gives the x-values of the points at
which the curve crosses the x-axis.

The curve on the right is the graph of the
function $f(x) = x^2 + 2x - 5$.

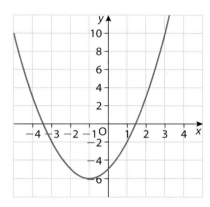

The roots of the equation $x^2 + 2x - 5 = 0$
are found by reading from the graph the
x-values of the points at which the graph
intersects the x-axis.

These values are $x = -3.5$ and $x = 1.5$.

2. Solving the equation $f(x) = k$, where $k \in R$

The graph of the function $f(x) = x^2 - 3x$ is drawn below.

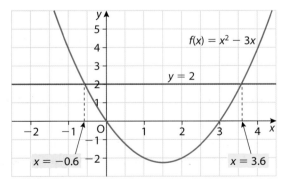

This graph can be used to solve the equation $f(x) = 2$ or $y = 2$ by drawing the line
$y = 2$ and then reading from the graph the x-values of the points where the
line $y = 2$ intersects the curve.
These values are $x = -0.6$ or $x = 3.6$.

3. When is a function positive or negative?

On the right is a graph of the function $f(x) = x^2 + x - 2$.

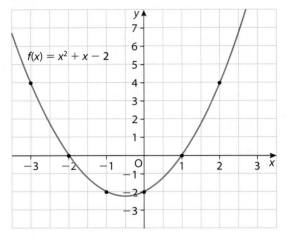

The function is said to be **negative** when the curve is **below** the x-axis. It is negative because the $f(x)$ values (or y-values) are negative.

Thus, the function is negative for $-2 < x < 1$.

The function is **positive** when $x < -2$ or $x > 1$.

4. Finding f(k) from a graph

The graph of the function $y = 6 + 2x - x^2$ is shown.

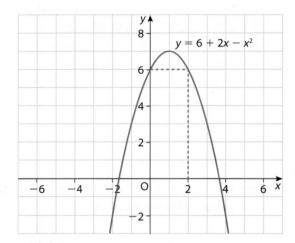

$f(2)$ is the value of y when $x = 2$.

To find $f(2)$, we draw the line $x = 2$ and then read the y-value of the point where this line intersects the curve. This y-value is 6, i.e. $f(2) = 6$.

5. Intersecting graphs

Graphed below are the functions,

$f(x) = x^2$ (i.e. $y = x^2$) and $g(x) = x + 2$ (i.e. $y = x + 2$).

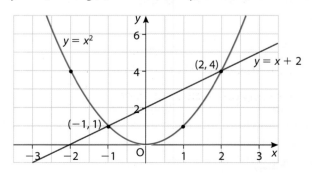

Notice that the curve $f(x)$ and the line $g(x)$ intersect at the points $(-1, 1)$ and $(2, 4)$. At these points of intersection, $f(x) = g(x)$, i.e. $x^2 = x + 2$.

We will now solve the equation $x^2 = x + 2$.

$$x^2 = x + 2 \Rightarrow x^2 - x - 2 = 0$$
$$\Rightarrow (x + 1)(x - 2) = 0$$
$$\Rightarrow x + 1 = 0 \text{ or } x - 2 = 0 \text{ i.e. } x = -1 \text{ or } x = 2.$$

Notice that these are the x-values of the points where the two graphs intersect.

Remember

If $f(x)$ and $g(x)$ are two functions, then the equation $f(x) = g(x)$ can be solved by drawing the graphs of the functions using the same axes and same scales and then writing down the x-values of the points of intersection of the graphs.

We can also use the curve above to solve the inequality **$f(x) < g(x)$**.
$f(x) < g(x)$ represents that part of the graph where the curve $f(x)$ is below the line $g(x)$.

From the graph, the curve is below the line from $x = -1$ to $x = 2$.
Thus, $f(x) < g(x)$ for $-1 < x < 2$.

6. Maximum and minimum values

On the right is a graph of the function

$$y = x^2 - 2x - 3.$$

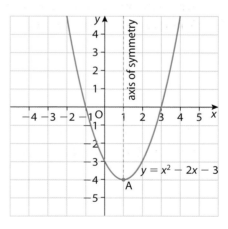

The point marked A is called the **minimum point** or **minimum turning point**.
This point is $(1, -4)$.
The y-value of this point is called the **minimum value**.
In this graph, the minimum value is -4.

The equation of the axis of symmetry of this curve is $x = 1$.

If the coefficient of x^2 is negative in a function, the curve will take the shape shown on the right.

This curve will have a **maximum turning point** (the point B).

481

Exercise 17.3

1. The curve on the right is the graph of the function

$$f(x) = x^2 - 1.$$

Use the graph to find
   (i) the value of $f(x)$ when $x = 2$
   (ii) the value of $f(x)$ when $x = -2$
   (iii) the minimum point of the curve
   (iv) the values of x when $f(x) = 0$
   (v) the values of x when $f(x) = 3$.

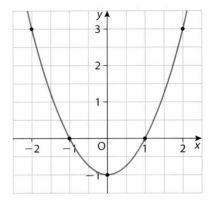

2. Shown below is the graph of the function

$$f(x) = x^2 - 3x - 4 \text{ in the domain } -2 \leqslant x \leqslant 5.$$

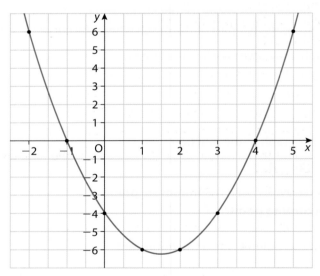

Use the graph shown to write down
   (i) the values of x for which $f(x) = 0$
   (ii) the values of x for which $f(x) = 6$
   (iii) the values of x for which $f(x) = -4$
   (iv) the value of $f(2)$
   (v) the value of $f\left(\frac{1}{2}\right)$
   (vi) the coordinates of the minimum point of the curve
   (vii) the minimum value of $f(x)$.

3. Drawn below is a graph of the function

$$f: x \rightarrow 3 + 2x - x^2, \text{ for } -2 \leqslant x \leqslant 4, \ x \in R.$$

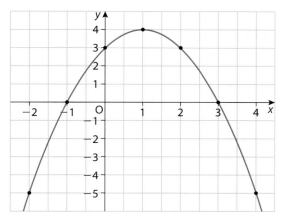

Use the graph to write down
   (i)   the roots of the equation $f(x) = 0$
   (ii) the values of x for which $f(x) = 3$
   (iii) the value of $f\left(2\frac{1}{2}\right)$
   (iv) the maximum value of $f(x)$
   (v)   the coordinates of the maximum point of $f(x)$
   (vi) the range of values of x for which $f(x)$ is increasing
   (vii) the range of values of x for which $f(x)$ is positive
   (viii) the equation of the axis of symmetry of the curve.

4. Draw the graph for the function $f(x) = 2x^2 - x - 3$ in the domain $-2 \leqslant x \leqslant 3$.
Use your graph to find
   (i)   the values of x for which $f(x) = 0$
   (ii) the values of x for which $f(x) = 6$
   (iii) the coordinates of the minimum point of the curve
   (iv) the values of x for which $f(x) < 0$.

5. The graphs of the functions $f(x) = x^2$ and
$g(x) = 2x + 3$ are shown on the right.

   (i)   Write down the coordinates of the points
         where the curve and line meet.
   (ii) Solve the equation $x^2 = 2x + 3$.
   (iii) What is the connection between the
         answers in (i) and (ii) above?
   (iv) Explain the meaning of the equation
         $f(x) = g(x)$.
   (v)   Use the graph to find the range of values
         of x for which $f(x) < g(x)$.

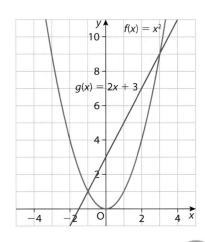

6. Here are two graphs:

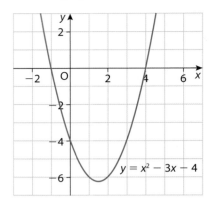

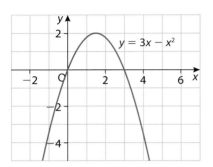

Use the graphs to solve these equations:
  (i) $3x - x^2 = 0$
  (ii) $x^2 - 3x - 4 = 0$
  (iii) $3x - x^2 = -3$
  (iv) $x^2 - 3x - 4 = -2.$

7. Using the same axes and the same scales, graph the functions $f: x \rightarrow x^2 + 3x - 3$ and $g: x \rightarrow x - 2$ in the domain $-4 \leqslant x \leqslant 2, x \in R.$

Use the graph to estimate
  (i)   the roots of the equation $x^2 + 3x - 3 = 0$
  (ii) the roots of the equation $x^2 + 3x - 3 = -2$
  (iii) the roots of the equation $f(x) = g(x)$
  (iv) the minimum value of $f(x).$

What is the meaning of $f(x) < g(x)$?
Now use your graph to find the range of values of x for which $f(x) < g(x).$

8. The equation of the given curve is $y = (x + 2)^2.$

  (i)   Solve the equation $(x + 2)^2 = 0.$
  (ii) Did you get one or two values for x?
  (iii) If you got one value only, the value for x that you found is called a **repeated root**.
         Explain how the graph reflects this repeated root.

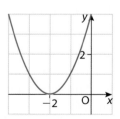

9. The diagram below shows the graphs of $y = x^2 + x - 2$, $y = x^2 - 6x + 9$ and $y = x^2 - 3x + 3$.

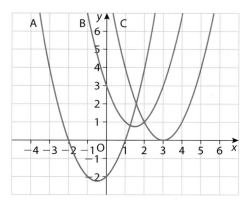

  (i) By substituting $x = 0$ (or any other value of x) into each equation, work out which graph corresponds to which equation.

  (ii) Which function has a repeated root?

  (iii) Use the graph to solve the equation

$$x^2 + x - 2 = x^2 - 6x + 9.$$

Section 17.4 Quadratic graphs and real-life problems ——

Many real-life situations such as the flight of a golf ball or maximising the area of a rectangle with a given perimeter can be modelled by quadratic equations.

The graph below shows the height above the ground of a ball that is thrown up in the air.

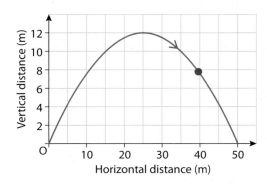

From the graph, it can be seen that
(i) the ball reaches a height of 12 m
(ii) the ball lands 50 m away from the position from which it was thrown.

Example 1

Given that $f(x) = 4 - 3x - x^2, x \in R$, copy and complete the given table.

Draw the graph of $f(x)$ in the domain $-5 \leqslant x \leqslant 2$.

If the graph represents the temperature, in °C, taken every two hours between 6 a.m. ($x = -5$) and 8 p.m. ($x = 2$) in a certain city, use the graph to estimate
  (i)   the temperature at 11 a.m.
  (ii) the time when the temperature was highest
  (iii) the times when the temperature was 3°C
  (iv) the number of hours the temperature was at or above freezing point.

x	4 − 3x − x²	y
−5	4 + 15 − 25	−6
−4		
−3		
−2		
−1		
0		
1	4 − 3 − 1	0
2		

The completed table is shown on the right.

The points on the graph are:
$(-5, -6), (-4, 0), (-3, 4), (-2, 6),$
$(-1, 6), (0, 4), (1, 0), (2, -6).$

x	4 − 3x − x²	y
−5	4 + 15 − 25	−6
−4	4 + 12 − 16	0
−3	4 + 9 − 9	4
−2	4 + 6 − 4	6
−1	4 + 3 − 1	6
0	4 + 0 + 0	4
1	4 − 3 − 1	0
2	4 − 6 − 4	−6

The graph is shown below on the right.

  (i)   11 a.m. is represented by $x = -2\frac{1}{2}$.
        The temperature at $x = -2\frac{1}{2}$ is the y-value of the point where the vertical line through $x = -2\frac{1}{2}$ intersects the curve.
        ∴ the temperature at 11 a.m. is 5.2 °C.
  (ii) The temperature is highest when $x = -1.5$.
        The time at $x = -1.5$ is 1 p.m.
        ∴ the temperature is highest at 1 p.m.
  (iii) The times when the temperature is 3 °C occur when $x = -3.3$ or $x = 0.3$.
        At $x = -3.3$, the time is 9.24 a.m.
        At $x = 0.3$, the time is 4.36 p.m.
        ∴ the temperature is 3°C at 9.24 a.m. and 4.36 p.m.
  (iv) The temperature is above freezing point when $y > 0$. $y > 0$ from $x = -4$ to $x = 1$.
        At $x = -4$, the time is 8 a.m.
        At $x = 1$, the time is 6 p.m.
        The temperature is above freezing point for 10 hours.

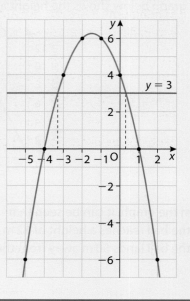

Exercise 17.4

1. On the right is the graph of the function
$f(x) = -x^2 + 4x + 12$.
Use the graph to write down

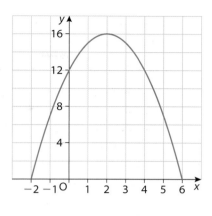

  (i) $f(1)$

 (ii) the values of x for which $f(x) = 12$

(iii) the equation of the axis of symmetry.

$f(x)$ represents the number of taxis at a taxi-rank
from 6 a.m. ($x = -2$) to 10 p.m. ($x = 6$).
Each unit on the x-axis represents 2 hours and
each unit on the y-axis represents one taxi.
Use the graph to estimate

 (iv) the number of taxis at the rank at 12 noon

  (v) the times when there were 14 taxis at the rank

 (vi) the number of hours during which there were 10 taxis or more at the rank.

2. Graphed on the right is the function

$$f(x) = 7 + 5x - 2x^2$$

in the domain $-1 \leqslant x \leqslant 4$.

Use your graph to solve

$$7 + 5x - 2x^2 = 0.$$

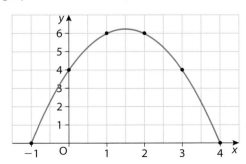

$f(x)$ is the height, in metres, reached by a particle
fired from level ground at the point where $x = -1$,
the x-axis representing level ground. From the time
of firing until it hits the ground again, the particle
was in flight for exactly 4.5 seconds.

Use your graph to estimate

  (i) the maximum height reached by the particle

 (ii) the height reached by the particle after 1.5 seconds of flight

(iii) the number of seconds the particle is 4 m or more above the ground.

3. Sketched below is the graph of $f(x) = 4 + 3x - x^2$ in the domain $-1 \leqslant x \leqslant 4$.

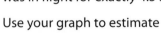

The graph represents the number of cars in a car park between 9 a.m. and 12 midnight.
Each unit on the y-axis represents 100 cars.
Each unit on the x-axis represents 3 hours, where
$-1 = 9$ a.m., $0 = 12$ noon, $1 = 3$ p.m., ... etc.

Use your graph to estimate
  (i)   the number of cars in the car park at 1.30 p.m.
  (ii) the times when the car park contained 400 cars
  (iii) the time the car park contained the greatest number of cars and write down this
        number
  (iv) the times that the car park contained no cars.

4. A farmer has 16 metres of fencing with which to make a rectangular enclosure for
   sheep. If one side of the enclosure is x metres long, show that the area A is given
   by $A(x) = 8x - x^2$.

   Draw the graph of $A(x)$ in the domain $0 \leqslant x \leqslant 8$.

   Use your graph to estimate
     (i)   the area of the enclosure when $x = 2.5$
     (ii) the maximum possible area and the value of x when this occurs
     (iii) the two values of x for which the area is 12 m².

5. Draw the graph of the function $f: x \rightarrow 6x - x^2$ in the domain $0 \leqslant x \leqslant 6$.

   $f(x)$ represents the height, in metres, reached by a golf ball from the time it was hit
   $(x = 0)$ to the time it hit the ground $(x = 6)$.

   If each unit on the x-axis represents 1 second and each unit on the y-axis represents
   5 metres, use your graph to estimate
     (i)   the greatest height reached by the golf ball
     (ii) the height of the golf ball after $1\frac{1}{2}$ seconds
     (iii) after how many seconds the ball was 10 metres above ground
     (iv) after how many seconds the ball reached its maximum height.

6. The area of a circle is given roughly by the formula $A = 3r^2$.
     (i)   Copy and complete the table given on the right
           and draw a graph of the function for $0 \leqslant r \leqslant 3$.
     (ii) Use your graph to find an estimate for the area
           of a circle of radius 2.5 m.
     (iii) If a circle has an area of 10 m², use the graph to
           estimate the length of its radius.
     (iv) Check your answers to parts (ii) and (iii) using the
           accurate version of the formula for the area of a circle (i.e. $A = \pi r^2$).

r	$3r^2$	A
0		
1	3	3
2		
3		

7. A farmer has 20 metres of fencing.
He wishes to use it to form a rectangular enclosure
in the corner of a field, as in the diagram.

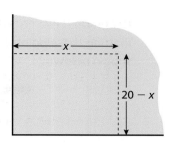

  (i) Write down an expression for the area,
A m², enclosed by the fencing.

 (ii) Plot the graph of A for values of x between
0 and 20.

(iii) For what values of x is the area 40 m²?

(iv) What range of values of x give an enclosed area greater than 90 m²?

 (v) What is the maximum area the farmer can enclose?
What are the lengths of the fencing for this maximum area?

Section 17.5 Cubic functions

A cubic function generally takes the form

$$f(x) = ax^3 + bx^2 + cx + d, \text{ where } a, b, c \text{ and } d \in R.$$

The graph of a cubic function $f(x) = ax^3 + bx^2 + cx + d$, generally consists of a smooth curve
with two turning points as follows:

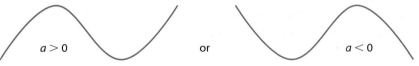

When drawing the graph of a cubic function, we are generally given a set of input values
called the domain.

We then construct a table to find the output (or y) values.

The steps involved in **constructing** the table and drawing the graph are illustrated in the
following worked example.

Example 1

Draw the graph of the function $f: x \rightarrow x^3 - 3x^2 - x + 3$, in the domain $-2 \leqslant x \leqslant 4$.

We construct a table of ordered pairs as follows:

x	$x^3 - 3x^2 - x + 3$	y
-2	$-8 - 12 + 2 + 3$	-15
-1	$-1 - 3 + 1 + 3$	0
0	$0 - 0 - 0 + 3$	3
1	$1 - 3 - 1 + 3$	0
2	$8 - 12 - 2 + 3$	-3
3	$27 - 27 - 3 + 3$	0
4	$64 - 48 - 4 + 3$	15

The ordered pairs are:
$(-2, -15), (-1, 0), (0, 3), (1, 0),$
$(2, -3), (3, 0), (4, 15).$

Plotting these points we get a smooth curve with two turning points as shown below:

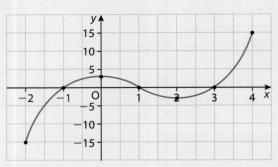

Features of a graph of a cubic function

Drawn below is a typical graph of a cubic function $y = f(x)$.

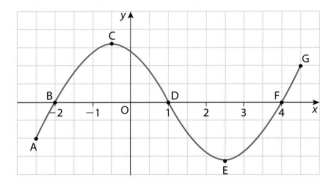

The following points are important when dealing with the graphs of cubic functions.

1. The point C is called a **maximum turning point**.
   The point E is called a **minimum turning point**.

2. The graph [i.e. $f(x)$] is **positive** when it is above the x-axis and **negative** when it is below the x-axis.
   $\Rightarrow f(x)$ is positive for the x-values from B to D and from F to G.
   The graph is negative for the x-values from A to B and from D to F.

3. Examining the graph from **left to right**, we say $f(x)$ is **increasing** when the curve is rising and **decreasing** when the curve is falling.
   (i) From A to B (i.e. from $x = -2\frac{1}{2}$ to $x = -2$), $f(x)$ is **negative and increasing**.
   (ii) From B to C (i.e. from $x = -2$ to $x = -\frac{1}{2}$), $f(x)$ is **positive and increasing**.
   (iii) From C to D (i.e. from $x = -\frac{1}{2}$ to $x = 1$), $f(x)$ is **positive and decreasing**.

(iv) From D to E (i.e. from $x = 1$ to $x = 2\frac{1}{2}$), $f(x)$ is **negative and decreasing**.

(v) From E to F (i.e. from $x = 2\frac{1}{2}$ to $x = 4$), $f(x)$ is **negative and increasing**.

(vi) From F to G (i.e. from $x = 4$ to $x = 4\frac{1}{2}$), $f(x)$ is **positive and increasing**.

4. The solutions to the equation $f(x) = 0$ are the x-values of the points at which the curve intersects the x-axis.

In the graph above, $f(x) = 0 \Rightarrow x = -2$, $x = 1$ and $x = 4$.

Exercise 17.5

1. Copy and complete the table given on the right.

   Use this table to draw the graph of the function $f(x) = x^3 + 3x^2 - x - 3$ in the domain $-4 \leqslant x \leqslant 2$, $x \in R$.

x	$x^3 + 3x^2 - x - 3$	y
-4	$-64 + 48 + 4 - 3$	-27
-3		
-2		
-1		
0		
1		
2		

2. Draw a graph of the function $y = x^3 - 2x^2 - 4x$ in the domain $-2 \leqslant x \leqslant 4, x \in R$.

3. Graph the function $f(x) = x^3 - 5x + 2$ in the domain $-3 \leqslant x \leqslant 3, x \in R$.

4. The diagram below shows the graph of a function $y = f(x)$.

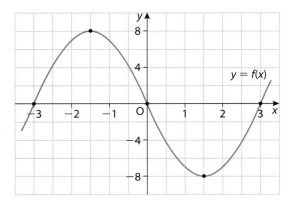

Use the graph to write down
   (i) the roots of the equation $f(x) = 0$
   (ii) the domain of values of x for which $f(x)$ is positive
   (iii) the values of x for which $f(x)$ is positive and decreasing
   (iv) the coordinates of the maximum turning point
   (v) the coordinates of the minimum turning point.

5. The diagram on the right shows the graph of the function $f(x) = x^3 + x^2 - 6x$.

Use the graph to write down

   (i)   the roots of the equation $f(x) = 0$

  (ii) the coordinates of the minimum turning point

 (iii) the values of x for which $f(x)$ is positive

 (iv) the values of x for which $f(x)$ is negative and decreasing.

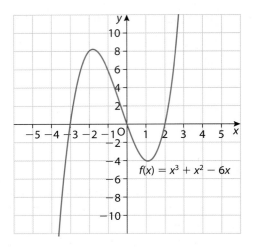

$f(x) = x^3 + x^2 - 6x$

6. If $f(x) = x^3 + 2x^2 - 7x - 3$, copy and complete the following table:

$x =$	-4	-3	-2	-1	0	1	2	3
$f(x) =$	-7					-7		21

Draw the graph of the function

$$f(x) = x^3 + 2x^2 - 7x - 3 \text{ in the domain } -4 \leqslant x \leqslant 3, x \in R.$$

Use your graph to estimate
   (i)   the roots of the equation $f(x) = 0$
  (ii) the domain of values of x for which $f(x)$ is decreasing
 (iii) the coordinates of the minimum turning point.

7. Copy and complete the table of values for $y = 6x + x^2 - x^3$.

x	-3	-2	-1	0	1	2	3	4
y		0	-4			8	0	

   (i)   Draw a graph of the function $y = 6x + x^2 - x^3$ in the domain $-3 \leqslant x \leqslant 4$.
  (ii) How is this graph different from the graphs you have drawn so far?
 (iii) Write down the roots of the equation $y = 0$.
 (iv) Use your graph to estimate the coordinates of the minimum turning point.
  (v) For what values of x is y negative and decreasing?

8. Here are the graphs of three cubic functions, $f(x) = \ldots$.

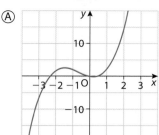 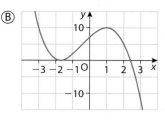 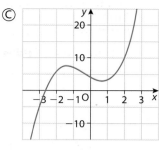

   (i) Which graph represents a function in which the coefficient of x^3 is negative?

  (ii) Which graph has only one real root for the equation $f(x) = 0$?

 (iii) In which graph is $f(x)$ positive for $-2.5 < x < 0$?

 (iv) Which graph is negative and decreasing for $x > 2.4$?

9. If $f(x) = -2x^3 + 3x^2 + 5x - 6$, complete the following table:

$x =$	-2	-1	0	1	2	3
$f(x) =$		-6				-18

Draw the graph of the function $f: x \rightarrow -2x^3 + 3x^2 + 5x - 6$ in the domain $-2 \leqslant x \leqslant 3$.

Use your graph to estimate

   (i) the roots of the equation $f(x) = 0$

  (ii) the coordinates of the maximum turning point

 (iii) the values of x for which $f(x) > 0$

 (iv) the values of $x < 0$ for which $f(x)$ is negative and decreasing.

10. Associate each sketch-graph below with one of the given equations:

$y = x^3 - x^2$ $y = 1 - x^2$ $y = x - x^2$ $y = -\frac{3}{4}x + 3$ $y = x^2 + 3x$ $y = 9x - x^3$

Ⓐ 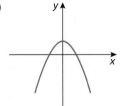   Ⓑ 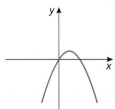   Ⓒ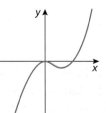

Ⓓ 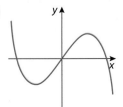   Ⓔ 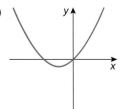   Ⓕ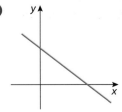

Section 17.6 Using graphs of cubic functions

The graph below represents the function $f(x) = x^3 - 9x$.

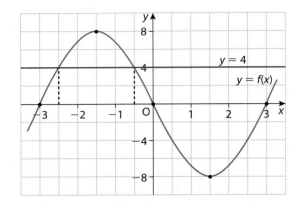

In the previous section, it was shown that the solutions of the equation $f(x) = 0$ are the x-values of the points at which the curve intersects the x-axis.

From the graph, the solutions to $f(x) = 0$ are $x = -3, 0$ and 3.

How to solve the equation $f(x) = 4$

We can use the given graph to solve the equation $f(x) = 4$ by drawing the line $y = 4$ and then reading from the graph the x-values of the points at which the line intersects the curve. From the graph, an estimate of these values are

$$x = -2.5 \text{ or } x = -0.5.$$

If another function $g(x)$ is drawn using the same axes and scales, then the solutions to the equation $f(x) = g(x)$ are the x-values of the points of intersection of the two graphs.

Solving related equations

If we have drawn the graph of $f(x) = x^3 - 2x^2 + 5x - 4$, how do we use the graph to solve the equation $x^3 - 2x^2 + 5x - 6 = 0$?

Notice that the second equation can be expressed as

$$\text{First equation} = 2$$
$$\text{i.e. } x^3 - 2x^2 + 5x - 4 = 2.$$

To find the solutions to this equation, we draw the line $y = 2$ and read off the x-values of the points where this line intersects the curve $y = f(x)$.

Example 1

Draw the graph of the function $y = x^3 - 3x^2 - 2x + 5$ in the domain $-2 \leqslant x \leqslant 4$.

Use your graph to solve the equations
(i) $x^3 - 3x^2 - 2x + 5 = -3$
(ii) $x^3 - 3x^2 - 2x + 5 = 2x - 4$

We set out the table of ordered pairs as follows:

x	$x^3 - 3x^2 - 2x + 5$	y
-2	$-8 - 12 + 4 + 5$	-11
-1	$-1 - 3 + 2 + 5$	3
0	$0 - 0 - 0 + 5$	5
1	$1 - 3 - 2 + 5$	1
2	$8 - 12 - 4 + 5$	-3
3	$27 - 27 - 6 + 5$	-1
4	$64 - 48 - 8 + 5$	13

The points on the curve are: $(-2, -11), (-1, 3), (0, 5), (1, 1), (2, -3), (3, -1), (4, 13)$.

The graph is shown below:

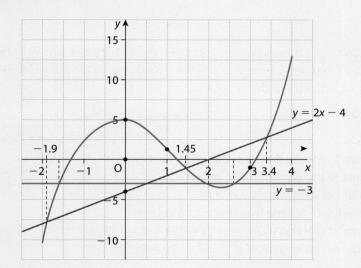

(i) The solution of the equation $x^3 - 3x^2 - 2x + 5 = -3$ is found by getting the x-values of the points of intersection of the curve and the line $y = -3$.
We now draw the line $y = -3$ and read the x-values of the points where it cuts the curve, as shown.

$$\Rightarrow x = -1.6, 2 \text{ and } 2.6.$$

(ii) The equation $x^3 - 3x^2 - 2x + 5 = 2x - 4$ is in the form $f(x) = g(x)$.

Here $g(x) = 2x - 4$.

We now draw the graph of $y = 2x - 4$.

Two points on the line are $(0, -4)$ and $(2, 0)$.

This line is shown on the graph.

From the graph, it can be seen that the curve and the line intersect at the points where

$x = -1.9, 1.45$ and 3.4.

Thus, $x^3 - 3x^2 - 2x + 5 = 2x - 4$

$\Rightarrow x = -1.9, \ x = 1.45 \ \text{or} \ x = 3.4.$

Exercise 17.6

1. Drawn below is the graph of the function $f(x) = x^3 - 2x^2 - 5x + 6$ in the domain $-2 \leqslant x \leqslant 3, x \in R$.

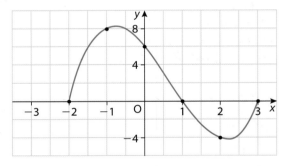

Use your graph to write down, in the given domain,

   (i) the roots of the equation $f(x) = 0$
  (ii) the values of x for which $f(x) \geqslant 0$
 (iii) the coordinates of the maximum turning point
  (iv) the roots of the equation $x^3 - 2x^2 - 5x + 6 = -2$
   (v) the roots of the equation $x^3 - 2x^2 - 5x = 0$.

2. Draw a graph of the function $f(x) = 2x^3 - x^2 - 8x + 4$ in the domain $-2 \leqslant x \leqslant 3$.
Find from your graph, as accurately as you can, the root(s) of the equations

   (i) $f(x) = 0$
  (ii) $2x^3 - x^2 - 8x - 4 = -3$
 (iii) $2x^3 - x^2 - 8x - 6 = 0$.

3. Here is the graph of the function

$$y = x^3 - x^2 - 8x + 12.$$

Use your graph to estimate

(i) the roots of the equation $y = 0$
(ii) the roots of the equation
$x^3 - x^2 - 8x + 12 = 5$
(iii) the values of x for which $y > 0$
(iv) the range of values of x for which y is positive and decreasing
(v) the repeated root of the equation
$x^3 - x^2 - 8x + 12 = 0.$

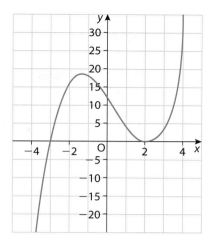

4. Graph the function $f(x) = x^3 + 4x^2 + x - 6$ in the domain $-4 \leqslant x \leqslant 2, x \in R$.
Find from your graph as accurately as you can,
(i) the roots of the equation $f(x) = 0$
(ii) the real root of the equation $x^3 + 4x^2 + x - 9 = 0$
(iii) the values of x for which $f(x) < 0$
(iv) the values of x for which $f(x)$ is decreasing
(v) the roots of the equation $x^3 + 4x^2 + x - 6 = 2x + 4.$

5. Here is the graph of the function

$$f(x) = x^3 - 3x^2 - 9x.$$

Use your graph to estimate
(i) $f(3)$
(ii) the maximum turning point
(iii) the roots of the equation $x^3 - 3x^2 - 9x = -20$
(iv) the range of values of x for which $f(x)$ is decreasing.

Explain why the equation $f(x) = 10$ has only one root.
Explain why the equation $f(x) = -10$ has three roots.

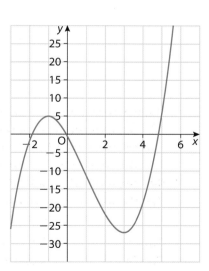

6. Draw the graph of the function $f(x) = 3x - x^3$ in the domain $-2 \leqslant x \leqslant 2$.
Use your graph to solve these equations
(i) $-x^3 + 3x = 0$
(ii) $-x^3 + 3x + 1 = 0$
(iii) $-x^3 + 3x = x + 1.$

7. A function $f(x)$ is of the form $f(x) = ax^3 + bx^2 + cx + d$, where a is positive. Draw a rough sketch of $f(x)$ given that $y = f(x)$ satisfies these conditions:
(a) $f(1) = 0$ and $f(9) = 0$
(b) $(1, 0)$ and $(5, -10)$ are turning points.

Use your graph to state
   (i) the range of values of x for which $f(x) < 0$ when $x > 1$
   (ii) the range of values of x for which $f(x)$ is negative and decreasing.

8. Let $f(x) = 2x^3 - 5x^2 - 4x + 3$ for $x \in R$.
Copy and complete the table below:

x	-1.5	-1	0	1	2	3	3.5
$f(x)$	-9						13.5

Draw the graph of $f(x) = 2x^3 - 5x^2 - 4x + 3$ in the domain $-1.5 \leqslant x \leqslant 3.5$.
Use your graph to write down
   (i) the coordinates of the minimum turning point
   (ii) the roots of the equation $f(x) = 0$
   (iii) the roots of the equation $2x^3 - 5x^2 - 4x = 0$.

Write the equation $2x^3 - 5x^2 - 6x + 6 = 0$ in the form
$$2x^3 - 5x^2 - 4x + 3 = ax + b, \ a, b \in Z.$$

Hence use your graph to estimate the solutions of the equation
$$2x^3 - 5x^2 - 6x + 6 = 0.$$

9. A canvas wind-shelter has two square ends, each of side x metres, and a rectangular back of length ℓ metres. The area of canvas is $9\,m^2$.

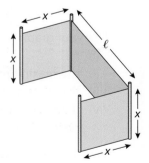

   (i) Show that $\ell = \dfrac{9}{x} - 2x$, and hence show that
   the enclosed volume, $V\,m^3$, is $9x - 2x^3$.
   (ii) Plot the graph of V against x for $0 \leqslant x \leqslant 3$.
   (iii) (a) Use your graph to find the value of x that gives the largest possible volume.
        (b) From your graph, what is this largest volume?

Section 17.7 Graphing exponential functions

Consider the function $f(x) = 2^x$.
In this function, the variable x appears as a power.
A function in which the variable appears as a power is called an **exponential function**.

Here are some more exponential functions:

(i) $f(x) = 3^x$ (ii) $f(x) = 3.2^x$ (iii) $f(x) = 2.3^{-x}$

To draw the graph of $f(x) = 2^x$, we set out a table of inputs and outputs from $x = -2$ to $x = 3$.

x	2^x	y
-2	$2^{-2} = \frac{1}{4}$	$\frac{1}{4}$
-1	$2^{-1} = \frac{1}{2}$	$\frac{1}{2}$
0	$2^0 = 1$	1
1	$2^1 = 2$	2
2	$2^2 = 4$	4
3	$2^3 = 8$	8

Any number to the power of zero is 1.

The graph of $f(x) = 2^x$, is shown below.

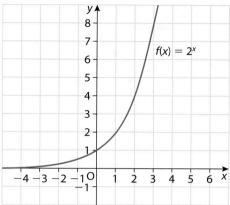

> Notice that the curve rises very steeply.
> If we take further values for x, e.g. $x = 4, 5, 6, \ldots$, we get these y-values:
>
> $$2^4 = 16; \quad 2^5 = 32; \quad 2^6 = 64, \ldots$$
>
> The curves of functions such as $f(x) = 2^x$, $f(x) = 3^x$, $f(x) = 4^x$ rise very quickly.

> The curve of any function of the form $f(x) = a^x$, will contain the point (0, 1) as any number to the power of zero is 1.

> The curve will move closer and closer to the x-axis but will never actually touch it.

Example 1

Draw the graph of the function $f(x) = 2.3^x$ in the domain $-2 \leqslant x \leqslant 3$.
(i) Use your graph to find an estimate for $f(2.5)$
(ii) Use your graph also to find the value of x for which $f(x) = 7$.

We set out a table of values for
$f(x) = 2.3^x$, $-2 \leqslant x \leqslant 3$.

x	2.3^x	y
-2	2.3^{-2}	$\frac{2}{9}$
-1	2.3^{-1}	$\frac{2}{3}$
0	2.3^0	2
1	2.3^1	6
2	2.3^2	18
3	2.3^3	54

The graph is shown on the right.

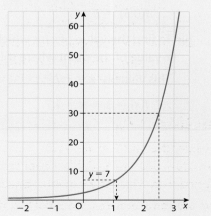

(i) To find $f(2.5)$, draw a vertical line from $x = 2.5$ until it meets the curve.
   The y-value of the point of intersection is 30.
   $\therefore \quad f(2.5) = 30$

(ii) To find the value of x for which $f(x) = 7$, draw the line $y = 7$ and read the
   x-value of the point of intersection of this line and the curve.

   This value is $x = 1.1$.

Example 2

Draw the graph of the function $f(x) = 10.\left(\frac{1}{2}\right)^{x}$ in the domain $0 \leqslant x \leqslant 4$.

(i) Use your graph to find an estimate of $f(0.5)$
(ii) Use your graph to solve the equation $f(x) = 3$.

We set out a table of input values for $x = 0$ to $x = 4$.

x	$10\left(\frac{1}{2}\right)^{x}$	y
0	$10\left(\frac{1}{2}\right)^{0}$	10
1	$10\left(\frac{1}{2}\right)^{1}$	5
2	$10\left(\frac{1}{2}\right)^{2}$	2.5
3	$10\left(\frac{1}{2}\right)^{3}$	1.25
4	$10\left(\frac{1}{2}\right)^{4}$	0.625

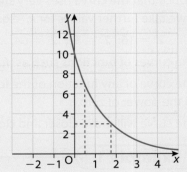

(i) To find $f(0.5)$, draw a vertical line from 0.5 on the x-axis until it intersects
   the curve.
   The y-value of the point is 7.
   $\therefore \quad f(0.5) = 7$

(ii) To find the value of x for which $f(x) = 3$, draw the line $y = 3$ and read the
   x-value of the point where this line intersects the curve.

   This value is $x = 1.7$.

   $\therefore \quad f(x) = 3 \Rightarrow x = 1.7.$

Exercise 17.7

1. This is the graph of $f(x) = 2^x$.

Use the graph to write down
  (i) $f(0)$ (ii) $f(1)$ (iii) $f(1.5)$.

$f(3)$ is not shown on the graph.

  (iv) What is $f(3)$?
  (v) For what value of x is $f(x) = 5$?

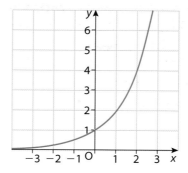

2. Copy and complete the table below and then draw the graph of the function $f(x) = 3^x$.

x	-2	-1	0	1	2	3
3^x		$\frac{1}{3}$				

Use your graph to write down
  (i) $f(1.5)$
  (ii) the value of x for which $f(x) = 4$.

3. Copy and complete the table below.

x	-2	-1	0	1	2
2^x	$\frac{1}{4}$				
4.2^x	1				

Use the table to draw a sketch of the function $f(x) = 4.2^x$ in the domain $-2 \leqslant x \leqslant 2$.
Use your graph to find an estimate for $f(0.5)$.

4. On the right is the graph of $f(x) = k \cdot 2^x$, where $k \in N$.

  (i) Write down the value of k.
  (ii) $f(2)$ is not shown on the graph.
      What is $f(2)$?
  (iii) Use this graph to estimate the value of x for
      which $f(x) = 1$.

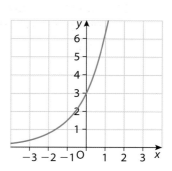

5. Three graphs Ⓐ, Ⓑ and Ⓒ are sketched on the right.

Associate each graph with one of the functions given below:

$f(x) = 2^x$ $f(x) = 3^x$ $f(x) = 3.3^x$

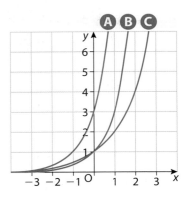

6. Copy and complete the table below and hence draw the graph of the function $f(x) = 3^{-x}$ in the domain $-2 \leqslant x \leqslant 3$.

x	-2	-1	0	1	2	3
$f(x) = 3^{-x}$						

Use your graph to estimate

(i) $f(-1.5)$ (ii) the value of x when $f(x) = 4$.

7. Graphed on the right is the function $f(x) = a \cdot b^x$.

Copy and complete the table below and use the table and the graph to find the values of a and b.

x	$f(x) = a \cdot b^x$	y
0		
1		

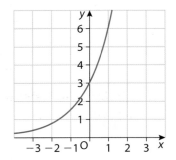

8. The diagram below shows the graphs of

$$y = 2^x, \ y = 5^x, \ y = \left(\tfrac{1}{2}\right)^x \ \text{and} \ y = 3^{-x}.$$

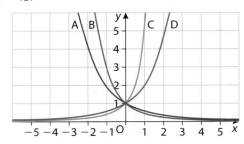

Use different values for x and the corresponding y-values to match each graph to its equation.

9. Anto is told that the given curve is the graph of either

   (a) $f(x) = k \cdot 2^x$ or   (b) $f(x) = k \cdot 3^x$.

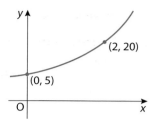

   (i) Find the value of k.

   (ii) Write down which of the two functions the
       curve represents.

10. The curve $y = a(2^x)$ passes through the point $(1, 3)$.

   Find the value of a.

11. The curve $y = a(b^x)$ passes through the points $(1, 10)$ and $(3, 250)$.

   Find the value of a and the value of b.

12. $f: x \rightarrow 2x + 3$, $g: x \rightarrow x^2 + 3$, and $h: x \rightarrow 3(2^x)$ are three functions.

Table A

x	y
0	3
1	6
2	12
3	24
4	48

Table B

x	y
0	3
1	5
2	7
3	9
4	11

Table C

x	y
0	3
1	4
2	7
3	12
4	19

   (i) Match the table of outputs with the correct function.

   (ii) Which function is increasing at the quickest rate?

13. A: $y = 2^x$; B: $y = 2x + 1$; C: $y = x^2 + 1$ are three functions.

   Match each graph below to its function.

(i)

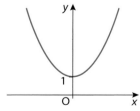

(ii)

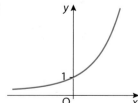

(iii)

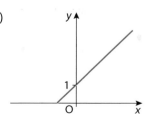

14. Here are three statements and three graphs:

   (i) A car worth €60 000 decreases in value by €10 000 each year.
   (ii) Property prices have fallen in value by 10% each year for the past four years.
   (iii) A bunjee jumper jumps off a bridge and her height above the ground is recorded every second.

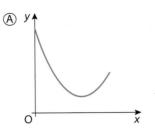 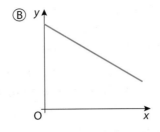 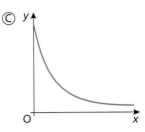

Match each statement with its graph and explain your answer in each case.

15. The functions f and g are defined as follows:

$$f\colon x \to 3^x \text{ and } g\colon x \to 4x^2 + 1 \text{ in the domain } 0 \leqslant x \leqslant 5.$$

   (i) What type of function is f?
   (ii) What type of function is g?
   (iii) Which function is increasing at the faster rate between $x = 0$ and $x = 3$?
   (iv) Which function is increasing faster between $x = 3$ and $x = 5$?

16. Two functions f and g are defined as follows:

$$f\colon x \to 2^x, \ g\colon x \to 9x - 3x^2 - 1.$$

Complete the table below and use it to draw the graphs of f and g for $0 \leqslant x \leqslant 3$.

x	0	0.5	1	1.5	2	2.5	3
$f(x)$							
$g(x)$							

   (i) Use your graph to estimate the value(s) of x for which

$$2^x = 9x - 3x^2 - 1.$$

   (ii) If $2^k = 6$, use your graph to estimate the value of k.

Test yourself 17

1. (a) Draw the graph of the function $f(x) = 3x - 1$ in the domain $-2 \leqslant x \leqslant 3$.
   Use your graph to estimate
   (i) $f(-1.5)$ (ii) the value of x when $y = 3.5$.

   (b) The diagram on the right shows the path of a
   rocket which is fired into the air.
   The height, h metres, of the rocket, after t seconds,
   is given by $h = 30t - t^2$.

   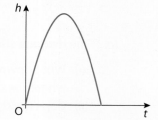

   (i) For how many seconds is the rocket in flight?
   (ii) What is the maximum height reached by the
   rocket?

   (c) If $f(x) = x^3 - 2x^2 - 5x + 4$, copy and complete the following table:

x =	−2	−1	0	1	2	3	3.5
f(x) =	−2					−2	4.9

   Draw the graph of the function $f(x) = x^3 - 2x^2 - 5x + 4$ in the domain
   $-2 \leqslant x \leqslant 3.5$.

   Use your graph to estimate
   (i) the roots of the equation $f(x) = 0$
   (ii) the values of x at which $f(x) < 0$ and $(x) > 0$
   (iii) the coordinates of the minimum turning point
   (iv) the values of x at which $f(x)$ is negative and decreasing
   (v) the roots of the equation $y = 4$
   (vi) the value of $f(-1.5)$.

2. (a) On the right is the graph of the function
   $f(x) = x^2 - 4x$.
   Use the curve to write down
   (i) $f(3.5)$
   (ii) the values of x for which $f(x) = -3$
   (iii) the minimum value of $f(x)$
   (iv) the equation of the axis of symmetry
   of the curve.

   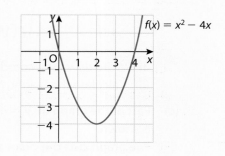

   $f(x) = x^2 - 4x$

   (b) Match each of the graphs on the next page with one of the equations given.

$y = kx$	$y = x^2 - k$	$y = k - x^2$	$y = k - x$

   In each equation, k is a positive number.
   (One of the equations is not needed.)

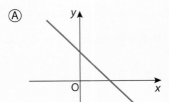
Ⓐ

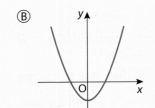
Ⓑ

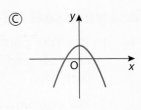
Ⓒ

(c) The diagram shows a sketch of the curve $y = 3^x$.

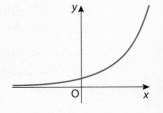

(i) Write down the coordinates of the point where the curve cuts the y-axis.

(ii) Copy the diagram and add sketches of the curves

(a) 2×3^x (b) 5×3^x.

3. (a) A straight line is represented by the equation $y = ax + b$.
Sketch a possible straight line graph to illustrate this equation when $a = 0$ and $b > 0$.

(b) The curved part of the letter A in the *Artwork* logo is in the shape of a parabola.

The equation of this parabola is $y = (x - 8)(2 - x)$.

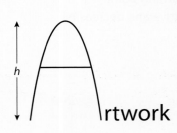

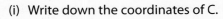
rtwork

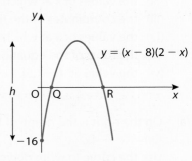

$y = (x - 8)(2 - x)$

(i) Write down the coordinates of Q and R.

(ii) Calculate the height, h, of the letter A.

(c) Part of the graph of $y = a^x$, where $a > 0$, is shown.
The graph cuts the y-axis at C.

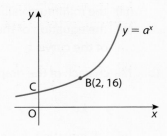

$y = a^x$

B(2, 16)

(i) Write down the coordinates of C.

B is the point (2, 16).

(ii) Calculate the value of a.

4. (a) A taxi fare consists of a €4 "callout" charge **plus** a fixed amount per kilometre. The graph shows the fare, f euro, for a journey of d kilometres.
The taxi fare for a 5 km journey is €12.
Find the equation of the straight line in terms of d and f.
Use the equation to find the cost of a journey of 20 km.

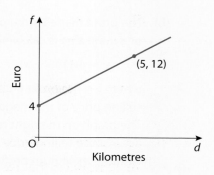

(b) Match the graphs below with their equations.
For the equation that is left over, sketch its graph.

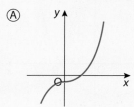 Ⓐ

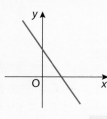 Ⓑ

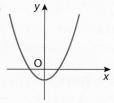 Ⓒ

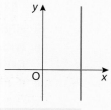 Ⓓ

$x = 4$

$y = 5$

$y = 3 - 2x$

$y = x^2 - x - 6$

$y = x^3 - 1$

(c) Copy and complete the following table.

x	−3	−2	−1	0	1	2	3	4	5
2^x	0.125			1		4			

(i) Use the values in your table to draw the graph of $y = 2^x$ using a scale of 1 cm for 1 unit on the x-axis, and 1 cm for 5 units on the y-axis.

(ii) Use your graph to solve the equation $2^x = 5$.

5. (a) Some graphs are drawn on the right. Use these graphs to find the approximate solutions of these equations:

(i) $x^2 - x - 2 = 2$

(ii) $x^2 - x - 2 = -1$

(iii) $x^2 - x - 2 = x + 1$

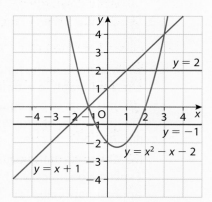

(b) The profit made by the publishing company of a magazine is calculated by the formula

$$y = 4x(140 - x),$$

where y is the profit (in euro) and x is the selling price of the magazine (in euro). The graph on the right represents the profit y against the selling price x.

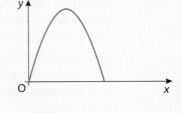

Find the maximum profit the company can make from the sale of the magazine.

(c) The curve on the right is the graph of the function

$$f(x) = x^2 - 2x - 3.$$

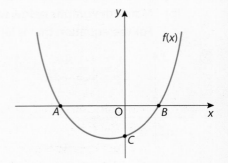

  (i) Find the coordinates of A, B and C.

  (ii) Write down the values of x for which $f(x) \leqslant 0$.

  (iii) If $f(k) = -3$, find two values for k.

6. (a) The following table gives the cost of hiring a surfboard for a number of days:

Days t	3	4	5	6
Cost €C	50	60	70	80

  (i) By using any two couples, write down the equation of the line that relates the cost €C to the number of days t.

  (ii) Use the equation to find the cost of hiring a surfboard for two weeks.

(b) Which sketch graph fits which equation? Give reasons for your answers.

Ⓐ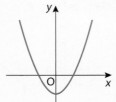

Ⓑ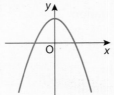

Ⓒ

$y = 2x$

$y = x^2 - 2$

$y = 2 - x^2$

$y = x^2 + 2$

(c) Draw a graph of the function $f(x) = x^3 - 5x + 1$ in the domain $-3 \leqslant x \leqslant 3$. Use your graph to estimate

  (i) the roots of the equation $f(x) = 0$

  (ii) the values of x for which $f(x) > 0$ when $x < 0$

  (iii) $f(-2.5)$

  (iv) the roots of the equation $f(x) = 1$.

Explain algebraically why one of the roots you have found in (iv) gives an approximate value for $\sqrt{5}$.

Summary of key points...

1. A function such as $f(x) = 3x + 2$ is called a **linear function** because its graph is a straight line.
   If the graph of a linear function is in the form $y = mx + c$, then **m** is the **slope** and the line crosses the y-axis at the point $(0, c)$.

2. A **directly proportional** graph is always a straight line through the origin.

3. A **quadratic function** is an expression of the form $ax^2 + bx + c$, where the highest power of x is x^2.
   The graph of a quadratic function is called a **parabola**. It has one of the following shapes.

   $y = ax^2 + bx + c,$
   $a > 0$

   $y = ax^2 + bx + c,$
   $a < 0$

   The **solutions** of a quadratic equation are the values of x where the graph cuts the x-axis.

4. A **cubic function** is an expression of the form $ax^3 + bx^2 + cx + d$, where the highest power of x is x^3.
   The graph of a cubic function has one of the following shapes.

A	A
a > 0 B	B a < 0

   The point A is called a **maximum turning point**.
   The point B is called a **minimum turning point**.

5. If $f(x)$ and $g(x)$ are two functions, then the equation $f(x) = g(x)$ can be solved by drawing graphs of the functions using the same axes and same scales and then writing down the x-values of the **points of intersection** of the two graphs.

6. An **exponential function** is a function of the form $y = a^x$ or $y = a^{-x}$, where $a > 0$.
   The **graph** of an exponential function has one of the following two shapes:

   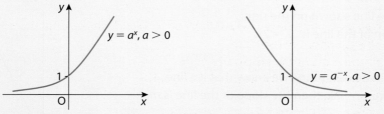

   $y = a^x, a > 0$

   $y = a^{-x}, a > 0$

   The graphs cross the y-axis at $(0, 1)$, since $a^0 = 1$ for all values of a.

18 Calculus

Key words

slope   rate of change   differentiation   derived function   slope function
tangents   maximum turning point   minimum turning point
second derivative   increasing function   decreasing function   velocity (speed)
acceleration   average rate of change

Section 18.1 The slope of a line

In this chapter we begin the study of a branch of mathematics called **calculus**.
Calculus was developed in the 17th century by two mathematicians working independently.
One, Isaac Newton, was an Englishman and the other, Gottfried Leibnitz, was a German.

Calculus involves the study of the rate of change where one quantity varies with
respect to another.

Here are some examples:

 (i) Petrol consumption varies with respect to size of engine.
 (ii) Distance travelled varies with respect to time.
 (iii) The area of a square varies with respect to the length of its side.

The speed of a car is the rate at which the distance travelled changes with respect to time.
If a car is accelerating, it is changing speed by the second.

If 60 km/hr is registered on the speedometer, this tells us the **instantaneous speed**.
Calculus is the mathematical tool that will enable us to find **instantaneous rates of change**.

The slope (gradient) of a line

Consider the line shown on the right.
The equation of the line is $y = 2x$.
The **slope** is $\frac{2}{1} = 2$.

From coordinate geometry, we know that if a line
is in the form $y = mx$, then the slope of the line is m.

Thus, if $y = 2x$,
$\Rightarrow$ the slope $m = 2$, as shown on the right.

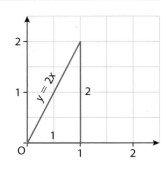

Rate of change is another name for slope.

In this case, the rate of change is 2.

This means that if x increases by 1 unit, y increases by 2 units.

The rate of change of y with respect to x is called the **slope**.

From now on we will use the notation $\dfrac{dy}{dx}$ to represent slope.

The slope (or rate of change) can also be obtained by a mathematical operation called **differentiation**.

Consider again the line $y = 2x$, as shown.

$$\frac{dy}{dx} = \text{slope} = \frac{\text{rise}}{\text{run}} = \frac{2}{1} = 2$$

For the line $y = 2x$, we will examine the table of inputs and outputs.

x	y	1st difference
0	0	
		+2
1	2	
		+2
2	4	
		+2
3	6	

The first difference between the outputs
(i) is constant
(ii) is 2 ... the same as the slope.

The diagram and the table above show that for a linear function –

$$\frac{dy}{dx} = \text{slope} = \text{1st difference}$$

Here is a selection of lines and their slopes:

(i) $y = 4x$ $\qquad \dfrac{dy}{dx} = 4 = \text{slope}$

(ii) $y = -3x + 5$ $\qquad \dfrac{dy}{dx} = -3 = \text{slope}$

(iii) $y = \frac{1}{2}x + 6$ $\qquad \dfrac{dy}{dx} = \frac{1}{2} = \text{slope}$

Rule $\qquad y = ax + b \qquad \dfrac{dy}{dx} = a = \text{slope}$
$\qquad\qquad$ ↑
$\qquad$ (Slope of line)

511

The given graph shows the line $y = 6$.

Here the slope of the line is 0 as there is **no change** in y for any change in x.

This illustrates that if $y = 6$, then $\dfrac{dy}{dx} = 0$.

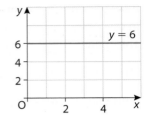

Rule   If $y = 6$ (a constant), $\dfrac{dy}{dx} = 0$

Exercise 18.1

1. Use the given grid to write down the rate of change of y with respect to x.

   Give another name for this rate of change.

   Now write down the value of $\dfrac{dy}{dx}$.

   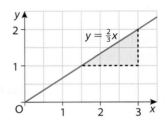

2. Write down the rate of change of y with respect to x $\left(\dfrac{dy}{dx}\right)$ in each of these grids:

   (i)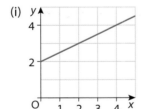
   (ii)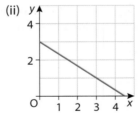
   (iii)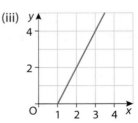

3. Write down $\dfrac{dy}{dx}$ for each of these linear functions:

   (i) $y = 3x$ (ii) $y = 2x - 1$ (iii) $y = 4x + 3$ (iv) $y = 5x + 6$

   (v) $y = -2x$ (vi) $y = -3x + 7$ (vii) $y = 7x - \frac{1}{2}$ (viii) $y = 2$

4. Find the rate of change of y with respect to x $\left(\dfrac{dy}{dx}\right)$ for the line joining

   (i) A and B   (ii) B and C

   (iii) C and D   (iv) D and E.

   Explain why $\dfrac{dy}{dx}$ is negative for the line joining D and E.

   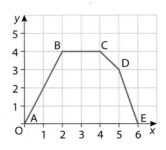

5. $y = 3x - 2$ is a linear function.

By completing the table of outputs on the right, write down the difference between the outputs.

Now write down the value of $\dfrac{dy}{dx}$.

What is the connection between the difference of the outputs and $\dfrac{dy}{dx}$?

x	y
0	−2
1	...
2	...
3	...

6. Make up a function of your own for the following rates of change. (The first one is done for you.)

$\dfrac{dy}{dx}$	Function
$\dfrac{dy}{dx} = 10$	$y = 10x$
$\dfrac{dy}{dx} = 6$	
$\dfrac{dy}{dx} = -4$	
$\dfrac{dy}{dx} = \dfrac{1}{2}$	
$\dfrac{dy}{dx} = 0$	

7. Copy and complete the table below by writing a function to suit the given information. (The first one is done for you.)

y-intercept	$\dfrac{dy}{dx}$	Function
3	2	$y = 2x + 3$
−2	4	
−3	2	
0	4	
2	$\dfrac{1}{2}$	
0	$\dfrac{2}{3}$	

8. (i) An aunt decides to give her niece €50 pocket money on the 1st January and she increases it by €10 per year from then on.
What is the rate of change of pocket money with respect to time (years)?

(ii) A train travels at a steady speed of 80 km/hr.
What is the rate of change of distance (km) with respect to time (hours)?

(iii) A sunflower is 5 cm in height when bought and grows 3 cm per week thereafter.
What is the rate of change of height (cm) in relation to time (weeks)?

9. The distance–time graph shows the journey of a motorcyclist who set out from town A.

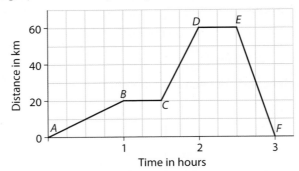

(i)   What is the rate of change of distance in relation to time for the journey from A to B?
(ii) What is the average speed from A to B?
(iii) What is the slope of the line BC?
(iv) What is the average speed between B and C?
(v)   What is the average speed between C and D?
(vi) What is the rate of change of distance in relation to time for the journey from E to F?
      Suggest another way of asking this question.

Section 18.2 The slope of a curve

Consider the curve $y = x^2$, sketched on the right.
$(2, 4)$ is a point on this curve.

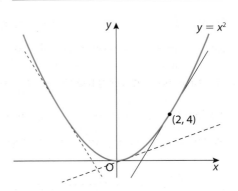

The slope of the curve at $(2, 4)$ is defined as the slope of the tangent at $(2, 4)$.

If the drawing is done accurately, the slope of the tangent will be 4.

The two broken lines on the graph show two more tangents to the curve.
The slopes of these three tangents are all different.
This illustrates that the slope of a curve varies as we move to different points along the curve.

To find the slope of a curve at a particular point, we would need to draw the curve and then find the slope of the tangent to the curve at that point. This will give only an estimate of the slope even if the curve and tangent are drawn accurately.

However, there is a shorter way to find the slope of a curve.
In the previous section we saw that when a linear function is given in the form of $y = f(x)$,
then $\dfrac{dy}{dx}$ represents the slope of the line.

How do we find $\dfrac{dy}{dx}$ for the function $y = x^2$?

The rule for finding $\dfrac{dy}{dx}$ of the function $y = x^n$ is given on the right.

> **1.** If $y = x^n$, then $\dfrac{dy}{dx} = nx^{n-1}$
>
> **2.** If $y = ax^n$, then $\dfrac{dy}{dx} = nax^{n-1}$

The rule for finding $\dfrac{dy}{dx}$ of a function may be described in words as follows:

> Multiply the coefficient of the variable by the power and reduce the power by 1.

We will now use the rule to find $\dfrac{dy}{dx}$ of the function $y = x^2$.

$y = x^2 \Rightarrow \dfrac{dy}{dx} = 2x^{2-1} = 2x^1 = 2x$, i.e. the slope $= 2x$.

What does 'slope $= 2x$' mean?

It means that the slope will change for different values of x.

Now if the slope is $2x$, then at $x = 2$, the slope is $2(2) = 4$.

So we have used differentiation $\left(\text{finding } \dfrac{dy}{dx} \right)$ to show that the slope of the curve is 4 when $x = 2$, as already stated above.

The process of finding the slope of a line or a curve at a point (x, y) is called **differentiation**.

If a function is in the form $y = f(x)$, we use the expression **differentiating y with respect to x** to describe the process of finding $\dfrac{dy}{dx}$.

Since $\dfrac{dy}{dx}$ is derived from the equation of the curve, it is often called the **derived function** or **slope function**.

If a function is in the form $f(x) = \ldots$, the derived function is generally represented by $\boldsymbol{f'(x)}$.

Functions with more than one term

If a function contains more than one term, we differentiate each term separately.

For example, if $y = 3x^2 - 5x + 4$

$\dfrac{dy}{dx} = 6x - 5$

Example 1

Differentiate each of the following with respect to x:

(i) $y = x^2 - 3x + 4$ (ii) $y = 3x^2 + 9x - 5$ (iii) $y = x^3 - 3x^2 + 6x - 7$

(i) $y = x^2 - 3x + 4 \Rightarrow \dfrac{dy}{dx} = 2x - 3$

(ii) $y = 3x^2 + 9x - 5 \Rightarrow \dfrac{dy}{dx} = 6x + 9$

(iii) $y = x^3 - 3x^2 + 6x - 7 \Rightarrow \dfrac{dy}{dx} = 3x^2 - 6x + 6$

Finding the value of a derivative

A function is defined by $f(x) = x^2 - 3x + 2$.

$f'(x) = 2x - 3$; $2x - 3$ is called the **derivative** of $f(x)$.

$f'(x)$ represents the slope of the tangent to the curve at any point.

At $x = 4$, then $f'(4) = 2(4) - 3 = 5$.

This means that 5 is the slope of the tangent to the curve at the point where $x = 4$.

Example 2

If $y = 3x^2 - 2x + 4$, find the value of $\dfrac{dy}{dx}$ at $x = -2$.

$y = 3x^2 - 2x + 4 \Rightarrow \dfrac{dy}{dx} = 6x - 2$

$\qquad\qquad = 6(-2) - 2 \text{ at } x = -2$

$\qquad\qquad = -12 - 2 = -14$

$\therefore \dfrac{dy}{dx} = -14 \text{ at } x = -2.$

Exercise 18.2

Differentiate with respect to x each of the functions in numbers **1–21**.

1. $y = 2x + 3$

2. $y = 3x - 4$

3. $y = 7x - 1$

4. $y = x^2$

5. $y = 2x^2 + 6x$

6. $y = 5x^2 - 3x + 4$

7. $y = x^2 - 8x - 4$

8. $y = \frac{1}{2}x^2 - 3x$

9. $y = 3x^2 - 4$

10. $y = x^3$

11. $y = x^3 + 2x - 3$

12. $y = 2x^3 - 5x^2$

13. $y = 3x^3 - 2x^2 - x$

14. $y = x^3 - x^2 + 2x + 5$

15. $y = \frac{1}{3}x^3 - x^2 + 4x$

16. $y = x^3 - 4x^2 + 9$

17. $y = 1 - 2x + x^2$

18. $y = -5 + 2x - 3x^2$

19. $y = -x^3 + 2x - 4$

20. $y = 5 - x^2 + 2x^3$

21. $y = 3x - 4x^2 + \frac{1}{3}x^3$

22. If $y = x^2 - 3x$, find the value of $\dfrac{dy}{dx}$ when $x = 2$.

23. If $y = 2 - 4x + x^2$, find the value of $\dfrac{dy}{dx}$ when $x = -1$.

24. If $f(x) = 4x^2 - 3x + 2$, find $f'(1)$.

25. If $y = x^3 - x^2 - 3x + 7$, find the value of $\dfrac{dy}{dx}$ when $x = 2$.

26. If $y = x^2 - 3x$, find the slope of the tangent to the curve at the point where $x = 3$.

27. If $f(x) = 4x - 3x^2$, find the slope of the tangent to the curve at the point where $x = -2$.

28. If $A = 2k^2 - 3k$, find the value of $\dfrac{dA}{dk}$ when $k = 1$.

29. If $V = 2h^2 + h + 5$, find the value of $\dfrac{dV}{dh}$ when $h = 3$.

30. If $F = 6 + 4t - 2t^2$, find the value of $\dfrac{dF}{dt}$ when $t = 4$.

31. Here is the graph of the function

$$y = 2x^2 - 4x - 3.$$

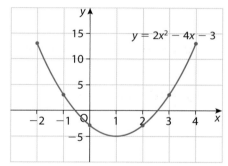

   (i) Find the slope of the tangent to the curve at the point where $x = 3$.

  (ii) Find the slope of the tangent to the curve at the point where $x = -1$. Explain why your answer is a negative number.

 (iii) What is the slope of the tangent to the curve at the point where $x = 1$? Explain your answer in the context of the graph.

Section 18.3 Tangents and curves

In the previous section, it was shown that $\dfrac{dy}{dx}$ represents the slope of the tangent to a curve at any point on the curve.

To find the equation of a tangent to the curve $y = f(x)$ at the point (x_1, y_1), follow these steps:

> $\dfrac{dy}{dx}$ is the slope of the tangent to the curve at any point (x, y) on the curve.

1. Find $\dfrac{dy}{dx}$.

2. Find the value of $\dfrac{dy}{dx}$ at the given value for x.
This value is the required slope.

3. Use the slope found in **2.** above and the given point to find the equation of the tangent using $y - y_1 = m(x - x_1)$.

Example 1

Find the slope of the tangent to the curve $y = 3x^2 + 4x - 5$ at the point $(1, 2)$.
Hence find the equation of the tangent at this point.

The slope of the tangent is $\dfrac{dy}{dx}$.

$\dfrac{dy}{dx} = 6x + 4$

$\qquad = 6(1) + 4 \;\; \dots x = 1$ at the point $(1, 2)$

$\qquad = 10$

$\therefore$ the slope of the tangent $= 10$.

Equation of tangent: $y - y_1 = m(x - x_1)$

$\qquad\qquad\qquad\quad y - 2 = 10(x - 1) \;\; \dots (x_1, y_1) = (1, 2)$

$\qquad\qquad\quad \Rightarrow y - 2 = 10x - 10$

$\qquad\qquad\quad \Rightarrow 10x - y - 8 = 0$ is the equation of the tangent.

Example 2

Find the coordinates of the point on the curve $y = x^2 + 2x + 1$ at which the slope of the tangent to the curve is 4.

Since the slope of the tangent $= 4$, then $\dfrac{dy}{dx} = 4$.

$\qquad \dfrac{dy}{dx} = 2x + 2$

$\Rightarrow 2x + 2 = 4$

$\Rightarrow \qquad 2x = 2 \Rightarrow x = 1$

To find the y-value of the point, we substitute 1 for x in the given equation.

$x = 1 \Rightarrow y = (1)^2 + 2(1) + 1$

$\qquad\quad \Rightarrow y = 4$

$\therefore$ the point on the curve is $(1, 4)$.

Example 3

Find the coordinates of the point on the curve $y = x^2 - 3x + 7$ at which the tangent to the curve is parallel to $y = 3x + 4$.

Slope of the line $y = 3x + 4$ is 3.
$\Rightarrow$ Slope of tangent to the curve is also 3.

Slope of curve is given by $\dfrac{dy}{dx}$.

$y = x^2 - 3x + 7 \Rightarrow \dfrac{dy}{dx} = 2x - 3$

Slope $= 3 \Rightarrow 2x - 3 = 3$
$\qquad\qquad \Rightarrow \quad 2x = 6 \Rightarrow x = 3$
When $x = 3$, $y = (3)^2 - 3(3) + 7$ i.e. $y = 7$

$\therefore$ the point on the curve is $(3, 7)$.

Exercise 18.3

1. Find the slope of the tangent to the curve at the given point in each of the following functions:
   (i) $y = x^2 - 2$ at $(2, 2)$
   (ii) $y = x^2 - 2x + 3$ at $(2, 3)$
   (iii) $y = x^2 - 2x$ at $(2, 0)$
   (iv) $y = x^2 - 4x + 5$ at $(3, 2)$
   (v) $y = 3x^2 - 24x + 48$ at $(3, -1)$
   (vi) $y = x^3 - 4x + 7$ at $(1, 4)$

2. Find the slope and hence the equation of the tangent to each of the following curves at the given point:
   (i) $y = x^2 - 3x + 2$ at $(3, 2)$
   (ii) $y = x^2 + 6x + 5$ at $(-1, 0)$
   (iii) $y = x^2 - 3x + 2$ at $(0, 2)$
   (iv) $y = 6 + x - x^2$ at $(2, 4)$
   (v) $y = 3x^2 + x - 7$ at $(-2, 3)$
   (vi) $y = 2x^2 - 3x + 4$ at $(1, 3)$

3. Find the x-value of the point at which the slope of the tangent to the curve $y = 8 + 2x - x^2$ is 6.

4. At what point on the curve $y = x^2 - x$ is the slope of the tangent equal to 1?

5. Find the point on the curve $y = 2x^2 - x - 4$ at which the slope of the tangent is 3.

6. The curve on the right is the graph of the function $f(x) = x^2 - 2x - 3$.

   If the value of $f'(x)$ at the point P is 2, find its coordinates.

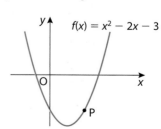

$f(x) = x^2 - 2x - 3$

7. Find the point on the curve $y = x^2 - 2x - 15$ at which the slope of the tangent is 0.

8. Find the point on the curve $y = 2x^2 - 3x + 1$ at which the slope of the tangent is 1.

9. Find the value of a if the slope of the tangent to the curve $y = x^2 + ax$, at the point where $x = -1$, is 3.

10. Show that the tangent to the curve $y = x^2 - 3x + 4$, at the point where $x = 1\frac{1}{2}$, is parallel to the x-axis.

11. The graph of the function
$$f(x) = x^2 + x - 2 \text{ is shown.}$$
The equation of the tangent to the curve at the point A is
$$y = -5x - 11.$$
Using the slope of the tangent, find the coordinates of A.

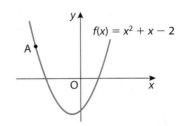

12. Find the point on the curve $y = 2x^2 - 2x + 3$ at which the slope of the curve is 6. Hence find the equation of the tangent at this point.

13. Find the point on the curve $y = 2x^2 - 8x + 3$ where the tangent is parallel to the line $4x - y + 2 = 0$.

14. Find the coordinates of the point on the curve $y = x^2 - 3x + 7$ where the tangent to the curve is parallel to the line $y = 3x + 4$.

15. If the slope of the tangent to the curve $y = kx^3 - 2x^2 - x + 7$ is 3 at the point where $x = 2$, find the value of k.

Section 18.4 Maximum and minimum turning points

The curve shown below has **turning points** at A and B.

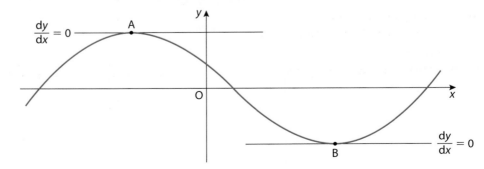

Notice that at A and B, the tangents to the curve are parallel to the x-axis.
Thus, the slope of each tangent is zero.

Since $\dfrac{dy}{dx}$ is the slope of the tangent to a curve, then $\dfrac{dy}{dx} = 0$ at the points A and B.

Remember At the turning point(s) on a curve, $\dfrac{dy}{dx} = 0$.

At the point A, we have a **maximum turning point**.
It is generally referred to as a **local maximum**.
At the point B, we have a **minimum turning point** (or **local minimum**).

Finding the turning point(s) of a curve

To find the turning point (or points) of a curve, we use the following steps:

1. Find $\dfrac{dy}{dx}$.

2. Let $\dfrac{dy}{dx} = 0$ and solve the equation to find the value(s) for x.

3. Substitute these value(s) for x in the given function to find the corresponding y-value(s).

4. If there are two turning points, the higher point (i.e. the point with the greater y-value) will be the maximum turning point. The other point will be the minimum turning point.

Note: Quadratic functions have one turning point only.
The function $y = ax^2 + bx + c$
(i) has a minimum turning point if $a > 0$.
(ii) has a maximum turning point if $a < 0$.

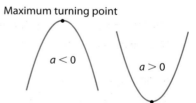

Maximum turning point

$a < 0$ $a > 0$

Minimum turning point

Example 1

The graph of the function $f(x) = x^2 - 2x - 5$ is shown on the right.

(i) Use the graph to write down the coordinates of the minimum turning point.

(ii) Now use calculus to verify your answer.

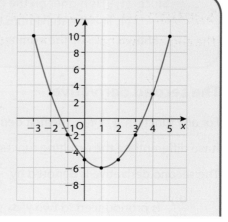

(i) The minimum turning point is $(1, -6)$.

(ii) Now we find the turning point using calculus:

$$f(x) = x^2 - 2x - 5$$
$$f'(x) = 2x - 2$$
$$2x - 2 = 0 \Rightarrow 2x = 2 \Rightarrow x = 1$$

When $x = 1$, $y = (1)^2 - 2(1) - 5 = 1 - 2 - 5 = -6$

$\therefore$ $(1, -6)$ is the minimum turning point, as found above.

Example 2

Find the coordinates of the local maximum and the local minimum of the curve $y = x^3 - 9x^2 + 15x + 2$.

1. Find $\dfrac{dy}{dx}$

$$y = x^3 - 9x^2 + 15x + 2 \Rightarrow \dfrac{dy}{dx} = 3x^2 - 18x + 15$$

2. When $\dfrac{dy}{dx} = 0$, $3x^2 - 18x + 15 = 0$

$\Rightarrow x^2 - 6x + 5 = 0$ ... divide each term by 3
$\Rightarrow (x - 1)(x - 5) = 0$
$\Rightarrow x = 1$ and $x = 5$.

$x = 1 \Rightarrow y = (1)^3 - 9(1)^2 + 15(1) + 2$
$\qquad = 9$
$x = 5 \Rightarrow y = (5)^3 - 9(5)^2 + 15(5) + 2$
$\qquad = -23$

$\Rightarrow (1, 9)$ and $(5, -23)$ are turning points.

Since $(1, 9)$ is higher on the graph than $(5, -23)$, then
$\qquad (1, 9)$ is the maximum turning point
and $(5, -23)$ is the minimum turning point.

The second derivative

For any function $y = f(x)$, the first derivative is $\dfrac{dy}{dx}$ or $f'(x)$.

It we differentiate the resulting function, we get the **second derivative**.

The second derivative is denoted by $\dfrac{d^2y}{dx^2}$ or $f''(x)$.

$\dfrac{d^2y}{dx^2}$ is pronounced 'd two y, dx squared'.

Example 3

(i) If $y = 3x^2 - 5x + 2$, find $\dfrac{dy}{dx}$ and $\dfrac{d^2y}{dx^2}$.

(ii) If $f(x) = x^3 - 2x^2 + 4x - 5$, find $f''(x)$ and hence $f''(-2)$.

(i) $y = 3x^2 - 5x + 2 \Rightarrow \dfrac{dy}{dx} = 6x - 5$

$\qquad\qquad\qquad\qquad \dfrac{d^2y}{dx^2} = 6.$

(ii) $f(x) = x^3 - 2x^2 + 4x - 5$

$\qquad f'(x) = 3x^2 - 4x + 4$

$\qquad f''(x) = 6x - 4$

$\qquad f''(-2) = 6(-2) - 4 = -12 - 4 = -16$

$\qquad \therefore \;\; f''(-2) = -16$

Using the second derivative to determine the nature of a turning point

In the given diagram, the positive signs (+) indicate where the slope of the curve is positive $\left(\text{i.e. } \dfrac{dy}{dx} > 0\right)$ and the negative signs (−) indicate where the slope of the curve is negative.

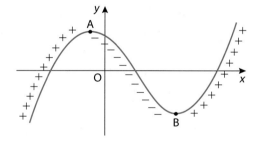

As the point A is approached from the left, the slope of the curve is positive but decreasing; at A, the slope is zero, and to the right of A, the slope is negative. Thus as we go through the point A, the slope of the curve changes from positive to negative, (i.e. is decreasing). Thus the rate of change of $\dfrac{dy}{dx}$, i.e. $\dfrac{d^2y}{dx^2}$, is negative.

This shows that $\dfrac{d^2y}{dx^2}$ is negative at a maximum turning point.

Similarly, $\dfrac{d^2y}{dx^2}$ is positive at the minimum turning point.

The second derivative test for turning points

At a maximum turning point, $\dfrac{dy}{dx} = 0$ and $\dfrac{d^2y}{dx^2} < 0$, i.e. negative.

At a minimum turning point, $\dfrac{dy}{dx} = 0$ and $\dfrac{d^2y}{dx^2} > 0$, i.e. positive.

Example 4

Find the coordinates of the turning points of the curve $y = x^3 - 3x^2 + 5$.
Use the second derivative test to determine whether each turning point is a
maximum or minimum one.

$y = x^3 - 3x^2 + 5$

$\dfrac{dy}{dx} = 3x^2 - 6x$

$3x^2 - 6x = 0 \Rightarrow x^2 - 2x = 0 \Rightarrow x(x - 2) = 0 \Rightarrow x = 0$ or $x = 2$.

$x = 0 \Rightarrow y = (0)^2 - 3(0) + 5 \Rightarrow y = 5 \Rightarrow (0, 5)$ is a turning point.

$x = 2 \Rightarrow y = (2)^3 - 3(2)^2 + 5 \Rightarrow y = 1 \Rightarrow (2, 1)$ is also a turning point.

We now find the values of $\dfrac{d^2y}{dx^2}$ at $x = 0$ and $x = 2$.

$\dfrac{dy}{dx} = 3x^2 - 6x \Rightarrow \dfrac{d^2y}{dx^2} = 6x - 6$.

At $x = 0$, $\dfrac{d^2y}{dx^2} = 6(0) - 6 = -6$ (negative)

Since $\dfrac{d^2y}{dx^2}$ is negative, $(0, 5)$ is a maximum turning point.

At $x = 2$, $\dfrac{d^2y}{dx^2} = 6(2) - 6 = 6$ (positive)

Since $\dfrac{d^2y}{dx^2}$ is positive, $(2, 1)$ is a minimum turning point.

Increasing and decreasing

Examining the given curve from left to right,
we can see that it is rising (or increasing) from
A to B and decreasing from B to C.

From A to B, the slope of the tangent $\left(\text{i.e. } \dfrac{dy}{dx}\right)$
is positive.

From B to C, the slope of the tangent is negative.

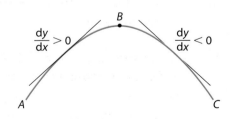

Remember

When the curve is increasing, $\dfrac{dy}{dx} > 0$.

When the curve is decreasing, $\dfrac{dy}{dx} < 0$.

Example 5

For what values of x is the curve $y = 2x^2 + 8x - 5$ increasing?

If the curve is increasing, $\dfrac{dy}{dx} > 0$.

$y = 2x^2 + 8x - 5 \Rightarrow \dfrac{dy}{dx} = 4x + 8$

$\dfrac{dy}{dx} > 0 \Rightarrow 4x + 8 > 0$

$\qquad\qquad \Rightarrow 4x > -8 \Rightarrow x > -2$

$\therefore$ the curve is increasing for $x > -2$.

Exercise 18.4

1. The graph of the function $y = x^2 - 1$ is shown.
   A, B and C are three points on the curve.

   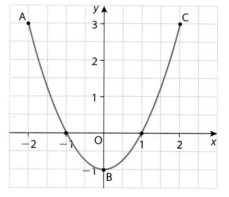

   (i) What is the slope of the curve at the point B?
   Explain your answer.
   (ii) What is the point B called?
   (iii) Use the graph to write down the coordinates of the minimum turning point.
   (iv) Now use calculus to verify your answer.
   (v) Copy and complete this sentence:
   "When the coefficient of x^2 of a quadratic function is ... , the curve will have a minimum turning point."

2. Find the turning point of each of the following quadratic functions and use the coefficient of x^2 to state whether the turning point is a maximum or minimum point.

   (i) $y = x^2 + 2x - 1$ (ii) $y = 3x^2 - 6x + 4$ (iii) $y = x^2 - 4x + 9$
   (iv) $y = 4 + 8x - 2x^2$ (v) $y = 5 + 6x - x^2$ (vi) $y = x^2 - x + 4$

Find the coordinates of the two turning points of the functions in numbers (**3–8**) and state if each turning point is a local maximum or a local minimum.

3. $y = x^3 - 3x^2$

4. $y = x^3 - 6x^2 + 9x - 10$

5. $y = x^3 - 3x^2 - 9x + 6$

6. $y = 2x^3 - 3x^2 - 12x + 7$

7. $y = 2x^3 - 9x^2 + 12x$

8. $y = x^3 - 6x^2 + 9x$

9. For the curve $y = x^2 - 4x + 4$,
  (i) state whether the curve has a maximum or minimum turning point
  (ii) find this turning point
  (iii) find the value of x at which the slope of the curve is 2.

10. Find the coordinates of the points on the curve $y = x^3 - 3x^2 - 9x + 12$ at which the tangents to the curve are parallel to the x-axis.

11. Given the function $y = x^3 - 3x^2 + 4x - 2$.

Find (i) $\dfrac{dy}{dx}$ (ii) $\dfrac{d^2y}{dx^2}$

12. Find the second derivative, $\dfrac{d^2y}{dx^2}$, for each of these functions:

  (i) $y = 3x^2 - 4x + 2$ (ii) $y = x^3 - 4x^2 + 6$ (iii) $y = \frac{1}{3}x^3 - 8x^2 + 3x$

13. The graph of the function
$y = 3 + 2x - x^2$ is shown.

  (i) Find the coordinates of the turning point of this curve.

  (ii) Find the value of $\dfrac{d^2y}{dx^2}$ at this turning point.

  (iii) How does your answer to (ii) indicate whether the turning point is a maximum or minimum one?

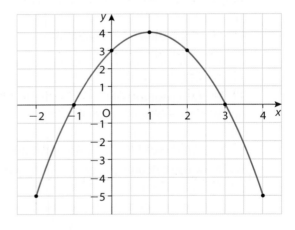

14. Find the turning point of the function $y = x^2 - 4x + 5$.
By finding the sign of $\dfrac{d^2y}{dx^2}$, state whether the turning point is a maximum or minimum one.

15. The function $y = x^3 + 3x^2 - 9x$ is graphed on the right.
  (i) Show that there is a turning point at $(1, -5)$ and find the coordinates of the other turning point.

  (ii) Find $\dfrac{d^2y}{dx^2}$.

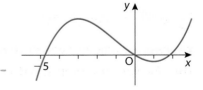

  (iii) Use the second derivative test to determine if each turning point is either a maximum or minimum.

16. Let $f(x) = x^3 - 3x^2 + 2$.
  (i) Find $f'(x)$, the derivative of $f(x)$.
  (ii) Hence find the coordinates of the local maximum and local minimum points of $f(x)$ by using the second derivative test.

17. Find the coordinates of the local maximum of the curve $y = 6x^2 - x^3$, given that the curve has a local minimum at $(0, 0)$.

18. Let $f(x) = x^3 - ax + 7$ for all $x \in R$ and for $a \in R$.
  (i) The slope of the tangent to the curve $y = f(x)$ at $x = 1$ is -9.
     Find the value of a.
  (ii) Hence find the coordinates of the local maximum point and the local minimum point of the curve $y = f(x)$.

19. Find the coordinates of the local maximum of the curve $y = 12x - x^3$.
  Verify that $\dfrac{d^2y}{dx^2}$ is negative at this point.

20. Let $f(x) = x^3 - 3x^2 + ax + 1, \ a, x \in R$.
  $f(x)$ has a turning point at $x = -1$.
  (i) Find the value of a.
  (ii) Find the coordinates of the two turning points of $f(x)$ and state if each point is a local maximum or a local minimum.

21. For what values of x is the curve $f(x) = x^2 - 6x - 7$ increasing?

22. For what values of x is the curve $f(x) = 14 - 8x - x^2$ decreasing?

Section 18.5 Graphical representation of the slope function

The curve on the right is the graph of the function
  $y = x^2 - 2x - 3$.

$\dfrac{dy}{dx}$ for this function is $2x - 2$.

$y = 2x - 2$ is the **derived** or **slope function**.

The blue line represents this slope function.

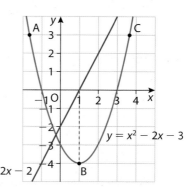

$y = x^2 - 2x - 3$

$y = 2x - 2$

From the two graphs, the following can be observed:
  (i) From A to B on the curve, the slope is negative.
     For this x-interval, the slope function (blue line) is also negative, i.e., the blue line is below the x-axis.

(ii) From B to C on the curve, the slope is positive.
For this x-interval, the slope function (blue line) is also positive, i.e., the blue line is above the x-axis.

(iii) The slope of the curve at the point B is zero, i.e., $\dfrac{dy}{dx} = 0$.

At the point B, $x = 1$.
Notice that the slope function is also zero at the point where $x = 1$.
This illustrates that $\dfrac{dy}{dx}$ (the slope function) is zero at a turning point.

The slope function of a cubic function

The red curve on the right is the graph of a cubic function, $y = f(x)$.
The blue curve is the graph of its slope function, $y = g(x)$.

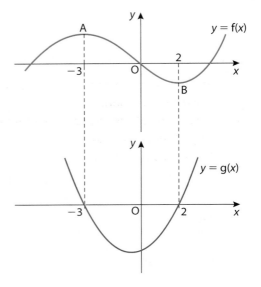

Some of the features of these curves are:

> In the function $y = f(x)$, for $x < -3$, the slope is positive.
This is represented in the slope function $y = g(x)$, where $g(x)$ is positive for $x < -3$.

> From A to B the slope of the curve is negative.
That is, from $x > -3$ and $x < 2$, the slope is negative.
It can be seen that the slope function is negative from $-3 < x < 2$.

> At $x = -3$ and $x = 2$, the slope of the cubic function is zero.
At these two x-values, the slope function is also zero.

> For $x > 2$, the slope of the cubic function is positive.
For $x > 2$, the slope function reflects this, since it is also positive for $x > 2$.

Example 1

The diagram shows the line $y = 3x + 2$.
Copy the diagram and draw the slope function.

$$y = 3x + 2 \Rightarrow \frac{dy}{dx} = 3$$

The slope function is $y = 3$.

The line (or slope function) $y = 3$ is shown on the diagram.

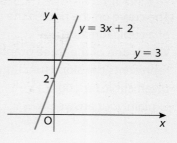

Example 2

The curve on the right is the graph of a quadratic function.
Which one of the lines below represents the slope function of the given curve?
Explain your answer.

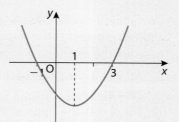

(A) 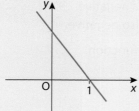 (B) 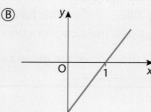 (C)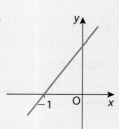

The line Ⓑ represents the slope function for these reasons:

(i)   For $x > 1$, the slope of the curve is positive and the y-value of the line is also positive for $x > 1$.

(ii) For $x < 1$, the slope of the curve is negative and the y-value of the line is also negative for $x < 1$.

(iii) At $x = 1$, the slope of the curve is zero.
      The y-value of the line is also zero at $x = 1$.

Example 3

The curve on the right is the graph of a cubic function.
Which one of the three graphs below represents the slope function of the given cubic function?
Explain your answer.

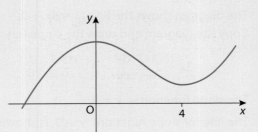

Ⓐ 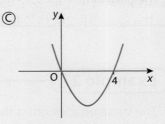 Ⓑ Ⓒ

Graph Ⓒ represents the slope function of the given cubic function.
These are the reasons:

(i)   At $x = 0$, the slope of the cubic function is zero and the slope function is zero at $x = 0$.

(ii) For $x < 0$, the slope of the cubic function is positive.
For $x < 0$, curve Ⓒ is also positive.

(iii) For $x > 0$ and < 4, the slope of the cubic function is negative.
Between these two x-values, the slope function is also negative.

Hence, graph Ⓒ is the slope function of the given cubic function.

Exercise 18.5

1. The graph of the function $y = f(x)$ is shown.

   (i)   For what value of x is the slope of the curve zero?

   (ii) For what range of values of x is the slope of the curve positive?

   (iii) For what range of values of x is the slope of the curve negative?

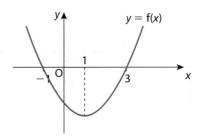

2. The graph of the function $y = f(x)$ is shown on the right.

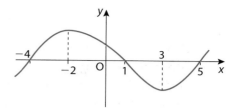

  (i) Explain what is meant by '$f'(x) > 0$'?

  (ii) For what range of values of x is $f'(x) > 0$?

  (iii) For what range of values of x is $f'(x) < 0$?

  (iv) For what values of x is $f'(x) = 0$?

3. Give three reasons why the given line represents the slope function of the given curve.

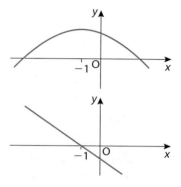

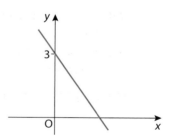

4. The graph of $y = -2x + 3$ is shown.

Which one of the three lines below represents the slope function of this line?
Explain your answer.

Ⓐ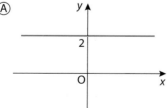

Ⓑ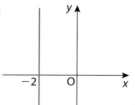

Ⓒ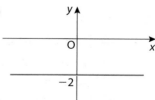

5. The graph of the function $y = f(x)$ is shown on the right.

Which one of the three lines below represents the graph of the function $y = f'(x)$?

Give a reason for your answer.

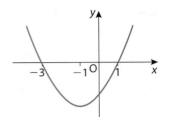

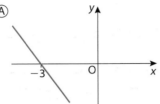

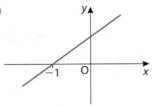

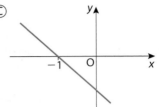

6. The diagram on the right is the graph of the function $y = f(x)$.

Which one of the three graphs below represents the graph of the slope function $y = f'(x)$?

Explain your answer.

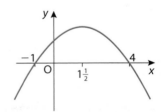

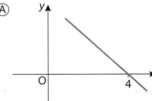

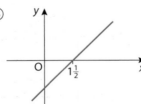

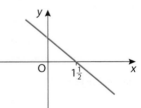

7. The graph of the function $y = f(x)$ is shown on the right.

Which one of the three graphs below represents the slope function of the given curve?

Explain your answer.

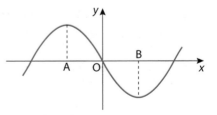

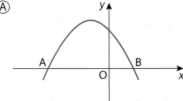

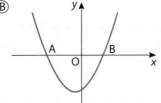

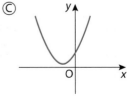

Section 18.6 Rates of change

In previous sections we have seen that $\dfrac{dy}{dx}$ represents the rate of change of y with respect to x.

If $\dfrac{dy}{dx} = 2$, this means that y is increasing by 2 units for every 1 unit that x increases.

We have also seen that for a linear function, the rate of change is constant and this rate of change gives the slope of the line.

If a car moves at a constant speed, the rate of change of distance with respect to time is also constant. However, most objects do not travel at a constant speed. If the speed of a car varies, then the rate of change of distance with respect to time will be constantly changing.

Consider the distance–time graphs shown on the right.
The straight line through A shows a constant speed of 60 km/hr.
By comparison, the graph through the points B, C and D shows the motorist travelling at varying speeds.

Although we do not know the actual speed of this car at any particular time, we can work out the average speed of the car travelling over a one-hour time period.

The average speed is given by $\dfrac{\text{distance travelled}}{\text{time taken}} = \dfrac{30}{1} = 30$ km/hr.

This average speed is the slope of the line OD.
If we require the average speed of the car between the points B and C, we find the slope of the line segment [BC].

In general, the **average rate of change** between two points on the graph of a function is the slope of the line joining these points.

For example, the average rate of change of y with respect to x between the points P and Q is given by the slope of [PQ]:

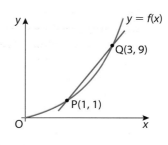

$$\text{Slope} = \frac{y_2 - y_1}{x_2 - x_1} = \frac{9 - 1}{3 - 1} = 4$$

The slope of the tangent to the curve at the specific point P is found by getting $\dfrac{dy}{dx}$ and finding its value when $x = 1$.

We refer to the rate of change at a specific point as the **instantaneous rate of change**.

Application of rates of change

We have already seen that $\dfrac{dy}{dx}$ represents the rate of change of y with respect to x for any function $y = f(x)$.

Similarly, $\dfrac{dV}{dr}$ represents the rate of change of V with respect to r,

and $\dfrac{dS}{dt}$ represents the rate of change of S with respect to t.

Example 1

Water is being collected in a water tank.
The volume, V cubic metres, of water in the tank after time t minutes is given by
$$V = 3t^2 + 4t + 2.$$
Find the rate of change of volume with respect to time when $t = 2$.

$$V = 3t^2 + 4t + 2$$
$$\frac{dV}{dt} = 6t + 4 \;\ldots\; \frac{dV}{dt} \text{ is the rate of change of volume with respect to } t$$
$$\quad\;\; = 6(2) + 4 \;\ldots\; \text{when } t = 2$$
$$\quad\;\; = 16$$
$$\quad\;\; = 16 \, \text{m}^3/\text{min}$$

Displacement, velocity and acceleration

One of the key applications of rates of change is in the study of the motion of a particle.

If an object moves in a straight line, the distance, s metres, travelled after t seconds, is generally given by a formula of the type –

$$s = 3 - 6t + t^3.$$

When a body is moving, we have two rates of change;
(i) **speed**, which is the rate at which distance travelled changes with respect to time.

$\dfrac{ds}{dt}$ represents this change, i.e. $\dfrac{ds}{dt} = $ speed (or **velocity**).

If $\dfrac{ds}{dt}$ is positive, the particle is moving away from a fixed point P.

If $\dfrac{ds}{dt}$ is negative, the particle is moving towards P.

(ii) **acceleration**, which is the rate of change of speed (v) with respect to time.

$\dfrac{dv}{dt}$ represents this change, i.e. $\dfrac{dv}{dt}$ = acceleration.

$\dfrac{dv}{dt}$ and $\dfrac{d^2s}{dt^2}$ both denote acceleration.

$\dfrac{d^2s}{dt^2}$ is got by differentiating $\dfrac{ds}{dt}$.

Thus, if $s = 3t^3 - t^2 + 4t$,

then $\dfrac{ds}{dt} = 9t^2 - 2t + 4$

and $\dfrac{d^2s}{dt^2} = 18t - 2$.

Remember

> If $s = 3 - 6t + t^3$ represents the distance s (in metres) travelled by an object after t (seconds) then,
>
> (i) $\dfrac{ds}{dt}$ = speed (in m/sec) after t seconds
>
> (ii) $\dfrac{d^2s}{dt^2}$ = acceleration (in m/sec²) after t seconds

Note:
> Acceleration is given in metres per second per second – written as m/sec².
> If $\dfrac{d^2s}{dt^2}$ is negative, then the speed is decreasing.

Example 2

A body moves along a straight line and its distance, s metres, from a fixed point on the line after t seconds is given by

$$s = 3t^3 - 4t + 6.$$

Find
(i) its speed after t seconds
(ii) its speed after 2 seconds
(iii) after how many seconds the body is at rest
(iv) its acceleration after 3 seconds.

(i) The speed is represented by $\frac{ds}{dt}$.

$$s = 3t^3 - 4t + 6$$

$$\Rightarrow \frac{ds}{dt} = 9t^2 - 4$$

$\therefore$ the speed is $(9t^2 - 4)$ m/sec.

(ii) To find the speed after 2 seconds, substitute 2 for t in $\frac{ds}{dt}$.

At $t = 2$, $9t^2 - 4 = 9(2)^2 - 4$
$$= 9(4) - 4 = 32 \text{ m/sec.}$$

(iii) The body is at rest when the speed is zero.

Speed $= 0 \Rightarrow 9t^2 - 4 = 0$
$$\Rightarrow 9t^2 = 4$$
$$\Rightarrow t^2 = \tfrac{4}{9} \Rightarrow t = \tfrac{2}{3}$$

$\therefore$ the body is at rest after $\tfrac{2}{3}$ of a second.

(iv) Acceleration is represented by $\frac{d^2s}{dt^2}$.

$$\frac{ds}{dt} = 9t^2 - 4 \Rightarrow \frac{d^2s}{dt^2} = 18t$$

At $t = 3$, $18t = 18(3) = 54 \text{ m/sec}^2.$

Example 3

A rocket is fired vertically upwards.

After t seconds, its height, h metres, is given by the formula $h = 100t - 5t^2$.

Find   (i) the height of the rocket after 2 seconds

       (ii) the velocity of the rocket after 3 seconds

      (iii) after how many seconds the rocket is momentarily at rest

      (iv) the maximum height reached by the rocket.

(i) To find the height of the rocket after 2 seconds, we substitute 2 for t in the given formula.

$$h = 100t - 5t^2$$
At $t = 2, h = 100(2) - 5(2)^2$
$$= 200 - 20 = 180 \text{ metres}$$

$\therefore$ the height $= 180$ metres after 2 seconds.

(ii) Velocity $= \dfrac{dh}{dt}$.

$$h = 100t - 5t^2 \Rightarrow \dfrac{dh}{dt} = 100 - 10t$$

$$= 100 - 10(3) \text{ after 3 seconds}$$

$$\Rightarrow \quad \text{velocity} = 70 \text{ m/s after 3 seconds.}$$

(iii) The rocket is at rest when the speed is zero.

$$\text{Speed} = 0 \Rightarrow \dfrac{dh}{dt} = 0$$

$$\Rightarrow 100 - 10t = 0$$

$$\Rightarrow \qquad 10t = 100 \Rightarrow t = 10$$

∴ the rocket is momentarily at rest after 10 seconds.

(iv) The maximum height is reached after 10 seconds, i.e., when the body is at rest.

When $t = 10$, $\quad h = 100(10) - 5(10)^2$

$$= 1000 - 500$$

$$= 500 \text{ metres}$$

∴ the maximum height reached is 500 metres.

Exercise 18.6

1. A body moves s metres in t seconds such that $s = 2t^2 - 4t + 4$.
   Find   (i)   the distance travelled after 4 seconds.
        (ii) the distance travelled after 6 seconds.
        (iii) What is the meaning of $\dfrac{ds}{dt}$?
        (iv) What is the speed of the body after 5 seconds?
        (v) What does $\dfrac{ds}{dt} = 0$ mean?
        (vi) After how many seconds is the body at rest?

2. A motorcyclist accelerates in a straight line away from a starting point P.
   The distance travelled, s (in metres), after t seconds is given by $s = t^2$.
   (i)   Find the distance travelled after 2 seconds.
   (ii) Find the distance travelled after 6 seconds.
   (iii) Find his average speed, in metres per second, between $t = 2$ and $t = 6$.
   (iv) Find his speed after 5 seconds.

3. A car, starting at $t = 0$ seconds, travels a distance of s metres in t seconds where

$$s = 30t - \frac{9}{4}t^2.$$

   (i) Find the distance travelled in the first 4 seconds.
   (ii) Find the speed of the car after 2 seconds.
   (iii) After how many seconds is the speed of the car equal to zero?
   (iv) Find the distance travelled by the car up to the time its speed is zero.

4. A particle is fired vertically upwards and its height, h metres, after any number of seconds, t, is given by the formula $h = 50t - 2t^2$.
   (i) Find the height of the particle after 2 seconds.
   (ii) Find the speed of the particle after 3 seconds.
   (iii) What does $\dfrac{dh}{dt} = 0$ mean in the context of the equation?
   (iv) After how many seconds does the particle stop rising?

5. If $s = t^3 - 3t^2 + 9t + 4$, find
   (i) the value of $\dfrac{ds}{dt}$ when $t = 2$
   (ii) the value of $\dfrac{d^2s}{dt^2}$ when $t = 3$.

6. A stone is thrown vertically upwards and the height, h metres, reached after t seconds, is given by the formula $h = 50t - 5t^2$.
   Find   (i) the speed of the stone after 3 seconds
          (ii) after how many seconds the speed is equal to zero
          (iii) the greatest height reached by the stone.

7. The distance, s metres, travelled by an object in t seconds is given by the formula

$$s = t^3 - 2t^2 + 3t.$$

   (i) Find the distance travelled after 2 seconds.
   (ii) Find the speed of the object after 3 seconds.
   (iii) Find $\dfrac{d^2s}{dt^2}$.
   (iv) What does $\dfrac{d^2s}{dt^2}$ represent?
   (v) Find the acceleration of the object after 4 seconds.

8. The distance travelled, s, in metres, by an object after any number of seconds, t, is given by the formula $s = 3t^3 - 4t + 6$.
   Find   (i) the speed of the object after 1 second
          (ii) the acceleration after 3 seconds
          (iii) after how many seconds the speed is equal to zero.

9. A projectile is fired vertically upwards and its height, h metres, after any number of seconds, t, is given by the formula

$$h = 48t - 2t^2.$$

Find   (i) the height of the projectile after 3 seconds
      (ii) its speed after 3 seconds
     (iii) its acceleration
    (iv) after how many seconds the projectile is momentarily at rest
     (v) the maximum height reached by the projectile.

10. A lorry is travelling along a motorway. Suddenly, the brakes are applied. From the time the brakes are applied $(t = 0$ seconds), the distance travelled by the lorry, in metres, is given by

$$s = 30t - \frac{t^2}{4}.$$

  (i) What is the speed of the lorry at the instant the brakes are applied?
 (ii) How many seconds does it take for the lorry to come to rest?
(iii) How far does the lorry travel in that time?

11. The area, A, of a circle of radius r is given by

$$A = \pi r^2.$$

Find, in terms of π, the rate of change of A as r changes when
  (i) $r = 2$ (ii) $r = 6$.

12. A marble is dropped from the top of a building 45 metres in height.
The height of the marble above the ground, in metres, after t seconds, is given by the formula

$$h = 45 - 5t^2.$$

  (i) After how many seconds does the marble hit the ground?
 (ii) Find the speed at which the marble hits the ground
    (a) in metres per second
    (b) in kilometres per hour.

13. The speed, v, in metres per second, of an object after t seconds is given by

$$v = 12t - 3t^2.$$

  (i) For what values of t is the speed 9 metres per second?
 (ii) What does $\dfrac{dv}{dt}$ mean in the context of the equation?
(iii) When is the acceleration zero?
(iv) Find the speed when the acceleration is zero.
 (v) Find the acceleration at each of the two instants when the speed is 9 metres per second.

Section 18.7 Maximum values

In a previous section of this chapter we learned that for any function $y = f(x)$, $\dfrac{dy}{dx} = 0$ at the maximum and minimum turning points. This is shown in the given figures.

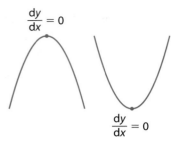

The result that $\dfrac{dy}{dx} = 0$ at a maximum or at a minimum turning point can be used very effectively in real-life problems where we are required to maximise (or minimise) functions defining area or profit, for example.

Example 1

The diagram on the right shows the path of a rocket which is fired into the air.

The height, h metres, of the rocket after t seconds is given by

$$h(t) = -2t^2 + 28t.$$

(i) For how many seconds is the rocket in flight?

(ii) What is the maximum height reached by the rocket?

(i) The rocket is in flight for the time represented on the x-axis between the origin and the point A, i.e., the points where the height is zero.
To find the point A, we solve the equation $-2t^2 + 28t = 0$.

$$-2t^2 + 28t = 0 \Rightarrow 2t^2 - 28t = 0$$
$$\Rightarrow t^2 - 14t = 0$$
$$\Rightarrow t(t - 14) = 0 \Rightarrow t = 0 \ \text{ or } \ t = 14$$

The point A is $(14, 0)$.

∴   the rocket is in flight for 14 seconds.

(ii) The maximum height is reached at the turning point P.

At P, $\dfrac{dh}{dt} = 0$.

$$h = -2t^2 + 28t$$

$$\frac{dh}{dt} = -4t + 28$$

$$-4t + 28 = 0 \Rightarrow 4t = 28 \Rightarrow t = 7$$

The maximum height is reached when $t = 7$.
To find the maximum height reached, we substitute 7 for t into the given equation.

$$h = -2t^2 + 28t$$
$$= -2(7)^2 + 28(7) \text{ when } t = 7$$
$$h = 98$$

∴ the maximum height reached by the rocket is 98 metres.

Exercise 18.7

1. A ball is thrown into the air.
The formula $y = 20x - 4x^2$ shows the height of the ball, y metres above the ground, x seconds after it is thrown.
The graph shown represents the flight of the ball.
Each unit on the x-axis represents 5 metres.

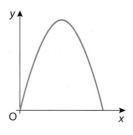

   (i) For how long was the ball in the air?
   (ii) How far from the point at which it was thrown did the ball land?
   (iii) Use $\dfrac{dy}{dx}$ to find the value of x when the ball reached its maximum height.
   (iv) Now find the maximum height reached by the ball.

2. A farmer has 20 metres of fencing.
He wishes to use it to form a rectangular enclosure in the corner of a field, as in the diagram.

   (i) Show that the area of the enclosure is given by the formula $A = 20x - x^2$.
   (ii) For what value of x is the area of the enclosure at its maximum?
   (iii) Find this maximum area.

3. The equation of the graphed function is
$$y = 8x - x^2.$$

The function represents the number of taxis (y) at a taxi-rank for eight consecutive hours.
$x = 0$ represents noon and $x = 8$ represents 8 p.m..

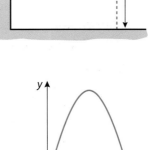

   (i) At what time is the number of taxis at the rank at its highest?
   (ii) Hence find the maximum number of taxis at the rank in this eight-hour period.

4. The function $f: x \rightarrow 12x - x^2$ represents the height, in metres, reached by a golf ball from the time, in seconds, it was struck $(x = 0)$ to the time it hit the ground $(x = 12)$.
   (i) After how many seconds did the ball reach its maximum height?
   (ii) Use your answer to find the maximum height of the golf ball.

5. The length of the given rectangle is x cm and its perimeter is 12 cm.

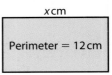

   (i) Show that the area, A, of the rectangle is given by $A = 6x - x^2$.
   (ii) For what value of x is the area of the rectangle at a maximum?
   (iii) Find this maximum area.

6. The equation $h = 15t - 5t^2$ gives the height, in metres, of a ball moving through the air t seconds after it was projected from ground-level by a machine.
   (i) How long does it take the ball to reach its maximum height?
   (ii) Find the maximum height reached.

7. A farmer is growing winter wheat. The amount of wheat he will get per hectare depends on, among other things, the amount of nitrogen fertiliser that he uses. For his particular farm, the amount of wheat depends on the nitrogen in the following way:

   $$Y = 7000 + 32N - 0.1N^2,$$

   where Y is the amount of wheat produced, in kg per hectare, and N is the amount of nitrogen added, in kg per hectare.
   (i) How much wheat will he get per hectare if he uses 100 kg of nitrogen per hectare?
   (ii) Find the amount of nitrogen that he must use in order to maximise the amount of wheat produced.
   (iii) What is the maximum possible amount of wheat produced per hectare?
   (iv) The farmer's total costs for producing the wheat are €1300 per hectare. He can sell the wheat for €160 per tonne. He can also get €75 per hectare for the leftover straw. If he achieves the maximum amount of wheat, what is his profit per hectare?

8. In the given right-angled triangle ABC, the sides [AB] and [BC] vary such that their sum is always 12 cm.
   (i) If the length of [AB] is x cm, write in terms of x, the length of [BC].
   (ii) Express the area of the triangle in the form $A = f(x)$.
   (iii) For what value of x is the area of the triangle at its maximum?
   (iv) Calculate this maximum area.

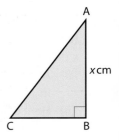

9. The number of salmon, s, swimming upstream in a river to spawn is approximated by $s(x) = -x^3 + 3x^2 + 360x + 5000$, with x representing the temperature of the water in degrees (°C).

(This function is valid only if $6 \leqslant x \leqslant 20$.)

Find the water temperature that results in the maximum number of salmon swimming upstream.

10. The profit made by the publishing company of a certain magazine is calculated by the formula

$$P = 50x - 5x^2,$$

where P is the profit (in thousands of euro) and x is the selling price (in euro) of the magazine.

   (i) At what price should the company sell the magazines in order to maximise profit?

   (ii) Hence find the maximum profit the company can make.

Test yourself 18

1. (a) Differentiate each of these functions:

   (i) $y = 3x - 4$ (ii) $y = 2x^2 - 4x$ (iii) $y = x^3$

  (b) The diagram shows the graph of the function $y = x^2 - 2x - 3$.

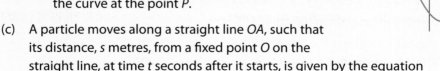

   (i) Find the slope of the curve at the point $P(2, -3)$.

   (ii) Hence find the equation of the tangent to the curve at the point P.

  (c) A particle moves along a straight line OA, such that its distance, s metres, from a fixed point O on the straight line, at time t seconds after it starts, is given by the equation

$$s = t^3 - 6t^2 + 9t + 7.$$

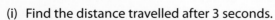

   (i) Find the distance travelled after 3 seconds.

   (ii) Find the speed of the particle after 4 seconds.

   (iii) After how many seconds is the particle at rest?

   (iv) Find the acceleration of the particle after 4 seconds.

2. (a) If $f(x) = 2x^2 - 3x + 5$, find $f'(-2)$.

    (b) Find the slope and hence the equation of the tangent to the curve
$y = 2x^2 - 5x - 2$ at the point $(1, -5)$.

    (c) The height, h metres, of a balloon is related to the time, t seconds after it is
released, by
$$h = 120t - 15t^2.$$

    Find   (i) the height of the balloon after 2 seconds

              (ii) the speed of the balloon after 1 second

              (iii) after how many seconds the balloon is momentarily at rest

              (iv) the maximum height reached by the balloon.

3. (a) Differentiate with respect to x each of these:

        (i) $3x + 2$ (ii) $\frac{1}{2}x^2 - 3x - 5$ (iii) $2x^3 - x^2 - 9x$

    (b) The graph of the curve $y = x^2$ is shown
on the right.

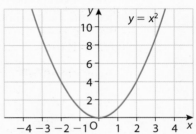

        (i) Find the slope of the tangent to this
curve at the point where $x = 2$.

        (ii) At what point on the curve is the slope
of the tangent -2?

       (iii) Find the coordinates of the point on
the curve at which the slope is zero.

    (c) A rectangular patch of ground is to be enclosed with
100 metres of fencing wire.

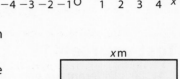

        (i) If the length of the patch is x metres, express the
width in terms of x.

        (ii) Express the area, $A\,\text{m}^2$, in terms of x.

       (iii) Find the value of x for which A is a maximum.

       (iv) Find this maximum area.

4. (a) State whether the slope of the given curve is positive,
negative or zero at the three points A, B and C.

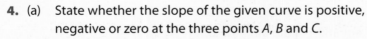

    (b) Find the point on the curve $y = 4x - x^2$ at which the
slope of the tangent to the curve is 1.

    (c) A marble rolls along the top of a table.
It starts to move at $t = 0$ seconds.
The distance that it has travelled after t seconds is given by

$$s = 14t - t^2, \text{ where } s \text{ is in centimetres.}$$

        (i) What distance has the marble travelled when $t = 2$ seconds?

        (ii) What is the speed of the marble when $t = 5$ seconds?

       (iii) After how many seconds is the speed of the marble equal to zero?

       (iv) How far has the marble travelled before it comes to rest?

5. (a) If $y = x^3 - 5x^2 + 2x - 1$, find

(i) the value of $\dfrac{dy}{dx}$ at $x = 1$

(ii) the value of $\dfrac{d^2y}{dx^2}$ at $x = -2$.

(b) A sketch of the function

$$f(x) = -x^2 + 3x + 4$$

is shown on the right.

Make a rough copy of this curve and using the same axes, draw a sketch of the slope function.

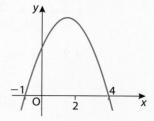

(c) The population density (number of residents per unit area) of many cities depends on the distance from the city centre. For a particular city, the population density P, in thousands of people per square kilometre at a distance of r kilometres from the centre, is given approximately by $P = 10 + 40r - 20r^2$.

(i) What is the population density in the centre of the city?

(ii) Write down $\dfrac{dP}{dr}$.

Explain what $\dfrac{dP}{dr}$ means.

(iii) Evaluate $\dfrac{dP}{dr}$ when $r = 5$.

(iv) Where is the population density greatest?

6. (a) The equation of the line shown is not given.
It intersects the y-axis at $(0, 2)$.

If $\dfrac{dy}{dx} = 1$, write the equation of the line in

the form $y = mx + c$.

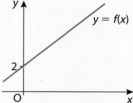

(b) The equation of a curve is $y = 2x^2 - 6x + 3$.

Find $\dfrac{dy}{dx}$ and hence find the coordinates of the point on the curve at which the tangent is parallel to the line $y = 2x + 4$.

(c) The distance, s metres, travelled by a body in t seconds, is given by the formula

$$s = 3 - 6t + 2t^3.$$

(i) How far does the body travel in the first 2 seconds?

(ii) How far does the body travel in the next 4 seconds?

(iii) Find the average speed of the body between the second and the sixth seconds.

(iv) Find the speed of the body after 2 seconds.

(v) After how many seconds does the body come to rest?

summary of key points...

1. For the function $y = f(x)$, the process of finding $\frac{dy}{dx}$ is called **differentiation**.

   For a linear function, $\frac{dy}{dx}$ = slope = 1st difference between outputs.

   If $y = ax + b$, then $\frac{dy}{dx} = a$ = slope.

2. If $y = x^n$, then $\frac{dy}{dx} = nx^{n-1}$; if $y = ax^n$, then $\frac{dy}{dx} = nax^{n-1}$.

   In words: Multiply the coefficient of the variable by the power and reduce the power by 1.

   Example: $y = x^3 - 2x^2 + 3x - 4 \Rightarrow \frac{dy}{dx} = 3x^2 - 4x + 3$.

3. If $y = f(x)$, then $\frac{dy}{dx}$ represents the **slope of the tangent** to the curve at any point on the curve.

4. At the point A, we have a **maximum turning point**.
   At the point B, we have a **minimum turning point**.

   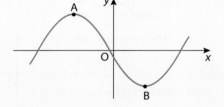

   At a maximum turning point,
   $\frac{dy}{dx} = 0$ and $\frac{d^2y}{dx^2} < 0$, i.e. negative.

   At a minimum turning point, $\frac{dy}{dx} = 0$ and $\frac{d^2y}{dx^2} > 0$, i.e. positive.

5. **Increasing and decreasing functions**

   (i) When a curve is increasing, $\frac{dy}{dx} > 0$.

   (ii) When a curve is decreasing, $\frac{dy}{dx} < 0$.

6. If $s = 3 - 5t + t^3$ represents the distance, s, travelled by an object after t seconds, then

   (i) $\frac{ds}{dt}$ represents **speed** after t seconds

   (ii) $\frac{d^2s}{dt^2}$ represents **acceleration** after t seconds.

Inferential Statistics

Key words

normal distribution   normal curve   the Empirical Rule   standard deviation
margin of error   sample   population   sample proportion
population proportion   confidence interval   hypothesis test
null hypothesis   alternative hypothesis   reject/accept

Section 19.1 The Normal Distribution and The Empirical Rule

When the physical characteristics, such as height or weight, of a large number of individuals are arranged in order, from lowest to highest, in a frequency distribution, the same pattern shows up repeatedly. This pattern shows that a large number of values cluster near the middle of the distribution, as illustrated by the symmetrical histogram shown below.

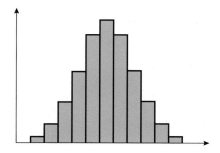

If the distribution is very large and continuous, and the class intervals become sufficiently small, the distribution forms a symmetrical bell-shaped smooth curve called **the curve of normal distribution** or simply **the normal curve**, as shown.

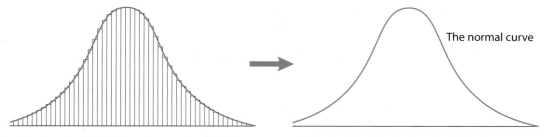

The normal curve

In Section 8.6 of this book, we dealt with a measure of spread called **standard deviation**, σ, which gives an indication of the distance the data is from the mean.

There is a very important relationship between the normal curve and standard deviations. It is called **the Empirical Rule** and it is given below:

The Empirical Rule

For any large population with mean $\bar{x}$ and standard deviation σ

(i) about 68% of the values will lie within one standard deviation of the mean, that is, between $\bar{x} - \sigma$ and $\bar{x} + \sigma$

(ii) about 95% of the values will lie within two standard deviations of the mean, that is, between $\bar{x} - 2\sigma$ and $\bar{x} + 2\sigma$

(iii) almost all (99.7%) of the values will lie within three standard deviations of the mean, that is, $\bar{x} - 3\sigma$ and $\bar{x} + 3\sigma$

The normal curve on the right illustrates the Empirical Rule.

Based on the Empirical Rule, the probability that a score, selected at random, will be within one standard deviation of the mean is 68% or 0.68.

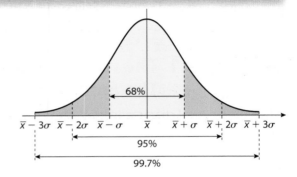

Example 1

The given curve represents a normal distribution with mean $\bar{x} = 80$ and standard deviation $\sigma = 10$.
P represents the mean, Q represents a value one standard deviation below P and R represents a value one standard deviation above P.

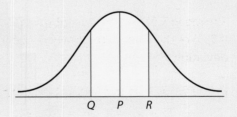

(i) Write down the values of P, Q and R.
(ii) What percentage of the data lies in the shaded area?
(iii) If a value is chosen at random from all the data, what is the probability that it comes from the shaded area?

(i) P represents the mean; so $P = 80$

$$Q = 80 - \sigma \qquad\qquad R = 80 + \sigma$$
$$= 80 - 10 \ldots \sigma = 10 \qquad = 80 + 10$$
$$Q = 70 \qquad\qquad\qquad R = 90$$

(ii) The shaded area represents all the values that lie within one standard deviation of the mean. Accordingly, the shaded area contains 68% of the data.

(iii) The probability that a value comes from the shaded area = 68% = 0.68.

Example 2

A normal distribution has mean $\bar{x} = 45$ and standard deviation $\sigma = 5$.
  (i) Find the range within which 68% of the distribution lies.
  (ii) Find the range within which 95% of the distribution lies.
  (iii) What percentage of the distribution lies within 3 standard deviations of the mean?

  (i) 68% of the distribution lies in the range $\bar{x} - \sigma, \ \bar{x} + \sigma$.
  $\bar{x} - \sigma = 45 - 5 = 40$ and $\bar{x} + \sigma = 45 + 5 = 50$
  $\therefore$ 68% lies in the range $[40, 50]$

  (ii) 95% of the distribution lies in the range $\bar{x} - 2\sigma, \ \bar{x} + 2\sigma$.
  $\bar{x} - 2\sigma = 45 - 2(5) = 45 - 10 = 35$
  $\bar{x} + 2\sigma = 45 + 2(5) = 45 + 10 = 55$
  $\therefore$ 95% lies in the range $[35, 55]$

  (iii) 99.7% of the distribution lies in the range $[\bar{x} - 3\sigma, \bar{x} + 3\sigma]$.

Example 3

The mean $\bar{x}$ of a normal distribution is 84.
If 95% of the values are between 72 and 96, find the value of σ, the standard deviation.

By the Empirical Rule, 95% of the values lie in the range $[\bar{x} - 2\sigma, \bar{x} + 2\sigma]$
$$\Rightarrow \quad [\bar{x} - 2\sigma, \bar{x} + 2\sigma] = [72, 96]$$
$$\Rightarrow \quad \bar{x} - 2\sigma = 72$$
$$84 - 2\sigma = 72$$
$$-2\sigma = -12 \quad \Rightarrow \quad 2\sigma = 12 \quad \Rightarrow \quad \sigma = 6$$
The standard deviation is 6.

Exercise 19.1

1. Copy and complete these sentences:
    (i) Approximately ____% of the data lies within one standard _____ of the mean.

    (ii) Approximately 95% of the data lies within _____ standard deviations of the _____.

2. The mean $\bar{x}$ of a distribution is 54 and the standard deviation σ is 3.
   (i) Find the range $[\bar{x} - \sigma, \bar{x} + \sigma]$.
   (ii) Find the range within which 95% of the data lies.
   (iii) If a value is selected at random from the distribution, find the probability that it is in the range $[\bar{x} - \sigma, \bar{x} + \sigma]$.

3. For each of the following normal curves, find the percentage of all the values that are in the shaded area:

   (i)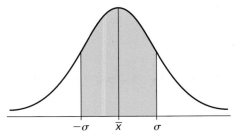
   (ii)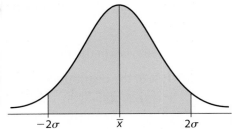

4. (i) In the given normal curve, complete the labels on the horizontal axis.
   (ii) If a value is selected at random, find the probability that it is in the shaded region.
   (iii) If $\bar{x} = 84$ and $\sigma = 7$, what are the values of the incomplete labels in the diagram?

   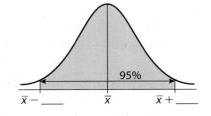

5. In a normal distribution, the mean $\bar{x} = 120$ and the standard deviation $\sigma = 15$.
   (i) Find the range within which 68% of the values lie.
   (ii) Find the range within which 95% of the values lie.

6. The standard deviation σ of the given normal curve is 4.
   (i) Write down the value of the mean $\bar{x}$.
   (ii) What percentage of the values lie in the shaded area?
   (iii) Write down the values of A and of B.

   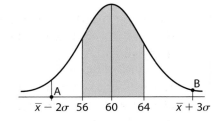

7. The mean speed of vehicles on a given road can be modelled by a normal distribution with mean 55 km/h and standard deviation 9 km/h.
   What would be the speed of a vehicle that was travelling at
   (i) one standard deviation below the mean
   (ii) two standard deviations above the mean
   (iii) three standard deviation above the mean?

8. A normal distribution has a mean $\bar{x} = 60$ and standard deviation $\sigma = 5$.
   (i) Find the range within which 68% of the distribution lie.
   (ii) Find the range within which 95% of the distribution lie.

9. The heights of students in a certain university are normally distributed with a mean of 180 cm and a standard deviation of 10 cm.

   The given diagram represents this distribution and each mark on the horizontal line represents 1, 2 or 3 standard deviations from the mean.
   Write down the values of a, b, c, d and e.

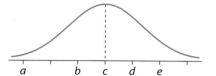

10. The heights of a large sample of adults are normally distributed with a mean of 170 cm and a standard deviation of 8 cm.
    Within what limits do
    (i) 68% of the heights lie
    (ii) 99.7% of the heights lie?

11. The distribution of the times taken by factory workers to get to their place of work can be modelled by a normal distribution.
    The mean time is 35 minutes and the standard deviation is 6 minutes.
    (i) What percentage of the workers take longer than 35 minutes?
    (ii) What percentage of the workers take between 29 minutes and 41 minutes?
    (iii) What is the range of the times it takes 95% of the workers to get to their place of work?

12. The lengths of time taken to complete a crossword puzzle are normally distributed with a mean $\bar{x} = 18$ minutes.
    If 68% take between 14 minutes and 22 minutes, find the standard deviation, σ, of the distribution.

13. The marks awarded in an examination are normally distributed with mean 74 marks.
    If 95% of the marks are in the range [62 marks, 86 marks], work out the standard deviation, σ.

14. The weights of a group of 1000 schoolchildren were normally distributed with a mean of 42 kg and a standard deviation of σ.
    950 of the children were in the range 30 kg to 54 kg.
    (i) Express 950 as a percentage of 1000.
    (ii) Complete the following sentence:
        "95% of the children lie in the range $[\bar{x} - \_\_, \ \bar{x} + \_\_]$".
    (iii) Use the information given to find the value of the standard deviation σ.
    (iv) If a child is selected at random, find the probability that the child's weight is in the range 30 kg to 54 kg.

Section 19.2 Margin of error – Confidence intervals ──────

When dealing with sampling in your earlier study of statistics, it was stated that the purpose of sampling is to gain information about the whole population by surveying a small part of the population. This small part is called a **sample**.

If data from a sample is collected in a proper way, then the sample survey can give a fairly accurate indication of the population characteristic that is being studied.

Before a General Election, a national newspaper generally requests a market research company to ask a sample of the electorate how they intend to vote in the election. This survey is generally referred to as an opinion poll.
The number is usually about 1000.
If the number of people surveyed was increased to 2000, you would get a more accurate picture of voting intentions.

The result of the survey might appear in the daily newspaper as follows:

> *40% support for* **The Democratic Right**.

The **40%** support is called the **sample proportion**, that is, the part or portion of the sample who indicated that they would vote for *The Democratic Right*.
The party could then expect to get somewhere around 40% of all voters in the general election.

The notation $\hat{p}$ is used to denote **sample proportion**.
The notation p is used to represent **population proportion**.
Since p is generally not known, $\hat{p}$ is used as an **estimator** for the true population proportion, p.

Of course everybody knows that sample surveys are rarely 100% accurate.
There is generally some 'element of chance' or **error** involved.

The newspaper might add to their headline the following sentence:

> *The margin of error is 3%.*

The **margin of error** of 3% is a way of saying that the result of the survey is 40% $\pm$ 3%.
That means that the research company is quite 'confident' that the proportion of the whole electorate who intend to vote for *The Democratic Right* could be anywhere between 37% and 43%.

How does the research company calculate **the margin of error**?

The margin of error, E, in opinion polls is generally calculated using the formula,

$$E = \frac{1}{\sqrt{n}}, \text{ where } n \text{ is the sample size.}$$

Margin of error
$E = \dfrac{1}{\sqrt{n}}$

If the sample size is 400, then $E = \dfrac{1}{\sqrt{400}} = \dfrac{1}{20} = 0.05$.

If the sample size is 1000, then $E = \dfrac{1}{\sqrt{1000}} \approx 0.03$.

If the sample size is 4000, then $E = \dfrac{1}{\sqrt{4000}} \approx 0.016$.

Notice that the error decreases as the sample size increases.

Confidence interval

The result of the opinion poll above was given as 40% $\pm$ 3%.

$$40\% - 3\% = 37\% \quad \text{and} \quad 40\% + 3\% = 43\%.$$

So, the result of the opinion poll is anywhere in the interval 37% to 43%.
More formally, it can be written as $37\% < p < 43\%$, where p is the population proportion.
$37\% < p < 43\%$ is called a **confidence interval**.
But how confident are we that the result will lie in this interval?
There are many levels of confidence, but for our course the **confidence level** is pitched at **95%**.

The 95% confidence level implies that the interval was obtained by a method which 'works 95% of the time'.
The confidence interval, $37\% < p < 43\%$, is a way of stating that if you surveyed numerous samples of 1000 people on the same day, the results would be in the interval 37% to 43% on 95 occasions out of 100, that is, in 95% of the samples.

The 95% confidence interval for a population proportion
is given on the right.

The confidence interval on the right may also be expressed

as $\hat{p} \pm \dfrac{1}{\sqrt{n}}$.

> Confidence interval is
> $$\hat{p} - \dfrac{1}{\sqrt{n}} < p < \hat{p} + \dfrac{1}{\sqrt{n}}$$

Example 1

A random sample of 400 persons are given a flu vaccine and 136 of them experienced some discomfort.

  (i)   Write down the sample size.
  (ii) Calculate the margin of error using $\dfrac{1}{\sqrt{n}}$.
  (iii) Find the sample proportion.
  (iv) Find the confidence interval.

(i) The sample size is 400.

(ii) The margin of error is $\dfrac{1}{\sqrt{n}} = \dfrac{1}{\sqrt{400}} = \dfrac{1}{20} = 0.05$.

(iii) The sample proportion, $\hat{p} = \dfrac{136}{400} = 0.34$.

(iv) The confidence interval is $\hat{p} \pm \dfrac{1}{\sqrt{n}}$

$$\hat{p} \pm \dfrac{1}{\sqrt{n}} = 0.34 \pm 0.05 \text{ ... from (ii) and (iii) above}$$

$$= 0.34 - 0.05 \quad \text{to} \quad 0.34 + 0.05$$

$$= 0.29 \text{ to } 0.39$$

The confidence interval may be written as $0.29 < p < 0.39$.

Example 2

What sample size would be required to have a margin of error of

(i) 0.05   (ii) $2\tfrac{1}{2}\%$?

(i) $\dfrac{1}{\sqrt{n}} = 0.05$

$\therefore \dfrac{1}{n} = (0.05)^2$ ... square both sides

$\therefore n = \dfrac{1}{(0.05)^2}$

$n = 400$

(ii) $\dfrac{1}{\sqrt{n}} = 2\tfrac{1}{2}\% = 0.025$

$\dfrac{1}{n} = (0.025)^2$ ... square both sides

$n = \dfrac{1}{(0.025)^2}$

$n = 1600$

Exercise 19.2

1. Work out the margin of error for each of the following random samples at the 95% confidence level:

   (i) 900   (ii) 1200   (iii) 2025   (iv) 800

Give your answer correct to 2 decimal places where necessary.

2. In a random sample of 500 households, 80 said that they had at least one pet.
   (i) What is the sample size?
   (ii) What is the margin of error?
   (iii) What is the sample proportion?

3. In a random sample of 200 students, 48 said that they spend at least one hour each day watching television.
   (i) Write down the sample size.
   (ii) What is the margin of error?
   (iii) What is the sample proportion, $\hat{p}$?
   (iv) If you increase the sample size to 400, what effect would this have on the margin of error?

4. A manufacturer tests a random sample of 300 items and finds that 45 are defective.
   (i) Write down the sample size, n.
   (ii) Calculate the margin of error.
   (iii) Work out the sample proportion, $\hat{p}$.
   (iv) Using $\hat{p} \pm \dfrac{1}{\sqrt{n}}$, work out a confidence interval for the proportion of defective items produced.

5. A survey was undertaken to find the level of use of the internet by residents of a city. In a random sample of 150 residents, 45 said that they log onto the internet at least once a day.
   (i) Write down the sample size.
   (ii) Calculate the margin of error.
   (iii) Work out the sample proportion.
   (iv) Construct a confidence interval for p, the population proportion that log onto the internet at least once a day.

6. In a random sample of 400 computer shops, it was discovered that 168 of them sold computers at below the list price recommended by the manufacturer.
   (i) Write down the sample size.
   (ii) Calculate the margin of error.
   (iii) Work out the sample proportion.
   (iv) Construct an approximate 95% confidence interval for the proportion of shops selling below the list price.

7. Copy and complete this sentence:
   "A 95% confidence level means that on _____ occasions out of _____, the proportion will be in this ____".

8. A college principal decides to consult the students about a proposed change to the times of lectures. She finds that, out of a random sample of 80 students, 36 of them are in favour of the change.
   (i) Calculate the margin of error.
   (ii) Work out the sample proportion, $\hat{p}$.
   (iii) Construct a confidence interval for the proportion of students who are in favour of change.

9. A survey was carried out in order to gauge the response to a new school "healthy eating" menu. A random sample of 200 schoolchildren was selected from different schools. It was found that 84 children approved of the new menu.
   (i) Write down the sample size.
   (ii) Calculate the margin of error, correct to 2 decimal places.
   (iii) Work out the sample proportion, $\hat{p}$.
   (iv) Establish a 95% confidence interval for the proportion of all students who approved of the new menu.

10. Write each of these percentages as a decimal:
    (i) 10%   (ii) 5%   (iii) 3%   (iv) 2.5%   (v) 6.5%

11. What size sample, n, is required to have a margin of error of 6%.
    The first two lines are done for you:

    $$\frac{1}{\sqrt{n}} = \pm 0.06 \ldots 6\% = 0.06$$

    $$\left(\frac{1}{\sqrt{n}}\right)^2 = (\pm 0.06)^2$$

12. What size sample is required to have a margin of error of
    (i) 5%   (ii) 4%   (iii) 12%   (iv) 3.5%   (v) 2.5%?

13. The results of a survey showed that 360 out of 1000 families regularly purchase the *Daily Bulletin* newspaper.
    (i) Write down the sample size.
    (ii) Calculate the margin of error, correct to two places of decimal.
    (iii) For this survey, what is the sample proportion, $\hat{p}$?
    (iv) Construct a confidence interval for the proportion of families that purchase the *Daily Bulletin*.

Section 19.3 Hypothesis testing

Many people believe that the average or mean height of Irish people is greater than the mean height of Spanish people.
To illustrate this belief, we could make the following statement:

"The mean height of Irish people is greater than the mean height of Spanish people".

In mathematics, this statement is called an **hypothesis**.
Having made this statement, we now need some evidence to show the truth, or otherwise, of the statement.
The process of proving the truth of the statement is called **hypothesis testing**.

The assumption or statement made is called the **null hypothesis**.
The null hypothesis is denoted by $\mathbf{H_0}$.
Usually, the null hypothesis is a statement of "no change", "no difference", or "no effect".

Suppose a drug company claims that a "new improved drug" is more effective that the existing drug, then the null hypothesis could be worded as follows:

H_0: There is no change in the effectiveness of the new drug.

The drug company would not like this hypothesis and so would put forward an **alternative hypothesis, H_1.**
This alternative hypothesis might read as follows:

H_1: There is a change in the effectiveness of the new drug.

We generally concentrate on the null hypothesis and carry out a **hypothesis test** to accept or reject the null hypothesis.

Here are some examples of null hypotheses and their corresponding alternative hypotheses.

H_0: The mean weight of adult males is 78 kg.
H_1: The mean weight of adults males is not 78 kg.

H_0: A football team is more likely to concede a goal just after it has scored a goal.
H_1: A football team is not more likely to concede a goal just after it has scored a goal.

H_0: The average marriage-age of men is higher than the average marriage-age of women.
H_1: The average marriage-age of men is not higher than the average marriage-age of women.

In Section 19.2 the results of a newspaper survey stated:

"40% support for *The Democratic Right*.

The margin of error was $\pm 3\%$.

40% $\pm$ 3% gives an **interval** 37% to 43%.

What this interval means is that in 95 samples out of 100, *The Democratic Right* would receive a percentage vote somewhere between 37% and 43%.
95 samples out of 100 is called the **95% confidence level**.

How do we prove the truth, or otherwise, of the newspaper's claim that the true percentage of people who intend to vote for *The Democratic Right* lies in the interval 37% to 43%.

To test the truth of the newspaper statement, or hypothesis, we carry out an **hypothesis test**.
To do this test, we select another sample of the same size and calculate the percentage of this sample who say that they will vote for *The Democratic Right*.

If the percentage of voters who intend to vote for the named party lies outside the interval 37% to 43%, we reject the null hypothesis; that is, we reject the claim made by the newspaper. If the percentage is within the interval 37% to 43%, we accept the newspaper's claim.

The steps involved in carrying out an hypothesis test are given on the next page.

Procedure for carrying out an hypothesis test

1. Write down H_0, the **null hypothesis**, and H_1, the **alternative hypothesis**

   For example, to test whether a coin is biased if we get 7 heads in 10 tosses, we could formulate the following hypotheses:

   H_0: The coin is not biased.

   H_1: The coin is biased.

2. Write down or calculate the sample proportion, $\hat{p}$.

3. Find the margin of error, $\dfrac{1}{\sqrt{n}}$.

4. Write down the confidence interval for the population proportion, p, using

   $$\hat{p} - \frac{1}{\sqrt{n}} < p < \hat{p} + \frac{1}{\sqrt{n}} \qquad \left[\text{or} \quad \hat{p} \pm \frac{1}{\sqrt{n}} \right]$$

5. (i) If the value of the population proportion stated is within the confidence interval, accept the null hypothesis H_0 and reject H_1.

   (ii) If the value of the population proportion is outside the confidence interval, reject the null hypothesis H_0 and accept H_1.

Example 1

The *Kennell Club* claims that 30% of households keep a dog.

To test this claim, a group of statistics students carry out a survey of 400 households.

The results of the survey found that 112 of the 400 households kept a dog.

(i) Write down the null hypothesis.

(ii) Write down the alternative hypothesis.

(iii) Write down the sample size, n.

(iv) Work out the margin or error, $\dfrac{1}{\sqrt{n}}$.

(v) Calculate the sample proportion, $\hat{p}$.

(vi) Calculate the confidence interval using $\hat{p} - \dfrac{1}{\sqrt{n}} < p < \hat{p} + \dfrac{1}{\sqrt{n}}$.

(vii) At the 95% confidence level, can we accept the *Kennell Club's* claim?

(i) H_0: 30% of households keep a dog.

(ii) H_1: The percentage of households who keep a dog is not 30%.

(iii) The sample size, n, is 400.

(iv) Margin of error is $\dfrac{1}{\sqrt{n}} = \dfrac{1}{\sqrt{400}} = \dfrac{1}{20} = 0.05$.

(v) Sample proportion, $\hat{p} = \dfrac{112}{400} = 0.28$

(vi) Confidence interval is $\hat{p} - \dfrac{1}{\sqrt{n}} < p < \hat{p} + \dfrac{1}{\sqrt{n}}$

$$= 0.28 - 0.05 < p < 0.28 + 0.05$$
$$= 0.23 < p < 0.33$$
$$= 23\% < p < 33\%$$

(vii) Since the claim, i.e. 30%, is within the confidence interval $23\% < p < 33\%$, we accept the null hypothesis.

Example 2

A school principal claimed that 45% of students were in favour of a change to the school uniform.

The students' council carried out a survey of 120 students to test the principal's claim.

The results of the survey found that 42 students were in favour of a change to the school uniform.

  (i) Write down the null hypothesis.
 (ii) Write down the alternative hypothesis.
(iii) Calculate the margin of error, correct to two decimal places.
 (iv) Work out the sample proportion, $\hat{p}$.
  (v) Calculate the confidence interval for the population proportion.
 (vi) At the 95% confidence level, is the principal's claim correct?

  (i) H_0: 45% of students are in favour of a change to the school uniform.

 (ii) H_1: The percentage of students in favour of a change is not 45%.

(iii) Margin of error is $\dfrac{1}{\sqrt{n}} = \dfrac{1}{\sqrt{120}} = 0.09 \ldots$ correct to 2 decimal places.

 (iv) Sample proportion, $\hat{p} = \dfrac{42}{120} = 0.35$

  (v) Confidence interval $= \hat{p} - \dfrac{1}{\sqrt{n}} < p < \hat{p} + \dfrac{1}{\sqrt{n}}$

$$= 0.35 - 0.09 < p < 0.35 + 0.09$$
$$= 0.26 < p < 0.44$$
$$= 26\% < p < 44\%$$

 (vi) Since the principal's claim, i.e. 45%, lies **outside** the confidence interval $26\% < p < 44\%$, we **reject** the null hypothesis H_0 and accept the alternative hypothesis H_1.

Exercise 19.3

1. A school principal claims that 95% of students are on time for the first class at 9.00 a.m.
    (i) Write down H_0, the null hypothesis when carrying out an hypothesis test.
    (ii) Write down an alternative hypothesis, H_1.
    (iii) Describe the next steps you would take in testing the principal's claim.

2. The manufacturer of *Chummy Bits* claims that 80% of dog owners choose this product for their dogs.
    In a random sample of 200 dog owners, 155 chose *Chummy Bits*.
    (i) Write down the null hypothesis, H_0.
    (ii) Write down the alternative hypothesis, H_1.
    (iii) What is the sample size, n?
    (iv) Calculate the margin of error, $\frac{1}{\sqrt{n}}$.
    (v) Calculate the sample proportion.
    (vi) Work out the confidence interval.
    (vii) At the 95% confidence level, is the manufacturer's claim correct?

3. A company states that 20% of the visitors to its website purchase at least one of its products. A sample of 400 people who visited the site is checked and the number who purchased a product is found to be 64.
    (i) Write down the null hypothesis, H_0.
    (ii) What is the sample size?
    (iii) Calculate the margin of error.
    (iv) Work out the sample proportion.
    (v) Work out the confidence interval.
    (vi) At the 95% confidence level, is the company's statement correct?

4. In a pubic opinion poll, 1000 randomly-chosen voters were asked whether they would vote for the *Purple Party* at the next election and 350 replied "Yes".
    The leader of the *Purple Party* believes that the true proportion is 40%.
    The random sample was used to test the party leader's belief.
    (i) Write down the null hypothesis, H_0.
    (ii) Write down the sample size.
    (iii) Find the margin of error, correct to two decimal places.
    (iv) Calculate the sample proportion.
    (v) Work out the confidence interval for the percentage of voters who say that they will vote for the *Purple Party*.
    (vi) Is the leader's belief justified at the 95% level of confidence?

5. A college claims that it admits equal numbers of men and women.
    The Student's Union took a random sample of 500 students to test the college's claim.
    It found that 270 were men.

(i) What percentage of those admitted did the college claim were men?
(ii) Write down the null hypothesis.
(iii) Write down the sample size.
(iv) Calculate the margin of error, correct to 2 decimal places.
(v) Work out sample proportion, $\hat{p}$.
(vi) Work out the confidence interval for the percentage of men admitted by the college.
(vii) Is the college's claim justified at the 95% level of confidence?

6. A seed company sells pansy seeds in mixed packets and claims that 20% of the resulting plants will have red flowers. A packet of seeds is sown by a gardener who finds that only 16 out of 100 plants have red flowers.
(i) Write down the null hypothesis, H_0.
(ii) Calculate the margin of error.
(iii) What is the sample proportion of plants with red flowers?
(iv) Work out a confidence interval for the percentage of seeds that will go on to have red flowers.
(v) Is the percentage claimed by the company within this confidence limit?
(vi) Based on your answer to part (v), do we reject the null hypothesis?

7. A drugs company produced a new pain-relieving drug for migraine sufferers and claimed that the drug had a 90% success rate.
A group of doctors doubted the company's claim.
They prescribed the drug for a group of 150 patients.
After six months, 120 of these patients said that their migraine symptoms had been relieved.
(i) Write down the null hypothesis, H_0.
(ii) Write down H_1.
(iii) Write down the sample size.
(iv) Calculate the sample proportion.
(v) What is the margin of error, correct to 2 decimal places?
(vi) Work out a confidence interval for the percentage of patients who said their symptoms had been relieved.
(vii) At the 95% level of confidence, can the company's claim be upheld?

8. A university library claimed that 12% of returned books were overdue.
The college President wanted to test this claim.
A random sample of 200 returned books revealed that only 15 were overdue.
(i) Write down the null hypothesis, H_0.
(ii) Calculate the margin of error, correct to 2 decimal places.
(iii) Write down the sample proportion.
(iv) Work out a confidence interval for the percentage of returned books that were overdue.
(v) At the 95% confidence level, can the library's claim by justified?

9. Jack rolled a dice 240 times and 52 sixes were recorded.
   Jack suspected that the dice was biased.
   He carried out a hypothesis test to see if the dice was biased.
   (i) Write down the null hypothesis H_0.
   (ii) Write down the alternative hypothesis H_1.
   (iii) What is the sample size?
   (iv) Calculate the margin of error, correct to 2 decimal places.
   (v) Work out the sample proportion, correct to 2 decimal places.
   (vi) If the dice was not biased, what percentage of sixes would Jack expect?
   Give your answer correct to the nearest whole number.
   (vii) Work out a confidence interval for the proportion of sixes obtained.
   (viii) Is Jack's suspicion justified at the 95% confidence level?

Test yourself 19

1. In the given normal curve, the mean $\bar{x}$
   is 60 and the standard deviation $\sigma = 4$.

   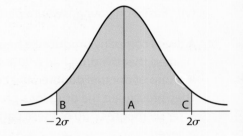

   (i) Write down the percentage of all
   the values that are in the shaded
   area.
   (ii) Write down the values represented
   by A, B and C.
   (iii) Use the Empirical Rule to find the range within which 68% of the values lie.
   (iv) If a value is selected at random, find the probability that it comes from the shaded
   area.
   (v) If there are 1000 values in the full distribution, how many of them lie in the shaded
   area?
   (vi) How many of the 1000 values are greater than 60?

2. (a) In a normal distribution, the mean $\bar{x} = 30$ and the standard deviation $\sigma = 3$.
   (i) Find the range within which 95% of the values lie.
   (ii) Find the range within which 99.7% of the values lie.
   (iii) What percentage of the values lie in the range [27, 33]?

   (b) In the given normal curve, the arrows
   indicate intervals of one standard
   deviation. If the mean $\bar{x} = 44$ and the
   standard deviation $\sigma = 6$, write down
   the values represented by A, B, C, D
   and E.

   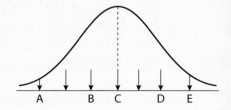

3. A political party claimed that it had the support of 23% of the electorate.
A newspaper carried out an opinion poll to test this claim.
In a random sample of 1000 voters, 250 stated that they support the party.
   (i)   Write down the null hypothesis.
   (ii) Write down the alternative hypothesis.
   (iii) What is the sample size?
   (iv) Calculate the margin of error.
   (v)   Work out the sample proportion.
   (vi) Work out a confidence interval.
   (vii) At the 95% confidence level, can the party's claim be accepted?

4. (a) The diagrams below show two normal curves.
        Write down the percentage of values in each of the shaded areas.

   (i)   (ii)

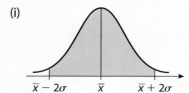
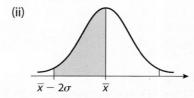

   (b) The lengths of roofing nails are normally distributed with a mean of 20 mm and a
        standard deviation of 3 mm.
        (i)   What percentage of nails lie between 17 mm and 23 mm?
        (ii) What percentage of nails lie between 14 mm and 26 mm?
        (iii) If 3000 nails were measured, how many of them would have a length
              between 17 mm and 23 mm?
        (iv) If a nail is selected at random, what is the probability that its length is greater
              than 20 mm?

5. The owner of a large apple-orchard claims that 10% of the apples on the trees in his orchard
   have been attacked by birds. A local wildlife organisation is looking to test this claim.
   A random sample of 2500 apples is picked and 275 are found to have been attacked by
   birds.
   (i)   Write down the null hypothesis.
   (ii) Write down the alternative hypothesis.
   (iii) What is the sample size?
   (iv) Work out the margin of error.
   (v)   Calculate the sample proportion.
   (vi) Work out a confidence interval.
   (vii) At the 95% confidence level, should the orchard-owner's claim be accepted by the
         wildlife organisation?

Answers

Chapter 1: Algebra 1

Exercise 1.1

1. 5
2. −4
3. −6
4. 8
5. 3
6. 4
7. 3
8. 4
9. 10
10. 2
11. −12
12. −3
13. 2
14. −7
15. −4
16. 72
17. −30
18. −42
19. 48
20. 63
21. −63
22. −36
23. 24
24. −24
25. 3
26. −3
27. 4
28. −9
29. −2
30. −27
31. −12
32. 9
33. 30
34. 21
35. 27
36. 1
37. 18
38. 72
39. 11
40. 0
41. 4
42. 4
43. −12
44. −6
45. −2
46. (i) −2 (ii) −4 (iii) 2
(iv) 5 (v) 2 (vi) 6

Exercise 1.2

1. $13x$
2. $3x$
3. $7a$
4. $6a$
5. a
6. $2y$
7. $5x^2$
8. $3x^2 - 2x$
9. $7a^2 - 2b$
10. $-2x + 2$
11. $4a + 4$
12. $6x^2 - 2$
13. (i) $x^2 + 7x + 12$ (ii) $2x^2 + 5x + 3$
(iii) $2x^2 + 5x - 12$ (iv) $2x^2 + 8x - 10$
(v) $6x^2 + 13x - 5$ (vi) $2x^2 - 15x + 18$
14. (i) $19x - 17$ (ii) $2x^2 - 17x$
(iii) $x - 10$ (iv) $2x^2 + 6x + 3$
15. (i) $x^2 + 4x + 4$ (ii) $x^2 - 6x + 9$
(iii) $4x^2 + 12x + 9$ (iv) $9x^2 - 12x + 4$
16. (i) $2x$ (ii) 2 (iii) $4x$, 15 (iv) $4x$, 8
17. $12x - 24$
18. (i) 3 (ii) $a + 6$
19. (i) $18ab + 6b^2$ (ii) $12a + 10b$
20. $x^2 + 19x - 24$

Exercise 1.3

1. 8
2. −2
3. 12
4. 4
5. 21
6. 24
7. 0
8. 22
9. 19
10. 21
11. 69
12. −15
13. (i) 33 (ii) −21 (iii) 7 (iv) 2
14. (i) A, D, F (ii) C, D, E
15. (i) 11 (ii) −4 (iii) 4 (iv) 2

Exercise 1.4

1. $x = 4$
2. $x = 5$
3. $x = 5$
4. $x = 8$
5. $x = 6\frac{1}{2}$
6. $x = 3$
7. $x = 2$
8. $x = 6$
9. $x = 5$
10. $x = 3$
11. $x = 6$
12. $x = 5$
13. $x = 7$
14. $x = 7$
15. $x = 5$
16. $x = 2$
17. $x = 5$
18. $x = 1$
19. $x = 10$
20. $x = 10$
21. $x = 5$
22. $x = 3$
23. $x = 3$
24. $x = 9$
25. $x = 2$
26. (i) 15 (ii) $60 - 2x$
(iii) $9\frac{1}{2}$ (iv) 10
27. $x = 35°$; 101°, 64°, 15°

Exercise 1.5

1. $x = 12$
2. $x = 1$
3. $x = 7$
4. $x = 21$
5. $x = 11$
6. $x = 6$
7. $x = 4$
8. $x = 3$
9. $x = 2$
10. $x = 5$
11. $x = -5$
12. $x = 7\frac{1}{2}$
13. $x = 4$
14. $x = 7$
15. $x = 7$
16. $x = 3$
17. $x = 6$
18. $x = 8$
19. $x = 8$
20. $x = 2$
21. $x = 24$
22. $x = 30$
23. $x = 2$
24. $x = 1\frac{1}{2}$
25. $x = 1$
26. $x = \frac{1}{2}$
27. $x = 11$
28. 8 cm
29. (i) $\dfrac{3(x + 6)}{5} = x - 4$ (ii) 15 cm

Exercise 1.6

1. $\dfrac{13}{12}$
2. $\dfrac{13}{10}$
3. $\dfrac{11}{24}$
4. $\dfrac{5x}{6}$
5. $\dfrac{9x}{4}$
6. $\dfrac{7x}{6}$
7. $\dfrac{10x + 9}{12}$
8. $\dfrac{9x - 17}{6}$
9. $\dfrac{17x - 24}{15}$
10. $\dfrac{-x - 6}{6}$
11. $\dfrac{3x + 5}{12}$
12. $\dfrac{13x + 7}{20}$
13. $\dfrac{2x + 3}{x(x + 3)}$
14. $\dfrac{5x + 15}{x(x + 5)}$
15. $\dfrac{5x + 14}{(x + 2)(x + 4)}$
16. $\dfrac{14x - 15}{(2x - 1)(2x - 3)}$
17. $\dfrac{25x - 7}{(4x - 1)(3x - 1)}$
18. $\dfrac{-x + 17}{(3x - 1)(x + 3)}$
19. $\dfrac{22}{(3x - 1)(2x + 3)}$
20. $\dfrac{-3x + 13}{4(3x - 5)}$

21. $\dfrac{-x + 20}{(2x - 7)(3x - 5)}$ **22.** $\dfrac{-x - 7}{(2x - 1)(x - 2)}$

23. $k = 34$

24. (i) $\dfrac{13a}{12}$ (ii) $\dfrac{9a + 4}{12}$ (iii) $\dfrac{7a - 5}{6}$

Exercise 1.7

1. A, F; B, D; C, H; E, G   **2.** D and E
3. A, D; B, G; F, H; C, E   **4.** $x \leqslant 3$
5. $x < -3$ **6.** $x \leqslant 4$
7. $x < 3$ **8.** $x \leqslant -3$
9. $x < -12$ **10.** $x \geqslant 4$
11. $x \leqslant 1$ **12.** $x \leqslant -5$
13. $x \leqslant -8$ **14.** $x \geqslant -1$
15. $x > 2$ **16.** $x \geqslant 1$
17. $-3 < x \leqslant 3$ **18.** $-\frac{1}{2} \leqslant x \leqslant 3$
19. $\frac{1}{2} < x \leqslant 8$ **20.** $x = 2, 3, 4$
21. (i) (b) is true   (ii) 9

Exercise 1.8

1. $x = 4, y = 1$ **2.** $x = 5, y = 2$
3. $x = 3, y = -2$ **4.** $x = 3, y = 1$
5. $x = -1, y = -2$ **6.** $x = 2, y = 3$
7. $x = 4, y = 2$ **8.** $x = 5, y = -2$
9. $x = \frac{13}{2}, y = 1$ **10.** $x = 3, y = 1$
11. $x = -2, y = 3$ **12.** $x = 6, y = 3$
13. $x = -2, y = 3$ **14.** $x = 4, y = -3$
15. $x = -1, y = -1$ **16.** $x = 1, y = 5$
17. $x = \frac{3}{2}, y = 2$ **18.** $x = 2, y = 1$
19. $x = 2, y = 3$ **20.** $x = 8, y = 3$
21. $x = 6, y = -4$
22. (i) $x = \frac{1}{2}, y = \frac{5}{2}$ (ii) 6.5 cm

Exercise 1.9

1. 7, 2   **2.** 10, 3
3. €9, €6   **4.** 28, 15
5. 196 g, 366 g   **6.** (ii) $a = 2\frac{1}{2}, b = 3$
7. 40 cows, 10 hens
8. (i) 80 g   (ii) 120 g
9. Rory – 9, Sarah – 3
10. (i) $x = 1, y = 2$ (ii) $x = 3, y = 0$
   (iii) $x = -1, y = -2$
11. (i) (a) $x = 1, y = 3$ (b) $x = 0, y = 4$
   (ii) Parallel lines $\Rightarrow$ no point of intersection
12. $\frac{14}{49}, \frac{15}{50}$
13. $|AB| = 21$ cm, $|BC| = 2$ cm

Exercise 1.10

1. (i) $x = \dfrac{y + 4}{2}$ (ii) $b = \dfrac{a + 6}{8}$

(iii) $d = \dfrac{c + 1}{4}$ (iv) $k = \dfrac{h + 2}{2}$

2. (i) $b = \dfrac{a + 5}{3}$ (ii) $w = \dfrac{b - 2}{4}$

(iii) $e = \dfrac{d + 12}{6}$ (iv) $h = \dfrac{-g + 18}{5}$

3. (i) $t = \dfrac{v - u}{a}$ (ii) $p = \dfrac{k - bq}{a}$

(iii) $g = 5(p - 3h)$

4. (i) $x = y + 2z$ (ii) $x = \dfrac{b + 4c}{3}$

(iii) $x = \dfrac{-6y + 7}{3}$ (iv) $x = 6y + 24$

5. (i) $a = \dfrac{2b + 1}{4}$ (ii) $a = \dfrac{5}{b - 3}$

(iii) $a = \dfrac{4b + 21}{7}$

6. (i) $a = b(k + 2)$ (ii) $v = \dfrac{u}{s - 10}$

7. (i) $a = 2(c + 4b)$ (ii) $a = \dfrac{4b + 3c}{2}$

(iii) $x = \dfrac{y + 1}{6}$ (iv) $b = \dfrac{a + 30}{10}$

(v) $z = \dfrac{-3x + y}{2}$ (vi) $b = \dfrac{4a + 3c}{2}$

8. (i) $a = \dfrac{mn}{m - n}$ (ii) $n = \dfrac{b - a + d}{d}$

9. (i) $y = \dfrac{3x}{20} - z$ (ii) $b = \dfrac{6c}{2a - 3}$

(iii) $y = \dfrac{x - tz}{2}$ (iv) $t = \dfrac{q^2}{p - q}$

10. (i) $a = \dfrac{b + xb}{x - 1}$ (ii) $x = \dfrac{y + 4}{y - 3}$

(iii) $r = \dfrac{pq}{p + q}$

11. $k = \dfrac{abe}{ab - d}$ **12.** D, E, F

13. (i) $b = x^2 - a$ (ii) $y = \dfrac{x}{a^2}$

(iii) $b = \dfrac{4a}{k^2}$

14. $F = \dfrac{9C + 160}{5}$

15. (i) $q = \dfrac{8p}{pt - 8}$ (ii) $b = \dfrac{am}{ac + m}$

Test yourself 1

1. (i) $x = 1$ (ii) $x = 3, y = 4$

(iii) $b = \dfrac{c - ax}{y}$

2. (i) $x = 2\frac{1}{2}$ (ii) A, B, D, E
   (iii) $2\frac{3}{10}$ (iv) $v = 23, w = -5$

3. (i) $-2x + 9$ (ii) $x = \frac{1}{4}$
   (iii) $x \leqslant -1$ (iv) $x = 3\frac{1}{2}$

4. (i) 10   (ii) $x = 4$ (iii) $2 < x \leqslant 5$
   (iv) (a) A: $x + y = 3$
            B: $y = 2x$
            C: $x - 2y = 3$
     (b) (i) $x = 1, y = 2$
         (ii) $x = 3, y = 0$
       (iii) $x = -1, y = -2$

5. (i) $x \leqslant -3$ (ii) B, E
   (iii) $a = 5, b = 2$ (iv) $\dfrac{9x - 13}{6}$; $x = 7$

6. (i) $x = 4$ (ii) $(2, -1)$ (iii) 1
   (iv) (a) $r = \sqrt{\dfrac{3V}{\pi h}}$ (b) $r = 3.5$ cm

7. (i) -1 (ii) Megan – 21, Olivia – 26
   (iii) $r = \dfrac{pq}{3q - p}$
   (iv) (b) $r = \dfrac{P}{\pi + 6}$ (c) $h = \dfrac{30}{\pi + 6}$

15. $x = \frac{1}{6}$ or $x = -3$ **16.** $x = 0$ or $x = 7$
17. $x = 0$ or $x = \frac{5}{2}$ **18.** $x = 0$ or $x = -\frac{4}{3}$
19. $x = 0$ or $x = \frac{9}{2}$ **20.** $x = 0$ or $x = -\frac{10}{3}$
21. $x = 0$ or $x = \frac{12}{5}$ **22.** $x = \pm 3$
23. $x = \pm 7$ **24.** $x = \pm\frac{3}{2}$
25. $x = \pm\frac{5}{2}$ **26.** $x = \pm\frac{4}{3}$
27. $x = \pm\frac{1}{2}$ **28.** $x = -2$ or $x = 7$
29. $x = -\frac{1}{2}$ or $x = 5$ **30.** $x = -\frac{5}{2}$ or $x = 6$
31. (ii) (a) $x = \frac{3}{2}$ (b) 4 cm, $3\frac{1}{2}$ cm
32. (i) (a) $(x^2 + 6x)$ cm²   (b) $(8x + 24)$ cm²
   (ii) $x = 6$; $l = 12$ cm, $w = 6$ cm;
        x must be positive
33. (i) $(3x + 4)^2 = (2x + 6)^2 + (x + 2)^2$
   (ii) $x = 3$
   (iii) 13 cm
34. (i) $x = 3$ or $x = 5$
   (ii) $x = -2$ or $x = -4$
   (iii) $x = -1$ or $x = 2$
35. (ii) $x = 3$, perimeter $= 30$ cm

Chapter 2: Quadratic Equations

Exercise 2.1

1. $(x + 6)(x + 1)$ **2.** $(x + 3)(x + 4)$
3. $(2x + 1)(x + 2)$ **4.** $(2x + 1)(x + 4)$
5. $(2x + 1)(x + 7)$ **6.** $(3x + 2)(x + 2)$
7. $(3x + 4)(x + 1)$ **8.** $(5x + 2)(x + 3)$
9. $(2k + 1)(2k + 3)$ **10.** $(4x + 1)(x + 3)$
11. $(10x + 7)(x + 1)$ **12.** $(3x + 10)(2x + 1)$
13. $(x - 3)(x - 4)$ **14.** $(x - 4)(x - 9)$
15. $(2x - 1)(x - 3)$ **16.** $(2x - 1)(x - 9)$
17. $(2x + 3)(x - 5)$ **18.** $(4x - 1)(2x + 3)$
19. $(3x - 1)(2x - 3)$ **20.** $(4x + 1)(2x - 3)$
21. $(4x - 1)(2x - 3)$ **22.** $(3x - 2)(x + 5)$
23. $(2x - 9)(x - 6)$ **24.** $(6x - 11)(x + 2)$
25. $(6x - 5)(4x + 3)$ **26.** $(6x - 1)(x - 3)$
27. $(5x + 2)(3x - 4)$ **28.** $x(x - 4)$
29. $x(x + 8)$ **30.** $x(2x - 3)$
31. $(x - y)(x + y)$ **32.** $(x - 5y)(x + 5y)$
33. $(4x - 1)(4x + 1)$ **34.** $(4x - 5y)(4x + 5y)$
35. $(7x - 10)(7x + 10)$ **36.** $(6x - 7y)(6x + 7y)$

Exercise 2.2

1. $x = 4$ or $x = -1$ **2.** $x = \frac{1}{2}$ or $x = -2$
3. $x = 0$ or $x = \frac{5}{2}$ **4.** $x = -1$ or $x = 3$
5. $x = 2$ or $x = 6$ **6.** $x = -1$ or $x = 5$
7. $x = -2$ or $x = 4$ **8.** $x = 3$ or $x = -5$
9. $x = \frac{1}{2}$ or $x = 2$ **10.** $x = \frac{2}{3}$ or $x = -\frac{1}{2}$
11. $x = \frac{1}{4}$ or $x = 7$ **12.** $x = -\frac{4}{3}$ or $x = \frac{7}{3}$
13. $x = \frac{1}{2}$ or $x = \frac{5}{2}$ **14.** $x = -\frac{2}{3}$ or $x = 5$

Exercise 2.3

1. $x = 1$ or $x = 4$ **2.** $x = 3$ or $x = 4$
3. $x = 2$ or $x = 3$ **4.** $x = -3$ or $x = 5$
5. $x = \frac{3}{2}$ or $x = 1$ **6.** $x = -1$ or $x = 3$
7. $x = 0$ or $x = 4$ **8.** $x = \frac{2}{3}$ or $x = 2$
9. $x = \frac{3}{2}$ or $x = -2$ **10.** $x = -3$ or $x = 4$
11. $x = \frac{2}{3}$ or $x = 1$ **12.** $x = 1$ or $x = 3$
13. $x = -2$ or $x = 4$ **14.** $x = 5$ or $x = \frac{3}{2}$
15. $x = \frac{3}{2}$ or $x = 6$ **16.** $x = \frac{1}{2}$ or $x = -3$
17. $x = 2$ or $x = -\frac{2}{3}$ **18.** $x = -1$ or $x = -\frac{1}{2}$
19. (i) $x = \frac{3}{5}$ (ii) $x = -2$ (iii) $x = 0$

Exercise 2.4

1. $-3.41, -0.59$ **2.** $-5.24, -0.76$
3. $-3.45, 1.45$ **4.** $-1.83, 3.83$
5. $-0.81, 0.31$ **6.** $-0.43, 0.77$
7. $0.42, 1.58$ **8.** $-2.91, 0.57$
9. $-0.35, 1.15$ **10.** $-2.39, -0.28$
11. $-0.36, 1.86$ **12.** $-2.59, 0.26$
13. $-1.55, 0.80$ **14.** $0.72, 2.78$
15. $-2.14, 0.47$ **16.** $0.3, 6.7$
17. $0.3, 3.2$ **18.** $-2.8, 1.3$
19. $-4.3, 3.3$ **20.** $-1.4, 1.8$
21. $-0.8, 3.5$
22. (i) $x^2 + 3x - 4$
   (ii) $x = 2.53$
   (iii) 6.53 cm

Exercise 2.5

1. $(2, 1), (1, 2)$ **2.** $(3, -1), (1, -3)$

3. $(3, 3), (-3, -3)$ **4.** $(1, 1), (-3, 9)$

5. $(4, 2), (-4, -2)$ **6.** $(-4, -3), (3, 4)$

7. $(3, 0), (0, 3)$ **8.** $(4, 3), (3, 4)$

9. $(1, 0), (6, 5)$ **10.** $(-2, -2), (1, 4)$

11. $(1, 2), (4, -4)$ **12.** $(5, 1), (-7, -5)$

13. $(1, 1), (-3, 9)$ **14.** $(1, 1)$; tangent

15. $(3, 5), (-4, 12)$

Exercise 2.6

1. $x^2 - 6x + 8 = 0$ **2.** $x^2 - 6x + 5 = 0$

3. $x^2 - 5x + 6 = 0$ **4.** $x^2 - 2x - 3 = 0$

5. $x^2 - 2x - 8 = 0$ **6.** $x^2 + 7x + 12 = 0$

7. $x^2 - 4x - 12 = 0$ **8.** $x^2 - 5x = 0$

9. $2x^2 + 3x - 2 = 0$ **10.** $x^2 + 9x + 20 = 0$

11. $2x^2 - 7x - 4 = 0$ **12.** $4x^2 - 33x + 8 = 0$

13. $x^2 + 4x = 0$ **14.** $4x^2 - 1 = 0$

15. $x^2 - 9 = 0$ **16.** $4x^2 - x = 0$

17. $a = -1, b = -2$

Exercise 2.7

1. (i) a^7 (ii) a^6 (iii) a^4 (iv) $6x^3$

    (v) $3a^5$ (vi) x^3 (vii) a^3 (viii) $3a^4$

    (ix) a^6 (x) 1

2. (i) 5^2 (ii) 8^2 (or 4^3 or 2^6)   (iii) 3^3

    (iv) 2^5 (v) 5^3 (vi) 9^2 (or 3^4)

3. A: 3^3, B: 3^{-2}, C: 2^{-6}, D: 6^{-3}, E: 1, F: 2^{-2},

    G: 3^2, H: 5^5

4. (i) 8 (ii) 4 (iii) -1

    (iv) 2 (v) -4 (vi) -2

5. (i) $5n^{11}$ (ii) $6n^3$ (iii) $21n^{13}$

    (iv) $30n^9$ (v) $16n^2$ (vi) $8n^3$

    (vii) $125n^6$ (viii) $32n^{15}$

6. (i) $2m^7$ (ii) $\dfrac{m^2}{5}$ (iii) $2m^{-4}$

    (iv) $\dfrac{2m^3}{3}$ (v) $\dfrac{3m^{-2}}{2}$

7. A & E; B & H; C & G; D & F

8. (i) 5 (ii) 3 (iii) 4 (iv) 4 (v) 6 (vi) 5

9. (i) 36 (ii) $\frac{1}{8}$ (iii) $\frac{4}{9}$ (iv) $\frac{1}{9}$ (v) 12

10. A & I; B & H; C & G; D & F

11. (i) $\frac{1}{4}$ (ii) 1 (iii) 8 (iv) $\frac{3}{4}$ (v) $\frac{2}{3}$

12. (i) $x^{\frac{1}{2}}$ (ii) $a^{\frac{1}{3}}$ (iii) $a^{\frac{1}{4}}$ (iv) $x^{\frac{2}{3}}$ (v) $a^{\frac{3}{4}}$

13. (i) $\sqrt{x}$ (ii) $\sqrt[4]{a}$ (iii) $\sqrt[3]{x^2}$

    (iv) $\sqrt{a^5}$ (v) $\sqrt[3]{\left(\dfrac{a}{x}\right)}$

14. (i) 2 (ii) 4 (iii) 8 (iv) 8

    (v) 9 (vi) 64 (vii) 16 (viii) 1000

    (ix) 27 (x) 25

15. (i) $\frac{1}{3}$ (ii) $\frac{1}{16}$ (iii) $\frac{1}{2}$ (iv) 2 (v) $\frac{1}{4}$

16. (i) $\frac{1}{4}$ (ii) 4 (iii) $\frac{1}{8}$ (iv) $\frac{1}{1000}$ (v) $\frac{1}{8}$

17. (i) 2^3 (ii) $2^{\frac{1}{2}}$ (iii) $2^{\frac{3}{2}}$ (iv) $2^{\frac{5}{2}}$ (v) $2^{\frac{1}{2}}$

18. (i) 5^2 (ii) $5^{\frac{1}{2}}$ (iii) $5^{\frac{3}{2}}$ (iv) $5^{\frac{5}{2}}$ (v) $5^{\frac{1}{2}}$

19. (i) 2^4 (ii) $3^{\frac{5}{2}}$

20. 5

Exercise 2.8

1. (i) 2^3 (ii) 2^4 (iii) 2^{-2} (iv) 2^{-3} (v) 2^{-5}

2. (i) 3^2 (ii) 3^3 (iii) 3^4 (iv) 3^{-3} (v) 3^{-4}

3. 3 **4.** 3 **5.** $\frac{5}{2}$ **6.** $\frac{3}{2}$

7. $\frac{3}{2}$ **8.** $\frac{3}{2}$ **9.** $\frac{5}{3}$ **10.** $\frac{5}{4}$

11. -2 **12.** -3 **13.** $-\frac{3}{2}$ **14.** -3

15. $-\frac{3}{2}$ **16.** $\frac{4}{3}$ **17.** -4 **18.** -3

19. $-\frac{5}{2}$ **20.** 3 **21.** 2 **22.** 3

23. (i) $2^{\frac{1}{2}}$ (ii) $2^{\frac{3}{2}}$ (iii) $2^{\frac{3}{2}}$ (iv) $2^{-\frac{3}{2}}$

    (v) $2^{-\frac{3}{2}}$ (vi) $2^{\frac{1}{2}}$

24. (i) $\frac{3}{2}$ (ii) $\frac{3}{2}$ (iii) $-\frac{1}{2}$ (iv) $-\frac{5}{3}$

25. (i) $x = -\frac{1}{2}$ (ii) $x = -\frac{3}{2}$

    (iii) $x = 2$ (iv) $x = \frac{5}{4}$

26. $3^{\frac{7}{2}}; \frac{3}{4}$ **27.** $2^{\frac{4}{3}}; \frac{4}{3}$ **28.** $3^{\frac{5}{2}}; 3\frac{1}{4}$

29. $2^{\frac{5}{2}}; \frac{9}{4}$ **30.** $3^{-\frac{5}{2}}; \frac{17}{4}$

31. (i) 2^4 (ii) $2^{\frac{7}{2}}; x = \frac{17}{4}$

Exercise 2.9

1. (i) 3 (ii) 6 (iii) 12 (iv) 5 (v) 4

2. (i) $2\sqrt{2}$ (ii) $2\sqrt{3}$ (iii) $3\sqrt{2}$

    (iv) $3\sqrt{3}$ (v) $3\sqrt{5}$

3. (i) $5\sqrt{3}$ (ii) $6\sqrt{2}$ (iii) $5\sqrt{5}$

    (iv) $12\sqrt{3}$ (v) $8\sqrt{3}$

4. (i) $8\sqrt{3}$ (ii) $5\sqrt{2}$ (iii) $5\sqrt{2}$

    (iv) $7\sqrt{2}$ (v) $5\sqrt{3}$ (vi) $3\sqrt{3}$

5. (i) 5 (ii) 18 (iii) 60 (iv) 21

6. (i) $5 - 2\sqrt{5}$ (ii) $6 - 4\sqrt{3}$ (iii) $6 - \sqrt{6}$

7. (i) $2\sqrt{10} - 10$ (ii) 1 (iii) 22

    (iv) -9 (v) -11 (vi) -3

8. (i) 2 (ii) $-7 - 13\sqrt{2}$ (iii) 1

9. $24 - 8\sqrt{5}$ **10.** $4\sqrt{15}$

Exercise 2.10

1. 5 **2.** 9 **3.** 5

4. 6 **5.** 7 **6.** 9

7. 6 **8.** 2 **9.** 5

10. 2 **11.** $1, 4$ **12.** 9

13. $\frac{3}{2}$ **14.** $10\frac{2}{3}$ **15.** 3

16. $x^2 - x; x = 3$

17. $x - \frac{4}{x}$; $x = 4$ **18.** $k = \frac{1}{10}$

Test yourself 2

1. (i) $(2x - 1)(x + 3)$; $-3, \frac{1}{2}$

   (ii) $(3, 4), (5, 0)$ (iii) (a) $\frac{3}{4}$ (b) 3

2. (i) $3x + 13$ (ii) $7.77, -0.77$

   (iii) $5\sqrt{2}$ (iv) $3^{\frac{3}{2}}$; $x = \frac{1}{2}$

3. (i) $b = -5$ (ii) $(5, -1), (-7, 5)$

   (iii) $8\,\text{cm}, 3\,\text{cm}$

4. (i) $4x^2$ (ii) $\frac{1}{3}, 2$ (iii) A, C, D, E

5. (i) $k = -3$ (ii) (a) $x = \frac{5}{2}$ (b) $x = \frac{1}{4}$

   (iii) $(1, 1), (4, 7)$

   (iv) $2 \pm \sqrt{3}$

6. (i) (a) 4 (b) 125 (c) $\frac{1}{27}$

   (ii) $(\frac{1}{4}, -\frac{1}{4}), (-\frac{1}{2}, -\frac{1}{2})$

   (iii) $3\sqrt{2}$

   (iv) $x = \frac{3}{4}$

7. (i) (a) $(x + 7)\,\text{cm}$ (b) $(x^2 + 7x)\,\text{cm}^2$

   (ii) (a) $x = 4$ (b) $30\,\text{cm}$

8. (i) $\frac{3}{5}$ (ii) $\frac{1}{x - 1}$; $\pm\sqrt{3}$

   (iii) $x = -\frac{1}{8}$ (iv) $4, 5$

Chapter 3: Coordinate Geometry – The Line

Exercise 3.1

1. A = $(5, 4)$, B = $(6, 1)$, C = $(3, 2)$, D = $(-4, 3)$,
    E = $(-4, 0)$, F = $(-3, -3)$, G = $(0, -2)$,
    H = $(4, -2)$, I = $(3, 0)$

3. (i) First   (ii) Third   (iii) Fourth

   (iv) Second   (v) Fourth   (vi) Third

4. (i) x-axis   (ii) x-axis   (iii) y-axis

   (iv) y-axis   (v) Both axes\origin

5. (i) A$(4, 2)$, B$(-3, 2)$, C$(-5, -2)$, D$(5, -3)$

   (ii) $1.3\,\text{km}$ (iii) $1.3\,\text{km}$

6. (i) $(0, 8), (9, -1)$ (ii) $(4, 11), (0, 15)$

   (iii) $(7, 1), (-3, 11), (10, -2)$

Exercise 3.2

1. (i) $\sqrt{34}$ (ii) $\sqrt{50}$ (iii) $\sqrt{53}$; No

2. (i) $|FE| = 6, |ED| = 3$ (ii) $\sqrt{45}$

3. (i) $\sqrt{10}$ (ii) $\sqrt{5}$ (iii) $\sqrt{13}$

   (iv) $\sqrt{89}$ (v) $\sqrt{53}$ (vi) 5

4. (i) $\sqrt{26}$ (ii) $\sqrt{8}$ (iii) $\sqrt{10}$ (iv) $\sqrt{8}$

6. $|XY| = \sqrt{65}$; $|XZ| = \sqrt{65}$; $|YZ| = \sqrt{26}$;

   $|XY| = |XZ| \Rightarrow \triangle XYZ$ is isosceles

7. A$(2, 0)$, B$(6, 7)$, C$(10, 0)$, D$(6, 0)$; $2\sqrt{65}$ units

8. $\sqrt{53}$

9. (i) $\sqrt{18}$ (ii) $\sqrt{34}$; No

10. $k = 1$ or $k = 3$

11. $k = 5$ or $k = -1$

12. $\sqrt{26}\,\text{km}$

Exercise 3.3

1. (i) $(4, 3)$ (ii) $(1, 3)$ (iii) $(3, 1)$

   (iv) $(1, 1)$ (v) $(1, -2)$ (vi) $(-2, 0)$

2. $(0, \frac{11}{2})$; y-axis

3. $(2, 4)$ **4.** $(1, \frac{1}{2})$

5. $(-1, -1)$ **6.** $(-1, 6)$

Exercise 3.4

1. (i) $a + c$ (ii) $b + d$

2. (i) b (ii) $\frac{2}{3}$ (iii) 2

3. Line is falling from left to right; $-\frac{1}{2}$

4. (i) 1 (ii) $-\frac{3}{2}$ (iii) 8

   (iv) 1 (v) 1 (vi) $\frac{2}{3}$

5. They are parallel

6. Yes, parallel

8. $a = \frac{1}{2}, b = 1, c = 2$

9. (i) $\frac{3}{4}$ (ii) $-\frac{4}{3}$

10. (i) $-\frac{3}{2}$ (ii) $-\frac{5}{4}$ (iii) $\frac{4}{3}$

   (iv) $\frac{5}{2}$ (v) 2

11. (i) 1 (ii) -1

12. (i) -1 (ii) 1

13. $k = 5$

14. $k = -\frac{8}{3}$

15. (i) $\frac{1}{2}$ (ii) $\frac{2}{k - 1}$ (iii) 5

16. (i) Each line is falling from left to right

   (ii) $\ell = -2, m = -1, n = -\frac{1}{2}, k = 0$

Exercise 3.5

1. (i) $2x - y - 2 = 0$ (ii) $4x - y + 1 = 0$

   (iii) $5x - y + 13 = 0$ (iv) $3x + y + 6 = 0$

   (v) $5x + y + 17 = 0$ (vi) $2x - 3y - 9 = 0$

2. (i) $3x - 4y - 19 = 0$ (ii) $3x - 5y + 22 = 0$

3. (i) $4x - y + 11 = 0$ (ii) $2x + y + 1 = 0$

   (iii) $3x - 4y + 18 = 0$ (iv) $2x + 3y - 5 = 0$

4. $3x + y = 0$

5. (i) $3x - y = 0$ (ii) $5x + y = 0$

   (iii) $x - 3y = 0$ (iv) $3x + 2y = 0$

6. -3; $3x + y - 5 = 0$

7. (i) $3x - 2y = 0$ (ii) $2x + y = 0$

   (iii) $x + 6y - 1 = 0$ (iv) $4x + 5y - 7 = 0$

   (v) $x - y + 5 = 0$ (vi) $2x - y + 1 = 0$

8. $5x + 4y - 2 = 0$

9. (i) A$(4, 3)$, B$(7, 5)$, C$(10, 3)$

   (ii) $\frac{2}{3}$ (iii) $2x - 3y + 1 = 0$

Exercise 3.6

1. (i) $y = -x + 4$; -1 (ii) $y = -3x + 5$; -3
   (iii) $y = -\frac{2}{3}x + \frac{7}{3}$; $-\frac{2}{3}$ (iv) $y = \frac{5}{2}x + \frac{3}{2}$; $\frac{5}{2}$
   (v) $y = -\frac{3}{4}x + \frac{1}{2}$; $-\frac{3}{4}$ (vi) $y = \frac{3}{4}x + \frac{3}{2}$; $\frac{3}{4}$

2. $y = -\frac{2}{3}x + \frac{7}{3}$;
   (i) $-\frac{2}{3}$ (ii) $-\frac{2}{3}$ (iii) $\frac{3}{2}$

3. -2

5. (i) $y = 3x + 6$ (ii) $y = -\frac{1}{3}x + 11$

6. Yes; parallel

7. (i) 3 (ii) $(0, -2)$

8. (i) $a + f$ (ii) $a + e$ or $b + d$
   (iii) e (iv) a

9. $x - 2y + 2 = 0$ or $y = \frac{1}{2}x + 1$

10. $k = 4$ 11. $k = 2$ 12. $k = 6$

Exercise 3.7

1. -2; $2x + y - 8 = 0$
2. $3x - y - 9 = 0$
3. $\frac{2}{3}$; $-\frac{3}{2}$; $3x + 2y - 10 = 0$
4. $2x - 3y + 7 = 0$
5. $3x - y + 12 = 0$
6. $x + 3y = 0$
7. $P(2, 4)$; $5x - y - 6 = 0$
8. $2x + y - 5 = 0$
9. $x + 4y - 28 = 0$
10. C
11. $x + 2y - 10 = 0$
12. (i) $\frac{5}{3}$ (ii) (b) $3x + 5y = 2$

Exercise 3.8

1. a: $y = 1$; b: $y = 3$; c: $x = 3$; d: $x = -1$
3. (i) $x = 3$ (ii) $(0, 6)$ (iii) 4
   (iv) 1 (v) 9 sq. units
4. x-axis: $(6, 0)$; y-axis: $(0, -3)$
6. x-axis: $(5, 0)$; y-axis: $(0, -\frac{5}{2})$
7. 9 sq. units
9. (i) A (ii) B
   (iii) Not perpendicular (iv) 7.5 sq. units
11. (i) d (ii) c (iii) a (iv) b
12. (iv) Not on line
14. $k = -6$
15. $k = 3$
16. (i) $k = 2$ (ii) $t = 5$

Exercise 3.9

1. $(4, 1)$ 2. $(1, 4)$ 3. $(2, 3)$
4. $(3, 1)$ 5 $(-2, 1)$ 6. $(-3, 1)$
7. $(-2, 3)$ 8. $(-3, -1)$ 9. $(-1, -2)$
10. $(3, -4)$ 11. $(-2, 5)$

Exercise 3.10

1. (i) $\frac{5}{2}$ sq. units (ii) $\frac{27}{2}$ sq. units
   (iii) $\frac{5}{2}$ sq. units (iv) 5 sq. units
   (v) 3 sq. units (vi) 9 sq. units
2. $B'(-7, -2)$; $C'(1, -2)$; 8 sq. units
3. (i) $\frac{9}{2}$ sq. units (ii) $\frac{33}{2}$ sq. units
   (iii) 15 sq. units (iv) 4 sq. units
4. 14 sq. units; 14 sq. units
5. 14 sq. units
6. 14 sq. units
7. 4 sq. units
8. Not a triangle, i.e. a straight line
9. $k = 1$

Test yourself 3

1. (i) $\sqrt{10}$ (ii) $\frac{1}{3}$
2. (ii) $-\frac{4}{3}$ (iii) $4x + 3y - 10 = 0$
3. (i) 2 (ii) $(0, -4)$
   (iii) $(2, 0)$ (iv) $-\frac{1}{2}$
4. (ii) $k = 3$
5. (i) $(0, 5)$; y-axis (ii) $\frac{4}{3}$
   (iii) $-\frac{3}{4}$ (iv) $3x + 4y = 0$
6. $\frac{1}{2}$; $y = \frac{1}{2}x + 1$
7. (i) -2 (ii) $(0, 4)$
8. (ii) $\frac{1}{2}$ (iii) $2x + y - 10 = 0$
9. (i) $k = 2$
   (ii) $A(3, 0)$, $B(0, 2)$; 3 sq. units
10. (i) $3x + y - 6 = 0$
    (ii) 6 m
    (iii) `6.3 m
11. $(2, 2)$
12. (i) $2x + y - 12 = 0$
    (ii) x-axis: $(6, 0)$; y-axis: $(0, 12)$
    (iii) 36 sq. units
13. (i) $2x - y + 1 = 0$
14. (i) b and c
    (ii) 2
    (iii) D, a; E, b; F, c
15. (i) $c = -7$
    (ii) $3x + 2y - 4 = 0$

Chapter 4: Collecting Data and Sampling

Exercise 4.1

1. (i) Discrete (ii) Discrete
   (iii) Continuous (iv) Discrete
   (v) Continuous
2. Continuous; time measured on a scale
3. Discrete

4. (i) Discrete (ii) Discrete
(iii) Continuous
5. Continuous; discrete
6. (i) Discrete (ii) Continuous
(iii) Discrete (iv) Continuous
(v) Discrete (vi) Continuous
(vii) Discrete

Exercise 4.2

1. (i) Numerical (ii) Categorical
(iii) Numerical (iv) Categorical
2. (i) Categorical (ii) Numerical
(iii) Numerical; number of buttons is discrete
3. (i) No (ii) Yes
(iii) Yes (iv) No
5. (ii) Number of eggs (iii) Amount of flour
6. Numerical … Categorical
7. (i) Categorical (ii) Numerical
(iii) Numerical
(iv) Categorical; Shoe-size is discrete; Bivariate continuous data
8. (i) True (ii) False
(iii) False (iv) False
(v) True (vi) False
(vii) True (viii) True

Exercise 4.3

1. (i) Primary (ii) Secondary
(iii) Primary (iv) Secondary
2. (i) Secondary data
(ii) Roy's; his results are more recent
3. Primary data
5. (i) No (ii) Primary

Exercise 4.4

1. (i) (c) (ii) (a) (iii) (b) (iv) (b)
2. Q(i); Q(ii) is a leading question
3. (i) Too personal (ii) Too vague
4. (i) Question too personal; Response boxes too vague
5. (i) Too personal
(ii) Leading question
(iii) (a) Numbers overlapping
6. B and D are leading or biased questions
7. Not suitable – too vague
8. (i) Too personal – may embarrass
9. QA: Too personal; QB: Leading question
10. (i) Too vague
11. (i) Too vague – may embarrass
(ii) Response boxes should be included
(iii) Too vague – open to different interpretations

15. (i) (a) Too vague; should provide appropriate choice of responses
(b) Too personal; may cause embarrassment

Exercise 4.5

1. B
2. B
3. People already at a cinema are probably interested in movies and would go more than the average sample.
4. Not representative as time frame too limited and confined.
5. People at a sports shop are already interested in sport and are more likely to play some sports
6. Gender-biased; only supermarkets surveyed; time too limited and so may be unrepresentative
7. Method 2; Totally random
11. (i) Not biased (ii) Biased
(iii) Biased
13. 300

Test yourself 4

1. (i) Numerical (ii) Categorical
(iii) Categorical (iv) Numerical
(v) Categorical (vi) Numerical
(vii) Categorical
2. (i) Discrete (ii) Discrete
(iii) Continuous (iv) Continuous
(v) Discrete (vi) Continuous
3. (i) Primary (ii) Secondary
(iii) Primary (iv) Seconday
(v) Secondary
4. (i) Univariate (ii) Bivariate
(iii) Bivariate (iv) Univariate
(v) Bivariate
5. (i) A (ii) A (iii) C
(iv) B (v) B (vi) A
(vii) B (viii) A (ix) A or C
(x) C
6. (i) B and C (ii) A and D
9. (i) 219

Chapter 5: Arithmetic

Exercise 5.1

1. (i) $\frac{3}{5}$ (ii) $\frac{4}{15}$ (iii) $\frac{3}{4}$ (iv) $\frac{5}{8}$
2. (i) $\frac{5}{8}$ (ii) $1\frac{5}{24}$ (iii) $\frac{19}{42}$ (iv) $1\frac{11}{18}$
3. (i) $5\frac{1}{4}$ (ii) $3\frac{11}{12}$ (iii) $4\frac{3}{10}$ (iv) $6\frac{1}{5}$
4. (i) $1\frac{3}{10}$ (ii) $2\frac{1}{6}$ (iii) $2\frac{1}{15}$ (iv) $2\frac{5}{24}$

5. (i) 10   (ii) 21   (iii) 39   (iv) 49

6. (i) $\frac{3}{2}$ (ii) $4\frac{2}{7}$ (iii) $\frac{3}{2}$ (iv) 10

7. (i) $\frac{1}{6}$ (ii) $\frac{5}{36}$ (iii) $\frac{5}{12}$ (iv) $\frac{5}{18}$

8. (i) 0.125   (ii) 0.625   (iii) 0.875
   (iv) 0.0625   (v) 0.4375

9. (i) 0.58, 0.6, $\frac{5}{8}$, $\frac{13}{20}$ (ii) $\frac{3}{10}$, 0.35, 0.4, $\frac{9}{20}$

10. (i) 750 m   (ii) 250 m

11. (i) 2.57   (ii) 2.6

12. (i) 1720.6   (ii) 8.1   (iii) 9.1

13. (i) 0.3   (ii) 0.4   (iii) 0.4

14. (i) 3   (ii) 2   (iii) 2   (iv) 3
   (v) 4   (vi) 3   (vii) 1   (viii) 3
   (ix) 4   (x) 3

15. (i) 3200   (ii) 650   (iii) 2900
   (iv) 29 000   (v) 41 000

16. (i) 7520   (ii) 294   (iii) 14.3
   (iv) 0.627   (v) 1.07

17. 1024 ℓ

18. 63

19. 90

Exercise 5.2

1. €56, €24   **2.** €104   **3.** €5508

4. 210   **5.** 81 kg   **6.** 6 : 3 : 1

7. €225   **8.** 2100 cm^2 **9.** 438

10. (i) 10 kg   (ii) 15 kg

11. 250

12. (i) 50 cm   (ii) 16 m

13. (i) 3 km   (ii) 18 cm

14. 80 m   **15.** 1.2 m

16. €10.00   **17.** 9.6 km\ℓ

18. (i) 86 : 5   (ii) 86   (iii) 80

19. (i) 80 km   (ii) 100 miles   (iii) 30 ft
   (iv) 360 cm   (v) 88 lb   (vi) 40 kg
   (vii) 70 pints   (viii) 48 ℓ

20. 500 m   **21.** 14 kg

Exercise 5.3

1. (i) 25%   (ii) 34%   (iii) 25%
   (iv) 40%   (v) 15%

2. (i) 0.75   (ii) 0.5   (iii) 0.64
   (iv) 0.06   (v) 0.025

3. (i) 11.25   (ii) 56   (iii) 54
   (iv) €31.50   (v) €221   (vi) 174 cm

4. (i) 7.5   (ii) €28.50   (iii) €480

5. (i) 25%   (ii) 15%   (iii) 25%

6. (i) 85%   (ii) 5%

7. 850

8. (i) 45   (ii) 112   (iii) 49
   (iv) 57.6   (v) 32 kg   (vi) €60.72

9. (i) 18   (ii) 161   (iii) 60
   (iv) 242.5   (v) 135   (vi) 42.75

10. €1600

11. (i) €245   (ii) €240

12. €650

13. (i) €320   (ii) 17%

14. (i) €4050   (ii) €370 000

15. 41%   **16.** 20%

17. $21\frac{1}{3}$%   **18.** €1104

19. (i) 12.5%   (ii) 4000 kg

20. (i) €800   (ii) €18 000

21. 84

22. Store A by €24.90

23. €479

Exercise 5.4

1. 8.7%   **2.** 7.7%   **3.** 4.7%

4. 7.4%   **5.** 1.3%

6. (i) 5.8%   (ii) 2.3%

7. 2.6%

8. (i) $F = 68°$ (ii) 2.9%

9. (i) 28.5 m   (ii) 27.5 m   (iii) $441\frac{3}{4}$ m^2

10. (i) 88 m   (ii) $410\frac{3}{4}$ m^2

11. (i) 2.85 kg   (ii) 165 kg   (iii) $555\frac{3}{4}$ kg

12. (i) 12.5 cm   (ii) $515\frac{5}{8}$ cm^3
   (iii) 179 cm^3 (iv) 14.6%

Exercise 5.5

1. (i) €1363.64   (ii) $3696

2. €2150.74

3. (i) €1764.71   (ii) £1700

4. (i) $1680   (ii) Y268 800
   (iii) €3409.09   (iv) €964.29
   (v) $450   (vi) Y636 363.64

5. 596 Swiss Francs

6. €57.89

7. €1625

8. 2%

9. €29 931; €3975 gain

Exercise 5.6

1. (i) €13 160   (ii) €9960

2. (i) €275.20   (ii) €231.20

3. €8080   **4.** €156.90

5. €7850   **6.** $r = 22$

7. €1000   **8.** €4950

9. €35 000   **10.** €46 000

11. (i) €3308.80   (ii) €53.40
   (iii) €3728.80   (iv) €70.90

12. (i) €11 200   (ii) €5600
   (iii) €5600   (iv) €14 000
   (v) €42 000

Exercise 5.7

1. (i) 0.04   (ii) 0.055   (iii) 0.12
   (iv) 0.145   (v) 1.12
2. (i) 1.06   (ii) 1.055   (iii) 1.1
   (iv) 0.96   (v) 1.125
3. (i) €61.50   (ii) €338.58
   (iii) €848.04   (iv) €848.00
4. €423.20   5. €9235.20
6. 4.5%   7. €6400
8. €8904; 4%   9. €800
10. €11 475; 4%   11. €8200
12. 11.5%
13. (i) €5434   (ii) $r = 4\%$
14. €8500
15. (i) 15%   (ii) €4500
16. 4.6%   17. 34.5%   18. 19.6%
19. (i) 31st May   (ii) €212.28
20. (i) €4664   (ii) 6%
21. $B = $ €8000
22. A – 78%, B – 93.2%, C – 103.9%, D – 112.9%
23. 5.5%
24. €10 837.50
25. (i) €11 776   (ii) €18 000
26. 16%   27. 39%
28. 458   29. €28 000
30. (i) 1 min 39 sec   (ii) Day 6
   (iii) 5 min 17 sec

Exercise 5.8

1. 70 km\hr   2. $4\frac{1}{2}$ hours
3. (i) 120 km\hr   (ii) 112 km\hr
   (iii) 136 km\hr   (iv) 112 km\hr
   (v) 128 km\hr   (vi) 135 km\hr
4. (i) 76 km\hr   (ii) $53\frac{1}{3}$ km\hr
   (iii) 65 km\hr
5. 72 km\hr
6. (i) 240 km   (ii) 260 km   (iii) 198 km
7. (i) 3 hr   (ii) $2\frac{1}{2}$ hr   (iii) 20 min
8. 5 hr 12 min   9. $53\frac{1}{3}$ km\hr
10. 12 m\s   11. 75 km\hr
12. (i) $1\frac{1}{3}$ hr   (ii) 1 hr 20 min
13. 2 hr 9 min   14. 125 m
15. 8.3 km\hr   16. 8.35 am
17. (i) 30 km   (ii) 1 hour
   (iii) 45 km   (iv) 75 km
18. (i) 20 km   (ii) $\frac{2}{3}$ km\min
   (iii) 40 km\hr   (iv) 30 km\hr
19. (i) 20 km   (ii) 30 min
   (iii) 30 km   (iv) 2 hours
20. (i) 55 min   (ii) 10 min
   (iii) 30 km\hr   (iv) 24 km\hr

21. (i) $1\frac{1}{2}$ m\s   (ii) It reduces
   (iii) $\frac{3}{4}$ m\s   (iv) 3 m\s
   (v) $1\frac{1}{2}$ sec   (vi) 4 m\s

Exercise 5.9

1. (i) 600   (ii) 450   (iii) 6800
   (iv) 51 000   (v) 67 000   (vi) 516
   (vii) 7050   (viii) 18 600
2. (i) 4×10^2 (ii) 5.8×10^2
   (iii) 6.2×10^3 (iv) 5.7×10^3
   (v) 6×10^4 (vi) 7.6×10^4
   (vii) 9.2×10^4 (viii) 7.2×10^5
3. (i) 0.25   (ii) 0.06
   (iii) 0.0048   (iv) 0.00092
4. (i) 4×10^{-2} (ii) 6.2×10^{-2}
   (iii) 7×10^{-3} (iv) 6.5×10^{-3}
5. (i) 8×10^{-3} (ii) 7.9×10^{-3}
   (iii) 6×10^{-4} (iv) 5.3×10^{-4}
6. A, D
7. (i) 2080   (ii) 660.6
   (iii) 8230   (iv) 570
8. (i) 5.4×10^5 (ii) 1.702×10^2
   (iii) 3.276×10^3 (iv) 1.44×10^2
9. (i) 7×10^3 (ii) 6×10^2
   (iii) 5.6×10^3
10. (i) 2.8×10^3 (ii) 8×10^2
11. (i) 1.62×10^8 (ii) 5×10^{-3}
   (iii) 8×10^{-4} (iv) 2×10^1
   (v) 5×10^{-1} (vi) 1.6×10^{-5}
12. (i) Earth   (ii) 5900 km
   (iii) 1.95×10^4
13. 2.4×10^4
14. 0.0005
15. (i) 340,000,000
   (ii) Christianity
   (iii) Confucianism
   (iv) Islam and Christianity
16. (i) 19.625   (ii) 78.4

Test yourself 5

1. (i) €2080   (ii) (a) €420   (b) $31\frac{1}{4}$%
   (iii) €9930
2. (i) A & I, B & H, C & G, D & F
   (ii) 5.5%   (iii) 192 cm
3. (i) 210
   (ii) (a) 824   (b) €168.92   (c) 21%
   (iii) 2%
4. (i) 252 cm²   (ii) €7806
   (iii) (a) €5040   (b) 5%
5. (i) (a) $\frac{7}{36}$ (b) 8
   (ii) She should accept B (marginally better)
   (iii) (a) €1080   (b) €56 000

6. (i) 124   (ii) (a) €8864.73   (b) 2.8%
     (iii) (a) €320   (b) €120   (c) €1100
7. (i) 150 km   (ii) No   (iii) €6000
8. (i) $\frac{7}{16}$ (ii) (b) 0.64
     (iii) (a) €6000   (b) €5250
         (c) €15 000   (d) €45 000
9. (i) 84 km\hr (ii) (a) $108\frac{1}{2}$ km   (b) 1.6%
     (iii) €8000

Chapter 6 : Probability

Exercise 6.1
1. (i) Impossible (ii) Evens   (iii) Certain
     (iv) Evens   (v) Impossible
2. (i) Impossible   (ii) Very likely
     (iii) Very unlikely   (iv) Very unlikely
     (v) Evens   (vi) Certain
     (vii) Unlikely
3. (i) Bigger than 5   (ii) Yes
5. (i) B   (ii) C   (iii) C
     (iv) A   (v) B   (vi) C
6. (i) 6   (ii) 4   (iii) 0   (iv) 2
7. (i) 6   (ii) 8   (iii) 2

Exercise 6.2
1. (i) $\frac{1}{6}$ (ii) $\frac{1}{3}$ (iii) $\frac{1}{2}$ (iv) $\frac{1}{2}$ (v) $\frac{1}{3}$ (vi) $\frac{1}{2}$
2. (i) $\frac{1}{4}$ (ii) $\frac{3}{8}$ (iii) $\frac{1}{4}$ (iv) $\frac{1}{8}$ (v) $\frac{3}{8}$
3. (i) $\frac{1}{8}$ (ii) $\frac{1}{4}$ (iii) $\frac{3}{8}$
4. (i) $\frac{1}{4}$ (ii) $\frac{3}{4}$ (iii) $\frac{1}{4}$; $\frac{3}{4}$
5. (i) $\frac{1}{2}$ (ii) $\frac{1}{4}$ (iii) $\frac{1}{13}$ (iv) $\frac{1}{26}$
6. (i) $\frac{5}{12}$ (ii) $\frac{1}{4}$ (iii) $\frac{3}{4}$ (iv) $\frac{2}{3}$
7. (i) $\frac{1}{4}$ (ii) $\frac{3}{8}$ (iii) $\frac{5}{8}$ (iv) $\frac{1}{4}$
8. (i) $\frac{1}{5}$ (ii) $\frac{1}{5}$ (iii) $\frac{2}{5}$ (iv) $\frac{1}{2}$
9. (i) $\frac{1}{7}$ (ii) $\frac{2}{7}$ (iii) $\frac{2}{7}$
10. (i) $\frac{1}{6}$ (ii) $\frac{1}{3}$
11. (i) $\frac{1}{5}$ (ii) $\frac{1}{21}$ (iii) 0
12. (i) $\frac{2}{15}$ (ii) $\frac{2}{5}$ (iii) $\frac{2}{3}$
13. (i) (a) $\frac{1}{4}$ (b) $\frac{1}{6}$ (ii) (a) $\frac{1}{4}$ (b) $\frac{5}{12}$
14. (i) $\frac{2}{5}$ (ii) $\frac{3}{10}$ (iii) $\frac{11}{25}$; $\frac{1}{6}$
15. $\frac{2}{5}$
16. (i) $\frac{1}{2}$ (ii) $\frac{8}{25}$ (iii) $\frac{8}{25}$
17. (i) $\frac{2}{5}$ (ii) $\frac{3}{5}$ (iii) $\frac{4}{25}$ (iv) $\frac{4}{15}$ (v) $\frac{2}{5}$
18. (i) $\frac{1}{7}$ (ii) 5 fours
19. (i) $\frac{3}{49}$ (ii) $\frac{12}{49}$
20.

Exercise 6.3
1. (i) $\frac{1}{12}$ (ii) $\frac{1}{4}$ (iii) $\frac{1}{3}$ (iv) $\frac{1}{6}$
2. (i) $\frac{1}{9}$ (ii) $\frac{1}{12}$ (iii) $\frac{1}{12}$ (iv) $\frac{5}{36}$
3. (i) $\frac{1}{8}$ (ii) $\frac{1}{8}$ (iii) $\frac{3}{8}$
4. (i) $\frac{1}{12}$ (ii) $\frac{1}{6}$ (iii) $\frac{1}{2}$; 9 most often; $\frac{1}{4}$
5. BBR, RBB; $\frac{2}{3}$
6. (i) (1, 5), (1, 6), (1, 7), (2, 5), (2, 6), (2, 7), (3, 5), (3, 6), (3, 7), (4, 5), (4, 6), (4, 7)
     (ii) 12
     (iii) (a) $\frac{1}{3}$ (b) $\frac{1}{6}$ (c) $\frac{1}{4}$
7. ABC, ACB, BAC, BCA, CAB, CBA;
     (i) $\frac{1}{6}$ (ii) $\frac{1}{3}$
8. (i) $\frac{1}{6}$ (ii) $\frac{2}{3}$ (iii) $\frac{1}{4}$
9. (i) $\frac{1}{8}$ (ii) $\frac{3}{8}$ (iii) $\frac{1}{8}$ (iv) $\frac{7}{8}$

Exercise 6.4
1. 50
2. (i) 10   (ii) 10   (iii) 20
3. (i) 50   (ii) 150
4. (i) $\frac{13}{20}$ (ii) 100   (iii) Yes
5. (i) 35   (ii) 70   (iii) 105
6. (i) (a) $\frac{1}{5}$ (b) $\frac{2}{15}$
     (ii) (a) $\frac{1}{6}$ (b) $\frac{1}{6}$
     (iii) No
7. If fair – 6 times; No
8. $\frac{7}{10}$
9. (i) 0.15   (ii) '1'   (iii) 50
10. Ben's; Joe's
11. (i) $x = 0.1$ (ii) 0.6   (iii) 200
12. (i) Ciara   (ii) 0.4, 0.3, 0.2, 0.1 (1, 2, 3, 4)
     (iii) Yes
13. Red dice is fair
14. (i) Bill's   (ii) Biased spinner
     (iii) $\frac{63}{290}$
15. (ii) 1   (iii) Yes
     (iv) Extremely unlikely   (v) Mint

Exercise 6.5
1. (i) $\frac{1}{6}$ (ii) $\frac{1}{2}$ (iii) $\frac{2}{3}$
2. (i) $\frac{1}{2}$ (ii) $\frac{1}{4}$ (iii) $\frac{3}{4}$
3. (i) $\frac{4}{9}$ (ii) $\frac{2}{9}$ (iii) $\frac{2}{3}$
4. (i) $\frac{1}{4}$ (ii) $\frac{3}{26}$ (iii) $\frac{19}{52}$
5. (i) $\frac{1}{2}$ (ii) $\frac{1}{3}$ (iii) $\frac{2}{3}$
6. (i) $\frac{1}{4}$ (ii) $\frac{1}{13}$ (iii) $\frac{4}{13}$
     (iv) $\frac{1}{2}$ (v) $\frac{1}{13}$ (vi) $\frac{7}{13}$
7. (i) $\frac{1}{36}$ (ii) $\frac{1}{6}$ (iii) $\frac{1}{6}$
8. (i) yellow 3 included twice   (ii) $\frac{3}{5}$
9. (ii) Yes   (iii) No   (iv) No   (v) Yes

Exercise 6.6

1. (i) $\frac{11}{20}$ (ii) $\frac{3}{10}$ (iii) $\frac{3}{40}$ (iv) $\frac{3}{8}$
2. (i) 35 (ii) $\frac{4}{7}$ (iii) $\frac{8}{35}$ (iv) $\frac{1}{5}$ (v) $\frac{6}{35}$ (vi) $\frac{4}{5}$
3. (i) $\frac{13}{41}$ (ii) $\frac{6}{41}$ (iii) $\frac{13}{41}$ (iv) $\frac{26}{41}$ (v) $\frac{15}{41}$
4. (i) 12 (ii) $\frac{3}{5}$ (iii) $\frac{1}{10}$ (iv) $\frac{21}{25}$ (v) $\frac{37}{50}$
5. (ii) $\frac{1}{5}$ (iii) $\frac{4}{15}$ (iv) $\frac{7}{15}$ (v) $\frac{8}{15}$
6. (i) $\frac{19}{30}$ (ii) $\frac{3}{10}$ (iii) $\frac{9}{10}$ (iv) $\frac{1}{15}$ (v) $\frac{1}{10}$ (vi) $\frac{14}{15}$
7. (i) 24
   (ii) They like both chocolate and ice-cream
   (iii) $\frac{3}{20}$ (iv) $\frac{3}{4}$

Exercise 6.7

1. (i) $\frac{1}{4}$ (ii) $\frac{1}{4}$
2. (i) $\frac{1}{12}$ (ii) $\frac{1}{4}$ (iii) $\frac{1}{6}$
3. (i) $\frac{1}{36}$ (ii) $\frac{1}{4}$ (iii) $\frac{1}{9}$
4. (i) $\frac{25}{81}$ (ii) $\frac{20}{81}$ (iii) $\frac{20}{81}$
5. (i) $\frac{1}{24}$ (ii) $\frac{1}{4}$ (iii) $\frac{1}{12}$
6. (i) $\frac{4}{49}$ (ii) $\frac{1}{49}$ (iii) $\frac{1}{49}$ (iv) $\frac{9}{49}$
7. (i) $\frac{1}{4}$ (ii) $\frac{1}{2}$ (iii) $\frac{1}{16}$ (iv) $\frac{1}{8}$
8. (i) $\frac{1}{5}$ (ii) (a) $\frac{1}{25}$ (b) $\frac{1}{5}$
9. (i) $\frac{2}{5}$ (ii) $\frac{2}{25}$ (iii) $\frac{4}{25}$ (iv) $\frac{8}{25}$
10. (i) $\frac{1}{7}$ (ii) $\frac{1}{49}$ (iii) $\frac{4}{49}$
11. (i) $\frac{1}{4}$ (ii) $\frac{1}{8}$
12. (i) $\frac{1}{6}$ (ii) $\frac{25}{216}$
13. (i) $\frac{8}{27}$ (ii) (a) $\frac{2}{9}$ (b) $\frac{2}{27}$
14. (i) $\frac{1}{64}$ (ii) $\frac{9}{16}$ (iii) $\frac{9}{64}$
15. (i) $\frac{2}{5}$ (ii) $\frac{18}{125}$
16. (i) $\frac{4}{25}$ (ii) $\frac{4}{125}$ (iii) $\frac{1}{125}$
17. (i) $\frac{7}{10}$ (ii) $\frac{9}{100}$ (iii) $\frac{147}{1000}$
18. (i) $\frac{1}{3}$ (ii) $\frac{2}{9}$ (iii) $\frac{2}{27}$
19. (i) $\frac{1}{4}$ (ii) $\frac{9}{64}$ (iii) $\frac{27}{64}$
20. (i) $\frac{1}{8}$ (ii) $\frac{3}{8}$ (iii) $\frac{3}{8}$
21. (i) $\frac{1}{5}$ (ii) $\frac{9}{50}$ (iii) $\frac{2}{25}$ (iv) $\frac{3}{25}$
22. (i) $\frac{1}{6}$ (ii) $\frac{1}{6}$ (iii) $\frac{1}{36}$
    (iv) 6, 6, 6, or 5, 6, 5 or 5, 5, 6 (v) $\frac{1}{72}$

Exercise 6.8

1. (i) 4 (ii) $\frac{1}{4}$
2. (i) $\frac{8}{15}$ (ii) $\frac{7}{15}$
3. (ii) (a) $\frac{4}{35}$ (b) $\frac{16}{35}$ (c) $\frac{19}{35}$
4. (ii) $\frac{13}{18}$ (iii) $\frac{5}{36}$
5. (ii) $\frac{9}{25}$ (iii) $\frac{12}{25}$
6. (i) $\frac{12}{35}$ (ii) $\frac{6}{35}$ (iii) $\frac{18}{35}$
7. (i) $\frac{9}{49}$ (ii) $\frac{16}{49}$ (iii) $\frac{12}{49}$

8. (ii) (a) $\frac{7}{60}$ (b) $\frac{1}{3}$
9. (ii) $\frac{4}{15}$
10. (i) $\frac{1}{8}$ (ii) $\frac{3}{8}$
11. (ii) $\frac{21}{50}$

Exercise 6.9

2. $5\frac{1}{2}$
3. €11.50
4. 8
5. €3.33 win
6. €1 loss
7. €4.50 loss
8. €0.55
9. (i) $\frac{1}{9}$; €1 win; Not fair
10. €2.38 loss; Not fair

Exercise 6.10

1. 12   2. 12   3. 504   4. 20
5. 12   6. 54   7. 20   8. 27
9. 90   10. 120   11. 336

Exercise 6.11

1. 120
2. 720; (i) 120 (ii) 24
3. 24
4. 60; (i) 12 (ii) 24
5. 720; (i) 240 (ii) 24 (iii) 48
6. 120
7. (i) 720 (ii) 120
8. 720; (i) 120 (ii) 360 (iii) 144
9. 96
10. 120; 48
11. 720; 240
12. 24; (i) 12 (ii) $\frac{1}{2}$
13. (i) 24 (ii) DABC, CABD, DBAC, CBAD
    (iii) $\frac{1}{6}$
14. (i) 120 (ii) 24 (iii) 6
15. (i) 120 (ii) 5040 (iii) 120 (iv) 144
16. (i) No (ii) No
17. (i) 8(7!) (ii) 56(6!)
18. $k = 11$

Test yourself 6

1. (i) $\frac{1}{4}$ (ii) $\frac{3}{4}$ (iii) $\frac{3}{8}$
   (iv) 0 (v) 1
2. (i) 50 times (ii) 150 times
3. (i) $\frac{1}{7}$ (ii) $\frac{4}{7}$
4. (i) $\frac{1}{6}$ (ii) $\frac{1}{3}$ (iii) $\frac{1}{2}$ (iv) $\frac{1}{2}$
5. (i) $\frac{1}{4}$ (ii) Lose money
   (iii) $\frac{19}{20}$ (iv) 60 times

6. (i) $\frac{11}{20}$ (ii) $\frac{1}{4}$ (iii) 18

7. 90

8. (i) $\frac{1}{12}$ (ii) $\frac{1}{36}$ (iii) $\frac{5}{18}$ (iv) $\frac{1}{6}$

9. $\frac{1}{3}$

10. $\frac{1}{6}$

11. (i) $\frac{1}{2}$ (ii) $\frac{1}{4}$

12. (i) $\frac{2}{7}$ (ii) $\frac{1}{2}$ (iii) $\frac{3}{4}$ (iv) $\frac{5}{7}$

13. (i) (a) 0.52 (b) Yes

14. (i) $\frac{1}{9}$ (ii) $\frac{2}{27}$

15. (i) $\frac{2}{15}$ (ii) $\frac{2}{5}$ (iii) $\frac{8}{15}$ (iv) $\frac{7}{15}$

16. 50c loss; Not fair

17. (i) 0.25 (ii) 60

18. (i) (a) (ii) $\frac{11}{15}$

19. (i) $\frac{1}{3}$ (ii) $\frac{1}{9}$ (iii) $\frac{4}{27}$

20. Yes; both have an even chance of winning

21. 60; (i) 12 (ii) 36

Chapter 7 : Complex Numbers

Exercise 7.1

3. (i) T (ii) T (iii) F (iv) T
(v) F (vi) T (vii) F (viii) T

4. (i) $\frac{7}{10}$ (ii) $\frac{6}{5}$ (iii) $\frac{13}{5}$
(iv) $\frac{41}{5}$ (v) $\frac{1}{20}$

5. (i), (iii), (iv), (v)

6. (i), (iii), (iv) all natural numbers.

7. (i) Natural (ii) Natural (iii) Integer
(iv) Rational (v) Irrational (vi) Irrational

8. $x = \frac{4}{9}$

9. (i) $\frac{7}{9}$ (ii) $\frac{16}{9}$ (iii) $\frac{7}{45}$

10. (i), (ii), (iv), (v)

11. (i) $\sqrt{17}$ (ii) $\sqrt{37}$ (iii) $\sqrt{0.75}$ (iv) $\sqrt{108}$

12. (i), (iii)

13. (i) -3 and -4 (ii) -3 and 4
(iii) 9 and 16 (iv) 16 and 9

Exercise 7.2

1. (i) $2i$ (ii) $10i$ (iii) $8i$ (iv) $7i$ (v) i

2. (i) 2, 5 (ii) 6, -2 (iii) -1, 9 (iv) -3, 1
(v) a, b (vi) $\frac{1}{2}, -3$ (vii) $-4, 0$ (viii) $0, -3$
(ix) 0, 1 (x) $x - 2$, 6

3. (i) $6 + 4i$ (ii) $0 + 11i$
(iii) $-2 - 10i$ (iv) $2 + 2\sqrt{2}i$

Exercise 7.3

1. (i) $8 + 5i$ (ii) $5 - 10i$ (iii) $3 - 4i$
(iv) $1 + 4i$ (v) $-2 - 7i$ (vi) $3 - 4i$
(vii) $8 - 6i$ (viii) $-2 - i$
(ix) $(a + 3) + (b + 2)i$
(x) $(a + x) + (b + y)i$

2. (i) $1 + 3i$ (ii) $-2 - 6i$ (iii) $-5 + 6i$
(iv) $-1 - 10i$ (v) $1 + 5i$ (vi) $-11 - i$
(vii) $-3 - 4i$ (viii) $-3 + 3i$
(ix) $(a - 5) + (b + 2)i$
(x) $(x - p) + (y + q)i$

3. (i) $6 + 9i$ (ii) $11 + 8i$ (iii) $17 + 0i$
(iv) $24 + 2i$ (v) $-7 + 15i$ (vi) $-16 + 10i$

4. (i) $2 - 5i$ (ii) $5 + 7i$ (iii) $3 + 3i$
(iv) $-1 + 0i$ (v) $-3 - i$ (vi) $-4 + 2i$

5. $8 + 13i$

6. (i) $4 + i$ (ii) $1 - 6i$ (iii) $5 - 5i$
(iv) $4 + 9i$

Exercise 7.4

1. $-2 + 3i$

2. $15 + 3i$

3. $-6 - 8i$

4. $11 - 10i$

5. $8 - i$

6. $-5 + i$

7. $10 - 10i$

8. $5 - 3i$

9. $13 + 0i$

10. $-2 + 11i$

11. $5 - 12i$

12. $12 + 16i$

13. (i) $3 + 11i$ (ii) $-8 + 14i$ (iii) $14 - 18i$
(iv) $7 + 17i$

Exercise 7.5

1. (i) $2 - 3i$ (ii) $-3 + 4i$
(iii) $4 + 6i$ (iv) $(x + 2) - yi$

2. (i) $2 - 3i$ (ii) $6 + 8i$ (iii) $5 + 7i$
(iv) $18 - i$ (v) $-6 - 17i$

3. (i) $3 + 2i$ (ii) $\frac{3}{2} - i$
(iii) $\frac{7}{4} + \frac{3}{4}i$ (iv) $-\frac{2}{3} + 2i$

4. (i) $\frac{6}{13} + \frac{4}{13}i$ (ii) $\frac{3}{5} + \frac{4}{5}i$ (iii) $\frac{18}{37} + \frac{3}{37}i$
(iv) $-\frac{4}{5} + \frac{7}{5}i$ (v) $\frac{6}{13} - \frac{17}{13}i$ (vi) $-\frac{1}{2} + \frac{1}{2}i$
(vii) $-\frac{3}{13} + \frac{28}{13}i$ (viii) $-2 - 6i$

5. (i) $25 + 0i$ (ii) $-2 + i$ (iii) $11 - 23i$
(iv) $-\frac{2}{25} + \frac{11}{25}i$ (v) $\frac{9}{5} + \frac{8}{5}i$

6. (i) $4 + 6i$ (ii) $-4 - 2i$ (iii) $\frac{2}{5} + \frac{1}{5}i$
(iv) $-2 - 3i$ (v) $-\frac{1}{13} + \frac{8}{13}i$

8. (i) 41 (ii) $\frac{9}{41} + \frac{40}{41}i$

9. $5 - 5i; a = \frac{1}{2}$

10. (i) $6 + 3i$

Exercise 7.6

2. (i) $2 + 2i$ (ii) $2 - i$
(iii) $0 + 3i$ (iv) $-1 - 3i$

3. (i) $2 - i$ (ii) $3 + 2i$
(iii) $5 + 5i$ (iv) $-3 + i$

4. (i) $6 - 4i$ (ii) $3 - 2i$ (iii) $1 + 5i$

6. Plot (i) $4 + 2i$ (ii) $-1 - 2i$
(iii) $8 + 0i$ (iv) $5 + 0i$

Exercise 7.7

1. 5   **2.** 10   **3.** $\sqrt{13}$ **4.** $\sqrt{5}$

5. $\sqrt{13}$ **6.** $\sqrt{26}$ **7.** $\sqrt{10}$ **8.** $\sqrt{37}$

9. 4   **10.** 5   **11.** 3   **12.** 5

13. (i) $2\sqrt{5}$ (ii) 2 (iii) $2\sqrt{10}$

14. $-3 + 4i, -3 - 4i, 3 - 4i, 0 + 5i$ etc

15. (i) $\sqrt{13}$ (ii) $\sqrt{10}$ (iii) $\sqrt{17}$ (iv) $\sqrt{130}$

16. (i) $\sqrt{34}$ (ii) $\sqrt{5}$ (iii) $\sqrt{53}$

17. (i) $\sqrt{13}$ (ii) $\sqrt{5}$ (iii) $8 + i$ (iv) $\sqrt{65}$

18. $13 + 0i$; 13

19. (i) $\sqrt{5}$ (ii) 5 (iii) $\sqrt{26}$; No

20. (i) $3 + 5i$ (ii) $\sqrt{34}$

21. $\sqrt{a^2 + 64}$; $a = \pm 6$

23. $\sqrt{26}, \sqrt{13}$

24. $-\frac{5}{13} + \frac{12}{13}i$; $k = \sqrt{13}$

Exercise 7.8

1. $x = 3, y = 3$ **2.** $x = 2, y = 4$

3. $x = 0, y = -1$ **4.** $x = -\frac{1}{3}, y = \frac{1}{9}$

5. $x = 1, y = 5$ **6.** $x = -\frac{5}{2}, y = \frac{15}{2}$

7. $x = 2, y = \frac{1}{2}$ **8.** $x = -1, y = -3$

9. $x = 2, y = -7$ **10.** $x = -2, y = 3$

11. $a = \frac{6}{5}, b = \frac{3}{5}$ **12.** $a = 2, b = -1$

13. $a = \frac{1}{2}, b = -\frac{1}{2}$ **14.** $x = -5, y = -10$

15. (i) $x = -1, y = 3$ (ii) $x = 3, y = 8$

Exercise 7.9

1. (i) $-2 \pm i$ (ii) $-3 \pm 2i$ (iii) $-1 \pm 3i$
(iv) $3 \pm 5i$ (v) $5 \pm 2i$ (vi) $1 \pm 4i$

2. $2 - 5i$ **3.** $4 + 3i$

4. $6 - i$ **5.** $k = 10$

6. $k = 34$ **7.** $a = -8, b = 17$

Exercise 7.10

2. $|3z_1| = 3|z_1|$

3. $z_1 = 4 + 3i, z_2 = -3 + 4i$; (ii) z_5 (iii) $4 + 3i$

4. (i) $a = 3$ (ii) $b = -1$

5. (i) $-2 + 6i$ (ii) $-6 - 2i$ (iii) $2 - 6i$

6. a translation

7. 360° rotation anticlockwise

9. $z_3 = 1 + 7i$

Test yourself 7

1. (ii) (a) $9 + 2i$ (b) $\frac{3}{25} - \frac{4}{25}i$ (c) $k = -3$
(iii) $x = 3, y = 2$

2. (i) $5 + 18i$ (ii) $k = 2$ (iii) $\frac{4}{5} + \frac{7}{5}i$; $\frac{\sqrt{13}}{5}$

3. (i) (a) $3 + 4i$ (b) $2 - 3i$ (c) $-2 + 2i$
(iii) $k = \pm 5$

4. (i) $2\sqrt{12}$ (ii) (a) $3 + 7i$ (b) $\frac{2}{5} + \frac{4}{5}i$
(iii) $18 + i$

5. (i) (a) F (b) T (c) T (d) F
(ii) $2 \pm 3i$
(iii) $|z_1| = 2\sqrt{5}, |z_2| = 2\sqrt{5}$; $-2 - 4i, 2 + 4i$

6. (i) $5 + 18i$
(ii) (a) $7 + 2i$ (b) $-3 + 4i$; Yes
(iii) $x = -3, y = -\frac{4}{3}$

7. (i) (a) $z^2 = -4 + 0i$ (b) $iz = -2 + 0i$
(ii) $3 + 3i; -3 + 3i; -3 - 3i; 3 - 3i$;
Anticlockwise rotations of 90°, 180°
and 270°
(iii) $k = 17$; $z_2 = -4 - i$; $t = \sqrt{17}$

8. (i) $3 + 3i$; $3\sqrt{2}$
(ii) $3 - 4i$; $k = -\frac{1}{2}, t = \frac{5}{2}$
(iii) $2 + i$; $p = -4, q = 5$

Chapter 8: Measures of Location and Spread

Exercise 8.1

1. (i) 10 (ii) 9 (iii) 8 (iv) 6

2. (a) (i) 8 (ii) 7
(b) (i) 7 (ii) 7

3. (i) 41 km\hr (ii) 39.5 km\hr

4. (i) 14 (ii) 14 (iii) 17

5. (i) 6 (ii) 9.5

6. Example: 2, 6, 9, 12, 13, 13, 22

7. (i) 28 (ii) 2

8. 14

9. €7.10

10. Example: 4, 4, 5, 8, 9

11. (i) $x = 2$ (ii) $k = 17$

12. 17

13. 90 g

14. 4 and 6

15. 6

16. (i) $14\frac{1}{4}$ hours (ii) $12\frac{1}{4}$ hours
(iii) Boys: 14.5; Girls: 12 (iv) Yes

17. $x = 19$

18. (i) 1320 cm (ii) $165\frac{1}{3}$ cm

19. (i) 195 (ii) 19

20. B − 40

21. (i) Mode (ii) Mean

Exercise 8.2

1. (i) 8 (ii) 57 (iii) 11

2. (i) 6 (ii) 8

3. (i) 33 (ii) 29
(iii) (a) 18.5 (b) 34 (c) 15.5

4. (i) 4 (ii) 11 (iii) 7

5. (i) 13 min (ii) 8
(iii) 15 (iv) 7

6. (i) 5   (ii) 14.5
7. (i) 25   (ii) 50   (iii) 64.5   (iv) 14.5
8. (i) 105 g   (ii) 19 g
9. (i)

3 5 6 6 7

(ii)

4 6 6 7

10. (i) 41 and 47   (ii) 8, 9, 13, 15, 25
11. (i) Football: 13, 13, 4; Hockey: 13.7, 14, 6
(ii) Football team

Exercise 8.3

1. (i) Mean   (ii) Mode   (iii) Mean
(iv) Mode   (v) Median
2. (i) 94 kg
(ii) $87\frac{4}{9}$ kg; Median best describes data
3. (i) $25\frac{6}{7}$ (ii) 15; Median
4. (i) $30\frac{4}{7}°C$
(ii) Closely-grouped data (no outliers)
5. (i) $26\frac{6}{11}$
(ii) Mode ($= 37$) is not a typical value
6. (i) 8.1   (ii) 6; Median
7. (i) 16   (ii) 16
(iii) 19.1   (iv) Mode or median
8. (i) €37 667   (ii) €24 500
(iii) No two salaries the same; median
9. 330 ml cans

Exercise 8.4

1. (i) 2 goals   (ii) 3
2. 3
3. (i) 25   (ii) 6 marks   (iii) 5.6
(iv) 14   (v) 6
4. (i) 4   (ii) 4   (iii) 4.25
5. (i) 30   (ii) 7   (iii) 13
(iv) 13   (v) 13
6. (i) 2   (ii) 2   (iii) 50   (iv) 10
7. $x = 2$
8. $y = 5$
9. (ii) 4   (iii) 4.6

Exercise 8.5

1. (i) $(4 - 6)$ (ii) 6.5   (iii) $(4 - 6)$
2. (i) $(12 - 14)$ (ii) 14 years (iii) $(12 - 14)$
3. 18.6
4. (i) 18 min   (ii) $(18 - 20)$
5. (i) 32 years   (ii) $(30 - 40)$
6. (i) $(5 - 9)$ (ii) $(0 - 4)$ (iii) 7

Exercise 8.6

1. (i) 1.9   (ii) 2.4   (iii) 2.8
(iv) 3.5   (v) 2.7   (vi) 3.9
3. (i) 10 is added to each number
(ii) Same (both $= \sqrt{2}$)
(iii) equal standard deviations
4. 1.6
5. 0.84
6. 2.3
7. Mean $= 4$; $\sigma = \sqrt{10}$
8. Mean $= 3$; $\sigma = 1.48$
9. (i) 25   (ii) 5.3
(iii) 30.3; 19.7   (iv) 3
10. Mean $= 2$; $\sigma = 1.14$
11. 2.3
12. (i) 6   (ii) 2
13. (i) Route 1 $= 14$; Route 2 $= 15$
(ii) Route 1 $= 2$; Route 2 $= 2.3$
(iii) Route 1 recommended

Test Yourself 8

1. (i) $x = 2$ (ii) $y = 9$
2. (i) 2   (ii) 1, 9   (iii) 8
3. (i) 60   (ii) 78
4. 2 or 45
5. (i) Mean $=$ €67 840; Mode $=$ €4500;
Median $=$ €45 000
(ii) Mean
6. 5
7. (i) 8   (ii) 9   (iii) 5
8. (a) False   (b) True
(c) False   (d) Could be true
9. (i) 42   (ii) 42   (iii) 42.5
10. (i) $(8 - 12)$ (ii) $(8 - 12)$ (iii) 11.7
11. (i) 9   (ii) 2.6
12. Mean $= 12.6$; $\sigma = 0.9$
13. (i) Rory, 81; Darren, 80
(ii) Rory, 6; Darren, 9.3; Rory is better

Chapter 9: Area and Volume

Exercise 9.1

1. (i) 48 cm²   (ii) 28 cm   (iii) 10 cm
2. (i) 56 cm²   (ii) 42 cm²   (iii) $25\frac{1}{2}$ cm²
3. 20 m²; 25 m²
4. (i) 6 units   (ii) 12 units   (iii) 8 units
5. (i) (a) 24 cm²   (b) 84 cm²   (c) 216 cm²
(ii) (a) $4\frac{4}{5}$ cm   (b) $10\frac{1}{2}$ cm   (c) $21\frac{3}{5}$ cm
6. (i) 112 cm²   (ii) 108 cm²   (iii) 132 cm²
7. (i) 10 cm   (ii) 160 cm²
8. (i) 102 cm²   (ii) $94\frac{1}{2}$ cm²   (iii) 68 cm²
9. (i) 70 cm²   (ii) $8\frac{3}{4}$ cm
10. (i) 110 cm²   (ii) 48 cm²   (iii) 56 m²

11. (i) 75 cm² (ii) 65 cm² (iii) 414 mm²
12. (i) $4x - 5$ (ii) $x = 8\frac{1}{2}$
13. (i) 7 cm (ii) 9 cm (iii) 11 cm
14. (i) 42 cm (ii) 34 cm (iii) 36 m
15. Largest P $-$ 12 cm, Smallest P $-$ 10 cm
16. 72 cm²
17. 4 cm

Exercise 9.2

1. (i) 88.0 cm (ii) 100.5 cm (iii) 37.7 cm
2. (i) 615.8 cm² (ii) 804.2 cm² (iii) 113.1 cm²
3. (i) 19.6 cm² (ii) 39.3 cm² (iii) 37.7 cm²
4. (i) 5.5 cm (ii) 6.3 cm (iii) 67.0 cm
5. $4(\pi + 3)$
6. (i) 154 m² (ii) 114 m
7. 74.6 cm²
8. 18.3 cm²
9. 193 cm²
10. (i) 10 848 m² (ii) €542.40
11. 14 cm
12. 180 cm²
13. (i) 188 m (ii) 0.24 m\s
14. 28 cm
15. 733 cm²
16. (i) 58 cm (ii) 235 cm²

Exercise 9.3

1. (i) 105 cm³ (ii) 60 cm³ (iii) 72 cm³
2. (i) 576 cm³ (ii) 432 cm²
3. 8.5 cm
4. (i) 3.5 cm (ii) 6 cm (iii) 4 cm
5. (i) 2112 cm³ (ii) 1116 cm³ (iii) 15 120 cm³
6. (i) 240 cm³ (ii) 450 cm³
7. 7 cm
8. (i) 156 cm³ (ii) 145 cm³
9. (i) 36 cm² (ii) 648 cm³
10. 157.5 m³
11. 1080 cm³
12. A, 5; B, 3; C, 6
13. (i) F (ii) [BC] (iii) [LK]
14.

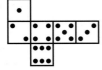

15. (i) 124 cm² (ii) 72 cm³
16. (i) Closed cylinder (ii) Cone
(iii) Triangular pyramid
18. E only
19. (i) Rectangle; 4 cm $\times$ 2 cm
(ii) [AL], [FG], [CD] and [JI] (iii) C
(iv) 4 cm $\times$ 3 cm $\times$ 2 cm (v) 52 cm²

Exercise 9.4

1. (i) 706.9 cm³ (ii) 4825.5 cm³ (iii) 9047.8 cm³
2. (i) 440 cm² (ii) 1608 cm² (iii) 3242 cm²
3. (i) 1540 cm³ (ii) 748 cm²
4. (i) $V = \pi r^2 h$ (ii) $350\pi = 14\pi r^2$
(iii) 5 cm
5. $2\pi rh$; 3.5 cm
6. 15 cm
7. (i) 523.6 cm³ (ii) 1436.8 cm³ (iii) 4188.8 cm³
8. (i) 314 cm² (ii) 616 cm² (iii) 1257 cm²
9. (i) $83\frac{1}{3}\pi$ cm³ (ii) 75π cm²
10. (i) 6 cm (ii) 144π cm²
11. 396 cm³ **12.** 8 cm
13. 3 cm
14. (i) 2155 cm³ (iii) 2 : 3
15. $1\frac{1}{2}$ cm **16.** 10 cm
17. $4\frac{1}{2}$ cm **18.** $42\frac{2}{3}\pi$ cm³; 14 cm
19. $10\frac{2}{3}$ cm **20.** $\frac{2}{3}$

Exercise 9.5

1. 301.6 cm³
2. 1407 cm³
3. (i) 65π cm² (ii) 90π cm²
(iii) 12 cm (iv) 100π cm³
4. 6 cm
5. 8 cm
6. (i) 6 cm (ii) 234.6 cm³
7. (i) 54π cm³ (ii) 12π cm³; 207 cm³
8. 9 cm
9. 24 cm
10. 192π cm³; $h = 36$ cm
11. 144π cm³; $2\frac{1}{4}$ cm
12. 8 cm
13. (i) 72π cm³ (ii) 6 cm
14. (i) 72 (ii) 6912 cm³
15. 811.6 cm³
16. 1592 cm³
17. (i) 15 cm; 180π cm³ (ii) 144π cm³
(iii) 5 : 4

Exercise 9.6

1. 1 : 8
2. 1 : 4
3. A $-$ 192π cm³, B $-$ 384π cm³;
(i) 1 : 2 (ii) 1 : 1
4. (i) 6600 cm³ (ii) 396 ℓ
5. 28π cm³; 75 min
6. $56\frac{1}{4}$ min
7. 14 cm
8. (i) 180π cm³ (ii) 18π cm³ (iii) 13.5 cm
9. (i) 3 cm (iv) 2 cm
10. (i) $\frac{2}{3}\pi r^3$ (ii) 3 m

Exercise 9.7

1. $810\,m^2$ **2.** $1932\,m^2$

3. $3560\,m^2$ **4.** $830\frac{1}{2}\,m^2$

5. $x = 18\,m$ **6.** $h = 7\,cm$

7. $x = 12\,m$

8. (ii) 34 sq. units   (iii) 2%

Test Yourself 9

1. (i) $56\,cm^2$ (ii) $2025\,g$
    (iii) (a) $720\pi\,cm^3$ (b) $15\,cm$

2. (i) $8\,cm$ (ii) $1350\,m^2$
    (iii) (a) $20\,000\pi\,cm^3$ (b) $160\pi\,cm^3$ (c) 125

3. (i) $30\,cm^2$ (ii) $6\,cm$ (iii) $308\,cm^3$

4. (i) $8.5\,cm$ (ii) $580\,cm^3$
    (iii) (a) $2592\pi\,cm^3$ (b) $144\pi\,cm^3$ (c) 18

5. (i) $462\,cm^2$ (ii) 63   (iii) $25\,m$

6. (i) $14\,cm^2$ (ii) $400\,cm^3$
    (iii) (a) $\frac{16\pi}{3}\,cm^3$ (b) $2\frac{2}{3}\,cm$

7. (i) $8224\,cm^2$ (ii) $h = 24\,m$

Chapter 10: Patterns and Sequences

Exercise 10.1

1. (i) 10, 12, 14   (ii) 9, 11, 13
   (iii) 13, 16, 19   (iv) 16, 32, 64
   (v) 81, 243, 729   (vi) $2, 1, \frac{1}{2}$
   (vii) 14, 12, 10   (viii) 54, 162, 486

2. (i) 16, 22   (ii) 17, 26
   (iii) 30, 42   (iv) 27, 38
   (v) 31, 46   (vi) 34, 47

3. (i) 21, 34   (ii) 47, 76
   (iii) 125, 216   (iv) $\frac{1}{81}, \frac{1}{243}$

4. (i) $6666 \times 9 = 59\,994$
   (ii) $9 \times 12\,345 = 111\,105$
   (iii) $66\,667 \times 66\,667 = 4\,444\,488\,889$

Exercise 10.2

1. (i) 5, 6, 7   (ii) 3, 5, 7
   (iii) 7, 11, 15   (iv) 1, 4, 7

2. (i) 3, 6, 9, 12   (ii) 5, 7, 9, 11   (iii) 1, 4, 7, 10

3. $-1, 5, 26$

4. (i) 1, 4, 9   (ii) 4, 7, 12   (iii) 3, 9, 19

5. (i) 1   (ii) 7   (iii) 49   (iv) 199

7. (i) 13, 15; $2n + 1$ (ii) 16, 19; $3n + 1$
   (iii) 22, 26; $4n - 2$ (iv) 21, 25; $4n + 1$

8. (i) $T_n = 3n - 1, T_{20} = 59$
   (ii) $T_n = 2n + 4, T_{20} = 44$
   (iii) $T_n = 5n - 1, T_{20} = 99$
   (iv) $T_n = 5n - 3, T_{20} = 97$

9. (i) $5n + 1$ (ii) 101   (iii) 501

10. T_9

Exercise 10.3

1. (i) 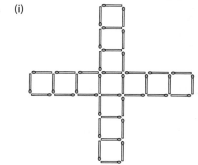   (ii) 3, 5, 7, 9, 11, 13
   (iii) $2n + 1$ (iv) 101

2. (i)
   (ii) 6, 11, 16, 21, 26, 31
   (iv) 101   (v) 10th pattern

3.

No. of squares	1	2	3	4	5
No. of m'sticks	4	7	10	13	16

   (i) 19   (ii) $3n + 1$ (iii) 151

4. (i)
   (ii) $4n - 3$ (iii) 117   (iv) 20th

5. (i)

Shape no.	1	2	3	4	5
No. of m'sticks	5	9	13	17	21

   (ii) 29   (iii) $4n + 1$ (iv) Shape 25

6. (i) 31   (ii) $6n - 4$

7. (i) 13   (ii) 23   (iii) $2n + 3$
   (iv) 203   (v) Pattern 49

8. (i) 18   (ii) $4n + 2$ (iii) 22

9. (i) $5\,cm, 8\,cm, 11\,cm, 14\,cm$
   (ii) $17\,cm, 20\,cm$ (iii) $3n + 2$
   (iv) $152\,cm$ (v) 30th

Exercise 10.4

1. (i) $a = 2, d = 3$ (ii) $a = 7, d = 5$
   (iii) $a = 0, d = 3$ (iv) $a = -2, d = 3$
   (v) $a = 60, d = -5$ (vi) $a = 6, d = -5$

2. (i) 14, 18, 22   (ii) $-4, -8, -12$
   (iii) 3, 6, 9

3. (i) 2   (ii) 4   (iii) $4n - 2; 78$

4. (i) $4n - 3$ (ii) $2n + 4$ (iii) $5n - 10$

5. (i) -1 (ii) 2   (iii) 38   (iv) 3

6. $3n + 9$;   (i) 39   (ii) 129

7. $T_1 = 4, T_2 = 9, T_3 = 14; a = 4, d = 5$

8. $a = 4, d = 3; T_n = 3n + 1; T_{20} = 61$

9. $T_1 = 3, T_2 = 7, T_3 = 11; a = 3, d = 4$

10. $T_n = 4n - 2; n = 12$

11. $T_n = 2n - 1; n = 44$

12. (i) 　　(ii) 21

(iii) 1, 3, 6, 10, 15, 21; no common difference

13.

No. of triangles	1	2	3	4	5
No. of m'sticks	3	5	7	9	11

(i) common difference present
(ii) $2n + 1$　　(iii) 61　　(iv) 40th term
14. $T_n = 11 - 3n$; $n = 15$
15. 42
16. T_{37}
17. T_{24}
18. 41
19. (i) 22　　　　　　(ii) $4n + 2$
(iii) 82　　　　　　(iv) 30th
20. $T_1 = 5, T_2 = 8, T_3 = 13$; not arithmetic

Exercise 10.5

1. $d = 7$; $T_n = 7n - 2$; $T_{20} = 138$
2. $a = 2, d = 4$; $T_{13} = 50$
3. $a = 5, d = 4$; $T_n = 4n + 1$; $T_{60} = 241$
4. $a = 24, d = -6$; $T_{100} = -570$
5. $a = 10, d = -3$; $T_n = -3n + 13$; $n = 20$
6. (i) $d = 3$　　　　(ii) $T_n = 3n$
7. (i) $a = -4, d = 2$　　(ii) Both = 8
8. $a = -3, d = -2$; $T_n = -2n - 1$; T_{40}
9. (i) 12　　　　(ii) 4, 6, 8, 10, …
(iii) $2n + 2$　　(iv) 162　　　(v) 120 km
10. $a = 4, d = 2$
11. $a = 5, d = 3$; $T_{100} = 302$
12. $x = 1$
13. (i) $x = 3$　　　　(ii) $x = -2$
14. (i)

(ii)
Fence length	1	2	3	4	5	6
No. of pieces	4	7	10	13	16	19

(iii) $3n + 1$　　　　(iv) 121
(v) Fence length 30

Exercise 10.6

1. (i) $a = 2, d = 3$　　　(ii) 222
2. 820
3. $S_n = \frac{n}{2}(3n - 1)$; 376
4. 140
5. $a = 16, d = -4$; -720
6. $a = 3, d = 5$; $S_{16} = 648$
7. 5050
8. (i) $a = -4, d = 2$　　(ii) $n = 12$

9. (i) 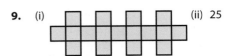　　(ii) 25

(iii) $T_n = 4n + 1$　　(iv) 860
10. (i) $a = -15, d = 6$　　(ii) 120
11. (i) $a = -4, d = 2$　　(ii) $S_n = n(n - 5)$; 9
12. $S_n = \frac{n}{2}(3n + 7)$; $n = 7$
13. (i) (a) $n + 1$　　(b) $2n$
(ii) $T_n = 3n + 1$　　(iii) 175
14. T_{20}; 1010
15. $S_1 = 7, S_2 = 16$; $T_1 = 7, T_2 = 9$
16. (i) 39　　　　　(ii) $T_n = 4n - 1$
(iv) 100　　　　　(v) 20 100
17. (i) $a = 48, d = -4$　　(ii) T_{13}
(iii) 312
18. (i) $a = -4, d = 8$　　(ii) 9
19. (i) $a = 29, d = -2$　　(ii) 200
(iii) $n = 30$
20. (i)
Pattern	1	2	3	4	5
No. of blue tiles	21	33	45	57	69

(ii) $T_n = 12n + 9$　　(iii) 129
(iv) $S_n = \frac{n}{2}(30 + 12n)$　　(v) 7

Exercise 10.7

1. (i) 18, 24　　(ii) 38, 51　　(iii) 47, 62
2. (i) Yes　(ii) No　(iii) Yes　(iv) Yes
3. (i) 5, 8, 13, 20, 29　　(ii) 0, 3, 8, 15, 24
(iii) 4, 11, 22, 37, 56
4. 116
5. 4　　7　　12　　19　　28; $a = 1$
　　　3　　5　　7　　9
　　　　2　　2　　2
6. (i) $T_n = n^2 + 4$　　(ii) $T_n = 2n^2$
7. $T_n = n^2 + 6$
9. $T_n = n^2 + 2n$
10. (i) 30　　　　　(ii) 55
(iv) 385
11. (iii) $T_n = \dfrac{n^2 + n}{2}$　　(iv) 210

Test Yourself 10

1. (i) (a) $a = 5, d = 3$　　(b) $T_n = 3n + 2$
(c) 20th
(ii) (a) $a = 3, d = 4$　　(b) 210
2. (i) (a) $d = -5$
(b) $T_n = 10 - 5n$; $T_{10} = -40$
(ii) (a)
Shape no.	1	2	3	4	5
No. of matches	8	15	22	29	36

(b) $T_n = 7n + 1$
(c) 85
(d) 1490

3. (i) $a = 8, d = -2$ (b) $T_n = 10 - 2n$
(c) 15th
(ii) $S_n = \frac{n}{2}\{2a + (n-1)d\}$; 6, 9, 12; 75

4. (i) (a) $a = 8, d = -4$ (b) 19th
(ii) (a)

Shape	1	2	3	4	5
No. of matches	8	13	18	23	28

(b) $T_n = 5n + 3$ (c) 103 (d) 426

5. (i) (c); $T_n = 2n - 7$
(ii) 1st: 7, 11, 15, 19, …;
2nd: 4; $T_n = 2n^2 + n + 5$

6. (i) $T_n = 4n + 5$; $T_{10} = 45$
(ii) (a) $T_n = a + (n-1)d$,
$S_n = \frac{n}{2}\{2a + (n-1)d\}$
(b) $a = -8, d = 3$

7. (i) (a) $d = 6$ (b) $T_n = 6n - 4$
(c) $n = 34$ (d) 1180
(ii) (a) 24 (b) 35
(c) 2nd difference = 2
(d) $T_n = n^2 + 2n$ (e) 120

Chapter 11: Geometry 1

Exercise 11.1

1. $a = 32°, b = 148°, c = 46°, d = 134°, e = 60°$,
$f = 120°, g = 110°, h = 70°, j = 140°, \ell = 80°$,
$m = 100°$
2. $a = 50°, b = 86°, c = 111°, d = 74°, e = 48°$,
$f = 112°$
3. $a = 65°, b = 40°, c = 52.5°, d = 60°, e = 30°$
4. $x = 65°, y = 50°$
5. $a = 62°, b = 110°, c = 55°, d = 34°$
6. 25°
7. (i) 55° (ii) 45°
8. (i) 76° (ii) 52°
9. $a = 95°, b = 115°, c = 39°, d = 85°$
10. (i) $x = 116°, y = 52°$
(ii) $x = 20°, y = 140°$
(iii) $x = 80°, y = 30°$
11. $x = 10, y = 5, z = 8$
12. $|AB| = 6$ units; Area = 13.5 sq. units
13. (i) 5 (ii) 13
14. (i) $\sqrt{76}$ (ii) $\sqrt{32}$ (iii) $\sqrt{44}$
15. $x = 5, y = 12$
16. RHS
17. SSS or SAS
18. SAS
19. $x = 10, y = 8$

Exercise 11.2

1. (i) 30 cm² (ii) 36 cm² (iii) 36 cm²
2. (i) 36 cm² (ii) 6 cm
3. (i) 4 (ii) 10 (iii) 6

4. (i) $4\frac{4}{5}$ cm (ii) $10\frac{1}{2}$ cm (iii) $21\frac{3}{5}$ cm
5. (i) 96 cm² (ii) 126 cm² (iii) 143 cm²
6. 308 cm²; $|BC| = 17\frac{1}{9}$ cm
7. $|DC| \times h$ is area of each
8. $2\frac{2}{3}$ cm
9. (i) (1, 3), (2, 4), (2, 5), (4, 5)
(ii) Interior angles or supplementary angles
10. (i) 30 cm² (ii) 30 cm²
(iii) 45 cm² (iv) 4 cm
11. (i) Alternate angles (ii) ASA
12. (i) 5 cm (iii) 8 cm
13. (i) $\frac{1}{2}|DC| \times h : |DC| \times h$ (ii) 10 cm²

Exercise 11.3

1. (i) [BC] (ii) [AC]
2. (a) (i) (b) (i) (c) (ii)
3. (i) $\angle$BAC (ii) $\angle$ACB
4. (i) 8 cm (ii) 7 cm
5. (i) 5 (ii) 6
6. (i) 2.5 (ii) 9 (iii) $6\frac{2}{3}$
7. (i) $6\frac{2}{5}$ (ii) $5\frac{5}{6}$ (iii) $2\frac{4}{7}$
8. 7
9. $6\frac{2}{3}$
10. (i) equal angles (ii) [DF]
(iii) $x = 13\frac{5}{7}, y = 9\frac{1}{7}$
11. (i) $1\frac{1}{2}$ times (ii) $x = 6, y = 4.5$
12. (ii) $x = 9, y = 10\frac{1}{2}$
13. (i) [XY] (ii) $x = 9, y = 13\frac{1}{2}$
14. $x = 4.5, y = 4$
15. (ii) 14
16. (i) $\angle$ABD + $\angle$BDC (iii) [DC]
(iv) [AD]
17. 6
18. (i) $\dfrac{|AE|}{|AC|} = \dfrac{|DE|}{|BC|}$ (ii) $x = \frac{48}{5}, y = \frac{12}{5}$

Exercise 11.4

1. $a = 90°, b = 90°, c = 45°$
2. As $|AO| = |OC| =$ radius;
(i) 43° (ii) 90° (iii) 47°
3. $a = 42°, b = 48°, c = 50°, d = 40°, e = 55°$,
$f = 35°$
4. (i) $\triangle$ABC (ii) [AO] + [OC]
(iii) 10 units (iv) 8 units (v) 24 sq. units
5. (i) 6 cm (ii) $\sqrt{61}$ cm
6. 48 cm
7. (i) 90° (ii) 50° (iii) 50° (iv) 80°
8. (i) 90° (ii) 35° (iii) 90° (iv) 55°
9. 30°
10. 12 cm
11. (i) 60° (ii) 120° (iii) 30° (iv) 30°
12. (i) 20° (ii) 30°

14. 20°

15. (i) 40°   (ii) 50°   (iii) 40°

Test Yourself 11

1. (i) Isosceles   (ii) $\angle ABC + \angle ACB$
(iii) 62°

2. 80°

3. (i) 84 cm^2 (ii) 126 cm^2 (iii) 84 cm^2

4. (i) 14 cm   (ii) 10 cm

5. (ii) 72 cm^2

6. (ii) $|OB| = |OA|$ (iii) 132°

7. (i) 90°   (ii) 25 cm   (iii) 24 cm

8. (i) $\angle ADC + \angle ABC$ (ii) 70°

9. Angle in a semicircle

10. (i) 90°   (ii) $2\sqrt{3}$

11. $3\frac{3}{5}$

12. 15 cm

13. $x = 2,\ a = 9\frac{1}{3}$

14. (i) $\angle CAB + \angle AOD$ (ii) 60°
(iii) 30°   (iv) 30°

15. (i) 15 units   (ii) 92 sq. units

16. (iii) 36 sq. units   (iv) 12 sq. units
(v) 24 sq. units   (vi) 60 sq. units

Chapter 12: Coordinate Geometry – The Circle

Exercise 12.1

1. (i) $x^2 + y^2 = 4$ (ii) $x^2 + y^2 = 9$
(iii) $x^2 + y^2 = 1$ (iv) $x^2 + y^2 = 25$
(v) $x^2 + y^2 = 2$

2. (i) $x^2 + y^2 = 8$ (ii) $x^2 + y^2 = 8$
(iii) $x^2 + y^2 = 18$ (iv) $x^2 + y^2 = \frac{4}{9}$
(v) $x^2 + y^2 = \frac{16}{9}$

3. 5; $x^2 + y^2 = 25$

4. (i) $x^2 + y^2 = 13$ (ii) $x^2 + y^2 = 5$
(iii) $x^2 + y^2 = 25$ (iv) $x^2 + y^2 = 16$

5. (i) $x^2 + y^2 = 25$ (ii) $x^2 + y^2 = 9$
(iii) (0, 5), (0, −5)   (iv) (3, 0), (−3, 0)

7. 36π

8. (i) 3   (ii) 7   (iii) 1
(iv) $2\sqrt{3}$ (v) $3\sqrt{3}$ (vi) $\sqrt{5}$

9. (i) $x^2 + y^2 = \frac{9}{4};\ \frac{3}{2}$ (ii) $x^2 + y^2 = \frac{25}{9};\ \frac{5}{3}$
(iii) $x^2 + y^2 = \frac{49}{4};\ \frac{7}{2}$

10. (i) (0, 0)   (ii) 5   (iii) $x^2 + y^2 = 25$

11. 18

12. $x^2 + y^2 = 20$

13. (i) $x^2 + y^2 = 6$ (ii) $x^2 + y^2 = 24$
(iii) $x^2 + y^2 = 18$ (iv) $x^2 + y^2 = 12$
(v) $x^2 + y^2 = 45$

14. $x^2 + y^2 = 36$

Exercise 12.2

2. Outside

3. (5, 0), (−5, 0); (0, 5), (0, −5)

5. (i) Outside   (ii) On
(iii) Outside   (iv) Inside

6. (iii)

7. (i) P(0, 4), Q(0, −4)   (ii) 8

8. $k = 2$

Exercise 12.3

1. (i) $(x − 3)^2 + (y − 1)^2 = 4$
(ii) $(x − 3)^2 + (y − 4)^2 = 9$
(iii) $(x − 1)^2 + (y + 4)^2 = 25$
(iv) $(x + 3)^2 + (y − 5)^2 = 16$
(v) $(x + 3)^2 + (y + 2)^2 = 1$
(vi) $(x − 3)^2 + y^2 = 36$
(vii) $(x + 3)^2 + (y + 5)^2 = 10$
(viii) $x^2 + (y + 2)^2 = 8$

2. (i) $\sqrt{10}$
(ii) $(x − 2)^2 + (y − 4)^2 = 10$

3. $(x − 5)^2 + (y + 2)^2 = 85$

4. $(x − 2)^2 + (y − 2)^2 = 10$

5. (i) (1, 3)   (ii) $\sqrt{8}$
(iii) $(x − 1)^2 + (y − 3)^2 = 8$

6. (2, 3); 4

7. (4, −3); 3

8. (−2, −5); 8

9. (−5, 1); 9

10. (0, 4); 5

11. (3, 0); 3

12. (1, −5); $\frac{4}{3}$

13. (0, 2); $2\sqrt{3}$

14. (3, 3); $(x − 3)^2 + (y − 3)^2 = 9$

15. (i) (4, 0)   (ii) $(x − 4)^2 + y^2 = 16$
(iii) 2   (iv) (4, 2)
(v) $(x − 4)^2 + (y − 2)^2 = 4$ (vi) (4, 4)

16. (i) 2   (ii) (4, −4)
(iii) $(x − 4)^2 + (y + 4)^2 = 4$ (iv) k_4

17. (2, 3); $(x − 2)^2 + (y − 3)^2 = 10$

18. (i) 3   (ii) $(x − 4)^2 + (y − 3)^2 = 9$

19. (i) (4, 0)   (ii) $(x − 4)^2 + y^2 = 4$
(iii) $(x − 4)^2 + y^2 = 36$ (iv) Yes, equal

20. (i) $(x − 1)^2 + y^2 = 1$ (ii) (2, 1)
(iii) $(x − 2)^2 + (y − 1)^2 = 1$
(iv) $\left(2 − \frac{\pi}{2}\right)$ sq. units

Exercise 12.4

1. (i) (−2, −3), (3, 2)   (ii) (3, 1), (1, 3)
(iii) (5, 0), (−3, −4)   (iv) (4, 2), (−2, 4)

2. (2, −1)

3. (i) (1, 1)   (ii) (1, −3)   (iii) (2, −2)

4. (3, 0), (0, −3); No; Two points of intersection

5. (4, 2), (−4, −2)

6. $x^2 + y^2 = 10$; $(-1, -3)$, $(-3, -1)$
7. $x + y - 3 = 0$; $(2, 1)$, $(1, 2)$
8. Point of contact $= (-2, 4)$
9. (i) $(3, 3)$ (ii) $(x - 3)^2 + (y - 3)^2 = 9$
    (iii) $y = 6$ (iv) $x = 6$ (v) $(6, 6)$

Exercise 12.5

1. (i) $(2, 0)$, $(-2, 0)$ (ii) $(5, 0)$, $(-5, 0)$
    (iii) $(9, 0)$, $(-9, 0)$
2. $(0, 7)$, $(0, -7)$
3. (i) $(2, 0)$, $(8, 0)$ (ii) $(6, 0)$, $(-2, 0)$
4. $(0, 1)$, $(0, -7)$
6. $(-4, 1)$; 3
7. Outside
8. $(x + 3)^2 + y^2 = 10$; 2
9. (i) 4   (ii) $(x + 2)^2 + (y - 4)^2 = 16$

Test Yourself 12

1. (i) $(0, 0)$; $r = 7$
2. $x^2 + y^2 = 25$; $(5, 0)$, $(-5, 0)$
3. (i) 6   (ii) $x^2 + y^2 = 144$
4. $(x - 2)^2 + (y + 3)^2 = 16$
5. (i) $(3, 4)$; radius $= 5$
6. Point of intersection $= (1, -3)$
7. (i) 6   (iii) $(0, 6)$, $(0, -6)$
8. (i) $A(-9, 0)$, $C(9, 0)$
    (ii) a: $(x + 9)^2 + y^2 = 36$; c: $(x - 9)^2 + y^2 = 36$
    (iii) $y = 6$, $y = -6$
9. (i) $A(2, 6)$, $B(6, -2)$
10. (i) $(1, -2)$; $r = \sqrt{5}$
    (ii) $(x - 1)^2 + (y + 2)^2 = 5$
11. (i) $C(2, 0)$; $r = 3$ (ii) $(x - 2)^2 + y^2 = 9$
    (iii) t_1: $y = 3$; t_2: $y = -3$
12. (i) $A = (3, 1)$, $B = (-3, -1)$
13. $(3, 4)$; $r = 2\sqrt{5}$; $A = (1, 0)$, $B = (5, 0)$; $|AB| = 4$
14. (i) $(4, -1)$; $r = 4$
    (ii) $(x - 4)^2 + (y + 1)^2 = 16$
    (iii) $\frac{5}{4}$; $AE \perp EB$ (angle in a semicircle)
15. (i) $(-2, 3)$; $r = 5$ (iii) $P = (-7, 3)$, $Q = (3, 3)$
    (iv) $x = -7$, $x = 3$ (v) $(x + 2)^2 + y^2 = 25$
17. k_1: $x^2 + (y - 2)^2 = 4$; k_2: $x^2 + (y + 2)^2 = 4$;
    k_3: $x^2 + y^2 = 16$; $y = 4$
18. (i) $(-4, 3)$; $r = 6$ (ii) $(-10, 3)$
19. $(x + 1)^2 + (y - 2)^2 = 25$

Chapter 13: Representing Data

Exercise 13.1

1. (i) 7   (ii) Brown   (iii) 22
2. (i) 25   (ii) 10   (iii) 3
    (iv) 5   (v) 9
4. (i) 6   (ii) 16   (iii) Can't tell
5. (i) 180   (ii) March and August
    (iii) 36

6. Mean $= 12.5$; line too low
7. (i) 15   (ii) 1   (iii) 5   (iv) 20%
8. (i) Conor (ii) Barry (iii) Dara (iv) Alan
9. (i) Monday   (ii) Saturday (iii) Saturday
    (iv) Friday   (v) 25
11. 88
12. (i) 40   (ii) 15; 15%
13. 90

Exercise 13.2

1. (ii) 12   (iii) $(20 - 40)$ km
    (iv) 40%
2. (i) 10   (ii) $(40 - 50)$ yr
    (iii) 12   (iv) 60
    (v) $(50 - 60)$ yr   (vi) $(40 - 50)$ yr
3. (ii) 38   (iii) $(12 - 16)$ min
    (iv) $(12 - 16)$ min   (v) 30
4. (i) 19   (ii) 54
    (iii) $(10 - 15)$ sec   (iv) $(10 - 15)$ sec
    (v) 20   (vi) 20
5. (ii) $(25 - 35)$ min   (iii) $(25 - 35)$ min
    (iv) $(15 - 25)$ min   (v) 48
    (vi) 29 min

Exercise 13.3

1. Symmetrical distribution;
    (i) Normal distribution
    (ii) People's heights
2. Negative skew
3. Positive skew
4. (i) (c)   (ii) (a)   (iii) (b)
    (iv) (b)   (v) (c)
5. Median
6. (i) Ⓑ   (ii) Ⓐ
    (iii) Normal distribution
7. (i) Negatively skewed
    (ii) Mode is generally higher when the
        distribution is negatively skewed
8. Negative skew; (i) Mean   (ii) Mode
9. (i) Positively skewed
    (ii) Mode < Median < Mean

Exercise 13.4

1. (i) 20   (ii) 5   (iii) 94   (iv) 51   (v) 8
2. (i) 4   (ii) 27
    (iii) 8   (iv) 36 years old
4. (ii) 8   (iii) 16
5. (i) 6   (ii) 4.3 sec
    (iii) 3.25 sec   (iv) 3.5 sec
6. (i) 62   (ii) 47   (iii) 67   (iv) 20
7. (ii) 16.5   (iii) 40   (iv) 23.5
8. (i) 19   (ii) (a) 66   (b) 49
    (iii) 55   (iv) 26

9. (i) 37   (ii) 44   (iii) 54
   (iv) 16   (v) 26; Brian
10. (i) Median = 76; Range = 27
   (ii) Median = 68; Range = 38
   (iii) The group who did not smoke
11. (i) 52 min
   (ii) (a) 52 min   (b) 69 min
   (iii) (a) 31 min   (b) 55 min
12. (i) 41   (ii) 41   (iii) 53
13. (ii) 55   (iii) 66.5   (iv) English

Exercise 13.5

1. (i) B   (ii) C   (iii) D
2. (i) C and F   (ii) A and E   (iii) B and D
   (iv) A; Perfect positive correlation
3. (i) 6   (ii) 8.2 years
   (iii) Weak positive
4. (i) Strong positive
   (ii) Strong or close relationship
5. (i) 100 kg   (ii) 170 cm
   (iii) 175 cm, 85 kg   (iv) Weak positive
6. (ii) Strong negative correlation; Yes, as you
       would expect positive correlation
7. (ii) Older bikes are cheaper
   (iii) Strong negative
8. (ii) Strong positive correlation
9. (i) B   (ii) C   (iii) A   (iv) D
10. (i) Strong negative   (ii) Strong positive
   (iii) No correlation   (iv) Strong negative
   (v) Strong positive

Exercise 13.6

1. Strong positive; 0.7
2. A: 0.1; B: −1; C: −0.4; D: 0.8
4. −0.9
5. −0.8
6. −1
7. 0.1
8. (i) 0.9   (ii) −0.8   (iii) 0
   (iv) −1   (v) −0.1   (vi) 0.2

Exercise 13.7

1. (i), (ii), (v) and (vi)
2. (i) 39 000 km
   (ii) Strong positive correlation
   (iii) Yes (Older implies more km travelled)
   (iv) (a) 2 years, 40 000 km
3. (i) Strong negative correlation
   (ii) Yes; Older implies less value
4. (ii) Strong positive correlation
   (iii) Yes; Sunshine causes higher temperatures
5. (ii) Strong negative correlation
   (iii) No

Test Yourself 13

1. (i) 47   (ii) 38   (iii) 29   (iv) 47   (v) 18
2. (i) 49   (ii) 30   (iii) 54   (iv) 24
3. (i) 32   (ii) €48 (iii) €25 (iv) €29
   (v) Males spent more
4. (i) €850   (ii) €300   (iii) €500   (iv) €150
5. (ii) Strong negative correlation
6. (i) D   (ii) C   (iii) A
   (iv) (a) B   (b) D   (c) C   (d) A
7. (i) Positive
   (ii) Positive
   (iii) No correlation
   (iv) Positive
   (v) Negative
8. (i) Bar chart or pie chart
   (ii) Scatter graph
   (iii) Back-to-back stem and leaf diagram
   (iv) Bar chart or pie chart
   (v) Pie chart or bar chart
   (vi) Scatter graph
9. (i) Symmetrical (or normal) distribution
10. (i) Higher concentration of values at lower
       end (or start) of the distribution
   (ii) Positively skewed
   (iii) Ages at which people learn to read
11. (i) Negatively skewed
   (ii) Ages at which people become
       grandparents

Chapter 14: Trigonometry

Exercise 14.1

1. 12 cm^2
2. 31 cm^2
3. Yes
4. $a = 3.6$ cm, $b = 9.2$ cm, $c = 9.5$ cm,
   $d = 4.5$ cm, $e = 15$ cm, $f = 12$ cm,
   $g = 9.4$ cm, $h = 6.4$ cm, $i = 8.9$ cm
5. 12.8 cm
6. 8.1 units
7. 2.6 m
8. 6.4 cm
9. (i) 3 cm   (ii) 5.8 cm
10. $c = 10$ cm, $d = 24$ cm
11. 25 cm
12. 25.7 m

Exercise 14.2

1. (i) tan A (ii) cos A (iii) sin A
2. $\frac{3}{5}, \frac{4}{5}, \frac{3}{4}, \frac{5}{13}, \frac{12}{13}, \frac{5}{12}, \frac{\sqrt{3}}{2}, \frac{1}{2}, \sqrt{3}$
3. 5; (i) $\frac{5}{13}$ (ii) $\frac{12}{13}$ (iii) $\frac{5}{12}$

4. $2; \dfrac{3}{\sqrt{13}}$ (ii) $\dfrac{2}{\sqrt{13}}$ (iii) $\dfrac{3}{2}$

5. (i) $\tan \theta$ (ii) $\sin \theta$ (iii) $\cos \theta$

6. $\sin B = \dfrac{12}{13}, \tan B = \dfrac{12}{5}$

7. (i) $\dfrac{1}{\sqrt{5}}$ (ii) $\dfrac{\sqrt{21}}{2}$

8. $\sin C = \dfrac{1}{2}, \cos C = \dfrac{\sqrt{3}}{2}$

9. 1

10. (i) 1   (ii) 1

Exercise 14.3

1. (i) 0.7431   (ii) 0.2756   (iii) 0.2679
    (iv) 0.9511   (v) 0.8788

2. (i) 0.5344   (ii) 0.7266   (iii) 0.5914
    (iv) 0.2773

3. (i) 48°   (ii) 69°   (iii) 55°
    (iv) 78°   (v) 42°   (vi) 12°

4. (i) 36.9°   (ii) 41.1°   (iii) 75.4°
    (iv) 74.2°

5. (i) 42°   (ii) 53°   (iii) 41°
    (iv) 24°   (v) 29°   (vi) 12°
    (vii) 35°   (viii) 58°

6. $A = 56.7°$; $\sin A = 0.84$

7. $A = 37°$; $B = 68°$; $C = 39°$

Exercise 14.4

1. (i) cosine   (ii) tangent   (iii) sine

2. $x = 3.8, y = 10.0, z = 10.2$

3. (i) 3.3   (ii) 16.7   (iii) 13.5

4. (i) 37°   (ii) 46°   (iii) 23°

5. $p = 67°, q = 24°, r = 37°$

6. $x = 9.4$

7. (i) 12.0   (ii) 15.9   (iii) 18.8

8. $x = 15, y = 20$

9. (i) 13.9   (ii) 44°

10. 12.5 cm

11. (i) 13 cm   (ii) 11°

12. (i) 4.2 cm   (ii) 25°

13. 20 m

14. 21 m

15. 40 m

16. (i) 4.0 m   (ii) 12.7 m

17. (i) 25°   (ii) 109 m
    (iii) 118 m   (iv) 357 m

18. Yes

19. (i) 37°   (ii) |BC| = 6 m, |DC| = 4 m

20. 3 cm

Exercise 14.5

1. (i) 24.1 cm²   (ii) 7.4 cm²   (iii) 11.4 cm²

2. (i) 12 cm²   (ii) 49 cm²   (iii) 85 cm²

3. 87 sq. units

4. 338 cm²

5. 139 cm²

6. $A = 75°$; $B = 22°$

7. 8.3

8. 10 cm

9. $\sin A = \dfrac{3}{5}$; 168 sq. units

10. (ii) 90°
    (iii) No; increases by a factor of four

11. 153 m

12. (i) $\dfrac{\sqrt{24}}{5}$ (ii) $6\sqrt{6}$; $k = 6$

Exercise 14.6

1. (i) 15.3   (ii) 11.3   (iii) 11.0

2. (i) $A = 34°$ (ii) $B = 51°$ (iii) 75°

3. (i) 40°   (ii) 22 cm

4. (i) 29 units   (ii) 302 sq. units

5. (i) 19.2 m   (ii) 15.3 m

6. (i) 94 m   (ii) 81 m

7. (i) 47°   (ii) 98 km

8. (i) 8 cm   (ii) 33 cm²

9. (i) 37 m   (ii) 23 m

10. (i) 60°   (ii) 74 m   (iii) 1899 m²

Exercise 14.7

1. (i) $a = 4.4$ (ii) $b = 11.1$ (iii) $a = 14.7$

2. $a = 6, b = 21, c = 9$

3. $A = 49°, B = 43°, C = 29°$

4. 29°

5. 45°

6. 66 m

7. (i) 13 m   (ii) 72°

8. 101 cm

9. 21 km

10. (i) 9 cm   (ii) 16.1 cm

11. (i) 23 cm   (ii) 39°

12. (i) 7.39   (ii) 10.61

13. 9 m

14. (i) 30 m   (ii) 177 m

15. (i) 13.7 cm   (ii) 69°

16. (i) 386 m   (ii) 363 m

17. (i) 37 m

18. (i) 58°   (ii) 79°

Exercise 14.8

1. $\dfrac{1}{2}$

2. 1

3. $\dfrac{1}{2}$

4. $\dfrac{1}{\sqrt{2}}$

5. $\dfrac{1}{4}$

6. $\dfrac{\sqrt{3}}{2}$

7. $\dfrac{\sqrt{3}}{2}$

8. $\frac{1}{2}$

9. $\frac{3}{4}$

10. $\frac{1}{3}$

12. $x = 3, y = 3\sqrt{3}$

13. $x = 3, y = 4$

14. $x = 4\sqrt{3}, y = 4, z = \dfrac{8}{\sqrt{3}} \left(\text{or } \dfrac{8\sqrt{3}}{3}\right)$

15. $400\sqrt{3}$

Exercise 14.9

1. (i) 34 cm²   (ii) 127 cm²   (iii) 44 cm²
2. (i) 8.4 cm   (ii) 23.0 cm   (iii) 17.5 cm
3. (i) 410.5 cm²   (ii) 58.6 cm
4. (i) 24 cm   (ii) 212 cm²
5. 14 cm
6. 15 cm
7. 115 m
8. 5.9 km²
9. (i) 170 cm²   (ii) 54 cm
10. (i) 25 cm   (ii) 23 cm   (iii) 226 cm²
     (iv) 160 cm²   (v) 66 cm²
11. (i) 106°   (ii) 18.5 m

Exercise 14.10

1. (i) 0.7660   (ii) −0.7660
     (iii) 0.6428   (iv) −0.6428
2. (i) 0.6691   (ii) −0.8480
     (iii) −0.9004   (iv) −0.9336
     (v) 0.2309   (vi) −0.8290
     (vii) 0.7314   (viii) 3.4874
3. (i) sin 50°   (ii) −cos 65°
     (iii) −tan 20°   (iv) −cos 40°
     (v) −sin 70°   (vi) −tan 60°
4. (i) $\dfrac{\sqrt{3}}{2}$ (ii) $-\dfrac{1}{\sqrt{2}}$ (iii) $-\dfrac{\sqrt{3}}{2}$
     (iv) $-\dfrac{1}{2}$ (v) $\dfrac{\sqrt{3}}{2}$ (vi) $\dfrac{1}{1}$
     (vii) $-\dfrac{\sqrt{3}}{2}$ (viii) $-\dfrac{\sqrt{3}}{2}$ (ix) $-\dfrac{1}{\sqrt{3}}$
5. 13° and 167°
6. (i) 147° and 213°   (ii) 129° and 309°
7. 30° and 150°
8. 1 and −1
9. $\dfrac{\sqrt{3}}{2}$ and $-\dfrac{\sqrt{3}}{2}$
10. $\frac{1}{2}$ and $-\frac{1}{2}$
11. 233°
12. $-\frac{3}{4}$
13. $-\dfrac{\sqrt{3}}{2}$
14. $-\dfrac{1}{\sqrt{5}}$

Test Yourself 14

1. (i) $\frac{3}{5}$ (ii) $\frac{3}{4}$; $A = 37°$
2. $x = 12$;   (i) $\frac{5}{12}$ (ii) $\frac{12}{13}$
3. 17.8 cm
4. (i) 8 cm   (ii) 22°
5. (i) 16 cm²   (ii) 6 cm   (iii) 41°
6. (i) 4.2 cm   (ii) 25°
7. (i) 32.0°   (ii) 43°
8. (i) 41 cm²   (ii) 11.6 cm
9. (i) 15 m   (ii) 9.6 m
10. (i) 22.3 cm²   (ii) 6.0 cm²
11. (i) 22 cm   (ii) 27 cm
12. (i) 240° and 300°   (ii) $\frac{3}{2}$
13. (i) 15 cm   (ii) 148 cm²
14. 12.7 m
15. (i) 13.1 cm   (ii) 39°
16. (i) 20 cm²   (ii) 18 cm
17. 9.1 cm; 50°
18. (i) Radar A   (ii) Radar A

Chapter 15: Geometry 2 – Enlargements and Constructions

Exercise 15.1

1. (i) 2   (ii) $x = 6$ cm, $y = 18$ cm
2. (i) 8   (ii) 12   (iii) 5
3. The point A
4. (i) 6 cm   (ii) 9 cm
5. (i) 2   (iii) (−2, 3)
6. (i) 2   (ii) (8, 9)
     (iii) A = 2 sq. units, B = 8 sq. units
7. (i) 2.5   (ii) 3.2 units
     (iii) 2 : 5; 25 sq. units
9. (i) A′B′C′
     (ii) (a) $\frac{1}{3}$ (b) $\frac{4}{3}$
     (iii) (a) 4 cm   (b) 16 cm
10. Yes; No
11. (i) (0, 2)   (ii) 2
     (iii) $\frac{1}{2}$ (iv) 60 sq. units
12. (i) 2.5   (ii) 10 units
     (iii) 2 : 5   (iv) 100 sq. units
13. (i) 104 mm   (ii) 42 mm
14. (i) 3
     (ii) Volume of image = k^3 times vol. of object
15. 10.8 cm
16. (i) 3   (ii) 14 cm by $9\frac{1}{3}$ cm
17. (i) 1 : 500   (ii) 60 m
     (iii) 1 : 2000   (iv) 50 cm

Exercise 15.2

7. 10.7 cm
9. 105°
11. Yes, same result

14. Point is equidistant from the two lines which form the angle

15. $|AG| : |GM| = 2 : 1$; $|BG| : |GN| = 2 : 1 : 1$

16. Point of intersection of perpendicular bisectors of [AB] and [BC]

Test Yourself 15

1. (i) 2
 (ii) 10 cm
 (iii) 10.5 cm
 (iv) N'N and L'L intersect at O
 (v) 32 cm

2. (i) (0, 2) (ii) 2 (iii) $\frac{1}{2}$ (iv) 96 cm²

3. (i) A (ii) $\frac{3}{2}$ (iii) 7.5 m (iv) 14.1 m
 (v) $\frac{2}{3}$

4. (i) 12 units (ii) 6 units
 (iii) 6 units; 45 sq. units

6. 7.8 cm

7. Sports field at circumcentre

8. (i) △ABE (ii) 11.25 cm (iii) $\frac{2}{5}$
 (iv) 28° (v) 26.25 cm²

9. (i) $\frac{3}{4}$ (ii) 4.5 cm (iii) 32 cm²

10. (ii) 2.2 km

11. (i) 1.5 (ii) 6 units (iii) 12 sq. units

12. (i) (a) $\frac{8}{5}$ (b) $\frac{4}{5}$ (ii) (a) 7.5 (b) 7.2

Chapter 16: Functions

Exercise 16.1

1. (i) 2, 10, 12 (ii) 12, 10, 8

2. (i) $y = 2x + 4$ (ii) $y = 8x - 7$
 (iii) $y = \frac{x}{4} - 3$ (iv) $y = 4(x + 3)$

3. (i) $x \rightarrow 3x + 2$ (ii) $x \rightarrow 5x - 2$
 (iii) $x \rightarrow \frac{x}{3} + 2$ (iv) $x \rightarrow 7(x + 2)$

4. (i) $(-1, 5), (0, 4), (1, 5), (2, 8)$
 (ii) $(-3, 9), (-2, 7), (-1, 5), (0, 3), (1, 1), (2, -1)$

5. (i) 'subtract 1' (ii) 'add 1'

6. (i) 5, 8, 20 (ii) 4, 8, 10

7. (i) {1, 2, 4, 5, 7}
 (ii) {3, 6, 4, 7, 9}
 (iii) {(1, 3), (2, 4), (4, 6), (5, 7), (7, 9)}
 (iv) $x \rightarrow x + 2$

8. (i) Yes (ii) No (iii) No (iv) Yes

9. As no two distinct couples have the same input

10. As the input 2 has two different outputs (5 and 10)

11. (i) Yes (ii) No (iii) Yes

12. (a) (i) {0, 1, 3, 5}
 (ii) {3, 4, 5, 8}
 (iii) {3, 4, 5, 6, 8}

(b) (i) {−2, 2, 3, 7}
 (ii) {−4, 6, 9}
 (iii) {−4, 2, 6, −3, 4, 9}

14. $a = 10, b = -26, c = 3, d = -2$

15. (i) $y = 2x - 4$ (ii) $y = 3x + 2$
 (iii) $y = 3x + 1$

Exercise 16.2

1. (i) −1 (ii) −3 (iii) 1 (iv) −5 (v) −9

2. (i) −3 (ii) −2 (iii) 1 (iv) 1 (v) 13

3. (i) $x = 2$ (ii) $x = 1$ (iii) $k = -2$

4. (i) $x = 2$ (ii) $x = 3$ (iii) $x = -2$

5. (i) −16 (ii) 0 (iii) $5k - 1$
 (iv) $10k - 1$ (v) $10k - 6$

6. 4

7. $\frac{8}{9}$

8. $\frac{1}{3}$

9. (i) $x = \pm\sqrt{2}$ (ii) $x = 15$
 (iii) $x = -1$ or $x = \frac{3}{2}$

10. (i) $\frac{1}{2}$, 11 (ii) 2 (iii) $\frac{5}{2}$

11. (i) $-4k - 3$ (ii) $k = -4$

12. (i) 1 (ii) 3 (iii) 11
 (iv) -2 ; $2x + 7$

13. {(2, 13), (5, 31), (7, 43)}

14. (i) 7 (ii) 25 (iii) −21
 (iv) $8x + 1$; 3

15. (i) 9 (ii) 9 (iii) 9 (iv) 81

16. (i) 9 (ii) −19 (iii) $6x - 1$ (iv) $6x + 3$

17. (i) 11 (ii) 2 (iii) $2x^2 + 3$
 (iv) $4x^2 - 4x + 3$; $x = 0$ or $x = 2$

18. (i) {4, 5, 6, 7} (ii) $2x + 6$
 (iii) {8, 10, 12, 14}

19. (i) −23 (ii) ±2

20. $2\sqrt{3}, 6\sqrt{2}$; $k = 12$

21. 36

22. (ii) (a) $18x^2 - 12x + 2$, $6x^2 - 1$ (b) $\frac{1}{2}$

Exercise 16.3

1. 2 **2.** 1 **3.** −2

4. 3 **5.** −4 **6.** 3

7. $a = -2, b = 4$

8. $a = 7, b = 5, c = -7$

9. $a = 2, b = -3$

10. $a = -1, b = 0$

11. $p = -2, q = 1$; $x = 1$

12. (i) $b = -2, c = -2$
 (ii) $y = -2$

13. $a = 7, b = 1$

14. (ii) $b = 2, c = -3$
 (iii) (1, 0)

15. $k = -2, p = -8$; $(-2, 0)$

Test Yourself 16

1. (a) (i) 7   (ii) 5
   (b) $a = 19, b = 49, c = 3, d = 3.5$
   (c) (i) 35   (ii) -33
       (iii) $15x - 3$ (iv) $15x + 5; x = 1\frac{7}{15}$

2. (a) (i) 'Subtract 3'   (ii) $\{-13, -10, -7, -4\}$
   (b) (i) 5
       (ii) $\frac{1}{2}$; 10; $h = -5$ or $h = 2$
   (c) (i) $2m + c = 7$ (ii) $4m + c = 17$
       (iii) $m = 5, c = -3$
       (iv) 5

3. (a) (i) -5 (ii) 11
   (b) (i) 49   (ii) 21; $x = 0$ or $x = -6$
   (c) (i) $f(0) = 0; \ell = 0$
       (ii) $k = 4$

4. (a) $a = -7, b = -1$
   (b) (i) 18   (ii) 2   (iii) 0; 9
   (c) $A(-5, 0), B(2, 0), C(0, 10)$

5. (a) (i) Yes   (ii) No
   (b) (i) 0   (ii) 23; $x = \frac{1}{2}, 1$
   (c) $A(-4, 0), B(2, 0), C(0, 8)$

6. (a)

x	-1	0	1	2
y	-5	-2	1	4

   (b) (ii) No, not equal
       (iii) 1
       (iv) Graph has x-axis as tangent
   (c) (i) $-b + c = -1, 3b + c = -13$
       (ii) $b = -3, c = -4$
       (iii) $f(x) = x^2 - 3x - 4$
       (iv) $D(4, 0), E(0, -4)$

Chapter 17: Graphing Functions

Exercise 17.1

1. $(-1, -5), (0, -3), (1, -1), (2, 1), (3, 3), (4, 5)$
2. $(0, -5), (1, -3), (2, -1), (3, 1), (4, 3), (5, 5)$
3. $(-1, -7), (0, -4), (3, 5)$
4. $(0, 6), (3, 3), (6, 0)$
5. $(-2, -6), (0, -2), (3, 4)$
6. (i) 4   (ii) 1   (iii) -3 (iv) -3
   (v) 5; slope $= 1$; increasing; as y increases,
        x increases
7. Slope $= 2; y = 2x + 1$
8. (i) $(3, 4)$
   (ii) x-value of point of intersection of lines
   (iii) $x = 3$; same
   (iv) Simultaneous equations
   (v) 3
9. $(3, 2)$
10. $(2, 0), (0, 4)$
11. $(0, 3), (2, 0)$

12. $(0, 0), (10, 1), (20, 2), (30, 3), (40, 4), (50, 5)$;
   (ii) Yes; through $(0, 0)$ and linear
   (iii) $x = 10y$ (iv) 7.5ℓ
13. (i) $(0, 2)$ is on each line
   (ii) 2 is the constant
   (iii) different slopes
   (iv) different x-coefficients
   (v) $y = -x + 2$
   (vi) $y = 2x + 2$
14. $(-2, -11), (-1, -7), (0, -3), (1, 1), (2, 5)$,
   $(3, 9), (4, 13)$; yes; same first difference
15. (i) $(0, -1), (1, -1.5), (2, -2), (3, -2\frac{1}{2})$,
   $(4, -3), (5, -3\frac{1}{2}), (6, -4)$
   (iv) $-3.75°$
   (v) $-3.75°$
16. (i) $H_1 : (1, 16), (2, 20), (3, 24), (4, 28), (5, 32)$,
   $(6, 36), (7, 40)$
   $H_2 : (1, 24), (2, 27.5), (3, 31), (4, 34.5)$,
   $(5, 38), (6, 41.5), (7, 45)$
   (ii) $H_1 = 4d + 12; H_2 = 3.5d + 20.5$
   (iv) (a) $(17, 80)$ (b) height the same
   (v) more accurate
   (vi) limit to growth

Exercise 17.2

1. $(-3, 5), (-2, 0), (-1, -3), (0, -4), (2, 0), (3, 5)$
2. $(-1, 5), (0, 0), (1, -3), (2, -4), (3, -3), (4, 0)$
3. $(-3, 4), (-2, 0), (-1, -2), (0, -2), (1, 0), (2, 4)$,
   $(3, 10)$
4. $(-2, 7), (-1, 0), (0, -3), (1, -2), (2, 3), (3, 12)$
5. $(-3, 5), (-2, -2), (-1, -5), (0, -4), (1, 1)$,
   $(2, 10)$
6. $(-2, 15), (-1, 4), (0, -3), (1, -6), (2, -5)$,
   $(3, 0), (4, 9)$;
   1st differences: $-11, -7, -3, 1, 5, 9$
   2nd difference: $4, 4, 4, 4, 4$
   The 2nd difference is twice the coefficient of x^2
7. 8
8. $(-2, -4), (-1, -1), (0, 0), (1, -1), (2, -4)$
9. $(-2, -5), (-1, 0), (0, 3), (1, 4), (2, 3), (3, 0)$,
   $(4, -5), (-1, 0), (3, 0)$

Exercise 17.3

1. (i) 3   (ii) 3   (iii) $(0, -1)$
   (iv) $-1, 1$ (v) $-2, 2$
2. (i) $x = -1, 4$ (ii) $x = -2, 5$ (iii) $x = 0, 3$
   (iv) -6 (v) -5.25 (vi) $(1.5, -6.25)$
   (vii) -6.25
3. (i) $-1, 3$ (ii) $0, 2$ (iii) 1.75
   (iv) 4   (v) $(1, 4)$
   (vi) $-2 < x < 1$
   (vii) $-1 < x < 3$
   (viii) $x = 1$

4. $(-2, 7), (-1, 0), (0, -3), (1, -2), (2, 3), (3, 12)$
   (i) $-1, 1\frac{1}{2}$ (ii) $2.4, -1.9$
   (iii) $(\frac{1}{4}, -3\frac{1}{8})$ (iv) $-1 < x < 1\frac{1}{2}$
5. (i) $(-1, 1), (3, 9)$ (ii) $-1, 3$
   (iii) same x-values
   (iv) x-values of points of intersection of $f(x)$
      and $g(x)$
   (v) $-1 < x < 3$
6. (i) $0, 3$ (ii) $-1, 4$
   (iii) $-0.8, 3.8$ (iv) $3.6, -0.6$
7. (i) $-3.8, 0.8$ (ii) $-3.3, 0.3$
   (iii) $-2.4, 0.4$
   (iv) -5.25; curve is below the line
   (v) $-2.4 < x < 0.4$
8. (i) $x = -2$ (ii) one
   (iii) x-axis is tangent to the curve at $x = -2$
9. (i) $A: y = x^2 + x - 2$; $B: y = x^2 - 3x + 3$;
      $C: y = x^2 - 6x + 9$
   (ii) $y = x^2 - 6x + 9$
   (iii) $x = 1.6$

Exercise 17.4

1. (i) 15   (ii) $0, 4$
   (iii) $x = 2$ (iv) 15 taxis
   (v) 11 a.m., 5 p.m.   (vi) 10 hours
2. $x = -1, 3.5$;
   (i) 10.1 m   (ii) 9 m   (iii) 3.5 secs
3. (i) 525
   (ii) 12.00 midday, 9 p.m.
   (iii) 4.30 p.m.; 625
   (iv) 9 a.m., 12 midnight
4. (i) 13.75   (ii) 16 m²; $x = 4$
   (iii) $2, 6$
5. (i) 45 m   (ii) 34 m
   (iii) 0.4, 5.7 secs   (iv) 3 secs
6. (i) $(0, 0), (1, 3), (2, 12), (3, 27)$
   (ii) 19 m²
   (iii) 1.8 m
   (iv) 19.6 m²; 1.78 m
7. (i) $(20x - x^2)$ m²
   (iii) 17.75, 2.25
   (iv) $6.8 < x < 13.2$
   (v) 100 m²; 10 m by 10 m

Exercise 17.5

1. $(-4, -15), (-3, 0), (-2, 3), (-1, 0), (0, -3),$
   $(1, 0), (2, 15)$
4. (i) $-3, 0, 3$ (ii) $-3 < x < 0; x > 3$
   (iii) $-1.5 < x < 0$ (iv) $(-1.5, 8)$
   (v) $(1.5, -8)$
5. (i) $-3, 0, 2$ (ii) $(1.1, -4)$
   (iii) $-3 < x < 0; x > 2$ (iv) $0 < x < 1.1$

6. $(-4, -7), (-3, 9), (-2, 11), (-1, 5), (0, -3),$
   $(1, -7), (2, -1), (3, 21)$;
   (i) $-3.7, -0.4, 2.1$
   (ii) $-2.3 < x < 1$
   (iii) $(1, -7)$
7. $(-3, 18), (0, 0), (1, 6), (4, -24)$
   (ii) decreases first
   (iii) $x = -2, 0, 3$
   (iv) $(-1.1, -6.7)$
   (v) $-2 < x < -1.1; x > 3$
8. (i) B (ii) C (iii) A (iv) B
9. (i) $-1.5, 1, 2$
   (ii) $(1.5, 1.5)$
   (iii) $-2 < x < -1.5; 1 < x < 2$
   (iv) $-1.5 < x < -0.5$
10. $A: y = 1 - x^2$; $B: y = x - x^2$; $C: y = x^3 - x^2$;
    $D: y = 9x - x^3$; $E: y = x^2 + 3x$;
    $F: y = -\frac{3}{4}x + 3$

Exercise 17.6

1. (i) $-2, 1, 3$ (ii) $-2 < x < 1$
   (iii) $(-0.8, 8.2)$ (iv) $1.4, 2.8$
   (v) $-1.5, 0$
2. (i) $-2, 0.5, 2$
   (ii) $-1.7, -0.1, 2.3$
   (iii) 2.55
3. (i) $-3, 2$
   (ii) $-2.8, 0.85, 2.9$
   (iii) $-3 < x < 2; 2 < x < 4$
   (iv) $-1\frac{1}{3} < x < 2$ (v) $x = 2$
4. (i) $-3, -2, 1$ (ii) 1.2
   (iii) $-2 < x < 1$ (iv) $-2.5 < x < 0$
   (v) $-3.45, -2, 1.45$
5. (i) -27 (ii) $(-1, 5)$
   (iii) $-2.8, 1.8, 4$
   (iv) $-1 < x < 3$; one point of intersection of
      curve and line $y = 10$; three points of
      intersection of curve and line $y = -10$
6. (i) $-1.7, 0, 1.7$ (ii) $-1.5, -0.35, 1.9$
   (iii) $-1.6, 0.6, 1$
7. (i) $1 < x < 9$ (ii) $1 < x < 5$
8. (i) $(2, -9)$ (ii) $-1, 0.5, 3$
   (iii) $-0.65, 0, 3.15$;
      $2x^3 - 5x^2 - 4x + 3 = 2x - 3$;
      $-1.35, 0.7, 3.15$
9. (iii) (a) 1.2 m   (b) 7.35 m³

Exercise 17.7

1. (i) 1   (ii) 2   (iii) 2.8
   (iv) 8   (v) 2.3
2. $(-2, \frac{1}{9}), (-1, \frac{1}{3}), (0, 1), (1, 3), (2, 9), (3, 27)$;
   (i) 5.2   (ii) 1.3

3.

x	−2	−1	0	1	2
2^x	$\frac{1}{4}$	$\frac{1}{2}$	1	2	4
4.2^x	1	2	4	8	16

; 5.7

4. (i) $k = 3$ (ii) 12   (iii) −1.6

5. $A : f(x) = 3.3^x$; $B : f(x) = 3^x$; $C : f(x) = 2^x$

6. $(-2, 9), (-1, 3), (0, 1), (1, \frac{1}{3}), (2, \frac{1}{9}), (3, \frac{1}{27})$;
   (i) 5.2
   (ii) −1.3

7. $a = 3$, $b = 2$

8. $A : y = (\frac{1}{2})^x$; $B : y = 3^{-x}$; $C : y = 5^x$; $D : y = 2^x$

9. (i) $k = 5$ (ii) $f(x) = k.2^x$

10. $a = 1.5$

11. $a = 2$, $b = 5$

12. (i) Table $A : h : x \rightarrow 3(2^x)$;
     Table $B : f : x \rightarrow 2x + 3$;
     Table $C : g : x \rightarrow x^2 + 3$
   (ii) $h : x \rightarrow 3.(2^x)$

13. A and (ii); B and (iii), C and (i)

14. $A = $ (iii); height will decrease, then increase
     $B = $ (i); decrease by the same amount each year
     $C = $ (ii); decrease by different amounts each year

15. (i) Exponential
   (ii) Quadratic
   (iii) $g : x \rightarrow 4x^2 + 1$
   (iv) $f : x \rightarrow 3^x$

16.

x	0	0.5	1	1.5	2	2.5	3
2^x	1	1.4	2	2.8	4	5.7	8
$9x - 3x^2 - 1$	−1	2.75	5	5.75	5	2.75	−1

   (i) 0.275, 2.15
   (ii) 2.6

Test yourself 17

1. (a) (i) −5.5   (ii) 1.5
   (b) (i) 30 sec   (ii) 225 m
   (c) $(-1, 6), (0, 4), (1, -4), (2, -6)$;
     (i) −1.85, 0.7, 3.2   (ii) $0.7 < x < 3.2$
     (iii) $(2, -6)$ (iv) $0.7 < x < 2$
     (v) −1.4, 0, 3.4   (vi) 3.6

2. (a) (i) −1.75   (ii) $x = 1, 3$
     (iii) −4   (iv) $x = 2$
   (b) $A : y = k - x$; $B : y = x^2 - k$; $C : y = k - x^2$
   (c) (i) $(0, 1)$

3. (b) (i) $Q(2, 0)$; $R(8, 0)$ (ii) $h = 25$
   (c) (i) $(0, 1)$ (ii) $a = 4$

4. (a) $5f = 8d + 20$; €36
   (b) $A : y = x^3 - 1$; $B : y = 3 - 2x$;
     $C : x^2 - x - 6$; $D : x = 4$

(c) $(-3, 0.125), (-2, 0.25), (-1, 0.5), (0.1),$
     $(1, 2), (2, 4), (3, 8), (4, 16), (5, 32)$
   (ii) 2.3

5. (a) (i) −1.6, 2.6   (ii) −0.6, 1.6
     (iii) −1, 3
   (b) €19 600
   (c) (i) $A = (-1, 0)$, $B = (3, 0)$, $C = (0, -3)$
     (ii) $-1 \leq x \leq 3$
     (iii) $k = 0, 2$

6. (a) (i) €$C = 10t + 20$
     (ii) €160
   (b) $A : y = x^2 - 2$; $B : y = 2 - x^2$; $C : y = 2x$
   (c) (i) −2.3, 0.2, 2.1   (ii) $-2.3 < x < 0$
     (iii) −2.1   (iv) −2.25, 0, 2.25
     (v) $x^3 - 5x + 1 = 1 \Rightarrow x^3 - 5x = 0 \Rightarrow$
       $x(x^2 - 5) = 0 \Rightarrow x = 0$ or $x = \pm\sqrt{5}$

Chapter 18: Calculus

Exercise 18.1

1. $\frac{2}{3}$; slope; $\frac{2}{3}$

2. (i) $\frac{1}{2}$ (ii) $-\frac{2}{3}$ (iii) 2

3. (i) 3   (ii) 2   (iii) 4   (iv) 5
   (v) −2   (vi) −3   (vii) 7   (viii) 0

4. (i) 2   (ii) 0   (iii) −1
   (iv) −3; as the line is falling (from left to right)

5. 3; 3; same

8. (i) €10/year   (ii) 80 km/hr
   (iii) 3 cm/week

9. (i) 20 km/hr   (ii) 20 km/hr
   (iii) 0   (iv) 0 km/h
   (v) 80 km/hr   (vi) 120 km/hr

Exercise 18.2

1. $\frac{dy}{dx} = 2$ **2.** $\frac{dy}{dx} = 3$

3. $\frac{dy}{dx} = 7$ **4.** $2x$

5. $4x + 6$ **6.** $10x - 3$

7. $2x - 8$ **8.** $x - 3$

9. $6x$ **10.** $3x^2$

11. $3x^2 + 2$ **12.** $6x^2 - 10x$

13. $9x^2 - 4x - 1$ **14.** $3x^2 - 2x + 2$

15. $x^2 - 2x + 4$ **16.** $3x^2 - 8x$

17. $-2 + 2x$ **18.** $2 - 6x$

19. $-3x^2 + 2$ **20** $-2x + 6x^2$

21. $3 - 8x + x^2$ **22.** 1

23. −6   **24.** 5

25. 5   **26.** 3

27. 16   **28.** 1

29. 13   **30.** −12

31. (i) 8   (ii) −8
   (iii) 0 ; tangent is parallel to x-axis